DOUGLAS
HAIG

WAR DIARIES AND LETTERS

1914–1918

DOUGLAS HAIG

WAR DIARIES AND LETTERS
1914–1918

Edited by Gary Sheffield
and John Bourne

Weidenfeld & Nicolson
LONDON

We respectfully dedicate this book to the memory
of two great Haig scholars, Robert Blake and John
Terraine, and to Lord Haig.

G.S. and J.B.

First published in Great Britain in 2005
by Weidenfeld & Nicolson

1 3 5 7 9 10 8 6 4 2

Previously unpublished extracts © 2005 the estate of Earl Haig
© 2005 in the selection, commentary, introduction and notes
Gary Sheffield and John Bourne

A CIP catalogue record for this book
is available from the British Library.

ISBN 0 297 84702 3

Typeset, printed and bound by
Butler and Tanner Ltd, Frome and London

Weidenfeld & Nicolson

The Orion Publishing Group Ltd
Orion House
5 Upper Saint Martin's Lane
London WC2H 9EA

www.orionbooks.co.uk

CONTENTS

LIST OF ILLUSTRATIONS

PREFACE

The First World War remains the most controversial war in British history. The reach of the conflict extends far beyond academe into the realms of literature, cultural studies, popular history, plays, films and television. The single most controversial figure of the period, whose reputation is central to many of the arguments, is Field Marshal Sir Douglas Haig (later Earl Haig of Bemersyde). Haig's voluminous writings, especially his diary, are an essential source for the study of Britain and the First World War. Given their importance, it is surprising that there has been only one published edition of Haig's private papers. Edited by Robert Blake, this appeared over fifty years ago and has long been out of print. Similarly, Alfred Duff Cooper's biography of Haig, which quoted from Haig's diary at great length (and some other passages are thin paraphrases of diary entries) is even older, being published in 1935–6. It too has been out of print for many years.

Since the early 1980s the study of the First World War has come of age with the production of a number of sophisticated works based on thorough examination of archival sources. We have been aware for some time of the need for a modern, more comprehensive edition of Haig's papers that takes account of recent research. At the beginning of the project, we had to make some fundamental decisions about the nature of the book. The first was the type of material that would be included and excluded. Given the importance of the diary as an historical source, we decided that the bulk of the book should be given over to the diary. The sheer volume of Haig's diaries meant that only a selection of entries could be reproduced. We also decided to include some of the letters written by Haig, but not, generally, those received by him. Official correspondence is excluded for the most part, although it is sometimes difficult to judge what is 'official' and what is not.

This book differs from Blake's in two significant respects: the version of the diary that we have used; and the balance between political and military material. First, there are two extant versions of Haig's diary. One is hand-written and contemporary (the manuscript, or Ms diary); the other was typed at a later date (the typescript, or Ts diary). The differences between the Ms and Ts diaries have been ignored by many writers, while others have made rather too much of them. Both Blake's and Duff Cooper's books were based on the Ts diary. Neither author properly differentiated between the two diary versions. We decided to base our version on the Ms diary, with significant additions and differences recorded in footnotes or incorporated in the text within square brackets [thus]. The Ms diary is inevitably less polished than the Ts diary, but what is lost in stylistic elegance is gained in accuracy, immediacy and authenticity.

Robert Blake's *Private Papers of Douglas Haig* reflected his expertise; he was one of the twentieth century's most distinguished political historians. Naturally enough, Blake emphasised those of Haig's writings that shed light on the politics of the First World War, and his introduction remains essential reading on such matters. We have approached the matter rather differently, and have sought to emphasise Haig's military role, without down-playing his importance as a political figure.

No one, it seems, can be entirely neutral on the subject of Douglas Haig. He is one of those historical characters who polarise opinion, and it seems appropriate that we make our position clear from the outset. Both of us have devoted our professional careers to the study of Britain and its Army in the First World War, and have arrived at a similar position, after years of study and immersion in primary sources. Originally, we shared the common view of Douglas Haig as the classic 'donkey'. Now, while we are not blind to Haig's faults and the mistakes he undoubtedly made, we recognise the 'donkey' image for the unfair and ludicrously inaccurate caricature that it is. We believe that Douglas Haig's career and achievements deserve sober consideration. It is our hope that this book, by providing an accurate and balanced selection of Haig's writings, supported by appropriate scholarly apparatus, will help to inform the debate.

Shrivenham and Birmingham
October 2004

Gary Sheffield   John Bourne
King's College London &   Centre for First World War Studies
Joint Services Command and   University of Birmingham
Staff College
Shrivenham

INTRODUCTION

This book is not another biography of Douglas Haig. Much less is it another history of the First World War. Rather, it presents a remarkable, almost day-by-day view of the war as seen from the perspective of one very important individual. Haig's career was unique. He commanded more British soldiers than any other general in history, and led them to the greatest victories ever achieved by a British army, in a war with unprecedented British casualties. Haig's reward was to be demonised. In popular memory, responsibility for the war's human costs has fallen principally on him, the chief 'butcher and bungler' among a generation of commanders seemingly inoculated against military genius. The very mention of the name Haig has the power to unleash paroxysms of unreason. What other British general could find himself, seventy years after his death, plastered across the front page of a tabloid newspaper with headlines demanding the demolition of his statue in Whitehall because of the 'shadow it casts over our war dead'?[1]

The reputation of the armies Haig commanded has risen dramatically during the last twenty-five years. The publication of Shelford Bidwell and Dominick Graham's *Fire-Power* in 1982 inaugurated a new era of scholarship.[2] Analysis of the war escaped from the debilitating focus on the alleged failings of a handful of senior commanders, chief of whom was Haig, and concentrated instead on the Army as an institution. The result has transformed our understanding of how the British Expeditionary Force (BEF) on the Western Front confronted, and eventually overcame, the difficult challenges it faced. The British Army was historically little more than a colonial police force trained and equipped to fight small wars against inferior opposition. By 1914 it had developed a capacity to intervene on a small scale in large wars. By November 1918 the BEF stood 1.8 million strong on the Western Front. It was generously equipped with the immense resources of British industry, which had been fully mobilised for war. It deployed state-of-the-art military

1 The *Express*, 6 November 1998. The assault on Haig, which was continued inside the newspaper, blamed him for the British Empire's war dead in all theatres of war, accusing him of leading a 'million men to their deaths'.
2 Shelford Bidwell and Dominick Graham, *Fire-Power: British Weapons and Theories of War 1904–45* (London: Allen & Unwin, 1982). For other key texts, see the Bibliography at the end of this volume.

technologies, many of them resulting from the work of the Empire's leading civilian scientists and engineers. And it was capable of successfully conducting, at short notice, 'all-arms deep battles' in high-intensity operations against a major military and industrial power. These changes have been described as constituting a 'revolution in military affairs'.[1] Despite the ending of the ice age of Great War scholarship Haig's reputation has been left behind by the retreat of the glaciers, marooned like a geological 'erratic' in a much changed historical landscape.

A reconsideration of Haig's part in this revolution is therefore not only timely but also necessary. Few documents provide a better insight into Haig's contribution than his wartime diary.

HAIG'S FICTIONS?

Haig's diary is a controversial document, though on close examination it is difficult to see why. Controversy partly arises because there are two versions of the diary. The first version was written by hand, almost on a daily basis, during the war. The second version was typed after the war. Haig included with this version a considerable number of supplementary papers, mainly letters and memoranda, and took the opportunity to make alterations, corrections and additions, though – significantly – very few major deletions. Both versions have been publicly available in the National Library of Scotland since March 1961 and may readily be compared.[2]

Each version of the diary has attracted its own legend. The manuscript diary is seen as a weapon in Haig's selfish rise to power and, especially, his campaign to undermine the authority and reputation of the British Expeditionary Force's first commander, Field Marshal Sir John French, and his chief potential rival for the supreme command, Sir Horace Smith-Dorrien. (Clearly, Haig's diary could not have performed this function if it was not a contemporary account.)[3] This is one of the themes of a recent study of the BEF in 1914.[4] The typed version is seen as Haig's attempt to rewrite history

1 Jonathan Bailey, *The First World War and the Birth of the Modern Style of Warfare* (Camberley: Strategic and Combat Studies Institute), Occasional Paper No. 22, 1996, especially pp. 17–21.
2 To be strictly accurate, there are three versions. Haig kept a carbon copy of the manuscript diary, to which he occasionally made corrections and additions after the original had been sent off. This is also in the National Library of Scotland (NLS).
3 Denis Winter, 'Haig's Fictions', in *Haig's Command: A Reassessment* (London: Viking, 1991) advances the theory that the Ms diary could have been a post-war fraud. For a counter, see John Hussey, 'A Contemporary Record or Post-War Fabrication? The Authenticity of the Haig Diaries for 1914', *Stand To! The Journal of the Western Front Association*, 42 (1995), pp. 29–31, and 'Sir Douglas Haig's Diary and Despatches. Dating and Censorship', *Stand To!*, 47 (1996), pp. 19–20.
4 Nikolas Gardner, *Trial by Fire. Command and the British Expeditionary Force in 1914* (London: Praeger, 2003), pp. 99–101.

to his own advantage and, by making it available to the British official historian, Sir James Edmonds, and the Australian official historian, C. E. W. Bean, to pollute the public record of the war.

Why did Haig keep a diary? The answer may in part be habit. Since his student days at Oxford, Haig had often kept a diary.[1] Keeping a diary is one way of maintaining control of one's life. Haig was orderly by temperament. His detractors often hold this against him, seeing in an ordered routine the sure sign of a second-rate mind and evidence of the 'authoritarian personality' identified by Norman F. Dixon as an explanation for 'military incompetence'.[2] Haig had been asthmatic as a child. Sufferers from the affliction require an unusual degree of self-control to maintain their health, not least in the matters of diet and exercise. It is not difficult to see why keeping a diary would appeal to such a personality.

Lady Haig was in no doubt, however, that Haig kept the diary for her.[3] She was certainly rather proprietorial about it. When, early in the war, Major Clive Wigram, King George V's Assistant Private Secretary, suggested that the diary might be sent to the King first and then forwarded to her, she immediately protested to her husband, who refused to comply with the Palace's request.[4] Diaries, of course, also develop a life of their own. Although Haig's diary has the reputation of a 'cool' document (and the bulk of it *is* an understated account of the day-to-day slog of high command), it does become 'warm', especially when referring to politicians and the French. Haig's exasperation with his own political leaders and with his allies becomes especially marked from the end of 1916 and the diary begins to perform the function of 'psychological release'. What it never becomes, however, is a confessional. Haig was not a man for reflecting on his own motives and performance.

Haig's diary was important to him. Writing it during the war and amending it after the war consumed a lot of time. Haig was concerned about his place in history. He knew he was living through historic events and that he was a major actor in them. Keeping a wartime diary was a way of recording systematically events that he and others would need to recall after the war. Robert Blake was in 'no doubt that [Haig] intended [his typescript diaries] to be his personal account of the war and it is clear from

---

1 Haig instructed his wife to destroy his pre-war diaries after his death, but she disobeyed him and they are available in the National Library of Scotland. His pre-1914 and post-1918 diaries, however, are generally very summary. Among Haig's military contemporaries, French, Rawlinson, Smith-Dorrien and Wilson also kept diaries.
2 Norman F. Dixon, *On the Psychology of Military Incompetence* (London: Futura, 1979), pp. 256–80.
3 The Countess Haig, *The Man I Knew* (Edinburgh and London: The Moray Press, 1936), p. 120.
4 Haig, *The Man I Knew*, pp. 120–21.

his will that he expected them to be published eventually, though not in his lifetime'.[1]

Lady Haig forwarded extracts from his diaries to Wigram at the King's request. His Majesty made similar requests to several other officers, including not only French and Smith-Dorrien,[2] but also Major General E. J. Montagu-Stuart-Wortley, Brigadier General Lord Loch, General Sir Hubert Gough and Lieutenant General the Earl of Cavan. General Sir Henry Rawlinson and Major General Sir Robert Whigham also regularly corresponded with Wigram.[3] On 28 April 1915 Haig wrote to his wife:

> As regards copies of my diary to Wigram – use your own judgement in this end and send him of course whatever *you think necessary* but I hope you will limit these extracts to past events and *not to future plans*. With this exception send him what you like – and if there is anything about which he wishes information of course tell him.

It does seem extraordinary for Haig to allow this apparently important weapon to be wielded by his wife, with very little supervision from him.[4] The extracts made by Lady Haig for Wigram have not survived, so there is no way of knowing exactly what she sent. But it would be remarkable if nothing of Haig's critical view of the conduct of operations on the Western Front and Sir John French's exercise of command was brought to the attention of the King by this means. Haig also wrote directly to the King and had opportunities to speak to him. He raised doubts about French to the King as early as 11 August 1914, during George V's visit to Aldershot.

How important this was in Haig's rise to power is debatable. If Haig was using his diary to undermine Smith-Dorrien this was a dangerous tactic: Smith-Dorrien was a great friend of King George V. In the event, it was French – not Haig – who did for Smith-Dorrien, whose royal connections did nothing to save him. As for French himself, he was quite capable of alienating powerful people without help from Haig. Those whom he alienated included Lord Kitchener and Sir William Robertson. By the end of 1915 French was a sick man and had lost the confidence of his closest subordinates and of leading figures in the Government who had far more say in military appointments than did the King.

---

1 Robert Blake, *The Private Papers of Douglas Haig 1914–1919* (London: Eyre & Spottiswoode, 1952), p. 13.
2 French was furious when he discovered from Smith-Dorrien that he was writing to the King.
3 Ian F. W. Beckett, 'George V and His Generals', in Matthew Hughes and Matthew Seligmann (eds), *Leadership in Conflict 1914–1918* (Barnsley: Leo Cooper Pen & Sword, 2000), pp. 247–66. Professor Beckett puts the King's influence in military appointments into its proper perspective.
4 Haig did, however, carefully mark in crayon items that were *not* to be typed up and passed on.

The changes made to the manuscript diary by Haig after the war are generally mundane. The following examples are typical:

1. 26 February 1917 – a tidying-up without significant changes:[1]
He then asked me my views. I said that, in my opinion, it would be madness to place the British under the French, and that I did not believe our troops would fight under French leadership. At the beginning of the war, there was much dissatisfaction [in the Army] with GHQ because there was an idea that British interests were sacrificed to those of the French.

2. 26 January 1918 – a clarifying gloss:
Letter received from Robertson from Paris stating that 'Versailles Military Council have just sent in a paper advocating an offensive in Palestine' – 'I have told the War Cabinet they cannot take on Palestine' and he says he will resign if overruled. [In this proposal Wilson is playing the tune called by Lloyd George.]

3. 3 April 1918 – a toughening of the original entry:
Before the meeting broke up, I asked the Governments to state their desire that a French offensive should be started *as soon as possible* in order to attract the Enemy's reserves and so prevent him from continuing his pressure against the British. Foch and Pétain both stated their determination to start attacking *as soon as possible*. [But will they ever attack? I doubt whether the French Army as a whole is now fit for an offensive.]

Two entries in the typescript diary, however, deserve closer examination. The first concerns Haig's account of the council of war called by Asquith on 5 August 1914 to consider what to do next. Haig left no substantial contemporary record of this meeting. His manuscript diary does not begin until 13 August.

As Britain went to war, Haig believed it might be more prudent to use the BEF as the cadre for building a mass army rather than immediately committing it to action on the Continent.[2] This idea is consistent with Haig's prescient belief that the war would be long and attritional, requiring the full mobilisation of Britain's resources.[3] However, this view ignored the

1 The post-war change is shown in square brackets.
2 See Haig to Howell, 4 August 1914, and Haig to Haldane, 4 August 1914, NLS: Haldane Papers, Acc. 5910. Haldane was sympathetic to this view: Samuel R. Williamson Jr, *The Politics of Grand Strategy* (London: Ashfield Press, 1990), p. 363.
3 While De Groot argues that at the War Council in early August, Haig wanted 'consideration of delaying full British mobilisation', it seems that Haig saw the importance of thorough mobilisation, which could not be rushed. See Gerard J. De Groot, *Douglas Haig 1861–1928* (London: Unwin Hyman, 1988), p. 148.

strategic reality that soon became evident: that France needed a small number of British troops on the ground immediately, not a large force at some point in the future. Haig had known, at least in outline, of the Anglo-French staff talks since November 1912, but it seems that discussions with Henry Wilson on 5 August put him fully in the strategic picture for the first time.[1]

At 4 pm on that day, Britain's senior military, naval and political leaders gathered in a council of war to decide Britain's wartime strategy. In his post-war memoirs, Sir John French claimed that Haig 'suggested postponing any landing till the campaign had actively opened and we should be able to judge in which direction our co-operation would be most effective'.[2] Haig was obviously sensitive to this charge, and it is suggestive that in 1919 Haig sought to enlist the support of men who had attended the meeting to rebut French's statement.[3] If Haig had believed that they were liable to contradict him, he would hardly have been likely to do this.

According to Henry Wilson's diary, in a meeting a short time before the council of war of 5 August, Haig argued for a delay of up to three months, in which to develop 'the immense resources of the Empire'.[4] He did indeed express similar views at the council of war itself.[5] This is not to say that Haig did not go on, as he claimed in the typescript diary and in subsequent conversations with his staff, to advocate the immediate dispatch of 'as strong an Expeditionary Force as possible ... and as soon as possible, to join the French Forces and to arrange to increase that force as rapidly as possible'.[6]

Perhaps Haig objected to French's implication that he had played a purely negative role at the council of war. John Charteris's biography gives a nuanced account. Charteris states that Haig had previously devised 'certain fundamental questions, and on their answers he believed the final decision must be based'. (That Haig needed to ask his perceptive questions at the meeting bears testimony to the muddle and confusion among the British politico-military elite: he helped to focus the debate.) Haig spoke of the need to mobilise the resources of the Empire and realised that the destruction of the BEF would gravely hinder this process; but he recognised the importance to

1 Williamson, *Politics of Grand Strategy*, p. 364; A. Duff Cooper, *Haig* (London: Faber, 1935), I, p. 129.
2 Field Marshal Viscount French of Ypres, *1914* (London: Constable, 1919), p. 6.
3 LHCMA: 13/49, Haig to Hamilton, 5 September 1919. Hamilton declined to support Haig.
4 Sir C. E. Callwell, *Field Marshal Sir Henry Wilson: His Life and Diaries* (London: Cassell, 1927), I, pp. 157–8.
5 TNA: PRO CAB 42/1/2: 'Secretary's Notes of a War Council' (5 August 1914); W. J. Philpott, *Anglo-French Relations and Strategy on the Western Front, 1914–18* (Macmillan: Basingstoke, 1996), p. 9.
6 Ts diary, 5 August 1914.

French morale of the arrival of a British force. Haig '*eventually*' (editors' emphasis) concluded that the realities of coalition warfare necessitated the dispatch of the BEF, and conformity to the plans of French High Command. This version seems plausible.[1] Charteris was Haig's confidant, and it is broadly consistent with the notes of the meeting provided by the Cabinet Secretary, Maurice Hankey, that make clear that Haig had qualified his views by referring to the importance of acting in accordance with the wishes of the French, something that Sir John French ignored in his memoirs.[2] It seems that Haig finally made up his mind as a result of the debate at the war council. Finally, there is the intriguing possibility that the confusion was due to Haig's notorious inarticulateness. Haig may have been convinced in his own mind that he had put forward clear recommendations, but perhaps the other members of the war council came away confused as to his precise views.

The entries from 29 July to 13 August 1914 survive in the typescript but not in the manuscript diary; there are, however, some brief and non-reflective entries in his pre-war diary. Gerard J. De Groot has asserted that Haig added the diary passages critical of Sir John French after the war, although he offers no convincing evidence in support of such a late date (or his statement that 'Haig's enmity towards French' was the cause of the supposed 'rewrit[ing]').[3] He suggests that Haig did so in order to justify his manoeuvrings against French in 1915. There is no evidence for the idea that the diary was *re*written. Most likely Haig simply did not keep a full diary for this period. If he did keep a diary at this time and later rewrote it and subsequently destroyed the original, one is left with the question, why? Haig's usual practice with the typescript diary was to expand upon, or occasionally alter, the manuscript, but not to destroy the original.

While the surviving typescript is clearly post-war, it is plausible that Lady Haig originally typed the entries for 29 July to 13 August 1914 from notes or from Haig's dictation, during the war, perhaps at the end of 1914; we simply do not know. We know that she did copy at least some parts of the diary while the war was in progress, although, as noted above, these have now been lost. Moreover, it is entirely possible that the typescript diary entries for 29 July to 13 August 1914 were not intended to deceive. Contrary to Haig's usual practice, several days are run together in a single entry to produce a narrative that has a retrospective 'feel', very different from later diary entries. One's interpretation of this matter depends on one's view of what Haig understood a 'diary' to be, and his motives in providing an expanded and sometimes

1 John Charteris, *Field Marshal Earl Haig* (London: Cassell, 1929), pp. 79–80.
2 Hankey did not agree that Haig had recommended the dispatch of the BEF, however. TNA PRO: WO 256, Hankey to Haig, 25 July 1919; De Groot, *Douglas Haig*, pp. 148–9.
3 De Groot, *Douglas Haig*, pp. 148, 151.

rewritten typescript version, while retaining the original manuscript as a potential 'smoking gun'.

The second example is perhaps more serious. It concerns Haig's account of the important meeting in the *mairie* at Doullens on 26 March 1918. For the bulk of the First World War, the Allied armies operated without the benefit of unity of command. The German Spring Offensive which opened on 21 March 1918 precipitated one of the gravest crises of Haig's career, leading to General Ferdinand Foch being appointed Supreme Allied Commander, or 'Generalissimo'. Haig claimed much of the credit for Foch's appointment. Fearing that Pétain was planning to retreat to the southwest to cover Paris – thus breaking contact with the BEF – Haig was instrumental in bringing about the Doullens conference. According to his typescript diary, Haig also proposed at the meeting that Foch should have wider powers as Generalissimo than Clemenceau had originally suggested.

There is little doubt that Foch's appointment was an extremely significant step, which made a material contribution to the Allied victory in 1918. However, recent work has cast doubt on the veracity of Haig's claims. No record survives of a telegram that Haig claimed be caused to be sent to London in the early hours of 25 March, summoning the CIGS and Lord Milner to France. There are also discrepancies in the written records that make it impossible to confirm Haig's claims about his activities at the Doullens conference. Haig influenced the official British record of the conference, which was used by Edmonds in the Official History, and defended his views after the war.[1]

There *are* striking differences between the manuscript and typewritten versions of Haig's diary, with the latter adding a good deal of material, much of it anti-Pétain, to the bare bones of the former. Elizabeth Greenhalgh dismisses the idea of a conspiracy, arguing that the two diary versions 'do not contradict each other on the whole ... The later additions and emendations are expansions.' As she suggests, there is evidence that by 21 April Haig truly believed the version that he had set down in the typescript diary.[2] To interpret Haig's motivations in expanding his diary is to enter the world of psycho-history. Some suggestions include Haig's sense of being used by God to bring about victory; and that his sense of pride meant that he had to adjust psychologically to the appointment of a Supreme Commander who could only be French. More prosaically, Haig may have feared that his job was in

---

1 Elizabeth Greenhalgh, 'Myth and Memory: Sir Douglas Haig and the Imposition of Unified Command in March 1918', *Journal of Military History*, 68 (July 2004), p. 814. See also Haig's correspondence with Pétain and Lawrence on this matter in 1920, in Acc. 3155, No. 216h, 228a), Haig papers, NLS and Acc. 3678, No. 7, Lawrence papers, NLS.
2 Greenhalgh, 'Myth and Memory', p. 817. See also H. Høiback, *Command and Control in Military Crisis: Devious Decisions* (London: Frank Cass, 2003), p. 56.

jeopardy. More prosaically still, one may surmise that Haig was tired and stressed, and let off steam in his diary, apportioning blame and giving himself the credit he believed he deserved.[1]

In reality, Pétain was not slow to support the BEF immediately following the German attack of 21 March, as Haig himself recognised in his diary entry for 23 March. Moreover, Pétain does not seem to have contemplated carrying out the sort of withdrawal that Haig feared. Haig, misled by German deception operations, miscalculated the weight and axes of the attack of 21 March. For the first two days of the battle, Haig was optimistic about the outcome, but on 23 March he realised the seriousness of the situation. Optimism was replaced by deep concern; one historian has gone so far as to describe a feeling of 'panic' at GHQ.[2] There is certainly some evidence that Haig was contemplating falling back on the Channel ports.[3] However, one of the key pieces of evidence, Haig's letter of 25 March sent via Weygand, is somewhat ambiguous. It asks for 'at least' twenty French divisions 'to operate on the flank of the German movement against the English Army which must fight its way slowly back covering the Channel Ports'.[4] Rather than meaning that Haig intended *heading for* the coast, it can be seen as an intention not to lose contact with it during the retirement. Elizabeth Greenhalgh makes the plausible suggestion that Haig and his Chief of Staff Lawrence simply misunderstood Pétain at their meeting on 24 March, and on the long drive back to their HQ 'convinced each other that Pétain was indeed intending "to abandon [Haig's] right flank"'.[5]

The overall authenticity of Haig's diary is, however, not in doubt. The diary does not construct (or reconstruct) the war according to an agenda designed to make Haig look good. If such an agenda existed it was surely laid down in his Final Despatch of 21 March 1919.[6] In this he argued that his strategy, which he characterised as 'ceaseless attrition', had been based on the fundamental principles of war. He emphasised that the 'stupendous and incessant struggle' on the Western Front could only be properly understood if considered as one long and continuous engagement involving four stages: the manoeuvre for position; the preparation or wearing-out battle; the decisive attack; and the final exploitation (a formula he had learned at Staff College). The diary does not conform to the superb clarity of this retrospective analysis.

1 Greenhalgh, 'Myth and Memory', pp. 817–18; Høiback, *Command and Control*, pp. 54–5.
2 Tim Travers, *How the War Was Won: Command and Technology in the British Army on the Western Front 1917–1918* (London: Routledge, 1992), p. 54.
3 Travers, *How the War Was Won*, pp. 66–70.
4 TNA: PRO WO 256. Haig to Weygand, 25 March 1918.
5 The idea of a basic misunderstanding is supported by the evidence of a French officer, Pierre Malleterre; see Greenhalgh, 'Myth and Memory', p. 793.
6 See below, Appendix Four.

The war, as seen by Haig from day to day, was a much more messy and uncertain business in which his own judgement, especially the confusion between the 'wearing-out' and the 'decisive battle', can often be brought into question according to his own account. If the diary was a post-war fabrication, written to a 'script', it would permit only one interpretation of Haig's actions. It does not do this. Haig's own words have often been used against him, not least by those – such as Denis Winter – who have most questioned the diary's authenticity and the author's motives in writing it. Read it and decide for yourself.

THE MAN

There is a sense in which Haig's private character is irrelevant to a consideration of his public conduct. 'We need no more books devoted exclusively to Sir Douglas Haig,' declared Robin Prior and Trevor Wilson in their devastating review of Denis Winter's *Haig's Command,* 'and least of all to trivialities such as his spitefulness or noble character, his callousness or grim forbearance, his sexual deviance or marital uprightness.'[1] There *is* no necessary connection between private virtue or vice and public success or failure. But few people in British public life in the twentieth century have had their private character, as well as their professional competence, more thoroughly denigrated than Haig. It is therefore important to consider some of the accusations made against him and what light the diary throws upon them.

Douglas Haig was born on 19 June 1861 at 24 Charlotte Square, Edinburgh. He was the youngest of the eleven children, nine of whom survived, of John Haig, a wealthy whisky distiller, and his wife Rachel Veitch. Haig was close to his mother, who died when he was eighteen, a bitter blow resulting in considerable emotional turmoil. His character gained in resolution after his mother's death, especially in the matter of religion. His father's death, a year earlier, while Haig was a schoolboy at Clifton College, left him with a comfortable private fortune that enabled him to go up to Brasenose College, Oxford, where he enjoyed a full social life but did not take his degree.[2] It was at Oxford that he decided on a military career. He entered the Royal Military College, Sandhurst, in February 1884. He was commissioned in the 7th Hussars in February 1885. The first part of his military career was confined to

1 Robin Prior and Trevor Wilson, 'Review of Denis Winter, *Haig's Command: A Reassessment'*, *Australian War Memorial Journal,* 23 (October 1993), p. 57. Prior and Wilson thoroughly demolish Winter's thesis.
2 Most of John Haig's fortune went to his elder sons who were junior partners in his business. The younger sons were granted reasonable settlements, but were not to have major sums unless they, too, entered the business.

regimental soldiering, but Haig's seriousness of professional purpose was always apparent. He confirmed this by seeking entrance to the Staff College in 1893. Graduation from Staff College was not, at this time, considered essential to professional success. Even so, Haig's failure to obtain entry was mortifying; when he did get in, three years later, it was on the nomination of the Duke of Cambridge, Commander-in-Chief of the British Army. After passing Staff College, Haig's career took its distinctive staff path that led him, by 1914, close to the summit of the British Army.[1] In 1905, while on leave from India, Haig met the Hon. Dorothy Vivian ('Doris'), twin second daughter of the 3rd Lord Vivian and Maid of Honour to Queen Alexandra. They married in the private chapel at Buckingham Palace after a whirlwind courtship, spent principally on the golf course. Haig was forty-four, Miss Vivian was twenty-six.

This bare outline of Haig's biography nevertheless contains most of the material for the charges made against his character. Perhaps the most important of these, and one of the most pervasive, is that he was stupid. His failure to take his degree, his failure to get into Staff College through the examination route, his apparent reliance on royal favour and deliberate cultivation of it through entering into an alleged marriage of convenience are often presented as evidence of Haig's stupidity.

It was unusual for pre-war Army officers to go to university (indeed, only relatively recently has it become the norm). Haig had, in fact, passed his examinations, but having missed a term at Oxford owing to illness he did not have sufficient 'residence' to entitle him to the degree. There were no career advantages in having a degree and considerable career disadvantages in delaying entry into the Army for three years. He decided that the Army could not wait. It is significant, however, that Haig chose to go to Sandhurst and not to pursue the back-door route into the Army through the militia, one that was not uncommon among university men. This was the route taken by the 'clever' Henry Wilson (who failed Sandhurst twice and Woolwich three times)! Haig was determined from the outset to pursue his career with professional seriousness. This meant undertaking a proper military training. He performed brilliantly at Sandhurst, passing out first and winning the Anson Memorial Sword. Haig was already identified by some as a future 'star'. Haig's failure to enter Staff College in 1893 was caused by a narrow failure in the mathematics paper.[2] But again, once he arrived in the institution, he excelled. The papers Haig wrote during the two-year Staff College course,

---

1 Haig's pre-war military career is further discussed below.
2 See John Hussey, ' "A Very Substantial Grievance", said the Secretary of State: Douglas Haig's Examination Troubles, 1893', *Journal of the Society for Army Historical Research*, 74 (299) (1996), pp. 169–80.

together with the instructors' comments in the margin, are preserved in the National Library of Scotland. They show a remarkable grasp of the subjects set, including a scheme for a Sudan expedition.

Haig was welcomed in royal circles, especially those of Edward VII, from early in his career. (His favourite sister, Henrietta Jameson, was a friend of the Prince of Wales.) He first stayed at Sandringham in 1898 and he became Edward's ADC in 1902. It is not immediately obvious why he should need to marry Miss Vivian in order to achieve 'royal favour'. If he did not have 'royal favour' already he would not have received the invitation to the Windsor Castle party at which he met his wife. The age gap between Haig and Doris was not unusual among the middle classes in general and Army officers in particular. Haig's father was nineteen years older than his mother. Among Haig's contemporaries, Charles Monro was fifty-two when he got married, Horace Smith-Dorrien was forty-six, Julian Byng was forty and Henry Horne was thirty-six. (Hubert Gough, precocious in all things, was only twenty-eight.) These marriages were invariably solid, loving and supportive. This was clearly so in Haig's case. Evidence for the 'instrumentality' of his marriage is very thin. It depends principally on Haig's reply to a friend who had commented on the speed with which he had become engaged and married: 'Why not: I have often made up my mind on more important problems than that of my own marriage in much less time.' This looks suspiciously like Haig's idea of a joke. The evidence of the diary and of Haig's letters to his wife show clearly that the marriage was a passionate one, which brought each of them constant love and support, of vital importance to him during the war. He showed great concern over his wife's welfare and comfort. He trusted her completely. He spent as much time as possible with her when he was on leave during the war. She usually drove him around to meetings when he was in London and they enjoyed playing golf. They had four children, on whom Haig doted, as men who marry late in life often do. Throughout his career Haig took demanding and difficult jobs that required long hours and intense effort. It is difficult to equate these actions with a man who thought that 'patronage' was enough. Haig was a meritocrat who admired professional merit in others and sought to advance it when he had the power to do so.

A second charge against Haig is that he saw himself as God's chosen instrument, that this sense of destiny fuelled a selfish ambition, reinforced the alleged 'rigidity' of his tactics, his 'mindless' determination to attack at all times, and made him careless of casualties. The religiosity that Haig got from his mother never left him after his late teens. Religious studies were his best subject at school. Under his mother's influence he developed the habit of prayer, a sense of 'divine oversight' and an easy familiarity with scripture. Because of the diary, in which Haig often comments on the sermons preached at GHQ during the war, and the subsequent memoir of Haig's favourite wartime preacher, the Rev. George Duncan, we know a lot about Haig's religion.[1] Because of this knowledge there is a tendency to regard Haig's religious views as unusual. They were, in fact, entirely typical of his Army generation. Religion has, to a remarkable extent, been airbrushed out of Army history and of the history of the war. Strong religious faith was common among senior military commanders, including Byng, Hubert Gough, Grierson, Horne, Plumer and Rawlinson.[2] Cavan underwent something of a religious renewal at a prayer meeting in Talbot House, Poperinghe, before taking command of XIV Corps in January 1916. All these men believed that religion was an important source of personal and Army morale, took an intimate interest in Army chaplaincy and supported the Church of England's National Mission. Haig's favourite chaplain, Duncan, was not a firebrand Old Testament preacher, but a sophisticated liberal academic theologian, trained – ironically – in the German tradition. Duncan himself was quite categorical that Haig was not a 'religious fanatic'. While recognising that Haig felt himself to be an instrument of providence, Duncan commented that Haig's conviction was held 'in all humility, not out of egotism or wishful thinking, but with a sober grasp of the situation as he saw it'. Duncan also rejected the view that 'spiritual conceit' had clouded Haig's military judgement:

> With some men, no doubt, belief in a divine 'call' leads easily to fanaticism. But Haig was no fanatic. There was about him a mental balance which was associated not a little with his stern sense of duty; and like other devout men down the ages he heard in the call of duty the voice of God. He takes his place with those heroic figures (like Moses and Joshua in the Scripture records, or like Cromwell and Lincoln in the story of the nations) who in some critical hour of history begin by recognising the need for action in the situation which confronts them, and then, in a spirit of obedience and faith in God, find themselves braced to meet it with courage and resolution, and in so doing draw strength from unseen sources.[3]

What does the diary reveal about Haig as a man? The first and most obvious thing is Haig's interest in people. The diary has a cast of thousands. Haig was

1 G. S. Duncan, *Douglas Haig as I Knew Him* (London: Allen & Unwin, 1966). See also Nigel Cave, 'Haig and Religion', in Brian Bond and Nigel Cave (eds), *Haig. A Reappraisal 70 Years On* (Barnsley: Leo Cooper Pen & Sword, 1999), pp. 240–59.
2 To this list should be added Second World War commanders such as Bernard Montgomery and Orde Wingate.
3 Duncan, *Haig*, p. 126. The editors would like to thank Dr Michael Snape for bringing this passage to their attention and for his general advice on religion in this period. Dr Snape's important book, *God and the British Soldier: Religion and the British Army in Two World Wars* will be published by Routledge in May 2005.

particular about recording the names of people he met and often provided some comment on them. It is difficult to see what advantage he derived from doing this. Haig's critical comments have attracted most attention, but he could deal in praise, too. His contact with people came principally during what Denis Winter has dismissed as Haig's 'innumerable' visits to subordinate formations. Haig's diary entry for 3 August 1915 is typical and instructive:

> On the way to Neuf Berquin I looked round the 24th Field Ambulance of the 8th Division at Doulieu. The Medical Officer in charge is a highly skilled lady's doctor from Exeter, and the personnel are all Territorials. The Ambulance was raised at Exeter. It has done excellent service. I thought their arrangements quite good. The officer in charge complained of the unnecessary number of returns which have to be sent in. His Sergeant Major is a Commercial Traveller; a number of the others were in the Post Office; one, in the operating tent, was an Assistant Manager of Timothy White's Chemist Stores . . .

Imagine the scene. General Haig enters the operating tent. Does the former assistant manager of Timothy White's rush up to him and say, 'Hello, General, my name is Snooks, I used to manage a chemist's shop before the war'? This is doubtful. Haig obtained the information because he was curious enough to ask the question and interested enough to record the information.[1] Haig often commented, and with increasing admiration, on the important work being done by 'civilians' in his Army, and took pride in drawing attention to this in his Final Despatch.[2] He remembered people, too. On 10 August 1917 Haig recorded a visit to the Base Depot at Le Havre:

> I spent about half an hour going round his office and talking to his assistants. I then visited the Convalescent Camp . . . on the ridge above the town. Much excellent work has and is done here. I saw several officers and others whose acquaintance I made on my visit last year. I noticed the Sergeant Major who had kidney trouble, but who is now fit and strong and has done magnificent work.

As we shall see, there is much evidence, too, that both during and after the war, Haig was concerned for the welfare of his soldiers when they returned to civilian life.

---

1 For an interesting comment on Haig's 'method' when visiting units, see J. Jellen, 'A Clerk in the First World War', *Journal of the Royal United Services Institution*, 105 (1960), pp. 361–9.
2 See also Haig's comments during a visit to the Machine Gun School at Camiers, Diary, 4 February 1918.

The second private virtue that emerges from Haig's diary is his courtesy. Robert Blake also commented on this. Part of Haig's job as Commander-in-Chief was to entertain visitors. These came in all shapes and sizes to visit GHQ: politicians, labour leaders, foreign dignitaries, journalists, newspaper barons, writers and painters as well as soldiers. He arranged a vegetarian breakfast for George Bernard Shaw, talked painting with Sir William Orpen and John Singer Sargent,[1] and watched – impressed – as Asquith demolished prodigious quantities of brandy. And all this from a man supposedly without culture, indeed without interests at all beyond merely military matters. Nor was Haig's charm deployed only on the great and the good. He was an excellent man to work for, demanding but appreciative. For this reason, his reproaches – when delivered – were accordingly stinging.

These insights into Haig's character must be set against those examples of lack of generosity towards others, touchiness, prickly pride and vanity. Such characteristics invariably surfaced when he was under extreme stress in his relations with politicians, especially Lloyd George, and with his French allies. Haig does not appear to his best advantage in his comments on the French. The publication of Blake's edition of the Haig diaries in 1952 caused great annoyance in France. This new edition will do little to smooth Gallic sensibilities. Haig often disparages French politicians, French generals, the French soldier and the French nation.[2] Diaries are often thought to be truthful because they record the moment – in private – uninhibited by social convention and unfiltered through later reflection. With Haig it is necessary to look at what he did as well as what he said. Haig's actions with regard to the French belie his words. He was essentially a loyal and co-operative ally, who recognised that such co-operation was fundamental if victory was to be achieved. It should also be remembered that the crass national stereotyping of the French by Haig and others was entirely reciprocated.[3] When it came to writing his Final Despatch, however, Haig paid handsome tribute to the 'gallant Army of France' and to the 'excessive burden' that it bore during the early years of the war. Less forgivable or understandable is the lack of generosity Haig showed in some of his comments about colleagues who were trying their hardest to help him, especially Lord Derby and Sir William Robertson.

1 According to Denis Winter, Haig actually watched Sargent paint *Gassed* and 'surprisingly' approved of the painting. It is only surprising if you hold the views of Haig that Mr Winter does.
2 It should be stressed that views of this kind were widely shared by the troops under Haig's command, among whom there grew a legend that the French charged rent for use of the trenches.
3 See, for example, General Huguet's *Britain and the War: An Indictment* (London: Cassell, 1928), which accuses the British of being animated principally by 'egoism'.

THE EDUCATED SOLDIER

Although Haig has borne the brunt of criticism among British commanders of the Great War, there is a sense in which his name is merely used by some critics as shorthand for a wider denunciation of the officer corps as a class. If Haig and his contemporaries were narrow and limited in their professional vision, it was because they were the typical products of a narrow and limiting institution, disproportionately recruited from an aristocratic class that was increasingly out of touch with the realities of modern, urban, industrialised civilisation, and for whom war was little more than fox-hunting carried on by other means. Tim Travers has been especially severe on the culture of the pre-war Army, portraying it as a professionally somnolent organisation, riven with petty jealousies and faction fighting.[1] This portrait is difficult to reconcile with what actually happened to the British Army between the end of the South African War and the outbreak of the Great War.

Nothing focuses the mind like embarrassment. The Army's difficulties in subduing a relative handful of Boer farmers had made the British Empire the laughing stock of the world. Something had to be done. There were significant changes at every level, from foreign policy downwards. Military reform was driven by the Elgin Commission and the Esher Committee, whose recommendations – accepted by the Cabinet – included the establishment of an Army Council, a general staff, reform of the Committee of Imperial Defence (founded by the Prime Minister, A. J. Balfour, in 1902), abolition of the office of Commander-in-Chief and promotion by selection board above the rank of captain. The Army's weapons and equipment were thoroughly overhauled and so was its training and fieldcraft. Military 'good practice' was codified in *Field Service Regulations, Parts I and II* (1909). A series of outstanding commandants – Henry Rawlinson, Henry Wilson and William Robertson – gave the Staff College a renewed sense of direction. The post-1905 Liberal governments addressed the politically sensitive issue of Britain's reserve forces. R. B. Haldane, the lawyer-philosopher who was Secretary of State for War from 1905 to 1912, established the Territorial Force and the British Expeditionary Force. Henry Wilson, Director of Military Operations at the War Office, and Adrian Grant-Duff, Secretary of the Committee of Imperial Defence, put in place the practical arrangements for the deployment of the BEF and for the establishment of the British state on a war footing. These were no mean achievements.

Douglas Haig was at the heart of the reforms. In his memoirs, Lloyd George declared that Haig's reputation was 'founded on his cavalry exploits'.[2]

1 Tim Travers, *The Killing Ground: The British Army, the Western Front and the Emergence of Modern Warfare, 1900–1918* (London: Allen & Unwin, 1987), *passim*.
2 David Lloyd George, *War Memoirs of David Lloyd George* (Watford: Odhams [nd]), I, p. 76.

This was not a compliment but shorthand for 'out-of-touch soldier from a technophobic military arm dominated by stupid aristocrats'. Haig was certainly at the forefront of modern thinking about the cavalry and he retained throughout the war, and beyond, a belief in the cavalry's utility and importance that was belied by the evolution of his army on the Western Front.[1] But in making such a statement, Lloyd George was not only prejudiced but also wrong. Haig was essentially, and self-consciously, a trained modern staff officer. As Director of Military Training (1906–7) and Director of Staff Duties (1907–9) at the War Office, he was responsible for establishing the Imperial General Staff and for drafting the British Army's first ever field service regulations. He worked closely with Haldane on the establishment of the Territorial Force. Haldane developed a high regard for Haig that he never surrendered. If to this is added Haig's experience in the Sudan and in the South African War, where he was Sir John French's Chief of Staff and in which he commanded a mobile column, his tour as Inspector General of Cavalry, India (1903–6), where his arrival had an electric effect, his period as Chief of Staff, India (1909–11), in which he laid the groundwork for an Indian Expeditionary Force, his extensive reading in military history, his deep knowledge of contemporary German military theory and his competence in foreign languages,[2] there were few men more ready to go to war in 1914.[3]

THE WESTERN FRONT, 1914–15

Haig entered the First World War with a very clear understanding of the gravity of the situation. He had long been convinced that war with Germany was inevitable, and paid close attention to the unfolding of events in the Balkans that followed the assassination of Archduke Franz Ferdinand in June 1914. Duff Cooper wrote that he greeted the news of a general European war

1 The cavalry constituted less than three per cent of the BEF's strength by September 1916: see J. M. Bourne, 'Haig and the Historians', in Bond and Cave (eds), *Haig: A Reappraisal,* pp. 4–5. See, also, Stephen Badsey, 'Bullets versus Horses? Douglas Haig, the Boer War, and the Development of Rifle-Armed Cavalry 1880–1914', *Osprey Military Journal,* 3 (2) (2001), pp. 41–9, and Lieutenant Colonel A. Echevarria, 'Combining Firepower and Versatility: Remaking the "Arm of Decision" before the Great War', *Royal United Services Institute Journal* (June 2002), pp. 84–91. Haig's diary entry for 11 April 1915, in which he records a discussion about the use of cavalry in the war, and especially his post-war gloss, is instructive. David Kenyon's forthcoming PhD makes a compelling case for the continued utility of cavalry.
2 Haig had passable German and good French. As Dr Stephen Badsey has amusingly remarked, 'Haig was at least as fluent in French as he was in English', a view confirmed by Haig's press officer the Hon. Neville Lytton in *Press and the General Staff* (Collins, 1920), p. 66.
3 For a contrary view, see Gerard J. De Groot, 'Educated Soldier or Cavalry Officer? Contradictions in the Pre-1914 Career of Douglas Haig', *War and Society,* 4 (2) (1986), pp. 51–69.

with no 'emotions save those of awe and dread'.[1] Charteris, who served on
Haig's staff, noted that Haig, 'although he gave no perceptible sign ... was a
prey to grave anxiety'.[2] He had no illusions about the strength of the enemy,
and unlike many other British senior officers and politicians, Haig anticipated
a long war. He knew 'how tremendous were the issues which were at stake',[3]
and was very properly conscious of the weight of responsibility that rested on
his shoulders. This is part of the heavy burden of High Command. It is
impossible to understand Haig's actions during the Mons campaign without
recognising that he was acutely aware that his decisions could determine the
fate not only of fifty per cent of the BEF, but possibly the security of his
country and even the outcome of the war.

Haig's opinion of three of the key players at GHQ further increased his
anxiety. He admired Field Marshal Sir John French's courage, but was convinced that French was not the right man to be Commander-in-Chief of the
BEF. Moreover, Haig feared that French's Chief of Staff, Major General Sir
Archibald Murray, would be too weak to stand up to the C-in-C; and he
thoroughly mistrusted the Francophile, intellectually able but scheming Sub-
Chief of the General Staff, Major General Henry Wilson.[4] On all three
accounts, Haig's assessment was correct. Historians have judged French as
brave but over-promoted.[5] Murray, who was in poor health, suffered a physical
collapse during the Mons campaign, and his performance in the crucial role
of Chief of Staff was indifferent. In any case, Murray's position verged on the
impossible. French had originally wanted his friend Wilson for this position,
Murray's immediate subordinates were Wilson men, and Wilson himself
subverted Murray's authority. Haig's suspicion of Wilson's judgement was
borne out by some aspects of the Sub-Chief's performance on the Retreat
from Mons.[6] This low opinion of the highest echelons of GHQ undoubtedly
influenced Haig's decision-making during the critical moments of the Mons
campaign.

Three of Haig's decisions in August 1914 can fairly be queried. The first is
the lack of support given by I Corps to Smith-Dorrien's II Corps during the
defensive Battle of Mons on 23 August. On this day, II Corps fought the

1 Duff Cooper, *Haig*, I, p. 127.
2 Charteris, *Field Marshal Earl Haig*, p. 82.
3 Duff Cooper, *Haig*, I, p. 127.
4 See Charteris's diary entry for 16 August 1914: John Charteris, *At GHQ* (London: Cassell,
1931), pp. 10–11.
5 Brian Bond, *The Victorian Army and the Staff College 1845–1914* (London: Eyre Methuen,
1972), p. 313; Richard Holmes, *The Little Field-Marshal: Sir John French* (London: Cape, 1981),
p. 367; George Cassar, *The Tragedy of Sir John French* (London: Associated University Presses,
1985), p. 292.
6 Bond, *Victorian Army*, pp. 310, 313–15; Gardner, *Trial by Fire*, p. 40.

BEF's first major action, a day when I Corps sustained a mere forty casualties. Two of Haig's earliest biographers stress that he was 'gravely concerned' that GHQ had paid insufficient attention to intelligence reports that the Germans were attempting to outflank the BEF. Haig was well-versed in German military doctrine, and knew the stress they laid on encirclement of the enemy. In historian Michael Orr's words, Haig was thinking like a modern, staff-trained officer. The absence of a major attack on I Corps, in the words of Charteris, an eyewitness, 'increased rather than diminished his anxiety'. If indeed the Germans were attempting to envelop the BEF, 'they would not attack the inner flank in force'. Haig turned down Smith-Dorrien's request for substantial support, although he eventually responded to a personal request by dispatching three battalions that did not, despite the optimistic entreaties of II Corps' Chief of Staff, result in the battle being won.

The news that arrived in the early hours of 24 August, that the French Fifth Army was retreating, forcing the BEF to follow suit, appeared to fulfil Haig's worst fears about the threat of envelopment. He ignored GHQ's instruction to cover Smith-Dorrien's retirement. To do so would have involved 'a flank march in the face of the enemy'[1] with its attendant dangers; there were two hours of darkness left, and he feared that I Corps would be attacked at dawn strung out on the line of march. Instead, Haig formed a rearguard and marched the rest of I Corps south. He firmly believed that the BEF had to avoid battle, to out-march their pursuers in order to give themselves a chance of regrouping and striking back, and to remain in contact with the French. To be forced into fighting a battle while on the retreat was to have failed.

This belief was reinforced by the action at Landrecies on the night of 25 August, when I Corps was involved in a small-scale clash between a German advance guard and one of Haig's brigades. There is no doubt that Haig was 'rattled', and sickness (stomach upset and diarrhoea) contributed to his loss of composure. He became personally involved in the defence of the town, declaring, according to Charteris, 'If we are caught, by God, we'll sell our lives dearly',[2] alarming Sir John French in the process. Landrecies was perhaps a more serious action than it is sometimes portrayed. Certainly, if I Corps HQ had been overrun, it would have been a severe blow to the cohesion of the BEF.

The chaotic fighting at Landrecies seems to have reinforced Haig's belief that to turn and fight while retreating was to court disaster. This undoubtedly coloured Haig's reaction to Smith-Dorrien's decision (which, under

1 Duff Cooper, *Haig*, I, p. 149.
2 John Terraine, *Douglas Haig, The Educated Soldier* (London: Hutchinson, 1963), p. 87; Charteris, *At GHQ*, p. 17.

the circumstances, was undoubtedly correct) to give battle at Le Cateau. I Corps' failure to support Smith-Dorrien resulted in II Corps having an open flank that the Germans proceeded to turn. On 26 August Haig was aware of gunfire from the direction of II Corps. But having ordered his corps to retreat, having for the second time exercised his judgement as the local commander to ignore GHQ's instructions on the route, he chose not to march towards the sound of the guns. The two corps were physically separated by the Forest of Mormal, and in a classic example of the 'fog of war' Haig was forced to make a decision based on fragmentary and incorrect information derived from rudimentary communications. Out of direct contact with II Corps, on 26 August he telegraphed to GHQ twice (the second time to Smith-Dorrien via GHQ) offering help. Haig received a reply to neither message. It seems that, having eluded the Germans on that day,[1] and achieved his primary aim of avoiding disaster to I Corps, Haig believed he was in a position to offer support to Smith-Dorrien. However, the tone of Haig's second telegram, sent at 11 pm – 'we could hear the sound of your battle, but could get no information as to its progress, and could form no idea of how we could assist you' – lends itself to a less charitable interpretation.[2] John Terraine argues that Haig's oft-stated conviction that Smith-Dorrien was wrong to fight at Le Cateau suggests that the I Corps commander 'was conscious of having fallen below his own standards'.[3] Alternatively, Haig simply continued to believe that on 26 August Smith-Dorrien took an unwarranted gamble.

Rather different interpretations have been placed on Haig's actions, in which rivalry and 'professional jealousy' towards Smith-Dorrien has been seen as a factor in his decision-making.[4] This is based in part on a suspect source, consisting of information passed on to Basil Liddell Hart many years after the event. His informant was Sir James Edmonds. Whatever his strengths as British official historian,[5] Edmonds was a fount of gossip that was sometimes unreliable and malicious. Moreover, as far as Haig was concerned, both

---

1 Actually the rearguard of I Corps had been overwhelmed, but Haig did not discover this until the 27th.

2 J. E. Edmonds, *Military Operations France and Belgium, 1914*, vol. 1 [hereafter OH] (Woking: Shearer, 1984), p. 201.

3 Terraine, *Douglas Haig*, pp. 87–8.

4 Gardner, *Trial by Fire*, pp. 14, 48–9. Ian F. W. Beckett, *Johnnie Gough VC* (London, Tom Donovan, 1989) p. 181, also uses Edmonds as a key source. According to Edmonds, there was also a long-standing rivalry between Gough, Haig's Chief of Staff, and George Forestier-Walker, Gough's opposite number at II Corps.

5 For differing views, see David French, ' "Official but not History"? Sir James Edmonds and the Official History of the Great War', *Royal United Services Institute Journal*, 131 (1986), pp. 58–63 and Andrew Green, *Writing the Great War. Sir James Edmonds and the Official Histories 1915–1948* (London: Frank Cass, 2003).

Edmonds and Liddell Hart had axes to grind. This is not to deny that Haig was ambitious, or even that he saw Smith-Dorrien, who was senior to him, as a rival. However, the editors find incredible the notion that Haig, who, as we have seen, was acutely conscious of his responsibility as a commander, would risk the destruction of half of the BEF in pursuit of a personal ambition. Haig's decisions in August 1914 are not above criticism, but they are perfectly explicable without recourse to conspiracy theories. They were decisions taken by a 53-year-old man, short of sleep, undergoing the privations of life on a mobile campaign, groping around in the fog of war, a man above all aware that were he to make a mistake, it could have catastrophic consequences.

The slowness of the BEF's advance to the Aisne has been fairly criticised and Haig cannot escape a share of the blame.[1] On 8 September, French's Operation Order No. 9 directed that 'The Army will continue the advance north tomorrow attacking rear guards of the enemy wherever met'.[2] On the following day, however, after I Corps had crossed the River Marne, Haig received information from aerial reconnaissance of a large German force to his front, and he ordered a halt. Roughly simultaneously, news reached Haig that caused him to suspect (erroneously) that the French had suffered a heavy defeat. Adding these two items of news to Haig's mindset discussed above, it seems that, far from being 'inexplicable',[3] his decision to order a halt was perfectly sensible and understandable. The Official History is also uncomplimentary about the speed of the BEF's advance to the Chemin des Dames ridge on 13 and 14 September. This criticism was sharpened by hindsight; the failure to secure these heights brought about the beginning of trench warfare on this sector, and arguably thwarted Joffre's plan for a decisive victory in open battle. While it is possible to detect some veiled criticism of Haig (as well as some praise), Edmonds principally blames GHQ.[4] It seems clear that given the terrain and the defenders, I Corps would have been hard pushed to advance any faster, and Haig's performance was sound.

Haig's I Corps played a critical role during the First Battle of Ypres, bearing the brunt of two major German attacks, on 31 October and 11 November. On the first occasion the Germans broke through the British defences and Haig undertook a celebrated ride to the front line. A counter-attack by 2nd Battalion Worcestershire Regiment at Gheluvelt, however, restored the situation.

1 B. H. Liddell Hart, *History of the First World War* (London, 1973), pp. 128–9.
2 Reproduced in Edmonds, *OH 1914*, I, p. 555.
3 David Ascoli, *The Mons Star* (London: Harrap, 1981), p. 160.
4 Edmonds, *OH 1914*, I, pp. 416, 65–6. For overt criticism of Haig, see Winter, *Haig's Command*, pp. 35–6.

Sir Douglas Haig emerged from First Ypres as the hero of the hour. 'On the moral side he was a rock,' declared one biographer.[1] Another wrote that although he gave no outward sign of worry, 'his burden of anxiety was heavier than the weariest of his weary men'.[2] Haig's demeanour was habitually imperturbable, but even he at moments of crisis let the mask slip a little. The degree to which he displayed his anxiety is, however, controversial. Edmonds claimed that Haig 'lost his head' on 31 October and drew up 'plans for a general withdrawal'; the orders subsequently being retrieved and destroyed.[3] While Haig certainly ordered a limited retirement, there are many problems with accepting Edmonds' post-war evidence relayed via Liddell Hart. A detailed analysis of the episode by John Hussey effectively rebuts the Edmonds version. Hussey points out that Haig gets the timings of events on 31 October wrong by about an hour – a fact that has interesting implications for the theory that the diaries were fabrications. For instance, Sir John French's visit took place at 2 pm, not at 'about 3 pm' as Haig records, but otherwise, Hussey says, 'the sequence of events is plain'.[4] It is clear that Haig was, not surprisingly, deeply anxious.[5] But he was a long way from panicking. Henry Horne, who was an eyewitness, declared in 1928 that the only sign of anxiety shown by Haig was a constant stroking of his moustache.

Haig's ride to the front on 31 October has also attracted attention. Denis Winter's strange theory that the ride took place in the morning, before the crisis of the battle, and was exaggerated by Haig 'to advance his own career' can be safely dismissed as flying in the face of the available evidence.[6] De Groot argues that Haig's ride took place after the crisis of the battle had passed, apparently as a public relations exercise. Gardner, rather more realistically, points out that the capture of Gheluvelt was but a temporary respite, and Haig sought to try to exert some control over the battle and help rally the troops. Whether or not it was wise for a corps commander to leave his headquarters to carry out the job of a regimental-level officer, disrupting (at least potentially) the command and control within the formation, is another matter.[7] In truth, the number of soldiers who would have seen Haig would have been limited, but in time of crisis, he instinctively behaved according

1 E. K. G. Sixsmith, *Douglas Haig* (London: Weidenfeld & Nicolson, 1976), p. 83. See also Anthony Farrar-Hockley, *Death of an Army* (London: Barker, 1967), p. 18.

2 Sir George Arthur, *Lord Haig* (London: W. Heinemann, 1928), p. 83.

3 Beckett, *Johnnie Gough*, p. 193.

4 John Hussey, 'A Hard Day at First Ypres – The Allied Generals and their Problems: 31 October 1914', *British Army Review*, 107 (August 1994), pp. 75–89.

5 Gardner, *Trial by Fire*, p. 218.

6 Winter, *Haig's Command*, pp. 36–7. See Gardner, *Trial by Fire*, pp. 219–20, and – more especially – John Hussey, 'Haig's Ride at 1st Ypres', *Bulletin of the Military Historical Society* (August 1995), for evidence to the contrary.

7 Gardner, *Trial by Fire*, pp. 219–20. See also Terraine, *Douglas Haig*, pp. 113–14.

to the credo of the late Victorian Army officer, leading by example and demonstrating his courage.

There is an interesting coda to the story of Douglas Haig at First Ypres. Brigadier General FitzClarence played a crucial part in the capture of Ghelu-velt but was killed eleven days later. It was not until August 1915 that Haig came to hear the story of FitzClarence's role, when he was instrumental in having documents, including sworn statements, placed in I Corps' War Diary that gave FitzClarence the credit he richly deserved.[1]

By the end of 1914 the war plans of all the powers were in disarray. The BEF faced a bleak winter in uncomfortable conditions for which it was – as yet – exceedingly ill equipped. Sir Douglas Haig took command of the newly created First Army on Boxing Day 1914 (Smith-Dorrien was given command of Second Army). The Army level of command had not existed before the war and there was no guidebook to follow other than the generalised arrangements advocated in *Field Service Regulations, Part I: Operations*, which Haig had done much to compile. These arrangements favoured what later became known as 'mission tactics'. Higher Command was responsible for choosing the time and place of attack and providing the necessary means for carrying it out, but the method of doing so was best left to the 'man on the spot'. Haig felt instinctively comfortable with these arrangements and operated them with great success in the second half of 1918. But in 1915 they begged many questions. What was to be done if Higher Command did not have the necessary means to carry out attacks? And what if the 'man on the spot' and his ill-trained, poorly equipped (though valorous) troops were not up to the job? Ian Beckett has drawn attention to Haig's repeated violation of his own principle of not interfering with the man on the spot,[2] the explanation for which has often been psychological. In reality, it was not Haig's psyche that was the problem, but the situation in which he found himself for most of 1915, 1916 and part of 1917. One of the themes of Haig's diary from the second half of 1917 onwards is his increasing confidence and pride in his subordinates and his sense of being able to trust them to carry out their jobs. This was not the case in 1915, as his remarkable encounter with the GOC 51st (Highland) Division, Major General Richard Bannatine-Allason, on 20 May, confirms.

The historiography of Haig in 1915 has been dominated by the disagreement with Sir John French over the release of the reserves to First Army during the Battle of Loos. This is unfortunate. It has left the impression that French's

---

1 TNA: PRO WO 95/588. See also FitzClarence's Personal File: PRO WO 138/25.
2 Ian F. W. Beckett, 'Hubert Gough, Neill Malcolm and Command on the Western Front', in Brian Bond, et al., *'Look to Your Front': Studies in the First World War by The Commission for British Military History* (Staplehurst: Spellmount, 1999), pp. 7–8.

removal was brought about principally as the result of a shabby conspiracy by a disloyal and ruthlessly ambitious subordinate, Haig, while disguising more significant underlying reasons for French's replacement and underplaying the role of other 'conspirators', notably Kitchener and Robertson. More seriously, the issue of the reserves has also disguised the underlying differences between French and Haig in the planning and execution of the attack at Loos. The reserves issue can only be fully understood in the context of these differences. The differences were also to resurface in 1916 between Haig, by then Commander-in-Chief, and his principal subordinate, Sir Henry Rawlinson. They get to the heart of the real debate about Haig's generalship.

The British battles of 1915, especially those conducted by First Army, have long been regarded as 'political' offensives fought for no great military reason but because of the compelling demands of the French alliance. There is much truth in this, but it is not the whole truth. Kitchener was the dominant force in the evolution of British strategy in 1915. He was an exceptionally clear-sighted statesman. The war for him was about achieving the long-term safety and security of the British Empire, which he – and virtually all other British statesmen of the period – believed was essential not only to maintain Britain's position in the world but also to maintain social peace and political progress at home. In order to realise this war aim Kitchener believed not only that Germany must be defeated but also that Britain must play a leading role in the defeat in order to be able to dictate the peace. In an ideal world Britain would play that leading role in 1917 when Kitchener's great volunteer armies would be fully trained and equipped and when the German Army would be rendered ripe for defeat by the combined effects of the French and Russian armies. Throughout 1915 Kitchener's strategic optimism contended with his operational pessimism. During a visit to the Western Front early in 1915 he cautioned the BEF's commanders against any thoughts of a breakthrough. This advice would appear to have been strengthened by experience of the spring battles at Neuve Chapelle, Aubers Ridge and Festubert which demonstrated how difficult a breakthrough was to bring about, given the state of the BEF's resources. Nevertheless, Kitchener was also adamant that an outcome to the war satisfactory to British interests could not be achieved if France or Russia was defeated.[1] Britain, and in practice the BEF, would have to collaborate 'to the utmost of its power' to ensure that France and Russia remained in the war. During 1915 French claims on British military support became ever more clamorous and demanding.

1 Kitchener, unlike some subsequent British commentators, was acutely aware that the war in Europe was being fought on more than one front and that the fighting power of Russia was essential to an Allied victory. He was much more concerned about Russia in 1915 than he was about France.

Neither Haig nor French showed any initial enthusiasm for the proposed British attack at Loos. Haig conducted a personal reconnaissance of the Loos battlefield before reporting discouragingly, on 23 June, that the ground was 'not favourable' and had 'very carefully sited' German defences.[1] Sir John French therefore offered to support the French through an 'artillery demonstration' that would pin down German forces on the Loos sector with benefit to the French attacks in Artois and the Champagne. The French response was hostile. Kitchener was compelled to come to France and order Sir John to 'co-operate vigorously' in the plans of the French Commander-in-Chief, General Joffre.[2] On 23 August Sir John ordered Haig to support Joffre's attacks 'to the full extent of your available resources, and not to limit your action in the manner indicated in the above quoted letter [the "artillery" plan]', adding, 'This instruction is not, however, to be taken as preventing you from developing your attack deliberately and progressively, should you be of the opinion that the nature of the enemy's defences makes such a course desirable.'[3] French then effectively abandoned control of the battle. He was very often ill and lethargic. He became the despair of his staff. Sir William Robertson, French's CGS, complained to Henry Wilson that he could not get the C-in-C to 'do anything'. Haig also confided to his wife the difficulties he had in getting hold of French, who was often only contactable by post! Haig was left to plan the Loos attack in what Nick Lloyd has called a 'command vacuum'.[4]

On 6 September Haig explained his views at a First Army conference.[5] The situation of the Russian armies on the Eastern Front required a major offensive on the Western Front. The BEF must support France in this attack to the 'full extent' of its power. It would do so by securing the line Loos–Hulluch, extending to Hill 70 and the Haute Deule Canal. The securing of this line would bring about a considerable victory. Haig stressed that the advance would be rapid and that it would not be enough to 'gain a tactical success. The direction of our advance must be such as will bring us upon the enemy's rear so that we will cut his communications and force him to retreat.'

1 Imperial War Museum (IWM): French Papers, 7/2 (1), Haig to GHQ, 23 June 1915.
2 During a visit to Haig's HQ on 19 August Kitchener reportedly said that 'He had heard, when with the French, that Sir J. French did not mean to co-operate to the utmost of his power when the French attacked in September. He (Lord Kitchener) had noticed that the French were anxiously watching the British on their left and he had decided that we "must act with all our energy, and do our utmost to help the French, even though, by doing so, we suffered very heavy losses indeed".' Haig diary, 19 August 1915.
3 TNA: PRO WO 95/157, GHQ to Haig, 23 August 1915.
4 The editors are most grateful to Mr Lloyd for allowing them to read his unpublished paper 'Sir Douglas Haig, Over-Optimism and the Battle of Loos' and for drawing relevant archival material to their attention.
5 TNA: PRO WO 95/158, *Précis of First Army Conference of Monday, 6 September 1915*.

This represented a considerable change since the pessimistic appreciation of 23 June.

In his Final Despatch Haig said nothing directly about the battles of 1915. His analysis is confined to the 'long succession of battles commenced on the Somme in 1916 and ended in November of last year on the Sambre', but presumably he would have placed the 1915 fighting in the 'wearing-out' period. However, there is no sense of his understanding this at the time of his planning for Loos. It is clear that he anticipated great outcomes from the battle. His letters to Lady Haig are full of confidence. On 15 August he explained that it would not be many months 'before the Germans are reduced to make peace on our terms'.[1] On 24 August he confided his hopes that 'the end may come [for an economically weakened Germany] by the direct result of a victory on this front', adding that he had 'great expectations from our next effort'.[2] On 22 September, three days before the infantry assault, he reaffirmed that he was 'pretty confident of some success' and that by October he hoped the BEF 'may be a good distance on the road to Brussels'.[3]

Haig's army was short of guns, high explosive and trained officers and men. It was about to attack over difficult ground, faced by a resolute enemy in formidable defensive positions. Why was Haig so confident? The answer appears to be 'gas'. He had been impressed by an initial demonstration of cylinder-released chlorine gas at Helfaut on 22 August. From then on his diary faithfully records his increasing interest in the work of Foulkes's engineers, his familiarity with the personnel involved, his appreciation of their efforts (which were, indeed, remarkably impressive), his increasing reliance on their success and his worries about the weather. He made it clear in his diary on 16 September that gas was vital to the prospect of 'decisive results', adding that 'On the other hand, without gas, the fronts of attack must be restricted, with the result of concentrated hostile fire on the attacking troops. Considerable loss and small progress! In my opinion the attack ought not to be launched except with the aid of gas!' On the same day Haig assured Sir William Robertson that 'with the *very extensive* gas and smoke arrangements which have been prepared, decisive results are almost certain to be obtained'.[4]

Decisive results, however, eluded First Army, despite an encouraging opening to the battle. It was at this point that the issue of the release of the reserves, and the unfortunate fate of the Reserve Divisions when they were eventually committed to the battle, surfaced.[5] It was important to Haig that

1 Haig to Lady Haig, 15 August 1915.
2 Haig to Lady Haig, 24 August 1915.
3 Haig to Lady Haig, 22 September 1915.
4 TNA: PRO WO 95/158, Haig to Robertson, 16 September 1915. Haig's emphasis.
5 For a thorough discussion of this episode, including other important issues not examined here,

the reserves (XI Corps) should be deployed close behind First Army's front, so that he could throw them speedily into the battle to exploit the break-through he was intending. He continually pressed French to allow this. French's refusal has usually been attributed to his unwillingness to yield authority to a subordinate commander. Nick Lloyd has, however, offered another explanation; the differing understanding of the battle by the two men. French was anticipating a more methodical offensive, in which there would be ample time to deploy the reserves when they were needed. This misunderstanding was French's fault, the outcome of his inaction and lethargy in the weeks preceding the attack. Haig's disappointment at French's actions was deepened by the early, optimistic reports of the attack on 25 September. He genuinely felt that his C-in-C had denied him the opportunity to win a significant victory.

THE COMMANDER-IN-CHIEF

Douglas Haig took command of the British Expeditionary Force at noon on 19 December 1915. He was fifty-four years old. He remained in command until April 1919, leading the BEF through the most sanguinary battles in British history: the Somme, Arras, Third Ypres ('Passchendaele'), the German Spring Offensive and the Hundred Days. Shortly after taking command Haig was given his instructions by Lord Kitchener.[1]

These instructions clearly established Haig's task. Few men have been more 'task oriented' than Haig. His determination to carry out his orders is the essential clue to his character and conduct for the remainder of the war. He viewed people and events in accordance with whether he thought they were helping or hindering him in his task. There is a marked softening in the comments in Haig's diary about other actors in the drama in 1918, when for virtually the first time everyone, in Haig's estimation, was pulling in the same direction.

Did Haig know what to do? At the strategic level, the answer is clearly 'yes'. Haig's analysis was incisive and unchanging. In order to carry out his task the military defeat of Germany was essential. Germany could not be defeated militarily except in conjunction with the French and Russian armies. Despite his denigration of the French, Haig understood this as one of the war's realities. And so, of course, did Kitchener, whose instructions to Haig were significantly different from those he gave to Sir John French, not least

see P. Bryant, 'The Recall of Sir John French', published in three parts in *Stand To!*, 22, 23, and 24 (1988).
1 See below, Appendix Two.

in the stress he placed on inter-Allied co-operation.[1] The German Army could only be defeated where its main forces were located and this was on the Western Front. In order to bring about this defeat every man and gun should be concentrated in the 'decisive theatre'. Despite Kitchener's pledge that Haig would receive the 'whole-hearted and unswerving support of the Government', in this matter Haig and his chief ally, Sir William Robertson (CIGS), found it difficult to prevail. There were actually more British troops stationed at home than there were deployed on the Western Front until the spring of 1917. And throughout that year Great Britain's new Prime Minister made it apparent that he did not support the 'Western' strategy, which he did his best to undermine. Haig's difficulties with Lloyd George did not represent a fundamental split between civilians and soldiers in the conduct of the war. Most senior political figures supported the 'Western' strategy. And so did the governments of Britain's allies. The real division over strategy was not between soldiers and statesmen or between 'Easterners' and 'Westerners' but between those who were prepared to adopt a 'win at all costs' strategy and those who were not.[2] Ironically, Lloyd George owed his rise to power to the dissatisfaction with Asquith's government of those who were prepared to 'win at all costs'. At home, Lloyd George showed a ready appetite for slaughtering sacred political, economic and cultural cows; but on the battlefield he balked at the human costs of 'attrition'. Like nearly all other leading wartime statesmen he also balked at the obvious alternative to 'attrition', peace through negotiations.

At the operational level, Haig's task was an unprecedented one. When the war began, no one could have predicted that Great Britain would become a major military power or that a British general, commanding more than 1 million men, would be required by the Government to launch them against the main forces of a first-class enemy. This was not the 'British way in warfare'. The task was also difficult. Although the German Army's failure to win a short war in 1914 would eventually prove as disastrous as many German military leaders feared, the battles of 1914 had left the German Army in the west in a very strong position. Its occupation of a tenth of the soil of France and most of Belgium meant that the German Army held the strategic initiative. At the same time, the soil of France had less mystic significance for the Germans and could be more readily abandoned for tactically advantageous ground, which was often the high ground. (This was characteristic of the German conduct of the war in the west between August 1916 – when Hindenburg and Ludendorff replaced Falkenhayn – and March 1918, when

1 See below, Appendix One and Appendix Two.
2 See David French, *British Strategy and War Aims 1914–1916* (London: Allen & Unwin, 1986) and *The Strategy of the Lloyd George Coalition 1916–1918* (Oxford: Clarendon Press, 1995).

Ludendorff launched his reckless attempt to strike a knockout blow.) Simply put, Haig would have to attack uphill against a powerful, tactically astute, well-led army endowed with high morale. The instrument that he inherited in December 1915 was not well developed for this task.

The Army of which Haig took command was essentially 'Kitchener's Army', one of the most remarkable and impressive pieces of improvisation in British history.[1] The rapid expansion of Britain's military numbers was achieved, however, at a great short-term cost in quality. The Army was 'de-skilled' at every level. The process of 'skilling' was a messy one, bottom up as well as top down, and one that took place in contact with the main forces of a powerful enemy. It was, in effect, 'on-the-job training', which began in earnest on the Somme in 1916. Haig has received little credit for his role in the 'skilling process'. A fair-minded reading of Haig's diary makes it difficult to sustain such a view. Its pages confirm, with new strength and under-standing, John Terraine's depiction of Haig as 'the educated soldier'. Haig's mastery of his Army – from the mechanics of the 3rd Echelon Base Depot at Rouen to the use of sound-ranging sets – is hugely impressive. His interest in new inventions and in finding technological solutions to tactical problems is apparent, as is his recognition of the importance of artillery, 'airoplanes' and tanks.

Haig's understanding of the relationship between 'strategy' and 'oper-ations', however, is more contentious. If his strategy was 'ceaseless attrition', what did that imply for his conduct of 'operations'? Does strategic attrition imply operational attrition and, if so, how was operational attrition to be achieved? 'Attrition' is historically the strategy of choice of those with superior resources, usually manpower. But Haig did not have manpower superiority. Nor did British industry supply him with the necessary firepower until the spring of 1917 at the earliest, and probably not until later. Only in 1918 could the BEF fight a 'rich man's war'. Although Haig's Armies undoubtedly inflicted huge damage on the German Army in 1916 and 1917, they did so at great cost to themselves. Haig argued in his Final Despatch that the great battles of 1916 and 1917 were essential to the eventual outcome in the west. But could they have been achieved at less cost in British lives if Haig had pursued a more cautious 'bite and hold' approach to operations? The current balance of scholarly opinion favours a 'yes' answer, but 'bite and hold' does not provide a panacea that Haig foolishly rejected. The BEF was no more capable of conducting, cheaply, 'bite and hold' operations in 1916 and for part of 1917 than it was Haig's optimistic 'breakthrough' battles.

1 See Peter Simkins, *Kitchener's Army. The Raising of the New Armies, 1914–16* (Manchester: Manchester University Press, 1988).

THE WESTERN FRONT 1916–17

In his despatch written at the end of 1916, Haig described the Somme as the 'Opening of the Wearing-Out Battle', arguing that it was always intended to be attritional.[1] However, it is evident that during the planning stages Haig hoped the battle would result in a breakthrough, leading to the reopening of mobile warfare. How can this circle be squared?[2]

Coalition warfare dictated that the BEF fought a major battle somewhere in 1916. Haig had to decide when and where, and as the junior partner he did not have a free hand in making these decisions. Allied strategy for 1916 called for concerted Russian, Italian, and Anglo-French attacks on three fronts. Joffre wanted a campaign in two stages. The first battle would wear out the enemy and force them to commit their reserves; the second would deliver a decisive blow. Initially, Haig favoured a battle around Ypres. On 20 January, Joffre agreed to a preliminary battle on the Somme in the spring, followed by a British summer offensive in Flanders. These plans foundered because of British uneasiness about casualties, the inability of Russia to attack before the summer, and the unwillingness of the Belgians to co-operate in an offensive in Flanders. On 14 February, Haig and Joffre agreed to attack on the Somme at the beginning of July, with the French Army as the senior partner. Seven days later, however, Falkenhayn launched a major attack at Verdun. As ever more French divisions became sucked into the battle, it became clear that the BEF would have to bear the major burden on the Somme.

Haig had a clear conception of the forthcoming battle from what he had learnt at the Staff College (see above). In January he had rejected the idea of a purely attritional battle, instead striving for decisive success.[3] The impact of Verdun on the French Army led to Haig and Joffre becoming less optimistic about the Somme. Joffre came to hope merely that the battle would relieve the pressure of Verdun, and aid the Russians by tying down German divisions in the west. By May 1916 Haig also had a much more modest view of the likely outcome of the Somme, as a wearing-out battle. The idea of an offensive in Flanders was revived, should the French Army be so battered at Verdun that it was unable to fight on the Somme. Haig's ambitious operational plans demonstrate that he still hoped for a breakthrough on the Somme. He wanted

1 J. H. Boraston (ed.), *Sir Douglas Haig's Despatches* (London: Dent, 1919; reprinted 1979), pp. 19–20.
2 The following account follows William Philpott, 'Why the British were Really on the Somme: A Reply to Elizabeth Greenhalgh', *War in History*, 9 (2002), pp. 446–71. For an alternative view, see Elizabeth Greenhalgh, 'Why the British were on the Somme in 1916', *War in History*, 6 (1999), pp. 147–73.
3 TNA: PRO WO 158/19, reproduced in *Journal of Military History*, 65 (October 2001), pp. 1061–5.

to dampen down expectations if the battle did turn out to be an attritional affair; but not to exclude the possibility of operations of a more decisive character. Haig's post-Somme despatch, which excluded mention of his hopes of open warfare, was to some extent *ex post facto* rationalisation, but he had certainly anticipated that the battle might be one of attrition and limited gains.

Haig's plan for the opening of the battle was highly ambitious. Lieutenant General Sir Henry Rawlinson's Fourth Army was to capture the three German defensive positions, and then Lieutenant General Sir Hubert Gough's Reserve Army, which included three cavalry divisions, could begin the exploitation phase, striking east and then north towards Arras.[1] Rawlinson had a very different concept of operations. He believed in 'bite and hold': bite off a section of the enemy's defences, hold it against counter-attack, and when the enemy had exhausted themselves, carry out the process again.

Rawlinson's scheme of attack resembled Haig's in that both saw weight of artillery fire as vital. Rawlinson believed that capture of the Somme ridges would force the Germans to counter-attack to regain key terrain. British guns would smash up the German attacks. Haig overruled this plan. That the two men differed so fundamentally, and Rawlinson lacked faith in the plan that was eventually imposed on him, did not augur well. When, on 1 July, the success of attacks in the southern sector of the battlefield opened the possibility of achieving a breakthrough, Rawlinson was not prepared in any sense to take advantage of it.

Historians have mainly sided with Rawlinson. The BEF's logistic system was incapable of sustaining a major breakthrough in 1916. Rawlinson's plan was to mount fairly limited attacks that could be supported by artillery. However, the width of front to be attacked, some 20,000 yards, and Haig's insistence on capturing trenches to an average depth of 2500 yards, diluted the available firepower. Too few guns were given too much to do. In general, Haig's plan was too ambitious, given the state of training and level of experience of his troops in July 1916.[2]

For all that, it is clear that the action of 1 July dealt the German defenders a heavy blow. Haig's optimism that a substantial advance was possible against a weakened enemy was not wholly unreasonable. Well-planned attacks such as those of 14, 23 and 27 July could bring success, although Haig was initially sceptical about the novel tactics used on 14 July. In early August, Haig recognised that the window of opportunity had closed, and began to work towards a major set-piece attack in mid-September.

1 TNA: PRO WO 95/518. WD Reserve Army, Appendix 1 to July 1916.
2 Robin Prior and Trevor Wilson, *Command on the Western Front: The Military Career of Sir Henry Rawlinson* (Oxford: Blackwell, 1992), pp. 166–70.

As Haig's diary shows, he placed considerable faith in the tank. Haig has been criticised for 'throwing away' the secret of the tanks on 15 September by using them before they were available in large numbers. On 22 August he wrote, 'It would be folly not to use every weapon at my disposal in what is likely to be our crowning effort for this year.'[1] Haig's critics overestimate how useful the primitive tank actually was on the battlefield. It was not a war-winning weapon in 1916, but it was a useful adjunct to the emerging all-arms weapons system. Given the importance Haig attached to the attack of 15 September, it is difficult to fault him for employing the tank just as he would have used a new type of shell or mortar.

Haig's command relationship with Rawlinson and Gough, the Reserve Army commander, was founded on the informal doctrine that the superior commander should set broad objectives but leave the details to his subordinates. Sometimes Haig adhered to this, but on other occasions he intervened, for good or ill. Haig can be fairly criticised for a lack of control over his subordinate commanders. Too often Rawlinson and Gough used 'penny-packets' of troops (and guns) rather than committing the sort of numbers that would make success possible, and failed to co-ordinate actions across formation boundaries. Such actions generally gained a little ground but at a high price. At times, Haig did give Rawlinson advice and even instructions on how to handle his command.[2] On other occasions he overruled 'the man on the spot', such as in the planning for 15 September. Overall, Haig's approach lacked consistency and 'grip'.

Haig did not abandon hope of a breakthrough until late in the campaign. He anticipated that 15 September would have more far-reaching results than actually transpired. Success was achieved at Morval on 25 September, as in earlier actions, by employing heavy firepower and sensible infantry tactics against a limited objective. However, Haig saw Morval as a signal that mobile warfare was at hand, a view that was to prove sadly mistaken. The failure of Haig (and Rawlinson) consistently to apply the lessons of successful operations is one of the more puzzling aspects of the Somme. Haig, only in his post for six months when the battle began, served his apprenticeship as an Army Group commander on the Somme. He was still learning.

Haig's prolongation of the battle when it was clear that a breakthrough was not going to occur is much more easily explained. In large part it was the consequence of coalition politics. Joffre pressurised Haig not only to continue fighting but also to carry out 'wide and deep offensive operations'.[3] While Haig refused to let Joffre dictate the precise nature of his battles, he

1 TNA: PRO WO 158/21, Haig to Robertson, 22 August 1916.
2 Prior and Wilson, *Command on the Western Front*, pp. 187–90, 203–7, 216–23.
3 J. Joffre, *The Memoirs of Marshal Joffre* (London: G. Bles, 1932), II, p. 485.

had no choice, whatever his personal preferences, but to carry on with offensive operations. As William Philpott has argued, 'Haig's claim that he mounted and prolonged the Somme battle for the broader interests of the alliance' was fundamentally correct.[1] As Haig stated in his diary for 12 November, if the Battle of the Ancre (13–18 November) was successful, it would show the French that the BEF was still pulling its weight on the Somme.

The Somme has frequently been judged a bloody failure.[2] At the other extreme, it has been acclaimed as a 'victory'.[3] The truth lies somewhere in between. The Somme was bloody, wasteful and at times poorly handled by the British High Command. It shattered the strategic consensus in Britain. Lloyd George, who was to become Prime Minister in December 1916, was appalled by the battle, a fact that had serious consequences for relations between Downing Street and GHQ for the remainder of the war.[4]

The Somme also dealt a heavy blow to the German Army, as its senior commanders candidly confessed. While it is best to avoid the emotional baggage associated with the word 'victory', the Somme was a British strategic success. This can be judged in a number of ways. German strategy in 1917 was in large part a reaction to the Somme. The Germans abandoned the 1916 battlefield by withdrawing to the Hindenburg Line, and opened unrestricted submarine warfare in an attempt to defeat Britain in the full knowledge that this was likely to bring the USA into the war, with ultimately disastrous consequences for Germany. This is a powerful vindication of Haig's attritional strategy.

While the campaign was going on, Haig came to set great store on counting German casualties, and noting signs of apparent deterioration in the quality and morale of German troops. Traditionally, John Charteris, Haig's Intelligence chief, has been seen as feeding Haig information that he thought the C-in-C wanted to hear, but recent research indicates that he shared Haig's optimism rather than being the cause of it. In his Final Despatch of 1919 Haig explicitly linked the attritional battles of 1915–17 to the final victory: they had 'worn out' the German Army. Just as in the case of the December 1916 despatch, there was an element of being wise after the event, as Haig had certainly hoped to achieve a breakthrough in earlier campaigns. But the evidence suggests that Haig's 'Plan B', of attrition, contributed mightily to the eventual defeat of the German Army. There are interesting parallels with

1 Philpott, *Anglo-French Relations*, p. 127.
2 e.g. Nigel Hamilton, *The Full Monty* (London: Allen Lane, 2001), p. 104.
3 Terraine, *Douglas Haig*, p. 229.
4 See Brock Millman's stimulating study, *Pessimism and British War Policy 1916–1918* (London, Frank Cass, 2001).

Montgomery in 1944. In Normandy, Montgomery won a major victory by carrying on attritional operations, wearing away the enemy before a breakthrough occurred (of course, in a much shorter time than on the Western Front in 1914–18). Montgomery liked to pretend that everything had gone according to plan, when clearly it had not.

The Somme was important for its impact on both German and British Armies. In spite of the very heavy British casualties (some 420,000), by the end of the battle the BEF was a more experienced and effective force than it had been at the beginning. Douglas Haig was far more than a battlefield commander. He presided over the BEF's expansion and development, taking a keen interest in diverse matters including reforming the logistic system, training and minor tactics. Improvements in administration and infra-structure were vital elements in the learning curve that transformed the BEF from the clumsy organisation of July 1916 to the formidable army of August 1918. While it is difficult to quantify his influence, it is clear that as C-in-C Haig deserves a share of the credit for the transformation of the BEF, just as he deserves a share of the blame for battlefield setbacks.

Douglas Haig's conduct of the campaigns of 1917 was, for a long time, the principal item on the charge sheet against him. Although the Somme, and especially the first day, 1 July 1916, has for most people come to symbolise the horror and waste of the First World War, in the 1920s and 1930s it was Third Ypres, popularly if inaccurately known from its final stage, which held that dubious honour. Certainly, Passchendaele was the stick that Lloyd George chose to beat Haig's reputation in the 1930s. There were many good reasons for attacking around Ypres in 1917. If the British could advance about seven miles, the Germans would be dislodged from the commanding heights that surrounded the city, and the BEF would be in a position to menace the vital German communications junction of Roulers, five miles further on. If Roulers fell to the Allies, the Germans would have faced a major crisis, with their lines of supply in Flanders disrupted. It might even have forced them to evacuate the area. For Britain, this prize was worth pursuing. In the first half of 1917, the German campaign of unrestricted submarine warfare appeared to be close to achieving its aim of severing Britain's Atlantic lifeline. The Admiralty was becoming increasingly nervous at the growing German naval threat based on the Channel coast. Indeed, on 20 June, a shocked Haig recorded that

> Admiral Jellicoe as First Sea Lord stated that owing to [the great shortage of shipping due to German submarines], it would be impossible for Great Britain to continue the war in 1918. This was a bombshell for the Cabinet, [and all present] and a full enquiry is to be made as to the real facts on which this opinion [of the Naval Authorities] is based.

Haig went on:

> No one present shared Jellicoe's view, and all seemed satisfied that the food reserves in Great Britain are adequate. [Jellicoe's words were, 'There is no good discussing plans for next Spring. We cannot go on.']

Haig had his own reasons for wanting to fight around Ypres. It would have been emotionally satisfying, for it was of course at Ypres in 1914 that his reputation with the wider British public had been secured. In many ways, his preference for fighting at Ypres in 1916 was sensible. Unlike on the Somme, there were real strategic objectives close to Ypres, and in 1916, the German defences in the area were not as powerful as they would be a year later.

The first of the major criticisms made of Haig's conduct of the 1917 Ypres battles is related to the Battle of Messines. This model set-piece action, conducted by Second Army, seized Messines Ridge on the first day of the battle, 7 June 1917. Following the success of this limited attack, on 8 June Plumer informed GHQ that it was impossible to redeploy Second Army's guns for a subsequent attack on the Gheluvelt plateau in less than three days. Haig transferred command of the second operation to Hubert Gough's Fifth Army. Gough promptly spent three days considering his options. He wanted an attack on a wide frontage; otherwise, he argued (probably correctly) that British gains would create a salient that would be difficult to defend. Some historians have therefore condemned Haig for failing to give Plumer the time for which he asked. However, research by Ian Brown has given a new twist to the debate. He argues that the Battle of Messines was successful largely because of the meticulous preparations, which had begun the year before. For Second Army to be in a position to attack on 7 June it had required three weeks of exhaustive efforts to get all the arrangements in place. Brown persuasively argues that suspension of major operations after the initial success 'was dictated by the need both to consolidate Messines's success and prepare a new battlefield, admittedly an adjacent one'.[1] That is not to deny that Haig made a mistake in refusing to allow Plumer the time to mount a *limited* assault on the Gheluvelt plateau; the German forces were badly disrupted by the attack of 7 June, and further pressure might have yielded some gains. However, the ideal of following up the major blow of Messines with a second substantial assault on a broad front, to capitalise on the success of 7 June, was logistically impossible. This assault would have to wait until 31 July.

After Messines, Haig sidelined Plumer and placed Gough in charge of the main attack for what was to become the Third Battle of Ypres. Haig seems

---

1 Ian Malcolm Brown, *British Logistics on the Western Front, 1914–1919* (London: Praeger, 1998), p. 164.

to have been operating on the principle of 'horses for courses'. Plumer, the cautious master of the limited offensive, had been right for Messines; but apparently believing that a breakthrough was possible, Haig selected Gough, the cavalryman, who in following up the enemy during the retreat to the Hindenburg Line earlier in 1917 had shown some flair for mobile warfare. In retrospect, most people agree that this was a mistake, but in the circumstances of June–July 1917, Haig's nomination of Gough for the principal role had a certain amount of logic.

Haig exacerbated this error by sending the Fifth Army commander confused signals about exactly what he wanted Gough to do. In the words of the American scholar Andrew Wiest, Haig 'hoped for a breakthrough but also understood the worth of a step-by-step attack to contribute to the wearing down of the German Army'. Unfortunately, Gough 'was not subtle enough to understand the dual nature of the offensive'. Haig offered Gough advice on the German defences and suggested that there should be a preliminary attack against the key ground of the Gheluvelt plateau on the right. Haig, true to his 'hands-off' conception of the role of commander-in-chief, did not give Gough a direct order; instead, in accordance with pre-war command doctrine, he deferred to the local commander.

Gough largely ignored the sensible advice he received from GHQ.[1] As a result, on the first day of the battle, 31 July 1917, only about 500 yards were gained on the vital ground of the Gheluvelt plateau. In other places, Fifth Army's assaulting troops often made good progress through the outer German defences – regarded as dispensable in German doctrine for elastic defence – only for German counter-attack formations to hit the attackers as their advance was losing impetus. In short, Gough's aspirations for a breakthrough proved to be hopelessly over-optimistic. In the weeks that followed, in spite of the fact that Haig continued to offer sensible advice, Gough's performance as an Army commander in the first stages of Third Ypres was deeply disappointing.[2] Haig's decision on 26 August to hand the main effort to Plumer was sensible if belated.

Plumer's methodical 'bite and hold' approach and limited objectives brought a rich harvest at the three battles of Menin Road (20 September), Polygon Wood (26 September) and Broodseinde (4 October). The British casualty lists were long, but these series of blows had an immensely damaging effect on the German forces. According to one modern German historian,

---

1 Andrew Wiest, 'Haig, Gough and Passchendaele', in G. D. Sheffield (ed.), *Leadership and Command: The Anglo-American Military Experience Since 1861* (London: Brassey's, 1997), pp. 77–92.
2 See NLS: Haig Papers, Acc. 3155 (116), for the advice on tactics in Kiggell to Army commanders, 7 August 1917.

'Against the new British approach to the battle, the Germans could find no remedy; the recapturing of ground lost was impossible.' German high commanders, aware that their forces were badly stretched fighting a multi-front war across Europe, began to consider limited withdrawals, while Crown Prince Rupprecht, the local Army Group commander, even began to prepare for 'a comprehensive withdrawal' that would have entailed giving up the Channel ports. If this had happened, the BEF would have achieved one of the major British objectives of the entire operation.[1]

This is the context in which Douglas Haig took the fateful decision to order his divisions to fight on in Flanders after the success of 4 October, despite the onset of unpredictably and unusually heavy rain that produced the mud by which 'Passchendaele' would forever be remembered. Inevitably, Haig has been criticised by subsequent writers for this decision. But as Charles Bean, the Australian official historian, a man who was the very opposite of an apologist for the British High Command, later reflected:

> For the first time in years, at noon on October 4th on the heights east of Ypres, British troops on the Western Front stood face to face with the possibility of decisive success ... Let the student ... ask himself 'In view of the results of three step-by-step blows [the battles of Menin Road, Polygon Wood and Broodseinde] all successful, what will be the result of three more in the next fortnight?'[2]

Haig could not see into the future. He was called upon to make a decision which, based on the information he had available at the time, involved a degree of acceptable risk. Indeed, had he decided to halt the Flanders offensive after 4 October 1917, historians would undoubtedly have had a field day in blaming Haig for throwing away the opportunity to capitalise on the crisis in the German Army created by Plumer's offensives. Haig decided to renew the offensive, with damaging consequences for his reputation.

Bad weather, and the artillery which had done so much to secure Plumer's successes, combined to reduce the battlefield to a shattered quagmire. With forces struggling to get guns and supplies to the front line, the next attack, the Battle of Poelcappelle (9 October), lacked the punch of previous attacks and the British found it difficult to achieve any sort of operational tempo. Haig fought on, aiming to take the Passchendaele Ridge and stop there for

1 Heinz Hagenlucke, 'The German High Command', in Peter H. Liddle (ed.), *Passchendaele in Perspective. The Third Battle of Ypres* (Barnsley: Leo Cooper Pen & Sword, 1997), p. 53. See also German Werth, 'Flanders 1917 and the German Soldier', in ibid., pp. 324–32.
2 C. E. W. Bean, *The Australian Imperial Force in France, 1917. The Official History of Australia in the War of 1914–1918*, vol. 4 (Sydney: Angus & Robertson, 1933), pp. 877, 881.

the winter, and to use this new position as a jumping-off point for renewing the offensive in 1918. While the continuation of the battle after Poelcappelle is much harder to justify, in truth it has some merit, given the degree to which the BEF had achieved operational, tactical and even psychological dominance over the Germans in September–October 1917. Careful planning, skilful tactics and extensive combat engineering enabled the Canadian Corps to capture Passchendaele Ridge, albeit at a high price. However, by the New Year the political climate in London and the strategic realities of the Western Front had changed to such an extent that Haig's 1918 Flanders offensive was stillborn.

In 1960 Cyril Falls, Great War veteran, official historian and one of the wisest of commentators on the war, wrote that 'popular verdicts on this battle, and on the British Commander-in-Chief's conduct of it, are too much simplified'.[1] That verdict remains true today. The implication underlying the (almost certainly untrue) story that Kiggell, Haig's Chief of Staff, on seeing the battlefield for the first time, tearfully cried out, 'Good God, did we send men to fight in that?' – that Haig and GHQ were unaware of the state of conditions at the front – is simply untrue.[2] Neither is it true that Haig's approach at Passchendaele consisted of 'blind bashing'; Andy Simpson has described the battle in the pithy phrase, 'good tactics, bad ground'.[3]

On 20 and 27 September and 4 October Haig's divisions inflicted heavy defeats on the Germans and, overall, the campaign had a serious impact on the enemy. Dennis Showalter has suggested that, arguably, if the pre-war German Army was destroyed on the Somme, 'the German citizen army, the reservists and wartime conscripts, was eviscerated at Passchendaele'.[4] This attrition contributed to the eventual defeat of the Germans in 1918 and also, it seems, worked on the minds of the German generals. Ludendorff, fearful of a repetition of Third Ypres, later claimed that this was a factor in deciding to attempt the gamble of a knockout blow in the west, a statement that had the ring of truth. These gains of Haig's 1917 Flanders offensive were substantial. His conduct of Third Ypres certainly deserves criticism but such criticism, to have validity, should be measured rather than shrill. A cool assessment of all the available evidence suggests, in Showalter's words 'that Haig's determination and the perseverance of the BEF was not altogether in vain'.[5]

1 Cyril Falls, *The First World War* (London: Longmans Green, 1960) p. 286.
2 Brian Bond, 'Passchendaele: Verdicts, Past and Present', in Liddle (ed.), *Passchendaele in Perspective*, pp. 482–3.
3 Andy Simpson, *The Evolution of Victory* (London: Tom Donovan, 1995) (title of chapter 6).
4 D. Showalter, 'Passchendaele', in D. Showalter (ed.), *History in Dispute*, vol. 8: *World War I: First Series* (Detroit: St James Press, 2004), p. 224.
5 Showalter, 'Passchendaele', p. 224.

THE ACCIDENTAL VICTOR?

The 'Hundred Days' of Allied victories between August and November 1918 pose an interesting problem of interpretation. How can it be explained that under Douglas Haig, roundly criticised by many for his handling of the Somme and Passchendaele offensives, the BEF won the greatest series of land victories in British history?

One approach is to contend that Haig was largely irrelevant to the Allied victory. Tim Travers has written the most sophisticated and influential version of this thesis. He argues that in 1918 Haig's power was curtailed by the appointment of Foch as Allied Generalissimo, Wilson as CIGS, and Lawrence as the BEF's CGS. The shock of the German breakthrough and the resumption of mobile warfare caused the rigid, hierarchical, British command system to break down: 'an increasingly mobile style of warfare dictated a decentralized command structure until the Armistice', with low-level commanders taking key decisions.[1] It 'appears that Haig and his GHQ ... did not have a critical influence on the victory in the last 100 days of the war. In fact it can be argued that in the second half of 1918, Haig and the senior staff at GHQ lost power to the army commanders, and retained only a symbolic form of leadership.'[2] Furthermore, Travers argues that in 1918 there was a dichotomy between 'mechanical warfare', involving the use of technology such as aircraft, tanks and guns 'to save lives and win the war' and 'traditional', infantry-centred warfare, favoured by Haig. Despite the success of 'mechanical warfare' at Amiens (8 August 1918), Travers argues, the BEF instead returned to 'traditional or semi-traditional open warfare' from the end of August 1918.[3]

Robin Prior and Trevor Wilson argue that as the BEF 'at every level became a more complex, sophisticated and above all specialist organization, any detailed intervention by the commander-in-chief became increasingly inappropriate'. The jobs of both C-in-C and Army commander 'were diminishing not expanding' as their forces 'grew in expertise and complexity'. However, this argument develops into something rather different from Travers's: that Haig 'proved far more effective as a commander once the sphere of his activities began to diminish to an extent that brought them within the limits of his capabilities'.[4]

This seems eminently fair. Haig had long wanted greater decentralisation in command, but recognised that the inexperience of his Army and subordinate

1 Tim Travers, 'The Army and the Challenge of War 1914–1918', in David Chandler and Ian F. W. Beckett (eds), *The Oxford Illustrated History of the British Army* (Oxford: Oxford University Press, 1994), pp. 220, 237.
2 Travers, *How the War*, p. 175.
3 Travers, *How the War*, p. 179.
4 Prior and Wilson, *Command on the Western Front*, p. 305.

commanders did not always make this possible. From 1916 onwards, British command and control became steadily less hidebound and inflexible, as new methods and effective leaders emerged from the hard school of combat experience.[1] By 1918 the greater experience of commanders and staffs enabled him in large measure to achieve his goal of 'arm's-length' command, although he was still prone to intervene, sometimes at unhelpful moments.[2] Haig has been rightly criticised for failing to 'grip' his Army commanders on the Somme in 1916, but tighter control of subordinate formations in the very different circumstances of 1918 would have been utterly inappropriate. As Haig told Henry Wilson on 20 September 1918, he commanded 'a surprisingly large number of *very capable* generals'.

This does not mean that Haig or GHQ were reduced to ciphers. Harris and Barr make a robust case for the critical importance of Haig's 'drive', 'resolution', 'determination' and 'force of personality' in the Hundred Days. He 'set the BEF as a whole in motion', overcoming potential inertia among some of his Army commanders, especially Horne and Byng (although not Rawlinson).[3] Haig correctly recognised early in August that there was a real possibility (although not a certainty) of winning the war in 1918. His was virtually a lone voice. Even in the face of the BEF's great victories, there was deep pessimism among other British decision-makers. 'Haig alone had realised how drastic was the disconnection between conception in London and reality in France ... For this he deserves more praise than he has yet received.'[4] However, Haig's optimism in previous years probably undermined his credibility.

Foch's importance in 1918 has sometimes been underestimated by British historians,[5] but neither should we go to the other extreme, of down-playing Haig's role. He was Foch's *de facto* principal subordinate, given the size and effectiveness of the BEF. Of particular importance was Haig's contribution to the sequential offensives of 26–29 September. As Dan Todman has pointed out, GHQ's Operations staff played a vital part in these critical battles by sequencing the offensives, a job for which the section was better suited than carrying out planning in detail for subsidiary formations. Similarly, the

1 See G. D. Sheffield and D. Todman, *Command and Control* (Staplehurst: Spellmount, 2004), *passim.*

2 Peter Simkins, 'Haig and the Army Commanders', in Bond and Cave (eds), *Haig: A Reappraisal,* pp. 94, 97; D. Todman, 'The Grand Lamasery revisited: General Headquarters on the Western Front, 1914–1918', in Sheffield and Todman, *Command and Control,* pp. 39–70.

3 J. P. Harris and N. Barr, *Amiens to the Armistice* (London, Brassey's, 1999), pp. 300–1.

4 Millman, *Pessimism and British War Policy,* p. 274.

5 See W. Philpott, 'Marshal Ferdinand Foch and Allied Victory', in Matthew Hughes and Matthew Seligmann, *Leadership in Conflict 1914–1918* (London: Leo Cooper, 2000), pp. 38–53, for an important corrective.

Adjutant General's (A) and Quartermaster General's (Q) branches of GHQ kept the BEF in supply under very difficult circumstances.[1]

The fact that Haig's optimism seemed to take a downturn in mid-October has puzzled some historians. On 19 October, Haig reported to the War Cabinet that, despite much success, the Allies had not yet inflicted a 'decisive defeat' on the Germans, who could pull back to their borders and hold out into 1919. He advocated that the Germans should be offered moderate terms for peace. In retrospect, Haig grossly underestimated the scale of the BEF's success and the effect on the Germans. He had consistently stated that the campaign might go on until 1919, and was anxious about the burdens the advance was placing on the logistic services. He was also influenced by intelligence that the Germans were holding back the 1920 class of conscripts. Haig feared that these might provide the German Army with a timely injection of manpower.

However, Haig's views were informed by political as well as by military factors. He, along with other members of the British elite, was suspicious of French motives and ambitions, and was painfully aware that British strength and influence would decline, and that of the United States increase, the longer that the war dragged on. Sidney Clive, Haig's Intelligence chief, also briefed him on the power struggle in Germany. Clive argued that if the Allies demanded harsh terms for an armistice, it would bring about the downfall of the newly installed reformist government of Prince Max of Baden. In Haig's words, 'The militarists would return to Power, and begin a life-and-death struggle.' This also needs to be placed into the wider context of Haig's fear of the spread of Bolshevism in Germany – and even beyond its frontiers – should all existing authority collapse. A lenient peace might avert the prospect of both prolonged fighting and Communist revolution. The BEF's victories of 4 November seem to have restored some of Haig's confidence, and in early November intelligence began reaching the British of the parlous state of Germany, where revolution was breaking out. But it was too late for the Government to change its mind about accepting terms that allowed the German Army to march home. This stored up trouble for the future, in that it nourished the myth of a 'stab in the back' that helped propel Hitler to power in 1933. As Sir Eric Geddes wrote on 12 November, 'Had we known how bad things were in Germany, we might have got stiffer terms; however, it is easy to be wise after the event.'[2]

---

1 Todman, 'Grand Lamasery' pp. 63–4.
2 David French, '"Had We Known How Bad Things Were in Germany, We Might Have Got Stiffer Terms": Great Britain and the German Armistice', in M. F. Boemeke, G. D. Feldman and E. Glaser, *The Treaty of Versailles: A Reassessment after 75 Years* (Cambridge: Cambridge University Press, 1998), pp. 69–86; TNA: PRO WO 158/25. Minutes of the War Cabinet, 19 October 1918,

CONCLUSION

Haig began his diary entry for 11 November 1918 in his usual way – 'Fine day but cold and dull'. His use of block capitals for November was the only hint of the triumph that he had a right to feel. At the moment the Armistice came into effect, he began a meeting with his Army commanders in the *mairie* at Cambrai. One of the issues he raised with them was

> the importance of looking after the troops during the period following the cessation of hostilities. Very often the best fighters are the most difficult to deal with in periods of quiet! I suggested a number of ways in which men can be kept occupied. It is as much the *duty* of all officers to keep their men amused as it is to train them for war. Staff officers must [attend to this]. If funds are wanted, GHQ should be informed, and I'll arrange for money to be found.

This is the authentic voice of the paternalist regimental officer that was never far from the surface of most British generals during the Great War.[1] Haig has acquired a reputation for callousness and indifference to the suffering of his men. This could not be further from the truth. His diary frequently records his admiration for the achievements of his 'amateur' soldiers and an appreciation of their suffering. He wrote in his diary for 31 March 1917 that

> No one can visit the Somme battlefield without being impressed with the magnitude of the effort of the British Army. For five long months this battle continued. Not one battle, but a series of great battles, were methodically waged by numerous divisions in succession, so that credit for pluck and resolution has been earned by men from every part of the Empire. And credit must be paid too, not only to the private soldier in the ranks, but also to those splendid young officers who commanded platoons, companies and battalions. Although new to this terrible 'game of war' they were able, time and again, to form up their commands in the darkness of night, and in spite of shell holes, wire and other obstacles, lead them forward in the grey of the morning to the attack of these tremendous positions. To many it meant certain death, and all must have known that before they started. Surely it was the knowledge of the great stake at issue, the existence of England as a free nation, that nerved them for such heroic deeds. I have not the time to put down all the thoughts which rush into my mind when

NLS: Acc. 3155; Haig Diary, 28 August 1917, 19, 25 October 1918. The editors are grateful to Jim Beach for his advice on Intelligence matters.
1 See Niall Barr and Gary Sheffield, 'Douglas Haig, the Common Soldier and the British Legion', in Bond and Cave (eds), *Haig: A Reappraisal*, pp. 223–39.

I think of all those fine fellows, who either have given their lives for their country, or have been maimed in its service. Later on I hope we may have a Prime Minister and a Government who will do them justice.

Haig was particularly anxious about the welfare of officers who had been maimed and disfigured, commenting in a letter to his wife on 19 July 1918:

Very pleased to get yours of Wednesday, and to see that the Government at last means to look after the claims of Disabled Officers, although they cannot yet decide how exactly they will proceed in the matter. The Officer Class is now very different to what it was in the case of the old regular Army. Now the Officer in many cases has risen from the ranks, and in most cases is quite without means outside his pay. They are also very numerous, about 90,000 in France alone. So you will thus see that the suffering after the war will be very great indeed unless something is arranged soon for their benefit. You are doing splendid work my darling, in interesting yourself so intensely in their claims...

It was this deep personal sense of duty and paternalism towards his men that motivated Haig's subsequent post-war work for the welfare of veterans, especially through his Presidency of the British Legion. This work inevitably involved him in making public speeches, an activity he detested. His last public act was to give a speech at the enrolment ceremony of the 20th Richmond (Earl Haig's Own) Boy Scouts, formed from the sons of disabled ex-servicemen employed at the British Legion Poppy factory. On the following day, 29 January 1928, he collapsed and died from a heart attack at his brother-in-law's house in London. He was sixty-six.

LIST OF ABBREVIATIONS

2 i/c	Second in Command
AA&QMG	Assistant Adjutant & Quartermaster General
ADC	Aide-de-Camp
AG	Adjutant General
ANZAC	Australian & New Zealand Army Corps
BEF	British Expeditionary Force
BGGS	Brigadier General General Staff
BGRA	Brigadier General Royal Artillery
CGS	Chief of the General Staff
CHA	Commander of Corps Heavy Artillery
CIGS	Chief of the Imperial General Staff
CO	Commanding Officer
CoS	Chief of Staff
CRA	Commanding Royal Artillery
CRE	Commanding Royal Engineers
CSO	Chief Staff Officer
DAN	Détachement d'Armée du Nord
DAQMG	Deputy Adjutant and Quartermaster General
DGMS	Director General of Medical Services
DGT	Director General of Transportation
DMI	Director of Military Intelligence [at the War Office]
DMO	Director of Military Operations [at the War Office]
DMS	Director of Medical Services
DMT	Director of Military Training [at the War Office]
DSD	Director of Staff Duties [at the War Office]
DSO	Distinguished Service Order
edn	Edition
EEF	Egyptian Expeditionary Force
FM	Field Marshal
FSR	Field Service Regulations
GHQ	General Headquarters
GOC	General Officer Commanding

GOC-in-C	General Officer Commanding-in-Chief
GCB	Knight Grand Cross of the Most Honourable Order of the Bath
GQG	Grand Quartier Général [French GHQ]
GS	General Staff
GSO	General Staff Officer
GSO1	General Staff Officer (1st Grade)
GSO2	General Staff Officer (2nd Grade)
GSO3	General Staff Officer (3rd Grade)
HLI	Highland Light Infantry
HQ	Headquarters
i/c	In command
IG	Inspector General
K	Lord Kitchener
KOSB	King's Own Scottish Borderers
KRRC	King's Royal Rifle Corps
LoC	Lines of Communication
LG	Lloyd George
LHCMA	Liddell Hart Centre for Military Archives
MGA	Major General i/c Administration
MGC	Machine Gun Corps
MGGS	Major General General Staff
MGO	Master General of the Ordnance
MGRA	Major General Royal Artillery
MS	Military Secretary
NCO	Non Commissioned Officer
NLS	National Library of Scotland
OC	Officer Commanding
QMG	Quartermaster General
PM	Prime Minister
RA	Royal Artillery
RAMC	Royal Army Medical Corps
RE	Royal Engineers
RFA	Royal Field Artillery
RFC	Royal Flying Corps
RHA	Royal Horse Artillery
SGSO	Senior General Staff Officer
TNA	The National Archives
WO	War Office

A NOTE ON THE TEXT

The text consists, for the most part, of extracts from Douglas Haig's manuscript war diary, supplemented by letters written by him. This diary was written on an almost daily basis during the Great War and sent by King's Messenger in batches to Lady Haig in England. After the war Haig and Lady Haig produced a typed version of the diary, to which Haig added various official papers, letters and memoranda. On completion, these were bound in thirty-eight volumes. The present Earl Haig deposited both the manuscript and typed versions of the diary in the National Library of Scotland in 1961. A copy of the typed version has been available in the National Archives (Public Record Office) since 1977. As explained in the Introduction, Haig took the opportunity to make additions and corrections to his manuscript diary (though *not* major deletions) when compiling the typed version. Where this text uses the typed version Haig's additions are shown in square brackets.

In selecting entries for publication the editors have been anxious to reflect the full range of Haig's activities, especially during his period as Commander-in-Chief (1915–19), and not only his dealings with senior political and military leaders. The balance between the years also reflects the increasing importance of the British Expeditionary Force to the Allied war effort, something not always reflected in the wider historiography of the war, which still underplays the importance of 1918. The complete diary contains in the region of 750,000 words. This edition, at *c*.200,000 words, is the most extensive version of the diary ever published.

The war's main actors are the subjects of Biographical Sketches, which appear at the end of the book. Such persons are identified by an asterisk (*) before their names the first time they appear in each year of the diary. Lesser figures have explanatory footnotes at the first mentions of their names in the text. In a small number of cases, the editors have found it impossible to provide firm identification, and they would welcome further information.

Although the diary is literate and generally easy to read in the original, the text is not here rendered exactly as Haig wrote it. His excessive use of capital letters has been brought more into line with current practice, though the editors found merit in retaining his distinctive capitalisation of 'Enemy' and 'Tanks' as well as his eccentric spelling of 'airoplane'. Haig was also somewhat promiscuous in his use of exclamation marks, a trait shared by many of his contemporaries, and these have been pruned. His habit of rendering surnames by their capital letter alone is sometimes confusing and except in the case of Kitchener (Lord K) and Lloyd George (LG) surnames have been generally spelled out. The description of military formations has been standardised for clarity, thus: First Army; I Corps; 1st Division; 1 Brigade. The names of regiments and battalions are either spelled in full or shown in standard abbreviations, such as KOSB or KRRC. Military ranks are shown in full and without hyphens (e.g., Major General *not* Maj.-Gen.). Full stops have been removed from abbreviations such as RFC, GOC, BEF, and so on. During the First World War the words 'moral' and 'morale' were used interchangeably. Haig uses both in the modern sense of 'morale', and we have retained that usage.

1914
CORPS COMMANDER

———————————————

Great Britain declared war on Germany on 4 August 1914, in response to the German invasion of Belgium. Although Britain, France and Russia had created a loose power bloc in the years before 1914, there was no formal alliance between Britain and the other two states. However, it was clearly in the British national interest to support France and Russia in resisting German aggression. To have deserted her Entente partners would probably have resulted in a German-dominated Europe, with Britain facing the German threat alone at some point in the future. Britain's motives in going to war in 1914 were those that had under-pinned British foreign policy for centuries. It aimed to prevent the Channel coast falling into hostile hands – thus posing a threat to British maritime security; and to defend the balance of power in Europe. Douglas Haig, for one, had for many years been expecting war with Germany.

In August 1914 Lieutenant General Sir Douglas Haig was General Officer Commanding Aldershot, and commander designate of I Army Corps. With the coming of war, Haig took command of his Corps, which consisted of the Aldershot-based 1st and 2nd Infantry Divisions and the only permanent Corps Staff in the British Army. The newly assembled II Corps (3rd and 5th Divisions) was commanded by Lieutenant General Sir James Grierson, with a hastily improvised staff. The overall commander of the British Expeditionary Force (BEF) was Field Marshal Sir John French. The BEF originally consisted of I and II Corps, plus Major General Allenby's Cavalry Division. A III Corps under Major General W. P. Pulteney formed in France at the end of August. By the end of 1914, the BEF had expanded to five corps (including the Indian Corps), plus the Cavalry Corps and an Indian Cavalry Corps.

The key relationship on I Corps Staff was Haig's partnership with his Chief of Staff (formally, the Brigadier General General Staff or BGGS), Brigadier General 'Johnnie' Gough VC. He was the brother of Hubert Gough, over whose career Haig was to exercise a decisive influence; the same could be said of I Corps' Brigadier General Royal Artillery, H. S. Horne, who had worked with Haig previously. Another important personality on I Corps Staff was Major John Charteris, Haig's aide-de-camp and Intelligence Officer, who was to play a controversial role in Haig's subsequent career.

Haig's I Corps saw relatively little action during the initial clash of arms, culminating in the battles of Mons (23 August) and Le Cateau three days later.

However, once the Retreat from Mons halted and the advance to the Marne commenced on 6 September, I Corps had plenty of fighting, taking a prominent role in the embryo trench warfare on the Aisne in September–October, and around La Bassée and Ypres in October and November. In part, this reflects the high level of trust that Sir John French placed in Haig, and the Field Marshal's dislike of the II Corps commander, Sir Horace Smith-Dorrien. Haig emerged from the defensive First Battle of Ypres with his reputation greatly enhanced.

Haig's wartime diary begins on 29 July, but no manuscript copy survives; it appears that it was written up from memory and, possibly, rough notes. The first manuscript entry is for 13 August. Material taken from the typed (Ts) diary is placed in square brackets.

[On the afternoon of Wednesday, 29 July 1914 I received an Order (as GOC Aldershot Command) by telegram from Secretary of State for War to adopt 'Precautionary Measures' as detailed in Defence Scheme.

All our arrangements were ready, even to the extent of having the telegrams written out. These merely had to be dated and despatched.

On 2 March last 'Mobilisation Orders' for the Aldershot Command, having been brought up to date, were sent out over the signature of Major General Robb,[1] my MGA, consequently when the telegram containing the one word 'Mobilise' and signed 'Troopers' (i.e., Secretary War Office) was received at 5.3 pm on 4 August, these orders were put in force and methodically acted upon without friction and without flurry. Everything had been so well thought out and foreseen that I, as 'C-in-C Aldershot', was never called upon for a decision. I had thus all my time free to make arrangements for my own departure for the front, to visit Field Marshal *French's GHQ now established at the Hotel Metropole in London, and to ponder over the terribly critical military situation as it gradually developed day by day.]

Tuesday 4 August. Letter to Major Philip Howell[2]

Very many thanks for your 2 letters.

I agree that we ought not to dispatch our Expeditionary Force in a hurry to France. Possibly had there been a chance of supporting her at the very

1 Major General Sir Frederick Spencer Robb (1858–1948), Major General i/c Administration, Aldershot, 1910–14; Inspector General of Communications BEF, 1914; Military Secretary to the Secretary of State for War, 1914–16.
2 LHCMA: Howell Papers, 6/2/14. This letter was written before receipt of the 'Mobilisation' telegram. Major (later Brigadier General) Philip Howell (1877–1916); BGGS Cavalry Corps, X Corps, XII Corps (Salonika), GHQ Salonika, 1915–16; BGGS II Corps, 1916; killed in action on 7 October 1916. Howell was Haig's protégé, hence the unusually close relationship between a junior and senior officer.

beginning, our help might have been decisive. That moment seems to have been allowed to pass. Now we must *make* an Army large enough to intervene decisively – say 300,000. With the necessary reserves at home for wastage say 200,000. On what principle would you set about incorporating the less regular forces with our existing 6 divisions? I know nothing about the policy at the WO at present...

How rapidly events move! I hardly liked looking at last week while our Government 'waited'!

How much longer will the German Empire last?

Haig's diary continued:

[At midnight, 4/5 August (Tuesday/Wednesday) Captain Harding Newman[1] DAQMG, telephoned from the Headquarters Office to Government House that War Office had wired 'War has broken out with Germany.' On the 5th I motored to London, was medically examined at War Office and passed 'physically fit for Active Service at home or abroad'.

At 4 pm I attended a War Council at 10 Downing Street. Mr *Asquith (the Prime Minister) was in the Chair. He began with a brief statement of the circumstances in which he had summoned this Council. The Germans had crossed their frontier into Belgium early yesterday (4 August). War had actually been declared between England and Germany, between Russia and Germany and between France and Germany, but as yet Austria was not technically at war with any country except Serbia. One unexpected factor in the situation was the neutrality of Italy. It must now be assumed that Italy would not stand in with Germany and Austria. A further unexpected factor in the situation was the action of Belgium and Holland. Belgium appeared to be offering a better resistance than had been anticipated. Germany was reported to have violated Dutch Limburg, and was apparently determined to overwhelm all resistance.

Sir John French gave in outline a pre-arranged plan which had been worked out between the British and French General Staffs. Briefly stated, it was hoped that the Expeditionary Force would mobilise simultaneously with the French, and would be concentrated behind the French left at Maubeuge by the fifteenth day of mobilisation. The intention then was to move eastwards towards the Meuse, and act on the left of the French against the German right flank. We were now, however, late in mobilising, and so this plan was

1 Captain (later Major General) John Cartwright Harding Newman (1874–1935), DAQMG XVII Corps and IX Corps in 1918. He was the author of *Modern Military Administration, Organization and Transportation* (Aldershot: Gale & Polden, 1933).

no longer possible. He spoke about his hopes of now going to Antwerp and operating with the Belgian and possibly Dutch Armies.

The alternative routes for reaching Antwerp were then discussed: viz., whether by sea or land.

The Navy, the First Lord (*Churchill) stated, could not protect the passage of our transports during the longer sea passage across the North Sea to the Scheldt.

Then the CIGS (Douglas)[1] pointed out that the military plans were worked out for an embarkation at Newhaven, Southampton and Bristol, with a landing at Havre, Boulogne, and other French ports in the Channel. The French had also arranged for rolling stock and prepared railway timetables for the movement of our units. A change of destination at the last moment would have serious consequences.

Personally, I trembled at the reckless way Sir J. French spoke about 'the advantages' of the BEF operating from Antwerp against the powerful and still intact German Army! So, when it came to my turn to speak I formulated a number of questions to bring out the risk we would run of 'defeat in detail' if we separated from the French at the outset of the campaign. 'Have we enough troops, with the Belgians, to carry on a campaign independently of the French, or do we run excessive risk, if we act separately, of defeat in detail?' and 'What does our General Staff know of the fighting value of the Belgian Army?' I also made these points:

1st. That Great Britain and Germany would be fighting for their existence. Therefore the war was bound to be a long war, and neither would acknowledge defeat after a short struggle. I knew that German writers had stated in their books that a modern war in Europe would not last more than a few months. In my opinion, that was what they hoped for and what they were planning to make it. I held that we must organise our resources for a *war of several years*.

2nd. Great Britain must at once take in hand the creation of an Army. I mentioned one million as the number to aim at immediately, remarking that that was the strength originally proposed for the Territorial Force by Lord Haldane.[2] Above all, we ought to aim at having a strong and effective force when we came to discuss peace at a conference of the Great Powers.

3rd. We only had a small number of trained officers and NCOs. These

1 General Sir Charles Whittingham Horsley Douglas (1850–1914). Douglas was CIGS from 6 April 1914 until his death from overwork on 25 October 1914.
2 Richard Burdon Haldane (1856–1928). As Secretary of State for War, 1905–12, Haldane had played a key role in the preparation of the British Army for war, including the creation of the Territorial Force, the British Expeditionary Force, the Officers Training Corps and the Special Reserve. Haig had worked with him at the War Office during the period 1906–9 and was a great admirer.

must be economised. The need for efficient instructors would become at once apparent. I urged that a considerable proportion of officers and NCOs should be withdrawn from the Expeditionary Force. (This latter suggestion met with much opposition from Sir J. French, with the result that only 3 officers per battalion were retained in England from the battalions now ordered to France.) *Lastly,* my advice was to send as strong an Expeditionary Force as possible, and as soon as possible, to join the French Forces and to arrange to increase that Force as rapidly as possible.

The conclusions arrived at by this War Council were: (a) take up transports at once, but our line of operations could be settled later. (b) A French Staff officer of high standing was asked for to come to London to confer with Lord *Kitchener. (c) India was to be asked to send a division to Egypt, and to retain another division and a cavalry brigade in readiness to start on receipt of orders. (d) The offers of contingents from the Dominions were accepted and their troops are to concentrate in England.

After the meeting broke up, Lord Kitchener came with me to the War Office in my car. I took him to the CGS's[1] room. The latter (Sir Charles Douglas) did not come in for some 15 or 20 minutes, so I had an opportunity of discussing the situation with Lord K. Two points struck me: first K.'s ignorance of the progress made by the Territorial Army towards efficiency, and secondly, his ignorance of the Military situation in German East Africa, and of the value, as soldiers, of the German Military settlers there. Personally, I was very intimately acquainted of course, with what the Territorials had been doing. I was well aware how hard some units had worked and of the splendid patriotic spirit which pervaded the whole Force. The position in German East Africa was only known to me as the result of talks with my BGGS (Johnnie Gough).[2] He had spent several years as Inspector General in the adjoining British Territory under our Colonial Office, and before I left Aldershot for the War Council he gave me a few notes on the military situation in those parts. He urged the immediate capture of Dar-es-Salaam. On the arrival of Sir Charles Douglas, I left. Lord Kitchener then took over the duties of Secretary of State for War, which since the Curragh disturbance in the spring of 1914 had been performed by Mr Asquith in addition to his other duties...

On Thursday afternoon, 6 August: I attended another War Council at 10 Downing Street. The Prime Minister again presided, and more or less the

---

1 A slip for CIGS.
2 Brigadier General (later Major General) John Edmond ('Johnnie') Gough VC (1871–1915), BGGS Aldershot, 1913–14; I Corps, 1914; MGGS First Army, 1914–15. Gough died from wounds inflicted by a ricocheting bullet in February 1915, shortly before he was due to return home to command a New Army division.

same gentlemen attended. The PM stated that today the Cabinet had decided on principle to send the Expeditionary Force. It remained to be decided its strength and where it was to concentrate.]

Tuesday 11 August

[The *King and Queen arrive at Aldershot at 12 noon. His Majesty joins me in an open car and we motor round the lines. The troops turn out and line the roads and give their Majesties a cheer as they pass along. Their Majesties, too, say goodbye to the senior officers as they pass along in front of their Headquarters. The King seemed delighted that Sir John French had been appointed to the Chief Command of the Expeditionary Force. He asked me my opinion. I told him at once, as I felt it my duty to do so, that from my experience with Sir John in the South African War, he was certain to do his utmost loyally to carry out any orders which the Government might give him. I had grave doubts, however, whether either his temper was sufficiently even, or his military knowledge sufficiently thorough to enable him to discharge properly the very difficult duties which will devolve upon him during the coming operations with Allies on the Continent. In my own heart, I know that French is quite unfit for this great Command at a time of crisis in our Nation's History. But I thought it sufficient to tell the King that I had 'doubts' about the selection.

Their Majesties lunch with *Doris and me, quite simply at Government House. The King seemed anxious, but he did not give me the impression that he fully realised the grave issues both for our Country as well as for his own house, which were about to be put to the test; nor did he really comprehend the uncertainty of the result of all wars between great nations, no matter how well prepared one may think one is.]

Haig began to keep a manuscript diary on 13 August.

Thursday 13 August

Haig met French and his Chief of the General Staff, Sir Archibald Murray, at the Hotel Metropole.

Informed where the Expeditionary Force was to concentrate ... [I play golf with Doris in the afternoon ... I felt the great uncertainties of the future lying before me and could not talk much. The situation which I had often pondered over had now come to pass ...

[I have also felt for many years dating from my stay in Berlin in 1896, that war between Germany and England was sure to break out as soon as Germany felt strong enough to hold her own on the sea ... I have also tried to think out many a time what the next Great European War is likely to mean for an Army engaged in it. But in all my dreams I have never been so bold as to imagine that when that war did break out, that I should hold one of the most important commands in the British Army. I feel very pleased at receiving command of the First Army (Corps)[1] and I also feel the greatest confidence that we will give a good account of ourselves, *if only* our Higher Command give us a reasonable chance!

[I have a first rate Staff and my troops are throughout well commanded. Major General Lomax[2] commands the 1st Division. He is an experienced and practical leader, much beloved by the men, most loyal to me, and I have a thorough trust in his ability to command his division well, even in the worst of difficulties. The 2nd Division has just been given a new Commander, viz. Major General *Monro in the place of Major General Archibald Murray[3] (who has been selected by Sir J. French to be the Chief of Staff of the Expeditionary Force). Monro proved himself to be a good regimental officer and an excellent Commandant of the Hythe School of Musketry, but some years with Territorials has resulted in his becoming rather fat. There is, however, no doubt about his military ability, although he lacks the practical experience in commanding a division.

[The brigades and battalions are also all well commanded, and the regimental officers are probably the best all round in any Army. The artillery and mounted troops are also highly trained and thoroughly well found. On the other hand, our numbers are very small indeed, and I have an uneasy feeling lest we may be thoughtlessly committed to some great general action before we have had time to absorb our reservists. Any precipitate engagement of our little force may lose us the inestimable value which our highly trained divisions do possess not only as a unit in battle, but also as a leaven for raising the moral of the great National Army which the Government is now proceeding to organise.[4]

[This uneasy feeling which disturbs me springs, I think, in great measure from my knowledge of the personalities of which our 'High Command' is composed. I have already stated somewhat briefly my opinion of Sir John

1 The designation was changed from 'Army' to 'Corps' in early August.
2 Major General (later Lieutenant General) Samuel Holt Lomax (1855–1915), GOC 1st Division, 1910–14. Lomax was wounded at Ypres on 31 October 1914; he died of his wounds on 10 April 1915.
3 Major General (later General) Sir Archibald ('Archie') James Murray (1860–1945), CGS BEF, 1914–15; Deputy CIGS, then CIGS, 1915; GOC-in-C Egyptian Expeditionary Force, 1916–17. Murray was an intelligent and able officer who lacked the physical and mental resilience necessary to be effective in the field.
4 Kitchener's appeal for 100,000 volunteers for his 'New Armies' was issued on 8 August.

French's ability as a Commander in the field. His military ideas often shocked me when I was his Chief of Staff during the South African War. In those days, with only mounted troops under him, he fortunately could not put into practice some special theories which he told me he had deduced from Hamley's *Operations of War*. A chance for this came to him, however, last autumn, when as Director of Manoeuvres, he handled a force (representing the Expeditionary Force) against a skeleton enemy. His instructions for moving along the front of his enemy (then halted in a fortified position) and subsequently attacking the latter's distant flank were of such an unpractical nature that his Chief of the General Staff (Grierson)[1] demurred. Some slight modifications in the orders were permitted but Grierson ceased to be his CGS in case of mobilisation and was very soon transferred to another appointment in the BEF. Major General Murray as already stated, replaced him. Murray had been Sir John's BGGS during the period of the latter's Command at Aldershot. Recently during certain divisional exercises I had had occasion to criticise Murray's handling of his division. There was not only lack of method in putting his troops into the fight, but his views on 'protection' and on fighting generally, were in my view quite unpractical. So I had a poor opinion of his qualifications as a General; and in some respects he seemed to me to be 'an old woman'. For example, in his dealings with Sir John, when his own better judgement told him that something which the latter wished put in orders was quite unsound, instead of frankly acknowledging his disagreement, he would weakly acquiesce, in order to avoid an outbreak of temper and a scene.

[With all this knowledge of the Chief and his CGS behind me, I have grave reason for being anxious about what happens to us in the great adventure upon which we are now to start this very night. However, I am determined to behave as I did in the South African War, namely, to be thoroughly loyal and do my duty as a subordinate should, trying all the time to see Sir John's good qualities and not his weak ones. For most certainly both French and Murray have much to commend them, although neither in my opinion are at all fitted for the appointments which they now hold at this moment of crisis in our country's history.]

Haig crossed to France on 15 August on SS Comrie Castle.

---

1 General Sir James ('Jimmy') Moncrieff Grierson (1859–1914), GOC II Corps, 1914. Grierson was a talented but notoriously corpulent officer. He died of a heart attack on 17 August 1914 on his way to the front.

Monday 17 August

About 9 am, on his way to the front, while the train halted at Serquex, Haig was informed that Grierson had died suddenly in the train at about 7.30, and was asked what should be done.

I said trains to continue the journey to Amiens and to report the matter to General Robb, commanding the communications, who was at Amiens. It seemed to me of no use for me to delay until the train with the II Army Corps Headquarters came up, as I could do nothing. I heard later that the cause of death was aneurism of the heart.[1]

Tuesday 18 August

Haig attended a conference at GHQ, now at Le Cateau.

General *Allenby and Vaughan[2] of the Cavalry Division and General Walker[3] (Chief Staff Officer of the II Army Corps) were among those present. Sir J. French explained the situation and indicated a possible line of action but refrained from giving definite orders until divisions had fully concentrated.

Wednesday 19 August

I gathered that the Belgian Army is falling back on Antwerp while the Germans are crossing [the Meuse] in considerable strength (at least 4 corps) about Huy and Liège [and marching with all speed westwards on Brussels and Namur.] They have a railhead at Warenne. This looks as if an effort is to be made to turn the French left, which rests on Namur fortress [by an advance through Belgium. In fact, the solution of the problem which was given as the most likely one when I was at Camberley Staff College in 1897.] The neighbourhood of Waterloo and Charleroi should then be the scene of another great battle.

1 According to Charteris, this incident was typical of Haig: he felt the loss of his friend 'acutely', but refused to let personal feelings disturb his professionalism. *At GHQ*, pp. 10–11. Grierson's replacement was General Sir Horace Smith-Dorrien.
2 Lieutenant Colonel (later Major General) John Vaughan (1871–1956), GSO1 Cavalry Division, 1914; GOC 3rd Cavalry Brigade, 1914–15; GOC 3rd Cavalry Division, 1915–18; a renowned horseman, polo player and huntsman.
3 Brigadier General (later Major General Sir) George Townshend ('Hooky') Forestier-Walker (1866–1939), BGGS II Corps, 1914; MGGS Second Army, 1914–15; GOC 21st Division, 1915. Haig had a low opinion of Forestier-Walker's abilities.

Thursday 20 August

Had conference at 10 am at Wassigny in my writing room ... I explained general situation as far as I knew it. Pointed to possibility of general action early next week, and made a few remarks on following lines:

1. Avoid excessive thickness in attacking lines.
2. Operations in open country and the 'rassemblement articule'.[1]
3. Advanced guards.
4. Attack on enemy's machine guns which are said to be well commanded.
5. Village and street fighting – necessity for keeping reserve.
6. Avoid woods if possible.
7. Make good one's hold on tactical points as the attack progresses. Use of RE, companies and machine guns for this.[2]

Friday 21 August

On this day II Corps was attacked by a larger German force at Mons.

Late last evening an order came from GHQ for my Corps to take up front from Mons (held by 3rd Division) to Peissant about 4 miles southwest of Binche. Movement to be completed without delay. This seemed to me to be an ill-considered order in view of the condition of the reservists in the ranks, because it meant a forced march by night ...[3]
  [I] went on to meet Sir J. French at a chateau near Blaregnies where II Corps HQ was situated. Here I met Sir H. *Smith Dorrien ... The meeting took place at 10.30 am. It was arranged that II Corps' right should extend to the southeast of Mons as far as and including up Hill 93 (about 1 mile north of Harmignies). The general situation as explained by Sir J. French on information given by General H. *Wilson from Air reconnaissances etc. showed at least 3 German corps suitably placed for an attack on Mons and neighbourhood ... [Little attention seemed to be paid to the reports which have been coming in for several days that the Enemy is moving in large masses on Tournai. The Commander-in-Chief had apparently not discussed the

1 'Marshalling in formation', i.e. co-ordination of forces in successive moves.
2 Charteris noted that Haig was 'much concerned about the general plan'. Fearing that the Germans might turn the BEF's flank, he aimed 'to keep liberty of manoeuvre'. *At GHQ*, p. 13.
3 Haig also criticised GHQ's decision in his diary entry of 22 August, adding 'Impossible' for Sir John French 'to command at distance of 30 miles from the scene of action'.

situation with his Intelligence Officer (Macdonogh)[1] because the latter, who was not in the conference room, told me after the Conference that aeroplanes reported all the roads running west from Brussels to Ath and Tournai were thickly covered with masses of German troops of all arms marching very rapidly westwards. This was indeed an alarming situation. Yet our C-in-C ordered my Corps to press on! Wilson had news that the French would re-establish the situation by a breakthrough in the Ardennes or in Alsace! De Castelnau[2] was about to deliver an enormous attack which must succeed!]

I spent the day at Le Bonnet and moved my HQ at nightfall to a chateau about $\frac{1}{2}$ mile west of Bettingues. About 1 o'clock I motored to HQ of 3rd Division ... and saw Hubert Hamilton[3] ... [he] seemed to me quite worn-out with fatigue: indeed so sleepy he scarcely paid attention to General Rice's[4] report.

In afternoon very heavy firing took place on Vellereille-le-Sec by high explosive. A battery in action near the 'Halte' was badly knocked about but the Berks in trenches scarcely suffered ... a motor car arrived to say that H. Hamilton was being seriously attacked and wanted support. His advanced troops had been driven back from the Canal north and northeast of Mons. I got into motor and went to crossroads about 3 miles north of Le Bonnet. Heavy firing was then going on to the north, and great columns of refugees were seen leaving Mons and advancing on Hamilton's position. I should have liked to have sent forward the 4 Guards Brigade and Haking[5] to counter-attack, but my right was still being attacked. I therefore ordered the 4 Guards Brigade to Hartweg with instructions to detach 2 battalions to Hill 93 ... so as to relieve two battalions of 3rd Division now on it. I also had Haking's

1 Lieutenant Colonel (later General Sir) George Mark Watson Macdonogh (1865–1942), GSO1 Intelligence, GHQ BEF, 1914; BGGS Intelligence GHQ BEF, 1914–16; DMI War Office, 1916–18; an able and cautious Intelligence Officer, whom Haig later in the war often characterised as a 'defeatist'.
2 General Noel Joseph Edouard de Curières de Castelnau (1851–1944), GOC French Second Army in 1914; a devout Roman Catholic, known as the 'Fighting Friar'.
3 Major General Hubert Ion Wetherall Hamilton ('Hammy') (1861–1914), GOC 3rd Division, 1914; killed in action 14 October 1914.
4 Rice had personally reconnoitred Hill 93: Brigadier General (later Major General Sir) (Spring) Robert Rice (1858–1929), Chief Engineer I Corps, 1914–15; First Army, 1915–16; Engineer-in-Chief France, 1916–17. Rice was a friend of Haig, with whom he had served in Aldershot Command before the war. Haig had great faith in him.
5 Brigadier General (later Lieutenant General Sir) Richard Cyril Byrne Haking (1862–1945), GOC 5 Brigade, 1914; GOC 1st Division, 1914–15; GOC XI Corps, 1915–18. Haking was, like Haig, an 'educated soldier', but as GOC XI Corps he acquired an unenviable reputation as a 'butcher' and organiser of pointless 'stunts'. He suffered a bad head wound on 14 September 1914 while GOC 5 Brigade.

Brigade and the bulk of the artillery of 2nd Division in readiness near the crossroads northeast of Bougnies to support in case of necessity. I wrote to Smith Dorrien at 5.30 pm telling him what I had done.[1]

About 6.30 pm Smith Dorrien and his CGS (Forestier Walker) came to Le Bonnet to see me and asked for troops to fill gaps between Hamilton's left and the right of 5th Division. Forestier Walker said 'The battle is won if you will only send us a battalion or two'.

I accordingly ordered General Haking to take 3 battalions of infantry to march at once in accordance with General Smith Dorrien's orders which would be given to him en route ... Haking reported later that he deployed a few men but no Enemy was met.

At 11 pm General Scott Kerr[2] Commanding 4 Guards Brigade came to see me regarding how point 93 ... is to be held. He said that 'George Morris[3] (Commanding Irish Guards) and others said the hill was another Spion Kop, a death trap' etc.[4]

I gave him a reply to GOC 2nd Division in writing stating that the hill must be held ...

The decision of French Fifth Army to withdraw forced the BEF to retreat in spite of II Corps' defensive victory.

Monday 24 August

At 2 am I am aroused by Captain Studd[5] with telegram from GHQ ordering retreat at once on Bavai where a defensive position would be taken up. I Corps to cover retirement of II Corps! ... This seemed impossible, as I was much further to east, and not being allowed to pass through Maubeuge had to make a flank march in the face of the enemy!

I decide:

(a) to organise a rear guard under General *Horne, consisting of 5 Cavalry Brigade, [2 battalions of infantry] ... 2 brigades RFA [to concentrate

1 A copy of this letter is appended to the Ts diary and is reproduced in Duff Cooper, *Haig*, I, pp. 144–5.
2 Brigadier General Robert Scott-Kerr (1859–1942), GOC 4 (Guards) Brigade, 1914. He never really recovered from the serious wound he received on 1 September 1914.
3 Lieutenant Colonel George Henry Morris (1872–1914), CO 1st Battalion Irish Guards, 1913–14.
4 On 24 January 1900, during the Second Boer War, a British force climbed Spion Kop (Look-Out Hill) only to find themselves exposed to heavy Boer fire from the surrounding hills. The British sustained heavy casualties.
5 An Intelligence Officer with I Corps.

near the crossroads south of Le Bonnet, and to take the offensive at daybreak, with the object of delaying and misleading the Enemy's leading troops.]

(b) under cover of this attack, 2nd Division to move to a position northwest of Le Bonnet: and 1st Division to draw westwards and hold the Villers–Sire–Nicole position (as arranged by me on the 22nd, but orders from GHQ upset this).

(c) meantime trains, Divisional ammunition columns, ambulances, etc., to move off by 2 roads to Bavai.[1]

I motored to Le Bonnet and dictated orders as above to Colonels Jeudwine[2] and Neil Malcolm,[3] then I went on in car ... to crossroads about 3 miles north of Le Bonnet. General Monro had his HQ here in a little shop or auberge by the wayside.

Having given Monro orders in above sense ... [I] marked his map, as he and his Staff officer (Colonel Gordon)[4] were very sleepy.

General Scott Kerr ... came in ... looking very pale. He said that the two Guards Battalions had left Hill 93 contrary to the orders which had been given them ... I replied that Monro must go into that question later: at present arrangements for retreat were most urgent.[5]

It was now about 3 am. [Baird[6] and I] motored by direct road to Givry. Owing to a barricade in the village we mistook turn in the dark to General Davies' HQ [(6 Brigade)][7] and went for a bit towards the Enemy's lines! We soon detected mistake. I saw General Davies [and some of his Staff;] all very tired and sleepy – told him to [cancel the orders which he had given for a move forward and instead] to be ready to carry out order to retire on Le Bonnet which would soon reach him from HQ 2nd Division. I then went

---

1 In the absence of Johnnie Gough at GHQ, Haig carried out his own staff work.
2 Colonel (later Lieutenant General Sir) Hugh Sandham Jeudwine ('Judy') (1862–1942), GSO1 I Corps, 1914; GSO1 1st Division, 1914–15; BGGS V Corps, 1915; GOC 41 Brigade, 1915; GOC 55th (West Lancashire) Division, 1916–19.
3 Properly Lieutenant Colonel (later Major General Sir) Neill Malcolm (1869–1953), GSO1 I Corps, 1914–15; an acerbic MGGS Fifth Army, 1916–17; badly wounded while commanding 66th Division on 29 March 1918.
4 Colonel (later Major General) Hon. Sir Frederick Gordon (1861–1927), GSO1, 2nd Division, 1911–14; GOC 19 Brigade, 1914–15; GOC 22nd Division, 1915–17 (Salonika).
5 As a consequence, Haig sent home the CO 2nd Grenadier Guards, Lieutenant Colonel N. A. L. Corry. Diary, 9 September 1914.
6 Major (later General Sir) Harry Beauchamp Douglas Baird (1877–1963), Haig's ADC, 1914.
7 Brigadier General (later Major General) Richard Hutton Davies (1862–1918), a New Zealander; GOC 6 Brigade, 1910–14; GOC 20th Division, 1914–16. Davies never really recovered from the physical and mental exhaustion he suffered in 1914; he committed suicide in a London nursing home on 5 May 1918.

on to General Lomax at the Chateau de Rouveroy. All still asleep here. I gave him and Colonel Fanshawe¹ (his CGS) full details. The road from Givry to Rouveroy was encumbered with transport but I was able to see General Bulfin² and Davies on my way back as I passed Givry, and was back at Le Bonnet before 4 am.

Thanks to the motor I was able to give personal orders to all the chief commanders concerned in the space of an hour, [and enable them to cancel the orders which their troops were on the point of carrying out for a forward movement.] Written orders reached them later, but the movement [in retreat] was started on certain lines in a way which would have been impossible before the days of the motor . . .

I spent the morning at Le Bonnet. Sir J. French came to see me. Evidently very anxious, but was reassured at seeing the orderly way in which the retreat was proceeding. I took him to some rising ground about ½ mile northwest of Le Bonnet whence the Enemy's shelling was plainly visible. The attack to the north seemed also very heavy . . .

General Davies returned to me at the crossroads just south of Malplaquet³ and reported that there were no prepared entrenchments and that it [the Bavai position] was a bad position! I at once ordered my HQ to move from Bavai to Vieux Mesnil (5 miles southeast of Bavai) and went in to Bavai to see Sir J. French . . . All seemed much excited but with no very clear plan beyond holding this wretched Bavai position.

I pointed out strongly to Sir John that if we halted for a day at Bavai the whole Force would be surrounded by superior numbers. [To this the Field Marshal replied that 'Smith-Dorrien had just stated that his troops could march no farther; that they could not march on the following day, but must halt for rest'. The Field Marshal, however, agreed with me as to the grave risk we would incur if we were to halt] and ordered the Force to continue its retreat. By Murray's request I arrange roads for retirement of my Corps on Landrecies, *giving the direct route to Le Cateau to the II Corps . . .*

When I got to my room I turned very sick with diarrhoea and continued for 2 hours, then went to sleep.

---

1 Colonel (later Major General Sir) Robert Fanshawe ('Fanny') (1863–1946), GSO1 1st Division, 1911–14; GOC 6 Brigade, 1914–15; GOC 48th (South Midland) Division, 1915–18.
2 Brigadier General (later General Sir) Edward Stanislaus Bulfin (1862–1939), GOC 2 Brigade, 1914 (wounded); GOC 28th Division, 1914–15 (sick); GOC 60th Division, 1915–17; GOC XXI Corps EEF, 1917–19. Haig greatly admired Bulfin's performance in 1914.
3 Scene of the Duke of Marlborough's victory over the French in 1709.

Tuesday 25 August

HQ I Corps was attacked at Landrecies.

I was much better in the morning but went in motor car ... I reached Landrecies about 4 pm and sent for GOC divisions and Cavalry Brigade.

Meantime, about 5 pm there is a panic in the town and country people rush in saying that the Germans are upon us. Our kit is waiting loaded on the waggons, [but the mess had been unpacked.] I prepare to go to the *mairie* as being more central. The mess, etc., is all bundled out. Soon matters quiet down. But at dusk (about 7 pm) the town is attacked on the north side, and shells burst in the main street. The 4 (Guards) Brigade [with 41 and 44 Howitzer Brigades and Army troops] are billeted in Landrecies. Their guard [north of the bridge] does not seem to have been very alert, for the Enemy suddenly advanced and managed to capture their 2 machine guns. It is stated that the Enemy came on dressed as French officers and knocked up the rifles of the Guard. If so, they were very plucky fellows! The inlying picket turned out and Enemy were checked until further support arrived [and pressed them back from the bridge.]

Then the whole town was organised for defence. General Gough thought the Guards were very sleepy and that the measures taken were rather half-hearted, so I went out myself – saw the GOC (General Scott Kerr) and impressed on him the necessity for rapid action. I ordered barricades at once, 2 guns in each; men to take off kits and fix bayonets ready for street fighting, machine guns to be suitably placed in windows to sweep streets. I then went to where Irish Guards were quartered near Infantry Barracks. I directed the latter to be organised as a 'reduit' in case Enemy should penetrate the other defences. The howitzers firing point blank from the barricades made the Enemy pause and inflicted great loss on him.

The 4 (Guards) Brigade seemed now fully alive to the necessity for exertion on their part, and the situation being more tranquil, I decide to go off to where I could best control the Army Corps. Gough, I and *Charteris accordingly got into my motor [about 11.30 pm]. We had had some difficulty in getting past the barricade ...

We motor to Le Grand Fayt where General Landon,[1] Commanding the 3 Brigade has his [HQ]. Baird and Secrett,[2] with the horses, join me later in the night. I got there about midnight ...

General Monro had come to Landrecies on receipt of order and was present

1 Brigadier General (later Major General) Herman James Shelley Landon (1859–1948), GOC 3 Brigade, 1910–14; GOC 9th (Scottish) Division, 1915; 33rd Division, 1915–16; 35th Division, 1916–18.
2 Sergeant T. Secrett, Haig's soldier-servant.

when the attack on the town began. I ordered him to move up his brigades to the support of the 4 (Guards) Brigade.

Wednesday 26 August

II Corps was attacked at Le Cateau. Smith-Dorrien hoped that Haig would move to support his right flank. However, I Corps eight miles away, continued to retreat and did not get involved in the battle. II Corps fought a model defensive battle and then disengaged, but with much heavier casualties than at Mons.

Major Dawnay[1] (communication officer between GHQ and my Staff) joined me about 6 am at Le Grand Fayt with a message from the C-in-C to the effect that I was to fall back southeast with the French and rejoin later by *rail*, or move on St Quentin. I could do as I judged best. GHQ had evidently given my corps up as lost from their control! [I felt that I could not do more than I had already done to comply with the spirit of these orders, and I considered it best to allow the movements of the Corps to proceed on the lines which I had already laid down.[2]

[Unfortunately direct communication with the II Corps was cut off, and touch was not regained until the I Corps reached Villers-Cotterets on the 1st September.]

Thursday 27 August

I was aroused about 2 am by 2 Staff officers who had come from General Vallabregue's HQ[3] who came to say that Corps wished to use the main Iron–Guise road. If I allowed them to use this road it would be impossible for my Corps to escape. I therefore insist on having the main road from Etreux through Guise to Mont d'Origny ... and I was prepared to fight them for the road because it was *the only one* available for my use[4] ...

At 7 am as the transport seemed to be moving back slowly, I ordered vehicles to be double banked. The road was a good wide one with grass on each side. No motors were to be driven up or down the columns; all officers were ordered to ride. I sent [Staff officers] on to Guise to reconnoitre 2 roads through that town. The result of all these arrangements was that the transport moved with the greatest smoothness and in perfect order, on to the hills

---

1 Major (later Major General) Guy Payan Dawnay (1878–1952), GSO2 and GSO1 GHQ BEF, 1914–15; MGGS GHQ BEF, 1918–19.
2 i.e. I Corps continued to retreat to the south.
3 Commander of the French Reserve divisions.
4 Haig considerably softened his language in his description of this episode in the Ts diary.

beyond Guise; and two divisions at war strength with all their transport, supply and ammunition columns were moved on one road for a march of 16 to 18 miles.

The 1st Division was in the rear and Maxse[1] 1 (Guards) Brigade acted as rear guard. By some error of judgement, this rear guard remained too long in its position north of Etreux, and the greater part of the Munster Fusiliers was surrounded in a village and killed or captured. Only some 7 officers [and] 250 men returned.[2]

Saturday 29 August

... I was awoken about 5 am by a despatch from GHQ asking why 'I had initiated operations with the French'. I replied that before asking my reasons they should find out if the statement was true![3] French officers from General Lanrezac[4] also arrived asking for support. I replied that my actual position covered their flank and I could not do more. My troops were very tired and must have rest ...

Gough and I ordered to GHQ at Compiègne – about 35 miles distant and road difficult to find and very hilly – arrive 4 pm. Sir J. French sees me first and apologises for the communication regarding corresponding with the French ...

General *Joffre arrives, looking very worried, so are his Staff. All the Fifth French Army has been defeated and is falling back.[5] Sir J. French decides that our Army must fall back changing its base from Havre to Nantes (or vicinity). Retreat to begin at once ...

1 Brigadier General (later Lieutenant General Sir) (Frederick) Ivor Maxse (1862–1958), GOC 1 Brigade, 1914; GOC 18th (Eastern) Division, 1914–17; GOC XVIII Corps (1917–18); Inspector General of Training, 1918–19. Maxse recovered from the ignominy of being sent home in 1914 to become a leading figure in the history of the BEF.
2 See Haig's damning comments on Maxse's report of 27 August 1914: TNA PRO: WO 95/588. Maxse certainly deserved some of the blame.
3 Based on a report from aerial reconnaissance, Haig saw an opportunity to strike the German flank, and suggested that I Corps co-operate with French Fifth Army. Sir John French refused permission. See Edward Spears, *Liaison 1914* (London, Cassell, 2000), pp. 256–9; for Haig's letter, see Duff Cooper, *Haig*, I, p. 162.
4 General Charles Louise Marie Lanrezac (1852–1925), GOC French Fifth Army. Clever, sarcastic and defeatist, he was a difficult and unreliable ally on the BEF's right flank; ruthlessly sacked by Joffre on 5 September 1914.
5 In reality, the Battle of Guise (29 August 1914) was a French victory. This passage illustrates the problems that even a commander of Haig's status experienced in trying to obtain accurate information.

Thursday 3 September. Letter to Lady Haig

It is too sad losing so many good fellows without materially affecting the result of the campaign. I should like to see the whole of our Expeditionary Force moved entirely forward to Ostend, where we could operate on our own against the German lines of communication which pass through Belgium. The French are most unreliable. One cannot believe a word they say as a rule!

I must tell you what a comfort the little spirit lamp and tin in the leather case has been. I use it for Maggi soup usually twice a day, and of course the luncheon box is always in use.

Friday 4 September

About 4 pm Sir J. French came to see me. I stated that our troops were tired out, that we could hold a position but that they could not attack or move at the 'double'. Smith-Dorrien arrived and concurred in all I had said. Sir J.F. agreed that Force must retire at once behind the Seine in order to refit.[1]

On 4 September Joffre, the French Commander-in-Chief, ordered a counter-offensive: the Battle of the Marne. The BEF was to advance into the gap that had developed between German First and Second Armies.

Saturday 5 September

The day was cooler: the troops marched with more life ... Major Dawnay arrived from GHQ with a note from Sir J. French asking me to pay particular attention to this message. The latter was to the effect that the French were really going to stand and attack! This time there was to be no doubt about it: they would fight to the death! ... About 1 o'clock the CGS (Sir A. Murray) came to see me on the same subject ... I pointed out two 'ifs': viz. *if* the French advance, and *if* the Germans don't attack before the French organise their forces for an attack, then the situation seems very favourable for us.

Wednesday 9 September

I Corps reached the River Marne.

About noon II Corps reported that an aeroplane had discovered large force

---

1 On 1 September Kitchener had forbidden French from withdrawing the BEF from the front line. Clearly, French had not entirely abandoned such ideas.

of the Enemy on the line Marigny–Château Thierry. I therefore ordered my advanced guard to halt and hold a position covering the crossings at Charly and Nogent.

About the same time officers arrived from the Sixth French Army saying that they were hard pressed on the Ourq and asking us to push on to their support. This report gave colour to the believe[1] that this army of the French had been beaten and that the Germans had brought up fresh troops which had been besieging Maubeuge.

I sent out special airoplane reconnaissance and soon I was able to send word to divisions to continue the march and that the Enemy seemed to be in full retreat ...

I met the 5 Cavalry Brigade moving at a walk and delay the advance of our infantry. I motored on and saw Chetwode.[2] At my suggestion he at once trotted on. I explained to him that a little effort now might mean the conclusion of the war. [The Enemy was running back. It was the duty of each one of us to strain every effort to keep him on the run.]

On 9 September 1914 German Second Army retreated, a move triggered in part by the BEF's crossing of the River Marne.

Friday 11 September

Orders were received last night from GHQ for the Expeditionary Force to wheel towards the right.[3] My Corps being on the right has a comparatively short wheel ...

The march was carried out without incident. Personally, I think it is a mistake to have changed direction now, because the Enemy on our front was close to us last night and was much exhausted. Had we advanced today on Soissons with cavalry on both flanks, large captures seemed likely. Bearing out this view is an intercepted wireless message from the German General commanding the Cavalry Corps in our front ... He wished infantry to cover his retirement across the river!

1 *sic.*
2 Brigadier General (later Field Marshal) Sir Philip Walhouse Chetwode Bt. (1869–1950), GOC 5 Cavalry Brigade, 1914–15; GOC 2nd Cavalry Division, 1915–16; GOC Desert Mounted Column EEF (1916–17); GOC XX Corps EEF (1917–19). Universally known as 'The Bart', he is now best remembered as father-in-law of the poet John Betjeman.
3 This movement was ordered by Joffre to make room for the French Sixth Army.

Monday 14 September

Army orders which reached me about 9 pm last night directed: 'The Army will continue the pursuit tomorrow at 6 am and will act vigorously against the retreating enemy ... Heads of Corps will reach the line Laon–Suzy–Fresne.'[1]

About 3 to 4 miles north of the river, a considerable ridge[2] (some 400 feet or more above the river) runs east and west with spurs running southwards to the river. It seemed to me very necessary to have a foothold on the ridge before putting our transport north of the river. I therefore ordered that the first objective of the Corps during today's march was to gain possession of this ridge, and that no movement (except reconnaissances) should take place beyond that line until we had ascertained progress [of] division (the 3rd) on my left. I also pointed out to General Lomax the advisability of getting possession of the ridge north of Vendresse village at daylight ...

At this time a young officer of the 15th Hussars[3] rode in to tell me that he had been reconnoitring on the left of the 6th Brigade toward Ostel village and Vailly; that he had seen a [British] gun limber and retreating infantry retreating hurriedly towards Vailly. These belonged to the 3rd Division ... [which] had come under hot shell fire just west of Chavonne. Fugitives said the 3rd Division had been driven back upon the river ...

Sir J. French and Staff arrived at this time. I explained the situation. How very fortunately situated we were until 3rd Division had run away back! It was impossible to rely on some of the regiments in the 3rd Division which had been so severely handled at Mons and Le Cateau ...

Shells now began to fall near where we were. High Explosive ones which make a great noise but do little damage beyond the actual spot hit. So I moved my Headquarters back about a mile to Canal Bridge south of Bourg village.

The situation remained very critical all afternoon. The 1st Division were heavily shelled and attacked by infantry, but the troops behaved magnificently and held their ground. Similarly on the left the 4 Guards Brigade repelled counter-attack after counter-attack ...

The 1st Division on the right gained ground, but could not maintain itself in the face of the opposition encountered. Only in the centre the 5 Brigade, moving along the eastern slopes of the Beaulne ridges, was able to get forward and to continue its advance until it reached the ridge about Tilleul de Courtacon. In the dark General Haking failed to get touch with the 1st Division, but his patrols found German outposts on both flanks. He con-

---

1 i.e. about 12 miles north of I Corps' position.
2 The Chemin des Dames ridge.
3 Lieutenant Guy Herbert Straker, who later became Haig's ADC. The time was around noon.

sequently drew back his troops under cover of darkness to the neighbourhood of Verneuil . . .

I then rode on to see Lomax . . . I told him that his action in capturing the ridge at daylight and the way his troops withstood the repeated attacks throughout the day was beyond all praise. At my request his troops had taken the offensive, about 5 pm 2 battalions [of] 3rd Brigade [pushed] up Chivy valley and then the whole line went forward. He then explained to me the situation. Practically all [his troops] were now extended and he had no reserve left. [The situation was indeed critical if the Enemy had any fresh troops to put into the battle!]

I told him to dig in, and hold on. I would arrange for French on my right and all [the British] on my left to take the offensive tomorrow.

The BEF came very close to capturing the Chemin des Dames ridge on 14 September, but its failure to do so marked the beginning of the end of mobile warfare. On 16 September French ordered his forces to entrench.

Tuesday 15 September. Letter to Sir John French[1]

The troops have done splendidly, and when one considers the continuous marching and the retreat, I believe it will be hard to find an instance in our annals in which troops have shewn a finer spirit, or fought with greater determination, at the close of such a trying period.

Prisoners have said that they intended to break through on my left, but owing to the splendid defence of the 2nd Division north of Soupir, and their severe losses they have abandoned the idea and are now entrenching in front of us. We spent all last night digging in, so I think our position will defy attack.

Wednesday 16 September

I arranged to work with an aeroplane helping to direct the guns today against one of the Enemy's concealed batteries and at 5 pm I arranged a bombardment by all the guns of the Army Corps (152) of the Enemy's position. The air reconnaissance had given us the dispositions behind the ridge. The firing was kept up for twenty minutes and seemed effective. The Enemy did not reply very effectively so I hope we warmed him up . . .

1 IWM: French Papers, 75/46/3.

Friday 18 September

I visited some of the wounded. The Ambulance personnel have been much overworked. Dressings are very short. *Horse* ambulance waggons no use; light motors (like what the French have) most necessary. Shortage of stretchers. The situation is quite unlike what the regulations anticipated!

I Corps settled into the routines of primitive trench warfare.

Sunday 20 September

Our troops have now been a week in the trenches. It is well nigh impossible for them to have a hot meal, and the weather has been very wet and cold. I am therefore most anxious to withdraw the men in turn from the trenches for rest and food. I therefore sent Gough to put my views before the officers at GHQ. In the meantime Sir J. French arrives and agrees with my request. He orders the remaining 2 brigades of 6th Division to join me, provided that I send 2 of my brigades into General Reserve . . .

About 1 o'clock a heavy attack begins on our right front in the section held by the new 18 Brigade (Brigadier General Congreve).[1] On the right was the West Yorkshire Regiment and the 2 Cavalry Brigade in the vicinity under General de Lisle.[2] The latter reported personally to me that West Yorks left their trenches and ran back to Paizy village headed apparently by the Colonel of the battalion. De Lisle and the 4th Dragoon Guards drove back a good many of the infantry at the point of their swords to the trenches . . . The Sussex Regiment . . . was in Paizy village as Divisional Reserve. This was hurried forward, and the situation was soon restored.[3]

Monday 21 September. Letter to Lieutenant Colonel Clive Wigram[4]

I am glad you already realise how wrong it was to have rushed the Army north to Mons by forced marches before our reservists had got their legs. GHQ had the wildest ideas at that time of the nature of the war and the rôle

1 Brigadier General (later Lieutenant General Sir) Walter Norris Congreve VC (1862–1927), GOC 18 Brigade, 1911–15; GOC 6th Division, 1915; GOC XIII Corps, 1915–17 (wounded); GOC VII Corps, 1918 (sick).
2 Brigadier General (later Lieutenant General Sir) (Henry de) Beauvoir de Lisle (1864–1955), GOC 2 Cavalry Brigade, 1911–14; GOC 1st Cavalry Division, 1914–15; GOC 29th Division, 1915–18; GOC XVIII Corps and XV Corps, 1918.
3 See also Haig's angry comments on Lomax's report of this incident: TNA PRO: WO 95/588.
4 Royal Archives: RA PS/GV/Q 2521/V/125. Later 1st Baron Wigram of Clewer (1873–1960), Assistant Private Secretary to HM King George V.

of the British Force. There are many too many in GHQ, and so friction and misunderstandings arise.

In mid-October I Corps began moving from the Aisne to Flanders, where the Battle of La Bassée had already begun. At first, the British advance encountered little resistance, but this changed when the Germans rushed troops to the area. On 16 October, Haig drove to visit the C-in-C at GHQ, St Omer.

Friday 16 October

I see Sir John French on my arrival. He seemed quite satisfied with the general situation and said that Enemy was falling back and that we 'would soon be in a position to round them up'. His intention is not to employ the I Corps until it has quite concentrated and units have had a day or two to pull themselves together after their trying time in the trenches.

Monday 19 October

I returned to St Omer at 6 pm.

Sir John stated that he 'estimated the Enemy's strength on the front Ostend to Menin, at about one corps, not more'. I was to march via Thourout and capture Bruges. Defeat Enemy and drive him on Ghent. My right would pass through Ypres. After passing that place, I was free to decide whether to go for Enemy on the north of me, or that part of him which was towards Courtrai. When I did advance, the French Cavalry would be on my left and *Byng's Cavalry Brigade on my right.

Wednesday 21 October

... All roads crowded with French Territorial troops ... Owing to block on roads, advance of 1st Division was delayed and advanced guard only reached Pilkem at 9 instead of 7 am. The attack of 2nd Division was consequently delayed ... 2nd Division moved east to attack Passendaele[1] in conjunction with advance of 1st Division ... Fighting was hard and came to bayonet work. Enemy seem to have been advancing when our attack took place. The 5 Brigade beat back an attack with much loss to the Enemy. And the Enemy was seen to be falling back from Poelcappelle village.

Now, without warning the French Cavalry guarding our left flank is ordered to retire west of the Canal![2] Reason Enemy is attacking from direction of

1 Properly, 'Passchendaele'.
2 At about 2 pm.

Clerken in strength about a division! The General commanding the French
Cavalry Division immediately on Lomax's left at once declined to obey the
order until it was repeated. He refused to uncover our flank without 'une
ordre formelle'. It was certainly a strange proceeding [to withdraw troops
supporting an ally's flank during a battle.] Lomax detached a few companies
to protect his own flank, and these were never attacked in force throughout
the afternoon!

About this time Sir H. *Rawlinson came to see me at the Hotel Châtelaine
where I had my HQ and reported that hostile infantry and guns were
advancing from Comine[1] up both sides of the Canal towards Ypres, and had
already forced back Gough's Cavalry Division in that part. He had only
Byng's Cavalry Brigade[2] (which was near Zonnebeke) as a reserve. He moved
a brigade of it to support his right near Zandvoorde. Then Rawlinson's 22
Brigade near Zonnebeke was attacked and the men left their trenches!

In view of all this uncertainty, excitement and despairing messages, I
decided that it was impossible to continue the offensive with the I Corps, so
I ordered 1st and 2nd Divisions not to go beyond the first stage of attack, viz.,
the capture of Poelcappelle and Passendaele. They were to fortify these points
and reconnoitre . . .

Sir J. French came to see me in the afternoon. He explained [that he would
soon be] taking the offensive and approved of the position I had taken up.
The advance was to be discontinued for the present.

*French's plan of 19 October was over-ambitious. The BEF was sucked into an
encounter battle, as units had to be committed piecemeal to shore up the line
against heavy German attacks. One important result of French's abortive attack
was that Haig's I Corps was now in position at the point of greatest danger,
around Ypres.*

Saturday 24 October. Letter to Major General S. H. Lomax[3]

I enclose herewith a wire from Military Secretary in reply to one from me
recommending Bulfin for promotion for service in the field.

The C-in-C told me more than a week ago that Lord Kitchener had
approved of yours and Landon's promotion and the announcement will
appear in an early gazette.

Again many thanks for your efforts, and generous support so freely given
to one at all times.

1 Properly, 'Comines'.
2 Actually, division.
3 IWM: Lieutenant General S. H. Lomax Papers, 90/1/1.

Monday 26 October

I ordered 2nd Division to push forward left and get Hill 27 ... By noon our left is progressing satisfactorily, when a report from IV Corps reaches me that the 7th Division which is holding line from crossroads southeast of Gheluvelt to Zandvoorde is giving way. I send Staff officer to find out whether they are being attacked by infantry or whether they are merely leaving their trenches on account of shell fire. He reports several battalions in great disorder passing back through our 1st Brigade...

By 4 pm the bulk of the 7th Division had retired from the salient about Kruiseik, most units in disorder. One brigade came back to the vicinity of Hooge Chateau where I had my 'reporting centre'. I rode out about 3 pm to see what was going on, and was astounded at the terror stricken men coming back. Still there were some units in the division which stuck to their trenches. I arranged for the necessary number of units from the 1st Division to support the latter, and hold a line from Poezelhoek to the left of the Cavalry Corps near Zandvoorde.

It was sad to see fine troops like the 7th Division reduced to inefficiency through ignorance of their leaders in having placed them in trenches on the *forward* slopes where Enemy could see and so effectively shell them.

On 29 October seven German divisions attempted to break through the Allied positions in the Ypres salient.

Saturday 31 October

About 7 General d'Urbal¹ came to see me. In the event of having to retreat I would cover Ypres from the east, and hold a line with Messines as my right, while the French held north of the town...

[Reports varied as to the strength of the Enemy's Forces now attacking my Corps. Early in the morning, however, a prisoner who had been captured during the night proved to be of the XV German Army Corps, and on his examination he stated that the whole of the XV Army Corps was present. This information was at once telegraphed to GHQ and telephoned to General Foch.]

At 10 am report reached me that situation in the trenches east and southeast of Gheluvelt was serious!...

2.30 General Lomax reported that 1st Division had broken and that he was trying to reform on the line east of Hooge. Soon after this 4 big shells fell into Hooge Chateau into a room which HQ 2nd Division occupied and

---

1 General Victor Louis Lucien D'Urbal (1878–1943), GOC French 7th Cavalry Division; later GOC French Eighth Army, 1914–15, Tenth Army, 1915–16.

killed Colonel Kerr, Senior GSO, 1st Division; Colonel Percival, GSO1 of 2nd Division; Lieutenant Colonel Paley, GSO2 1st Division.[1] Wounded General Lomax and General Monro was stunned.

About 3 pm Sir John French [came to the White Chateau to see me just as I was on the point of mounting my horse to go forward to the 1st Division. Owing to the congestion to traffic in Ypres, Sir John left his motor and walked the last half mile to my chateau. I told the Field Marshal of the serious condition of affairs on the 1st Division front. Sir John was full of sympathy and expressed his gratitude for what the Corps, as well as I myself, had done since we landed in France.] He was most pleasant[2] but he had no reinforcements to send me, [and viewed the situation with the utmost gravity. After a few sharp words of criticism about 'French help', he left me to go to his motor and visit Foch.]

I got on my horse and rode forward to see if I could do anything to organise stragglers and push them forward to check Enemy. I ride to Veldhoek and see Generals Landon, Capper[3] and FitzClarence,[4] and find that 'Gheluvelt has been retaken by the Worcesters' and the situation has been restored.[5] Troops very exhausted and 2 Brigadiers assure me that if the Enemy makes a push at any point, they doubt our men being able to hold on. Fighting by day and digging to strengthen their trenches by night has thoroughly tired them out.

[The recapture of Gheluvelt released the 6 Cavalry Brigade, till then held in support of the 1st Division; two regiments of this brigade were sent at once to clear the woods to the southeast, and closed the gap by my instructions in the line between the 7th Division and 2 Brigade. I saw some of the squadrons go forward. They advanced with much dash, partly mounted and dismounted. Their appearance seems to have taken the Enemy by surprise in the woods, and they succeeded in killing large numbers of the Enemy. This

1 Colonel F. W. Kerr, Lieutenant Colonel A. J. B. Percival, Major G. Paley. Three other officers were also killed.
2 In the Ts diary, Haig adds, 'No one could have been nicer at such a time of crisis.'
3 Major General Sir Thompson 'Tommy' Capper (1863–1915). GOC 7th Division, 1914–15. Died of wounds received during the Battle of Loos, 27 September 1915.
4 Brigadier General Charles FitzClarence VC (1865–1914), GOC 1 (Guards) Brigade, responsible for ordering the counter-attack of the 2nd Worcesters at Gheluvelt on 31 October 1914; killed in action on 12 November 1914.
5 In the Ts diary, Haig gives a slightly different version of events: 'As I was riding out of the gate, General Rice suddenly galloped up to say that on his way to 1st Div. HQ he had met an officer who stated that "Gheluvelt had been recaptured. The 1st Division had rallied!" The C-in-C also got this good news before going off.' This fuller version of events, written when Haig had had time to collect his thoughts, largely agrees with other witnesses. See Charteris, At GHQ, p. 53, and John Hussey, 'A Hard Day at First Ypres – The Allied Generals and their Problems: 31 October 1914', British Army Review, 107 (August 1994), pp. 75–89.

advance of the cavalry materially helped to restore the line. About 5 pm the French Cavalry Brigade also came up to the crossroads just east of Hooge, and at once sent forward a dismounted detachment to support our 7 Cavalry Brigade. I watched the smart dapper little fellows march off. Several had 'jemima' boots, most unsuited for war and mud such as we soon encountered in Flanders. They went off in great spirits to take on the German infantry, though the little carbine with which they were armed was not much better than an ordinary rook rifle!]

I ride round by Zillebeke and see General Moussy.[1] The little town had been terribly bombarded and most houses greatly destroyed. General Moussy has not advanced far owing to the hot fire of Enemy's guns ... About 11 pm Captain Requin[2] came to see me regarding Foch's orders for tomorrow.

Sunday 1 November

8 am Landon (Commander 1st Division)[3] came to report that the Division so disorganised that no organised attack could really be withstood. Rifles jammed owing to mud and soil and no opportunity for cleaning and oiling ...

Tuesday 3 November. Letter to Leopold de Rothschild[4]

The cigars arrived this morning – many thanks for them. I almost feel I shall have to take to smoking as some of my Staff are so delighted with them and say I miss so much as a non-smoker.

We have had terribly hard fighting during the last week, but we have held our ground and the Germans seem to be almost more tired than we are. Our casualties I regret to say have been very heavy, but we have had to hold our ground until French reinforcements could be brought forward. Our men are very tired: they fight hard by day and then during the night dig all they can to strengthen their position so they get very little sleep. We ought to have more men. Even Territorials would do splendidly against the present German infantry ... Of course *officers* are also badly needed as our casualties in officers have been very heavy.

1 Commander of French 33 Brigade, 17th Division, IX Corps.
2 An officer on Foch's staff.
3 Landon had taken over command vice the wounded Lomax.
4 NLS: Haig Papers, Acc. 3155, No. 214a. Leopold ('Leo') de Rothschild (1845–1917), racehorse owner and member of the banking family. Haig met Rothschild in 1906 while taking a cure at a spa, and they became firm friends.

Thursday 5 November

I motored to Bailleul to see Sir J. French and lunched with him. [The table was laid in a room at the back of a chemist's shop.] The Corps Commanders were present at the meeting, viz. Smith-Dorrien, Pulteney,[1] Sir James Willcocks[2] and Allenby. The II Corps (Smith-Dorrien) is to relieve my I Corps, so that my divisions may have a rest in which to refit. [I was very astonished to find that the point which attracted most interest was, 'Winter leave' for the Army! Personally, my one thought was how soon I could get my battle-worn troops relieved and given a few days' rest out of the trenches and shell fire!][3]

Saturday 7 November

The Lincolns, Northumberland Fusiliers and the Bedfords leave their trenches on account of a little shell fire. Several pass Divisional Headquarters while I am there. I order [all] men to be tried by [Court Martial] who have funked in this way, and [the abandoned] trenches to be re-occupied at once.

Sunday 8 November

Aroused soon after 2 am by General Wing,[4] Commanding the 3rd Division, to say that he could not get his men to charge to retake the old line of trenches...

Lord Cavan[5] wrote in at 8 this morning asking for relief. 'I feel bound to report that the units of the 3 Brigade, 22 Brigade and Irish Guards are not at the moment fit to make offensive movements. Relief of the units, if only for 24 hours, would I am sure re-establish confidence, which is at the moment much shaken, as officers left in command say they have nobody to see their

1 Lieutenant General (later Sir) William Pulteney ('Putty') (1861–1941); GOC III Corps, 1914–18.
2 Lieutenant General (later General) Sir James Willcocks (1857–1926), GOC Indian Corps, 1914–15.
3 On 6 November Haig wrote to Field Marshal Sir Evelyn Wood that 'Our troops have had and are having terribly hard times. This high explosive of the Germans is most disturbing. We have much to learn from their artillery and machine-gun methods. We want many more machine guns, but organised into batteries or units.' Sir E. Wood, *Winnowed Memories* (London: Cassell, 1918), p. 388.
4 Major General Frederick Drummond Vincent Wing (1860–1915). Wing took over command of 3rd Division on 29 October 1914. He was killed in action at Loos on 2 October 1915.
5 Brigadier General (later Field Marshal) Earl of Cavan ('Fatty') (1865–1946), GOC 4 (Guards) Brigade, 1914–15; GOC Guards Division, 1915–16; GOC XIV Corps, 1916–18; GOC-in-C British Forces, Italy, 1918–19.

orders carried out. The men are physically exhausted etc.' I saw Cavan about 4.30 pm and arranged to relieve part of his line with the London Scottish . . .

I gather from the bombardment of Ypres last night that the Kaiser has given up the idea of a triumphal entry!!

Wednesday 11 November

About 8 am reports from the 3rd and 7th Divisions say that the trenches are being shelled more heavily than ever experienced before . . .

[The night had been a quiet one, but at 9.30 am a heavy attack, preceded by extremely heavy shelling by a large number of guns along the whole front of the 1st and 2nd Divisions, suddenly developed. The line which we held was pierced just north of the Menin road and consequently the Royal Fusiliers, whose trenches were immediately south of the road, were enfiladed and this regiment lost very heavily. Its Colonel – McMahon,[1] was killed, and the strength of the regiment was reduced to two subalterns and about 100 men . . . To meet the situation, reserves were at once moved up . . . our line was eventually re-established.] . . .

[Soon after 9 am] I rode to the White House near the railway crossing on the Menin road. Sent Gough on to Landon to organise counter-attack to regain trenches on south and north of Menin road . . . I sent Straker to General Monro to ask where his reserves were and to say I was anxious about my right, as French had given way on Lord Cavan's right near Zillebeke. Monro had the Oxfords and Irish Guards (each only about 300) available north of Menin road near Hooge.

Cavan reports situation satisfactory, though shelling severe. No infantry attack had yet developed.

General Horne goes to see Vidal (who had his Headquarters in farm about a $\frac{1}{4}$ mile from where I was). He said he had asked [his own chief] for reinforcements, and wanted me to support him. I, however, have no troops available.

[Towards noon, Lord Cavan reported that General Vidal's detachment on his right were being heavily shelled, and were leaving their trenches, and that General Vidal had applied to him for help, which, however, Lord Cavan was unable to afford. The situation, therefore, at this point was extremely critical, most of the Divisional and Corps reserves had been used up to re-establish the position in the vicinity of the Menin road, and the lack of the five battalions which had been withdrawn from General Vidal was now very severely felt, as the attack on our extreme right progressed. Every effort was

1 Lieutenant Colonel Norman Reginald McMahon (1866–1914), CO 4th Royal Fusiliers; killed in action 11 November 1914.

made to re-establish a corps reserve ready to meet this new danger on the right by the withdrawal of such troops as could be spared from the firing line.]

I return to Chateau de Trois Tours about 2 pm and find General Harper[1] from GHQ. I impress on him the seriousness of the situation: because –

1. Owing to retirement of French on our right, our communications [through Ypres] are endangered.
2. German Guard Division has arrived in our front as we took prisoners from them today. Enemy has been reinforced by 15 fresh battalions.
3. Our troops have had terribly hard fighting for over 10 days and many casualties. Our numbers therefore greatly reduced.

French reinforcements must be hurried up without delay. The I Corps and 3rd Division are in a false position, and unless immediate action were taken to support us, both we and the French IX Corps would be in great risk of being cut off. This would be an irreparable loss to England at the present time.

In afternoon, reports come in pointing to critical situation north of Menin road owing to gap in 1 Brigade line. All Divisional and Corps reserves are moved to block it and drive back a force of 1200 Germans who are advancing on it.

I send General Gough to see Landon and find out what General Fitz-Clarence (of 1 Brigade) has been doing. Baird to Monro to find out what line he proposes to take up in event of Germans not being driven out.

[At 3 pm] Colonel Davies[2] with Ox. and Bucks advances southeast from Westhoek [and] clears the Nonne Boschen Wood [with the bayonet] while Northants move northeast from Hooge. The Irish and Grenadier Guards support. The Germans are driven back with heavy loss, and the Oxfords reach the old trenches near the Polygon Wood. But owing to French guns shelling the ground, our troops cannot occupy the old line as far as the Menin road.

Many prisoners of the Guard Division are taken. They say that they have been specially brought up from Arras to break our line because the other Army Corps had failed to do so. Our losses are heavy. The 1 Brigade is reported to have no formed body left.

1 Brigadier General (later Lieutenant General Sir) (George) Montague Harper ('Uncle') (1865–1922), GSO1, then BGGS Operations GHQ BEF, 1914–15; GOC 17 Brigade, 1915; GOC 51st (Highland) Division, 1915–18; GOC IV Corps, 1918–19.
2 Lieutenant Colonel (later Major General) Henry Rodolph Davies (1865–1950), CO 2nd Oxfordshire and Buckinghamshire Light Infantry, 1911–15; GOC 3 Brigade (1915–16); GOC 11th (Northern) Division, 1917–19 (wounded September 1918).

About 9 pm, 1st Division reports that arrangements being made to attack and regain trenches at 1 am.

Sir J. French sends up De Lisle's Cavalry Division to arrive at daylight.

For the second time, the BEF had survived a major German attack that had appeared to be on the point of breaking through to Ypres.

Saturday 14 November

When I was with the 1st Division a note from the Colonel of the London Scottish reached me. He stated his 'Battalion was not in a fit state to take the field – the men are thoroughly broken. What is urgently required for the Battalion is a period of rest behind the guns. – Without the required rest it might be disastrous for the Battalion.'

It struck me that the Colonel (Malcolm by name)[1] wanted the rest more than his men. So I told Landon to see the Battalion and make them as comfortable as possible in 'dugouts' in reserve...[2]

Message from Sir J. French that he had recommended me for 'Immediate promotion to General for distinguished service in the field'. I reply thanking him and add 'Whatever success the I Corps has gained is mainly due to untiring zeal of my Staff and to the fine soldierly spirit fostered by Commanders of Divisions, Brigades and Battalions in their units during peace'.

The relief of I Corps began during 15 November.

Wednesday 18 November

The French proposed that the BEF take over more of the front line.

... I wired to GHQ that unless the numbers of the British Force in this theatre were greatly increased, it would be madness for us to take over such an extended line.[3] It would mean that our troops could not be given proper rest, and the Expeditionary Force would soon cease to be of fighting value. With the disappearance of this Force, the voice of Great Britain in European politics would be diminished. It will be many months before the new forces forming in England can take the field. Our policy ought therefore to be to

1 Lieutenant Colonel G. A. Malcolm, commander of 1/14th London Regiment (London Scottish).
2 For Haig's positive views on the battalion, see his letter to Lieutenant Colonel G. A. Malcolm, 9 November 1914: IWM: Special Miscellaneous, J5.
3 As proposed by the French.

husband the strength of our present field army as much as possible and get the French to do a fair share! The latter seem ready to drain the last drop of blood out of the British Force and Henry Wilson (now called Sub-Chief of the General Staff) seems quite ready to acquiesce and fails to uphold the interests of the British Forces. He seems to pander to Foch and is more French than the French!!'

Saturday 21 November

We (Gough, Baird, Straker and I) lunched with Sir John French. The latter told me that he had had a severe attack of heart, and doctors ordered him to take things easier. He looked rather pulled down.

He wished me to go home on a 'special mission' to see Lord Kitchener and tell him how things were going here. Sir J.F. understood people at home were despondent and knew little of [what tremendous opposition we had suffered and what had] been done here. He also considered that time for forming the Expeditionary Force into 2 Armies had arrived and he wished me to put that to Lord K.

Monday 23 November

At the War Office I was shown into Lord Kitchener's room at once, and we discussed the situation generally and the equipment and armament of the Force in France for fully two hours.

He agreed that it was time to divide the Expeditionary Force into 2 Armies, but said his scheme was to have Armies of 6 divisions each, [for instance the First Army would comprise the 1–6 original divisions. The Second Army would have the 7th and 8th Divisions with the 27th, 28th and 29th Divisions ...] and also the two Indian Divisions, i.e. an Army of seven divisions.

Tuesday 24 November

At 4 pm I was received by the King at Buckingham Palace. It was past 5 pm before the interview was over. Queen Mary came [into the King's study] to see me [and was very friendly ...]

The King was most complimentary today. He stated that on all sides (and he got reports, [he said,] from 'a large number of officers of all ranks') my work with the I Corps was highly spoken of. He said that more Territorials could not be spared to go abroad and join us because they had (until now)

1 In spite of some difficulties, the relief was completed by dawn on 21 November.

no trained troops at home to resist invasion. Now, [His Majesty considered that] the New Armies were wonderfully efficient. [I remarked that the surest way to prevent the Enemy from attempting to invade Great Britain was to engage and press him hard on the Continent! If that were done, the Germans could not spare any troops to take part in a landing expedition against this country.]

Thursday 26 November

I walked to the War Office with Doris. I saw General Sclater (Adjutant General)[1] and discussed the class of man sent out as drafts. Latterly the special reservists had neither the will, nor the physique for fighting.

I said we wanted patriots who knew the importance of the cause for which we are fighting. The whole German people have been impregnated from youth up with an intense patriotic feeling, so that they die willingly for their country. There are not many of our men who will do this unless well led. Now we are short of officers to lead them. I said send out young Oxford and Cambridge men as officers; they understand the crisis in which the British Empire is involved . . .

At 1 o'clock we lunched at Princes Gate with the children, and spent a happy afternoon at the Zoo. The Houses were locked up before we came away, so that they did not see the monkey house, [great] disappointment [to both Xandra and Doria],[2] but they saw every other kind of animal very well and fed them.

Haig returned to France on 27 November. In December, King George V visited the BEF.

Friday 4 December

In the evening I motored to St Omer and dined with the King . . .

I sat between the King and Prince of Wales. The King seemed very cheery but inclined to think that all our troops are by nature brave and is ignorant of all the efforts which Commanders must make to keep up the 'morale' of their men in war, and of all the training which is necessary in peace in order to enable a company for instance to go forward as an organised unit in the face of almost certain death. I told him of the crowds of fugitives who came back down the Menin road from time to time during the Ypres battle having thrown everything they could, including their rifles and packs, in order to

1 General Sir Henry Crichton Sclater (1855–1923), Adjutant General to the Forces, 1914–16.
2 Haig's daughters, Alexandra (b. March 1907) and Victoria (b. November 1908).

escape, with a look of absolute terror on their faces, such as I have never before seen on any human being's face. I felt certain that all who had been rewarded, had won their rewards most thoroughly. It was impossible adequately to reward some for what they had done because their glorious deeds were beyond earthly reward. This seemed to interest him.

He expressed the opinion that the grant of the Victoria Cross for carrying a wounded man out of action was justified and was beneficial. I replied that each case must be judged on its merits but, as a rule in *civilised* war such efforts did the wounded man harm and also tended to increase loss of valuable lives. On the other hand, in the case of a building containing wounded catching fire, and troops going [forward] under fire to remove the wounded, they would merit the VC. As a matter of fact we have to take special precautions[1] to prevent more unwounded men than are necessary from accompanying a wounded man back from the trenches. With *motor* ambulances this difficulty is lessened, because these vehicles can run up closer to the front, than can horse vehicles.

Saturday 12 December

I inspected some trench mortars [which we are making in our Engineer workshops.] They are made of steel piping [which we obtain in the district,] about 2 feet long, with a movable support near the muzzle to alter the elevation. A kind of spade is fixed to the base to prevent the gun from sinking in to the ground. They fire a bomb of 2lb weight. This can be thrown up to 300 yards by means of gunpowder charges . . . Each division has already made four of these guns and about 100 rounds of ammunition . . .

I offered my trench guns, and 4 are to be sent to the II Corps and 4 to the III Corps. Neither Corps had apparently started to make any. They seemed to me rather slovenly in their methods of carrying on war.

Tuesday 15 December

Very little energy displayed by the 8 Brigade (Bowes)[2] of the 3rd Division, II Corps in pressing the attack. Their methods are much the same as at Spion Kop and Vaal Krantz in South Africa where the whole Army looked on at a couple of battalions attacking. So at Le Petit Bois the attack was made by the Royal Scots and Gordon Highlanders, and when the latter lost some 200 casualties, operations ceased, and the Gordons fell back to their original trenches! In my opinion there are only 2 ways of gaining ground either, (a) a

1 In the Ts diary Haig added 'to post police'.
2 Brigadier General William Hely Bowes (1858–1932), GOC 8 Brigade, 1914–15.

general offensive all along the front, with careful preparation of artillery at special chosen points in order to dominate the Enemy's artillery at specially chosen points, [and] use of trench guns, mortars, hand grenades, etc. to occupy the Enemy's attention everywhere, and press home in force at certain points [where not expected.] The other method (b) is to sap up, as in siege warfare. This is a slow business especially in wet ground. It is sad to see the offensive movement by the British Army 280,000 strong resolve itself into an attack of two battalions!

Thursday 17 December

I ... saw Sir A. Murray at GHQ report centre. He said the C-in-C had gone to see *Foch. Murray was well aware of the effect on the troops of the results of the attack against Messines. After so much talk and so many preparations beforehand, the only conclusion arrived at was that 'They (GHQ) did not mean business'.

Forestier Walker's orders were most ridiculous. He spoke about 'taking the offensive by defensive measures'.

Late on the night of 17 December, Haig received orders from GHQ. Field Marshal French intended to 'attack vigorously all along the front, with the II, III, IV and Indian Corps' but later the orders stated that 'III, IV and Indian Corps will demonstrate and seize any favourable opportunity'. On the following day Haig visited French's CGS, Murray.

Friday 18 December

I asked him why he had put in the word 'demonstrate', because it makes the sense of the second para quite contrary to the intention expressed in the first para which orders Corps to 'attack vigorously'. He said that he had great difficulty in getting the orders passed by Sir John last night, that the C-in-C had ordered the word 'demonstrate' to be left in and that he (Murray) did not get dinner till nearly 10 pm. He quite agreed that no definite results could be expected from ambiguous orders of that nature.

I then went in and saw Sir John. I thought him looking tired. We discussed the attacks made on Monday and Tuesday by II Corps. He agreed that Smith Dorrien was at fault in not employing more troops, especially on Monday afternoon (when only 2 battalions were employed) and also in not having artillery officers forward to observe. But he said it would be impossible [for the British] to go forward until the French captured the high ground north of Wytschaete. I told him the general criticism was that the 'Higher Leaders did not mean business, etc.' He seemed grateful for my telling him what was going on, and he said he was greatly troubled by the friction which existed in the General Staff at his HQ. Billy Lambton[1] had gone to London this morning to see Lord K. and arrange for Henry Wilson to succeed Murray. He also said that he had no faith in Harper. On being asked my views I said Wilson was an intriguer, [and had up-to-date subordinated the interests of the British Army to those of the French]. I knew the Army had every confidence in *Robertson. French said the latter could not be spared from his post as QMG ...

Sir J. seemed relieved and pleased at having had a good talk with me, and I felt sorry for him being in the present plight. He said I had been a great help to him, and he was going to form two Armies at once ... 'This arrangement would at any rate give me an easier time,' he said, 'I can't go on as things are now.'

Saturday 19 December. Letter to Lady Haig

Henry Wilson has been intriguing to get poor Murray moved on, so that he might take his place. H.W. is very cunning but has no military knowledge for such an appointment and I am sorry that he should have succeeded in his disgraceful plotting.[2]

Monday 21 December

I went to Hinges – HQ of Indian Corps in a large chateau ... Sir James [Willcox][3] was not so cheery and confident as last time I saw him. He said the Indian troops were 'quite tired out, and unable to fight any more'. They must be relieved at once or the consequences would be disastrous. We discussed the situation further, and I then wired to the CGS at St Omer recommending immediate relief of Indian Corps and arranged to move remainder of I Corps to Béthune tomorrow.[4]

1 Major General Hon. Sir William 'Billy' Lambton (1863–1936), Military Secretary GHQ France, 1914–15; GOC 4th Division, 1915–17.
2 In fact, Wilson's appointment was blocked because of the opposition of Asquith and Kitchener. Robertson was appointed in place of Murray, who became Deputy CIGS in London. Churchill and Kitchener suggested Haig as a successor to Murray but Asquith, in a letter of 10 January 1915, described Haig as 'irreplaceable as first fighting Commander'. M. and E. Brock (eds), *H. H. Asquith, Letters to Venetia Stanley* (Oxford: Oxford University Press, 1985), p. 368.
3 Properly Sir James Willcocks.
4 Haig had also commented adversely on Indian Corps HQ after a previous visit: Diary, 29 November 1914.

Thursday 24 December

At 11 am I presided over a meeting of GOC Divisions and CRA, CRE and General Gough to consider best method of carrying on operations under the new conditions. We discussed:

(1) a) Trenches. [Size, depth and state, nature of revetment etc.]
    b) Care of men. Not to put into wet trenches up to their knees in water as has been done [in parts of this front.]
(2) Nature of Defence.
    It must be active, otherwise enemy will advance and blow in our trenches with 'minen werfer'[1] as he did to the Indians.
(3) Trench Mortars. Personnel to be gunners or specialists.
(4) Hand Grenades. Keep enemy at a distance as long as possible. Use outposts entrenched.
(5) Local Attack. As in the old days
    Bomb throwers
    Bayonet party
    Attacking body, with flank detachments etc.
(6) General attack. I asked GOCs to get to know the ground so as to be ready for a general advance when the time comes . . .

Tomorrow being Xmas day, I ordered no reliefs to be carried out, and troops be given as easy a time as possible.

Alan Fletcher,[2] Straker and Secrett [helped me to tie up and address my] Xmas parcels. Doris sent [me a nice present] for everyone on my Staff: some 36 [in all, including the] servants. And Leo Rothschild sent me 50 odd pairs of fur-lined gloves! All sent out with a line 'Best Wishes for Xmas from Lady Haig', or from Leo Rothschild, as the case might be. [This kept me employed till past midnight. But what an amount of pleasure it gave me to distribute Doris' Xmas gifts in the midst of all my anxiety!]

Friday 25 December

I lunched today with Sir J. French at St Omer. Smith Dorrien also present. We were ordered to form Armies tomorrow. I am to command the First: Smith Dorrien the Second.

---

1 *sic*
2 Lieutenant Colonel Alan Francis Fletcher, Haig's ADC, best remembered for the cigarette he smoked on 25 September 1915 to see if the wind was right for the use of gas at Loos. See below, Diary, 25 September 1915.

1915
ARMY COMMANDER

By the end of 1914 the British Expeditionary Force had expanded to nine infantry divisions and three cavalry divisions. The Indian Corps had also begun to arrive in October. A further infantry division, the 28th, would deploy to France in January 1915. Behind these Regular formations there were the Territorial and New Army divisions, completing their training at home, and which would be ready for deployment progressively in the new year. This scale of expansion required changes to the BEF's command structure. A new level of command, Army, was created. This had no precedent in British pre-war organisation or planning. The two Army commands were given to the most senior and experienced of the British corps commanders. Sir Douglas Haig became GOC First Army and Sir Horace Smith-Dorrien GOC Second Army. Both men had to improvise staff and command arrangements and learn how to do the job by doing it. Haig soon lost his Chief of Staff, Major General John Gough VC. Gough was chosen to go home and command a division, but before he could do so a chance ricochet fatally wounded him while he was making a farewell visit to his old battalion. Richard Butler became Haig's new Chief of Staff, a post he held throughout 1915. There were also staff changes at GHQ, where the formidable Sir William Robertson succeeded the ineffectual Archie Murray as Chief of the General Staff. The relationship between Haig and Robertson became increasingly important in the conduct of the war.

The British Government opened two new theatres of war in 1915: at Gallipoli in April and at Salonika in October. Both were to divert scarce resources from the BEF. In May Herbert Asquith, Liberal Prime Minister since 1908, was forced to bring Unionists (i.e. Conservatives) into his government; at the same time David Lloyd George became Minister of Munitions, a new post intended to galvanise the British war effort at home.

Sir John French, the British Commander-in-Chief, had a history of bad relations with Smith-Dorrien that pre-dated the war. Smith-Dorrien's unsanctioned stand at Le Cateau on 26 August 1914, which French increasingly perceived as recklessly threatening the existence of the BEF, did nothing to improve them. It was not surprising, therefore, that French looked to Haig rather than Smith-Dorrien to conduct the first British attack since the onset of trench warfare, at Neuve Chapelle (10–13 March). Nor was it surprising that when Smith-Dorrien wished to make a sensible withdrawal in the face of the infamous German gas

attack on Second Army near Ypres on 22 April French would not countenance the
'retreat', using the request instead as an excuse to replace Smith-Dorrien. (French
approved the withdrawal when Smith-Dorrien's successor, Sir Herbert Plumer,
requested it.) Smith-Dorrien's dismissal left Haig without rival as an operational
commander on the Western Front and made him the leading candidate to replace
Sir John French, if such replacement was required. All subsequent British offensives
in 1915, at Aubers (9 May), at Festubert (15–25 May) and at Loos (25 September–
8 October) were carried out by Haig's First Army. Haig's time and his diary were
dominated by the planning and execution of these offensives and by the aftermath
of the Battle of Loos that resulted in the resignation of Sir John French and Haig's
elevation to command of the BEF, a post he retained for the rest of the war.

Friday 1 January

The New Year began worryingly with German attacks against the First Army
near Givenchy.

I told General *Monro to organise a heavy artillery fire on the German
position and the Railway Triangle. To bring up armoured train, and 60 pdr.
guns for which I have plenty of ammunition. This should have been done,
in my opinion, before launching the infantry to the attack last night.

Monday 4 January

*Sir John *French called a meeting, attended by Haig, *Allenby and Archie Murray.*

Lord *Kitchener has recently published in the Press that 6 armies will be
formed each of about 3 corps! We all think that these new formations with
[rather elderly] doubtful Commanders and untrained staff a great mistake . . .
It was[1] folly to send out 'the New Army' by divisions and armies. Much better
to send out battalions, or even brigades, for incorporation in our existing
divisions and corps. C-in-C wished to say he had the Army Commanders in
agreement with him on this. We all quite concurred, and thought that the
new corps and new armies [which are insufficiently trained] might readily
become a danger!
    French also read a letter from Kitchener in which the latter hinted that his
New Army might be used better elsewhere than on the eastern frontier of
France. A suggestion was made of co-operating with Italy and Greece.[2]
    I said that we ought not to divide our military force . . . but *concentrate on*

1 That is, 'would be' folly. The New Armies were yet to be deployed.
2 This is not an early reference to the Dardanelles/Gallipoli campaign.

the decisive front which was on this frontier. With more guns and ammunition, and more troops we are bound to break through.

Monday 18 January

I receive report on the defences of Givenchy from Lieutenant General Monro Commanding I Corps. The general scheme of the defence is:

(1) *Fire trenches* with support trenches within bomb-throwing distance (15 to 25 yards).
(2) A *second line*, called the 'Village Line', embracing the buildings along the main roadway of Givenchy village, and continued in a southerly direction to the canal.
     In close support of this are the
     (a) 'Keep' (near the church) and the
     (b) Redoubt to be constructed just north of canal in soil heap with minor work between them.
(3) A *third line* along the road running north from Pont Fixe to road junction 800 yards north of Pont Fixe.

Wednesday 20 January

General Hobbs' reported on the results of his visit to GHQ yesterday ... The intention is to enlarge my Staff so as to enable me to control a second line of communications ... About 11 officers are now to be added to my Staff including a senior officer as Provost Marshal who will be responsible to me for the supervision of Military Law in the area occupied by the First Army.

My total Staff of officers is now 33 with every chance of becoming larger still ...

Leave to private soldiers, to the extent of 50 per Corps a day, has also been approved for 7 days to England. Only those of good character who have been in the field three months can obtain leave ...

Haig then met Sir John French.

I gathered that Sir John had addressed the War Cabinet ... with the result that the New Army will not come out in larger bodies than divisions ... Sir J. seemed very satisfied with his visit, and he hazarded the opinion that 'the

---

1 Brigadier General (later Major General) Percy Eyre Francis Hobbs (1865–1939), Deputy Adjutant and Quartermaster General (chief logistics officer) at First Army, 1914–17; previously he had held a similar post at I Corps.

New Army was not likely to be here before June by which time, he thought, the war would be over'.

I called on Major General Fanshawe[1] Commanding 1st Cavalry Division of 2 the Indian Cavalry Corps ... He showed me a letter from General Leader[2] Commanding Sialkot Cavalry Brigade recommending that Colonel Tilney[3] should be kept at home as he was too excitable to command in the field.

Thursday 21 January

Conference with Generals Gough[4] and Hobbs regarding the organisation and location of the HQ First Army. We already number 32 officers so I said the first thing was to find a suitable locality for HQ. Lillers had not sufficient accommodation and in view of the French taking over the right of our line (as far as Richebourg St Vaast), was too far to the right. I therefore wished Aire to be reconnoitred with the object of establishing ourselves there. Once established I would decide where to have an advanced 'poste de commandement' ... I was opposed to having the several branches of the Staff kept apart: HQ Messes should therefore have a mixture of all branches.

Friday 22 January

Haig spent the morning carrying out various inspections.

I got back to Lillers about 5 pm and found Colonel Repington[5] (*Times* Correspondent) waiting to see me. He was anxious to know whether I thought we could advance on this front. I replied that as soon as we were supplied with ample artillery ammunition of High Explosive, I thought we could walk through the German lines at several places. In my opinion the reason we were

1 Major General (later Lieutenant General) Sir Hew Dalrymple Fanshawe ('Fanny') (1860–1957), GOC 1st Indian Cavalry Division, 1914–15; GOC Cavalry Corps, 1915; GOC V Corps, 1915 (sacked and replaced by his brother, Edward). He later commanded 58th Division (from which he was also sacked) and 18th Indian Division (in Mesopotamia), 1917–19.
2 Major General Henry Peregrine Leader (1865–1934), GOC 2 Indian Cavalry Brigade, 1912–15; GOC 4th Cavalry Division, 1915–16.
3 Lieutenant Colonel William Arthur Tilney, OC 17th Lancers, 1911–15. Haig was Regimental Colonel of the 17th Lancers and always took a special interest in it.
4 Brigadier General John Gough.
5 Colonel Charles à Court Repington (1858–1925), Military Correspondent of *The Times*, 1903–18. Repington was to play a key part in the 'shell scandal' of May 1915 that resulted in the formation of a new Ministry of Munitions, headed by Lloyd George. Repington was a former Regular soldier who had been forced to resign his commission following his involvement in a messy divorce case. He and Henry Wilson had long been personal enemies.

here was primarily due to want of artillery ammunition and then to our small numbers last November.

He told me that Henry *Wilson had got Huguet[1] (the head of the French Mission) to get *Joffre and French Government to ask that HW should be appointed CGS instead of Sir A. Murray! Such an intrigue greatly astonished me.

Saturday 23 January. Letter to Leopold de Rothschild[2]

We are not making much progress – but that is not to be expected until we get an ample supply of High Explosive ammunition for our guns, and a few more troops. Given lots of artillery ammunition I think that there are several points at which we might advance as soon as the ground dries up a bit...

Sunday 24 January

I motored to Bailleul in the forenoon and attended a conference with Sir John French. He first of all saw *Smith-Dorrien and myself and told us that Sir A. Murray (CGS) was ill and would be sent home for a month, but he did not intend to have him back again. Sir William *Robertson (now QMG) would be CGS permanently. Brigadier General J. Du Cane[3] was to be CRA vice Lindesay.[4] He had not yet decided on the successor to Robertson as QMG.[5]

Monday 25 January

At 7.55 am Haig received reports of enemy shelling of Béthune. Further reports of enemy attacks followed during the morning.

I ... went by motor to Hinges (as I had heard that I Corps were leaving

1 Victor Jacques Marie Huguet (1858–1925), French Liaison Officer at British GHQ. Huguet, who was close to Sir Henry Wilson, was replaced when Haig became Commander-in-Chief. He was the author of a post-war memoir, *Britain and the War. A French Indictment* (London: Cassell, 1928), that was highly critical of Britain.

2 NLS: Haig Papers. Acc. 3155, No. 214a.

3 Brigadier General (later General Sir) John Philip ('Johnny') Du Cane (1865–1950), BGGS III Corps, 1914–15; MGRA GHQ BEF, 1915; GOC XV Corps, 1916–18; Senior British Military Representative HQ Allied Armies, 1918–19. Du Cane was what would now be called 'laid back'. This was not a trait likely to endear him to Haig.

4 Actually Major General (later Sir) Walter Fullarton Lodovic Lindsay (1855–1930), MGRA BEF, 1914–15.

5 Robertson was replaced as QMG by Lieutenant General (later Sir) Ronald Charles Maxwell (1852–1924), who held the post until the end of 1917.

Béthune on account of the shelling) and then into Béthune where I found
General Monro looking perturbed and his Staff anxious as to whether the 3
Brigade would hold on to Givenchy. It was difficult to know exactly what
was going on because the telephone wires had been broken by artillery fire.

As usual in such chaos the first reports were very alarming indeed, but
there is no doubt that the Welsh abandoned their trenches and did not wait
for the bayonet attack of the Germans, and that hand to hand fighting took
place in the village.

But for the numerous orders I issued on the subject of fortifying Givenchy
and that 'a whole company of RE be permanently detailed for the defence of
Givenchy' I think that the place would have been captured . . .

General Hobbs went on to St Omer, Sir William Robertson has taken over
as CGS. Brigadier General Percival¹ is to be 'Sub-Chief' vice Henry Wilson!
General Hobbs is to become Director of Supplies & Transport for the
whole Expeditionary Force vice Clayton² who becomes Inspector General of
Communications.

Tuesday 26 January

In the forenoon I motored to Hinges and saw General Monro . . . I gathered
that the line south of the Canal was held by 2 companies of the Coldstreams
and 2 of the Scots Guards – that under a heavy artillery fire . . . they left their
trenches – that the Enemy followed them for over 300 yards to beyond the
'keep' – the latter held out – and the supports formed on that line.

As the circumstances did not seem very creditable to the Scots and Coldstream Battalions nor to the Brigadier of the 1 Guards Brigade (Lowther)³ I
told Monro to enquire fully into the circumstances, and to find out especially:

1. Why the Guards left their trenches?
2. What were the nature of the trenches, and supporting trenches?
3. Why did so much delay occur in making a counter-attack? . . .

General Gough went to St Omer this morning to see the new CGS (Sir
William Robertson) who has taken over. Major General H. Wilson is to be
'Officièr de Liaison' with General Joffre. He may still 'intrigue' and cause

1 Actually Brigadier General (later Major General Sir) Edward Maxwell Perceval ('Perks') (1861–
1955), BGGS (Sub-Chief of the General Staff) GHQ, 1915; GOC 49th Division, 1915–17.
2 Lieutenant General (later Sir) Frederick Thomas Clayton (1855–1933), Inspector General of
Communications BEF, 1915.
3 Brigadier General (later Major General Sir) (Henry) Cecil Lowther ('Meat') (1869–1940),
GOC 1 (Guards) Brigade, 1914–15; Military Secretary GHQ, 1915; BGGS Home Forces, 1915–
19. Unionist MP, 1915–18 and 1921–22.

trouble to GHQ in that appointment! General Murray writes that he 'goes home on Saturday'.

Wednesday 27 January

I sent General Gough to HQ I Corps to hasten the enquiry which I had ordered General Monro to make. The latter and his SGSO (Brigadier General Whigham)[1] came to see me at 5 pm. The report furnished by Brigadier of 1 [Guards] Brigade (Lowther) was not complete so I withheld my opinion and asked for information on certain points.

In forwarding the report to CGS I pointed out that the 1 Brigade had been unlucky since it was reconstituted after its great losses at Ypres. Before the Brigade had got together, it was heavily engaged and lost severely in retaking Givenchy on 22–23 December. These 2 battalions lacked officers and NCOs, and so companies were in by no means a really satisfactory state. Hence this must be considered one of the main causes of the companies leaving their trenches.

I recommended that 1st Division should be withdrawn for training, and if possible replaced by a new formation for 3 weeks.

Thursday 28 January

General Sir Stanley von Donop,[2] Master General of Ordnance came to see me. I explained to him our wish for 'High Explosive shell'. He said that every round that was possible to make is being sent out – that he hoped that by April we would have an ample supply.

As regards trench mortars, I recommended a larger shell say 50lb in place of 2lb of High Explosive ... The charge should also be smokeless ...

I received a letter from Lieutenant Colonel Tilney Commanding 17th Lancers saying that he had been poorly in France (a chill) and had gone to England on leave. Three days before he had been due to return he received a wire to say his leave had been extended and not to return till further orders. He wants me to help him get back. Having been so ill at Sialkot and off his head, I expect the Brigadier had probably a very good reason for keeping him at home ... I thought it best to ride out to Rély where the 17th are in billets,

1 Brigadier General (later General Sir) Robert Dundas Whigham ('Whigwam') (1865–1950), BGGS I Corps, 1914–15; BGGS (Sub-Chief) GHQ, 1915; Deputy CIGS, War Office, 1915–18; GOC 59th Division, 1918; GOC 62nd Division, 1918–19. Cyril Falls, the historian, considered Whigham the best divisional commander with whom he served.
2 Major General Sir Stanley Brenton von Donop (1860–1941), Master General of the Ordnance, 1913–16; the butt of Lloyd George's scorn for his 'failure' to increase British munitions production.

and find out what some of the officers thought of it. I saw Carden¹ (in temporary command) who seemed to think that Tilney was [no] madder than he was before the sunstroke...

On getting home about 5 pm I found Sir James Willcocks waiting to see me regarding the composition of the brigades in the Indian Corps. He said the Native Battalions were quite unable to face German troops unless stiffened with an extra battalion of British infantry per brigade ... Willcocks also proposed to form 4 inefficient battalions into a 6th brigade as they were quite unfit for fighting – these he will use to dig and make entrenchments etc. This I agreed to as a temporary measure.

I told Sir James that, in order to rest 1st Division I proposed to give him a larger section of our front to hold ... and that he would take command of it. He had a lot of things to say, but I pointed out that they had done nothing since 23 December, and finally he went off saying that he was glad to be doing active service again 'though the Indians are sure to be *attacked*! The Enemy always goes for the Indians.'²

Friday 5 February

Sir J. French has been laid up with 'flu and in bed. I thought him looking pulled down. He spoke to me about General H. Wilson. He knows that he is an intriguer, but he thinks he can do no harm in his present position which is 'Senior Officier de liaison' with the French.

Sir J. also said that Sir H. Smith-Dorrien is a weak spot, and that he ought not to be where he is in command of an Army, but that he could not pass him over at this stage of the campaign. I said I could not give an opinion about SD as I did not know enough of the facts, but in my opinion his Chief Staff Officer (Forestier-Walker) was useless, and had not enough of the fighting spirit. Sir J. agreed and said he knew it.

I also had a long talk with Sir William Robertson. In talking to him, one gets a great feeling of confidence in what he takes in hand.

Saturday 6 February

After lunch I motored to Merville and saw Sir Henry *Rawlinson Commanding IV Corps who returned from leave in England last night ... I told him ... that my plan was to operate against Neuve Chapelle ... I told him to prepare a scheme and put forward proposals for the capture of Neuve

1 Major R. J. W. Carden, 17th Lancers.
2 The Germans were outraged by the British use of Indian and the French use of Senegalese ('black') troops to fight them.

Chapelle. I hoped to be ready for this operation in about 10 days' time. He was to treat this as very secret.

Tuesday 9 February

After lunch I motored to Chocques and saw General Monro Commanding I Corps, then on to HQ 2nd Division at Béthune where General *Horne (Commanding 2nd Division) and General Lord Cavan (Commanding 4 Brigade) and Fanshawe (Commanding 6 Brigade)[1] met me. I wanted information regarding the Enemy's position opposite our lines at Rue du Bois. Ground is very flat and at present wet and next to impossible to attack over for that reason just now. But in a few weeks it is hoped this difficulty will disappear . . .

The conclusion I arrived at is that the advance from Rue du Bois has many advantages and is quite feasible provided careful preparations are made. And that when the big guns arrive, we should be able to destroy the Enemy in Neuve Chapelle at the same time.

Wednesday 10 February

Sir William Robertson CGS called to see me. I told him we wanted:

(a) Some pack artillery guns, or preferably howitzers. 1 Battery per Division would be found valuable.
(b) Some battalions of specially enlisted men for mining operations. If possible 1 Battalion per Brigade. A separate set of muscles are required for digging, and moreover if men are required to fight it is a mistake to fatigue them with digging, unless absolutely necessary . . .

On return I saw General Mercer[2] (CRA) regarding the action of the artillery against Neuve Chapelle. He proposed bombarding it by compartments, and to take 4 days over it. In my opinion such action would lose much of the effect of the heavy shells. Much better compress this fire into a terrific outburst for 3 hours . . . This will take advantage of the element of surprise!

1 Brigadier General (later Major General Sir) Robert Fanshawe ('Fanny') (1863–1946), GSO1 1st Division, 1914; GOC 6 Brigade, 1914–15; 48th Division, 1915–18; GOC 69th Division (UK), 1918–19. A good divisional commander who got to know his men; brother of Lieutenant General Sir Edward Fanshawe and Lieutenant General Sir Hew Fanshawe.
2 Major General (later Sir) (Harvey) Frederick Mercer (1858–1936), MGRA First Army, 1915–18.

Thursday 11 February

A letter received from the CGS calling my attention to the amount of ammunition expended by the artillery on Saturday and Sunday last when we advanced our line from Cuinchy. The 9.2 ('Mother') fired 91 rounds in the 2 days. But decisive results were produced and we advanced our line to points which has rendered it almost impregnable. On the other hand 10 days ago the Enemy fired 183 equally large shell at the Canal Lock Gate and has [only] succeeded in damaging it. They also fired large quantities of other kinds of shell! ... The 4.5 howitzer, which is our best gun, is reduced to less than 5 rounds a day. The CGS said that the output of ammunition in January was only half of what was expected. This is doubtless due to the New Year holidays which our unpatriotic workmen at home insisted on taking!

Saturday 13 February

Haig met Sir John French.

He asked me regarding my proposal for taking the offensive. I explained my plan for taking Neuve Chapelle ... He agreed, and said that he would prefer to take the offensive on my front, rather than at Ypres because 1) He wished me to carry out the operation as he could never be certain of getting satisfactory results from Smith Dorrien, and 2) my troops were better ...

Sunday 14 February

At a meeting between French, Haig and John Gough, it was agreed that Gough would go home to command a division.

As regards his successor I said that there were 3 officers who would suit. *Kiggell (now at War Office), Whigham (now SGSO I Corps) and *Butler (Commanding 3 Brigade). I should be glad to have any one of them. The first has been sent for to go to Smith Dorrien;[1] the second cannot be taken away from Monro ... – So it has been decided to send me Butler when Gough goes. This may not be for some weeks.

[1] Kiggell actually remained at home until he became Haig's Chief of Staff at GHQ in December 1915.

Tuesday 16 February

I also saw Major Trenchard[1] today ... I told him the plan and asked for his proposals as to disposal of airoplanes[2] for reconnaissance and also for artillery observation. Some new lamps are required to supplement the wireless in case the latter is damaged by the heavy explosions of the shells and big guns.

Thursday 18 February

At 11 o'clock I motored to Merville and saw Sir Henry Rawlinson Commanding IV Corps. I impressed on him the necessity for keeping plan secret. He agreed and said he was doing all he could to divert attention [from Neuve Chapelle] to an attack at Fauquissart and Trivelet. He handed me two papers marked 'Secret' – 'Notes on the attack on Neuve Chapelle', and 'Points for consideration in the attack on Neuve Chapelle'.

I went on by motor to Estaires and went to the top of the church tower from which a good view is obtained of Aubers village and the surrounding countryside. Major *Charteris (who is in charge of the Intelligence Service of the First Army), Brigadier General Mercer CRA and Straker ADC were with me. One gets a good idea of the nature of the country. Aubers village stands out very clearly and is on a ridge which seems to rise gradually up to it.

Friday 19 February

Second Army report that the 28th Division will be replaced by other brigades from III Corps. I gather because 28th Division is in baddish way – men suffering from 'cold feet' (frostbite) and fever etc. Owing to better management the health of this Army has greatly improved. The total sickness is *under* 3 per cent...

The CGS (Robertson) came to see me about 1 o'clock to tell me that full approval had been given by C-in-C for the operations I had suggested so I could push on now as fast as possible. In reply to question as to possible date, I said that all depended on the weather. The rain of last Sunday flooded the country again, and threw operations back a week. But I said the end of the 2nd week in March probably would find us ready [and the ground in a fit state for attacking over it].

He said General Joffre had written suggesting the same move as I was

---

1 Major (later Marshal of the Royal Air Force) Hugh Montague Trenchard ('Boom') (1873–1956), 'The Father of the Royal Air Force', OC 1st Wing RFC, 1915; GOC RFC, 1915–18; Chief of the Air Staff, 1918. Trenchard had one of the most meteoric rises of the war. He and Haig greatly admired one another.
2 This eccentric spelling is indicative, perhaps, of the novelty of aircraft.

engaged in preparing; to be made in co-operation with a move of the French Tenth Army from Arras towards Lens and Douai. This would mean that we will not relieve the French Corps about Ypres. This is very satisfactory.

Saturday 20 February

Gough received letter about breakfast time from Colonel Stephens[1] Commanding 2/Rifle Brigade asking him to go and lunch with his brother officers near Fauquissart. I raised no objection but told him to be careful . . .

After lunch a message reached me by wire from OC 2/Rifle Brigade saying 'General Gough dangerously wounded'.

Charteris was at once sent off with Medical Officer to 8th Division to find out particulars. Next General Davies[2] Commanding 8th Division wired that he had arranged for Sir Anthony Bowlby[3] to see Gough and he was taking charge of the case. Wound in abdomen . . .

After dinner Charteris arrived and reported that Sir Anthony Bowlby had examined Gough and thought that the bullet had not entered the intestine and that there was every chance of recovery.

Monday 22 February

About 6 am telegram was brought that Gough had died at 5 am from heart failure. 'End was painless and peaceful' . . .

At 10 am I motored to Merville and held conference there regarding plans for offensive . . . I went into the plans sent in at some length, and insisted on the necessity for methodical preparation, and that every individual man should know exactly what his task was. Thanks to the wonderful map of Enemy's trenches which we now had as the result of the airoplane reconnaissance it was now possible to make our plans very carefully beforehand . . .[4]

. . . after lunch we rode to Estaires and attended General Gough's funeral . . . Colonel Stephens came to see me, and said he hoped I did not consider him to blame, that it was a chance shot, and many officers and men regularly

1 Lieutenant Colonel (later General Sir) Reginald Byng Stephens ('Stiff 'un') (1869–1955), CO 2nd Battalion Rifle Brigade, 1914–15; GOC 35 Brigade, 1915–16; GOC 5th Division, 1916–18; GOC X Corps, 1918.
2 Major General (later Lieutenant General Sir) Francis John ('Joey') Davies (1864–1948), GOC 8th Division, 1914–15; GOC VIII Corps and IX Corps, 1915–16; Military Secretary to the Secretary of State for War, 1916–19.
3 Sir Anthony Bowlby (1855–1929), Advising Consultant Surgeon, British Armies in France, 1916–18. He was instrumental in bringing surgery closer to the front line.
4 The battlefield of Neuve Chapelle was the first in the history of war to be surveyed in its entirety by aerial photographic reconnaissance.

walk on the road where the accident happened. He also said that General Gough at the time thought that he was seriously wounded, and asked him to tell me 'how grateful he (Gough) was for all my kindness to him' . . .

By Gough's death the Army loses a very capable soldier. Active in mind and body and with a charming manner, he made everything go smoothly and ensured orders being cheerfully obeyed. Only once throughout the whole war did I have to say a sharp word to him. It was during the retreat, on the night after the action at Villers-Cotterets. After dinner at Mareuil he in his impetuous way grumbled at my going on retreating and retreating. As a number of the Staff were present I turned on him rather sharply and said 'That retreat was the only thing to save the Army, and that it was his duty to support me instead of criticising' . . . He was very sorry, poor fellow.

Tuesday 23 February

Haig visited IV Corps.

I saw Brigadier General Dallas[1] . . . I asked what action had been taken as a result of my conference yesterday. He replied that at a meeting yesterday afternoon the problem of an attack on Neuve Chapelle had been given to GOC 7th as well as the GOC 8th Division to work out! I said that the time for setting schemes had passed. It was now for the Corps Commander to order a certain Divisional general to give his plan of attack . . . If any Commander did not do what was required he should be dismissed. If each problem is given to 2 Commanders where are we to stop? Why not give the Brigadiers' scheme to 2 Brigadiers and so on. The idea is ridiculous.

Friday 26 February

We went on to Fleurbaix to HQ 21 Brigade, Brigadier General Watts.[2] A plucky hard little man, with no great brains, I should judge from his doings at Ypres last November. Thence I walked down the street to HQ 22 Brigade (Brigadier General Lawford).[3] The latter lives in the Doctor's House. Although most of the houses in Fleurbaix have been much damaged by shell

---

1 Brigadier General (later Major General) Alister Grant Dallas (1866–1931), BGGS IV Corps, 1915 (sacked). He later commanded a brigade and a division in the Egyptian Expeditionary Force.
2 Brigadier General (later Lieutenant General Sir) Herbert Henry Watts ('Teeny') (1858–1934). Watts was 'dug out' of retirement in 1914. He was GOC 21 Brigade, 1914–15; 7th Division, 1915–17; and XIX Corps, 1917–19.
3 Brigadier General (later Major General Sir) Sidney Turing Barlow Lawford ('Swanky Sid') (1865–1953), GOC 22 Brigade, 1914–15; 41st Division, 1915–19 (the only man to command the division); father of the film star, Peter Lawford.

fire, this has not been troubled. Lawford's Brigade suffered heavily near Zonnebeke (east of Ypres) through their trenches being sited on the top of the ridge 'so as to have a good field of fire'! The hostile artillery was able to range exactly on them and knocked them out without much difficulty. I was at Sandhurst with Lawford. He went into the 7th Fusiliers. Though endowed with no great ability, he is a hard-fighting, plucky soldier.

Saturday 27 February

Haig visited HQ Meerut Division.

Lieutenant General Anderson[1] is still on leave (unwell) so Major General Scott[2] (CRA of Indian Corps) is in command ... We rode on to Le Touret, HQ of Brigadier General Blackadder's Brigade.[3] This brigade has been chosen by GOC Division to attack Neuve Chapelle. I therefore went into the operation in some detail and explained the necessity of giving each one a certain definite responsibility and a clearly defined objective. Brigadier General Blackadder recently commanded a battalion of the Leicesters: that battalion is now in his brigade and he says all ranks are keen to go on.

Sunday 28 February

Haig met General De Maud'huy at St Pol, HQ French Tenth Army, in order to explain the plan for Neuve-Chapelle.

De Maud'huy is a small active man: about 58, sandy coloured hair, probably dye![4] Quite the old type of French man seen on the stage of the Louis XIV period...

I received Rawlinson's proposals for the operation. I wired for him and General Holland[5] (Commanding the artillery of the 8th Division). They arrived about 9 pm. It is difficult to estimate the proper number of howitzers to employ to batter in a line of trench. We don't want to run any risk of

1 Lieutenant General (later Sir) Charles Alexander Anderson (1857–1940), GOC Meerut Division, 1913–15; Indian Corps, 1915; XV, XVII and XI Corps, 1915–16; I Corps, 1916–17.
2 Brigadier General (later Major General Sir) Arthur Binny Scott (1862–1944), CRA Indian Corps, 1915; MGRA Third Army, 1915; GOC 12th Division, 1915–18.
3 Properly Brigadier General (later Major General) Charles Guinand Blackader (1869–1921), GOC Garwhal Brigade, 1915; GOC 38th (Welsh) Division, 1915–18.
4 General Louis Ernest de Maud'huy (1857–1921), GOC French Tenth Army, 1914–16.
5 Brigadier General (later Lieutenant General Sir) Arthur Edward Aveling Holland (1882–1927), CRA 8th Division, 1914–15; BGRA VII Corps, 1915; GOC 1st Division, 1915–16; MGRA Third Army, 1916–17; GOC I Corps, 1917–19.

failure, so I decided to ask for 2 more batteries of 6 inch howitzers (siege) making 28 in all.

Tuesday 2 March

About 11 the CGS (Robertson) came to see me ... In case we succeed in breaking the Enemy's line, I asked for a division of cavalry to be moved up close to Chocques and that a Cavalry Commander (Hubert *Gough for choice) be attached to my Staff during the operations so as to be able to take advantage of [any] suitable opportunity which might arise. The CGS agreed.

I motored to Merville and had meeting with Sir H. Rawlinson at 12.30 regarding his proposed plan. As to the general scheme I said that our objective was not merely the capture of Neuve Chapelle. Our existing line was just as satisfactory for me as if we were in Neuve Chapelle! I aimed at getting the line Illies–Herlies and the line of the La Bassée road to Lille, and then to break the Enemy's front. It seemed to me desirable to make our plans with the definite objective of advancing rapidly, (and without any check) in the hope of starting a *general advance*. The scheme of the 8th Division, and that sent in by General Capper of 7th Division seemed to indicate a very limited objective. As to the proposal of the 8th Division to employ 3 brigades in attacking Neuve Chapelle, I considered that even from an administrative point of view it would be better not to mix up the 3rd Brigade in the same trenches as the others – and having in view the possibility of several days fighting it was important to keep troops as fresh as possible.

After lunching at Merville I rode to Calonnes to HQ of Jullundhur Brigade (Brigadier General Strickland)[1] and rode with the Brigadier through his billets to Robecque ... Strickland seems a hard and capable soldier with considerable foreign experience of Africa etc. He recently commanded the Manchester Regiment.

Brigadier General Walker[2] commands the Sirhind Brigade. He was in the Gurkhas and is a VC ...

General Mercer came to see me about 6 pm. He had been to see some practical Battery Commanders of recent experience. He now considered a bombardment of half an hour sufficient. I told him that in my opinion it was a question of calculation. For instance there were certain houses to be demolished. How many shells would it require in each case? How long would it take to fire these? Then there was the bombardment of trenches! The

1 Brigadier General (later General Sir) (Edward) Peter Strickland ('Hungry Face') (1869–1951), GOC Jullundhur Brigade, 1915; GOC 98 Brigade, 1915–16; GOC 1st Division, 1916–18.
2 Brigadier General (later Major General) William George Walker VC (1863–1936), GOC Sirhind Brigade, 1915; 2nd Division, 1915–16; Assistant Censor, 1917–18.

number of shell required must be worked out, time required for firing etc. When all this has been totalled up we might then give a decision. Tomorrow he is going into it with Colonels Franks[1] and Uniacke[2] and will tell me at night the conclusion arrived at.

Wednesday 3 March

I recommended that 3 men of the Loyal North Lancs who had deserted deliberately (one found in Paris) and after being arrested again, should be shot.[3] The state of discipline in this battalion is not very satisfactory...

I motored to Béthune and met Brigadier General Hudson CGS of Indian Corps,[4] and Major General Scott in temporary command of the Meerut Division. Sir J. Willcocks and Lieutenant General Anderson (Commanding Meerut Division) are in England on leave. Their proposals were to attack Neuve Chapelle in *two* bounds, and they (like 8th Division) had a different brigade holding the 'starting' trenches to the attackers. I explained my reasons ... against these two proposals. In other respects I thought their scheme well worked out and possible difficulties foreseen and provided against...

General Mercer came to see me about 6 pm. He has gone thoroughly into the artillery question with Colonels Franks and Uniacke and the CRAs concerned. The conclusion they have arrived at is that 35 minutes in all of a bombardment should suffice. I am to have a detailed statement of the rôles assigned to the several guns and batteries by tomorrow morning. There is a considerable difference between the $2\frac{1}{2}$ hrs bombardment first recommended by IV Corps and the present proposal!

Thursday 4 March

About 3 am report came in that 22 Afridis and a native NCO of the 58th (Vaughan's) Rifles had deserted to the Enemy. The remainder of the Afridis in that company were at once disarmed and marched under the escort of a

1 Colonel (later Major General Sir) George MacKenzie Franks (1868–1958), MGRA Second Army, 1915–17; GOC 35th Division, 1917–18; Inspector General of Artillery, 1918–20; Franks was responsible for the artillery fire plan used at Messines in June 1917.
2 Colonel (later Lieutenant General Sir) Herbert Crofton Campbell Uniacke (1866–1934), BGRA Heavy Artillery Reserve BEF, 1915; BGRA V Corps, 1915–16; BGRA III Corps, 1916; MGRA Fifth Army, 1916–18; a 'scientific gunner' and a leading figure in British artillery development on the Western Front.
3 The executions were not, in fact, carried out.
4 Brigadier General (later General Sir) Havelock Hudson ('Huddie') (1862–1944), BGGS Indian Corps, 1914–15; GOC 8th Division, 1915–16. Returned to India at the end of the Somme fighting to become Adjutant General.

company of Seaforths to Locon Prison. It is thought that the bombardment of the Dardanelles and the prospective attack on Constantinople have been magnified by some German agents so as to make them think that Great Britain is attacking Islam and the Mahomedan religion...[1]

Sir James Willcocks returned from England this afternoon and called about 6 pm. I told him to consider the question, and let me know tomorrow, whether the Indian Corps is fit to attack on Wednesday or not. If he has any doubt about their advancing I won't employ them. Incidentally he expressed his sorrow at having wasted so much of his life with such a wretched lot as the Indians! And much more in the same vein. It is a serious matter for the future of the Native Army, if the Imperial Commanders judge the regiments here unfit for offensive operations.

Friday 5 March

Haig went to Béthune to meet key commanders and staff involved in the forth-coming attack at Neuve Chapelle.

The following is a summary of my remarks –

1. We are embarking on a serious offensive movement with the object of breaking the German line. There is no idea of merely taking a trench here, or a trench there. My object is to surprise the Germans, and push forward to the Aubers ridge *with as little delay as possible,* and exploit the success thus gained by pushing forward mounted troops as quickly as possible so as to threaten La Bassée from the northeast in which direction there are no fortifications.

    The keynote of all the work is *offensive action.* Bombing parties must act offensively trying to get forward on to the flanks. Infantry will advance first to Enemy's front trenches, then beyond the village, next to the Bois de Biez and Aubers ridge.

    Commanders must therefore carefully consider the *employment of their reserves* so as to maintain the forward movement.
2. At the same time, the principle of securing the ground already gained must not be overlooked...
3. It may be necessary to advance the operations to a date before the 10th either on account of the French situation on our right, or on account of Germans anticipating in attacking first ...

1 Haig, of course, knew the Indian Army very well. He served there from 1886 to 1893 with the 7th Hussars, he was Inspector General of Cavalry in India from 1903 to 1906 and Chief of the General Staff India from 1909 to 1912.

4. I Corps and 7th Division must be ready to push in at any period, even in the first morning of the attack. Arrangements must be made for artillery support with a view to this eventuality . . .

Rawlinson and Davies thought it would be well to stop for the day after reaching east edge of village – I said 'No'. The effect of this great mass of artillery which we have, must be most demoralising, consequently the advance must be as rapid as possible to take advantage of the demoralisation caused by a heavy bombardment.

Saturday 6 March

General Allenby is to arrange about two Cavalry Divisions being handy to support me if circumstances are favourable. At first Sir John wished to employ the cavalry on the right flank, i.e. south of Béthune.

Sunday 7 March

General H. Gough and Colonel Greenly[1] came to see me regarding the part the cavalry was to take in the operations. I gave them all information thinking they had come by Allenby's orders, but they told me it was a mere chance that they had come! . . .

General Sir Locke Elliot[2] came to see me . . . He considered that there was no religious question involved in the desertion of the Afridis . . . The remainder . . . now begged a chance to retrieve their good name. He was strongly of opinion that they should be given this chance.

Tuesday 9 March

. . . General Monro . . . said his Corps was in splendid condition. Considerable reinforcement had been received . . . I rode to HQ 2nd Division in Béthune. General Horne . . . was quite confident of obtaining success tomorrow . . . General Haking Commanding 1st Division . . . said his division was in fine order and much improved by the period of rest . . . General Anderson . . . seemed in good spirits and most confident but remarked that he was anxious

1 Colonel (later Major General Sir) Walter Howorth ('Bob') Greenly (1875–1955), GSO1 2nd Cavalry Division, 1914–15; GOC 9 Cavalry Brigade, 1915; BGGS XIII Corps, 1915–16; GOC 2nd Cavalry Division, 1916–18. Greenly was a protégé of Haig's. He collapsed with nervous exhaustion in 1918 while commanding 14th (Light) Division during the German March Offensive.
2 General Sir (Edward) Locke Elliot (1850–1938), Military Adviser Indian Army. Haig had succeeded Elliot as Inspector General of Cavalry India in 1903. Elliot had a reputation as something of a military pedant, devoid of wider vision.

about his right flank . . . Sir James Willcocks and Hudson . . . assured me that Indians were much fitter and would fight excellently.

Wednesday 10 March

The Battle of Neuve Chapelle was launched at 7.30 am on 10 March with a 35 minute artillery bombardment. The infantry attack met with initial success, carrying four lines of German trenches and capturing the village, but then lost its momentum owing to communication difficulties. Reserve troops were not brought forward quickly enough to exploit the success. The Germans regained their composure, brought up their reserves and re-formed their line, which the British had insufficient ammunition to break. The attack was broken off on 13 March. This experience, with varying degrees of success, was common to most British attacks of 1915.

Sun rises about 6.30 am. About 6, the day seemed uncertain. General Butler saw Trenchard . . . An airoplane had made a short reconnaissance and reported clouds low but day fairly satisfactory. By 6.30 clouds seemed to be lifting so I ordered the plan to be carried out as arranged namely, bombardment to begin at 7.30 and attack by infantry at 8.5 am.

Thursday 11 March

After lunch I rode to HQ of 8th Division . . . I saw Major General Davies. Apparently he had got his brigades much mixed up . . . Capper's left[1] is hung up in Pietre Wood . . . His right not getting on as he would like . . . So much uncertainty regarding position of units of 8th Division that Rawlinson himself went up . . . to see what was going on.

Friday 12 March

At night although our flanks had progressed to right and left no forward move had been made today. Enemy seems now to have *greatly* strengthened his front opposite Neuve Chapelle so that it is no easy job to break through. I therefore saw Mercer with a view to surprising Enemy and breaking through his front at a point *not* expected!

1 i.e. the left of 7th Division.

Saturday 13 March

I saw Rawlinson at 7 am and told him of the new plan. He asked me to arrange for a new GOC for his 8th Division and for the artillery of 7th Division . . .

Monday 15 March

I saw Lieutenant General Alderson[1] Commanding Canadian Division and explained to him the scope of intended operations . . . I directed him to exercise his men . . . in attacking houses and localities . . . The chief obstacle to our advance is the Enemy's machine guns . . . it is important that all ranks should think out the best method for attacking buildings which are sure to be protected by machine guns.

India Office wired for names of Indian units which had done well in the fighting about Neuve Chapelle. In sending in this information I added that, to prevent misconception (in India) and false conclusions it should be stated that though Indians had done very well the task accomplished by them was not so difficult as that of the British . . .

After lunch I rode to Estaires and Neuf Berquin where I saw the brigade of the North Midland Division (Territorial) commanded by Brigadier General Shirley,[2] the 5th, 6th, 7th and 8th Battalions of Sherwood Foresters. A fine keen looking lot of men . . .

After lunch General Capper discussed with me plan of attack from Fauquissart. I told him the extent of the penetration depended on the amount of artillery ammunition available . . .

Tuesday 16 March

Sir H. Rawlinson came to see me at 8 am and handed me a letter which he had written about Major General Davies. He did not consider him a good Commander of a Division on the field of battle. In forwarding the letter on I concurred in Rawlinson's opinion; and said that he (Davies) had done well in preparing the attack but that he had failed to advance from the village of Neuve Chapelle *at once* after its capture. I thought that he was unfit to command a Division at this critical period of the operations in France, but should be employed at home.

I went to Hazebrouck about 10 am and saw Sir John French. He approved

1 Major General (later Lieutenant General Sir) Edwin Alfred Harvey Alderson (1859–1927), GOC Canadian Division, 1914–15; GOC Canadian Corps, 1915–16.
2 Actually Brigadier General Charles Tyrell Shipley (1863–1933), GOC 139 Brigade, 1911–17. It was most unusual for Haig to get someone's name so completely wrong.

of my plan of operations; but there was no ammunition at present, as the expedition to the Dardanelles had to be supplied! It would be necessary to wait a fortnight. Sir Ian Hamilton[1] has gone to command expedition against Constantinople.[2] This lack of ammunition seems serious. [It effectively prevents us from profiting by our recent success and pressing the Enemy before he can reorganise and strengthen his position.] . . .

On return to Merville about noon I received a letter from Rawlinson enclosing one from Davies. As a result of this Rawlinson at once wrote that he 'took all responsibility for having delayed the advance from the village until 3.30 pm'. This at once showed that Rawlinson was himself to blame for the delay and not Davies. I wrote at once to Sir John French and withdrew the letter from Rawlinson on the subject which I had left with him. After lunch I rode to Estaires and saw Davies who was overjoyed that I had discovered the truth, viz. that Rawlinson was trying to put the blame on him for the delay. I am afraid Rawlinson is unsatisfactory in this respect, loyalty to his subordinates!

Tuesday 17 March

Went to Hazebrouck at 11.30 am to see Sir John French. When I was shown into his room Sir William Robertson (CGS) followed. Sir J. said would he kindly wait as he had something to say to me alone! Then when Robertson had gone he said he had nothing further to say, and he wished to make it clear to Robertson that he (French) meant to see his Army Commanders alone occasionally; because Robertson had tried to insist that French should not see any of his subordinate Commanders unless he (Robertson) was present as CGS! Robertson was then summoned; and it was agreed that Rawlinson had behaved badly to Davies – and the latter was to retain command of the Division and I was to tell Rawlinson that Sir John thought that he (Rawlinson) had treated Davies badly and told me to tell Rawlinson that he was to consider this as a warning. In fact for some time French was doubtful whether it would not be best to send Rawlinson home.

Haig then went to Merville to see an experiment in wire-cutting using 13-pounder and 18-pounder field guns and machine guns.

1 General Sir Ian Standish Montieth Hamilton (1853–1947) commanded the Mediterranean Expeditionary Force from March to October 1915. Hamilton was close to Kitchener and one of Britain's leading soldiers. His appointment to command the ill-fated Dardanelles campaign removed another potential rival to Haig as a future GOC-in-C BEF.
2 This expedition resulted in the Gallipoli landings of 25 April 1915.

... I told Rawlinson Sir J. French's views regarding his action towards Davies and told him to take it as a warning from Sir John, and that next time he will lose his Corps. He quite understood.

Thursday 18 March

Sir John French, having told me that owing to shortage of ammunition active operations could not be resumed for 2 to 3 weeks, suggested that I should run over to England for a few days.

Haig was in England from 21 to 26 March 1915.

Saturday 27 March

Brigadier General Butler (my SGSO) said all was quiet, and that nothing had happened in my absence. As regards our report on the action at Neuve Chapelle, he had been ordered to substitute 'C-in-C' for 'GOC First Army' in one of the early paragraphs. Report now reads as if the action taken was on the orders of the GHQ! This is as it should be, but the actual orders received by me from GHQ were dated after the whole plan had been worked out by us in detail. The whole thing is so childish, that I could hardly have credited the truth of the story had I not seen the paper. The main thing, however, is to beat the Germans *soon*, and leave to the British public the task of awarding credit for work done after peace has been made.

Wednesday 31 March

At 11 am I motored to the Canal basin at Aire and inspected the motor boat Flotilla. It is commanded by Capt Eyres RN.[1] He is away on leave and in his absence a Captain Sharp or Smart is in charge. The latter lives in Harley Street and is a specialist bone setter. A quick little Scotchman. The Flotilla consists of three 60ft gun boats ...

I heard that Major General Johnnie Du Cane had written home that he had 'been complimented by the CGS on his work with the Artillery at Neuve Chapelle'. As a matter of fact he did nothing but get in the way of General Mercer and his subordinates when they were very busy. Du Cane is Artillery Adviser to the C-in-C, but had absolutely nothing to do with the placing or handling of the guns at Neuve Chapelle. This was all arranged by General Mercer (my CRA), Colonels Uniacke and Franks, and the Divisional CRAs,

1 Captain (later Admiral) Cresswell John Eyres (1862–1949).

First Army, Holland chiefly. It seems stupid¹ to wish to take credit which really belongs to others!

Friday 2 April (Good Friday)

Surgeon General Sloggett,² [who has recently taken over duties of Director General Medical Services] came to see me. Very pleased with the success of all the medical arrangements. Says he is much troubled by Lord Kitchener listening to wishes of certain titled ladies and sending out ambulance cookers and other appliances, which are only encumbrances. This seemed to me [to paint] Lord Kitchener in a new light: but Sloggett assured me that Kitchener wishes to become a Duke and a great political power, like the Duke of Wellington in his later years, and so 'he is moving in political circles' and is much influenced by Lord *Derby!...

After dinner, I received back a letter I had sent to the CGS stating what I proposed to do in the way of exploding mines and harassing the Enemy during the next few weeks. The C-in-C approved of my proposals but, with reference to the last paragraph of the letter, in which I 'requested that the Second Army might be directed to make similar arrangements to mislead the Enemy (i.e., to build shelters, etc., along the whole front, in the same way as the First Army is doing)', he wrote a long story to the effect that the GOC First Army was not to give orders to other parts of the Force: that he (Sir John) would direct what they should do, and that the GOC First Army was to carry out the orders given him by C-in-C, etc. In reply, I merely noted on the letter that the 'C-in-C seemed to have overlooked the point to which the paragraph in question referred!' I infer that something must have upset Sir John's balance of mind. Some think Lord Kitchener has found him out, as he has gone out of his way to *assert his position*! However, the only thing that one ought to consider is how best to act so as to end the war.

Saturday 3 April

Colonel Hankey,³ Secretary of the Committee of Imperial Defence, arrived to see me. He is over in France for 3 days. He states Lord Kitchener is more hopeful as regards the ammunition. As to the Dardanelles operations I asked

---

1 In the Ts diary, this is changed to 'unmanly'.
2 Lieutenant General Sir Arthur Thomas Sloggett (1857–1929), Director General of Medical Services BEF, 1915–18.
3 Colonel Maurice Pascal Alers Hankey (1863–1963), Secretary to the Committee of Imperial Defence, 1912–38, and to successive war committees and cabinets.

why the naval bombardment had taken place[1] before the military part of the expedition was on the spot [to take advantage of it and co-operate.] He quite agreed with my view, and said the 'operation had been run like an American Cinema Show' – meaning the wide advertisement which had been given to every step long before anything had actually been done.

Sunday 4 April

Lord Esher[2] . . . told me that he had met an American during the winter who had just returned from Berlin where he dined with the Kaiser. The former[3] said that 'the First Army Corps under Douglas Haig is the best in the world'. This was after our retreat [from Belgium,] the Battle of the Aisne, and the Battle of Ypres. Esher said [the Kaiser] emphasised 'DH in command'. In my opinion however 'the Command' greatly depended on the excellent Staff which had worked together [in peace] and been trained with the troops at Aldershot.

Sunday 11 April

Brigadier General MacAndrew[4] and Major Baird[5] (Indian Cavalry Corps) came to dinner. MacAndrew very amusing about the orders issued to the cavalry [during the Neuve Chapelle operations] by the Field Marshal, and, of course, [he was] very critical. Allenby and Howell (Staff officer now) of Cavalry Corps seem to be despondent regarding the possibilities of cavalry action in future. MacAndrew thinks that if these two had their way, Cavalry would cease to exist as such. In their opinion, the war will continue and end

1 The first bombardment took place on 3 November 1914 (two days before Britain declared war on the Ottoman Empire). There was a second, prolonged bombardment, much interrupted by bad weather, from 19 February until the first week in March. A third bombardment took place on 18 March. The original date for the landing was 14 April, changed to 23 April and actually carried out on 25 April.
2 Viscount Esher (1852–1930), the *éminence grise* of Edwardian politics, exercising great influence in military affairs, especially through his chairmanship of the Esher Committee that began the post-South African War reform of the British Army; a strong admirer of Haig.
3 Presumably a slip for 'latter'.
4 Brigadier General (later Major General) Henry John Milnes MacAndrew (1866–1919), BGGS Indian Cavalry Corps, 1915; GOC 5th Cavalry Division, 1916–19 (in Palestine from 1917–19). MacAndrew was a fellow Scot and was Haig's Brigade Major while Haig was Inspector General of Cavalry India (1903–6). He was accidentally burned to death.
5 Major (later General Sir) Harry Douglas Beauchamp Baird (1877–1963), GSO2 Indian Cavalry Corps, December 1914–September 1915, CO 1/8 Argyll and Sutherland Highlanders, October 1915–June 1916, GOC 75 Brigade, November 1916–February 1918. Baird was Haig's ADC at Aldershot before the war.

in *trenches*. [I told them that we cannot hope to reap the fruits of victory without a large force of mounted troops.]

Monday 12 April

Trenchard (Commanding Flying Corps) came to see me. He has recently been to England to hasten the provision of airoplanes etc.... We have succeeded in making bombs weighing 600lbs (containing about 500lb weight of High Explosive). Special airoplanes are being constructed for them. It is feared that they won't be ready till July. Their chief value will be for destroying some large fortification, or big factory of guns and ammunition...

I motored to St Omer and dined with Sir J. French. An American, Mr Howard, head of a group of journalists was there. A quick-witted active little man, with a big top to his head. 3 years ago he is said to have been a paper boy in the street! He recently returned from Germany and Russia, and has toured in France. He stated that the French now have a genuine admiration for the British Army. I sat next Lord Curzon.[1] We discussed the value of the Indian Army, I told him that its administrative system was antiquated, and many changes would be necessary after the war. Lieutenant General H. Wilson was also dining. Brinsley Fitzgerald[2] told me that the C-in-C had asked Wilson to join his Mess – a very great mistake, we both agreed: because he is such a terrible intriguer, and is sure to make mischief. Wilson's face now looks so deceitful! By having Wilson in his Mess, while Robertson (the Chief of the Staff) is only able to see him at stated times, the Commander-in-Chief is courting trouble. Billy Lambton (the Military Secretary) is weak, and quite under the influence of Wilson it seems. Luckily Lambton is stupid, and more than once has unconsciously given away what H. Wilson has been scheming for. Brinsley is fully alive to the situation, so I hope no great harm may come of Wilson getting himself into such a position that he has the ear of the Commander-in-Chief constantly.

Wednesday 14 April

After lunch I motored the plateau northwest of St Omer and saw some experiments with a rocket. Its range is 500 to 1200 yards; it carries 50lb of HE, and it makes a crater of 6 feet in depth. The fault is that if there is a wind, the rocket is inaccurate. Still it will be most useful against large targets such as a wood (e.g. Bois du Biez) or a village. I arranged with CGS to start

1 Earl (later Marquess) Curzon of Kedleston (1859–1925), former Viceroy of India (1898–1905) and later Foreign Secretary (1919–24), but out of office and unemployed at this time.
2 Lieutenant Colonel Brinsley Fitzgerald (1859–1931), Sir John French's private secretary.

a class of 9 officers tomorrow for instructions in use of rocket (three from each Corps).

Sunday 18 April

I saw Gough[1] at 9.30 and ordered him to take over his new Command[2] at once. I also told him the facts of the case in which Rawlinson had asked for Major General F. Davies to be removed from command of 8th Division on account of his failure to carry out orders at Neuve Chapelle, but that, on Davies putting forward a statement of orders received and issued by him, Rawlinson had written in to say that he (Rawlinson) accepted all the blame for the delay which had occurred. I gave Gough this information because Davies had told me privately that neither he nor his Staff had full confidence in Rawlinson because they felt that if his personal interests required it, he (Rawlinson) would throw over his subordinate Commanders and that he would not hold to any [verbal] order which he had given.

Tuesday 20 April

After lunch I motored to Vertbois Farm (between Forêt de Nieppe and Merville) to see experiments with 18 pdr. field gun firing high explosive against earth parapets. A very strong breastwork seven to eight feet high, six feet at top, and about 14 to 15 feet at the base was built up with rammed earth, and was revetted with sandbags ... On examining the breastwork ... many said ... it was much stronger than any breastwork which the Germans had erected in our front.

The field gun was placed at about 1500 yards range. The gun was securely anchored and telescopic sights were used. Range was found with percussion shrapnel. First shot was about 100 yards over, the next was short and the 3rd and 4th hit the parapet.

High Explosive shell was then fired. The first burst in the parapet making a great furrow. The next shot struck almost on the same spot, and made a passage right through! The aim was then changed to about a couple of yards further to the right, and two more shots were fired. The result was a complete breach right through the parapet on a front of about 15 feet. That is roughly 1 shell per yard of front!

The lessons I deduce are (1) the importance of *anchoring* the gun when great accuracy is required and (2) the tremendous power of our High Explosive 18 pdr. shell. Up to the present only the 6-inch and 4.5-inch howitzers have

1 That is, Hubert Gough.
2 7th Division, vice Capper, who had been wounded.

been used against the Enemy's trenches. Consequently the front of Enemy's trench which could be broken was limited by our number of howitzers. Now our field gun has been shown to be the most useful against parapets.

Looking at the experiment from the Engineer's point of view the lessons seem to be (1) High parapets are a mistake (2) concealment of a line of defence is more than ever necessary to avoid bombardment of hostile artillery.[1]

Tuesday 27 April

Held conference at Béthune of Corps and Divisional Commanders and their senior GS officers and CRAs – Corps had previously sent in their plans on which I had commented. Plans were then returned for amendment. The object of today's conference was to co-ordinate the action of the several attacking divisions and detachments . . . I explained the objective of the First Army . . . as follows:

Firstly. (a) First and Indian Corps *break through* German line near Richebourg l'Avoué and secure line Rue de Marais–Lorgies–Ligny le Petit. (b) IV Corps *break through* about Rouge Bancs and secure Fromelles and the Fromelles–Aubers road.

Secondly. Secure la Cliqueterie Ridge.

(a) Indian Corps advances on Ligny le Grand.
(b) IV Corps advances on la Cliqueterie Farm.
(c) I Corps advances on Illies.

Thirdly. General advance through Illies and Herlies upon Don.

The artillery is being disposed with these objectives in view and certain heavy batteries have been ordered to push forward to the Aubers ridge as soon as possible after the Divisional Artillery has pushed on.

I then asked the GOC Meerut Division and 7th and 8th Divisions how they proposed to deal with the Enemy who would be enveloped by our advance on to the line Fromelles–Aubers on the one hand, and to Bois de Biez–Ligny le Grand–la Cliqueterie on the other hand. Some 6 or 7 battalions (say 7000 men) will be probably cut off in this section. All stated that they

---

1 This passage shows Haig's strengths and weaknesses: on the one hand, his willingness to experiment and to deduce relevant lessons; on the other, his willingness always to draw the most optimistic conclusions. The 18-pounder field gun may have been able to destroy German breastworks under test conditions, but in reality the BEF had at this stage of the war neither the quality of High Explosive nor an effective fuse nor the number of guns nor the ability to fire them accurately under combat conditions. As Commander-in-Chief, however, Haig was able to do something about concealment, giving great encouragement to the art of camouflage and its often unmilitary practitioners.

had warned their Brigadiers to occupy certain localities for hemming the Enemy in, while they had other units ready to make a counter-attack.

I then discussed several points connected with the proposed action of Corps, and directed as follows:

1. Units to collect prisoners, and hold positions gained to be pushed forward from the Supports and not left behind by leading battalions so as to prevent attacking line from becoming reduced in numbers early in the action.
2. Prevention of gap between Meerut Division and 1st Division during the advance on le Biez Farm and Rue de Marais respectively. The Brigadier *on the spot* must push up troops at once.
3. Advance of Meerut Division and the protection of its left flank by occupying the Bois de Biez. As soon as possible one or two companies to extend and advance into Bois from the south. If opposition encountered, two battalions should be ready to support them. In any case la Russie and the northeast corner of the Bois must be secured in order to prevent the left flank of the brigade during its advance on la Cliqueterie from being fired upon at point blank range.
4. '*Infantry* Artillery' – i.e. batteries of bomb guns, 3 pdr. Hotchkiss, pack guns, will be attached to Infantry Brigades – guns will then be detached to battalions as circumstances require. In fact we are returning to the 'canons de Bataillons' of Napoleon.
5. The necessary barbed wire and other stores to be collected ready for the new flank from la Cordonnerie Farm to Fromelles by 8th Division.
6. As soon as the latter Division gains the road near Rouges Bancs an advanced guard to be pushed out at once, and an attempt made to capture Le Clereq's Farm by a 'coup de main'.

The Conference finished about 12.45. An artillery conference was then held by General Mercer to settle some points of detail.

Thursday 29 April

Yesterday Generals Mercer and Butler (my SGSO) met General Basse (the CRA French Tenth Army) and arranged details of the co-operation of the detachment of French artillery on my right. Altogether they will have 16 heavy guns available for our support.

I requested Captain Gemeau (Liaison Officer)[1] to ask for use of captive balloon from Tenth Army to assist observation of the French heavy batteries.

---

1 Commandant A. M. E. Gemeau remained with Haig for the rest of the war. He oversaw the French translation of Haig's despatches in 1919.

We cannot arrange for a second wireless station near the latter guns, and our own station is so distant that delay must result.

*The Second Battle of Ypres began on 24 April when the Germans attacked, using, for the first time in warfare, poison gas. Smith-Dorrien, Second Army commander, sensibly recommended withdrawing to a new position. Sir John French used this as an excuse to get rid of Smith-Dorrien but afterwards allowed Smith-Dorrien's successor, Herbert *Plumer, to carry out the withdrawal.*

Friday 30 April

At 11.30 Sir John French came to see me to tell me of the situation generally, and to ask my opinion regarding the withdrawal from the Ypres salient. Lee, MP,[1] arrived while we were talking, with a letter from CGS (Robertson) and enclosing one for Sir J's. signature to *Foch. Sir J. read me the latter. It was of the nature of an ultimatum, and stated that the withdrawal of the British troops from the salient would commence tonight, unless the French had succeeded in advancing their line. As regards the line to be occupied, it will run from Hill 60 on the south, through Hooge Chateau and Verlorenhoek, and join the French right. Practically the same line as I had organised as an intermediate defence line in case of being forced to retire last November. My main line was to run from Zillebeke to the east side of the road to Potijze, thence to Canal.

As to the policy of retiring, I said that I had no doubts in my mind as to the wisdom of such a step if the French [did not regain the old front] but continued in their present position. [Our troops are now in a very sharp salient] and if the Enemy did attack in force, they will find it most difficult to withdraw, when forced to do so. They would also suffer most terribly from hostile artillery, *which almost envelops them at the present moment.* [I considered that it was the C-in-C's duty to remove his men from what was really a 'death trap'.]

Sir John also told me Smith Dorrien had caused him much trouble. 'He was quite unfit [(he said)] to hold the Command of an Army' and so Sir J. had withdrawn all the troops from his control except the II Corps. Yet Smith

1 Arthur Lee (later Viscount Lee of Fareham) (1868–1947), MP (Unionist) Fareham, 1900–18. Lee served in the Royal Artillery after passing out top of the RMA Woolwich. Served as British Military Attaché with the US Army during the Spanish–American War. Rejoined the Army in 1914. He was Parliamentary Secretary to the Ministry of Munitions, 1915–16, and Personal Military Secretary to the Secretary of State for War (Lloyd George), 1916. He was Director General of Food Production, 1917–18. He is now principally remembered for bequeathing his country house estate, Chequers in Buckinghamshire, to the nation in 1917.

D. stayed on! [He would not resign!] French is to ask Lord Kitchener to find him something to do at home.

As regard my operations, it will be 15 May before we can begin. I then told the C-in-C that in my opinion we had not enough troops to *sustain* our forward movement and reap decisive results. It seems likely that by the time we have secured the Aubers ridge and destroyed the Enemy between our line and that ridge, we shall only have sufficient troops to maintain our positions until the tired brigades have reformed. That is to say that apart from the troops holding the line outside the area of attack, the following will be the only fresh troops available on the evening of the first day:

1. One Brigade 7th Division
2. One Brigade Indian Corps
3. Two Brigades 2nd Division

2 is doubtful. One Brigade must remain in Army Reserve. This leaves only *two* brigades belonging to different Corps to go on!! The Cavalry Corps will not suffice, because hostile infantry will be found, for certain, in prepared positions in rear. In my opinion more good divisions are required in addition to my eight divisions in a position to *sustain* our attack and prevent us from being held up after we have really broken the line . . .

I thought the Field Marshal looking very well, though he said he had [several] bad nights as the result of the anxiety [regarding the Ypres situation]. He added he could not express what he felt for the staunch support and help I had been to him throughout the war. [He had never had any anxiety about my Command.] He also alluded to Smith Dorrien's conduct on the retreat, and said he ought to have tried him by Court Martial, because (on the day of Le Cateau) he 'had ordered him to retire at 8 am and he did not attempt to do so [but insisted on fighting in spite of his orders to retire'].

Sunday 2 May

As soon as I heard of the Enemy having used gas against Hill 60 I sent Straker to the 15 Brigade . . . to get details as to what happened. Apparently the Enemy forced a jet of liquid into the air which immediately became vapour. This vapour being heavier than air falls on to the ground like a cloud. The best form of mask is one which comes up to the eyes and over nose and mouth. A tabloid of bicarbonate of soda should be placed in the mask, and the lint moistened with water.

Wednesday 5 May

After lunch I motored to Lestrem and saw Willcocks Commanding Indian Corps. I was anxious to ascertain state of Corps, and the fitness of the Indian troops to attack at the end of the week. He said the Meerut Division had been in the trenches over a fortnight and had had much work at night to execute in preparing the trenches for troops to assemble in prior to the attack. Still he felt that the Division would do well, and on no account should the attack be postponed.

Thursday 6 May

Haig held a conference with his Corps and Divisional commanders and their senior staff officers and CRA, Trenchard of the RFC and Allenby of the Cavalry Corps.

I indicated again general plan and emphasised principles. *1st*. Break through and then as soon as possible enlarge the gap. That is to say the two attacks must combine and establish themselves on la Cliqueterie ridge before advancing further towards Fournes. *2nd*. Extend defensive flank from Fromelles to Fournes, and then start offensive movement with left in Don and right towards Beauvin.

I discussed arrangements to mislead Enemy and by means of mines, gun and rifle fire etc. to make him fear an attack along his *whole* front if possible.

Local action. Attacking troops must not be deflected from their objectives through having to provide for their own flank protection . . .

Artillery arrangements. All were satisfied with the adequacy of artillery fire provided them.

Friday 7 May

Left at 8.30 am and attended Conference at Sir J. French's house in Hazebrouck at 9 am. There were present GOCs III Corps (Pulteney), Cavalry Corps (*Byng, as Allenby has taken over V Corps vice Plumer who now commands Second Army) and Indian Cavalry Corps (Rimington)[1], besides CGS, AG and QMG. Sir John placed me in the chair on his right. (I had sat down somewhere on his left!) Sir J. (who had been in London for the previous 24 hours!) explained the general situation in Europe, which he said

---

1 Major General (later Lieutenant General Sir) Michael Frederic ('Mike') Rimington (1858–1928), GOC 1st Indian Cavalry Division, 1914; GOC Indian Cavalry Corps, 1914–16.

was most favourable to the Allies, and then situation on this frontier, which he thought was still more favourable for us . . .

I gave Sir John tables of artillery timings and two maps, showing the [preliminary disposition] of my troops. The attack is to begin tomorrow morning, as I had arranged.

The Battle of Aubers Ridge actually began on 9 May, after the French requested a 24-hour delay. The aim of the attack was to support the major French offensive in Artois. As at Neuve Chapelle, in March, First Army used a short (forty-minute) bombardment, but this time it failed badly. Many rounds fell short, inflicting heavy casualties and preventing the infantry from getting into their attack positions. At the end of the bombardment the German infantry manned their parapets and repulsed the British attackers, who were unable to reach their objectives. The German counter-bombardment on the British front line interdicted British reserves and led to the battle being called off in the afternoon. Haig's analysis of the failure had an important influence on his plans for the Somme campaign (see diary entry for 11 May below).

Sunday 9 May

Bombardment began 5 am, and our infantry advanced to attack at 5.40. The assault by the 1st Division was well carried out. Men advanced with great dash and apparently in some places got into the Enemy's front trenches, but owing to machine gun fire sweeping down the leading line and supports, the attack of I Corps and Indian Corps failed. Our bombardment seems to have been accurate but the Enemy had placed machine guns under his parapet to fire just above level of ground . . . The muzzles could not be seen or hit by shell fire.

By 6 pm it was clear that roads were so encumbered that fresh brigades for the attack at dusk could not be got forward in time, also Enemy's artillery prevented rapid movement in rear of our line in the open. I therefore cancelled order for the attack . . .

Tuesday 11 May

The conclusions I arrived at are:

1. The defences in our front are so carefully [and so strongly made], and mutual support with machine guns is so complete, that [in order to demolish them a] long methodical bombardment will be necessary [by heavy artillery (guns and howitzers) before infantry are sent forward to attack].

2. To destroy the Enemy's 'material' – 60 pdr. *guns* will be tried, as well as the 15-inch, 9.2 and 6-inch siege howitzers. Accurate observations of each shot will be arranged so as to make sure of flattening out the Enemy's 'strong points' of support before the Infantry is launched.

3. To destroy the *physical* power of the Enemy, and shatter the nerves of the men who work his machine guns, the bombardment will be carried [on] during the night...

The immediate impact of this analysis was the abandonment of the short pre-paratory bombardment before the renewal of the infantry attack on 15 May. More than 100,000 shells were fired, beginning on 12 May, but these were almost entirely shrapnel; the heavier howitzers were notably inaccurate, with a high percentage of 'duds'. The infantry attack began at 11.30 pm on 15 May. The battle continued until 25 May; a gain of about half a mile was made. Haig spent much of the battle visiting his subordinate commanders at their Headquarters and keeping them 'focused'.

Wednesday 12 May

Horne wishes to attack on his present front with 2 brigades in front line ... To start not later than 1 am Saturday. Meantime methodical bombardment to knock out Enemy's strong points. The object of the night attack will be to gain first two lines of German trenches, and establish ourselves before daylight...

7th Division (Gough) will attack at dawn on Saturday – a converging attack on P4.[1] ...

Meantime our guns have begun to [methodically] bombard Enemy's first and 2nd lines – 28 nine point two inch shells were put into V6 today.

After lunch I rode to Sailly and saw Major General Davies Commanding 8th Division who gave me details of the fighting last Sunday. The Rifle Brigade got well through up to the road as ordered, and found that there was no obstacle between their position and Fromelles.

The East Lancs were on the right of the Rifle Brigade. It seems that they did not advance with the same dash as the Rifle Brigade and they did not get in. The Northamptons further on right pierced Enemy's line, and a young officer was in a German dugout all day and returned at dark with only five men...

On the left of the Rifle Brigade the 13th Middlesex[2] (a Territorial battalion) did splendidly, and pressed on as ordered; but Enemy were able to bring

1 A map reference.
2 Actually, the 1/13th Londons (Kensington).

Maxims to bear on ground in their rear, and it was impossible for reinforcements to get forward to them so a detachment was unfortunately cut off by the Enemy.

Friday 14 May

At 1 am the following programme of bombardment was carried out:

(a) 3 minutes by all 4.5-inch howitzer, 6-inch howitzer, 5-inch howitzer. And infantry kept up heavy rifle fire.
(b) 2 minutes dead silence.
(c) 2 minutes heavy shrapnel and rifle fire. The heavy artillery also shelled certain localities.

The Enemy evidently expected an attack because during the pause they manned their parapets, and poured a heavy rifle fire against our trenches. Our shrapnel bombardment then suddenly started so it is hoped that a good many were hit!

Saturday 15 May

About 10 am sent for Sir J. Willcocks to make sure that General Anderson (Meerut Division) would after capture of V6 establish himself securely in that position, with ample machine guns, before sending on a skirmishing line; because, from V6, a considerable area of ground can be covered by machine gun fire. Such a point would be a great support to the advance of the 2nd Division...

I also commented strongly on the error of Lieutenant General Anderson ... in keeping so many men in his front trenches and supporting trenches which resulted in a considerable number being wounded by our own shells. Willcocks said he could not say how many because the Enemy was shelling our trenches also...

After lunch I motored to Lestrem and saw Willcocks, and arranged that if night attack failed, a general offensive would start at 3.15 am tomorrow at same time as 7th Division's attack. If that failed, a bombardment of at least 6 hours would take place, and fresh troops organised for a third attack. The time at which this latter would be made would be ordered by me.

Sunday 16 May

At 1 am General Butler reported to me that the Garwhal Brigade had failed to capture V6 and that the Worcesters which was the next battalion (but belonging to 2nd Division) on the right had also failed and suffered considerably. The rest of the attacking line had however succeeded ...

At 2.45 am bombardment commenced and at 3.15 am the further advance began by 2nd Division and the attack of the 7th Division (Gough) was launched against P4. This latter was successful.

Monday 17 May

Our guns opened a heavy fire about 1.45 am on Enemy's communication trenches, and points where his reserves might be concentrated ...

Fire began as ordered at daylight (2.45 am) on the triangle of ground in front of the gap between the 2nd and 7th Divisions. Three 9.2-inch dealt with P8 and P14 and numerous other guns also bombarded this zone, which is not more than 1000 yards long and 500 deep. It was fired upon most of yesterday in the same way, so I was surprised last night that the Enemy were able to hold out there, and expressed my opinion strongly to my CRA (Mercer) in consequence: 'the guns surely could not have been hitting the mark!'

By 9 am a somewhat curious situation seemed to have arisen. Opposite Horne's troops, near Ferme du Bois, about a thousand or more Germans wished to surrender and advanced towards our troops carrying white flags. Our guns at once opened on them with shrapnel and so did the German guns. There were not many left to surrender.

Thursday 18 May

Slow bombardment by all artillery was kept up 2 pm till 4 pm and an intense bombardment from 4.20 pm to 4.30 pm. Infantry attacked at 4.30 pm.

Wednesday 19 May

General Bannatyne Allason Commanding 2/Highland Division, now called 51st,[1] came to see me soon after 9 am. He seemed a little anxious about putting his men straight into trenches! I told him that we want them to take the offensive, and press the Enemy hard as he is already showing signs of demoralisation.

1 Properly Major General (later Sir) Richard Bannatine Allason (1855–1940), GOC 51st Division, 1914–15 (sacked). The Highland Division, like all pre-war Territorial divisions, was numbered in 1915.

Thursday 20 May

1st Canadian Division took over part of the front.

Alderson seemed scarcely to realise that we were engaged in an *offensive* battle, and seemed anxious to delay until his troops had consolidated their trenches...[1]

I also saw Major General Bannatyne Allason ... On his remarking that his men were not yet fully trained, I replied that infantry peace training was little use in teaching a company how to capture a house occupied by half a dozen machine guns! What he wanted was grit and determination combined with the abilities of the stalker. He had a number of good shots in his division. He should urge his men to operate at wide intervals, and use cover: and try and bring a converging fire on the locality to be attacked. He should also use our machine guns as much as possible.

Sunday 23 May

The cause of guns bursting is faulty ammunition, and also excessive rate of fire by which guns get so very hot that High Explosive exploded in the gun!...

The Canadians are splendid men but Alderson, his Staff and the Brigade Staff are very sketchy in their methods of Command to say the least! I spoke firmly both to Alderson and his SGSO Romer[2] yesterday on the methods.

Wednesday 26 May

Letter reached me tonight from Major Wigram. He states that there was an organised conspiracy in the Press controlled by Lord Northcliffe[3] against Lord Kitchener; and that Sir J. French's personal Staff are mixed up in it.[4] Brinsley

---

1 Haig went to see Alderson to spur him into activity.
2 Brigadier General (later General Sir) Cecil Francis Romer ('Romeo') (1869–1962), GSO1 5th Division, 1914–15, and 1st Canadian Division, 1915; BGGS III Corps, 1915–17; GOC 59th (2nd South Midland) Division, 1917–18.
3 Viscount Northcliffe (1865–1922), newspaper baron, whose titles included the *Daily Mail* and *The Times*.
4 This is a reference to the so-called 'shell scandal' provoked by Repington's *Times* despatch, published on 14 May. The article blamed recent British military difficulties on the lack of artillery ammunition. The source of Repington's information is generally understood to have been Sir John French. On 21 May the *Daily Mail* launched a scathing attack on Kitchener, who had the political responsibility for munitions production, accusing him of perpetrating 'a tragic blunder'. The effect was counter-productive where Kitchener was concerned. Circulation of the *Daily Mail* fell by 200,000 copies; it was banned in West End clubs and burned on the floor of the Stock Exchange. But the incident did lead to the formation of the Ministry of Munitions under Lloyd George and was an element, though not perhaps the key element, in Asquith's decision to bring Unionists into his government.

Fitzgerald and Moore, the American (with whom Sir J. lives when in London) approached the editors of the daily Press and asked them to write up Sir J. and blackguard Kitchener!

A most disgraceful state of affairs. Wigram thinks I have influence with Sir J. and can keep him from quarrelling with Kitchener! I have always put in a word, when I get a chance, advising that we all ... should pull together, and think about nothing but beating the Enemy! I fear such advice from me had no effect. The truth is that Sir J. is of a very jealous disposition.

Sunday 30 May

Letter from CGS. Foch has been to see the C-in-C and an advance on Loos has come up again.[1] Foch does not mind whether we attack on north or south of Canal as long as we attack somewhere *soon*. 'It is the C-in-C who hankers after Loos.' 'I have told him he *must* decide one way or the other, and this is what he wants to see you about tomorrow morning.'[2]

'The two alternatives are:

1. Go on as now, when time comes go in where you are ... combined with attack on Haisnes, if ammunition suffices for both.
2. Stop present operations entirely, and transfer bag and baggage to opposite Loos.'

No. 2 means throwing away such advantage as we have already gained, and then if the French do not succeed in gaining Vimy plateau, we shall be unable to do anything at all!

Monday 31 May

Haig attended a conference with the C-in-C.

Sir John considered my estimate for ammunition for the attack on Rue d'Ouvert excessive...

Haig's figure was arrived at from artillery sources. Eventually, a compromise estimate was reached.

This based on the several objectives, and the number of rounds calculated as

1 Foch commanded the northern group of French armies at this time and as such was a key figure in the French military leadership.
2 These words are Robertson's.

necessary for destroying certain houses, blocking communications, for counter-batteries, etc.

Saturday 12 June

Sir William Robertson (CGS) came to see me about midday regarding future operations. It seemed possible that the French near Arras would only be able to gain the Vimy plateau with the troops at present concentrated there. He understood however that in a month's time some 60 divisions would be collected on that front with the object of making a strong attack on a *wide* front. It was desirable for the British to break through either alongside of or very close to the French left. He asked me to view the situation and if necessary extend my right with the object of getting ground suitable for artillery positions for the attack against Loos.

Robertson was anxious I have some definite proposal to put before Sir J. French – otherwise the latter would whisk off the main bulk of the troops for an attack about Ypres.

Sunday 20 June

After lunch I motored to Saines-en-Gohelle and then rode to the high ground north of Ablain to the Bois de Bouvigny when I got a very good view of the country towards Loos, and the two lines of defences. To the east of Aix-Noulette the country is covered with coal pits and houses. The towns of Liévin, Lens etc. run into one another. This all renders the problem of an attack in this area very difficult.

Tuesday 22 June

Order received from GHQ (OAM 443) to 'submit a project for the attack of the Enemy's front between your right and the La Bassée Canal. It is proposed to make the attack between 10 and 15 July, and in as close co-operation as possible with the French so that each of the Allied Armies may derive the full advantage from the attack of the other' . . .

Horne and Haking have also looked at the front in detail.

Since the French attacked at Loos the Enemy has greatly strengthened his position. A second line with wire entanglement is distinctly visible here.

After full discussion, and consideration of their reports on the ground and hostile defences, I came to the conclusion that it would be possible to capture the Enemy's first line of trenches (say a length of 1200 yards) opposite Maroc (i.e. west of Loos) but it would not be possible to advance beyond, because our own artillery could not support us, as ground immediately in our front cannot be seen from any part of our front. On the other hand the Enemy has excellent observing stations for his artillery.

The main attack should be made from the 'triangle' southwards on a front of about 2000 yards with the object of getting the line of the railway. An attack on the Hohenzollern Redoubt might be made as a subsidiary operation.[1] A simultaneous attack should also be made from Givenchy against Chapelle St Roch.

The Enemy's defences are now so strong that they can only be taken by siege methods – by using bombs, and by hand to hand fighting in the trenches – the ground above is so swept by gun and machine gun and rifle fire that an advance in the open, except by night, is impossible.

Friday 25 June

General Philips[2] (a Welsh MP) Assistant to Mr *Lloyd George (Minister for Munitions of War)[3] with General Du Cane came to lunch. We discussed the nature of guns and ammunition most required. I said large numbers of heavy guns because Enemy's defences had become so strong. We ought to aim at having enough heavy guns to engage Enemy on a front of 25 to 30 miles, while retaining a strong central reserve . . .

I suggested a small calibre gun for counter-battery work, like naval 12 pdr., to save the large heavy shells.

We have 14 types of hand bombs: only 2 types should be provided.

Develop the bomb mortars so as to supplement the heavy artillery. Produce a trench mortar to throw a 100lb shell of High Explosive up to 500 yards.

A *lighter* machine gun, with tripod and gun in one part is a necessity. Mobility is most important.

Captive balloons to supplement airoplane observation.

Daggers or short bayonet for use in trenches.

---

1 The 'Hohenzollern Redoubt' was the name given by the British to an intricate network of strongly fortified trenches that protruded from the German first line at Loos. It was taken by the British on 25 September but recaptured by the Germans two days later.
2 Major General (later Sir) Ivor Philips (1861–1940), later GOC 38th (Welsh) Division. Following the debacle at Mametz Wood at the beginning of the Somme campaign, he was removed from command.
3 Lloyd George had been appointed Minister of Munitions in the new Coalition Government at the end of May.

Wednesday 7 July

At 11 o'clock Lieutenant Colonel Fowkes[1] RE called on me from GHQ regarding the use of asphyxiating gas. I said better wait until we can use it on a large scale, because the element of surprise is always greater on the first occasion. I thought the best plan to use it would be against the Aubers ridge on a front of 5 miles.

Wednesday 14 July

Haig was on leave in England between 9 and 17 July. On 14 July he had an audience with *King George V.

The King was waiting for me, and received me most cordially. He thanked me for coming to see him when I only had so few quiet days at home. He then handed me the GCB and 'collar' saying that no one had more thoroughly earned it than I had.

He referred to the friction between Sir John and Lord Kitchener and hoped I would do all I could to make matters run smoothly. He said he visited the Grand Fleet last week where all the Admirals were on the most friendly terms with one another. In the King's opinion the Army would be in the same satisfactory state and there would be no back-biting and unfriendly criticism of superiors if the officer at the head of the Army in the field – a most splendid body of troops – was fit for his position! He (the King) criticised French's dealings with the Press: *The Times*, Repington and Lord Northcliffe, etc. All most unsoldierlike and he (the King) had lost confidence in French. And he had told Kitchener that he could depend on his [(the King's)] support in whatever action he took in the matter [of dealing with French]. The King's one object was efficiency [and to ensure the Army being in as fit a state as possible to end the war.]

I pointed out that the time to get rid of French was immediately after the retreat. Now the Army was stationary and could practically be controlled from London!

The King hoped that I would write to Wigram, and said that no one but he and Wigram would know what I had written. He quite agreed with all I had said in my last letter, especially with my view that if it was necessary to give a general a good Staff officer to enable him to command, then the Staff officer should be appointed to the Command! . . .

1 Properly, 'Foulkes': Lieutenant Colonel (later Major General) Charles Howard Foulkes (1875–1969), Director of Gas Services BEF, 1917–19. For Haig's variations of his name, see diary entries for 14 July, 21, 22, 26 August 1915.

Later, Haig had a meeting with Lord Kitchener.

Kitchener wished me to write to him on any subject affecting the Army and in which I thought he could be of assistance. He would treat my letters as secret, and would not reply, but I would see my proposals given effect to and must profess ignorance when that happened!

As regards the present situation, he thinks the Germans will attack us in Flanders. I ventured to disagree, because *at present* no troops could be spared from Russia. And I thought the Germans found campaigning away from railways more difficult than they had anticipated. So reinforcements are really required in Russia...

At both my interviews today, I was urged to write regarding the situation and doings of the Army in Flanders to Lord Kitchener. The King quite realised the nature of such conduct on my part, because he told me he had said to Lord Kitchener with reference to it 'If anyone acted like that, and told tales out of school, he would at school be called a "sneak".' Kitchener's reply was that we are beyond the schoolboy's age!

Wednesday 21 July

Sir W. Robertson came to me about 11 o'clock. He stated that the French would not be able to attack before the end of August probably, and he wanted to know whether I had altered my views as to the most suitable point on my front for attack.

I replied that the Enemy's position in my front is very strong all the way along, and that the conclusion to attack immediately in the south of the Canal (Béthune–La Bassée) was arrived at because I was told it was necessary to attack as close as possible to the French flank, but in order to support their attack, and also to take advantage of the success which it was hoped they might gain. Further south on my front the Enemy's position is still less favourable for attack.

I still think that the capture of the Aubers ridge will have the greatest tactical results. By using gas it seems possible to make sure of gaining this position in spite of the greatly improved defences which the Enemy has erected on it.

Thursday 22 July

I received this morning OAM 582 from CGS asking if I had any modifications to make in the opinions expressed on 23 June relative to an attack by First Army on left of the French and to give my views on the tactical situation in regard to my front north of the Canal.

I replied that my views are still the same regarding the merits of an attack south of the Canal, viz. that that front is not favourable for attack, but if it is necessary for some reason to attack on that part of our front, then my previous proposals hold good.

As regards an attack elsewhere I recommend that an attack be made on the Aubers ridge . . .

Friday 30 July

Haig went to French's GHQ at St Omer to dine with Sir John French and meet Lord Haldane.

I sat next to Lord Haldane. He was anxious to know how to win the war! I said by applying the old principles to the present conditions. Engage the Enemy on a wide front; the wider the better, 100 miles or more; then after 5 or 6 days, bring up a strong Reserve of all arms to break through where the Enemy had shown that he was weak! One lesson of this war was that troops could stand 4 days' hard fighting and then must be relieved. Apparently the Germans had not very numerous reserves on this front. It must be our objective to engage the Enemy all along his line so as to induce him to throw in his Reserve.[1] Then by means of railways, buses, etc., bring up our big General Reserve by *surprise* against some point where the Enemy has shown weakness, and strike hard with much ammunition.

Sunday 1 August

General d'Urbal (Commanding Tenth French Army) came to see me in the afternoon. I had been pressing for the point of junction between my right and his left to be as strong defensively as possible because the Enemy very often attacks where the two Allies join. After some discussion we agreed to leave the decision as regards the details ... to GOC Corps (i.e. General Maistre Commanding XXI [French] Corps)[2] and Sir H. Rawlinson Commanding IV Corps. As regards the general operations d'Urbal has had 2 corps withdrawn from him, and his troops are resting, but he is ready to start attacking again as soon as he receives the necessary ammunition.

I gather that the next attack will be made against numerous points between the Swiss frontier and the sea on our left, followed by a decisive attack by strategical reserves against some point where the Enemy has shown weakness.

1 'Use up his reserves' is the phrase in the Ts diary.
2 General Paul André Maistre (1858–1922), GOC French XXI Corps, 1915–16.

Monday 2 August

Sir William Robertson CGS came to see me in the forenoon. Sir J. French is in England. As regards our co-operation with the French, Foch is again going to attack the Vimy plateau with the Tenth Army and is anxious that we co-operate *on the south* of the La Bassée Canal. Sir John apparently accepted my view, that the Aubers ridge would be a better objective: and has written to General Joffre putting forward his views, but saying the British will do whatever Joffre thinks best. Sir John seems now to have gone to the other extreme, and has put himself and the British Forces unreservedly in Joffre's hands!

No reply has yet been received from Joffre, but in the meantime Robertson has asked me to be ready to support the French by bringing heavy artillery fire against the Enemy's guns south of the La Bassée Canal, so as to prevent them from interfering with the French attacks on our right. At the same time only small infantry attacks need be launched in this part of our front. The main effort to be made as recommended, namely against the Aubers ridge, with the object of consolidating our position on it and extending our right to Violaines and La Bassée . . .

In consequence of the situation about Ypres I have been ordered to send a brigade of 8 inch howitzers, tractor drawn, which recently arrived from England and is now with the III Corps, to be attached to the Second Army.

Tuesday 3 August

On the way to Neuf Berquin I looked round the 24th Field Ambulance of the 8th Division at Doulieu. The Medical Officer in charge is a highly skilled lady's doctor from Exeter, and the personnel are all Territorials. The Ambulance was raised at Exeter. It has done excellent service. I thought their arrangements quite good. The officer in charge complained of the unnecessary number of returns which have to be sent in. His Sergeant Major is a Commercial Traveller; a number of the others were in the Post Office; one, in the operating tent, was an Assistant Manager of Timothy White's Chemist Stores. There were 11 cases of self inflicted wounds from the 8th Division.

Friday 6 August

Haig visited 15th Division.

I saw Major General McCracken Commanding.[1] He reported that the

---

[1] Major General (later Lieutenant General Sir) Frederick William Nicholas McCracken (1859–1949), GOC 7 Brigade, 1912–14 (wounded); GOC 15th Division, 1915–17; GOC XIII Corps, 1917–18.

new troops were doing very well in the line, and all were very keen.

I then rode on to ... HQ of IV Corps where I saw Sir H. Rawlinson. I asked him how the arrangements with General Maistre for the protection of the zone of country where the flanks of the two Armies meet, are progressing and how he came to recommend taking over more front. He stated that Maistre had told him that General d'Urbal and I agreed to extend my front. (This of course was not the case, because I could not take over more front without reference to GHQ.) After looking at the ground which the French wanted us to take over, Rawlinson said that he quite saw the reason for their wishing us to take it. 'The line was commanded from the Enemy's side and was not a nice place to hold!'

I have sent Gemeau to tell General d'Urbal that there is no question of my taking over more front trench, but only of the arrangements between the two Armies for defending the country in rear. These negotiations are yet another example of how the French try to work for their own hand in their dealings with the British.

Saturday 7 August

Haig attended a conference with Sir John French and Sir William Robertson at St Omer. They discussed Joffre's plans.

The latter[1] now wishes the British Army to attack between the Canal to La Bassée and our right opposite Loos with the object of taking Hill 70 and the ridge to the north of it near Hulluch. This will cover the left flank of the Tenth French Army in its attack on the Vimy plateau.

Sir John has decided to comply with General Joffre's wishes, even though he disagrees with the plan. I am therefore to work out proposals for giving effect to the decision, but my attack is to be made chiefly with artillery and I am not to launch a large force of infantry to the attack of objectives which are so strongly held as to be liable to result only in the sacrifice of many lives. That is to say, I am to assist the French by neutralising the Enemy's artillery, and by holding the hostile infantry on my front.

Friday 13 August

Held conference with Generals Rawlinson (IV Corps) and Gough (I Corps), Mercer (CRA) and Butler (my SGSO). I explained that the French would soon take the offensive on a large scale. I had been ordered by GHQ to support the French Tenth Army on my right which would attack with the

1 i.e. Joffre.

object of gaining the Vimy plateau and the plain of Douai. Our objective would be first the line Loos–Hulluch, and then Pont à Vendin. The thickly populated district about Lens, which is a mass of workman's houses and factories, would thus be turned on the south by the French and the north by the British.

In the first instance we will assist the French by neutralising the hostile artillery and by holding the Enemy's infantry in our front. At the same time all available troops will be held in readiness to advance, as soon as an opportunity for doing so is afforded . . .

The GOC IV Corps will submit proposals for:

(a) securing the German front system of trenches west of Loos, joining up the captured trenches with our present line, and consolidating the position gained.
(b) a subsequent advance with a view to capturing first Loos and then Hill 70, on the assumption that the progress of the French makes such an attack possible.

The GOC I Corps will submit proposals for:

(a) the capture of the Hohenzollern Redoubt and of such of the German defences in that locality as might be included in that attack, and the consolidation of the position gained.
(b) a subsequent advance on Hulluch.

The employment of asphyxiating gas in connection with these attacks is also to be considered.

Some additional heavy artillery will also be available – about 48 guns and howitzers. This will be a valuable reinforcement provided adequate ammunition comes also!

Arrangements for these attacks should be completed by the first week in September, but from my experience of the French I did not think that they would be ready before 15 September.

Saturday 14 August

Colonel Dufieux, Chief of the Staff of the Tenth French Army (General d'Urbal) came to lunch. He seems an intelligent and quick witted little man . . . He seems to be highly thought of in the French Army.

General Butler brought me back from St Omer copies of further correspondence between Sir J. French and General Joffre. The latter in a letter of 12 August seems to fear that the British Field Marshal is not going to attack sufficiently vigorously to do any good. He says 'You will certainly agree with me that this support can only be effective if it takes the form of a large and powerful attack, composed of the maximum force you have available, executed with the hope of success and carried through to the end.'

'You are aware of the importance of the effort which the French Army is performing.'

I sent to GHQ my proposals for supporting the French on the lines indicated in my diary of yesterday.

Monday 16 August

Last night I received a letter from the CGS (Robertson) regarding the forthcoming operations. He considered that the 'attack was not a very satisfactory matter from any point of view'. 'There is just a possibility of the Aubers plan being thought about again.' He wishes to know how long I would require to prepare for it. I replied 'two weeks', but would like longer if possible, on account of the arrangement of reliefs, and the necessity for taking new photographs of the Enemy's lines.

Tuesday 17 August

Lunched with Sir John French at his château in the country near Arques. Only us two, Alan Fletcher and the 2 ADCs present. French said he had been 'anxious to warn me not to talk to Lord Kitchener (who is to arrive today) about the forthcoming operations. If Lord Kitchener were to know, he would tell the others in the Cabinet and then all London would know! And the Germans would also get to hear of the prepared attack' . . .

I discussed the forthcoming attack with Sir John, and said that the front on which we attacked, and distance to which we go will depend on the orders which he gives me . . .

Sir John then said that he wished me to attack on as wide a front as possible and that he knew we must have big losses . . . to achieve any result.

I sent for General H. Gough to see me regarding . . . the attack on the Hohenzollern Redoubt by the I Corps. He has completed his reconnaissance of the area but is not quite clear as to the extent of his attack. I told him to arrange to take the redoubt first of all; then to make an attack astride the railway to the north of it and capture Enemy's front line trenches there. Next attack Fosse No. 8[1] and finally go for the trenches south of Fosse No. 8. That is to say that he must 'arrange to attack on as wide a front as possible'.

Thursday 19 August

Haig was visited by Lord Kitchener.

After washing his hands Lord Kitchener came into my writing room upstairs saying he had been anxious to have a few minutes talk with me. The Russians, he said, had been severely handled and it was doubtful how much longer their Armies would withstand the German blows. Up to the present he had favoured a policy of an active defence in France until such time as all our forces were ready to strike. The situation which had arisen in Russia had caused him to modify these views. He now felt that the Allies must act vigorously in order to take some of the pressure off Russia if possible. He had heard, when with the French, that Sir J. French did not mean to co-operate to the utmost of his power when the French attacked in September. He (Lord Kitchener) had noticed that the French were anxiously watching the British on their left and he had decided that we 'must act with all our energy, and do our utmost to help the French, even though, by doing so, we suffered very heavy losses indeed'.

Saturday 21 August

I saw Lieutenant Colonel Fowke [RE (gas expert)]. I said we should want enough for 6300 yards by 15 September. He said that he could furnish that amount now and would be able to let us have a good deal more by the date I mentioned.

Sunday 22 August

After lunch I motored to a place about 3 miles southwest of St Omer where Lieutenant Colonel Ffoulkes gave a demonstration with gas for asphyxiating the Enemy. I arranged for the IV Corps Commander and Staff officers to be present as well as certain Divisional Generals concerned. The gas is contained in cylinders about 30 inches high and 8 inches in diameter. It is liquified under pressure but comes out of the cylinders in the form of steam, which turns to a brownish colour about a few feet from the pipe and soon becomes invisible. A flexible pipe ... is attached to the cylinder, and connected with

1 The Loos battlefield was littered with mine workings. The principal mines were known as *fosses*, and the smaller mines as *puits*.

it using an ordinary $\frac{1}{2}$ inch iron pipe about 8 to 10 feet long which is placed on the top of the parapet from which the gas is emitted.

The gas which we saw yesterday was chlorine, and is poisonous unless some protection in the way of gas helmets or respirators are used. We discussed the question of how to get the cylinders into the trenches: each one is carried by two men, and how to store them in a trench. We decided to dig places under the front parapet below the firing step so as to prevent them from being damaged by gun fire. The effect of the gas is felt at 800 or 1000 yards down wind ... Some smoke candles were also shewn us. But the smoke emitted was too light in colour. The French have invented a smoke producing bomb which is fired from an ordinary trench mortar. I ordered Colonel Wardrop RA[1] to go to England tomorrow and arrange for some similar bombs to be made ... I wish to use them for the purpose of covering the flanks of our attack from the Enemy's machine guns on the flank. Most of our attacks have suffered from enfilade fire in this way.

Wednesday 25 August

Charteris went to GHQ today to get full information regarding roads leading from front of IV and Indian Corps southeast towards Pont à Vendin, so that in the event of piercing the Enemy's line they may be able to advance without delay. Each of these 2 Corps have also been directed to prepare for an attack by one brigade, supported by the other 2 brigades of the same division. One complete division per corps will thus be in a position to advance at once, if the situation becomes favourable.

Thursday 26 August

Lieutenant Colonel Foulkes[2] (gas expert from GHQ) arrived from England this morning and reported that by 4 September almost half the amount of gas upon which we had calculated would be received, owing to the manufacturers having disappointed. This disappointment affects my plans seriously. Either we must delay the attack until the required amount of gas can be provided,

---

1 Colonel (later General) Sir Alexander Ernest Wardrop ('W') (1872–1961), CRA Guards Division, 1915–16; BGRA XIV Corps, 1916–18; MGRA Third Army, 1918–19. Wardrop wore a monocle and was devoted to big-game hunting and pig-sticking (on which he published the classic account in 1914), but he was also a modern scientific gunner who played an important role in the development of smoke shells for the 4-inch mortar. He was fluent in Urdu and several Indian dialects.

2 It is, perhaps, indicative of the increasing importance of gas to First Army's plans that Haig finally managed to spell Foulkes's name correctly!

or we must curtail our scheme to suit the reduced amount of gas available . . . Foulkes is to let me know tomorrow the amount of gas which can reasonably be expected to reach us during the next 3 or 4 weeks. I urged that a special officer be sent home at once in order to hasten the dispatch of the gas. In my opinion it would be better to delay a week or 10 days in order to have an adequate supply of gas, because 'surprise' is always greatest on the first occasion of having some new instrument of war! Moreover up to the present on my front all prisoners taken have had most inefficient respirators. This looks as if the Enemy did not anticipate a gas attack here. His machine gunners are said to have oxygen inhalers which are good for half an hour.

In order thereupon to deal with them it will be necessary for the gas attack to last over half an hour. We can arrange this by giving (say) 10 minutes of gas, then a pause of 10 minutes, and then continue at intervals of 10 minutes. It is most unlikely that the Enemy would take off his apparatus, especially if the gas is invisible.

Saturday 28 August

Prisoner of 13 Regiment (VII Corps) surrendered this morning near Marquissart stated that gas cylinders were in position along this part of the Enemy's front, and that attack would take place on 30th. I at once ordered to bombard a portion of the Enemy's trench in order to verify the statement regarding the gas cylinders. Bombardment will begin at 2 pm tomorrow . . . The prisoner had a fairly good gas mask which he said was issued on 25th for those using the gas. The Enemy does not expect us to employ gas.

After lunch Sir H. Rawlinson came to see me re. the attack in Loos. I told him that as soon as he had broken the Enemy's front he was free to use the 1st Division which is in reserve for an attack against Loos and vicinity of Hill 70 from the north . . .

Lieutenant Colonel Foulkes reported that by 6 September we would have 5100 cylinders available and by the 11th 8500.

Sunday 29 August

In the afternoon I rode to Chocques, HQ of I Corps and saw Generals H. Gough and Horne (Commanding 2nd Division). Their arrangements for the attack are progressing satisfactorily. General Landon Commanding 9th Division is in bed with lumbago. His Division is to make the main attack for I Corps. Gough said he daily goes down in his estimation as a Commander, on account of his indecision and lack of thoroughness in making his plans.

Landon has also been given an indifferent GSO1 Buzzard by name.[1] I told Gough to write to the CGS and have the latter changed. As regards Landon he should get a medical opinion at once as to when he is likely to be fit . . .

In the evening (9 pm) I received a letter from Brigadier General Maurice[2] for CGS (who returns tonight) that 'Joffre after seeing Castelnau has decided that the attack cannot take place before the 15 September'.

Monday 30 August

A most discouraging document received last night from General Willcocks in reply to my orders to submit proposals for carrying out an attack on a small scale on the front of the Indian Corps, with the object of misleading the Enemy as to which attack is the main one. Willcocks sees objections to attacking anywhere! I therefore write on it 'This is a most discouraging document! The situation in Europe requires the Allies in the Western theatre therefore to attack with all their power, and the First Army has been ordered "to support the French attack to the full extent of its resources". The Indian Corps must do its share!' . . .

Bombardment began at 2.30 pm on point in Enemy's trenches where deserter stated gas cylinders were stored. This continued methodically till 6.30 pm. Two big explosions were caused . . . But no signs of gas cylinders!

Report from GHQ that the supply of 'gas' will be much better than was expected. Fifteen tons of phosphorus etc. for filling smoke bombs arrived Boulogne today.

My SGSO (Butler) received a letter from Sir J. Willcocks expressing his delight at the order of the Indian Corps to prepare to attack! I understand that quite a contrary feeling existed at Indian Corps HQ when my order arrived. This letter is apparently to counteract the impression which the first report may have produced on me!

Tuesday 31 August

I am to have 1000 'lachrymator gas' shells for certain and possibly 2000 for 4.5 inch howitzers. The gas makes the eyes and nose water to such an extent

1 Lieutenant Colonel F. A. Buzzard.
2 Brigadier General (later Major General Sir) Frederick Barton ('Freddy') Maurice (1871–1951), BGGS (Operations) GHQ, 1915. Maurice was close to Robertson. In May 1918 he published a letter in the press accusing the Prime Minister, David Lloyd George, of lying to the House of Commons about the strength of the British Army on the eve of the German Spring Offensive. Lloyd George managed to survive the ensuing 'Maurice Debate'. The index entry for Maurice in Lloyd George's *War Memoirs* is a triumph of character assassination.

that it is impossible to serve the guns or see, but it is not death dealing in effect.

Wednesday 1 September

The CGS (Robertson) came to see me – most anxious to assist in every way. I urged that Haking should be put in command of the XI Corps at once and not after the forthcoming operations, because if we succeeded the 3 divisions forming the XI Corps must have a Commander. CGS quite agreed and he intended to propose it to Sir John, but the latter is in bed and has not been able to see him . . .

I received a letter from General Foch. He has ordered two French heavy batteries (6 inch) to remain, but asks for the 105mm battery as it is required for counter-battery work. This is satisfactory . . .

I then rode . . . to HQ I Corps where Generals Gough and Birch[1] showed me in detail their proposals for the first two days' bombardment . . . I thought their arrangements very good and felt what an advantage it is to have two keen active, energetic officers engaged in this work. What an advantage it is too to have a Corps Commander able to command his Corps himself and who knows what he wants to do without the intervention of a Staff officer!

Thursday 2 September

Haig decided to replace Major General H. J. S. Landon (GOC 9th Division) as he was 'unwell'. Landon's successor was Major General G. H. Thesiger.

At noon I motored to HQ IV Corps at La Buissière and saw Sir H. Rawlinson and Brigadier General Budworth,[2] Commanding Artillery 1st Division who is to command the artillery of this Corps in the attack. All seems to have been most thoroughly worked out. I discussed the use of some lachrymator shells against the Enemy's artillery before the infantry assault and argued that the Enemy's front line of trenches should have shrapnel fired on them at intervals during the gas attack, to prevent the Enemy from rallying . . .

In the afternoon I motored to Busnes and saw Major General Capper Commanding 7th Division. His preparations are progressing well, and he is

---

1 Brigadier General (later General Sir) (James Frederick) Noel ('Curly') Birch (1865–1939), BGRA I Corps, 1915–16; MGRA, GHQ and Fourth Army, 1916–19. Birch, together with Budworth, Franks and Uniacke, was one of the leading figures in British artillery development. Haig was a great admirer and did much to advance Birch's career.
2 Brigadier General (later Major General) Charles Edward Dutton ('Buddy') Budworth (1869–1921), CRA 1st Division, 1915; BGRA IV Corps, 1915–16; BGRA X Corps, 1916; MGRA, Fourth Army, 1916–18.

fully satisfied that everything will be ready in time. I also saw Major (Brigadier General) Trefusis[1] Commanding 20 Brigade. He commanded the Irish Guards with great success, and though only 'Captain' I had him promoted to command a Brigade.

Owing to a telegram from London re. 'gas' that 'plant had again broken down', Lieutenant Colonel Davidson[2] GSO2 proceeded to GHQ to find out what this meant. He reports that there would be enough for my requirements south of the La Bassée Canal.

Friday 3 September

General Willcocks ... had an interview with me. He said that he felt that I had not much confidence in him, and if that were so he would rather go. I said that I had expressed my opinion regarding the memorandum which he had sent me on the scheme of operations, and as regards what he had now said I would think it over and let him know my decision ...

I have from time to time felt that Willcocks is no support whatever when operations are in progress – and in December last (before the formation of First Army) his conduct of the operations at Givenchy deserved dismissal. Luckily for him no one from GHQ was present or had any idea of what a mess Sir James had made of things!

Sir James Willcocks was replaced as GOC Indian Corps by Lieutenant General Sir Charles Anderson on 6 September.

Saturday 4 September

The CGS (Robertson) arrived ... He came to let me know at once, very secretly, that the operations had been postponed by the French for another ten days. The reason given is that Castelnau's Army is not ready. This extra delay may well jeopardise the success of what I am undertaking, because at present we know that the Enemy's troops have no further protection against gas – only small 'respirators'. They may hear of our getting up the gas cylinders and issue effective 'gas helmets'. On the other hand it would be foolish for

1 Brigadier General Hon. John Frederick Hepburn-Stuart-Forbes-Trefusis ('Jack Tre') (1878–1915), GOC 20 Brigade, 1915. He was killed in action by a sniper on 24 October 1915.
2 Lieutenant Colonel (later Major General Sir) John Humphrey ('Tavish') Davidson (1872–1954), GSO1 First Army, 1915; BGGS (Operations) GHQ, 1915–18; MGGS (Operations) GHQ, 1918–19. Another Scotsman. He was the rising force in the General Staff and very close to Haig. Conservative MP, 1918–31; author of *Haig: Master of the Field* (1953), which is in many points a straight reprint of sections of the 'Memorandum on Operations 1916–1918' written at the war's end and deposited by Haig in the British Museum.

a portion of the Allies to attack until the whole are ready for a combined effort.

General Gough came to see me about the amount of gas available. I told him to arrange to provide the whole of his front south of the Canal with sufficient gas for 40 minutes' attack before giving any cylinders to the Givenchy section; and that his Corps, and IV Corps, would attack simultaneously *along the whole front* from the 'Double Crassier'[1] on Rawlinson's right, up to the Canal on the left.

Later in the morning General Rawlinson arrived and asked me regarding the front on which the 1st Division is to attack. After discussion I agreed that one brigade should move east with its left on the Vermelles–Hulluch road. All the Enemy's communication trenches run in that direction, so that the troops would, whether they were ordered or not, move against Hulluch! That another brigade of the 1st Division should advance against Puits No. 14 and the north end of Loos, so as to maintain communication between the attacks against Hulluch and Loos . . .

I motored to La Buissière (HQ of IV Corps) as I had arranged for Lieutenant Colonel Foulkes (gas expert) to meet me there. The gas cylinders had not yet been off-loaded at Béthune Station, so I was able to send them back to Boulogne at once. The 'gas companies' also went back to St Omer without having mixed with our troops, so I hope the fact that we are able to use gas will remain a secret from the Enemy . . .

We arranged for several officers of the Cavalry Corps to go forward to our lines and reconnoitre the country with a view to advancing.

Monday 6 September

At 10.30 am I held a conference of all Corps Commanders, CRAs, CGS and other Staff officers of Corps, Commanders of Divisions (and SGSOs) which are attacking, were present. These with my senior Staff officers made up a total of 53! We just managed to get them into my dining room. Behind me I had a map showing the main German communications in France, and another map of the front of my Army and the country as far east as Carvin and Lille.

I explained that the situation in Russia *obliged* the Allies to abandon their defensive attitude in the west and to attack before all their resources had been organised. I told them what orders I had received and what I understood the

1 *Crassiers* were heaps of mining waste, usually found alongside *fosses* on the Loos battlefield. The Double Crassier (southwest of Loos) and the Dump (near the Hohenzollern Redoubt) were the largest and most important. The Double Crassier enfiladed any advance on Loos. It was almost impossible to destroy machine-gun positions dug into them.

French were going to do; namely a general attack on the whole front, including two main efforts, one near Arras, the other near Rheims. Thus the German salient will be attacked on its two flanks. Looking at the map and trying to apply strategical principles, 'to get on the Enemy's rear and cut his communications,' I argued that the French Army on my right, after reaching Douai, would move on Valenciennes and eastwards on Liège: while the Army from Rheims must advance in the direction Hisson–Namur so as to be able to shatter the Enemy between them.

My orders are to break the Enemy's front and reach Pont à Vendin. With this objective the IV and I Corps attack south of the La Bassée Canal. The Indian Corps and III Corps must also attack to the full extent of their power, with the objects of:

(a) holding as many of the Enemy as possible in their front and so preventing him detaching troops to counter-attack the I Corps left and
(b) finding out when the Enemy begins to weaken in order to pursue as vigorously as possible.

If the Enemy still holds on in their front in strength, then the concentrated divisions must be ready to march and support the I and IV Corps by the gap which it is expected they will make. There must be the greatest energy and determination everywhere.

I also considered the possible troops which the Enemy could bring against us from day-to-day, and gave some instructions regarding the use of gas.

Wednesday 8 September

Generals Rawlinson and Gough visited me after lunch. They were anxious to know which of their two Corps should be allotted the task of taking Pont à Vendin. I said that the IV Corps on the right had for main objectives Loos–Hill 70 – and the spur which runs out eastwards towards Haisnes and Courrières. Similarly the I Corps with its left must take Haisnes and the spur which runs eastwards to Billy Berclau. The right of I Corps moves on the Vermelles–Hulluch road inclusive. It will take Hulluch and if troops are still available will press on and occupy Pont à Vendin. In any case I propose that a division of the 'General Reserve' should be pushed in rear of the point of junction of the I and IV Corps so that when required it can push forward on Pont à Vendin. I also hope to have a brigade or two of cavalry ready to go forward to seize the rising ground northeast of Pont à Vendin. Corps Commanders must also have the mounted troops of divisions, machine guns, and cyclists ready to exploit the success and to cover the flanks of their divisions. Cavalry officers to command the Divisional mounted troops of the 7th and 8th Divisions were asked for...

At night received letter from CGS pointing out the necessity of attending to matters which have already had attention e.g.

(1) Commanders to study country in our front.
(2) Mobility of force in view of large amount of trench equipment which has been accumulated.
(3) Difficulties of marching with troops which have been stationary so long.
(4) Movement of tractor drawn artillery.

Friday 10 September

I saw an experiment this forenoon with some small wireless sets for use during the attack towards Pont à Vendin to connect the leading divisions (or brigades) with Corps HQ when artillery shells render ordinary telegraph lines impossible. The range is 4 to 8 miles...

General Rice reported today on the manufacture of phosphorus bombs. We have now so many of them that it will not be necessary to light any large quantity of phosphorus to give the necessary amount of smoke. There is always the danger of having a large tin of phosphorus in a trench that a bullet may ignite it.

Saturday 11 September

After lunch I motored to St Venant where the 'Bomb School' is located. I saw Captain Grey in a neighbouring building, where the filling of bombs with red phosphorus was going on. Captain Grey brought over 15 tons of red phosphorus from London about a week ago, and as the authorities on the Lines of Communication would have nothing to do with the phosphorus, thinking it was dangerous, we had to undertake the work ourselves. Over 8 tons has already been made into bombs. The whole will be finished by Monday night ... Altogether a very fine performance.

I also saw at St Venant Captains Lister and Trelawney who arrived from London this morning with 19 Stokes' bomb guns and the materials for making up 10,000 smoke bombs for me in these guns. Lister said that it was just a week ago since he was asked to make a smoke bomb for use from the Stokes' gun! Lister is a civil engineer (with a chemical knowledge) in ordinary times. 100 more guns will soon follow, with 50,000 High Explosive shells.

Sunday 12 September

Foch visited Haig.

He explained the nature of the French operations, which I already knew. And I showed him on the map what I had arranged to do. He said that he relied on me, as I relied on him to cover my right etc. I asked him where the left of the Tenth French Army would be, and he pointed on the map that I would be able to use the road Lens to Douai, exclusive of the latter town, and thence to Orchies. My main effort should be directed on Carvin. I gathered that the real object of Foch's visit was to find out whether we British meant *really* to fight or not. I reassured him on that point, and told him that Joffre's orders were the same to me as those of 'Marshal French' ... I told him that they¹ were never in better heart and longing to have a fight. As regards the date, Foch said that he would see me again and arrange details with me. He is to see General Joffre this evening.

Monday 13 September

In the afternoon, I rode to our line of trenches near St Venant and saw some experiments carried out with Stokes' guns and phosphorus bombs, and other types of trench mortars. The success of our smoke bombs is highly satisfactory...

Airoplane photos of the Canal near Pont à Vendin show that there are some new canal basins, and marsh land along the Canal which will render the rapid passage of it on a broad front a matter of some difficulty. On the other hand the existence of these obstacles in rear of the Enemy's lines will render his escape difficult!

Tuesday 14 September

At 10 am I attended a demonstration of smoke bombs between St Venant and Robecq. All Corps and Divisional Commanders were present, plus those Brigadiers chiefly concerned in the attack and Staff officers. Altogether between 60–70 officers. We saw:

1st – 2 Stokes' mortars firing to place a curtain of smoke in front of machine gun emplacement about 400 yards distance.

2nd – 2 inch trench mortar firing a large spherical shell of phosphorus. Most effective but range not so long as the 1st.

---

1 i.e. British troops.

3rd – Two 'gas pipes' (i.e. 95mm trench mortar) firing the bombs we had made at St Venant.

4th – Two Gamage catapults made a flank curtain of fire by dropping bombs from close to our trenches up to the Enemy's lines.

5th – 8 men threw three phosphorus grenades each and made a dense line of smoke which blew slowly forward from our trenches.

6th – ditto with smoke candles. This latter is preferable to 5, if it is intended to advance over the ground on which the bombs are burning.

The whole of the experiment was extremely successful.

I explained to the Corps Commanders that they must each consider the particular problem which confronted him and adopt the kind of smoke producer which was most suited to the case.

All seemed highly delighted with the results of what they had seen. Considering that the men who worked the guns etc. only saw them yesterday for the first time, the results were most creditable.

In the afternoon I motored to . . . HQ 9th Division and saw Major General Thesiger Commanding.[1] He explained to me the arrangements for the attack of his Division. I impressed on him the principle that the men must go in as fast and as far as possible once the attack was launched!

I went to HQ 22 Brigade (Brigadier General Steele)[2] at Noyelles-les-Vermelles. All their trenches have been completed very satisfactorily.

Wednesday 15 September

I motored in the morning to HQ at Aire . . . and then went on to St Omer where I called on the CGS (Robertson) at 2 pm. Sir J. French has not yet got over his attack of fever. He attended a conference with General Joffre at Chantilly yesterday, but he has not yet been able to see Army Commanders to explain the general plan. The information I now got from the CGS was given *privately* and he begged me not to mention to the C-in-C that he had discussed the matter at all! He is to see Army Commanders at 10.30 am on Saturday.

The plan is generally on the lines I had worked out and explained to Conference on Monday 6th. I now learnt that our left were to move on Frasnes (northwest of Ath) and right of Tenth Army on Le Quesnoy (southeast of Valenciennes). The Cavalry Corps is to pass through near Arras, and move so as to gain possession of some crossings over the Scarpe.

I stated that it is most necessary some cavalry should be under my

1 Major General George Handcock Thesiger (1868–1915), killed in action at Loos, 27 September 1915.
2 Brigadier General Julian McCarty Steele (1870–1926), GOC 22 Brigade, 1915–18.

command – at least one brigade – to protect and scout on my left flank. Robertson agreed.[1] As regards date, the French have laid stress on the importance of all attacks going in on 25th whether the day is favourable for the use of gas or not. I stated that in my opinion it would be a mistake not to take advantage of the gas, for using which all arrangements had been made. If gas were not used, the fronts on which we attack will have to be restricted, and our prospects will be much more difficult. I advised that we should arrange to attack on 24th, if the wind was favourable. The French would be bombarding the Enemy on that day in any case, and would so be in a position to cover our right flank.

Thursday 16 September

Received a letter from Robertson saying that a brigade of cavalry and a battery RHA will be sent me ... 'The Chief will talk to you on Saturday about taking advantage of the 24th if favourable weather prevails. But he finds it difficult to decide.' 'Chief has just retired to bed till Saturday.'[2]

At 10 am I had a meeting with Rawlinson and Gough. I put the question to them 'If we have to attack on the 25th without gas, what modifications will it be necessary to make in your plans?' They both agreed that we must reduce the front of our attack and only go for the salient of Enemy's line i.e., Fosse No. 8, and the first line of trenches north of the Double Crassier. But they are to work out details and give me their plans in writing.

I also gave them a 'Timetable of Gas' for:

A. Main attack south of the La Bassée Canal, and
B. Subsidiary attack north of the La Bassée Canal.

A is for 40 minutes using 15 cylinders and B is for 6 minutes using 3 cylinders.

Our resources in bridging material were also given to them in the form of a memorandum. For the crossing of the Haute Deule Canal we must rely on the resources of the Army. GHQ will arrange for large bridges further forward.

Major General Butler went to GHQ today to make sure that steps were being taken to join up our railways with those now in German hands, at the first possible moment. Similarly the canals must be opened up ...

1 Sir John French agreed to place a cavalry division (less one brigade) at Haig's disposal after their meeting on 18 September.
2 Field Marshal Sir John French was quite often ill and incapacitated during the preparations for the Battle of Loos.

I wrote to Robertson in reply to his letter and said I did not understand the difficulty which was being experienced in deciding as to the gas. On the one hand, with gas, decisive results were to be expected. On the other hand, without gas, the fronts of attack must be restricted, with the result of concentrated hostile fire on the attacking troops. Considerable loss and small progress! In my opinion the attack ought not to be launched except with the aid of gas!

Hearing that the gas cylinders were not coming forward as rapidly as expected, I wrote to Robertson at 10 pm asking him to send a special officer to London to (a) insist on gas factory working *night* and day – at present they only work 8 hours daily and (b) make *special* arrangements to get the gas brought out and sent up to the troops. The situation was entirely a *special* one and *special* measures must be taken to ensure success.

Saturday 18 September

I attended meeting at St Omer presided over by Sir John French . . .

I gave a short outline of the attack which the First Army was carrying out for the information of the meeting. I urged the importance of having the General Reserve (which is under GHQ) with the lead divisions at Noeux Les Mines and Verquin respectively by the morning of the 25th. Sir John seemed to think that was too close up . . .

At the meeting I explained that if the 25th was unfavourable for gas and an attack had to be made notwithstanding, the scope of my offensive would be much curtailed because we only had enough guns to cover the attack of 2 divisions. In that case only the Hohenzollern Redoubt and the Loos salient could be attacked at the same time. So I emphasised the importance of being able to use gas with our attack . . .

Wind changed to the northeast in the afternoon.[1]

Sunday 19 September

Written instructions at last received from GHQ regarding the attack. The reserves are not to reach the area south of Lillers till 24th. This is too late! So I send Butler with a letter to the CGS on the subject, and repeat what I said at the C-in-C's Conference yesterday – The head of the two divisions of the Reserve Corps should be at Noeux-Les-Mines and Verquin by the night of 24/25 September. Butler got back about 3 pm and reported that the CGS

---

1 Haig began to record details about the change of wind from this time. Throughout the period of positional warfare he regularly began his diary entry with a note on weather conditions.

would arrange for the divisions to be disposed as desired by me, and would issue orders accordingly . . .

Orders were issued tonight for the forthcoming operations. Butler made the first draft yesterday and I amended it last night. Then, on receipt of the GHQ instructions, I amended them still further this afternoon.

Wind is in the east and northeast so it is unfavourable for our operations. It seems likely that by the end of the week the wind will change.[1]

Monday 20 September

Haig had a meeting with Kitchener.

We lunched at Hinges. Afterwards I explained the nature of our offensive operations. Last Saturday Sir J. French had said that he did not wish me to touch on this subject, but when the Secretary of State for War asks a Commander for certain information the Commander is bound to give it to the best of his ability. Kitchener did not realise how congested the whole front of attack becomes, and how difficult it is to get fresh troops forward to reinforce or replace those which have been engaged . . .

As regards the forthcoming operations, he told me that it is of very great *political* importance to gain a success at the present time. I told him that if the wind were only favourable on the 25th, we had *all of us* every confidence . . .

Personally I also felt the advantage of having a talk with him, and getting to know first hand, what the Government really expects of the Army. I can then give my orders with much more confidence that efforts on a large scale are really needed of us at the present moment . . .

Both Boulogne and Calais are closed today on account of mines. This has caused us trouble – we expected more gas cylinders to arrive. We have urged that a special boat be sent to Dieppe and a special train onwards from there.

Tuesday 21 September

Glass steady. Cold night – morning bright but a little foggy at first. Wind from northeast so it would not be possible to use gas today.

But day fairly favourable for bombardment which we began this morning.[2] The fog of the morning and afternoon somewhat interfered with observation, but artillery shooting reported to be very good and most satisfactory. The Enemy made very little reply to our fire. During the day both the I and IV

1 Gas was carried by the wind on to the enemy positions.
2 This was the preliminary bombardment before the infantry attack, which began on 25 September.

Corps simulated attacks by bombarding Enemy's front lines heavily: then lifting onto his second line: after allowing 5 minutes, in which Enemy manned his front trenches, several rounds of rapid fire with shrapnel were directed at his front trenches. The same arrangement will go on tomorrow at different points in the Enemy's line. Steady fire will be kept up on the Enemy's communication trenches each night (one round every five minutes) to stop his rations and reliefs from coming up and his working parties from repairing the damage done by our guns during the day.

After lunch I motored to Vaudricourt where Sir H. Rawlinson has established his advanced HQ in some huts under trees in the château grounds. In the orders which he issued to IV Corps I thought he failed to recognise the tactical value of the ridge which runs east and west on the north side of the Canal from Lens to Haisnes. He had ordered the 1st Division on his left on Pont à Vendin, while the 15th Division (next on the right) was to take Hill 70 and then move southeast on hill north of Loison. I directed Rawlinson to have the right of his 1st Division on the spur just south of Annay and to make certain of capturing the ridge in question.

Wednesday 22 September

Lieutenant General Gough, I Corps, came to see me. I spoke to him regarding the action of his Corps, and the need for having 2 or 3 officers at his HQ ready to fill the places of Brigadiers who might become casualties . . .

General Haking's XI Corps of 3 divisions will be close up ready to support.

Sir J. French came to see me about midday. He looked a little better, but older and fatter. He seemed in very good spirits. He said that he would release the XI Corps to support me on the first possible moment.[1] He seemed afraid that I might push the cavalry forward too soon. On Friday at 5 pm he is to see General Foch and will come on to see me afterwards. Foch will probably not attack till 9 or 10 am because of the fog in the mornings. If we are not able to use gas, he thought that we should delay our main attack to the same hour as the French.

Thursday 23 September

Reports of the bombardment yesterday show that Fosse 12 and 8 were set on fire, also Aubers village and Moulin du Pietre . . .

Enemy replied very little to our fire, but casualties amounted to 170 for the 24 hours, instead of the usual 90 to 100 . . .

General Robertson (CGS) came to . . . lunch. It seems that Sir J. French

---

1 This is the beginning of the confusion over the control of the Reserve.

does not realise the size of the units which he is fighting the forthcoming battle. He still clings to Haking's 3 divisions with which he, in his mind, is about to fight the battle, when really he is fighting with 3 Armies and 2 Cavalry Corps!! However the 3 divisions will be close up in the places where I have arranged to put them, and will go forward as soon as any opportunity offers.

Friday 24 September

At 2 pm I saw Generals Rawlinson and Gough. I told them that I would let them know (according to the weather report) by 10 pm whether to put their men in the trenches or not. If impossible to use gas Rawlinson would put in his attack against the Loos salient at the same time as the French which would certainly *not* be before 10 am. Gough's attack against the Hohenzollern Redoubt would however be made at 3.30 am.

Mr Gold (the weather expert)[1] arrived – I introduced him to Rawlinson and Gough. His weather charts were most interesting, but his forecast for a favourable wind was not very encouraging ...

I took a ride and walked the last 2 miles home. I got back about 5.30 pm to meet Sir J. French. He and his CGS arrived about 7.30 pm. They had been to see Foch. The latter would attack, if he possibly could, tomorrow but the hour would be 11 am. I told Sir John what I had arranged about the timings of my attacks viz. the III Corps at 3.30 am, and all the rest, if gas possible, as early as possible. I would fix zero by 10 pm if it were possible to do so.

If no gas, the timings would be as I told Gough and Rawlinson this afternoon ... Rawlinson before leaving said that he was glad for England's sake that the fighting of the coming battle was in my hands.

Mr Gold at 6 pm reported telegrams from Finisterre and Norway were more favourable.

At 9.20 pm forecast midnight to midnight '*wind* southerly then changing to southwest or west, probably increasing to 20 miles per hour'.

'Weather unsettled and showery at first, probably improving later.'

On this I ordered the troops to be put into the trenches. About 10 pm I walked out and the wind seemed from southwest but very light.

After much delay and uncertainty the great offensive at Loos was launched on 25 September. Loos was the biggest land battle in British military history to that time. It also marked the first use by the British of poison gas and the debut of New

1 Ernest Gold FRS (1881–1976), Fellow of Trinity College, Cambridge, Britain's leading meteorologist. Gold's staff rose from 3 to 120 during the war.

Army divisions in a major battle on the Western Front. The gas was intended, in part, to make up for artillery weakness which otherwise would have further constricted the front. Although the gas disappointed expectations, the initial infantry assault, especially on 15th (Scottish) Division's front, went well. But such opportunity as may have existed to achieve a breakthrough was lost because of the failure to bring up reserves. As at Neuve Chapelle the Germans acted swiftly, brought up their own reserves, counter-attacked and drove the British back to their start line. The issue of the release of the British reserves became contentious between Haig and French and led, ultimately, to French's 'resignation'.

Saturday 25 September

An anxious night – wondering what the wind would be in the morning. The greatest battle in the world's history begins today – some 800,000 French and British troops will actually attack today.

At 2 am General Butler reported Mr Gold was waiting for a telegram from War Office before making a forecast. Wind had fallen.

At 3 am I saw Mr Gold. Wind in places had fallen to 1 mile per hour. He could not say anything definitely beyond that the wind would probably be stronger just after sunrise (5.30) than later in the day. The Indian Corps required $2\frac{1}{2}$ hours' notice as they had a mine to explode. I therefore fixed Zero for 5.30 am which would mean the main attack going in 6.30 am.

I went out at 5 am – almost a calm. Alan Fletcher lit a cigarette and the smoke drifted in puffs towards the northeast. Staff officers of Corps were ordered to stand by in case it was necessary to counter order to attack. At one time owing to the calm I feared the gas would simply hang about *our* trenches! However at 5.15 I said 'Carry on'. I went to top of our lookout tower. The wind came gently from southwest and by 5.40 had increased slightly. The leaves of the poplar gently rustled. This seemed satisfactory. [But what a risk I must run of gas blowing back upon our dense masses of troops!]

At 5.45 I heard III Corps had got Enemy's front trenches.

About 7 am I Corps reported that attack from Givenchy had advanced unopposed. IV Corps said gas going in right direction. A little later, the whole front from the Double Crassier to Fosse No. 8 had been captured and our troops were advancing.

Soon after 7 am Colonel Barry[1] left my HQ with news for Sir J. French. I urged the necessity of having Haking's Corps ready to advance in support. I ordered Briggs's[2] Cavalry Division to move to Vaudricourt.

1 Lieutenant Colonel (later Colonel) Stanley Leonard Barry (1873–1943), a Northamptonshire landowner; ADC to Sir John French; later served in the Military Secretary's Office.
2 Major General (later Lieutenant General Sir) Charles James Briggs (1865–1941), GOC 3rd Cavalry Division, 1915. He later commanded XVI Corps at Salonika.

8.45 Dawnay arrived from C-in-C with congratulations. I sent him back at once to Philomel to tell Sir John that the Reserve Brigades of the I and IV Corps had already reached the German trenches, and to tell him to place Haking's Corps under my orders. Reserves must be pushed on at once.

9.45 I saw Gemeau and asked him to telephone General Foch urging him to attack at once. Our troops had reached already Cité St Elie, the eastern side of Loos and were attacking Hill 70 and Cité St Auguste – Puits 14 bis taken 9.30 about.

At 10.30 am Cavalry Division ordered to move on Noyelles (south of Vermelles) in readiness to advance on high ground between Pont à Vendin–Haisnes as soon as Cité St Auguste captured.

Hill 70 taken by 15th Division about 11. Also Hulluch by 1st Division.

Sir J. French came to see me about 11.30 am and then went to Noeux Les Mines to see General Haking Commanding XI Corps. He said he will arrange to put Haking under my orders less the Guards Division. Gough reported about 11 that his left north of Fosse 8 is hard pressed. I order the leading brigade of 24th Division (Ramsay)[1] XI Corps to come under his orders as soon as it reaches Vermelles. 21st Division (Walker) to march on Mazingarbe.

2 pm. Haking wired that his Corps less Guards Division has by Sir J. French's orders, been placed under my orders. I direct him to advance between Hulluch, and Cité St Auguste, and occupy the high ground between Pont à Vendin and Haisnes with the crossings over the Canal to the east and south of that line. If Hill 70 is in need of support Haking will give it. At 1.30 I wired to GHQ asking what D'Urbal's army was doing because Enemy were counter-attacking Hill 70, and Rawlinson was in doubt whether 15th Division could hold on.

3 pm. I Corps reports that St Elie has not been captured and IV Corps states that we have not got Hulluch yet, and that a party of Germans still hold a portion of their front line trench near 'Lone Tree'.

Airoplanes report Enemy's reinforcements arrived from Lille ... this morning in 'every kind of vehicle'. This was due no doubt to the attack of the 8th Division of III Corps which started at 3.30 am – considerable numbers of the Enemy's troops have consequently been drawn off from our main attack by III Corps.

By dark the Germans about 'Lone Tree' had surrendered. The two new Divisions (24th and 21st) were so slow in coming forward. It was 6 pm before they began to cross our old trenches. I accordingly ordered Haking to relieve

1 Major General Sir John George Ramsay (1856–1920), dug out of retirement in 1914 to raise and train 24th Division. At fifty-seven he was old to command a division in the field and was replaced after the Loos battle.

with them the IV Corps troops from near Hill 70 to Hulluch, and to prepare to attack Cité St Auguste tomorrow morning.

The day has been a very satisfactory one on the whole. We have captured 8000 yards of German front, and advanced in places 2 miles from our old front line. This is the largest advance made on the Western Front since this kind of warfare started.

Sunday 26 September

During the night the Enemy counter-attacked and retook 'The Quarries'. They were held by a brigade of the 9th Division under Brigadier General Bruce.[1] Our troops were driven back to the old German front line. The 9th Division failed to regain the lost ground. The 7th Division on its right, re-established itself with a counter-attack.

The I Corps had apparently no reserves, and appealed to Army HQ for help. I only had a brigade of cavalry to place at his disposal. The rear battalion of the 21st Division ... was ordered to move to Gough's support: apparently a whole brigade went.

About 9 am I saw Generals Rawlinson, Gough and Haking at Vaudricourt. Rawlinson is to capture the work on Hill 70. Haking with 5 brigades of his XI Corps will, as soon as Hill 70 is taken, advance on Cité St Auguste and the German 2nd line which runs north of Bénifontaine. The 1st Division will attack Hulluch.

About noon Sir J. French came to see me. The Guards Division comes under my orders today, and I am to place the 15th Division in GHQ Reserve at Noeux Les Mines, in its place. The 28th Division is on the march from Béthune and will replace the 9th Division which similarly will go into GHQ Reserve ...

Prisoners reported to date 2235. I saw some 6 or 800 in a field this morning. They looked of good physique. A considerable number belong to the 2nd Guard Reserve Division which recently returned from Russia. 8 guns have been captured.

About lunch-time reports arrived that 21st Division (Ramsay) and 24th (Forestier-Walker) which had been ordered to attack on the line Hulluch–Hill 70 had broken, and were coming back in great disorder. The left of IV Corps about Hill 70 and Loos was thus exposed, and the right of the 1st Division which had got a footing in the south end of Hulluch village had to bend back and conform to the retirement of the 21st Division. The Guards Division was still too distant to intervene – Indeed its leading brigade did not reach the line of our old trenches till 4 pm.

1 Brigadier General Clarence Dalrymple Bruce (1863–1934), GOC 27 Brigade, 1915 (captured).

On hearing of the alarming situation of the 21st and 24th Divisions I placed Brigadier General Campbell[1] and the 6 Cavalry Brigade (less 1 regiment) at disposal of IV Corps with orders to place Campbell in command of Loos, and be responsible for its defence. The 15th Division which had fought splendidly for 2 days, had suffered very severely and only existed in fragments, was being collected west of the town of Loos. This was done by telephone and I then motored to Vaudricourt; saw Rawlinson, impressed on him importance of always indicating clearly the officer responsible for the defence of a captured locality etc. Got the reports of the situation which he had received from his subordinates on the ground near Loos and then motored on to Noeux Les Mines HQ of XI Corps. While waiting for General Haking a message arrived from 24th Division stating that the whole mass of infantry of the two new divisions was running away in great disorder and had abandoned the guns. I said that if the report was untrue the writer of the message should [be] tried by Court Martial for sending in an alarmist report.

I at once ordered Briggs with the 3rd Cavalry Division (less Campbell's detachment) to move out quickly, clear up the situation, and connect the left of the IV Corps with the right of the I Corps, until relieved by the Guards Division. Lord Cavan, Commanding Guards Division, came into Haking's HQ when I was there. His leading brigades only reached our old trenches about 4 pm, and his next brigade was 2 hours behind it. I told him to push forward troops as soon as possible to hold a position between the IV and I Corps, consolidate it and send out patrols to report how the Enemy was situated.

About 4 pm I Corps organised an attack with 2nd Division to recapture 'The Quarries' (about 500 yards west of Cité St Elie). Brigadier General Bruce's Brigade were in occupation of this last night and were surprised during the night. The General and Staff were captured. The brigade belongs to the 9th Division (New Army). Fine men, and did well in capturing Hohenzollern Redoubt and Fosse No. 8 on Saturday, but it seems careless to have gone to sleep in a quarry so close to the Enemy! The 7th Division attack against the Quarry met with stubborn resistance, and lost heavily but was successful in carrying the Enemy's position.

About 7 pm the Enemy delivered a strong counter-attack first against the Quarries, and then against Fosse No. 8. The Enemy came on in large masses. We were able to bring the fire of artillery of the 1st and 7th Divisions as well as of some 40 heavy guns. The attack was driven back with great loss.

The orders for tomorrow are that 28th Division relieves the 9th, and

1 Brigadier General (later Major General Sir) David Graham Muschet ('Soarer') Campbell (1869–1936), GOC 6 Cavalry Brigade, 1914–16. He inherited 21st Division in the aftermath of Loos and commanded it for the rest of the war.

Guards the 1st Division. Position to be consolidated. In afternoon Haking to arrange to capture Hill 70.

Major General Sir T. Capper Commanding 7th Division was wounded in chest with shrapnel bullet during the attack on the Quarries. Brigadier General Watts the senior Brigadier took his place. Capper is a great loss as he combined great pluck and straightforwardness with a thorough knowledge of war.

Monday 27 September

Another anxious day solely on account of the initial mistake of the C-in-C in refusing to move up the Reserve Divisions close to the rear of the attacking troops before the commencement of the operations.

The reason for the debacle of the 21st and 24th Divisions yesterday is said to be that the men had not been fed. The divisions were so far back that when wanted, they had to be pushed forward without waiting for food, and being new divisions, the battalions did not know how to look after themselves. I sent General Hobbs to see the divisions which are now collected west of Vermelles and find out how they were situated and how far the Divisional Commanders can be held to blame for the want of management.

Sir J. French came to see me about 11 o'clock. I showed him how long it had taken for the reserves to come up, even with the greatest energy on the part of everyone concerned. I urged the importance of the French on my right pressing on . . .

Later in the day I received letter from d'Urbal that he had arranged to mass guns on his left to assist it forward as well as to support my right.

About 1.30 pm I received report from I Corps that the 73 Brigade had been driven out of Fosse 8. General Bulfin's 28th Division had been placed at the disposal of I Corps as soon as it had arrived in our area. It marched from Strazeele yesterday . . . a long march, and the troops were tired. The original arrangement made by HQ Staff was to move one brigade by bus, another by train, and the third which was close, to march. But C-in-C refused to sanction and ordered the division to march to Merville!! This was cancelled later, when the urgency of the case was realised by him, and so the troops had a long fatiguing march and arrived too late to save Fosse 8. This morning 2 brigades were moved forward by motor bus. But as events showed, too late!

On getting the report of the loss of Fosse 8 I motored at once to Gough's HQ . . .

Ritchie[1] and some 600 men of his brigade counter-attacked at once when

1 Brigadier General (later Major General Sir) Archibald Buchanan Ritchie (1869–1955), GOC 26 Brigade, 1915–16; GOC 11th Division, 1916–17 (wounded); GOC 16th Division, 1918–19.

he found the 73 Brigade rushing back. Bulfin was put in charge of the section, and said he would regain Fosse 8 by tonight.

Some of Bulfin's troops having arrived and made situation on my left more satisfactory, I ordered the attack which had been arranged to take place at 4 pm by XI Corps (i.e., by the Guards Division) to continue. It was nearly midnight before I learnt the result. Communications back are so difficult owing to shell fire and telephone wires getting cut. The Guards got one end of Hill 70 and also the 'Chalk pit' but not Puits 14 bis.

About 8 pm copy of a German intercepted wireless was sent to me. It stated that 'The English have broken through – wireless station is falling back (from Loison) to Oignies'.

I at once ordered Briggs who was in Loos with 3rd Cavalry Division to get in touch with Guards in his front and if report was correct to move to Pont à Vendin before daylight and I would support him with infantry.

Tuesday 28 September

French on my right (X Corps) made no progress yesterday.

Bulfin made small progress towards regaining Fosse 8. Pereira commanding 13 Brigade was wounded.[1] To assist the attack last night on Fosse 8 the 2nd Division opposite Cuinchy let off gas which we were arranging for an effort later against Auchy and La Bassée from the west. The gas was let out at 5 pm but had very little effect. The Germans wore smoke helmets – so our attack was not pressed home.

This morning I ordered all our positions to be consolidated, and tired troops to be withdrawn.

Sir J. French came to see me this morning. He arranged with me to withdraw the 21st and 24th Divisions at once for training and to replace them with the 12th and 46th Divisions ...

Haking who will have 3 divisions viz. the Guards, 12th ... and 46th will take Hulluch and press between that place at Cité St Auguste and advance at once and capture crossings over Canal at Pont à Vendin.

Gough (also with 3 divisions) 2nd, 7th and 28th will protect the left flank. The moment Hulluch has been taken he will put brigade into it to hold it, and send a couple of brigades to capture and hold Wingles.

Rawlinson (with 1st, 15th and 47th) will protect right flank. He will hold Hill 70 and as Haking's troops advance he will push a detachment towards Loison.

---

1 This appears to be a slip by Haig. Brigadier General (later Major General Sir) Cecil Edward ('Pinto') Pereira (1860–1942) was wounded on 26 September 1915, but this was while he was commanding 85 Brigade, 28th Division, not 13 Brigade. He commanded 2nd Division, 1916–18.

Haking should thus be able to advance straight ahead. Unfortunately, the Enemy has had time to construct defences at Pont à Vendin! It was quite undefended last Saturday and the Enemy had no troops in his second line! It is thus certain, that even with *one* division in reserve and close up, as I had requested, we could have walked right through his second line! And all our present preparations would have been unnecessary! When the C-in-C remains blind to the lessons of the war in this important matter (handling of reserves) we hardly deserve to win . . .

Sir John French at his interview with me today said that it was most serious that Tenth Army could not make any progress. He seemed tired of the war, and said that in his opinion we ought to take the first opportunity of concluding peace otherwise England would be ruined! I could not agree, but said we cannot make peace till the German military party[1] is beaten.

Wednesday 29 September

Letter from CGS that the 46th Division is 'unlikely to reach area of First Army complete in less than a week from now'. Sir John yesterday said it might be here tomorrow or next day.

From the prisoners taken we find that the Enemy has been obliged to bring up detachments and units of various divisions to oppose our advance. Indeed he was so hard pressed to find troops on Saturday and Sunday that all servants of officers etc. in Lens were collected and sent forward to the trenches (2nd line) . . .

Sir J. French and his CGS came to see me at noon. General Foch is to send the IX Corps to cover my right flank and I am to arrange details with d'Urbal regarding its position.

At 1 o'clock telegram received that French have passed through the last German line with 3 divisions in Champagne. Tenth Army on my right has gained the crest of Vimy, from the Bois de Givenchy to the Ferme de la Folie.

At 5 pm I met General d'Urbal at the mairie at Noeux Les Mines and arranged that French IX Corps should take over the line on my right now held by IV Corps from near Double Crassier past the south side of Loos to the west summit of Hill 70, then north to the Puits 14 bis road from Loos (inclusive). The relief to take place tomorrow night.

This move is due to a change of plan on the part of Foch. Thanks to our success at Loos, the French can now place guns near Hill 70 to support their advance from the Vimy plateau to Douai. At the same time they will protect my right flank on our advance eastwards.

I had a conference at Vaudricourt Chateau at 6 pm. Present, Generals

---

1 'military power' in the Ts diary.

Rawlinson, Haking and Gough and Staff officers. I explained arrangement with French about taking over our right. IV Corps will be in reserve now, in rear of Haking. The attack on German 2nd line will take place on Saturday 2 October but will depend on French co-operation near Hill 70. Will they be ready?

Wednesday 29 September. Letter to Kitchener [1]

You will doubtless recollect how earnestly I pressed you to ensure an adequate reserve being close in rear of my attacking divisions, and under my orders. It may interest you to know what happened. No reserve was placed under me. My attack, as has been reported, was a complete success. The Enemy had no troops in his second line, which some of my plucky fellows reached and entered without opposition. Prisoners state the Enemy was so hard put to it for troops to stem our advance that the officers' servants, fatigue-men, etc., in Lens were pushed forward to hold their end line to the east of Loos and Hill 70.

The two Reserve Divisions (under C-in-C's orders) were directed to join me as soon as the success of the First Army was known at GHQ. They came on as quick as they could, poor fellows, but only crossed our old trench line with their heads at 6 pm. We had captured Loos 12 hours previously, and reserves should have been at hand *then*. This, you will remember, I requested should be arranged by GHQ and Robertson duly concurred in my views and wished to put the Reserve Divisions under me, but was not allowed.

The final result is that the Enemy has been allowed time in which to bring up troops and to strengthen his second line, and probably to construct a third line in the direction in which we are heading, viz. Pont à Vendin.

I have now been given some fresh divisions, and am busy planning an attack to break the Enemy's second line. But the element of surprise has gone, and our task will be a difficult one.

I think it right that you should know how the lessons which have been learnt in the war at such cost have been neglected. We were in a position to make this the turning point in the war, and I still hope we may do so, but naturally I feel annoyed at the lost opportunity.

Thursday 30 September

Held conference at 9.30 am. Generals Gough, Haking and Butler present. Owing to Fosse No. 8 commanding the ground to the south and southeast it is difficult to place guns for wire cutting of Enemy's second line south of

1 TNA PRO 30/57/53: Kitchener Papers, WD/15, 1915.

Hulluch without having them knocked out. I therefore decided that I Corps must arrange to take Fosse 8 and (by using gas) to advance line south of the Canal to the triangle.

XI Corps (Haking) to take the woods along Puits 14 bis (with a view to attacking Hulluch from the south later). This move must be made in co-operation with an attack by the French to capture the rest of Hill 70, and the front line of Enemy's trenches to the south and southeast. The date to be Saturday 2 October *but* French would be ready by then?

Haking will also gradually extend his line from the 'Chalk pit' north of Puits 14 bis to the Vermelles–Hulluch road . . .

Report about 2 pm that Germans were concentrating near Haisnes to attack our position in the Hohenzollern Redoubt. I at once went to HQ of I Corps. Enemy's attack was stopped by artillery fire. I impressed on Dick Cunyngham[1] (GSO2) necessity for Corps Staff keeping up map showing position at a glance of all reserves and time required to reach important points. Germans having brought troops by train to Lens, and also to vicinity of La Bassée, I told Corps to be prepared to resist a night attack. Horses met me at St Pry Château and I rode to GHQ IV Corps at Vaudricourt. I saw Rawlinson and ordered him to have a good reserve near Loos in case of a night attack. The French are delayed (as usual!) and finish taking over our line on Hill 70 till tomorrow night. I rode through Drouvin and saw some of the 15th Division which took Loos. All very cheery and pleased with themselves. Some battalions only 300 strong. General Wilkinson[2] (44 Brigade) told me that his men rushed through Loos and suffered comparatively small losses until they had gained Hill 70. They then came under machine gun fire in the open. Nothing could stop his men: they ran on so fast that some of the officers could not keep up until Hill 70.

Saturday 2 October

The CGS Robertson came to lunch. Sir John French returns to St Omer today. Robertson tackled him on the question of reserves. The reply was 'the 2nd day of the battle was the correct time to put them in and not the 1st'. It seems impossible to discuss military problems with an unreasoning brain of this kind! At any rate, no good result is to be hoped for from so doing.

---

1 Major (later Major General) James Keith Dick-Cunyngham (1877–1935), GSO2 I Corps, 1915–16; GSO1 51st Division, 1916–18; GOC 152 Brigade, 1918 (captured on 12 April during the German Spring Offensive).
2 Brigadier General Montagu Grant Wilkinson (1857–1943), GOC 44 Brigade, 1914–16.

Monday 4 October

French telephoned to express his 'surprise and regret' at the cancellation of an attack on Fosse 8.

I sent back a fairly straight reply, pointing out the continuous fighting which had been going on . . . and stating that the troops want rest, time to consolidate the positions gained, and time in which to reconnoitre before making a further advance. The Enemy's positions on my front are now so strong that an attack as carefully prepared as the previous one will be required to ensure success. Really Sir John is very ignorant of the nature of the fighting which has taken place ever since Neuve Chapelle!

Tuesday 5 October

About 7.30 pm Brigadier General Maurice arrived from GHQ with a letter from CGS asking if we could not attack on the 9th. I handed him my reply to the previous letter from Sir John French . . . And I told him verbally that it was impossible to attack before the 10th with any real chance of success. And further, in my opinion, we will have a great fight to retain Fosse 8, once we have captured it.

Wednesday 6 October

A letter arrived from the CGS, Robertson.

C-in-C directs 'that the 10th is definitely to be the day of the attack', and asked for an outline of my plan. I sent him a copy of my orders, and said that everything possible was being done to complete arrangements by the 10th, but that Fosse 8 was really a fortress and that 'parallels', starting trenches, and communication trenches had all to be dug. I would let him know later what is possible.

Friday 8 October

I motored to St Omer and saw Sir J. French at 11 o'clock. He seemed in a chastened mood! and was evidently anxious to make amends for the fiery letters which had been sent me by his orders.

    I explained the progress made in our arrangements for the attack [against the Hohenzollern Redoubt]. He expressed himself as in full agreement with my views that the attack should not be delivered until all was ready. This, I said would not be till the 13th. He wished me to try and hurry things up so as to attack on the 12th. [I said I would do my best.]

Sir John read me a letter which he had received from Lord Kitchener asking for a report on the action of the 21st and 24th Divisions. Some of the wounded had gone home and said that they had been given impossible tasks to accomplish, and that they had not been fed!

Saturday 9 October

Lord Haldane came to lunch. General H. Gough came to meet him. After-wards Lord Haldane came to my room and asked me to give him my views on the action of the reserves, i.e. of the 21st and 24th Divisions during the 25 and 26 September. He said that feelings were so strong on the subject in England, that he had come to France to help in arriving at the truth. I gave him all the facts. The main criticism to my mind is the fact that the reserves were not at hand when wanted. The causes for this seem to me to be:

1. Neither the C-in-C, nor his Staff fully realised at the beginning (in spite of my letters and remarks) the necessity for reserves being close up before the action began.
2. The two divisions were billeted in depth a long distance from where they would be wanted, and no attempt was made to concentrate them before the battle began.
3. When the course of the fight showed that reserves were wanted at once to exploit the victory, the two divisions were hurried forward without full consideration for their food etc., with the result that the troops arrived worn out at the point of attack and unfit for battle.
4. But the 21st and 24th Divisions having only recently arrived in France, with Staffs and Commanders inexperienced in war, should not have been detailed for this work. It was courting disaster to employ them at once in fighting of this nature.

There were other divisions available as shewn by the fact that they arrived three days later upon the battlefield, namely, the 28th Division, the 12th Division and the Guards Division.

I also felt it my duty to tell Lord Haldane that the arrangements for the Supreme Command during the battle were not satisfactory. Sir J. French was at Philomel (near Lillers) 25 miles nearly from his CGS who was at St Omer [with GHQ.] Many of us felt that if these conditions continued, it would be difficult ever to win!

Monday 11 October

Another German airoplane was captured today in the III Corps area, near Sailly. One of the officers stated that the Germans are feeling the shortage of men! This is the first mention from prisoners we have had of this. Another officer said that the German officers could not think why the English had not pressed forward on the 26 September, as they had broken through their line! A notebook of a man of the Prussian Guard also indicates this. 'In passing through Lens on the 27th, we were told that the British had pierced our line.' Captured documents show that the Germans are hard put to it to find sufficient men for the Army. The 1918 class is being registered.

Wednesday 13 October

On 13 October XI Corps (Lieutenant General R. C. B. Haking) attacked the Hohenzollern Redoubt. The attack was a failure, achieving (in the later words of the British official historian) nothing but a 'useless slaughter of infantry'. The 46th (North Midland) Division suffered especially badly.

General Haking came to see me about 9.30 am. I told him *conditions seemed likely* to become favourable, but I would decide about 10 am and notify him at once of my decision.

About 11 o'clock the meteorologist reported that he had not received the Scandinavian reports but those from Paris indicated that the westerly wind reported about Havre and northwest France was likely to move eastwards. He also thought that the wind was not likely to be more favourable tomorrow.

Reports from the trenches indicate favourable southwest wind blowing towards the Quarries and Fosse 8. At Cuinchy the wind is along the trenches.

On receipt of these reports I ordered attack to be delivered at 2 o'clock as arranged with gas and smoke, except near Cuinchy where the officers on the spot must decide whether it is possible to use gas...

At 2 pm the assault was delivered and the Field Artillery created barrages beyond and on the flanks of the positions assaulted...

Up to 4 pm reports indicated that the advance was making good progress ... After this the fighting seemed to be general and the situation was most confused...

The 46th Division held the west side of the Hohenzollern Redoubt. The shelling had been very hard and the trenches had been much destroyed. Only 2 battalions remained in the Divisional General's hand. He had apparently used up his reserves before they were really required.

Saturday 16 October

A communication received from GHQ asking for an explanation of certain statements which I had made in my report on the operations of 25th and subsequent days regarding the want of reserves at certain points, and [my opinion] that our troops had pierced the Enemy's rear line of defence. Statements from COs of battalions and also captured diaries of prisoners and killed bear out all I said in my report. I am glad that the facts should be elicited now when it is possible to get more or less at the truth.

Sunday 17 October

About 2 pm Lieutenant General Robertson, CGS, came to see me. He returned 2 days ago from a week in London, where he went at Lord Kitchener's bidding to assist the General Staff on matters connected with plans for conducting the war in view of the new situation in the Balkans.[1] He attended several meetings of the Cabinet. Apparently there is considerable dissension. One section (including Lloyd George) wishes to send troops to Salonika. Another section (including Kitchener) wish to throw more troops on to Gallipoli.

The General Staff in London produced a paper on the subject. It was really written by Kiggell. The opinion arrived at was that all efforts should be devoted to securing a victory in France which is the main theatre of war. After the paper was written, Lord Kitchener told Murray who is now 'Chief of the Imperial Staff', that whatever conclusion the General Staff arrived at in this paper, one recommendation must be that eight British divisions are sent from France to Gallipoli! Sir Archibald Murray was weak enough to comply, and added a paragraph to the desired effect! This clearly shows that he (Murray) is quite unfit for any responsible position as military *adviser*! . . .[2]

As regards Sir J. French, Robertson told me that when he was in London, Lord Stamfordham[3] called him up on the telephone from Sandringham and asked him by the King's orders whether he did not consider the time had come to replace Sir J. French. Robertson did not answer. He saw the King afterwards in London, and now he came to discuss the point with me. I told him at once that up to date I had been most loyal to French and did my best to stop all criticisms of him or his methods. Now at last, in view of what had

1 Bulgaria had entered the war on the side of the Central Powers and invaded Serbia.
2 Archie Murray succeeded Sir James Wolfe Murray as CIGS on 25 September 1915. Despite this comment General Staff appreciations of the military situation greatly improved under Archie Murray.
3 Lord Stamfordham (1849–1931), Principal Private Secretary to HM King George V, 1910–31. Stamfordham was the main channel through which the King corresponded with his generals.

happened in the recent battle over the reserves, and in view of the seriousness of the [general military] situation, I had come to the conclusion that it was not fair to the Empire to retain French in command [on this the main front.] Moreover, none of my Officers Commanding Corps had any opinion of Sir John's military ability or military views: in fact, they find no confidence in him. Robertson quite agreed, and left me saying 'he knew now how to act, and would report to Stamfordham'. He also told me that the members of the Cabinet who had up to the present been opposed to removing French had come round to the other opinion. French does not get on with the French: Joffre seems to have no great opinion of his military views and does not really consult with him. It is most important at the present time to have someone to put the British case and combine with the French in aiming at decisive results in their plans of operations.

Monday 18 October. Letter to Leopold de Rothschild[1]

We won quite a big success here ... great opportunity missed ... all we wanted was some reserves at hand to reap the fruits of victory and open the road for our cavalry to gallop through!

The main lesson I learn from all this is that we must take more pains to train our divisions before sending them to fight the Germans.

Sunday 24 October

Sir William Robertson came to see me and stayed to lunch. He was anxious that I should write to some of my friends in the Government and urge the importance of not sending troops to the Balkans. I said I hated intriguing in such a way, and that (except for him) I had no official knowledge of what was intended. I would express my views to the King with whom I was dining tonight, but the best solution in my opinion was that he (Robertson) should go home as Chief of the General Staff. The Government seems quite incapable of deciding on a sound military policy and sticking to it. [A sound military adviser, a man of character, must be found to advise them.] Two vital points must be attended to before we can hope to be victorious: (1) We must have a larger Army, and (2) Units must be trained.

Robertson said French was in London with views more unsettled than usual ...

After dinner the King asked me to come to his room, and asked me about Sir J. French's leadership. I told him that I thought the time to have removed French was after the Retreat, because he had so mismanaged matters, and

1 NLS: Haig Papers, Acc. 3155, No. 214a.

shewn in the handling of the small Expeditionary Force in the field a great ignorance of the essential principles of war. Since then, during the trench warfare, the Army had grown larger and I thought at first there was no great scope for French to go wrong. I have therefore done my utmost to stop criticisms and make matters run smoothly. But French's handling of the reserves in the last battle, his obstinacy, and conceit, showed his incapacity, and it [seemed to me] impossible for anyone to prevent him doing the same things again. I therefore thought strongly that for the sake of the Empire, French ought to be removed. I personally was ready to do my duty in any capacity, and of course would serve under anyone who was chosen for his military skill to be C-in-C. The King said that he had seen Generals Gough and Haking that afternoon, and that they had told him startling truths of French's unfitness for the Command. General Robertson also told him that it was 'impossible to deal with French: his mind was never the same for two consecutive minutes!'.

Thursday 28 October

During an inspection of First Army by the King, His Majesty was thrown from his horse. Haig was considerably discomfited by this.

It was a most unfortunate accident. We were within 50 yards of the place at which he [the King] was to dismount and look round the airoplanes [on foot, and come to Hinges for lunch with me.] The mare was so quiet all through the day, too, but the waving caps and the sudden cheering would have upset any horse at such a close distance . . .

A very wet afternoon. About 5 pm a telephone message was received from Sir Derek Keppel[1] to say that the result of the consultation of surgeons is that the King has no bones broken, but is to remain in bed for a day or two to recover from the stiffness and bruises. He was also desired by the King to say that His Majesty knew very well that the mare had never done such a thing before, and that I was not to feel perturbed at what had happened, (or words to that effect).

Tuesday 2 November

The Times today published a despatch from Sir J. French dealing with operations of 25 September. It is full of misstatements of fact. My Staff are

---

1 Hon. Sir Derek Keppel (1863–1944), Master of the King's Household, 1912–36. Keppel was the second son of the 7th Earl of Albemarle. Mrs Alice Keppel, mistress of King Edward VII, was his sister-in-law.

comparing the Despatch with the orders and telegrams received from GHQ and will make out a note on the subject. It is too disgraceful of a C-in-C to try and throw dust in the eyes of the British people by distorting facts [in his Official Reports].

Thursday 4 November

I sent in letter to GHQ today calling attention to two paragraphs in Sir J. French's recent Despatch which are incorrect. Para. 11 – I enclosed copies of 3 telegrams, which showed that the 21st and 24th Divisions were not placed under my orders as stated, nor did I issue orders to GOC XI Corps as he was not under my Command. Para. 13 (9) – The Guards Division was not placed under my orders till 4.15 pm *not* 'on the morning of the 26th', as stated.

Saturday 6 November

Letter received from Robertson (CGS) who returned from London on Wednesday. 'Matters don't improve much at home – in fact, not at all.' The papers today announce that Lord Kitchener has left the War Office and is replaced by the Prime Minister. Some seem to think Kitchener has left the War Office for good.[1]

Sir J. French has returned from England and is in bed with a heart attack. We wonder whether that is the result of my letter to GHQ asking that paras. 11 and 13 (9) of his last Despatch may be corrected.

Monday 8 November

I received two letters from CGS. One commenting on my reports on the papers which I had forwarded re. the 21st and 24th Divisions and [the] action of the reserves [at Loos]. This correspondence the C-in-C directed to cease. The other letter was in reply to mine of 4th inst. calling the Field Marshal's attention to certain inaccuracies in his Despatch which was published on 2 November. The CGS is directed to state that the statements in question are 'substantially correct' and call for no amendment. In reply I state that the paras. of the Despatch to which I take exception 'convey the impression that at 9.30 am on the 25th September I was able to use the 21st and 24th Divisions in support of the attacking troops, and similarly that I could make use of the

---

1 Kitchener had, in fact, gone to visit the Gallipoli peninsula, the evacuation of which he was forced to accept. He did return to the War Office and remained Secretary of State for War until his death in June 1916.

Guards Division on the *morning* of the 26th. This was not the case, and I beg to request that this fact may be placed on record.'

Wednesday 10 November

After the Conference I saw Sir John in his own room regarding the correspondence which I have had on the subject of reserves and his recent Despatch. He promised to send all my letters on the subject to the War Office, and to let me see his covering letter which will accompany the correspondence. I said all I wanted was that the *true facts* of the operations should be placed on record. He was most anxious that I should know that he had had nothing to do with an article by Repington in *The Times* of 2 November. I said that my only thought was how to win the war, and that my duties as GOC First Army took up all my time. I gather that no one of importance takes much notice of Sir J. when he goes to London, and that he feels his loss of position.

Sunday 14 November

Lord Esher came to lunch. We had a long talk afterwards on the general situation at home, and agreed that he should go to London tomorrow and recommend:

1. That General Robertson should be appointed CIGS and to advise the War Committee of the Cabinet direct (not through Secretary of State for War).
2. That the DMO and DSD directorates be removed from the War Office and placed in the Horse Guards under General Robertson. This to be the 'Imperial General Staff'.
3. That the DMT (which deals with Home Defence and Training) be reorganised as a local General Staff, and be placed under a C-in-C of the United Kingdom. Sir A. Murray could remain as the Chief of this General Staff.

The effect of these proposals, it is hoped, will be to strengthen the Imperial General Staff; and keep it free from the administrative details carried out in the War Office. The CIGS can then devote his whole time to thinking over the war and its problems – will advise the Cabinet, and will be in a position to keep in closer touch with the French General Staff.

On the other hand the War Office will become purely an Office of Administration with the AG, QMG, and MGO responsible for the provision of men, supplies, and ordnance on the lines indicated by the General Staff.

Lord Esher asked what should be done with Lord Kitchener. I replied 'appoint him Viceroy of India'. Trouble is brewing there and in Burma. Some blood letting will become necessary for the health of the body politic! The Germans are doing their best to land arms in Burma and also to send them by land from China. Disaffection is also being encouraged. No great harm can happen if the authorities in India and Burma are alert and take precautions in time. If Lord Kitchener won't go to India then let him be the 'business manager' at the head of the War Office, with a seat and vote on the War Committee. In my opinion, it is important to remove Lord Kitchener from the Mediterranean and Egypt because wherever he is, by his masterful action he will give that sphere of the operations an undue prominence in the strategical picture.

Wednesday 24 November. Letter to Asquith[1]

Lieutenant Colonel J. C. Wedgwood MP had compiled a report on the attack of 46th (North Midland) Division at the Battle of Loos. Wedgwood's constituency covered some of the area from which this Territorial formation was recruited. He sent it to Asquith, who forwarded it to Haig. Haig replied:

I return the paper on the 46th Division which you were good enough to send me for my 'private information only'.

I have already caused enquiries to be made into the failure of the 46th Division on the 13 October. I was induced to do this because I heard from two *independent* sources that the men of the 46th Division had not advanced to the attack as ordered.

One of my informants was an officer in charge of the Gas detail who stated that for nearly an hour after the release of the gas had ceased there was no *hostile* fire in the ground about Fosse 8 and the 'Dump': Yet the Territorials in question only advanced to our old trench line and held! and that the attack on the 'Dump' was made by officers and NCOs but few rank and file followed them.

The other source was Lord Cavan, who happened to mention to me that the detachment of Guards which had been sent into the trenches to help the 46th Division with 'smoke bombs', gas, etc. reported that the companies of the 46th Division who had been ordered to attack towards the line of the Dump–Quarries did not go forward 40 yards.

1 IWM: J. C. Wedgwood Papers, PP/MCR/104. This collection also contains Wedgwood's report, some (probably post-war) comments by Wedgwood on the affair, and Asquith's covering letter to Wedgwood in passing on Haig's reply. As Wedgwood was required to return Haig's original to Asquith, he copied it; it is from this copy that the above excerpt is taken.

The conclusion I arrived at as to the result of my enquiries was that:

(1) The preparations for the attack with gas bombardment was highly satisfactory, but that
(2) The troops did not take advantage of the favourable situation created for the attack.
(3) This was due to want of *discipline* in the 46th Division and general ignorance of war conditions![1]

I do not think much of Major General Stuart-Wortley[2] as a Divisional Commander and have already spoken to the GOC XI Corps (Haking) on the subject. You will see that I arrived at my conclusions by a different line of reasoning to your correspondent!

Friday 3 December

Haig had a meeting with Kitchener at the War Office in London.

As regards myself nothing had been definitely settled but today he had written to the Prime Minister recommending that I should be appointed to succeed Sir J. French. If the PM did not settle the matter today, he would again press for a settlement tomorrow, but in any case he had taken the matter in hand and I must not trouble my head over it. As soon as I was in the saddle he would see me again. Meantime he said that I must not be afraid to criticise any of his actions which I found unsatisfactory: he had only one thought, viz. to do his best to end the war.

I was also to keep friendly with the French. General Joffre should be looked upon as the C-in-C, in France where he knew [the country and] general situation well. It was different elsewhere, e.g., the Balkans and Egypt, etc. But in France we must do all we can to meet the [French C-in-C's] wishes whatever may be our personal feelings about the French Army and its Commanders. I would have a free hand as to my Staff. He said he was taking Sir William Robertson as his Chief of Staff. Would I like Murray? I said no, but I wished to bring Butler along with me as he knew the character of the war in which we were engaged better than anyone at GHQ or at home.

1 Haig's comments, made before all the facts were available, were unfair to 46th Division, which attacked bravely but faced an impossible task. See British Official History, *1915*, II, pp. 383–8.
2 Major General Hon. Edward James ('Eddie') Montagu-Stuart-Wortley (1857–1934), GOC 46th Division, 1914–16. He was sacked after the 46th Division's attack at Gommecourt on 1 July 1916.

Thursday 9 December. Letter to Leopold de Rothschild[1]

These are terrible times that we have been passing through, and our difficulties and anxieties here have been greatly added to by having at the head of the Army in France a general who is not only very ignorant of the principles of the higher leading of a large Army but is also lacking in the necessary temperament! He is so hot tempered and excitable – like a bottle of soda water in suddenness of explosion – that he is quite incapable of thinking over a serious situation and coming to a reasoned decision.

Friday 10 December

About 7 pm I received a letter from the Prime Minister (Asquith) marked 'Secret' and enclosed in *three* envelopes! It was dated 10 Downing Street, 8 December 1915 and ran as follows: 'Sir J. French has placed in my hands his resignation of the Office of Commander in Chief of the Forces in France. Subject to the King's approval, I have the pleasure of proposing to you that you should be his successor. I am satisfied that this is the best choice that could be made in the interests of the Army and the Country.'

Sunday 12 December

Haig conferred with Robertson.

The difficulty of finding a place for General Henry Wilson was discussed. I said he must command a division before being given a corps, and Robertson thought he would do less harm in France than in England! I raised no objection to giving Archie Murray (now CIGS) a corps, because he is quite fit to command a corps on a defensive front, and is an educated soldier, though [rather] lacking in decision and judgement. He thought General Butler too junior to be my CGS but I pointed out that no one had had such experience in practical Staff work in the field as Butler, or had done so well.

As regards my successor as GOC First Army, I recommended Sir Henry Rawlinson. Though not a sincere man, he has brains and experience. Robertson agreed that he was the best choice.

Tuesday 14 December

At 9 am the Military Secretary (Brigadier General H. Lowther) came to see me at my request. He knew that Sir J. French had resigned his Command

1 NLS: Haig Papers, Acc. 3155, No. 214a.

and I told him privately that I had accepted the appointment as his successor. I offered him to continue on with me as Military Secretary which he gladly accepted.

I stated that I had only one idea, namely to do my utmost to win the war: that in my eyes only those who had proved their fitness for advancement should be promoted. I had no 'friends' when it came to military promotion, and I would not tolerate a 'job' being done. Lowther fully understood and agreed. He told me that Sir John wished to give an infantry brigade to Winston Churchill![1] I said that was impossible until Winston had shewn that he could bear responsibility [in action] as CO of a battalion. I also added that I had no wish to change anything for change's sake, and that if Sir John had already selected some *good* officers for appointments which were vacant, by all means let them be appointed forthwith and not delay on my account.

Haig took command of the BEF on 19 December 1915 at noon.

1 Churchill, having been marginalised in the Government, had resigned and joined the Army. He commanded 6th Battalion Royal Scots Fusiliers from January to May 1916.

1916

THE YEAR OF THE SOMME

Douglas Haig spent the early months of 1916 adjusting to his new post of Commander-in-Chief of the BEF. This period coincided with the expansion of the British Army on the Western Front as numbers of fresh divisions of volunteers arrived in France. This necessitated the creation of new armies and corps, although Haig did not always get his first choice of commander for these formations. Haig's other major concern in this period was the preparations for the Battle of the Somme. One of Sir John French's last acts as C-in-C had been to participate in the Chantilly Conference of 6–8 December 1915, when the Allies agreed to launch 'co-ordinated offensives' across the battle fronts. The precise nature of the Anglo-French contribution was thrashed out in conference in the early months of 1916, a process complicated by the German attack at Verdun in February. As a result of Verdun the British rather than the French Army took the lead in the projected combined offensive, and the French pressed Haig to bring forward the date of the attack. Once the decision was taken to attack on the Somme, Haig played an active role in formulating the plan of attack. His ideas did not always coincide with those of his principal subordinate, General Sir Henry Rawlinson, commander of Fourth Army.

The Battle of the Somme raged from 1 July until mid-November 1916. Haig's diary gives an excellent indication of the perspective of the higher commander. Often the information that Haig received from the front line was inaccurate, but nonetheless he had to make decisions based upon it. Although Haig had frequent meetings with subordinate commanders, only part of his time was spent focusing on the day-to-day fighting. Otherwise, he was concerned with operational forward planning, logistics, the Royal Flying Corps, the organisation of the Army, pro-motions and sackings of commanders, and dealing with British politicians and newspapermen. The keen interest that Haig took in technology, especially aircraft and tanks, is noteworthy. Coalition matters took up much of his time: both the high politics and the very real problems of fighting a combined battle as the junior partner.

During 1916, the British command chain underwent significant changes of personnel. Kitchener drowned when HMS Hampshire was sunk on 5 June, and David Lloyd George grew in influence and authority within the Government. Haig had an uneasy relationship with Lloyd George as Secretary of State for War, which worsened after the latter replaced Asquith as Prime Minister in December.

The year ended with Haig, newly appointed Field Marshal, adjusting to working with Robert Nivelle, Joffre's replacement as French Commander-in-Chief.

Saturday 1 January. Letter to *Kitchener[1]

*Haig gave details of his visit to *Joffre at Chantilly on 29 December 1915.*

The chief question under discussion was the defence against a German attack ... There are indications of the Enemy preparing to attack in the direction of Roye-Montdidier. The Tenth Army say they think in south of Arras also. Also against the Ypres salient ... In view of the possibility of an attack of the Enemy in force, the formation of a fair sized Reserve, or Fourth Army, becomes a necessity. As soon as *Monro arrives I shall recommend that *Rawlinson be given command of it, and hope that you will concur.

Saturday 8 January

I left in motor at 9.30 am for Hinges where I held Conference with the 3 Army Commanders ... I stated that I intended to hold these meetings every week at the HQ of Armies in turn. The object of these meetings is to develop mutual understanding and closer touch not only between Army Commanders and myself but also between our Staffs ...

Offensive Operations. I outlined the general principles and directed each Army to work out schemes for (a) preliminary operations to wear out the Enemy and exhaust his reserves and (b) for a decisive attack made with the object of piercing the Enemy's lines of defence.

I also spoke on [the importance of good] Staff work and the need for adhering to the principles of FSR Part II.[2] Each branch of the Staff must confine itself to its own duties! This will prevent friction.

Tuesday 18 January

Spent much of the day discussing with Kiggell and *Butler our future plans, and reading and writing notes on the subject.

The principles which we must apply are:

(1) Employ sufficient force to wear down the Enemy and cause him to use up his reserves.

1 TNA PRO 30/57/53: Kitchener Papers, WD/15, 1916.
2 *Field Service Regulations*; Haig had played a major role in writing them.

(2) Then, and not till then, throw in a mass of troops (at some point where the Enemy has shown himself to be weak) to break through and win victory.

For (1) to be really effective, all the Allies must start at once. But Russia may not be ready till later, say July. In that case Germany may turn on and defeat her – she (Russia) may then make peace! We must be ready for this possible move of Germany, and arrange our plans so as to be ready to attack at once, the moment we hear of a German offensive in the Eastern theatre.

As regards (1), it will probably fall into two phases. First, the present winter activity will develop into a series of larger attacks, and secondly a more general engagement will be organised with a view to drawing in the Enemy's reserves.

Friday 28 January

Discussed with *Kiggell nature of the reply to General Joffre's letter received 2 days ago in which he proposes that British should make two preliminary attacks in April and May to wear out Enemy's reserves *before* the general offensive. I decide that we must let Joffre know at once my views, namely that such attacks . . . will be of the nature of *attacks in detail,* will wear us out almost more than the Enemy, will appear to the Enemy, to our troops and to neutrals . . . as 'failures', thereby affecting our 'credit' in the world which is of vital importance as money in England is becoming scarcer.

Saturday 12 February

I had 1½ hours talk with Lord K. . . . He also spoke very freely about his difficulties in the Cabinet. How 'rightly or wrongly, the people believe in me (K). Probably quite wrongly' he said. But 'in any case it is not me that the politicians are afraid of, but what the people would say to them if I (K) were to go'.

He told me how the politicians are constantly intriguing against one another, and have come to him to join them against *Asquith. He has always declined because he feels that Asquith is the best man for Prime Minister and he has found that Asquith can be trusted. Then the plot has always failed.

Recently a dangerous combine was made by Runciman[1] and the Chancellor

---

1 Walter Runciman (later Viscount Runciman of Doxford) (1870–1949), President of the Board of Trade, 1914–16; Runciman and Reginald McKenna, Chancellor of the Exchequer, were opposed to Britain's prosecuting 'total war', believing that this would dissipate British economic strength without equivalent gain.

of the Exchequer.[1] They were against Compulsory Service, and having failed in their efforts against the bill, they thought they could block its effect by saying the Country could not afford to pay for the Army and it must be reduced. K. was prepared to resign on that. The Premier defeated the attempt by means of a committee![2]

15 February. Letter to *King George V[3]

I had a conference with General Joffre yesterday ... The French raised two very important questions for us: One was that they wished the British to commence attacking in end of April with the object of, they said, 'wearing out' the German reserves (a 'bataille d'usure' as they are pleased to call it) – while they intend to do nothing until the enemy's reserves had disappeared! The other point was that they wanted me to take over the whole of their Tenth Army front. I am glad to say that on both points they gave way and agreed to my arguments. I have however accepted the principle that the British Army would take over the Tenth Army front when it was able to do so – and I added that would probably be 'next winter'!

Friday 18 February

*Haig visited *Plumer, commander of Second Army, and criticised the state of its defences.*

He then said that he was quite ready to go if I thought it desirable. He was only anxious to do what was best.

Altogether he behaved in such a straightforward way, and is such a thorough gentleman, that I said I would think over the matter and let him know tomorrow. I added that it is a matter of no small importance to get rid of an Army Commander. At the same time this is no time for having any *doubts* about anyone's capacity to discharge his duty ...

After thinking over the matter I wrote to Sir H. Plumer that I wished him to continue in his Command, and to do his utmost to strengthen his defences with as little delay as possible. If however, after a reasonable time I found but little improvement in the general arrangements and conditions of the Second

1 Reginald McKenna (1863–1943), Home Secretary, 1911–15; Chancellor of the Exchequer, 1915–16; responsible for putting Britain's war finances on a secure footing.
2 In January 1916 the first of several conscription acts was introduced, against the wishes of a number of Liberals.
3 RA: PS/GV/Q 832/118.

Army, I should feel it my duty in view of the great task which lies before this Army, to ask him to resign his Command . . .

Privately I feel that Plumer is too kind to some of his subordinate Commanders who are, I fear, not fit for their appointments, e.g. General Pilcher 17th Division,[1] Fanshawe V Corps,[2] Haldane 3rd Division.[3]

In the morning I received a reply from Plumer, thanking me for my letter, and saying he would do as I wished and also act on my advice to press his Corps Commanders to necessary action.

On 21 February the German Army attacked the French at Verdun. The battle turned into an attritional struggle, sucking in an ever-larger number of French troops, and cast a shadow over the preparations for the forthcoming Franco-British offensive.

Friday 25 February

Haig had a meeting with Admiral Bacon and Lieutenant General Hunter-Weston at Dover, and discussed a plan for an amphibious assault on Ostend.

We agreed that it was not a feasible operation until the Enemy's reserves had been drawn off. I had always held that view. I now directed that the whole scheme should be worked out in the most complete detail, but that the moment for execution of the scheme must depend on the military situation. The Admiral expressed himself as very pleased that I had come to this decision, and said that he would set to work and make his preparations in co-operation with Hunter-Weston . . .[4]

Haig then met Kitchener in London.

I told him that I thought we ought to be prepared for one of three situations arising as a result of the fighting at Verdun:

1. *A kind of stalemate.* Both sides having lost very heavily, and the French

1 Major General Thomas David Pilcher (1858–1928), GOC 17th Division, 1915–16 (wounded July 1915).
2 Lieutenant General (later Sir) Edward Arthur Fanshawe (1859–1952), CRA 1st Division, 1914–15; GOC 11th Division, 1915–16; GOC V Corps (1916–18).
3 Major General (later General Sir) (James) Aylmer Lowthrop Haldane (1862–1950), GOC 10 Brigade, 1912–14; GOC 3rd Division, 1914–16; GOC VI Corps, 1916–19.
4 Lieutenant General (later Sir) Aylmer Gould Hunter-Weston ('Hunter-Bunter') (1864–1940), GOC 11 Brigade, 1914–15; GOC 29th Division (Gallipoli), 1915; GOC VIII Corps, 1915–19. Hunter-Weston had commanded an amphibious assault at Gallipoli in 1915.

(owing to lack of reserves of men and ammunition) unable and unwilling to carry out a vigorous offensive again.

In my opinion, our action should then be to ask the French to take over some of the front from us so as to set free as many troops of ours as possible for a large offensive. In this case, our attack should be on the front from Ypres to Armentières in the direction of the Dutch frontier north of the Lys.

If, however, the French have sufficient troops left for the general attack, then we should make our attack alongside of theirs, say, astride the Somme [as already proposed by Joffre].

2. *In the case of success*: We must attack at once on the front of the Third Army. The Enemy will probably have had to reduce the numbers of his troops holding the front if he has suffered a check at Verdun.

3. *In the case of disaster*: We must counter-attack at once close to the French. I do not think an attack on the front of our Third Army in such case would do any good. This attack cannot be ready to start at once because there must be delay in preparing for it, which people would attribute to a determination to do nothing! Also the German line would not have been weakened, as would most likely be the case in the event of the Germans receiving a check.

Lord Kitchener agreed and said an offensive towards Cambrai had been proposed by General Maurice, War Office, but he felt that that would not produce an effect soon enough. To this objection, I added that having taken over the largest part of the Tenth Army front, I would not have sufficient troops to produce a decisive result.

Wednesday 15 March

Lieutenant General H. *Gough came to stay. I am appointing him to command 'the Reserve Corps'. My command will now consist of *four* Armies and the Reserve Corps. This latter will vary in strength to suit the situation. At one time it may consist of several infantry divisions, at another (e.g. in cases of an advance) of a large force of cavalry with infantry divisions, machine guns etc. in support.

Friday 24 March

I drafted instructions for training of cavalry divisions (which are now under Army Commanders except one in my hands). The keynote is co-operation with the other arms. When a break in [the Enemy's] line is made, cavalry and mobile troops must be at hand to advance at once to make a bridgehead (until relieved by infantry) beyond the gap with the object of checking hostile reserves which Enemy might rush up, and so give time for our own divisions to deploy.

At the same time our mounted troops must co-operate with our main attacking force in widening the gap both by

(a) Operating offensively in rear, of that part of the Enemy's defences which may still be holding out as well as
(b) By extending the flank of the 'bridgehead' as a protection to our attacking Forces' outer flank.

Wednesday 29 March

Lord Kitchener arrived . . . As regards the Conference in Paris, there were, [he said,] a very large number of people present at it. M. Briand' presided and succeeded in giving to the Conference an air of importance which was desirable for neutral countries and the world generally to show that the Allies were united. All the same, the British had an unfortunate passage of arms with the French over the question of withdrawing troops from Salonika . . . When the French refused, instead of the British withdrawing, *Robertson pressed his argument in bulldog way, with the result that the French spoke freely and said 'They had lost severely in men, and it was now time for the British to play their part' or some such words. Altogether Lord K. thought it was an unfortunate occurrence, except that it shows French intentions. He thinks the French are aiming at a development of their dominions in the Eastern Mediterranean, and will not now fight actively to beat the Germans in France. Consequently it is possible that the war will not end this year. Lord K. wished me for that reason to beware of the French, and to husband the strength of the Army in France.

I said that I had never had any intention of attacking with all available troops except in an emergency to save the French, and Paris perhaps from capture. Meantime, I am strengthening the long line which I have recently taken over, and training the troops. I have not got an Army in France really, but a collection of divisions untrained for the field. [The actual fighting Army will be evolved from them.]

---

1 Aristide Briand (1862–1932), France's longest-serving wartime Prime Minister, October 1915–March 1917.

Wednesday 5 April

I studied Sir H. Rawlinson's proposals for attack. His intention is merely to take the Enemy's first and second system of trenches and 'kill Germans'. He looks upon the gaining of 3 or 4 kilometres more or less of ground immaterial. I think we can do better than this by aiming at getting as large a combined force of French and British across the Somme and fighting the Enemy in the open![1]

Friday 14 April

I saw Lord Kitchener at the War Office . . . Sir William Robertson was present at the first part of my interview. I asked them definitely, 'Did His Majesty's Government approve of my combining with the French in a general offensive during the summer'? They both agreed that all the Cabinet had come to the conclusion that the war could only be ended by fighting, and several were most anxious for a definite victory over German arms, viz., the Secretary for Foreign Affairs (Grey)[2] and the Chancellor of the Exchequer (McKenna). I explained to Lord K my general plan . . .

I . . . saw Colonel Swinton with Generals Butler and Whigham (the Deputy CIGS) regarding the 'Tanks'. I was told that 150 would be provided by the 31 July. I said that was too late. 50 were urgently required for 1 June. Swinton is to see what can be done, and will also practise and train 'Tanks' and crews over obstacles and wire similar to the ground over which the attack will be made. I gave him a trench map as a guide and impressed on him the necessity for thinking over the system of leadership and control of a group of 'Tanks' with a view to manoeuvring . . .

Saturday 15 April

Kitchener summoned Haig to a meeting at Downing Street.

This Sub-Committee of the Cabinet had drawn up a report stating that the number of men available by the ordinary recruiting methods was more than the Army Council had asked for. To this the CIGS replied that the demand which he had put forward was for every available man! For the first hour of the meeting, the 'Civilians' and the 'Military' wrangled over certain figures. This really did not interest me, and I felt that the real issue of the war in the

1 This passage neatly summarises the differences between Rawlinson's 'bite and hold' philosophy and Haig's desire for mobile warfare.
2 Sir Edward Grey (later Viscount Grey of Fallodon) (1862–1933), Britain's longest-serving Foreign Secretary, 1905–16, and architect of pre-war foreign policy.

'Civilians'' minds was votes, and not the destruction of the German military party.

Finally, about 1.30, the Prime Minister who was dressed for golf and evidently anxious to get away for his weekend, gave to the Army Council a question to answer, namely, how they proposed to find the drafts which were necessary for the maintenance of the Army in France during the summer. Then Mr Chamberlain[1] made an appeal to the Army Council. He said that Britain was bearing the burden of the expense of the whole of the Allies. Recently, the French had told us that they were unable to meet their share of the subsidy which the French and Great Britain had jointly undertaken to pay to Russia (some 300 million).[2] In addition to this, France last week asked us for 60 million and would probably ask for more. In order to keep the war going, we must subsidise the Allies, and in order to provide the money for this, our trade must not be impaired. With this object in view, it was of vital importance not to interfere with the labour market.

To this Lord K. remarked that the demands made by the WO had never varied and that they should have been and could have been provided for, with proper foresight.

We adjourned at 1.40. I felt . . . sad at the sight of the inner Cabinet of this great Empire being so wanting in decision and public spirit. Real war and the basic principles of success seemed to hardly enter into the calculations of these 'politicians' . . .

Thursday 4 May

*Haig met *Clemenceau, former French Prime Minister and now chairman of the Senate Military Committee.*

His object in coming to see me was to get me to exercise a restraining hand on General Joffre, and prevent any offensive on a large scale from being made until all is ready, and we are at our maximum strength. We cannot expect that Russia will be able to do much towards the defeat of Germany, so we must rely on ourselves (British and French). If we attack and fail, then there will be a number of people in France who will say that the time has arrived to make terms, the French Government would certainly go out and M. Caillaux[3] would be the only alternative to M. Briand. He stated that there is

1 (Joseph) Austen Chamberlain (1863–1937), member of a great political dynasty (son of Joseph and half-brother of Neville); Secretary of State for India, 1915–17; famously too gentlemanly to assert his claims to become Prime Minister.
2 Pounds sterling.
3 Joseph Marie Auguste Caillaux (1863–1944); French Prime Minister, 1911; believed to be pro-German and pacifist; imprisoned by Clemenceau in 1918.

nothing to be lost by delaying; the French people are in good heart, but if there was a failure, after a big effort, it is difficult to say what the result on their feelings might be. Quick changes are apt to take place in their modes of thought! It is M. Briand and the present Government who are urging Joffre to act soon.

I assured him that I had no intention of taking part prematurely in a great battle, but, of course, I was making ready to attack to support the French in case anything in the nature of a catastrophe were to happen at Verdun. But such a situation seems most unlikely to arise now. My divisions, I told him, want much careful training before we could attack with hope of success. He asked me was I under Joffre's orders? I said Certainly NOT – at the same time it must be realised that there can be only one man responsible for the *plans*. These Joffre and his Staff worked out for France, and I did my best to co-operate with them; but *I* was responsible for the method of employment of the British Forces, so that if anything unfortunate happened, I am responsible and must bear the blame, not General Joffre! Clemenceau assured me that he had only one objective, to serve his Country and help the Allies to win.

Tuesday 9 May. Letter to King George V[1]

I inspected the Australian and New Zealand Divisions.[2] They are undoubtedly a fine body of men, but their officers and leaders as a whole have a good deal to learn ... A portion of their front was shelled last Thursday night and a small party of Germans entered their trenches. I understand that the severity and accuracy of enemy's artillery fire was a revelation to them! ...

Another day I visited the Canadians. Their 2nd Division (General Turner)[3] has had a hard time at St Eloi. But all were in the best of spirits, and determined to give the enemy more than they had received in hard knocks from him. Although Turner is not the best possible Commander of a Division, I think it would be an error to change him at this moment.[4] ...

The South African Brigade is as fine a unit as there is in the Army, and is well commanded by General Lukin.[5] I know him well, as he served under me

1 RA: PS/GV/Q 832/121.
2 Australian and New Zealand formations had arrived in France from the Middle East in late March 1916. Some had fought at Gallipoli in 1915.
3 Major General (later Lieutenant General Sir) Richard Ernest William Turner (1871–1961), GOC 3 Canadian Brigade, 1914–15; GOC 2nd Canadian Division, 1915–16.
4 German troops captured the St Eloi mine craters from 2nd Canadian Division in an action of 6–19 May 1916. Haig turned down Plumer's subsequent request to sack Turner: Diary, 21 April 1916.
5 Brigadier General (later Major General Sir) Henry Timson ('Tim') Lukin (1860–1925), GOC South African Brigade, 1915–16; GOC 9th Division, 1915–18.

in South Africa when he was CO of the Cape Mounted Rifles.

Wednesday 10 May

I saw General Hunter-Weston[1] ... I impressed on him that there must be no halting attacks at each trench in succession for rear lines to pass through! The objective must be as far as our guns can prepare the Enemy's position for attack – and when the attack starts it must be pushed through to the final objective with as little delay as possible. His experiences at Gallipoli were under very different conditions: then he landed from ships, a slow proceeding: now his troops can be forward in succession of lines in great depth, and all can start at the same moment!

Sunday 21 May

We had quite a large party of clerics at lunch ... In reply to a question, I told the Archbishop[2] that I had only two wishes to express, and I had already explained them to Bishop Gwynne and these are:
  First that the Chaplains should preach to [the troops] about the objects of Great Britain in carrying on this war. We have no selfish motive, but are fighting for the good of humanity.
  Second: The Chaplains of the Church of England must cease quarrelling amongst themselves. In the field we cannot tolerate any narrow sectarian ideas. We must all be united. The Archbishop thought his people were very united now, but possibly six months ago some were troublesome!

Thursday 25 May

Robertson visited GHQ.

After dinner, we discussed whether the British Army should comply with the French Generalissimo's request to attack in the month of July, or wait till August 15th when we would be much stronger.
  I had gone fully into the various aspects of the question and what might be the results if we did not support the French. I came to the conclusion that we *must* march to the support of the French. Robertson entirely agreed, and took my notes away to study.

1 Commanding VIII Corps.
2 Randall Thomas Davidson (1848–1930), Archbishop of Canterbury, 1903–28.

Friday 26 May

General Joffre explained the general situation. The French had supported for three months alone the whole weight of the German attacks at Verdun ... If this went on, the French Army would be ruined! He therefore was of opinion that 1 July was the latest date for the combined offensive of the British and French.

I said that before fixing the date I would like to indicate the state of preparedness of the British Army on certain dates and compare its condition. I took 1 and 15 July, and 1 and 15 August. The moment I mentioned 15 August, Joffre at once got very excited and shouted that 'The French Army would cease to exist, if we did nothing till then'! The rest of us looked on at this outburst of excitement, and then I pointed out that, in spite of the 15th August being the most favourable date for the British Army to take action, yet, in view of what he had said regarding the unfortunate condition of the French Army, I was prepared to commence operations on the 1st July or thereabouts. This calmed the old man, but I saw that he had come to the meeting prepared to combat a refusal on my part, and was prepared to be very nasty. Castelnau on the other hand was most anxious to put Joffre straight.

Finally, I asked them, once the date was fixed, not to postpone it at the last moment as had happened 3 times last year with *Foch!! We agreed on having 3 weeks' notice of the exact date of the attack ... They are, indeed, difficult Allies to deal with!

Saturday 27 May

Haig met his Army commanders.

I asked the First, Second and Third Armies to put forward plans of operations for misleading the Enemy as to the real point of attack. These operations should be ready to take place at the end of June ...

General Plumer then explained to me the state of the preparations which were made for a big attack on the Second Army front in accordance with my orders ... I gave him till beginning of August, and told him to expect possibly 200 new heavy guns after 1 July.

Lastly, I spoke to General *Monro regarding the situation on the IV Corps front west of the Vimy ridge ... The IV Corps was the most efficient one in the Army when Sir H. *Wilson took over the Command. Since then it had much decreased in military value. He (Monro) must go into the matter at once, and get things right without delay. [Monro criticised Sir H. Wilson very severely. There is no doubt that he has failed as a Commander in the field.][1]

Monday 5 June. Letter to Lord Bertie of Thame[2]

It is a great help to me in my dealings with the French over military plans to know how you gauge the political situation in Paris. My policy is briefly to

1. Train my divisions, and to collect as much ammunition and as many guns as possible.
2. To make arrangements to support the French ... attacking in order to draw off pressure from Verdun, when the French consider the military situation demands it.
3. But while attacking to help our Allies, not to think that we can for a certainty destroy the power of Germany this year. So in our attacks we must also aim at improving our positions with a view to making sure of the result of campaign next year.[3]

Friday 9 June

At a meeting at Downing Street attended by Briand and Joffre, the British continued to resist French pressure for the expansion of the commitment in Salonika.

I remained with the PM and Grey and Hankey who were drafting the report and gave them some notes on the nature of the offensive which the British Army in France is about to undertake to relieve the pressure on Verdun. It is to be a battle of 'durée prolongée' and Joffre had urged me to be ready to carry out frequent reliefs of the divisions engaged. All our resources in men and ammunition should be sent to the decisive points, viz., France and not wasted against Bulgars in the Balkans.[4]

1 The Germans had captured some trenches near Vimy, and IV Corps failed to retake them. As Haig commented in his diary for 28 May, Wilson lacked any experience of field command.
2 NLS: Haig Papers, Acc. 3155, No. 214c. Viscount Bertie of Thame (1844–1919) was the British Ambassador in Paris, 1905–18.
3 Haig expressed similar views to Rawlinson, adding to point 3: 'I mean don't forget the difficulties of the Ypres Salient while we attack on Fourth Army front: nor go down into the mud beyond the Pozières ridge unless we have enough fresh troops to take us on to a line on the ridge beyond the le Sars Valley!' Diary, 29 May 1916.
4 Haig was correct in seeing Salonika as militarily futile. However, the campaign was sustained largely for reasons of French domestic politics, and Britain had to acquiesce for reasons of Coalition harmony; see David Dutton, *The Politics of Diplomacy: Britain and France in the Balkans in the First World War* (London: I. B. Tauris, 1998), pp. 186, 188.

Monday 12 June

Haig had a meeting with Admiral Bacon.

The Admiral[1] thought the situation at Ostend had changed since our last meeting and that owing to 'land mines', a surprise from the sea was unlikely to succeed. I therefore said that the objective of our combined operations must be to envelop Ostend on the land side, while a military force on board ships worked along the coast and disembarked either in the harbour of Ostend or on the beach opposite the town. The object being to open up Ostend and organise it as a base with as little delay as possible. The troops prior to embarkation to be camped near Calais and Dunkirk ... These could be carried on 'monitors'.

Now that the plan depending on surprise had been given up, the operation could be carried out on any day independent of 'tides' or 'moon'. Ten days' notice would be necessary in the Admiral's opinion to concentrate the shipping for the expedition.

Thursday 15 June

Haig held a conference with the Army commanders.

After the general situation had been dealt with, I explained the scope of the offensive by the Fourth and two divisions of the Third Armies, and enunciated certain principles.

The length of each bound forward by the infantry depends on the area which has been prepared by the artillery. The *infantry* must for their part, capture and hold all the ground which the artillery has prepared with as little delay as possible.

The effect of the artillery depends on (a) 'Accuracy of fire' and (b) 'concentration'. Commanders must insist on these points.

The advance of *isolated detachments* [except for reconnoitring purposes] should be avoided. They lead to loss of the boldest and best without result: Enemy can concentrate on these detachments. Advance should be uniform. Discipline and the power of subordinate Commanders should be exercised in order to prevent troops getting out of hand.

As regards the objective of the Fourth Army attack, it was,

Firstly, to gain the line of the Pozières heights, organise good observation

1 Admiral Reginald Hugh Spencer Bacon (1863–1952), commander of the Dover Patrol, 1915–17. Bacon's co-operation would be essential to any amphibious operations on the Belgian coast; Haig was an admirer.

posts, and consolidate a strong position. Then, *secondly*, (a) If Enemy's defence broke down, occupy Enemy's third line (on line Flers–Miraumont), push detachment of cavalry to hold Bapaume and work northwards with bulk of cavalry and other arms so as to widen the breach in Enemy's line, and capture the Enemy's forces in the re-entrant south of Arras. The hill at Monchy le Preux (5 miles southeast of Arras) with intermediate points between it and Bapaume, seems a suitable line for the cavalry to hold as a flank guard for covering the operations of the other arms.

(b) *If Enemy's defence is strong* and fighting continues for many days, as soon as Pozières heights are gained, the position should be consolidated, and improved, while arrangements will be made to start an attack on the Second Army front.

Saturday 17 June

Joffre visited Haig.

Then we discussed the date for starting our offensive. He wished it to be 1 July. I pointed out that we had arranged to be ready on the 25th[1] to please him. The 29th ought to be the latest date; in my opinion it was unwise to run the risk of the Enemy discovering our area of concentration and then attacking where our lines were thin and ill provided with artillery. Finally we agreed that the attack should be fixed for 29th but Rawlinson and Foch will be given power if the day is bad to postpone the attack from day to day till the weather is fine.

Wednesday 21 June

I discussed the question of the Command of Fifth Reserve Army (General Gough) during the forthcoming operations, and whether he should be under GHQ or Fourth Army. I decided that to begin with he must be under the latter, for the following reasons. The Fourth Army has seven units to control. This is possible during the prepared operation of attacking the enemy's trenches, but, once a break is effected, a Commander and Staff is necessary to take charge on the spot. Thus once the Pozières ridge is taken, an effort should be made to push the cavalry through, covered with advanced guards and supported by as many divisions as Rawlinson can collect. The objective will be Bapaume. As soon as that place is secured the front of the Fourth Army will be pushed forward to the Bapaume–Péronne road.

The Fifth Reserve Army Staff (Gough) will be required to direct the

---

1 i.e. 25 June.

advance on Bapaume. As soon as that place is secured, one of the Corps Commanders of Fourth Army will hold the position, while Gough with all available cavalry and such Infantry Divisions as Rawlinson can spare will move northwards to clear the salient south of Arras by attacking the troops holding the front in flank and rear.

Rawlinson can employ two divisions of cavalry which are now in GHQ Reserve, and which with his own Cavalry Division makes a total of 3 Cavalry Divisions under him. He cannot however rely on being reinforced by the Infantry Corps of three divisions (under Jacob)[1] which I have in GHQ Reserve. These may be wanted to reinforce the Third Army which is organising an attack on the south of Arras and which will be pushed in as soon as the Fourth Army attack has produced its effect, that is, has possibly caused Enemy to thin his troops in the part just south of Arras. Also the whole Reserve Corps (Jacob) might have to be sent forward to act under Gough at a later stage. In this case it might be necessary to control Gough direct from GHQ.

Tuesday 27 June

Gough explained his plans.

I thought he was too inclined to aim at fighting a battle at Bapaume, forgetting that it was at the same time possible for the Enemy to attack him from the north and cut him off from the breach in the line! I therefore insisted on the offensive move northwards as soon as Bapaume has been occupied.

I then visited Rawlinson at Querrieu. He has ordered his troops to halt for an hour and consolidate on the Enemy's last line! Covered by an artillery barrage! I said this must depend on whether Enemy had reserves available and on the spot for counter-attack. I directed him to prepare for a rapid advance: and, as soon as the last line had been gained, to push on advanced guards of all arms as 'a system of security' to cover his front.

I told him to impress on his Corps Commanders the use of their Corps Cavalry and mounted troops, and if necessary supplement them with regular cavalry units. In my opinion it is better to prepare to advance beyond the Enemy's last line of trenches, because we are then in a position to take

1 Lieutenant General (later Field Marshal Sir) Claud William Jacob, GSO1 Meerut Division, 1914–15; GOC Dehra Dun Brigade, 1915; GOC Meerut Division, 1915; GOC 21st Division, 1915–16 (wounded); GOC II Corps, 1916–19. Jacob was an Indian Army officer. Haig supported Sir Charles Anderson's request, in 1915, that Jacob should be retained for service on the Western Front.

advantage of any breakdown in the Enemy's defence. Whereas if there is a stubborn resistance put up, the matter settles itself! On the other hand if no preparations for an advance are made till next morning, we might lose a golden opportunity.

He told me that he had not yet put Gough in command of any corps because he felt that it was impossible to say now which units would be able to advance after the attack: but he was ready to send him on 'with the cavalry' and support him with certain divisions which would be in reserve ...

After dinner I sent Kiggell to Querrieu to meet Rawlinson and Gough and fix up exactly how the latter was to get control over his Command once the battle had started. I favoured giving Gough the two left corps *at once*, but would like to hear what Rawlinson and Gough had worked out as the result of my talk. Kiggell returned after midnight, and stated Gough would have his HQ at Albert as soon as the Pozières heights were taken; he is then to be given certain divisions from Rawlinson's reserves. With these he will move on Bapaume in co-operation with the cavalry (3 divisions) which is now under him. I agree to this arrangement.

Wednesday 28 June. Letter to King George V[1]

Mr Hughes, the Australian Premier,[2] wrote to me regarding forming the Australian Divisions into an 'Australian Army'. I told him, when he was staying with me, that to do so would upset the organisation of the Army in France because the units which he wishes to dub 'an Army' don't amount to half the number which we have in our Army organisations. Moreover, GHQ have now quite as many Armies as they, and I, can conveniently deal with unless 'Groups of Armies' were formed ... But if an opportunity arose of using the 2 Australian Corps independently under *Birdwood[3] for any operation I would try to do so, and then call the force the 'Australian Army'. I understand that the Australian Premier is as keen about the name as anything else ...

Everywhere I found the troops in great spirits, and full of confidence of their ability to smash the Enemy when the moment for action arrives. Several officers have said to me that they have never known troops in such enthusiastic spirits. We must, I think, in fairness, give a good deal of credit for this to the Parsons ...

1 RA: PS/GV/Q 832/123. Haig misdated the letter as 28 July.
2 William Morris ('Billy') Hughes (1862–1952), formidable and belligerent Prime Minister of Australia, 1915–22. Hughes' enthusiastic support for the Imperial war effort and his willingness to introduce conscription, defeated in two divisive referendums (October 1916 and November–December 1917), have made him one of the most controversial figures in Australian history.
3 The commander of I Anzac Corps.

The French are still anxious about the German attack on Verdun, and General Joffre is of opinion that the Enemy will not desist until he is attacked in force elsewhere. This, as I think Your Majesty knows, we are in a position to do.

Thursday 29 June

General Hunter Weston came to see me and stayed to lunch. He seemed quite satisfied and confident. I gave him a kind message for his Divisional Commanders. I told him that I fully realised all the difficulties and hard work which they had had in training their divisions and in preparing their trenches etc. for attack, also that I have full confidence in their abilities to reap success in the coming fighting etc.

After lunch I motored to HQ X Corps at Senlis and saw General Morland.[1] He is quietly confident of success. Then I went on to HQ III Corps at Montigny and saw General Pulteney. He also is quite satisfied with the artillery bombardment and wire cutting...

After dinner my CRA (Birch) came to report on his visit to VIII Corps today. The conclusion I come to is that the majority are amateurs, and some thought that they knew more than they did of this kind of warfare because they had been at Gallipoli. Adversity, shortage of ammunition and fighting under difficulties against a superior enemy, has taught us much![2]

Friday 30 June

I left by motor soon after 9 am for HQ XV Corps ... I saw General *Horne and his CGS Vaughan[3] (Indian Army) ... They both are very pleased with the situation and are in high hopes. Preparations were never so thorough, nor

---

1 Lieutenant General Sir Thomas Lethbridge Napier Morland (1865–1925), GOC 5th Division, 1914–15; GOC X Corps, 1915–18; GOC XIII Corps, 1918–19. Morland achieved a certain notoriety by climbing a tree in order to get a better view of the Somme fighting on 1 July 1916.
2 This entry is one of the few examples from 1916 of Haig making substantive alterations to his Ms diary, no doubt because of the calamitous failure of VIII Corps on 1 July 1916. In the Ts diary, at the end of the sentence in which he states that he has confidence in VIII Corps' higher leadership, Haig adds 'but I still was anxious regarding the leading of the small units (platoons and companies) because their raids had failed'. He also makes his criticism more specific: 'Hunter-Weston and the majority of his officers' are 'amateurs in hard fighting', and says that he has come to this opinion after listening to Birch's story 'and as the result of my own observation'.
3 Brigadier General (later Lieutenant General Sir) Louis Ridley Vaughan ('Father') (1875–1942), GSO2 2nd Division, 1914–15; GSO1 2nd Division, 1915–16; BGGS XV Corps, 1916–17; MGGS Third Army, 1917–19; an Indian Army officer (7th Gurkha Rifles), he rose from major to lieutenant general during the course of the war.

troops better trained. Wire very well cut, and ammunition adequate. (NB This Corps expended twice as much as was allowed!)[1] ...

The weather report is favourable for tomorrow. With God's help, I feel hopeful for tomorrow. The men are in splendid spirits: several have said that they have never before been so instructed and informed of the nature of the operation before them. The wire has never been so well cut, nor the artillery preparation so thorough. I have seen personally all the Corps Commanders and one and all are full of confidence.[2]

Friday 30 June. Letter to *Lady Haig

The attack is to go in tomorrow morning at 7.30 am ... I feel that everything possible for us to do to achieve success has been done. But whether or not we are successful lies in the Power above. But *I do feel* that in my plans I have been helped by a Power that is not my own. So I am easy in my mind and ready to do my best what ever happens tomorrow.

Saturday 1 July

The Battle of the Somme began. On the first day the British Army incurred 57,000 casualties, 19,000 of them being fatalities. Some gains were made in the southern sector and by the French; elsewhere, the British attacks mostly failed.

Glass rose slightly during night. A fine sunny morning with gentle breeze from the west and southwest. At first some mist in the hollows. This very favourable because it concealed the concentration of our troops. The bombardment was carried out as usual, and there was no increase of artillery fire but at 7.30 am (the hour fixed for the infantry to advance) the artillery increased their range and the infantry followed the barrage.

Reports up to 8 am most satisfactory. Our troops had everywhere crossed the Enemy's front trenches.

By 9 am I heard that our troops had in many places reached the 1.20 line (i.e. the line fixed to be reached 1 hour and 20 minutes after the start).

They were held up (29th Division) just south of Hawthorn Ridge but 31st

1 Horne's optimism was well founded, as XV Corps proved to be successful over the beginning days of the Battle of the Somme. The extra expenditure of ammunition may have been relevant to this success.
2 In the Ts diary, Haig added a last sentence: 'The only doubt I have is regarding the VIII Corps (Hunter-Weston) which has had no experience of fighting in France and has not carried out one successful raid.' See also footnote to diary, 28 June.

Division was moving into Serre village. This was afterwards proved to be incorrect.

The Gommecourt attack was also progressing well. 46th Division had northern corner of Gommecourt Wood. 56th Division by 8 am were in Enemy's third line trench. But eventually right brigade of 46th Division did not press on.[1]

At 9 am it was reported that our troops were held up north of Authuille Wood but on their left were entering Thiepval village. This did not prove to be the case.

St Sauveur station in Lille, which is said to be an important ammunition store, was bombed by us early today. Our machines returned safely, though attacked by 20 Fokkers. 2 of these were destroyed and 2 damaged as the result of the fight.

I wired Admiral Bacon last night suggesting that he should demonstrate on Ostend coast. By 10 am a young naval officer was at my HQ with the Admiral's proposals for my concurrence. I arranged for French also to co-operate in attacking the Tirpitz Battery from near Nieuport.

Hard fighting continued all day on front of Fourth Army. On a 16-mile front of attack varying fortune must be expected! It is difficult to summarise all that was reported.

After lunch I motored to Querrieu and saw Sir H. Rawlinson. We hold the Montauban–Mametz spur and villages of those names. The Enemy are still in Fricourt, but we are round his flank on the north and close to Contalmaison. Ovillers and Thiepval villages have held our troops up, but our men are in the Schwaben redoubt which crowns the ridge north of the last named village. The Enemy counter-attacked here but were driven back. He however got a position with a few men in the river valley.

North of the Ancre, the VIII Division[2] (Hunter-Weston) said they began well, but as the day progressed their troops were forced back into the German front line, except 2 battalions which occupied Serre village and were, it is said, cut off. I am inclined to believe from further reports that few of the VIII Corps left their trenches!

The attack on Gommecourt salient started well, especially the 56th Division under General Hull.[3] The 46th Division (Stuart-Wortley) attacked from the north side but was soon held up. This attack was of the very greatest assistance in helping the VIII Corps, because many of the Enemy's guns and troops were directed on it, and so left the VIII Corps considerably free. In spite of this the VIII Corps achieved very little.

1 In the Ts diary Haig amended this to 'did not progress further'.
2 A slip for VIII Corps.
3 Major General (later Sir) (Charles Patrick) Amyatt Hull (1865–1920), GOC 10 Brigade, 1914–

After seeing Sir H. Rawlinson I motored to Villers Bocage (on Amiens–Doullens road) and called at HQ II Corps in Reserve. I left orders for Divisions 38th and 23rd in GHQ Reserve to march in 2 hours (7 pm) and close up nearer to the front, as the Fourth Army was getting through its reserves.

Sir William Robertson, CIGS arrived from England.

At 7 pm as the result of my talk, Sir H. Rawlinson telephones that he is putting the VIII and X Corps under Gough at 7 am tomorrow. The VIII Corps seems to want looking after! [Gough's command will be the Fifth Army.]

Sunday 2 July

A day of downs and ups! . . .

The news about 8 am was not altogether good. We held Montauban in spite of a counter-attack delivered at dawn. This was good, but the Enemy was still in Fricourt, La Boiselle,[1] Thiepval. It was also said that we had 2 battalions cut off in the 'Schwaben Redoubt' (on the hill north of Thiepval) and also that the VIII Corps (Hunter-Weston) had 2 battalions cut off in the village of Serre . . .

After church I and Kiggell motored to Querrieu and saw Sir H. Rawlinson. I directed him to devote all his energies to capturing Fricourt and neighbouring villages, so as to reduce the number of our flanks, and then advance on Enemy's second line. I questioned him as to his views of an advance from Montauban and his right, instead of from Thiepval and left. He did not seem to favour the scheme . . .

General J. Du Cane (who is here on behalf of the Minister of Munitions) came to lunch. I am anxious about the supply of heavy ammunition (9.2 especially),[2] as we have used so much owing to the two extra days of bombardment . . .

I also visited two Casualty Clearing Stations at Montigny, one under Major Thomas, the other under Colonel Macpherson. They were very pleased at my visit. The wounded were in wonderful good spirits . . .

The AG[3] reported today that the total casualties are estimated at over 40,000 to date. This cannot be considered severe in view of the numbers engaged, and the length of front attacked . . .

16; GOC 56th Division, 1916–17 (sick); GOC 16th Division, 1918; GOC 56th Division, 1918–19.
1 Correctly, La Boisselle.
2 i.e. for 9.2-inch howitzers.
3 The Adjutant-General, Lieutenant General (later Sir) George Henry Fowke (1864–1936).

... I hear that the Enemy had only a few patrols in Bernafay Wood (north of Montauban) and that they were surrendering freely. I therefore directed Kiggell to urge Rawlinson to greater activity in the direction of Longueval. My CRA (Birch) also went to HQ Fourth Army to [go] into the artillery situation with the same objective.

At night situation was much more favourable than when we started today!

Monday 3 July

By request I received Generals Joffre and Foch about 3 pm today. The object of the visit was to 'discuss future arrangements'.

Joffre began by pointing out the importance of our getting Thiepval hill. To this I said that in view of the progress made on my right, near Montauban, and the demoralised nature of the Enemy's troops in that area, I was considering the desirability of pressing my attack on Longueval.[1] I was therefore anxious to know whether in that event the French would attack Guillemont.

At this, General Joffre exploded in a fit of rage. 'He could not approve of it.' He 'ordered me to attack Thiepval and Pozières'. 'If I attacked Longueval, I would be beaten,' etc., etc. I waited calmly till he had finished. His breast heaved and his face flushed! The truth is the poor man cannot argue, nor can he easily read a map. But today I had a raised model of the ground before us. There were also present at the meeting Generals Kiggell and Foch and Renouard (from GQG) and Foch's Chief Staff Officer (Weygand).[2] Only Joffre, Foch and I spoke.

When Joffre got out of breath, I quietly explained what my position is as regards him as the 'Generalissimo'. I am *solely* responsible [to the British Government] for the action of the British Army; and I had approved the plan, and must modify it to suit the changing situation as the fight progresses. I was most polite. Joffre saw he had made a mistake, and next tried to cajole me. He said that this was the 'English Battle' and 'France expected great things from me'. I thanked him but said I had only one object, viz. beat Germany. France and England marched together, and it would give me equal pleasure to see the French troops exploiting victory as my own! ...

I soothed old Joffre down. He seemed ashamed [of his outburst] and I sent him and Foch off to Amiens. All present at the interview felt ashamed of Joffre ... However, I have gained an advantage through keeping calm! My views have been accepted by the French Staffs and Davidson is to go to lunch

---

1 In a letter to his wife of the same date, Haig commented that 'Things are going quite satisfactorily for us here, and the Enemy seems hard pushed to it to find any reserves at all'.

2 General Maxime Weygand (1867–1965). Foch and he were inseparable: 'Weygand, c'est mois,' Foch declared.

with Foch tomorrow at Dury to discuss how they (the French) can co-operate in our operation!

Tuesday 4 July

I visited Sir H. Rawlinson soon after noon. I impressed on him importance of getting Trones Wood to cover right flank, and Mametz Wood and Contalmaison to cover left flank of attack against the Longueval front.

I told him that Joffre would not attack Guillemont when we attacked Longueval so it might be necessary for us to cover our own right flank...

... I proceeded to HQ XIII Corps, where I saw Generals Congreve and Greenly. I complimented them on their work but urged greater rapidity. Also asked GOC to insist on his divisions patrolling widely, especially after a counter-attack had been beaten back. I insisted, too, on the importance of gaining Trones Wood before Enemy could wire it up.

I next visited HQ XV Corps at Heilly, calling at a Main Dressing Station en route. General Horne was dissatisfied with 17th Division under General Pilcher. He could not get it to advance quickly...

I reached Montigny, HQ III Corps about 5 pm and saw Generals Pulteney and Romer. I urged them to press their advance, because by delaying, the Enemy was given more time to strengthen his second line. The 34th Division (Ingouville-Williams)[1] had fought splendidly. The losses were severe, but it was anxious to remain in the Corps. The 8th Division (Hudson) had been withdrawn, and will be sent to First Army to replace the 1st Division...

General Headlam[2] visited the captured positions about Fricourt yesterday. Some of the 'dugouts' were 30 feet below ground, and in places a double tier! Also there were places arranged for shooting upwards from below at anyone in the trenches. [He considered] the effect of the artillery shooting was good and the fire accurate.

Thursday 6 July

General Foch and Colonel Weygand (his CSO) came to lunch. I had a short talk with him before. All questions regarding the co-operation of the French XX Corps and our XIII Corps have been arranged for tomorrow's action. The French will take Hardecourt and knoll to north, and put barrage in front of Guillemont.

1 Major General Edward Charles Ingouville-Williams ('Inky Bill') (1861–1916), GOC 16 Brigade, 1912–15; GOC 34th Division, 1915–16; killed by a shell, 22 July 1916.
2 Major General (later Sir) John Emerson Wharton Headlam (1876–1964), CRA 5th Division, 1913–15; MGRA Second Army, 1915; MGRA GHQ, 1915–16.

As regards the next step, when we attack Longueval and west of it to Bazentin-le-Petit, he has not sufficient troops on the spot to take Maurepas, because his communications north of river won't admit of feeding more than his present number. He will support us with counter-batteries as much as possible. Then when we attack Guillemont he will extend his position eastwards and take Maurepas, also on left bank of Somme to Villers Carbonnel (on the Amiens–St Quentin road). This latter as soon as possible.

In the subsequent advance, we will take Ginchy and Morval: and the valley of Combles will be the dividing line.

I confirmed the promise which we have several times given, viz. to hand over communications south of Albert–Bapaume road as soon as we have secured the heights of Pozières-Longueval. He assured me that he will do all that is possible to support us in our efforts to gain the latter ridge.

Lunch went off most satisfactorily. After it, Foch and I walked in the garden for about an hour, and he then left quite delighted with his reception. He seemed to be doubtful of how I would combine with him in these operations in view of his past difficulties with the British in Sir John French's time.

Friday 7 July

After lunch I visited HQ Fourth Army and saw General Rawlinson. I directed him to get Mametz Wood, and push on towards Pozières. At the same time Gough would connect between Ovillers and Bailiff Wood, and between Leipzig Redoubt and Ovillers; reconnaissances would be pushed forward towards Pozières with a view to attacking it in co-operation with III Corps.

I then went to HQ Fifth Army and saw General Gough. I then learnt that his troops had not yet captured the whole of Ovillers. His first objective is therefore to get that place and connect with III Corps.

Lord Esher arrived from Paris. He says all are very pleased with work of British Army. Our success has just made the difference of the French continuing the war, if necessary, for another winter.

Saturday 8 July

Correspondents are given a free pass to go anywhere and write what they like provided they do not divulge anything of value to the Enemy. Amongst the correspondents is Repington of *The Times* . . . He was yesterday received by General Foch who compared French and British artillery methods to the advantage of the former!

I was requested from London to receive Repington for the good of the Army. So I did so this morning at about 10.30. I told him he could go where he liked, and see who he liked, and write what he liked. Only one restriction, that he submits any *tactical* criticism he makes to the censor so as to prevent anything useful to the Enemy being published. I hated seeing such a dishonest individual, but I felt it was my duty to the Army to do so – otherwise he would have been an unfriendly critic of its actions...

Sir H. Rawlinson stated that his plan was now to pierce the Enemy's second line near Bazentin le Grand. I pointed out the necessity for having possession of Mametz Wood before making any attempt of the kind. The moment for taking the Enemy by surprise here had passed, and the fighting in the Mametz Wood showed that the Enemy's 'morale' was still good. I therefore gave Rawlinson an order to consolidate his right flank *strongly* in the south end of Trones Wood, and to capture Mametz Wood and Contalmaison before making any attempt to pierce the Enemy's second line. This was later confirmed in writing.

Saturday 8 July. Letter to Lady Haig

The troops are fighting very well and the battle is developing slowly but steadily in our favour.

In another fortnight, with Divine Help, I hope that some decisive results may be obtained.

In the meantime we must be patient and determined.

Sunday 9 July

We then visited HQ XV Corps at Heilly and saw General Horne. He was very disappointed with the work of the 17th Division (Pilcher) and 38th Welsh Division (Phillips). Both these officers have been removed. In the case of the latter division, although the wood had been most adequately bombarded the division never entered the wood, and in the whole division the total casualties for the 24 hours are under 150! A few bold men entered the wood and found little opposition. Deserters also stated Enemy was greatly demoralised and had very few troops on the ground.[1]

Monday 10 July

Two brigades of 38th Division (Welsh) had succeeded in entering Mametz Wood, and 2 battalions were pushing on and clearing it...

After lunch I visited Querrieu and saw Rawlinson and his Chief of Staff

---

1 For a more balanced judgement on 17th and 38th Divisions, see C. Hughes, *Mametz* (Norwich: Gliddon Books, 1990), pp. 143–51.

(Montgomery).[1] I questioned him about the plan of attack against Longueval ridge. He proposed to form up two divisions in the dark and attack at dawn over an open maidan[2] against the front Bazentin le Grand Wood to Longueval. Farther to the west the attack will be made by the XV Division.[3]

As regards the first day of the bombardment, I said Mametz Wood and Contalmaison must be in our hands to secure our left flank, while Trones Wood must be held on our right. At present the enemy is in Trones Wood, but we'll recapture the whole of it tonight. Progress in Mametz Wood is satisfactory; and we should capture Contalmaison this afternoon . . .

Monday 10 July. Letter to Lady Haig

The battle is being fought out on lines which suit us. That is to say the Enemy puts his reserves straight into the battle on arrival, to attack us, thereby suffering big losses.

Tuesday 11 July

I am not quite satisfied with Rawlinson's plan of attack against Bazentin le Grand–Longueval. His proposal to attack at dawn over an open plateau, for 1000 yards distance, after forming up 2 divisions in mass in the dark, and this with a force of two divisions, appears to me a manoeuvre which one cannot do successfully against flags in time of peace! So I proceeded to Querrieu with Kiggell about 11 am. Rawlinson explained his plan, and I gave him my opinion that it was unsound. He at once, in the most broad-minded way, said he would change it, making, as I suggested, the main attack against the line Contalmaison Villa–Bazentin le Grand Wood from Mametz Wood, while threatening from the rest of our front, namely from Ovillers to Trones Wood. General Montgomery was most anxious to adhere to the original plan but I declined to discuss the matter further . . .

About 3 pm Rawlinson spoke to CGS on telephone, stating he still thought his old plan the best. I considered that the experience of war, as well as the teachings of peace are against the use of *large masses* in night operations, especially with inexperienced Staff officers and young troops. Rawlinson was accordingly ordered to attack the line Contalmaison Villa–Bazentin le Grand

---

1 Major General (later Field Marshal Sir) Archibald Armar ('Archie') Montgomery (later Montgomery-Massingberd) (1871–1947), GSO2, 4th Division, 1914; GSO1 4th Division, 1914–15; BGGS IV Corps, 1915–16; MGGS Fourth Army, 1916–19; Rawlinson's inseparable right-hand man.

2 From the Urdu for an open space.

3 A slip for XV Corps.

Wood with XV Corps, reinforced by a brigade or division, as Horne might desire, and to be prepared to reinforce him. To establish a good flank on west of Bazentin le Petit Wood, and then work eastwards and capture Longueval, Ginchy, Guillemont etc. The XIII Corps to organise supporting points just under the slopes opposite Longueval, Bazentin etc. and be ready to push in when the XV Corps begin to work towards Longueval.

The whole question of the attack of the German second line is a difficult problem.

After dinner Rawlinson rang Kiggell up with a further proposition based on my discussion with him this morning. The XIII Corps is constructing supporting points, and the divisions will form on them by brigades. I said I would carefully go into the proposals and reply in the morning...

Today is the anniversary of my marriage. I could not get a telegram through to Doris. But everyone is working at highest pressure.

Wednesday 12 July

I thought carefully over Rawlinson's amended plan and discussed it in detail with Kiggell, Butler and Davidson. General Birch also gave me his opinion of the artillery situation, which was satisfactory, viz. that advancing certain guns he felt fairly sure that we could dominate the Enemy's artillery.

I put four questions to the General Staff:

1. Can we take the position in the manner proposed?
2. Can we hold it after capture?
3. What will be the results in case of a failure?
4. What are the advantages, or otherwise, of proceeding methodically, viz. extending our front and sapping forward[1] to take the position by assault?

They all agreed that Rawlinson's new plan materially altered the chances of success, and there seemed a fair chance now of succeeding. They thought we could both take the position and hold it. In the case of failure, the supporting points must be held, and we can then proceed by deliberate methods – extending our front and sapping up. The disadvantage of the deliberate method at once is that we must hold the German troops in our front. If the attack was allowed to die down, they might continue the attacks at Verdun or elsewhere. The news this morning shows the Germans again attacking at Verdun. Also to encourage the French, we must keep on being active. They lost severely in trying to take Barleux village (on left of Somme).

For the above reasons, I concurred in Rawlinson's amended plan, and I

---

1 i.e. digging trenches towards the Germans.

sent General Kiggell to discuss certain details with him, and to emphasise the necessity for constructing good supporting points on the front of XIII Corps, and for holding Trones and Mametz Woods firmly to cover our flanks . . .

QMG was anxious about our expenditure of ammunition, at our present rate of expenditure we will soon have exhausted our reserves, and be dependent on daily income for all except 18 pounder. I hope the expenditure in heavy ammunition will not be so great in future, because we have passed through the Enemy's first line of very deep dugouts and specially strong defence.

Thursday 13 July

I visited Sir H. Rawlinson after lunch. I spoke about the use of the cavalry. The divisions were not to go forward until we had got through the Enemy's fortifications, except a few squadrons to take 'High Wood'. For this he had the 2nd Indian Cavalry Division under his orders. As soon as he judged the situation favourable the 1st and 3rd Cavalry Divisions were available. I also stated his objectives as,

1. Occupy position Longueval–Bazentin le Petit, and consolidate it.
2. Take High Wood, and establish right flank at Ginchy and Guillemont.
3. At same time (if possible, as there are ample troops) extend left and take Pozières ridge and village of Martinpuich . . .

I saw General Pulteney at Montigny . . . [he] had not thought of how to employ his divisions to capture Pozières village. I said he should not attack direct, but take it from the rear to avoid loss. For this he should arrange plan with General Horne.

In the evening General Birch CRA said he was not satisfied with the handling of artillery of the Reserve Army. Guns were too far back. He had spent most of the day with General Gough and his guns were now being pushed as far forward as possible. He proposed sending Gough's CRA (Strong)[1] to the VIII Corps in exchange for Tancred,[2] the Corps CRA.

Friday 14 July

The 'dawn attack', a well-planned, well-executed operation with plenty of artillery support, succeeded in capturing Bazentin Ridge without difficulty. Delays in

1 Brigadier General William Strong (1870–1936), BGRA Reserve Corps; he took over as BGRA VIII Corps on 13 July 1916 and held the post until May 1917.
2 Brigadier General (later Major General) Thomas Angus Tancred (1867–1944), BGRA VIII Corps, March–July 1916; Tancred was moved to III Corps, where he was BGRA until May 1918.

committing reserves, especially cavalry, meant that the success was not fully exploited.

Very heavy artillery bombardment about 2.30 and then at 3.30 am. I looked out at 2.30, it was quite light but cloudy. Just the weather we want. The noise of the artillery was very loud and the light from the explosion of the shells was reflected from the heavens on to the ceiling of my room . . .

At 3.25 am today, after 5 minutes' intense bombardment we attacked enemy's second line from west of Bazentin-le-Petit Wood to Longueval with the 21st, 7th, 3rd, and 9th Divisions. Attack went right through and by 9 am we were holding the whole of Bazentin-le-Petit Wood and village, and the whole of Bazentin-le-Grand village and Wood. Also all Longueval village except part of the north end. Most of Delville Wood. Trones Wood is all in our hands.

At 7.40 am cavalry advanced to seize High Wood, but ground very slippery: it was difficult to get forward. General MacAndrew commanding the division had two falls. So High Wood was shelled and infantry was pushed on to take it. Fierce fighting continued all day, and we increased our gains of the morning. Enemy retook Bazentin-le-Petit, but it was retaken by the 7th Division. High Wood was taken by the XV Division[1], and was connected up with Bazentin-le-Petit in the evening . . .

I saw General Foch at Querrieu. He is very pleased with result of our attacks. French openly said their troops could not have carried out such an attack, not even the XX Corps!

Friday 14 July. Letter to Lady Haig

This morning very early our troops surprised the enemy, and have captured some 4 miles of his *Second Line.*[2]

This is indeed a very great success. The best day we have had this war and I feel what a reward it is to have been spared to see our troops so successful! There is no doubt that the results of today will be very far reaching. Our men showed that they have the superiority to the Germans in the fighting, and the latter are very much disorganised and rattled.

---

1 A slip for 'Corps'.
2 At 10.55 am Haig's private secretary, Sir Philip Sassoon MP, had sent, on Haig's behalf, a telegram to Lady Haig summarising events and stating 'hope to get cavalry through'. Travers, *Killing Ground*, p. 153, misdates this telegram as 1 July, and he has been followed by other historians, including Gary Sheffield in *The Somme* (London: Cassell, 2003), p. 65. For a corrective, see the article by Gary Sheffield and Stephen Badsey in *Journal of the Society for Army Historical Research*, vol. 82, no. 330 (Summer 2004), pp. 179–81.

Saturday 15 July

Today the whole of Delville Wood was taken.[1] Enemy counter-attacked wood in force from north and northeast at 2.45 pm and was repulsed. Waterlot Farm was occupied by us. Enemy still holds northern apex of High Wood where there is a very strong machine gun position . . .

I visited General Horne (XV Corps) about 3 pm. He told me that the 7th Dragoon Guards charged last night and killed with lances 16 Enemy and took over 30 prisoners. All the cavalry are much heartened by this episode and think that their time is soon coming.

Sunday 16 July

. . . I discussed our future plans with Kiggell, Butler and Davidson. I stated as our several objects

1. Consolidate the Longueval–Bazentin le Petit position so as to make it absolutely safe against counter-attack.
2. Establish our right flank in Ginchy and Guillemont.
3. Take Pozières village.

Kiggell then went to HQ Fourth Army to arrange details.

About noon I heard our troops withdrew from High Wood at dawn in accordance with orders. That point makes our position too extended until our flanks are safe, in General Horne's opinion.

The attacks made yesterday were within an ace of being successful. Unfortunately in the mist of the morning the Enemy managed to push forward a few machine guns into the northwest corner of Bazentin-le-Petit Wood. These enfiladed the troops advancing parallel with the trenches which run towards the windmill between Pozières and Martinpuich. This attack was consequently delayed, and the attack against the new trenches which run from High Wood towards the windmill was in its turn enfiladed from the before-named trenches. Had the other attack been able to go in as arranged, these machine guns would have been fully occupied in their own front.

Monday 17 July

I saw General Rawlinson about 3 pm. He is as much dissatisfied as I am with the action of the 9th Division in failing to occupy *the whole* of Longueval. I also think that there has been a lack of close co-operation between XIII and

1 The South African Brigade of 9th (Scottish) Division played a leading role.

XV Corps. The latter occupied High Wood with cavalry on right on night of 14th inst. and the latter dug a trench from that wood towards Longueval, while infantry (7th Division) dug line from High Wood to Bazentin-le-Petit. I think the XIII Corps should have at once connected up with the XV Corps in the direction of High Wood.

Tuesday 18 July. Letter to Major General Sir Stanley von Donop[1]

In reply to your letter of the 15 July, on the question of the supply of guns and ammunition to Russia.

Personally, I do not agree that the most probable development is an attack on Russia in great force in the autumn. I do not think the Germans will then have 'great strength' left for such an attack and such reserves as they may have available are, in my opinion, far more likely to be employed on the Western than on the Eastern Front. The point is one for the General Staff at the War Office to advise on.

The events of the last fortnight have again proved conclusively that the British troops are capable of beating the best German troops. They are fully confident, and so am I, that they can continue to do so, provided we are kept supplied with men, guns, and munitions.

Our present success has been gained before we have reached our full strength, and the exploitation of this success is limited only by the extent of our resources.

So far the Russians have had great success against the Austrians, but it remains for them to prove that they are capable of defeating the Germans proper; and however that may be, I can see no doubt that the most patriotic and the wisest policy is to provide all that we require ourselves before we give to others.[2]

On 19 July 5th Australian Division and 61st Division suffered heavy losses in a diversionary attack at Fromelles.

Thursday 20 July

GOC First Army reports that Haking's attack only partially successful, and after visiting the Corps HQ at dawn, he (Monro) decided to withdraw the

---

1 LHCMA: Kiggell Papers, KIGGELL 4/30. Von Donop was Master General of the Ordnance.
2 Haig, however, agreed to the limited transfer of some 4.5-inch howitzers to Russia if certain conditions were fulfilled. For the argument that Haig underestimated the importance of Russia, see Keith Neilson, *Strategy and Supply: The Anglo-Russian Alliance, 1914–17* (London: Allen & Unwin, 1984), p. 311.

units which had got into Enemy's trenches. The troops seem to have somewhat become disorganised. The reality of the fighting and shelling seems to have been greater than many had expected! So the experience must have been of value to all, and the enterprise has certainly had the effect of obliging the Enemy to retain reserves in that area. Besides, by merely bombarding the Enemy's front on similar lines again, we will compel him to mass troops to oppose a possible attack . . .

I also saw General Gough at Toutencourt (HQ Reserve Army). The Australians went in last night opposite Pozières . . . He proposes to attack Pozières with them on 22nd early, 1.30 am. I told him to go into all details carefully, as 1st Australian Division had not been engaged [in France] before, and possibly overlooked the difficulties of this kind of fighting.

Friday 21 July

In the afternoon I visited Querrieu and saw Sir H. Rawlinson. We discussed the manner and time of attacking Enemy's line north of the Bazentin–Longueval position . . . It was decided that the attacks will take place as simultaneously as possible, and I went on to HQ Reserve Army to arrange with General Gough to attack Pozières at the same time as Fourth Army attacked on their right. The hour of attack is still under discussion. It depends to some extent on the time taken to get the troops into position.

Lord Northcliffe arrived today and stayed the night. I was favourably impressed with his desire to do his best to help to win the war. He was most anxious not to make a mistake in anything he advocated in his newspapers, and for this he was desirous of seeing what was taking place. I am therefore letting him see everything and talk to anyone he pleases.[1]

Saturday 22 July

I visited General Gough after lunch to make sure that the Australians have only been given a simple task. This is the first time that they will be taking part in a serious offensive on a big scale [against the German Forces].

General Gough does not think very much of General Morland commanding the X Corps. This is no time for having 'doubts'; so I told him that I will arrange to withdraw Morland into Reserve and give him General Jacob in his place. [Personally, I found Morland one of our best brigadiers at Aldershot.]

1 Haig later reported that Northcliffe described Lloyd George as a ' "a shirt-sleeved politician" and he told me that LG does whatever he (Lord N) advises!' See letter to Lady Haig, 11 September 1916.

The major result of the attack of 23 July was the capture of Pozières by 1st Australian Division. Elsewhere the results were patchy.

Sunday 23 July. Letter to Lady Haig

My name is beginning to appear in the papers with favourable comments! You must think I am turning into an Advertiser! But that is not so. All sorts of people beg for interviews; Senators and others from Paris; some, the War Office ask me to see, in order to assist their Propaganda in neutral States. So I see these people for the good of the Army, and then they put some personal touches into their stories. But it is not with my approval.

Admiral Bacon is here tonight. He is a capital fellow . . .

Tuesday 25 July

After lunch I visited HQ Reserve Army and HQ Australian Corps at Contay . . . The situation seems all very new and strange to Australian HQ. The fighting here and shell fire is much more severe than anything experienced at Gallipoli! The German too, is a different enemy to the Turk! The hostile shelling has been very severe against Pozières today, and owing to clouds observation was bad, and our counter-battery work could not be carried out effectively.

I spoke to Birdwood about his CRA, Brigadier General Cunliffe Owen.[1] The latter had served with me at beginning of war, but soon left France and so had no experience of our present artillery or the methods which had developed during the war. I therefore wished to give him an up to date CRA. He thanked me and said he would take anyone I selected . . . I also saw Cunliffe Owen and explained how sorry I was to have to move him, but in the present situation I would be failing in my duty to the country if I ran the risk of the Australians meeting with a check through faulty artillery arrangements.[2]

Thursday 27 July

2nd Division attacked Delville Wood from the south and 5th Division the north end of Longueval village. By evening we were in possession of all Delville Wood, driving out the famous 5th German Division (Brandenburgers). We

1 Brigadier General Charles Cunliffe-Owen (1868–1932). He spent much of the rest of the war as an infantry brigade commander.
2 Cunliffe-Owen's replacement was Brigadier General William James Napier (1852–1925), who retained the post until October 1917.

also have one company in the northwest corner of wood which cuts off the approach of the Enemy to the village. We also have a company of Norfolks in the centre of that part of the village which the Enemy holds . . .

Friday 28 July

The 5th Brandenburg Division, the crack corps of Germany, was driven from its remaining positions north of Longueval village this morning, and also from the whole of Delville Wood. This is a fine performance. Two counter-attacks made yesterday by the Enemy on the wood were repulsed with great loss. 3 officers and 158 men were captured in the wood; and some officers in the village surrendered. They said they were the only survivors. They were greatly depressed and said 'Germany is beaten'. This is the first time we have taken German officers who have arrived at that opinion . . .

I visited General Horne at Heilly (XV Corps). He thought that the 51st Division under Harper was a little slow, but the Divisional Commander knew his work. They were opposite High Wood. The 5th Division under General Stephens had done well in retaking Longueval village and the strong points to the north of it . . .

At Senlis HQ II Corps I saw Generals Jacob and Howell (his BGGS). They explained their plan for working towards Thiepval and attacking it from the east. All very sound, and every detail had been most carefully thought out . . .

General Birch in the evening reported that the Australians[1] had at the last moment said that they would attack without artillery support and that 'they did not believe machine gun fire could do them much harm'! Birch at once saw Gough who arranged that the original artillery programme should be carried out. The Australians are splendid fellows but very ignorant.

Saturday 29 July

The attack by the 2nd Australian Division upon the Enemy's position between Pozières and the windmill was not successful last night. From several reports I think the cause was due to want of thorough preparation. Amongst the main causes were

1. The attacking troops were not formed up square opposite their objective. Troops started from the railway line and attacked against 3 fronts . . . Gaps occurred between the flanks of the 3 attacks. This must happen unless special detachments are made to fill the larger front.

---

1 i.e. the relatively inexperienced 2nd Australian Division.

2. The advance was made in the dark for a distance of 700 yards (over ground covered with shell holes and Enemy had thrown out 'knife rests' of wire) and then the men were expected to charge home against the Enemy's trench. Our experience is that about 150 yards is the limit for a successful charge. In this case it was hoped to advance unobserved in the dark to that distance and form up prior to the charge.

3. One of the brigades had spent the day 2 miles in rear and only marched up to Pozières after dark so, although the officers had reconnoitred their objective, the bulk of the troops were quite ignorant of the task before them.

4. The artillery bombardment was only for 'one minute' before the attack, which was made soon after midnight.

These facts alone in my opinion were sufficient to make the attack miscarry. Some of the battalions did actually get into the Enemy's first trench, and 2 companies reached the second trench, and the battalion on the left gained its objective, but withdrew as its right was in the air.

After lunch I visited HQ Reserve Army and impressed on Gough and his SGSO (Neil[1] Malcolm) that they must supervise more closely the plans of the Anzac Corps. Some of their Divisional Generals are so ignorant and (like many Colonials) so conceited, that they cannot be trusted [to work out unaided the plans of attack].[2]

I then went on to HQ Anzac Corps at Contay and saw Generals Birdwood and (his BGGS) White.[3] The latter seems a very sound capable fellow, and assured me that they had learnt a lesson, and would be more thorough in future. Luckily, their losses had been fairly small considering the operation and the numbers engaged – about 1000 for the whole 24 hours.

I pointed out to Birdwood that Pozières village had been captured thanks to a very thorough artillery preparation. Last year, the French had spent often a fortnight in taking such villages (Neuville St Vaast, Souchez etc.). Still, the capture of Pozières by the Australians would live in history! They must not however underestimate the Enemy or his power of defence, machine guns etc. I had given him a very experienced and capable CRA in Napier, and he must trust him.

1 Actually, 'Neill'.
2 Haig similarly warned Major General Cox, an Indian Army officer commanding 4th Australian Division, 'against Colonial ignorance and conceit' and that the Germans were a tougher enemy than the Turks: Diary, 31 July 1916.
3 Brigadier General (later General Sir) (Cyril) Brudenell Bingham White (1876–1940), GSO1 1st Australian Division, 1914–15; BGGS Anzac Corps, 1915–18; MGGS Fifth Army, 1918–19. Birdwood and White were a team throughout the war; Birdwood invariably left the day-to-day running of the formations he commanded to White.

Birdwood was very grateful for my visit and remarks.[1]

Sunday 30 July

I reminded Rawlinson that my plan is to do all possible to bring the French
on my right forward into line. [At present their troops are echeloned back in
rear of my right.] The [British] front to the north [(that is on the line
Longueval–Bazentin–Pozières)] must be stationary, and only pushed forward
to observation points to improve our position, but no big attack northward
is to be undertaken at present.

Monday 31 July

General Trenchard reported regarding the Flying Corps. More German
machines were seen yesterday than at any time previously during this battle,
but not more than 20 crossed our line, and none got very far. The previous
day 8 crossed our line. On the other hand we made 451 separate flights over
the Enemy's front two days ago, and some 500 flights yesterday.
    The Germans have concentrated nearly all their airoplanes on the Somme
front. Very few now remain at Verdun; and very few opposite our 1st, 2nd
and 3rd Army fronts. We are now operating towards Ghent, Brussels etc. in
the hope of forcing the Enemy to detach [airoplanes] to guard his important
depôts in rear.
    It is now impossible to say how many [air] fights take place in a day. So
many of our machines fight 4 or 5 Germans in one flight: also it is impossible
to know how many hostile machines our men really do bring down, because
there is no time for our victorious airmen to watch a machine crash to earth
before another enemy is upon him, and has to be engaged!

Tipped in at the end of the July 1916 portion of the diary is a note in Haig's hand:

OBJECTIVE
The war must be continued until Germany is vanquished to such an extent
as to be obliged to accept whatever terms the Allies may dictate to her.

DH
(July 1916)

1 For a recent assessment, see G. Sheffield, 'The Australians at Pozières' in D. French and B.
Holden Reid (eds), *The British General Staff: Reform and Innovation, c. 1890–1939* (London: Frank
Cass, 2002).

Tuesday 1 August

General Foch came to see [me] soon after 2 o'clock. He stated that their recent attack against Maurepas had not been well arranged. Not enough artillery support, and the morning fog had hampered the operation. His Tenth Army was now on too large a front to secure certain success both on the south as well as on the north of the Somme. He had accordingly reorganised his Command, and given General Fayolle[1] the sole objective of advancing on the north of the Somme on the English right. He would just have sufficient ground on the south of the Somme for artillery positions. Up to date Fayolle, he thought, rather hankered after an operation on the south bank: now he would have nothing to do on the south bank. This arrangement would enable a very powerful artillery to operate on our right, and progress should be certain . . .

I thanked him and said that I thought it was the best thing to do, and that our immediate objective must be to place the Anglo-French Army on the line Pozières–Morval–Sailly Saillisel with the view of then making a combined advance northwards. For this advance the 'Tanks' would be most useful, and I asked when Foch's Army would have them. Foch did not seem to know about these machines, but he is to press for them.

Note on letter received from CIGS dated 29 July[2]

1. '*The Powers that be*' are beginning to get a little uneasy in regard to the situation.
2. Whether a loss of say 300,000 men will lead to really great results, because if not, we ought to be content with something less than what we are now doing.
3. They are constantly enquiring why we are fighting and the French are not.
4. It is thought that the primary object – relief of pressure on Verdun – has to some extent been achieved.

I replied in OAD 90, dated 1 August:

(a) Pressure on Verdun relieved. Not less than six Enemy divisions besides heavy guns have been withdrawn.
(b) Successes achieved by Russia last month would certainly have been

---

1 General Marie-Émile Fayolle (1852–1928), GOC French Sixth Army on the Somme; he skilfully used his superior artillery resources and infantry tactics to inflict a substantial defeat on the Germans opposite him on 1 July 1916.
2 These next two entries are in Haig's hand, to be found after the diary entry of 1 August 1916.

stopped had Enemy been free to transfer troops from here to the Eastern theatre.

(c) Proof given to world that Allies are capable of making and maintaining a vigorous offensive and of driving Enemy's best troops from the strongest positions has shaken faith of Germans, of their friends, of doubting neutrals in the invincibility of Germany. Also impressed on the world, England's strength and determination, and the fighting power of the British race.

(d) We have inflicted very heavy losses on the Enemy. In *one* month, 30 of his divisions have been used up, as against 35 at Verdun in 5 months! In another 6 weeks, the Enemy should be hard put to it to find men!

(e) The maintenance of a steady offensive pressure will result eventually in his complete overthrow.

2. Principle on which we should act. *Maintain our offensive.* Our losses in July's fighting totalled about 120,000 more than they would have been, had we not attacked. They cannot be regarded as sufficient to justify any anxiety as to our ability to continue the offensive.

It is my intention:

(a) To maintain a steady pressure etc.

(b) To push my attack strongly whenever and wherever the state of my preparations and the general situation make success sufficiently probable to justify me in doing so, but not otherwise.

(c) To secure against counter-attack each advantage gained and prepare thoroughly for each fresh advance.

Proceeding thus, I expect to be able to maintain the offensive well into the autumn.

It would not be justifiable to calculate on the Enemy's resistance being completely broken without another campaign next year.

Thursday 3 August

Haig, having recognised that the Germans had 'recovered to a great extent from the disorganisation' of early July, issued instructions to the Army commanders that stated that enemy positions could not be attacked 'without careful and methodical preparation'. He was now looking towards securing good starting positions for a major attack in the future.[1]

1 OAD 91, 2 August 1916, in British Official History, *1916*, II, Appendix 13.

I saw General Monro about 11 am, told him of Secretary of State's decision.[1] He did not at all want to go to India. As regards his successor, he recommended General Haking. I said I hoped it would be a *temporary appointment* and that he would be back by spring...

I met General Gough near Toutencourt ... He said that the Australian Corps had again put off their attack. I thought cause was due to the ignorance of the 2nd Australian Division Staff and that the GOC Legge[2] was not much good. [Gough] had called for his reasons in writing as to why the delay had occurred.

Saturday 5 August

The Australians gained all their objectives north of Pozières and beat off 3 counter-attacks. A fine piece of work. Front taken is about 2000 yards.

The 12th Division also took about 1000 yards of trench on the left of the Australians.

The general principle of these attacks has been a steady and accurate bombardment with heavy shells throughout 48 hours, or more, with occasional intensive bursts of 18 pounder to make the Enemy expect an attack and man his trenches. Then at 9 pm or thereabouts an intensive barrage with 18 pounder shrapnel is opened behind which our infantry advanced, close up to our shells, and entered Enemy's trench before he had become aware of the attack. In some cases the Enemy was engaged in repairing the damage caused by our bombardment during the day when our real attack and barrage caught him...

Sir Mark Sykes MP[3] came to lunch ... he mentioned that the present Government was not likely to last over a month on account of the mistakes made over Ireland...

Sunday 6 August

Between 2 and 3 pm General Joffre came to see me ... It was a much more chastened Joffre than on 3rd July! He was in very good spirits, not so tired as hitherto, and with a beard of four days' growth! Extremely pleased with everything we had done, and full of compliments. He was also greatly

1 Monro, commander of First Army, was appointed as Commander-in-Chief India, a post in which he performed admirably, greatly augmenting Indian military strength and efficiency.
2 Major General (later Lieutenant General) James Gordon Legge (1863–1947), GOC 2nd Australian Division, 1915–16; Chief of the Australian General Staff, 1917–20.
3 Sir Mark Sykes (1879–1919), British diplomat, architect of British policy in the Middle East and co-signatory of the notorious Sykes-Picot Agreement of May 1916 for the post-war partition of the Ottoman Empire between France and Britain.

delighted at the remarks which I had made about him in my message to the French on the third anniversary of the war. 'As long as I got on well with him there was nothing to be feared from the politicians', he said. My message is in the *Matin* of 2 August. He brought me a box of 50 Croix de Guerre for me to distribute as I thought right. A nice little attention on his part, and a sort of 'peace offering' after the previous interview between us here! I managed to get together 10 officers who had rendered 'good service under fire' and he presented the crosses himself to them.

A letter from Robertson CIGS acknowledging receipt of my review of the situation of 1 August says 'I read it to the War Committee today (5 August) and it pleased them very much indeed. It is to be printed and circulated to the Cabinet as a rejoinder to a memorandum recently put before the Cabinet by Winston *Churchill.[1] Your paper is an adequate reply to what he said.' Then in a private letter he says 'Winston, French, Fitzgerald, and various "dégommé'd people"[2] are trying to make mischief,' but, 'they have not a friend in the War Committee or anywhere else amongst honest men'.

Tuesday 8 August

The King visited GHQ.

I visited Sir H. Rawlinson about noon . . . He thought attack was progressing fairly well, but King's Liverpools of 2nd Division had been driven out of the trench which they had captured between Delville Wood and Guillemont. About 7 am, our artillery had the mastery of the Enemy's guns, but at 9 am the latter seemed to revive for a time, and placed a heavy barrage between Guillemont and Trones Wood. As it was already past noon, I did not like the absence of reliable news, and did not share Rawlinson's optimistic view of the situation . . .

The King then came into my writing room, and I explained the situation etc. to him. He then spoke a great deal about a paper which Winston Churchill had written and given to the Cabinet, criticising the operations in France, and arriving at the conclusion that nothing had been achieved! . . . He [the King] also said that Viscount French had been very nasty and that he was 'the most jealous man he had ever come across'.

I said that these were trifles and that we must not allow them to divert our

---

1 This critique of the Somme is in W. Churchill, *The World Crisis* (London, Thornton Butterworth, 1938 edn), II, pp. 1084–9. Churchill had returned to his parliamentary duties in May, although he was to have no formal position until Lloyd George appointed him Minister of Munitions in 1917.
2 i.e. commanders who had been sacked from the Western Front.

thoughts from our main objective, namely 'beating the Germans'! I also expect that Winston's head is gone from taking drugs.[1]

The King also said that much harm was being done at home by the generals who had been sent back as useless from France. They formed a regular 'Cabal' and abused everything that was done [by the British HQ on the Western Front]. He thought best that I should refer home to the War Office every case of the appointment of Corps or Army Commanders for decision by War Committee before I acted. I then gave the King an instance to show that this procedure would be dangerous.

I had this morning seen Sir John Keir at 10 am.[2] General *Allenby had reported that his (Keir's) defensive arrangements were unsatisfactory, and that he had no real plans worked out for offensive action. As the Enemy showed signs of activity near Arras where Keir's sector of defence was, I felt it would be highly dangerous to retain him in command, so I *at once* relieved him of his Command and ordered him to England on leave pending orders of WO. This morning Keir came to see me, quite beside himself with rage against Allenby, and said that he had been wronged. He meant to go home and make a row; he was not done with the Army yet, etc. I had the CGS in the room as witness while I spoke to him. I was sorry for the old man as he is over 60, but I felt I had done right in relieving him of his Command. It would have been too great a risk to wait until the War Office had settled the question! No one who is any good at all as a Commander is ever sent home by me.

Friday 11 August

Letter from 'Munitions' stated that 'accessories for Tanks' will not be delivered till 1 September. This is disappointing as I have been looking forward to obtaining decisive results from the use of these 'Tanks' at an early date.

Examination of prisoners and other reports show that Enemy has lost heavily in his counter-attacks since we took the German second line northeast of Pozières on night 4/5 August . . . Causes of Enemy's failure seem to be

(1) Enemy's units are still so mixed up it is impossible to organise a counter-attack on a large scale and methodically.
(2) No assembly trenches suitable distance [from the objective].

1 In the Ts diary this is altered to 'I also expect that Winston's judgement is impaired from taking drugs'.
2 Lieutenant General Sir John Lindesay Keir (1856–1937), GOC 6th Division, 1914–15; GOC VI Corps, 1915–16. Keir was nicknamed 'The Matador' because of his ability to handle 'The Bull' (Allenby), but the bull gored him fatally in the end.

(3) No communication trenches so attacking troops must advance across the open in view of our guns etc.

After lunch I visited HQ Reserve Army and saw General Gough. I explained that my plan remained the same; viz. capture ridge Pozières–Longueval–Morval, with French in line on our right: *then*, a general advance northwards in close touch with one another. At present our main effort is to capture Guillemont and Ginchy and assist the French to come up into line.

As regards an attack north of the Ancre. All preparations should be made for such an attack. If the French come up on our right, such an attack will not be required, but if the French do not manage to work forward then it will be necessary to widen our own front by attacking north of the Ancre. Meantime Gough is to carry on his operations against Thiepval, and I congratulated him on the daily progress made ...

I then motored to Contay, HQ of the Anzac Corps. I saw General White, the BGGS and congratulated the Corps on the splendid way it was operating. The 4th Australian Division under General Coxe,[1] Indian Army, is now in the line. He is doing well. Also their new CRA Napier[2] is fully appreciated. Their success is in very great measure due to his arrangements ...

Letters dated 10 August from Military Secretary, War Office and CIGS (Robertson) telling me that War Committee do not sanction General Haking's appointment to command First Army 'in succession' to General Monro. I did not appoint him in succession, but to 'act temporarily' in Monro's absence! No other Corps Commander, who is fit for it, is available, e.g., *Byng, Birdwood, Cavan. The MS sends me four names to select from, Birdwood, H. Wilson, Horne and Cavan.[3]

I reply, pointing out misunderstanding. I am afraid that the WO wilfully misread my letter and telegram, as a desire to limit my powers of appointment are noticeable.

Saturday 12 August

*Haig had lunch with the King and the French President, Raymond *Poincaré.*

We had 15 at lunch and by the King's desire, only water of various kinds was served.[4] Many of us will long remember General Joffre's look of abhorrence,

---

1 Actually Major General (later Sir) (Herbert) Vaughan Cox (1860–1923), GOC 4th Australian Division, 1916–17.
2 For Napier, see p. 209, fn 2.
3 Haig selected his protégé, Horne.
4 At the beginning of the war George V had pledged to abstain from alcohol to set an example to his people.

or annoyance, when Shaddock handed him a glass jug of lemonade and a
bottle of ginger beer, and asked him which he preferred!

By the President's request, the King gave him 10 minutes private conversation. I gave up my writing room for the purpose. They sent and asked
me to join them. M. Poincaré[1] then pointed out the importance of continuing
to press the Enemy vigorously; and, in his opinion, a general attack on a wide
front should be made as soon as possible. I agreed, but said the first object
must be to get the French up into line with us, and that General Foch and I
were agreed as to our future plans. (I hear from other sources that the Russians
have been reproving M. Poincaré on the small progress made by the French,
and for allowing three divisions of Germans to be withdrawn from France to
Russia!) M. Poincaré thought the whole situation very favourable for the
Allies, but was most anxious, before the approach of winter, that we should
have made some decisive advance in order to keep the people of France and
England from grumbling. I said that we had yet at least 10 weeks of good
weather, probably more, and that I believed much will be done by us in that
time . . .

His Majesty knighted Kiggell, and, before he left, he expressed himself
most satisfied with all he had seen, and with the state of the Army. He said I
had his full confidence as well as that of the Cabinet. He then handed me the
GCVO[2] as a mark of his own personal appreciation. 'That Order had nothing
to do with any of the others,' and he thanked me for what I had done for his
'family'. He had given the same to Jellicoe[3] when he visited the Grand Fleet.

After the King left, I had a talk with Generals Joffre and Foch. I was in full
agreement as to the necessity for attacking on a wide front, say from the
Somme on the right of the French to the Bois de Fourneaux (High Wood)
on my left, so as to prevent the Enemy from placing a barrage which might
stop us if we attacked on a small front. The date for this attack can only be
settled after the result of today's attack by the French is known. I shall be
ready to attack on the 18th. This was agreed to . . .

At about 4.30 pm Mr *Lloyd George[4] arrived by motor from Amiens. He
had been to Paris to ascertain the views of the French Government on the
advisability of coming to terms with the Bulgarians. He said the Czar and all
the Crowned heads were against the proposal, and he asked me my view. 'I

1 Raymond Nicolas Landry Poincaré (1860–1934), President of France, 1913–20.
2 Grand Cross of the Royal Victorian Order: awards within the Royal Victorian Order were in
the personal gift of the sovereign.
3 Admiral of the Fleet Sir John Rushworth Jellicoe (1859–1935), Commander-in-Chief British
Grand Fleet, 1914–16; First Sea Lord, 1916–17; Haig was not an admirer of Jellicoe, dismissing
him as an 'old woman'.
4 Lloyd George was appointed Secretary of State for War in July 1915 in the aftermath of
Kitchener's death.

said beat the Germans as soon as possible is our objective: so I recommended making terms with Bulgaria and bringing in Roumania on our side as soon as possible!"[1]

LG was very pleasant ... He assured me that he had 'no intention of meddling' and that his sole object was to help.

Monday 14 August

After lunch I visited HQ II Corps at Senlis and saw General Jacob and his SGSO Philip Howell. Jacob was full of confidence and had arranged careful plans for capturing certain parts of trenches tonight, and a larger piece tomorrow and next day when the 48th Division have been able to look round and make a plan.

I impressed two points on Jacob.

1. Not to allow divisions to employ so many men in front line. Use Lewis guns and detachments.
2. Information from divisions frequently reaches HQs of Corps, Armies and GHQ very slowly. Too slowly!

So I desired Jacob to see that intercommunication between subordinate units in a division and Divisional HQ was efficiently kept up. I further pointed out that Staff officers must be able to explain the plans of their General, as well as to see that the actual orders are carried out. I have noticed lately that in many divisions, the Staff does not circulate sufficiently amongst the brigades and battalions when operations are in progress . . .

Sunday 20 August

About 10.30 I saw Colonel Swinton who has come from England about the 'Tanks'. 12 are now on the sea: – delay has been due to Enemy's submarines holding up our traffic to Havre recently. We may expect two companies (50) by 5th September.

Foch and I came to the agreement that our next combined offensive should take place on the 24th. The attack following should come off *about* the 26th. The objective of the Sixth French Army will then be to advance as far as possible against the Enemy's defences between the Somme and the Combles ravine. We are to fix the exact date on the 25th after the results of our attacks on the 24th are known . . .

1 Romania entered the war on 27 August 1916.

I saw General Horne. I told him that the Cabinet had approved of his appointment to command First Army, but in my opinion it was in the interest of the operations that he should continue to command the XV Corps until a decision in this battle had been reached. He quite agreed and said he would prefer to finish this fight as Corps Commander, but was ready to do whatever I judged the best.

Sunday 20 August. Letter to King George V[1]

The XX French Corps has been relieved on our right. They had been in the line so long that the men had lost most of their dash. The result of this was that on Friday, the French between our right and the Somme accomplished nothing, although *The Times* says they did wonders. Indeed poor Foch came in for a reprimand from Joffre, and General de Castelnau also visited him to urge him to make progress. But the fault lay with the troops and not Foch. I thought the latter was having a baddish time so I wrote and asked him to lunch. He came today and seemed grateful for my little attention. The French troops on our right are now fresh, and Foch expects great things of them when next we advance to attack.

Monday 21 August

I visited Reserve Army in afternoon and saw General Gough. I understand that French intend to attack *vigorously* on 27th or 30th and go as far as possible. We ought also to be ready for any eventuality and therefore the Cavalry Divisions should be brought up to within a day's march by the 29th.

Tuesday 22 August

A return compiled by my Intelligence Branch shows that whereas a German Division is worn out in $4\frac{1}{2}$ days opposite the British, opposite the French they last very much longer, sometimes 3 weeks! This clearly shows how regular and persistent is the pressure by the British.

The total number of German Divisions engaged on the Somme front amounts to 42, and possibly 45 because it is thought that 3 more are in process of being relieved.

Since 30 July 12 divisions have been exhausted on north of the Somme; of them the British have dealt with 9. The French 3.

1 RA: PS/GV/Q 832/124.

I visited Sir H. Rawlinson after lunch. He explained why he thought the 24th Division had failed at Guillemont, and stated that on the 24th he wished to attack with the XV Corps north of Delville Wood ... Between that attack and Guillemont he proposed to advance with a brigade to the Ginchy–Guillemont road and take also the north edge of Guillemont.

The latter village would be kept under fire but would not be attacked, but on the south of the place our line would be advanced from Angle Wood on the south along the road which runs north-north-west from Angle Wood to Guillemont. Our left flank would be turned back westwards under the crest of the ridge to our old (present) line. Rawlinson also said that he proposed, if all went well to then, advance (on the 24th) to attack Falfémont Farm and the Enemy's line to the north as far as the crest immediately south of Guillemont.

I disapproved of this last part of his plan because the whole advance would be under the Enemy's machine gun fire from the Guillemont Ridge. Numerous shell holes afforded excellent cover for his machine guns. In fact I thought the scheme doomed to failure.

Wednesday 23 August

Joffre has ordered the Tenth Army to attack south of the Somme in the first week September or thereabouts. He wishes the British to put in a big attack then instead of waiting till the middle of September. I said that I would do what was possible to meet General Joffre's wishes, but I could not attack northwards until I had established my flank eastwards of Ginchy in conjunction with the French. Thiepval, I expected, would be taken by the Reserve Army about 1 September.

I did not much like Rawlinson's scheme for attack by one brigade of 20th Division tomorrow between Ginchy and Guillemont. From our present line the length of advance is 650 yards, and the troops have to attack outwards to a salient ... a new trench ... is to be dug tonight as a starting trench. General Kiggell went by my orders to Fourth Army HQ and explained my views ... that unless the necessary starting trench had been finished, this part of his attack for tomorrow must be modified ...

General Trenchard reported on work of Flying Corps. Owing to clouds Enemy's aircraft have had an easier time so are showing more activity, but the first fine day, Trenchard is confident that they will be knocked out again. Today numbers of hostile airoplanes were engaged with most satisfactory results. Fighting was continuous to dark. We suffered no casualties, though Enemy in several cases was pursued back to his airodrome.

Thursday 24 August

Sir Eric Geddes,[1] for the last 7 months in Munitions Branch, and before that Manager of N.E. Railway, arrived from England. He is sent out by Mr Lloyd George to assist over the question of communications. A most pleasant and capable man. He is afraid that the Inspector General of Communications (General Clayton) resents his visit! I said that I am glad to have practical hints from anyone capable of advising!

Friday 25 August

After I left Foch's HQ I was handed a letter from General Joffre in which, after expatiating on what the French Army had done at Verdun and on the Somme etc., I was asked to attack in force on 6th September at latest ... I presume that Joffre has pledged himself to this owing to pressure from Russia, but before fixing the date, he should have ascertained what the British Army can do!

After talking to Kiggell I decided to enlarge the scope of our operations on the 30th by attacking with the Reserve Army against Thiepval and astride the Ancre, and to follow up any success gained. Allowing for hard fighting and the time required to bring up fresh divisions, it will be the 15th September before we can organise another attack on a large scale ...

Sir George Arthur stayed the night. He is writing Lord Kitchener's life. He stated that Winston Churchill is allowed to go in and out of War Office at will. This, he thinks, is very wrong as Churchill is openly very hostile to me, and the [Headquarters Staff of the] Army in France.

Saturday 26 August

At 3 pm I was present at a demonstration in the use of 'Tanks'. A battalion of infantry and 5 Tanks operated together. Three lines of trenches were assaulted. The Tanks crossed the several lines with the greatest ease, and one entered a wood, which represented a 'strong point' and easily walked over fair sized trees of 6 inches through! Altogether the demonstration was quite encouraging, but we require to clear our ideas as to the tactical handling of these machines. Officers and men had been working for the last 24 hours

1 Eric (later Sir Eric) Campbell Geddes (1875–1937). Geddes was appointed General Manager of the London North Eastern Railway in 1914 (aged only thirty-nine). In 1916 he was brought in to sort out the BEF's chaotic logistics, effecting dramatic improvements. Haig was originally dubious about his appointment, but soon came to appreciate Geddes' abilities. Geddes became First Lord of the Admiralty in 1917.

without a break to get their Tanks together. I complimented them on their good work, and self denial.

Sunday 27 August

Haig attended a conference held on President Poincaré's train.

A memorandum had been prepared dealing with the strengths in men, guns etc. of each of the Allies, and of each of enemy countries ... Our object was to be as strong as possible by next spring.

M. Poincaré mentioned that the Pope had stated that the Enemy would be forced to ask for an armistice by October. He should advise that the reply should be the same as that given by the Romans. 'No talk of peace so long as one enemy remained on the soil of the Republic.' ...

We lunched about 12.30 and continued the discussion afterwards. I sat at a little table opposite General Joffre. He mentioned that he had that moment received my reply to his letter requesting me to attack on the 6th. He would like to talk the matter over with me. We fixed next Friday 1st September, and he is to lunch with me. I mentioned that we could not attack before the 15th September. He replied 'C'est trop tard! C'est la mort.' But could give me no reason! ...

Afterwards at the Conference General Foch explained to M. Poincaré the scope of his next operations. I followed and stated that on the 30th I would attack in co-operation with Foch with 10 divisions. That after that a fortnight would be required in which to prepare for another big attack which I hoped to make with 14 divisions. I had every hope of success then, but was anxious that ample French reserves should be available to exploit our success. Both Poincaré and Briand said that was most important. Joffre insisted on an earlier date for my attack, but I pointed out the time required for

(a) Fighting after attack of 30th
(b) Relief of tired divisions by fresh ones
(c) Time for the fresh divisions to get acquainted with the ground
(d) Time for placing heavy and other artillery to deal with the new objectives.

The President said that the attack should not be later than 15 September on account of the Equinox, when the weather breaks on 25 September, and is usually bad for some weeks. I said I would do my best to arrange for our attack not to be later than the 15th.

Monday 28 August

Commandant Gemeau informed me that the reason French GQG was urging me to attack in force soon, was that reports from Russia showed that Germany was trying to bribe her to make separate peace by offering her more than she can get from the Entente! Also, that Russia would not attack until the French had done something!

Personally, I don't think Russia could leave the Allies now. Things have developed too far. [Allied officers are employed in all branches of her Services and are helping at her base ports, on the railways, etc. etc.]

Tuesday 29 August

The Australians are to attack the trenches about Le Mouquet Farm tonight. Gough thinks the Commanders of the Australians are becoming less offensive in spirit! The men are all right...

I studied Rawlinson's proposals for the September attack and for the use of the 'Tanks'. In my opinion he is not making enough of the situation and the deterioration of the Enemy's troops. I think we should make our attack as strong and as violent as possible, and go as far as possible.[1]

Saturday 2 September

Between 1 July and 31 August 30 German Divisions have been engaged on the British front and a total of 46 divisions by the French and British together (= 457 battalions). Some divisions have been engaged twice but have not been counted twice.

General Birdwood and the CGS of Australian Corps (General White) came to lunch. The latter is a sound capable soldier: Birdwood is useful too, though [at present] he is not much use for directing *operations*. His taste lies in making speeches to the Australian rank and file and so keeps them contented. He is wonderfully popular with them, but seems rather to do work which his subordinate generals should perform. I told Birdwood how satisfied I was with what the Australians had done, and though they were now going to Ypres, I had no intention of leaving them there all winter. The Canadians under General Byng replace the Australians. He takes over from Birdwood on Monday.

1 Once again, Haig and Rawlinson had fundamentally different ideas about the forthcoming battle.

Sunday 3 September

A combined British–French attack commenced.

XIV Corps with parts of 5th, 16th and 20th Divisions took Wedge Wood, the whole of Guillemont village, and ground eastwards to the hollow road south of Ginchy. XV Corps attacked Ginchy with part of 7th Division. Village was captured, enemy counter-attacked, and fighting was still going on in village up to 10 pm.

III Corps attacked High Wood ... with 1st Division: at first most successfully, and our men followed up Enemy on east over the ridge. Germans then counter-attacked but our guns could not turn on Enemy in open as they and our men were mingled together. So our troops were forced back to their original trenches near the wood ... At 10 pm I ordered Fourth Army to put in reserves to make sure of our hold on Ginchy and join up with French towards Bois de Louage. If possible, Ginchy Telegraph should be captured ...

Monday 4 September

General Trenchard reported on Flying Corps ... Trenchard is quite satisfied that we can hold our position of superiority in the air till next spring, but he is anxious lest the Germans bring out by then some new type of swift machine thanks to their better engines.[1] He has for long urged our Authorities at home to concentrate their efforts on our best type of engine, the Rolls Royce. Apparently only 300 of these are on order – while there are 3000 of an inferior Factory Experimental type also being produced, which will be of little use to us![2] ...

Later I visited Toutencourt and saw General Gough. The failure to hold the positions gained on the Ancre is due to the 49th Division (Percival).[3] The units did not really attack, and some men did not follow their officers. The total losses of this division are under a thousand! It is a Territorial division from the West Riding of Yorkshire. I had occasion a fortnight ago to call the attention of the Army and Corps Commanders (Gough and Jacob) to the slackness of one of its battalions in the matter of saluting when I was motoring through the village where it was billeted. I expressed my opinion that such men were too sleepy to fight well, etc.! It was due to the failure of the 49th

1 In reality, from mid-September German aircraft began to challenge the Allies' control of the skies.
2 This is a good example of the way that Haig would come to trust the judgement of an expert within a specialised field, of which he himself had little knowledge.
3 Properly Perceval.

Division that the 39th (which did well, and got all their objectives) had to fall back.

Tuesday 5 September

I also saw General Byng commanding Canadian Corps at Contay about 5 pm. His Corps is now called the 'Bing Boys' and various comic posters are put about – 'The Bing Boys are here' etc. etc.¹ I told him that in view of our main effort being about to be made towards Flers–Le Boeufs, I wished him to economise his men so as to be fresh when an opportunity offered to exploit our success. I told Gough this yesterday.

Wednesday 6 September

Lord *Derby left about 10 am on his return to England. He was anxious as to how I would find the Prime Minister. From several things, Derby is afraid Asquith would be willing to discuss peace in November or December, if Germany were to offer to give up Alsace, Lorraine, etc. . . .

Mr Asquith and I had a long talk after dinner. He said he and the Government are well pleased with the way the operations have been conducted here, and he is anxious to help me in every way possible.

Thursday 7 September

Mr Montagu, Minister of Munitions,² came to see me . . . I thought him a capable and agreeable man. He seemed to understand his job though he has only recently taken it over, and he is full of determination to help the Army as much as he possibly can. He is to come back and see me later when he is less busy. [He is apparently a Jew.]

Mr Asquith came to dinner. He sat on my right and was most pleasant. At 9.30 I went to deal with the evening reports and left him sitting at table. About an hour later he came to see me and thanked me for all my kindness and he said what a change for the better he found everywhere. A very great improvement all round, he said, and I have to thank you for it. [I found no grounds for the fears which Derby expressed to me (see 6 September).]

1 *The Bing Boys are Here* was a popular musical playing in London.
2 Edwin Samuel Montagu (1879–1924) succeeded Lloyd George as Minister of Munitions in June 1916, retaining the post until his resignation in December 1916.

Friday 8 September. Letter to Lady Haig

You would have been amused at the Prime Minister last night. He did himself fairly well – not more than most gentlemen used to drink when I was a boy, but in this abstemious age it is noticeable if an extra glass or two is taken by anyone! The PM seemed to like our old brandy. He had a couple of glasses (big sherry glass size!) before I left the table at 9.30, and apparently he had several more before I saw him again. By that time his legs were unsteady, but his head was quite clear, and he was able to read a map and discuss the situation with me. Indeed he was most charming and quite alert in mind.

Friday 8 September

I visited HQ Fourth Army at Querrieu at 3 pm and met General Foch. He explained that owing to the German 3rd line being so strong it was necessary to prepare the attack on it most thoroughly. The attack could therefore not take place as arranged, but on the 11th or 12th. (He arranged to continue his attacks along with ours on the 9th.) I said that the important date was the 15th, and I wished my troops to reach suitable positions from which to start that attack as soon as possible; I therefore could not postpone our attack on Ginchy, etc., which would take place tomorrow. He was quite apologetic and said he would give us as strong artillery support as possible especially on the hostile artillery. In reply to my question, he also said that he would have ample fresh troops to exploit any success we might gain on 15th.

After Foch had gone I discussed with Rawlinson his attack on the 9th and 15th. On the latter date I wish him to capture and hold the houses at the south end of Martinpuich. While Gough will go for the 'Sucrerie'. This was necessary to attract the Enemy's attention, and prevent him from con-centrating artillery fire on the right of our attack where the majority of the 'Tanks' will be. For this attack he must arrange to detail an extra brigade without interfering with the division per corps which he is keeping in reserve.

Saturday 9 September

General Kavanagh,[1] whom I have appointed (temporarily) to command the Cavalry Corps came to see me and stayed to lunch. I explained that the Enemy seemed to have exhausted his reserves, and that I thought that after the next attack the crisis of the battle is likely to be reached, and the moment

---

1 Lieutenant General (later Sir) Charles Toler McMurrough Kavanagh ('Black Jack') (1864–1950), GOC Cavalry Corps, 1916–19. Kavanagh was described by J. F. C. Fuller as 'probably the worst cavalry general in history'. Given Haig's belief in the continuing importance of cavalry, Kavanagh's retention in command, despite repeated failures, is surprising.

might possibly be favourable for cavalry action. Circumstances seemed to require the cavalry to operate, to start with, in three main groups. *Everyone must put forth the greatest effort and be ready to suffer privation for several days in order to reap the fruits of victory* . . .

I spoke to QMG re. the supply of troops in the event of a pursuit. The difficulty is due to the broken state of the ground and roads from shell fire . . .

Admiral Bacon's Flag Lieutenant arrived with a letter from the Admiral who is at Dunkirk, saying that by tonight he will have all [available] small boats across the Channel in Dunkirk. So [an infantry brigade with guns and transport] is ordered by me to Dunkirk with a view to embarkation for an attack (supposed) on Ostend. [By the rumour of this operation, we hope to make the enemy strengthen his garrisons on the coast.]

Thursday 14 September

It is interesting to see how the French have kept on delaying their attacks! Their big attack south of the Somme which was to have gone in on the 3rd has not yet been launched, and will probably not go in till the 15th. While the attacks of the 6th Army which were to have gone in with such vigour at the beginning of the month have not yet materialised!

The fact is that the French infantry is very poor now and lacks the offensive spirit. On the other hand such progress as the French have made has been achieved against a much smaller concentration of artillery [than the Enemy has collected against the British,] and judging by a comparison of the German prisoners working on the roads, those taken by the French are very much inferior in physique . . .

Friday 15 September

The Battle of Flers–Courcelette was the BEF's largest-scale operation since 1 July. It marked the debut of the tank and, once again, Haig hoped to break though the German defences and commence open warfare. Although the offensive made some gains and dealt the Germans a heavy blow, the results of 15 September were a disappointment to Haig.

Attack began at daylight as arranged. From reports received up to 8.30 am 'all three Corps appear to have reached their first objectives' (6.45). One 'Tank' reached northeast corner of Bouleaux Wood and one was seen 500 [yards] west of Flers signalling 'OK' (all correct!).

At 8.40 am three Tanks were seen entering Flers and south end of Flers reached.

10.15 am, 14th Division has apparently got the third objective and a Tank has been seen marching through the 'High Street of Flers, followed by large numbers of infantry cheering'![1]

Certainly some of the Tanks have done marvels! and have enabled our attack to progress at a surprisingly fast pace.

But progress on our right was not satisfactory. The 56th Division got on and formed a defensive flank opposite Combles in Bouleaux Wood etc., but the division on its left, the 6th Division (under Major General Ross)[2] did not take the Quadrilateral and was held up all day. An attack is being prepared to advance against the Quadrilateral from north and south.

As our attacks seem to be held up on the right I went soon after 2 o'clock to Querrieu and impressed on General Rawlinson the necessity for getting forward to Les Boeufs and Gueudecourt tonight if possible. The Guards were within 500 yards of the first place, but said there was a strong line in their front with good wire. On the other hand an airplane (which flew low) reported seeing our men running up a trench from Flers towards Eaucourt l'Abbaye which was lightly held by the Enemy.

I told Rawlinson to send on this message at once to Lord Cavan and Horne, and direct them to send out patrols (if that had not already been done) to probe the situation. [Rawlinson] thought Cavan slow and that he saw too many Germans in his front. His III Corps must also attack Martinpuich at once in order to allow Gough to proceed to capture Courcelette . . .

I also called at HQ Reserve Corps[3] and explained to the Major General General Staff (Malcolm) that Fourth Army were taking Martinpuich as soon as possible. He said Canadians would attack Courcelette at 6.30 pm.

Martinpuich and Courcelette were both taken in the course of the afternoon and evening. At 9 pm Generals Gough and Malcolm, and Pitt Taylor (GSO1 Fourth Army)[4] came to see me. I ordered Gough to:

(1) Extend northwest along ridge to get point of observation above Thiepval. This will prevent Enemy overlooking Courcelette slopes, will open the Bapaume road past Pozières, and will practically cut the communications of Thiepval.

(2) Push out mounted troops towards Grandcourt if possible.

(3) Co-operate with III Corps which will operate towards Le Sars.

The Fourth Army is continuing its advance tomorrow towards Les Boeufs, Gueudecourt etc.

---

1 This incident appeared in the press as 'A tank is walking up the High Street of Flers with the British Army cheering behind'.
2 Major General Charles Ross (1864–1930), GOC 61 Brigade, 1915; GOC 6th Division, 1915–17.
3 Actually, Reserve Army.
4 Lieutenant Colonel (later General Sir) Walter William Pitt-Taylor (1878–1950), GSO1 Fourth Army, 1916–17.

Today the French attacks against Rancourt and Frégicourt failed. I don't think there was much vigour in them. These were made by I and V Corps. The VII Corps is further south. The latter suffered heavily yesterday. It attacked before the I Corps, viz. at 1 pm, while the I Corps did not attack till 5 pm. The former corps was consequently unsupported, and though it gained ground had eventually to withdraw again.

Saturday 16 September

Owing to the disorder and mixing up of units which is inseparable from every fight, and in the case of an inexperienced Army is more difficult to straighten out, the attacks proposed for 9 am today did not take place ...

The attack north of the Somme will be renewed however about the 19th. Time is required to relieve troops and prepare. How different the French talk today, to last week! Then they were making such dispositions in depth that there would be no delay – once the attack started, it would be continuous until the line was pierced. Now the experience of the reality has shown the folly of their previous ideas! A delay of four days is wanted to prepare for the next attack.

Sunday 17 September

After church I presented French decorations to 2 officers in the General Staff here; saw Colonel Swinton, and congratulated him on the success of the 'Tanks' ... I then discussed our future Tank policy, and decided to ask the Home authorities to send us out quickly as many as possible; at the same time, to improve the armour of the present type, and to work out an improved design of a heavier nature (68 ton).

Major Stern[1] (who supervises their manufacture) promises 40 more of present pattern by October 14th and *after 12th November* about 20 per week with turtle top and thickened side plates can be sent us. General Butler goes to England tomorrow to press my views ...

In the afternoon, General Foch came to see me. He explained failure of French attacks on 15th against Frégicourt and Rancourt ...

Then he asked me to leave the others and go into the garden. He then spoke to me of Mr Lloyd George's recent visit to his (Foch's) HQ. Lunch was at 12 noon, and LG said he would bring 2 or 3 with him. He actually arrived at 1.45 and brought 8 persons! After lunch, LG, using Lord Reading as

1 Albert Stern (1878–1966), Chairman of the Tank Committee, 1916; Director of Tank Supply at the Ministry of Munitions from December 1916; he never succeeded in producing tanks in the quantities he or Haig would have liked.

interpreter, had a private talk with Foch. He began by saying that he was a British Minister, and, [as such, he considered] that he had a right to be told the truth! He wished to know why the British who had gained no more [ground] than the French, if as much, had suffered such heavy casualties!

Foch replied that the French infantry had learnt their lesson in 1914, and were now careful in their advances. He often wished that they were not so well instructed!! He would then have advanced further and more quickly. In reply to questions about our artillery, Foch said that the British had done wonders.

LG also asked his opinion as to the ability of the British generals. Foch said 'LG was sufficiently patriotic not to criticise the British Commander-in-Chief' but he did not speak with confidence of the other British generals as a whole! Foch's reply was that he had had no means of forming an opinion.

Unless I had been told of this conversation personally by General Foch, I would not have believed that a British Minister could have been so ungentlemanly as to go to a foreigner and put such questions regarding his own subordinates.

Foch thought Lord Reading was a cunning individual![1]

Monday 18 September

I spoke to Admiral Bacon regarding preparations for landing on Belgian coast. In view of the successes obtained by the 'Tanks', I suggested that he should carry out experiments with special flat bottomed boats for running ashore and landing a line of Tanks on the beach with object of breaking through wire and capturing Enemy's defences. This is to be done in co-operation with troops from Lombartzyde, attacking eastwards.

The Admiral was delighted with the idea, and is to go to Admiralty with a view to having special boats made.

I asked him also to urge the loan of personnel from Navy for manning 100 'Tanks' . . .

Trenchard reported on work of Flying Corps . . . By taking the offensive and carrying the war in the air beyond the Enemy's lines, our artillery airoplanes are free to carry on their important duties of observation and photography unmolested. Our communications too on which so much depends are undisturbed.

Sunday 24 September

In the afternoon I motored to HQ Third Army . . . and saw General Allenby

---

1 Lord (later Marquess of) Reading (1860–1935), Lord Chief Justice of England, 1913–21.

and Bols (his CGS).[1] I directed Allenby to make preparations to attack Gommecourt with the object of holding that place and the ridge running southeast to cover the left of an attack by General Gough eastwards from the 'Sunken Road' through Serre and Puisieux upon Achiet le Grand. Allenby should move on Bucquoy village if things develop satisfactorily.

The enemy has no reserves now, so the situation is different as to what it was at the beginning of the battle. Now Corps must move boldly forward against the Enemy's communications, and run risks. For this operation [Allenby] would have 3 divisions, and if necessary a 4th; and 12 to 25 (a company) of Tanks. My intention is (if the attack comes off) to make it by surprise with a line of 50 or 60 Tanks and no artillery bombardment.[2]

I then went to HQ Reserve Army at Toutencourt and urged the importance of taking the Beaumont Hamel valley as soon as possible after the Thiepval ridge is taken. Guns to be pushed up at once to enfilade the valley.

Monday 25 September

The Battle of Morval began. By concentrating sufficient force on limited objectives, the attack achieved considerable success.

The XIV Corps (Cavan) attacked Morval and Les Boeufs in 3 stages and gained all objectives. The 5th and 6th Divisions took Morval and the Guards Les Boeufs. Casualties reported by divisions to be 'slight'. By 5 pm we had detachments 500 yards to the east of these places, and also on the south of Morval to cut off the communications with Combles which lies in a deep valley.

The XV Corps (Horne) advanced against village of Gueudecourt and road southeast of it (towards Les Boeufs). The 21st Division got first objectives, but was held up by some trenches on its right and did not get into Gueudecourt until nightfall. The 55th and New Zealand Divisions attacked on the west of Gueudecourt and got objectives up to Factory Corner.

The III Corps advanced with 1st and 50th Divisions on the left of the NZ and gained objectives to north of Martinpuich. The 23rd Division from the latter village to the Bapaume–Pozières main road, did not get on.

1 Major General (later Lieutenant General) Louis Jean Bols (1867–1930), son of a Belgian diplomat; MGGS Third Army, 1915–17. Bols was effectively downgraded during the Battle of Arras and became GOC 24th Division, but his old chief Allenby secured his services again as Chief of Staff in the Egyptian Expeditionary Forces, where they formed an ideal partnership.
2 Against this paragraph in the Ms diary, Haig noted 'please do not copy'. This is presumably an instruction to Lady Haig not to put it into the versions of the diaries that she sent to the King. Haig presumably did not want to heighten expectations. This passage does, however, appear in the Ts diary.

The total front of attack was about six miles, and in several places we advanced over a mile in depth. Morval stands high and is strongly fortified . . .

Tuesday 26 September

Thiepval, an objective of 1 July, was captured by Maxse's 18th Division in a carefully planned attack.

The battle was continued on the Fourth Army front and at 12.30 the Reserve Army began an attack on Thiepval ridge by parts of 4 divisions. Our troops were everywhere successful . . .

The whole Thiepval ridge was very strongly fortified, and was defended with desperation . . .

Lord Cavan Commanding XIV Corps (whom I visited at Méaulte this afternoon) told me that the Enemy only put up a good fight on the first line which was attacked. After that was taken: they held up their hands and surrendered on the advance of our troops to the succeeding lines. The losses were comparatively small in consequence. The Guards had only 800 to 900 losses . . .

General Horne reported that General John Du Cane who had been living at XV Corps HQ for a fortnight was quite fit to take over command of the Corps now. Horne thought the moment favourable for handing over, so, on return home, I told CGS to arrange it.

Southeast of Gueudecourt today Enemy counter-attacked in force – over 100 guns were turned on him and he literally ran away, throwing down his arms. We now have the observation which makes so much difference to the success of our operations.

Wednesday 27 September

The AG came to report this morning. The total casualties for the last two days' heavy fighting are just 8000. This is very remarkable, and seems to bear out the idea that the Enemy is not fighting so well, and has suffered in moral. We have had 14 divisions engaged and the front of attack was altogether 23,000 yards . . .

Number of German Guns About twice the normal number of guns per division seem now to be allotted to divisional sectors.

Thursday 28 September

General Foch came to see me at 2.30 pm . . . He is prepared to continue the battle into November or until the bad weather stops all chance of attacking.

On 29 September Haig issued ambitious orders for future operations. However, strong German defences and bad weather helped to ensure that the British advance was piecemeal, with ground taken at heavy cost.

Saturday 30 September

Our position is difficult from artillery point of view, as our troops are on the forward ridge of the slope, time is required to bring guns forward to new positions from which to deal with hostile artillery, and further, concealed positions for guns are difficult to find on forward slope![1] When Le Sars is taken, situation will become better.

General Kavanagh (Commanding Cavalry Corps) and his CGS (Home)[2] came to lunch. Afterwards with General Kiggell I discussed disposition of Cavalry Corps for October attack.[3] I pointed out that the attack on north side of Ancre might take Enemy by surprise and at any rate it turns the lines of trenches which he is now making to envelop our left on the Ancre...

As regards the direction of the pursuit, if the Enemy breaks, I told him that I would aim at getting the Enemy into a trap with the marshes to the east of Arras (about Hamel) on his north side and the Canal du Nord on the east of him. The latter is a broad new canal running in deep cuttings in places 150 feet deep.

With the object of carrying out this manoeuvre, I hope to arrange for Allenby to attack on the south side of Arras and capture Monchy le Preux ridge.[4] On the south side Rawlinson (if the Enemy breaks) would press on and occupy the ridge near Beaumetz. Kavanagh must think over the best dispositions for his Cavalry Corps under the conditions arising which I outlined...

General Allenby (Commanding Third Army) came to see me later in the afternoon. His first objective is as stated by me to him on Sunday 24 September, namely, to cover the left flank of Gough's attack. We ... discussed details of his attack on the Gommecourt Ridge, so as to ensure that his arrangements and those of Gough (Reserve Army) are in conformity. Bombardment should commence now and be carried out methodically at different hours by day and night, cut wire, keep gaps open etc. Attack will then come

1 Correct employment of artillery was the key to success on the Western Front. Haig rightly identified a major problem with gunnery at this stage of the Somme.
2 Brigadier General (later Sir) Alexander Fraser ('Sally') Home (1874–1953), BGGS Cavalry Corps, 1915–16, and 1916–19.
3 In the Ms diary, the following section on future military plans is marked, in Haig's hand, 'please do not copy this part'.
4 Moreover, Haig ordered First Army to prepare to attack Vimy Ridge, which was also in the Arras sector.

as a surprise and will be preceded by a line of Tanks; only a barrage at zero hour, no preliminary bombardment . . .

Monday 2 October

After lunch I motored to Contay (HQ Canadians) and saw General Byng. He was disappointed that the Canadians had failed to hold the trench which they gained yesterday, and also to occupy another piece of trench which they attacked. I think the cause was that in the hope of saving lives they attacked in too weak numbers. They encountered a brigade of the German Marine Corps recently arrived from Ostend, and had not the numbers to overcome them in a hand-to-hand struggle.

They (the Canadians) have been very extravagant in expending ammunition! This points rather to nervousness and low moral in those companies which are frequently calling for a 'barrage' without good cause.

Byng hopes for good results when his 4th Division arrives. The 1st, 2nd and 3rd Canadian Divisions have suffered heavily, and no sufficient drafts have yet joined them. Sir Sam Hughes[1] wants the glory of having a Canadian *Army* in the field, and is forming a 5th division with the reinforcements . . .

Casualties since 25 September (estimated, the actual casualties are usually less):

Officers	Other Ranks	Total
552	18,473	19,025

This must be considered small judging by the results gained, the number of divisions engaged and the wide area over which fighting is now taking place.

Thursday 5 October. Letter to King George V[2]

Haig reflected on operations since 15 September.

I venture to think that the results are highly satisfactory, and I believe the Army in France feels the same as I do in this matter. The troops see that they are slowly but surely destroying the German Armies in their front, and that their enemy is much less capable of defence than he was even a few weeks ago. Indeed there have been instances in which the enemy on a fairly wide

1 Sir Sam Hughes (1853–1921), Canadian Minister of Militia and Defence, 1911–16; his manic energy was instrumental in raising and training the Canadian Expeditionary Force, but also made him an increasingly querulous and difficult colleague.
2 RA: PS/GV/Q 832/126.

front (1400 yards) has abandoned his trench the moment our infantry appeared!

On the other hand our divisions seem to have become almost twice as efficient as they were before going into the battle, notwithstanding the drafts which they have received. Once a division has been engaged, all ranks quickly get to know what fighting really means, the necessity for keeping close to our barrage to escape loss and ensure success, and many other important details which can only be really appreciated by troops under fire! The men too having beaten the Germans once gain confidence in themselves and feel no shadow of doubt that they can go on beating him.

Reinforcements have been coming in satisfactorily, and as regards ammunition, with the exception of 18 pounder, the provision keeps well abreast of the expenditure. I am still a little anxious however about the 18 pounder. It has again become most popular with divisions for barrages, and the expenditure is quite surprising. I therefore have to keep a close watch on this class of ammunition.

The recent wet weather has been very hard on the roads. To relieve pressure on them, we have been hurrying on the construction of railways (both normal and narrow gauge) in rear of the battle front. We already have 2 60C.[1] (illegible) up to Pozières cemetery from Albert, and a third line is running up the valley to Mouquet Farm. The broad gauge branch line from Dérnancourt reached Trones Wood yesterday. This is most important because this railway has to serve both ourselves and the French on the Morval front . . .

M. Poincaré came to see me here last Monday morning. He was most complimentary at what the British Army had achieved, and seemed very pleased with the general situation, but somewhat sad that General Foch's troops were so far behind my right, and unable to make full use of the large reserves which are available (owing to having to pass the defile forward of the hills north of Combles which the Enemy now commands).

He asked my views about continuing the fight. I pointed out that we had already broken through all the Enemy's prepared lines and that now only extemporised defences stood between us and the Bapaume ridge: moreover the Enemy had suffered much in men, in material, and in *moral*. If we rested even for a month, the Enemy would be able to strengthen his defences, to recover his equilibrium, to make good deficiencies, and, worse still, would regain the initiative! The longer we rested, the more difficult would our problem again become, so in my opinion we must continue to press the enemy to the utmost of our power. The President quite agreed, and assured me that the French Army would continue to act with energy.

1 60 centimetre (gauge).

The New Zealand Division came out of the line 2 days ago. They have been in over 3 weeks and have done extremely well. I sent a message through the War Office to the NZ Government to let them know of the grand service their division has rendered.

I had to send home General Barter (Commander 47th London Division) on Pulteney's recommendation.[1] He mishandled his division so on the 15th and 16th at High Wood. Two brigades were actually sent into the wood, when 2 battalions would have sufficed to engage the Enemy in it, while the others might have pushed on to the next objective.[2] General Gorringe is now in command of this division, and should I think do well.[3]

Saturday 7 October

Later in the day, I learnt from Lord Derby that Field Marshal *French is visiting Joffre at the instigation of the Secretary of State for War,[4] for the purposes of reporting on the French artillery and French tactics!! How unnecessarily difficult these authorities of ours at home seem to make things for one, struggling to do one's best against the Enemy. If Lloyd George wishes to know about French guns, tactics etc., he should ask me. But he has already got my reasoned opinion on the matter of guns, and doubtless wants another opinion differing from mine.

But the mystery of French's visit is still further heightened by Colonel Cavendish[5] from Chantilly saying that Sir William Robertson spoke to him of the visit, and French's instructions, when he was in France 2 weeks ago. But Robertson never said a word to me or to any of my Staff on the subject! And yet he tells me that he is 'wholeheartedly anxious to help' me in my difficult task! French's visit to Joffre at this time can do no good to anyone, but only tend to make discord. Personally, I feel I have done the right thing in sending an invitation to visit the battle front, and I have no intention of allowing the tactlessness of the War Office authorities to interfere with my peace of mind. Luckily, matters are going well with the British Army here;

1 Major General (later Lieutenant General Sir) Charles St Leger Barter (1856–1931), GOC 47th Division, 1914–16.
2 In fact, Barter seems to have been scapegoated by Pulteney. See Terry Norman, *The Hell They Called High Wood: The Somme, 1916* (London: William Kimber, 1984), pp. 235–6. Barter's plan, which was rejected by III Corps' staff, was actually sounder than the one he was compelled to execute.
3 Major General (later Lieutenant General) Sir George Frederick Gorringe ('Blood Orange') (1868–1945), GOC 47th Division, 1916–19.
4 Lloyd George.
5 Lieutenant Colonel (later Brigadier General) Frederick William Lawrence Sheppard Hart ('Caviare') Cavendish (1877–1931), British Liaison Officer at French GQG.

the French HQ Staff have volunteered the opinion to an outsider that 'the British Army has nothing to learn from *them*', and our heavy artillery (being modern) is very much better than what the French have. I can imagine the 'esprit moqueur'[1] of these gentlemen when the dismissed Field Marshal arrives amongst them. How few people are able to retire from a big position gracefully! But French is very thick skinned, and will probably not realise the humiliating position which he now occupies [in French opinion]. As far as I am concerned, he will be received with every mark of respect due to a British Field Marshal ...

... I am considering the reorganisation of our rearward services in view of the possibility of an advance, and the extension of our lines of communication. At 12 o'clock I had a meeting with Generals Kiggell, Butler and Sir Eric Geddes on this subject and decided on the general lines of the change which will be introduced gradually. Geddes will be 'Inspector General of Transportation', with 5 directors under him, viz. –

1) Broad Gauge Railway
2) Narrow Gauge Railway
3) Inland Water Transport
4) Roads
5) Ports.

After lunch I visited HQ Fourth Army and saw Rawlinson. The attack started at 1.45 pm and had done well. Le Sars village had been taken. The French had also done well, and had got near to Sailly Saillisel. General Fayolle had copied our system of artillery barrages, viz. one 'fixed' and one 'creeping', all carefully time-tabled.[2] It is interesting to see that the French have taken a leaf out of our tactical book!

Sunday 8 October

... Gough ... was of opinion that the Canadians (3rd Division) had not done well. In some parts they had not left their trenches for the attack yesterday. The Canadian 1st Division, which had attacked northwest of Le Sars and gained some trenches, had been driven out again.

I discussed with Gough the necessity for putting on a barrage after the

---

1 Spirit of mockery.
2 A barrage literally means a barrier. A creeping barrage was a curtain of shells that moved forward at a prescribed speed ahead of the infantry. The development of artillery tactics was a major factor in the BEF's improved performance in combat: see G. Sheffield, *Forgotten Victory: The First World War – Myths and Realities* (London: Headline, 2001), pp. 106–8.

capture of a trench, where the real objective lies a considerable distance further on. By putting on this barrage, the further advance of patrols and attacking line is checked. In view of the deterioration of the Enemy's fighting qualities, I thought that the barrage was not required then, but that reserves should advance as fast as possible to the next objective. Gough quite agreed.

I also advocated holding back from the fight the best of the drill sergeants in a battalion because they cannot be replaced now.

Gough told me how Philip Howell (Brigadier General General Staff in V Corps) had been killed instantaneously by a splinter of a shell which struck him in the back when walking through Authuille village. He was a fine capable officer of progressive ideas and is a terrible loss to the Army at this time.

Tuesday 10 October

I sent my senior ADC (Lieutenant Colonel Fletcher) to meet Field Marshal French at Boulogne today, to see that the Guard of Honour and other arrangements for his arrival were satisfactory, and to say that if the Field Marshal desired to see the work of the British Army arrangements would be made for him to do so. Fletcher was told by me privately that I would not receive Viscount French *in my house.* I despise him too much personally for that, but he would receive every attention due to a British Field Marshal. French was very pleased at being received with a Guard of Honour, and at my sending an ADC. He told Fletcher that he had *received orders from the Secretary of State for War to report* on certain matters in the French Army, and he did not expect to be able to visit the British area.

This employment of Field Marshal French on a mission [to General Joffre's HQ nominally regarding French guns by the Secretary of State] coupled with the desire which he (Lloyd George) expressed of sending Robertson to Russia for two months, seems to indicate a definite desire to have a puppet like French in the War Office as CIGS instead of Robertson. How it will all end is difficult to foresee, but meantime I gather that Robertson has a difficult task as CIGS.

Thursday 12 October

After lunch I had a long talk with Foch ... Foch is pleased with his success on south of Somme 2 days ago ... Foch is prepared to continue to press the enemy on north of the river in co-operation with the British. He spoke to Joffre about our taking over the front next the coast with a view to preparing for a landing in co-operation with the fleet on the Belgian coast. I gathered that Joffre is not willing to allow us to come next to the Belgians, and said he could not tell what the situation might be next spring!

Saturday 14 October

In afternoon I motored to HQ XIV Corps at Méaulte and saw Lord Cavan. His attack on the 12th was not altogether a success, because

1) *Surprise was lacking.* To please the French we have recently invariably attacked between 12 and 3 pm, so Enemy is ready for us!
2) *Observation* has been bad owing to cloudy weather. Airoplanes have therefore not been able to render the great help they have on previous occasions.
3) *Enemy fought better.* He has had time to recover since previous attack. Our advance has been delayed by wet and so Enemy has been given time.
4) *Enemy used machine guns at distant ranges* at 500 to 800 yards in rear of their front line (a) to obviate this it is proposed to put 'creeping barrage' *behind* and *not* in front of the first objective. The 'fixed' barrage will be on it as usual. (b) Smoke shells to block the view will also be valuable.

In view of above our line of departure is being straightened out, and departure trenches carefully made ...

General Sir J. Cowans,[1] QMG arrived from England this evening. We had a talk after dinner. Lloyd George has imported an element of distrust into the War Office so that one wants 'eyes in the back of one's head' now in that building.

As regards my proposal for reorganising the 'rearward services', Cowans said that the Army Council only wanted to know what my wishes were in order to assist me to the best of their power. He also thinks that Lloyd George wishes to put civilians into the military machine wherever he possibly can to replace soldiers. This is especially the case in the QMG's Branch.

Monday 16 October

Major General Maxse Commanding 18th Division came to lunch. He had heard from his brother [Leo] (Editor of the *National Review*) that Sir F. E. Smith[2] and others have banded themselves together with the object of having

---

1 Lieutenant General Sir John Steven Cowans (1862–1921), Quartermaster General of the British Army throughout the First World War.
2 Sir Frederick Edwin Smith (later Earl of Birkenhead) (1872–1930), Attorney General of England, 1915–19. Smith was a leading supporter of Lloyd George and of the Lloyd George Coalition Government formed in December 1916.

me removed from the Command of the Armies in France. General Maxse wished to know whether I thought he ought to urge his brother to take action in the matter. I saw him along with General Kiggell and I said that I had no dealings with the Press personally. That my policy had always been to give the Press as free a hand as possible. To show them everything, to allow them to talk to anyone they chose, and to write what they liked, provided no secrets were given away to the Enemy. In the present case, I saw no reason to depart from this policy. If his brother chose to come to France and go round the Army and see whether F. E. Smith's statements were true or false he was free to do so in the ordinary way. I at any rate could take no part in a Press campaign against anyone. All my time was taken up in thinking out how to beat the enemy of Great Britain [– I mean Germans].

Colonel Lee and Mr Murdoch (an Australian)[1] arrived from England and stayed the night. The latter is helping Mr Hughes, Premier of Australia, to carry through his proposals for Universal Service in that country. The Secretary of State for War had sent them to see me and get me to help by sending a telegram to Mr Hughes urging the importance of keeping the Australian Divisions up to full strength.

Unless Universal Service is passed the divisions in this country will fall much below strength. Only 3000 men per month are likely to be sent out to France. I sent a message as requested.

I was also asked to allow the Australian Divisions to pass a resolution in favour of Universal Service: at present it is thought that opinion is divided on the question. I replied that I will do everything possible to help Mr Hughes and Australia. That in view of the maintenance of discipline, political meetings at which officers or men addressed their comrades could not be allowed. On the other hand, I saw no objection to civilians going round and expressing Mr Hughes' views (or any other Australian views) and getting opinions expressed in a resolution.[2] Murdoch was quite satisfied and leaves for Paris to see General Joffre, M. Briand etc. tomorrow morning.

Fourth Army launched an attack on the Transloy Ridges in poor weather that hampered artillery observation. Like previous efforts, on 7 and 12 October, the troops made only modest gains at a heavy cost.

1 Keith Arthur Murdoch (1885–1952), Australian journalist and father of media tycoon Rupert Murdoch.
2 In the referendum of 28 October 1916, Australians narrowly rejected conscription. A small majority of troops in France voted in favour.

Wednesday 18 October. Letter to King George V[1]

Since I last wrote, the weather has been unfavourable, and so little has really been done. The Fourth Army attacked in places this morning at 3.45 am to straighten up their line with a view to getting into a more suitable position for a more serious effort later on ... the ground was very slippery and unfavourable for the advance of infantry. However, the majority of the objectives for this morning's attack were at no great distance, and about 60 per cent of them were taken. In many places the enemy is reported as running away as soon as our infantry were seen advancing!

The French too have got on a little on our right but they have not yet taken the whole of the village of Sailly Saillisel. It is very important that they should occupy the whole of that place, because the enemy's next line of trenches is on the far slope beyond the village (i.e. east and northeast of it) and can only be observed from it.

I went over to Villers Bretonneux to see General Foch yesterday. I heard that he was being unfavourably criticised for his operations on our right ... There is no doubt that the French have not really exerted themselves on the north of the Somme: but then they rather meant to save their troops and avoid casualties in view of their losses at Verdun, and previously.

I thought I might be able to help Foch in the matter of the latest criticism – his narrow front of attack – by handing him over the village of Les Boeufs, and the roads running back from it, through Ginchy and Guillemont. I could also spare him 2 railways which now run into the last named village ... Foch was most grateful for my offer, but said that he had so many guns still on the south of the Somme that time would be lost in getting them forward...

Haig related that Foch had told him that, during a recent visit to the front, Sir John French met Clemenceau at a French divisional HQ.

The latter had recently been studying *British* methods in the Somme battle: he had spent a full week on the ground and had gone into every detail. On being introduced to Lord French, he at once *expatiated* on what the English had done: the skill of everyone and the accuracy of the artillery etc. etc. I understand that it was quite amusing to see the critical Frenchman who had come to the British front to find arguments wherewith to chastise the French Higher Command, brought face to face with the British Field Marshal who had the exact contrary rôle! I expect that neither will succeed in doing much harm.

Last week I saw the greater part of the 11th and 18th Divisions, which did so

1 RA: PS/GV/Q 832/127.

well in the capture of the German defences on the Thiepval ridge. Lieutenant General Woollcombe[1] commands the former and has done very well in spite of 32 years spent in India, and some 40 years' service. He is really wonderfully active in mind and body. Maxse commands the 18th. In view of what he has done with his division, I think his misdeeds as a brigadier at the beginning of the war should be forgotten.

Wednesday 18 October

Mr John Masefield came to lunch. He is a poet but I am told that he has written the best account of the landing in Gallipoli. Now he wishes to write about the deeds of our men in the Battle of the Somme. To this I readily accorded permission, and said I would gladly put him in the way of meeting those most concerned with the various actions so that he could get first hand information.

Thursday 19 October

Bad weather forced the postponement of Reserve Army's attack.

Letter received yesterday from General Joffre. He now has abandoned his attempts to give me detailed instructions, but instead enclosed a copy of what he has sent to General Foch.

Haig attended an Anglo-French conference at Boulogne on 20 October, when the main topic of discussion was the Balkans.

Saturday 21 October. Letter to Lady Haig

I get on very well with Lloyd George, and yesterday he began to explain to me regarding his conversation with Foch which I noted in my diary. I would not let him go on with his explanation, but merely said I had never paid the smallest attention to it and I told him that he (Lloyd G) might rely on me to do my utmost to help him. He used Oliver's[2] words about some people trying to 'drive a wedge in between him and the soldiers'. So he seemed quite alive to the danger. On the other hand, he complained that the General Staff at the War Office don't let him know *everything*, but only feed him with what

1 Lieutenant General Sir Charles Louis Woollcombe (1857–1934); accepted command of 11th Division in 1916, despite holding the rank of lieutenant general; commanded IV Corps, 1916–18; was replaced after the Battle of Cambrai.
2 Frederick Scott Oliver (1864–1934), influential pro-Conservative businessman and author.

they think is suitable for him to know. That of course is quite wrong, and I will mention it to Robertson who is staying here tonight.

Sunday 22 October

At 11 am Sir William Robertson had a talk with me till close on lunch time. We discussed:

1. *The question of men.* He reminded me that I had strongly advised him when he became CIGS that he should aim at raising two million. He hoped soon to complete the first million but the Universal Service Act required revision.
2. *The general strategy of the war.* We agreed that the war was only to be won by defeating the Germans. This could not be done in the Balkans but only in France. So all possible means should be sent to France, and the Enemy should be pressed continuously – right through the winter whenever the weather permitted.
3. *Heavy artillery* which had been intended for this Army was being sent to Russia before the ports closed for the winter. This would not interfere with the completion of our programme by next spring.
4. *November Conference at Chantilly.* General Joffre had suggested postponing a general offensive till next May because Russians and Italians could not advance till then. We both agreed that such a late date was quite unsound.

Mr Balfour[1] and his 2 secretaries also lunched. After lunch we had a good talk. He seemed most pleased with all he had seen, and was quite sure that our offensive in France should be supported to the utmost of our power. At one time he had favoured an effort in the Balkans, because he then thought the German front in France could not be pierced. [Now our successes proved that his opinion was wrong.]

Monday 23 October

At 10 am General des Vallières[2] came to see me. He was on his way to meet General Joffre who is lunching with me today. He was afraid that Joffre, being an 'underbred individual' might make a scene on account of my last letter to him. The latter had written to me on the 18th stating that from information

1 Arthur James Balfour (1848–1930), Prime Minister, 1902–5; Leader of the Unionist Party, 1902–11; First Lord of the Admiralty, 1915–16; Foreign Secretary, 1916–19.
2 General Jean Des Vallières, succeeded Huguet as chief French liaison officer at British GHQ in December 1915.

which he had got from General Foch, I had evidently changed my plans and he called on me 'instamment de maintenir intégralement plans primitifs, etc., etc.'[1] I at once replied that his letter seemed to have been written under a misapprehension on several points: viz., that I am losing time; that scale of my attacks has been reduced; that my plans have been modified or changed. 'Not one of these suggestions is justified in fact.' – 'Meanwhile to the utmost extent of the means at my disposal, and so far as weather conditions render possible, I will continue to co-operate with you in exploiting to the full the successes already gained. But I must remind you that it lies with me to judge what I can undertake, and when I can undertake it.'

It was the last sentence which had upset General Joffre's equilibrium. I told des Vallières that it was most desirable for our good relations in the future that both General Joffre and his Staff should know that I could only receive orders from my Government. And I also told him that I knew as a fact that a certain number of French statesmen were anxious that the British Army in France should be placed *under* Joffre's orders. This could never be, neither the people at home nor the British Army in France would submit to such a thing.

About 12.30 Joffre arrived, evidently in a chastened frame of mind, and with a very good appetite. He also brought me a nice photo of himself on which he had written my name, and added, 'En souvenir de notre collaboration confiante et cordiale. Votre tout devoue. J. Joffre, October 23rd, 1916.'

He did full justice to a good lunch and then we had a talk for an hour or more. He gave me his views on the general situation and agreed with me that we must *continue* to press the Enemy here on the Somme battle front throughout the winter. There must be no reduction of strength on this battle front, so that whenever the weather is fine, we can carry out an attack without any delay to concentrate troops etc. As regards his letter, he begged me 'to pay no attention' to any letter which I received from him, the contents of which were not in accord with my own views! The meeting was most friendly all through.

Tuesday 24 October. Letter to Lady Haig

Yes I liked Mr Oliver's letter, and particularly your tactful reply. It was nice of him too to think of the country presenting me with Bemersyde, that old place on the Tweed that has never belonged to anyone but Haig. We must finish the war first before we think of any such things. Besides it is sufficient reward for me to have taken part in this Great struggle, and to have occupied

---

1 i.e. Joffre firmly asked Haig to stick to the original plans.

Right Haig was an excellent man to work for, demanding but appreciative. For this reason, his reproaches – when delivered – were accordingly stinging.

Below left General Sir Horace Smith-Dorrien: his unsanctioned stand at Le Cateau on 26 August 1914 is now generally recognised to have 'saved' the BEF.

Below right Field Marshal Sir John French: in time of crisis, he instinctively behaved according to the credo of the late Victorian army officer, leading by example and demonstrating his courage. By the end of 1915 French was a sick man who had lost the confidence of his closest subordinates and of leading figures in the government.

Left General Sir Charles Monro (second left) 'proved himself to be a good regimental officer and an excellent Commandant of the Hythe School of Musketry, but some years with Territorials has resulted in his becoming rather fat. There is, however, no doubt about his military ability, although he lacks the practical experience in commanding a Division.'
The key relationship on I Corps Staff was Haig's partnership with his Chief of Staff (formally, the Brigadier General General Staff or BGGS), Brigadier General 'Johnnie' Gough VC (second right).

Below right Few men exercised more influence over the British conduct of the war than Lord Kitchener. It was Kitchener who insisted on the raising of a mass volunteer army. This decision, made even before the professional BEF had been deployed, fundamentally changed the nature of the war for Britain.

Above The formidable Sir William Robertson succeeded the ineffectual Archie Murray as Chief of the General Staff. The relationship between Haig and Robertson became increasingly important in the conduct of the war.

'Monash is a most thorough and capable
Commander who thinks out every detail and
leaves nothing to chance.'

Hubert Gough was the son, brother, nephew and
cousin of Victoria Cross winners. Haig admired
Gough's high sense of professionalism, optimism
and aggression and seemed more comfortable in
his company than that of his other Army
commanders, responding warmly to the younger
man's energy and wit.

Foch was one of France's leading military
intellectuals, a man of boundless courage and
energy, vital to the Allied victory.

In 1914, Pétain was an elderly colonel of infantry and
his career appeared to be moving towards an
un-dramatic conclusion; by the end of 1916 he had
become 'the hero of Verdun' and 'the saviour of
France'. By 1917 Haig found Pétain 'businesslike,
knowledgeable, and brief of speech'. But he also
described him as 'defeatist', a view shared by the
French prime minister, Georges Clemenceau.

Above left When Asquith resigned as Prime Minister in 1916, Haig wrote: 'I am personally very sorry for poor old Squiff. He has had a hard time and even when "exhilarated" seems to have had more capacity and brain power than any of the others. However, I expect more action and less talk is needed now.'

Above right Haig: 'I get on very well with Lloyd George' (far right). Joffre (second from right) was a formidable man and a demanding ally.

Left Principal responsibility for planning the Somme campaign fell to Rawlinson (on the left), the first Army commander to be appointed under Haig. He favoured a cautious approach, based on the method of 'bite and hold', but this found little favour with Haig, who wished to leave open the possibility of a more decisive advance.

'His Corps is now called the "Bing Boys" [after a current West End revue] and various comic posters are put about "The Bing Boys are here".' As GOC Canadian Corps, Byng captured the Vimy Ridge in April 1917, the first really striking British success in trench warfare. As GOC Third Army at Cambrai in November 1917, he pioneered important artillery techniques that restored surprise to the battlefield and used tanks en masse for the first time in war.

Currie (left), commanding the Canadians, 'is suffering from a swollen head Horne thinks!' wrote Haig.

'He lodged a complaint when I ordered the Canadian Divisions to be brought out of the line in order to support the front and take part in the battle elsewhere. He wishes to fight only as a "Canadian Corps" and got his Canadian representative in London to write and urge me to arrange it. As a result, the Canadians are together holding a wide front near Arras, but they have not yet been in the battle!'

Pershing (right), Commander-in-Chief of the American Expeditionary Force, 1917–19, was a cold professional soldier, acutely aware of his responsibilities as a 'national contingent commander'. Haig was impressed by Pershing, being 'much struck with his quiet gentlemanly bearing – so unusual for an American.'

Above 1918: 'I spent some time today with the Canadians. They are really fine disciplined soldiers now and so smart and clean.'

Below 'I am sorry to say that the Australians are not nearly so efficient [as the Canadians]. I put this down to Birdwood [GOC I ANZAC Corps], who, instead of facing the problem, has gone in for the easier way of saying everything is perfect and making himself as popular as possible. We have had to separate the Australians into Convalescent Camps of their own, because they were giving so much trouble when along with our men and put such revolutionary ideas into their heads!'

Left British troops in a former German trench. The Front Line was never far from Haig's mind, as this vignette from May 1917 shows: 'At 11 am I met General Plumer at the village of Pernes (between Lillers and St Pol) and discussed the action to be taken if the Germans vacated their front Trench on the front of our attack … We agreed that the Germans were holding their front trenches lightly (in accordance with their Regulations).'

Above A meeting of British and French High Command. Haig wrote in August 1918: 'HM the King . . . then presented the KCB to General Debeney . . . We were then photo'd – Marshal Foch in his new hat, the King, self, Pétain, Fayolle and a host of others. The Cinema running all the time while we were forming up.'

Above By 1918, when this photograph was taken, the tank had become an accepted feature of the landscape of battle, but in August 1916 Haig recorded a conversation about a combined Anglo-French operation: 'For this advance the "Tanks" would be most useful, and I asked when Foch's army would have them. Foch did not seem to know about these machines, but he is to press for them.'

Left Haig with Clemenceau, at Doullens railway station, France, in April 1918. Clemenceau's return as prime minister, in November 1917, at the age of 76 and at the end of a traumatic year for France, was a political expression of French determination to see the war through to a victorious conclusion.

Haig, with British Army commanders at Cambrai, France, on Armistice Day, 'fine . . . but cold and dull'. Haig then continued: 'Reports from Foch's HQ state that meeting with the German delegates (which took place in train in the Forest of Compiègne, not in Château as previously reported) began at 2 am and at 5 am the Armistice was signed. The Germans pointed out that if the rolling stock and supplies of the Army (which have to be handed over by the terms of the armistice) are given up, then Germans East of the Rhine will starve. Report says Foch was rather brutal to the German delegates, and replied that that was their affair!'

France, 16 November 1918. Foch and Haig enter the advanced General Headquarters train. The day before, Haig reported: 'Marshal Foch came to lunch . . . Foch explained very graphically how the Conference with the German Delegates regarding an Armistice went off. They said that they expected "hard terms, but these were very hard".'

no inconsiderable position amongst those who have helped our country to weather the storm.

Wednesday 25 October

Mr Ben Tillett came to see me.[1] He calls himself a 'Socialist Revolutionary' but has rendered very valuable service in keeping the dockers and other operatives at work, and has inspired them with determination to beat the Germans. It seems extraordinary how he can impress his audiences, although he knows very little about his subject. To please 'Ben', I was photographed alongside of him!

Thursday 26 October

General Sir C. Fergusson,[2] Commanding XVII Corps, came to lunch. I gave him instructions. He will have his HQ at St Omer and be in reserve ready to reinforce any part of the front which may be threatened, or act offensively at some point where an attack has been prepared, e.g. Beauvaisnes, Vimy, Messines–Wytschaete Ridge. Meantime while divisions are resting he will supervise their training...

After lunch I ... saw General Gough. We arranged that he should watch the weather and be able to put his plans into execution after 3 fine days. I then ... rode round the billets of the 25th Division with General Bainbridge.[3] I also saw the three brigadiers, Onslow,[4] 7 Brigade, Bethell[5] 74 Brigade and Pratt,[6] 75 Brigade, and most of the Battalion Commanders. I also shook hands with and congratulated four or five NCOs and men in each battalion who were brought to my notice as having performed specially good service. I finished with Bethell's Brigade in Beauval; he and his brigade took Stuff Redoubt. Bethell is a Brevet Major in 7th Hussars having gone from the Indian infantry (Gurkhas) to that corps. I was much struck with the small

1 Ben Tillett (1860–1943), labour leader; founder of the Dockers' Union; a whole-hearted supporter of the British war effort.
2 Lieutenant General (later General) Sir Charles Fergusson Bt. (1865–1951), GOC 5th Division, 1913–14; GOC 9th Division, 1914; GOC II Corps, 1914–16; GOC XVII Corps, 1916–18.
3 Major General (later Sir) (Edmund) Guy Tulloch Bainbridge (1867–1943), GOC 110 Brigade, 1915–16; GOC 25th Division, 1916–18.
4 Brigadier General Cranley Charlton Onslow (1869–1940), GOC 7 Brigade, 1916–17.
5 Brigadier General (later Major General Sir) (Hugh) Keppel Bethell ('Beetle') (1882–1947), GOC 74 Brigade, 1916–18. He took over the shattered 66th Division in March 1918 and led it for the rest of the war; he was – at thirty-five – the youngest British divisional commander of both world wars.
6 Brigadier General Ernest St George Pratt (1863–1918), GOC 75 Brigade, 1916. Gas poisoning, incurred in March 1916, contributed to his death on 24 November 1918.

size and generally poor physique of the men in this division, yet no division has done better or seen more hard fighting than the 25th . . .

A letter received from Sir William Robertson CIGS, stating that Government had decided to send another division to Salonika. It will have to start from here end of November. In my opinion, it is not 'men' who are wanted at Salonika, but 'a man'! From all accounts, Sarrail, the French GOC there is quite useless.[1]

Thursday 26 October. Letter to Leopold Rothschild[2]

Mr Balfour spent a couple of days with me after the Boulogne Conference. I think he was much interested in all he saw. The sad thing is the competition which exists between the Naval Air Service and the Military Branch. They might belong to rival nations! I had hoped Curzon might have done something to lessen the evil, but apparently he has not got the power to compel the Naval people to co-operate. Mr Balfour is so full of sound sense that I am hoping that he will put this part of the matter right, and from what I know of the Military Air Service they are only too willing to go hand in hand with their Naval brothers if allowed by the Naval authorities to do so.

Friday 27 October

Major General Geddes, Director General of Transportation . . . reported that everyone was in agreement now regarding the principles of organisation of his new department. The main difficulties are
a) want of rolling stock. 16,000[3] more trucks are wanted and locomotives.
b) rails. He proposes to order 500 more miles and insists on getting it.

There is a good deal of criticism apparently being made at the appointment of a civilian like Geddes to an important post in the Army. These critics seem to fail to realise the size of this Army and the amount of work which the Army requires of a civilian nature. The working of the railways, the upkeep of the roads, even the baking of bread and a thousand other industries go on in peace as well as in war! So, with the whole Nation at war, our object should be to *employ men on the same work in war as they are accustomed to do in peace.* Acting on this principle, I have got Geddes at the head of all the railways and

1 In the Ts diary Haig added his objections to this 'folly' but concludes 'that he must obey orders'. It seems that Clemenceau, who dismissed Sarrail in 1917, shared Haig's view of the general's competence.
2 NLS: Acc. 3155.
3 The Ts diary reads '1600'.

transportation, with the best practical engineers under him. At the head of road directorate is Mr Maybury,[1] head of the road board in England. The docks, canals etc. are being managed in the same way, i.e. by men of *practical* experience. To put soldiers into such positions, merely because they are generals and colonels, would be to ensure failure![2]

Saturday 28 October

The 33rd Division ... captured this morning several important trenches northeast of Les Boeufs ... General Pinney[3] was recently transferred to the 33rd Division vice General Landon. The 33rd has done well since the change in command was made, and affords another example of the principle that the fighting of a division depends on the qualities and spirit of its commander!

All Brigadiers and COs agree that the barrage for the attack was excellent both on this occasion, as well as on the 23 October, when an attack on a larger scale was made.

The difficulties of the long carry to this part of our front are such that all reserve troops have to be employed. Otherwise necessities such as water, food, ammunition, bombs of all kind etc. cannot be kept up. The carry is roughly 5000 yards each way. Some pack horses have had to be destroyed owing to being hopelessly bogged. One man does one round journey carrying a load per 24 hours.

Lord Cavan estimates a pause of 'at least four days' necessary between each offensive operation, in order to keep up!

Tuesday 31 October

In the afternoon I rode to HQ Fifth Army at Toutencourt, and saw General Neil Malcolm. Gough was out with the Duke of Connaught.[4] I wanted definite information as to the state of the front trenches, and whether the winter leather waistcoats had yet been issued, also whether an extra blanket

1 Brigadier General (later Sir) Henry Percy Maybury (1864–1943), a civil engineer who was appointed the BEF's Director of Roads on 20 October 1916, retaining the post for the rest of the war.
2 A few days later Haig had to smooth over a dispute between Geddes and Lieutenant General R. C. Maxwell, the QMG, over their respective responsibilities in the new organisation, the QMG having threatened to resign. Diary, 30 October 1916.
3 Major General Reginald John Pinney (1862–1943), GOC 33rd Division, 1916–19. Pinney's reputation has suffered at the hands of Private Frank Richards and Captain J. C. Dunn, 2nd Battalion Royal Welch Fusiliers, but Haig had a high regard for Pinney and for 33rd Division, claiming that when this division was in the line he 'could be sure'.
4 Prince Arthur William Patrick Albert (1850–1942), Queen Victoria's third son; described by Haig as 'oh so stupid'. Diary, 30 October 1916.

per man had been sent up. Malcolm assured me that everything possible was
being done for the men, but the mud in front was quite terrible. Today, being
fine, things were fast improving, and where the 5th Canadians are (north of
Le Sars), the ground is fit to attack over . . . The Reserve Army has been given
the extra services and staff to place it on the same footing as the other armies.
It will now be called the 'Fifth Army'.

Thursday 2 November

The Enemy seems to be feeling a shortage in men. Captured correspondence
shows that a number of sailors at the depôts at Cuxhaven have been medically
examined with a view to being incorporated in the Army . . .

The Prime Minister of New Zealand (Massey)[1] and the late PM (Sir Joseph
Ward)[2] with General G. Richardson came to lunch.[3] They told me that New
Zealand has 100,000 men available as reserves for the division which they
have put in the field.

After lunch I rode round by Toutencourt and saw General Gough Commanding Fifth Army. I told him to have patience, and not to launch the main
attack until the weather was better and the ground dry. It was better to wait
than to start a series of small operations which would not have the same
decisive results . . .

Mr McKenna (Chancellor of the Exchequer) arrived about 10.30 pm from
England. He seems most friendly, and takes quite the right view of the
importance of the Western Front. 'Everything possible should be sent to
France' he said. He also told me that 'if the war ended in March, England
could take the cost of the war in her stride'! And this, in spite of the fact that
we give France and Russia each 300 millions a year. Italy, Roumania, Portugal,
etc., another 200 million, making a total of 800 million pounds a year handed
over by England to our Allies in addition to our own expenses!

Saturday 4 November

XIV Corps reported that attack by 33rd Division on Boritska and Zenith
trenches yesterday afternoon failed and Lord Cavan writes that in his opinion
the attack ordered to take place on the 5th *from our present line eastwards*

1 William Ferguson Massey (1856–1925), Prime Minister of New Zealand, 1912–25.
2 Sir Joseph Ward (1856–1930), Prime Minister of New Zealand, 1906–12. Although political
opponents, Massey and Ward collaborated so closely during the war that they were nicknamed
the 'Siamese Twins'.
3 Major General George (later Sir George) Spafford Richardson (1868–1938), a senior figure in
New Zealand's military forces.

against Le Transloy has no chance of succeeding. He thinks that that village should be attacked *from the south*. This is because of the heavy enfilade fire of machine guns and artillery from the north, and the great distance our troops have to advance against a strongly prepared position, owing to the failure to advance our line in the recent operations. He continues: 'No one who has not visited the front trenches can really know the state of exhaustion to which the men are reduced. The conditions are far worse than in the First Battle of Ypres, and my General Officers and Staff Officers agree that they are the worst they have seen, owing to the enormous distance of the carry of all munitions, food, water and ammunition.'

The question is how not to leave the French left in the air! Their situation is much easier owing to having the concealed main road up the Combles valley to Sailly Saillisel which is on the ridge, whereas we are a long way beyond the crest north of Ginchy and down the forward slope beyond Les Boeufs.

I sent at once and fixed a meeting with General Foch and Sir Henry Rawlinson at Querrieu. We met at 2.30 pm. We arranged the nature of our co-operation for tomorrow, namely we attack Boritska and Mirage trenches *from the south* and also bombard Le Transloy and counter-batter Enemy's guns as if we were about to attack Le Transloy.

Then Foch and I with our Staff officers (viz. Weygand and Davidson) had a talk about future operations. Foch laid great stress on the dangerously exposed position in which his troops would be north and northeast of Sailly Saillisal if we did not also press on, and asked me to give him a date when I would put in the attack with my Fifth Army. I said the attack was all ready to go in, but the wet weather had destroyed our communications. My plan was to get these into a proper state and after four fine days to dry the ground, then to put in the attack. But if by the 15th the attack, for one reason or another, had not gone in, then I proposed to commence an operation to capture the same objectives little by little.[1]

As regards the Fourth Army, the offensive would be continued as the weather permitted with the object of taking trench by trench and so keeping the Enemy in doubt as to where the next blow would fall. He would thus be unable to withdraw divisions from this front.

Foch gave me the impression that he was not very keen to carry on fighting during the winter!

---

1 Haig reiterated his instructions not to attack until the ground was dry to Gough, when the latter enquired whether he should attack on 8 November 'if the military situation required him' to do so 'even if the weather made success doubtful'. Diary, 6 November 1916.

Sunday 5 November

Kavanagh came to lunch. As regards the Cavalry Corps, I said that owing to
the state of the ground, the cavalry in the Fourth Army area could not hope
to break through this winter, unless a hard frost came! So they might now be
withdrawn to more comfortable billets. The Fifth Army (Gough) would still
want a division to co-operate in his operations. Kavanagh also mentioned
that he would probably have to report that Brigadier General Seely was unfit
to command the Canadian Cavalry Brigade.[1] [I told Kavanagh that he must
only think of him as a cavalry brigadier in the field responsible for the
efficiency and handling of his command and not as an MP and Ex-Secretary
of State for War][2] ...

   German casualties. German official casualty lists published up to the 14
October, give the following analysis:

   In 523 infantry battalions engaged there were:
      16% of total establishment killed, died and missing
      3%   "   "   "   prisoners
      27%   "   "   "   wounded
      46% total

This fully justifies the estimate of 50% loss of infantry for every German
battalion engaged in the Somme battle. It is noteworthy that the total of

killed, died, missing and prisoners $=$ 41% of the total casualties, and 19% of
total establishment.

   1158 battalions have been engaged by the Germans in the Somme battle.
Each has probably lost 500 = 579,000.
   The losses of the artillery and other arms must also be added, so that a *low
estimate* of the Enemy's total casualties since the battle must be *well over*
600,000.[3]

1 Brigadier General (later Major General) John Edward Bernard Seely (later Baron Mottistone)
(1868–1947), former Secretary of State for War, 1912–14; resigned as a result of the Curragh
Incident (March 1914).
2 In the event, Seely commanded the brigade, with a two-month break, from January 1915 until
May 1918.
3 Recent estimates of German casualties by historians range from 465,000 to 600,000: Sheffield,
The Somme, p. 151.

Monday 6 November

General Allenby came to see me about 11 am. I told him to continue his preparations for an attack on his front southeast of Arras. If it was not possible to carry it out this year, we would certainly make use of his preparations next spring. It was particularly important to improve the railway communications, making new lines and perhaps doubling the main line to Arras.

Wednesday 8 November

I then motored to Méaulte and saw Lord Cavan. We had a good hour's talk. I told him that the *main position of defence* would be the main Thiepval ridge–Flers–Les Boeufs. As our advanced or first position there would be the front line which we were now holding. This must be made very strong. Our next position for defence would be the main ridge. That is to say, no intermediate continuous line is to be constructed but existing villages are to be organised as 'strong points'; and obstacles and flanking fire by machine guns arranged [to provide mutual support].

It would be labour lost to make an intermediate line, besides it seemed to me sound policy to make the Enemy fight (if he attacked in force) on the forward slope while we have good unexposed communications in rear of the ridge.

As regards training, Lord Cavan said that his divisions are well off for instructors, and the staffs of the various schools are now quite excellent. The new regulation giving them the necessary rank and pay had made all the difference in getting good and experienced officers to leave battalions.

The communications are still very bad. In fact we are fighting under the same conditions as in October 1914, i.e. with rifle and machine guns only, because bombs and mortar ammunition cannot be carried forward as the roads are so bad.

Saturday 11 November

I sent a letter to General Joffre offering to take over on January 1 (about) the front from Les Boeufs round Sailly Saillisel and St Pierre Wood to a point 1000 yards north of Bouchavesnes.

In reply to my letter inviting Lloyd George to spend a few days with me he writes on November 10 that he will be very happy to do so, and will bring Sir William Robertson with him and adds, 'It is so important that soldiers and politicians should work together in this war. It is only by the most complete understanding and co-operation between the military and civilian elements that we can hope to win.' I hope he will practise what he preaches!

I invited him to stay in order to check some idle tales which have been going about regarding his last visit, and to show that at least those at the HQ of the Army in France have no feelings of ill-will towards him.

Sunday 12 November

General Kiggell visited HQ Fifth Army this morning to ascertain whether Gough felt satisfied that the chances of an attack succeeding tomorrow were sufficiently good to warrant my approving it being carried out. Gough was of opinion that the troops now in position should either attack tomorrow or then should be relieved and a new lot prepared for the operations say in a month's time. The present lot of divisions had been waiting on so long for fine weather that we could not keep them hanging on any longer with any prospect of success. He thought that the chances of success tomorrow 'were quite good', but he would go round some of the divisions, and be back at 4 pm to see me . . .

Afterwards I rode to Toutencourt and saw General Gough. He had been round all the divisions and most of the brigades detailed for the attack. Their Commanders all now thought that we had a fair chance of success. He himself recommended that the attack should go on. I told him that a success at this time was much wanted – firstly, on account of the situation in Roumania, we must prevent the Enemy from withdrawing any divisions from France to that theatre.[1] Next the feeling in Russia is not favourable either to the French or to ourselves. We are thought to be accomplishing little. The German party in Russia spreads these reports. Lastly on account of the Chantilly Conference which meets on Wednesday. The British position will doubtless be much stronger (as memories are short!) if I could appear there on the top of the capture of Beaumont Hamel for instance, and 3000 German prisoners. It would show too that we had no intention of ceasing to press the Enemy on the Somme.

But the necessity for a success must not blind our eyes to the difficulties of ground and weather. Nothing is so costly as a failure! But I am ready to run reasonable risks. I then discussed with Gough what these risks were, and why he thought our chances of success were good. Finally, I decided that the Fifth Army should attack tomorrow. Gough fixed the hour at 5.45 am.

---

1 The Germans and Austrians were engaged in conquering Romania. Bucharest fell on 5 December.

Monday 13 November

The Battle of Ancre began and Fifth Army achieved considerable success. The fighting continued until 18 November, when the Somme campaign came to an end.

Awakened at 5.30 am by terrific artillery fire. It increased, if possible, at 5.45 am, the hour fixed for the attack by the Fifth Army astride the Ancre, and continued till 6.30 when it slackened but it was still heavy all forenoon. By 7.30 I heard that the attack was going well and that our men were in all the Enemy's front line trenches, from opposite Serre to Thiepval. In many places our troops were said to be still further forward. The only doubt was on the left, where the 3rd Division had not apparently progressed very far.

By 1 pm it was reported that the whole of the ridge from Beaumont Hamel to Beaucourt was in our possession except a small portion of the ridge, and there were two or three pockets about Beaumont Hamel where the Germans were still holding out.

South of the Ancre all objectives had been gained and our troops were in touch across it near St Pierre d'Ivion. [By lunch time] I heard that 2000 prisoners had already been through the cages.

The attack was made with 43 battalions, i.e. parts of seven divisions. A great artillery concentration was effected: that is to say, about the same number of guns were firing today on the spurs about Beaumont Hamel, as we had firing on our whole front on 1 July! By noon Gough's 18 pounders had fired 240,000 rounds! The result was good because in spite of the wet ground our troops took the position without much difficulty: and the Enemy surrendered much more readily than on any previous occasion. The Enemy's front line was very strong and the villages of Beaumont Hamel, Beaucourt sur Ancre, and St Pierre d'Ivion were very strongly fortified, and strongly garrisoned. By 7 pm it was stated that 67 officers and 3227 prisoners (unwounded) had passed through the cages, and more were on the way. It is estimated that they number over 4000. This is more than were taken in two days' fighting at Loos. Our losses are estimated at 5000 to 6000.

After lunch I rode to HQ Fifth Army and thanked Gough and his Staff for all their efforts. The success has come at a most opportune moment...

On 15 November Haig participated in an inter-Allied conference at Chantilly.

Thursday 16 November

At 3 pm we assembled at the Quai d'Orsay ... General Joffre read the conclusions of the Chantilly Conference. Lloyd George asked several questions with a view to having more troops sent to Salonika! But he was crushed both by the French and the information which Robertson gave regarding the nature of communications in the Balkans...

The main conclusions are:[1]

1. That all are unanimously of opinion that the Western theatre is the main one, and that the resources employed in the other theatres should be reduced to the smallest possible.
2. That all the Allies will continue to press the Enemy throughout the winter as far as climatic conditions permit.
3. That if one of the Allies is attacked, the others will at once take the offensive to relieve the pressure elsewhere. With this object all agreed to complete their offensive preparations early next year.
4. If the Enemy leaves the initiative to the Allies, the date of the general offensive will be settled later to meet the general situation. With this in view, C-in-Cs will arrange to keep in the closest touch.

Saturday 18 November

I attended Conference with GOC Armies at Bryas Château (3 miles north of St Pol) at 11 am. [These conferences were suspended during the Battle of the Somme.]

After *Charteris had explained the general situation as regards the Enemy and showing that his losses have been most severe – at least 680,000 in the Somme battle alone,[2] I indicated our objectives as follows:

1) To be ready for the unforeseen, i.e. either for an attack (a) on the British or (b) on one of the Allies. In the case of (a), we hold our ground and not allow our general plans to be upset – so most essential to see our positions and system of defence. In the case of (b) it is possible that we may have to attack to withdraw pressure from an ally. [Consequently] several points suitable for an attack should be prepared.
2) Prevent Enemy from recovering from his demoralised condition by methodical pressure when and where possible, according to our means.
3) Prepare for general combined offensive by all the Allies simultaneously. Training most important. Railways must be seen to at once. Sir Eric

1 The Ts diary has a note before this section: 'Note added subsequently. This was not typed by me at the time owing to dangers of the post. Douglas did not send it me.' The Ms version of these conclusions is extant.
2 In the Ts diary, Haig amended this figure to 600,000.

Geddes (Director General of Transportation) explained a few of our difficulties. Shortage of steel, waggons, etc. etc.

Saturday 18 November. Letter to Lady Haig

I leave all the questions connected with the Press to 'John' who has a section in his office which deals with them. I only receive some of the principal ones, like Northcliffe and Robinson of *The Times*,[1] Strachey of the *Spectator*, the *Saturday Review* and such.

But I tell them all that they can go anywhere, and see whoever and whatever they like – there are no secrets. They also can write what they like, but I beg them to remember that we all have the same objective, viz., beat the Germans so they must not give anything away which can be of use to the enemy. I must say that the Correspondents have played up splendidly. We never once had to complain of them since I took over command.

When I come over I'll try and get Lord Northcliffe to come and lunch with us one day as he has been such a help latterly to the Army and myself.

As regards Lord Esher – I expect you are quite right, but he has a good head and knows the British public and is at times most helpful. But he has not come between me and old Bertie.[2] The latter is quite a friend and only two days ago said he hoped I would always tell him if he could help in any way, but he feared there was not much in which he could assist. He is furious with Esher, of course, for being in Paris.

Monday 20 November

I then went on to Gézincourt and inspected the 99 Brigade (Kellett) consisting of 22nd and 23rd Royal Fusiliers and 1st Royal Berks and the 1st KRRC at Beauval.[3] I rode round the battalions and spoke to many of the officers. The two Regular battalions left Aldershot with me in the 6 Brigade at the beginning of the war. I saw several sergeants who had been all through the war, but no original officers were present – 2 or 3 were on leave however. General Walker (commanding 2nd Division now) and these battalions greatly distinguished themselves in the recent fighting. One officer told me that on Monday

1 (George) Geoffrey Robinson (1874–1944), assumed name of Dawson in 1917, editor of *The Times*, 1912–19 and 1923–41.
2 Viscount Bertie of Thame, British Ambassador in Paris.
3 For a junior officer's view of this inspection, see G. D. Sheffield and G. I. S. Inglis, *From Vimy Ridge to the Rhine: the Great War Letters of Christopher Stone DSO MC* (Marlborough: Crowood, 1989), p. 76.

13th the Enemy was quite surprised and many were not fully dressed, when our men entered their trenches. The Germans readily surrendered if our troops were in sufficient numbers. 'They held up their hands, saluted once, and "then readily rushed down to their dugouts to pack their kit for London".'

I rode to Valvion. Admiral Bacon came from Dover to see me and stayed the night. He considers that the situation in the Channel is much less satisfactory than it was. The German sailors have learnt much and their recent raid has shown them that they can interfere with our communications without much danger or difficulty. He (the Admiral) cannot prevent these raids. I gather from this that our command of the Channel is precarious, and that our ports may be closed oftener in the future than in the past . . .

Wednesday 22 November

Haig visited Robertson in London.

He told me of the Peace Party in the Cabinet, and showed me a memorandum by Lord Lansdowne advocating coming to terms with the Enemy![1]

Friday 24 November

I had a conference with General [Sir Francis] Davies (Military Secretary, War Office) and my MS (Peyton)[2] regarding the Honours Gazette. I was anxious that all officers who had proved their fitness for promotion to Major General etc., should now be promoted. I had put forward 27 Colonels for promotion [to Major General.] The War Office view is to wait till the war is over! I entirely disagree and say that we ought to promote as soon as possible in order to have good officers well forward on the list from whom Commanders can be chosen . . .

At 5.30 pm I attended Buckingham Palace and was received by the King. We discussed many topics until 7 pm. He is to see FM Viscount French tomorrow morning, and intends to tell him that if he (French) does not cease from criticising adversely the doings of the Army in France, it will be necessary to sever his connection with the Army.

1 Lord Lansdowne, a former Conservative Foreign Secretary, made his views public a year later, in December 1917. He was fearful of the social and political consequences of total war.
2 Major General (later General Sir) William Elliot Peyton (1866–1931), Military Secretary GHQ 1916–18.

Saturday 25 November

Lloyd George visited Haig in London.

He told me that he considered the political situation serious. Lord Lansdowne had written a terrible paper urging that we should make peace now, if the Naval, Military, Financial and other Heads of Departments could 'not be certain of victory by next autumn'.

Wednesday 6 December. Letter to Lady Haig

Asquith had been forced out of office on 5 December. Lloyd George replaced him as Prime Minister.

I am personally very sorry for poor old Squiff. He has had a hard time and even when 'exhilarated' seems to have had more capacity and brain power than any of the others. However, I expect more action and less talk is needed now.[1]

Wednesday 6 December

This morning the AG brought me Court Martial proceedings on an officer charged with desertion and sentenced by the Court to be shot.[2] After careful consideration, I confirmed the proceedings. This is the first sentence of death on an officer to be put into execution since I became C-in-C. Such a crime is more serious in the case of an officer than of a man, and also it is highly important that all ranks should realise that the law is the same for an officer as a private.

Friday 15 December

It is a year since I took over the Chief Command in France . . .
    At 2.45 I visited Sir William Robertson in his office by appointment. He told me of the new Prime Minister's attitude. How he was in real earnest to leave nothing undone to win the war. At the same time, he seemed to wish to pose as the prime instrument and mainspring of the actions of the Allies.

1 In a letter to Philip Sassoon on 8 December 1916, Haig went further, expressing satisfaction at Lloyd George's elevation, and hoping that Asquith would offer support to the new Prime Minister. Quoted in P. Stansky, *Sassoon: The Worlds of Philip and Sybil* (London: Yale University Press, 2003), p. 67.
2 Lieutenant E. S. Poole, 11th Battalion West Yorkshire Regiment.

With this object, he was now anxious to help Italy with guns, and also Russia, so as to get a hold over these countries.

At 3.30 pm Robertson and I attended at 11 Downing Street, and were received by the Prime Minister in the drawing-room. He had a bad throat and a slight cold, but he talked a great deal to start with. He pointed out the need for an early success, and was anxious to make an attack from Egypt on El Arish and so towards Jerusalem. For this, he wanted two divisions from France. He was also anxious to help Italy with 200 heavy guns and take Pola. I was to provide these guns during the winter and get them back in the spring.

After patiently waiting, I was eventually asked to state my views. I asked Mr Lloyd George to look at the Western Front as a whole, before going into details, so that he might realise the tremendous efforts which were necessary before next season's attacks could be launched. He, incidentally, stated that, although he recognised the West as the principal theatre, he 'could not believe that it was possible to beat the German Armies there – at any rate, not next year'. I also urged that it was a waste of power to send guns and munitions to Russia until it was certain that she was able to use them, and I put in a plea for the Belgians to be given the heavy guns which had been promised them. As regards sending divisions to Egypt from France, I protested strongly against the proposal, because:

1. Divisions in France were in no state to fight, and were hard at work training.
2. We had recently taken over new line from the French, and we were still in hopes of pressing the Enemy all winter.
3. All were engaged in preparing for next year's attacks.
4. Health of some of the troops (Australian) obliged me to spare them as much as possible. This meant fewer troops being available at present.

As regards guns for Italy, I also protested against any going, for the following reasons:

1. Time was too short. We would never get them back in time for our offensive in the spring.
2. Wastage. Many guns show signs of wear.
3. Gun teams want rest after Somme battle. New teams require training, and were being divided amongst old teams for this purpose.

Arrangements for next year's operations were now in progress. It was 5 pm before I left the Prime Minister. He seemed less determined, I thought, to withdraw troops from France to go elsewhere. I rubbed in that 'to obtain great successes, we must endure minor ills'.

I then proceeded to the Admiralty and saw Admiral Jellicoe . . . I liked very much what I saw of Jellicoe though I should not look on him as a man of great power or decision of character.

Wednesday 20 December

Haig met Nivelle, who had replaced Joffre as the French Commander-in-Chief.

He was, I thought, a most straightforward and soldierly man . . . As regards operations, *Nivelle stated that he is unable to accept the plans which had been worked out for the French Armies under Joffre's directions. He is confident of breaking through the Enemy's front now that the Enemy's morale is weakened, but the blow must be struck by surprise and go through in 24 hours. This necessity for surprise after all is our own conclusion. Our objective on the Somme was the relief of Verdun, and to wear out the Enemy's Forces with a view to striking the decisive blow later, when the Enemy's reserves are used up. Altogether I was pleased with my first meeting with Nivelle. He is in his 61st year. Is alert in mind, and has had much practical experience in this war as a gunner, then in turn a Divisional, Corps, and lastly, Army Commander. He is to write to me his views. Nivelle also mentioned that Lloyd George had said to him at Verdun that 'the British are not a military people'. I said, LG had never studied our military history.

Friday 29 December. Letter to King George V[1]

Sir,

I beg leave to express my most grateful thanks for the very special honour which Your Majesty has conferred on me by appointing me to be a Field Marshal. The very charming letter in which the news was conveyed to me by Your Majesty adds still more to the honour and makes me still more grateful. At the same time I must confess that I realise that I have attained this great position in the Army, not by my own merits, but thanks to the splendid soldierly qualities of our Officers and men. And I cannot find words to express the pride I feel at having Your Majesty's confidence, and at the privilege which has been given me to command such Officers and such soldiers.

1 RA: PS/GV/Q 832/128.

1917
CALAIS TO CAMBRAI

Nineteen seventeen was one of the most important years of the twentieth century. Russia experienced two revolutions, the first – liberal – in March and the second – Bolshevik – in November. The March revolution produced a temporary revival in the Russian war effort, though at great political cost to the Provisional Government, but by the autumn the decline of Russian military power was palpable. A German victory in the east was only a matter of time. Worse still, the very existence of the Bolshevik regime threatened the survival of the European old order, both monarchical and parliamentary. The United States entered the war on the Allied side in April, though only as an Associated Power, a clear statement that the Americans would have their own agenda in any peace settlement.

American military power was fairly negligible, however, and it would be some time before a greatly expanded US Army could compensate for the loss of the Russian Army. In October, Austria-Hungary, reinforced with German troops, came close to knocking Italy out of the war at the Battle of Caporetto. The capture of Baghdad in March by British and Indian forces under General Sir Stanley Maude marked the start of the Ottoman Empire's collapse. Jerusalem fell in December to British, Dominion and Indian forces under Haig's erstwhile Third Army commander, General Sir Edmund Allenby. The British Government had declared its support for the Arab uprising against Ottoman rule in June 1916; in November 1917 it was also to declare its support for the establishment of a 'homeland for the Jewish people' in Palestine. The modern Middle East was beginning to take shape.

The events of 1916 had finally punctured 'the short war illusion'. There was awareness among political leaders that the European Great Powers were standing on the edge of the abyss. The possibility of a negotiated settlement began to be openly (and covertly) discussed, but in the event Germany, France and Great Britain chose the path of victory rather than the path of peace.

In February the German Government announced 'unrestricted submarine warfare'. Allied shipping losses rose calamitously, jeopardising Britain's food supplies and lines of communication. On the Western Front the German Army shortened its lines by retreating to the Hindenburg Line (Siegfried Stellung), a deep defensive position characterised by thousands of concrete machine-gun positions, interlocking arcs of fire and dense belts of barbed wire, that ran south from Arras to Laon. The German Army would stand on the defensive in the west, using the new operational doctrine of 'elastic defence in depth', while it sought a decision in the east.

France put its faith in a new military commander, General Robert Nivelle, who promised victory without tears. The Nivelle Offensive was launched in the middle of April but led only to tears without victory. Sections of the French Army refused to take part in further offensive operations. The burden of the 'wearing-out fight' against the German Army in the west fell increasingly on the British Expeditionary Force.

Britain's determination to win the war 'at all costs' was reflected in David Lloyd George's Government, which came to power in December 1916. Lloyd George immediately created a small executive War Cabinet and proclaimed his determination to strike a 'knockout blow' against Germany.

Nineteen seventeen was, perhaps, the most difficult year of the war for Sir Douglas Haig. It was certainly the year whose events, especially his conduct of the Third Battle of Ypres ('Passchendaele'), did most to damage his post-war reputation. Haig's difficulties are apparent from his diary.

The first of these was his relationship with the new Prime Minister. Haig greeted Lloyd George's elevation with anxiety. It promised a more ruthless prosecution of the war on the home front. But it also promised greater interference in matters of strategy and military operations than was apparent under Lloyd George's acquiescent predecessor. Haig's fears were spectacularly confirmed at the Calais Conference in February, when Lloyd George attempted to subordinate the BEF to French military command. Although the attempt failed, it left a legacy of bitterness and suspicion among the British military. Haig's diary often portrays his sense of being beleaguered, a feeling reinforced by the increasing pessimism, even defeatism, of his close allies, Sir William Robertson (Chief of the Imperial General Staff) and Lord Derby (Secretary of State for War).

Haig's second source of difficulty was with his French allies. He was concerned, even before the failure of the Nivelle Offensive, at the apparent decline in French military power and increasing French political and social instability. His diary for 1917 is full of complaints about the French Army and the French nation, but Haig typically remained a good and reliable ally, despite his private frustrations.

Amid these uncertainties Haig retained a clear and unshakeable belief in the need to attack the German armies in the west. To remain passive was to yield the initiative to the enemy and risk losing the war. Haig also became increasingly confident of the fighting quality of his armies and their commanders. His diary testifies to his optimism about the purpose, conduct and outcome of British military operations. These were on a scale greater even than those of 1916. Arras, Messines, Third Ypres and Cambrai showed impressive improvements at the operational and tactical levels, but they remained costly in human terms and were barren of obvious strategic success. The dramatic German counter-attack at Cambrai on 30 November did much to lower Haig's prestige and he ended the year more vulnerable perhaps than at any time in his period of command.

Saturday 6 January

Lord Northcliffe left for England this morning. He visits the Red [Cross] hospital at Boulogne en route. He is fully alive to his responsibility for putting *Lloyd George into power, and means to do his utmost to insist on him taking the advice of the General Staff. But he admitted that the CIGS[1] had not impressed him. He said 'you call him "Wully", I think "Wooly" would suit him better because he is not firm enough.'

Thursday 11 January

Davidson also brought me Courts Martial for my consideration from the AG.[2] These included 11 cases of the 35th Division (the Bantams). These were all death sentences as the Third Army Commander had already commuted all the cases for which he thought a smaller punishment adequate. Of the 11 cases sent to me I confirmed the proceedings on three, namely 1 sergeant and 2 corporals. The sentences on the remaining 8 I commuted to 15 years penal servitude and suspended the sentences.[3]

Monday 15 January

... I attended at 10 Downing Street by appointment and was received by the PM (Lloyd George). There were also present Generals *Robertson and Davidson (the latter with me) and Colonel Hankey, secretary of the Committee of Imperial Defence. After I had explained the general plan for the offensive, and General *Nivelle's proposals and wishes made to me, the PM proceeded to compare the successes obtained by the French Army during the last summer with what the British had achieved. His general conclusion was that the French Army was better all round, and were able to gain success at less cost in life.

I listened politely for some time, and then told him briefly a few of my experiences with the French in the field during the past $2\frac{1}{2}$ years. The general opinion amongst the British Army that the French infantry lacks discipline and thoroughness. On a number of occasions *we know* they did not attack

---

1 Sir William Robertson.
2 Adjutant General.
3 The men on whom Haig confirmed the death sentence were Lance Corporal Peter Goggins, Lance Corporal John McDonald and Lance Sergeant Joseph Stones, all 19th Battalion Durham Light Infantry. They were executed on 18 January 1917. Haig, like most senior commanders, believed that the death penalty was essential to the maintenance of discipline and that the maintenance of discipline was essential to morale. Despite this, Haig (like his predecessor Sir John French) commuted c. 89 per cent of the death sentences imposed by courts martial.

though *ordered* to do so. Gemeau and Des Vallières[1] have repeatedly said to me 'the French infantry does not exist'.[2]

Tuesday 16 January

At 11 am the War Committee assembled with Robertson and myself.

The PM then said that the War Cabinet had considered by themselves the 2 questions now before us. They felt that we must agree to take over the Roye road for the following reasons:

1. We had refused to send more divisions to Salonika though strongly pressed by the French Government. We must if possible oblige them now.
2. We were fighting in France and the [C-in-C of the French Army] had elaborated a plan which we must do our utmost to make successful.
3. The French Army was the largest force.

We must also agree to the date which the French wished. Their country was invaded and they wished to clear the Enemy out as soon as possible. Lastly by attacking early, we would be able, if the attack by the French failed, to launch another attack later in the year.

At 11.30 am General Nivelle and the other French officers arrived ... He was then questioned by various members of the War Committee as to the French method of holding the line and in reply came a regular lecture on how he thought it ought to be done and he hinted that the British line was being held too strongly.

I was able to tell the committee that 4 British Divisions had recently relieved $5\frac{1}{2}$ French Divisions!! ...

As we left the conference room, General Nivelle handed me a draft in French of the conclusions which he wished the Conference to arrive at. I translated this to the War Committee, and we were able to agree to it except that 'the first week in March' was substituted for '15 February'. The date of the attack was left at 'not later than the 1 April'.

I must say that these 'conclusions' were hastily considered by the War Committee.

We then returned to the Conference Room, the PM then announced the Cabinet's decision, and said they now accepted Nivelle's 'conclusions' modi-

---

1 French Liaison Officers at British GHQ. Des Vallières, during his time at GHQ, appeared well disposed to the British. In his messages to the French authorities, however, he was bitterly critical. This seems to have been an occasion when he was trying to get the British to do more to support the French but was understood as indicating that the French were totally exhausted.
2 The Ts diary reads 'no longer exists' ('n'existe plus').

fied as given above. The latter was signed by Nivelle, Robertson and myself.

Tuesday 23 January

Haig continued to plan for a future amphibious assault on the Belgian coast.

Admiral Bacon motored from Dover to Folkestone to see me off and had a talk with me in my cabin regarding future operations. He is having a special gangway made. It is some 600 ft long and by using 3 of them, he calculates that an infantry division and a few guns may be landed in 15 minutes.

Wednesday 7 February

General Maurice[1] came to lunch. General Maurice had stayed at HQ of First and Second Armies since he was here. After lunch I had a talk with him. From being an admirer of Mr Lloyd George he has got to distrust him, since he has got to know him better. He says that LG is so sketchy and goes into nothing thoroughly. He only presses forward the measures which he thinks will meet with popular favour. Further, Maurice does not think he really cares for the country or is patriotic: in fact he does not trust him! It is indeed a calamity for the Country to have such a man at the head of affairs in this time of great crisis. We can only try and make the best of him!

I reminded Maurice of what I told the PM before the Nivelle Conference in London, that by employing British Divisions to extend the line to the Roye road, we deprived the British Army of its chance of attacking in force and reaping a decisive success. We willingly play a second rôle to the French, that is, we are to make a holding attack to draw in the Enemy's reserves so as to make the task of the French easier. We shall at any rate have heavy losses, with the possibility of no showy successes, whereas the French are to make the decisive attack with every prospect of gaining the fruits of victory. I think it is for the general good that we play this rôle in support of the French, but let the future critics realise that we have adopted it with our eyes open as to the probable consequences.

I also pointed out to Maurice that in urging us to commence offensive operations before things were fully prepared and troops adequately trained, the War Committee were incurring a grave responsibility for [possible] failure. I spoke to the CIGS about this before I left London, and he was to write a paper for the Cabinet embodying my views. I have not seen a copy of it. Maurice said he would send me one. I also told Maurice that I am going to

---

1 Haig on this occasion spelt this name correctly. On others he rendered it as 'Morris'.

write a note on the subject to the War Office, so that my views may be on record.

Monday 26 February

10.45 am I left with General Geddes for Calais.¹ He had compiled an excellent summary of the Transportation case, and questions to be settled. We talked over this in the car, and took a walk together on reaching Calais . . .

I sat next LG at lunch. He agreed to see Geddes and me for ¼ hour before the Conference, on the matter of the Railway Transport question. As soon as he had finished lunch, he hurried off to see M. Briand, [in order, he said, to] settle the programmes of the meeting. He had a talk with Briand for over half an hour, and then sent word to say that we would go to the Conference straight away without the preliminary talk with [me and] Geddes. No doubt at the meeting with Briand, the whole arrangements which developed later were decided upon . . .

After a few general words from LG and Briand, Geddes was asked to give the several points in dispute. He spoke about our requirements in tonnage, and trains . . . and the discussion entered into points of technical detail. LG thereupon broke in, and said that he thought that it would be better if the Railway authorities withdrew, and settled their differences together, while the more important question of 'Plans' was dealt with at once. For me, [this was quite a new and] unexpected development! But doubtless it had all been planned by LG [with Briand beforehand] . . .

General Nivelle with the aid of a map, [at Lloyd George's request] indicated his plan of operations. He started by saying that he took over Command on 15 December, and on 17th, came to see Sir DH at Cassel: that I had 'after reflexion, concurred in his proposals and helped him in every way' and, on several occasions later in his address, he emphasised the 'accord' which existed between us.

The plan is the one which he had on several occasions explained [to Lloyd George], and for which we are now preparing. So it is not necessary to give it again here. Nivelle concluded by saying that he would answer any question LG cared to put to him. But LG said, 'That is not all – I want to hear everything,' and to Briand he said, 'Tell him to keep nothing back' and so forth, as to his disagreements with 'Marshal Haig'. This was quite a surprise to me, and apparently to Nivelle to some extent . . .

I now explained in French why I rejected Nivelle's suggestion [not to attack] the Vimy Ridge. [Briefly, I said that for tactical reasons my] left must

---

1 The Calais Conference was necessitated by a shipping accident at Boulogne that closed the port for twenty-six days and caused logistical chaos.

either be on the south side of Monchy le Preux ridge (south of the Scarpe) [or must be north of and include the Vimy Ridge. If our left were placed south of the Scarpe, then, with the number of attacking divisions agreed upon], my right would extend towards Gommecourt. If we pierced the front in this position we entered a pocket formed by the Hindenburg Line.

On the other hand, with my left on the Vimy Ridge, I had a secure flank and my attack would bring me *in rear* of the Hindenburg Line ... Lyautey said that my explanation was quite clear, and was sound.[1]

I then explained that I was doing my utmost to comply with the strategical requirements of Nivelle's plan, but in the matter of tactics I alone could decide. That is to say, Nivelle having stated that his plan required the British to break the Enemy's front north of the Somme and march on Cambrai, I decided *where* and *how* I would dispose of my troops for that purpose.

Lloyd George at once said he did not understand about strategy and tactics, he would like it clearly stated what [the respective] responsibilities were. It was then about 6.45 pm; he therefore asked the French to draw up their proposals for a system of command before dinner, so that he, Robertson and I could discuss it after dinner and a subsequent conference with the French Government would then be held tomorrow morning to finally decide. This was agreed to.

Robertson and I walked about till time to dress for dinner. LG said he was ill and did not come to dinner. At table I sat opposite Briand, with Lyautey on my right, and Nivelle on my left. We had quite a cheery talk.

After dinner, I went to Robertson's room and found him most excited over a typed paper which LG had given him containing the French proposals. These were briefly to organise a British CGS and Staff at Beauvais (French GQG) with what they called a 'Quartermaster General'. The CGS to report to the War Committee at home. The C-in-C would apparently only administer the discipline [and look after reinforcements].

Robertson and I then went into LG's room. [The latter now] told us that the War Cabinet had decided last week that since this was likely to be the last effort of the French, and they had the larger numbers engaged, 'in fact, it was their battle', the British Army would be placed under the French C-in-C's orders.

He then asked me my views. I said that, in my opinion, it would be madness to place the British under the French, and that I did not believe our troops would fight under French leadership. At the beginning of the war,

---

1 General Louis Hubert Gonzalve Lyautey (1854–1934) had become Minister of War in Briand's Government in December 1916. He was never convinced by Nivelle's plans. His resignation on 14 March 1917 brought down the Government but did not prevent the Nivelle Offensive from going ahead.

there was much dissatisfaction [in the Army] with GHQ because there was an idea that British interests were sacrificed to those of the French.

He agreed that the French demands were absurd¹ but insisted on Robertson and myself considering a scheme for giving effect to the War Cabinet's decision.

I went with Robertson to his room. He seemed thoroughly upset with the attitude of our Prime Minister. Colonel Hankey (Secretary War Committee) further added to our dissatisfaction by saying that LG had not received full authority from the War Cabinet for acting as he was doing.

General *Kiggell took part in our discussion and we agreed we would rather be tried by Court Martial than betray the Army by agreeing to its being placed under the French. Robertson agreed that we must resign rather than be partners in this transaction.

And so we went to bed, thoroughly disgusted with our Government and the Politicians.

Tuesday 27 February

[In the course of the morning of Tuesday, 27 February, 1917 and before the Conference assembled, General Lyautey sent his personal Staff officer to beg me to go to his room as he had something very important to tell me. On going to his room I found Nivelle with him. They both spoke of the 'insult offered to me and the British Army by the paper which Briand had produced'. They assured me that they had not seen the document until quite recently. Indeed, as regards Lyautey, he had not seen or heard of it until he entered the train at Paris to come to Calais today. I understand that the paper was drawn up in Paris with Lloyd George's approval and of course, that of Briand.]²

About 9.30 Robertson sent to ask me to come to his room. He had a paper [ready] giving LG's solution.

This distinguished between the period intervening between signing the document, and the date of commencing the battle. In the first period, I should conform to Nivelle's instructions as regards preparations for the battle, but am free to depart from these if I think the safety of the Army endangered or success prejudiced. In this case I am to report action taken to War Cabinet.

In the second period the Army is to act entirely as Nivelle orders. At an interview with Lloyd George I objected to this and insisted on having added 'that I have a free hand to choose the means and methods of utilising the

1 The Ts diary says 'excessive'.
2 Sir Edward Spears, in *Prelude to Victory* (London: Cape, 1939), Appendices, presents evidence that the French had been concocting the 'Calais plot' since the end of 1916 and that Nivelle's expressions of astonishment and ignorance were feigned.

British troops in that sector of operations allotted by the French C-in-C in the original plan'. This was concurred in by Nivelle. A document was then drawn up embodying these points. As it stands, the way in which I have worked with the French is not changed. I have always acted on General *Joffre's 'General Instructions' as if they had been orders, but retained absolute freedom of action as to how I carried them out. This power remains to me. I am however relieved of responsibility for the plan of the battle now being prepared for as well as for the [details of the] execution of the plan.

To settle the above there was much going to and fro between the parties interested. Robertson did the going to and fro: he seemed to have passed a restless night – indeed, it seems he could not sleep, and at 2 or 3 am knocked up his assistant (Major General Morris) to come and discuss the situation with him.

Finally, we all met at 11.30 about – that is, the members of British and French Governments with the 4 soldiers and 1 interpreter.

The document was considered and passed with a small addition, that the British and French War Cabinets should each judge when the operations shall be deemed to have terminated, so far as its own Army is concerned.

The battle is expected to last *about* a fortnight, and after that the normal state of arrangements will be reverted to . . .

The 2 documents were then signed by all of us, and a copy taken by each Government. I am to receive a copy of the 'proces verbal' of the proceedings . . .

Briand asked me to lunch, but having many matters to arrange[1] I left at once with Kiggell and Sassoon.

We lunched at Boulogne and got back about 4 pm to Beaurepaire.[2]

Davidson came to dinner. He has recently visited the French Armies which are preparing for the offensive and was full of his experiences. All most kind and hospitable. General Michelère[3] incidentally stated that it does not matter what the politicians may decide, the French soldier is not going to fight after the autumn!

Wednesday 28 February

The letter[4] arrived about 6 pm. Its language was couched in very commanding tones. It asked for a copy of my orders to my Armies for the forthcoming

1 The Ts diary was changed to 'I felt I had seen enough of him for the time being'.
2 The Château Beaurepaire, Haig's GHQ.
3 Properly, 'Micheler'. General Joseph Alfred Micheler (1861–1931), GOC French Reserve Army Group at the time of the Nivelle Offensive, about which he had grave reservations and which he voiced.
4 From General Nivelle.

offensive: stated that French personnel would be withdrawn and must be replaced by British by degrees: and that we must be ready to run our communications, etc., up to the Lille–Maubeuge line (this is at variance with previous agreements). Finally, he *desired* that Sir H. *Wilson should be detailed as head of the British Mission at Beauvais as soon as he returns from Russia.

Briefly it is a type of letter which no gentleman could have drafted, and it also is one which certainly no C-in-C of this great British Army should receive without protest.

By the Calais agreement I only come under his orders *after* the battle commences, and then only for operations in the sector assigned to me already. I intend to send a copy of the letter with my reply to the War Committee, with a request to be told whether it is their wishes that the C-in-C in command of this British Army should be subjected to such treatment by a junior *foreign* Commander.

It is too sad at this critical time to have to fight with one's Allies and the Home Government, in addition to the Enemy in the field!

Monday 12 March

At 9.30 am I went to Derby House and had a long talk with Lord Derby, Secretary of State for War. He looked more pulled down with worry over the Calais Conference than even Robertson did last night! He condoled with me, said Government had treated me disgracefully. I assured him that though I realised that fact, I felt no ill-will against any of them! That I wanted nothing more in the way of reward and that if the Government had anyone else whom they wished to put in my place, let them do it at once – and I would try and retire gracefully without causing the Government of the country any trouble or loss of prestige. He (like the *King) assured me that the last thing they wanted was that I should retire. I told him that I had no objection to appointing Sir H. *Wilson to be head of British Mission at French GQG provided the duties of the appointment were first settled [and in accordance with the needs of GHQ.]

Between 12 and 1 I saw Sir H. Wilson who came to the flat at my request. I showed him all the papers connected with the Calais Conference. He agreed that the difficulty arose from the French trying to work on the 'Projet d'Organisation, etc.' (which had been rejected) while I worked loyally on the Calais Agreement! We had a long talk and I came to the conclusion that it would be best for me to trust him, and appoint him as head of the reorganised mission at French GQG. In the meantime I asked him to go at once to Downing Street and see Lord *Milner, and impress on him what the French real intentions were, and the necessity for him to oppose them.

I lunched with *Doris at the flat and soon after Wilson arrived to tell me that he had seen Milner, that the War Cabinet was entirely in my favour, and that I could therefore appear before them confident that the Prime Minister (Lloyd George) would support me.

The French representatives arrived about 3 pm. Between 3.30 and 4 pm Robertson and I saw the Prime Minister at 10 Downing Street. The War Cabinet had accepted the conclusions at which I had arrived in my letter of this morning, and Lloyd George had had a copy from them extracted which he proposed to put to General Nivelle on his arrival.

Shortly after this Nivelle arrived and LG saw him, settled the points of divergence, and then asked Robertson and myself to join them. After a short talk, we [soldiers] adjourned to War Office and discussed the details of the 'Conclusions' for submission to Conference tomorrow, as well as the general situation and the nature of the plans, as affected by the Enemy's withdrawal from the front of our Fifth Army.[1]

With slight modifications Nivelle accepted the English document put before him by Robertson. As to plans, we agreed that it was most important to go forward with the plans of attack as soon as possible without change, i.e., the attacks near Arras, and that toward Laon (the French Reserve Group of Armies). At the same time to be prepared to move divisions from Franchet d'Esperey[2] to Champagne if the Enemy was found to be retiring in his present front. [As to] our Fifth Army (*Gough) I had already disposed of his reserves behind my First and Third Armies, while the heavy guns would reinforce my Third Army instead of bringing other guns from our Second Army front as arranged in original programme.

When Nivelle, Robertson and I left the Prime Minister's room, the rest of the French Mission arrived – M. Cambon (Ambassador in London)[3] begged me to dine at [his] Embassy tonight. I regretted that I was engaged. Then General Lyautey asked me to dine, and if I could not, at any rate to come to the French Embassy after dinner. I said I would be there at 9.30 pm but it was impossible to dine.

Before I left the War Office, Lyautey called. Robertson then went to see [the] King, so that I had 15 minutes quiet talk with Lyautey [alone. He is a thorough gentleman whom I can trust.]

I dined with Doris at the flat and at 9.30 pm, I went to French Embassy. The party there had finished dinner and were in drawing-room upstairs. I

1 The Germans began to retreat to the Hindenburg Line in mid-March. Their retirement made large parts of Nivelle's plan irrelevant and inoperable.
2 General Louis Felix Marie François Franchet d'Esperey (1856–1942), GOC Army Group North and Army Group East, 1916–17; a leading advocate of offensive operations.
3 Paul Cambon (1843–1924), French Ambassador to Great Britain, 1898–1920.

found myself to be the only Englishman present, and was most warmly welcomed. Lloyd George had declined the French Ambassador's invitation, and I expect that [our other Ministers] felt that the situation was strained!

I talked to Lyautey and A. Thomas.[1] I told them exactly the facts, how after the Calais Conference many young French officers had behaved as if the British Army was a subordinate force, how in aiming at 'Unity of Command' they had mistaken the *means* for *the end*, which was 'unity of effort'. The friction which had thus begun might have far-reaching evil consequences [unless the French War Office and GQG took proper steps to stop it at once.]

I then went into private room with Lyautey who asked me *very privately* whether I was satisfied with the French officers at [GQG]. I said I was quite satisfied, but I felt that Colonel D'Alençon, [Nivelle's confidential Staff officer,] was a cause of friction; he disliked every Englishman.[2] He quite agreed and said he was most disagreeable even to himself. We parted the best of friends. The Ambassador came downstairs to the door to see me off and bid me goodnight. It was 11.15 pm when I left the French Embassy. [I felt that I had been very forgiving and only the need of working with the French Army in order to win had dragged me there.]

Wednesday 14 March

Major Lucas[3] (ADC to CIGS) called for [the copy of the] Agreement between Nivelle and myself which I was asked to sign at once, as Nivelle was leaving at 11 am. I sent it back with a note to CIGS and eventually went to see him. I told him that we seemed to be always *giving in* to the French in all their demands, that we trusted in their good faith without any written documents, while they invariably wanted 'an agreement in writing' duly signed.

Finally I signed the Agreement, but wrote above my signature: 'I agree with the above on the understanding that while I am fully determined to carry out the Calais Agreement in spirit and letter, the British Army and its C-in-C will be regarded by General Nivelle as Allies and not as subordinates, except during the particular operations which he explained at the Calais Conference. Further, while I also accept the Agreement respecting the func-

1 Albert Thomas (1878–1932), French Minister of Munitions, August 1914–September 1917.
2 Properly Colonel D'Alenson. He was terminally ill (with tuberculosis) and was determined that his final efforts should bring victory. He despised many in the French military hierarchy and was *very* anti-British.
3 Major (later Brigadier General) Cecil Courtenay Lucas ('The Monument') (1883–1957), Royal Horse Artillery, Robertson's faithful ADC.

tions of the British Mission at French HQ, it should be understood that these functions may he subject to modifications as experience shows to be necessary.'

The above was approved by the War Cabinet at 12.30 before I signed. I was present at its meeting and explained the general plan agreed upon by Nivelle and myself. This is to:

1. Continue pressing Enemy back with advanced guards wherever he is giving way.
2. To launch our main attacks as soon as possible.
   But in view of the possibility of these attacks falling in the air, at once to prepare for attacks elsewhere.

As to the British Army, my plan based on foregoing is

1. To continue to make all preparations (as arranged) for attacks by First and Third Armies, keeping adequate reserves available either to support Second Army (Ypres) or to exploit success of attacks near Arras. These reserves are obtained from the Fifth Army.
2. *If successful,* at Arras, exploit with all reserves and the cavalry.
3. *If not successful,* prepare to launch attacks near Ypres to clear the Belgian coast. All cavalry will be required probably if this attack is successful.

The attack on Messines Ridge might be made in May if desirable.

Saturday 24 March

After dinner I had a long talk with Painlevé.[1] He is a pleasant bright little man. Said to be a great mathematician [and an extreme socialist.] He is most anxious to keep on the most friendly terms with the British. Hence his visit to me the day after he took over his office. I thought it was nice of him coming to see me so soon [and I was most friendly.] I gather that General *Pétain is a favourite of his. He questioned me closely about Nivelle. I was careful to say that he struck me as a capable general, and that I was, of course, ready to co-operate with whoever was chosen by the French Government to be their C-in-C. I said my relations with Nivelle are and always have been *excellent.* The Calais Conference was a mistake, but it was not Nivelle's fault.

On Easter Monday, 9 April, the BEF launched its attack at Arras, spearheaded

1 Paul Painlevé (1863–1933) succeeded Lyautey in March 1917 as Minister for War in the new Government of Alexandre Ribot.

*by the Third Army (*Allenby) and the First Army (*Horne). The attack began in
a snowstorm; atrocious weather had been a feature of the build-up to the battle.
This was designed to draw German reserves away from the Nivelle Offensive on
the Aisne, planned for later in the month. The battle opened well, including the
capture of Vimy Ridge by the Canadian Corps, and a four-mile advance by the
9th (Scottish) Division. Later, however, fighting descended into an attritional
slogging match with heavy casualties on both sides (British per diem casualties
were among their heaviest of the war).*

Monday 9 April. Letter to King George V[1]

Your Majesty will be pleased to hear that I found the troops everywhere in
the most splendid spirits and looking the picture of health. The marching
and the joy of operating in the open at last and above all, the fact that the
Army was *advancing* made everyone happy! ... The change to open warfare
has especially benefited the Australians: indeed they seem 50 per cent more
efficient now, than when they were in the trenches ...

I am writing this at Heuchin (near St Pol) while the Battle for Vimy Ridge
etc. is going on. Everyone is so busy today that I have managed to get a leisure
hour for writing a letter! I came here last night so as to be near the HQs of
Generals Horne and Allenby ...

The attack was launched at 5.30 am, and has progressed most satisfactorily.
Indeed at the time of writing (3 pm) the several lines have been captured
according to the timetable and a large number of prisoners have been taken;
probably 10,000 when all are counted! Our success is already the largest
obtained on this front in *one* day.

Tuesday 10 April

About 10.30 am I saw Generals Allenby and Horne at St Pol. They each
explained the situation on their respective fronts.

The Canadian Corps had consolidated its front and captured Hill 145 with
32 Germans out of a garrison of 300. Patrols have been sent to Vimy village
and Willerval. Canadian Corps has now taken all its objectives.

The Third Army is attacking Monchy le Preux at 12 noon from the
northwest and west.

I urged on Allenby the importance of keeping the Enemy on the move
during the next 24 hours, before he can bring up reserves to meet our
advance ...

If the Third Army is held up from the west of Monchy le Preux, I urged

1 RA: PS/GV/Q 832/137.

Allenby to push forward on the north of the Scarpe and then move southeast in the rear of Monchy so to turn the Enemy's flank...

At 2 pm I travelled to Noyelle-Vion (Headquarters of 6th Division[1]). General Haldane had gone forward to see his Divisional Commanders so I saw Lord Loch[2] his CGS and congratulated the Corps on the results achieved yesterday. I then rode across country to Duisans (HQ Cavalry Corps). I discussed the situation with General Kavanagh. He said the infantry were not as far forward as he had been led to believe. Monchy le Preux had not been taken. He had 3 brigades of cavalry on the Brown line south of the Scarpe with patrols pushing forward. I explained that if the First Army required a cavalry division the whole of the 1st Division must be detached and placed under General Horne.

Wednesday 11 April

Haig visited Arras.

General Haldane Commanding VI Corps also came to see me. He had been close to Monchy. His difficulty was to get the Commanders of Divisions to go forward, and take control of the operations. They had been accustomed to sit behind trenches and command by the aid of telegraph. Now their wires in the open soon get broken, and they lost connection with their brigades who were fighting. He had seen all the Division Generals of his Corps and he felt things were moving better.

I then got on my horse and rode to HQ Cavalry Corps ... where I saw General Kavanagh. His said the infantry had not progressed as hoped owing to machine gun fire from north bank of Scarpe. Early in the morning the 15th Division had gone forward in splendid style, and had advanced to the ridge east of Monchy. A brigade of cavalry was then sent up to pass through. Meanwhile the Enemy counter-attacked and forced our infantry back on Monchy village. The cavalry then had to come back. 2 cavalry regiments were now holding Monchy village dismounted along with an infantry battalion. General Bulkeley-Johnson[3] commanding the 8 Cavalry Brigade (Vaughan's division) was killed near Monchy by machine gun bullet from north bank of the Scarpe. He was well behind with his reserve regiment at [the] moment. Kavanagh also feared that a good many horses had been hit.

I then went to HQ 12th Division in the Place Ste Croix and saw General

1 Actually, 'Corps'.
2 Brigadier General (later Major General) Edward Douglas, Lord Loch (1873–1942), BGGS VI Corps, 1915–17.
3 Brigadier General Charles Bulkeley Bulkeley-Johnson (1867–1917).

Scott. He said that his division had suffered wonderfully few casualties in the battle. The men were in grand form but tired. The arrangements for collecting the wounded had worked very well indeed. They were all collected and sent off by 2 am.

I next visited General McCracken (Commanding 15th Division) in a dugout in the east of the town. His losses on the Monday were very small: he was next the Scarpe but on the south of it: but he feared that his losses today were heavy. His men had returned early today to Monchy from the north, and had come under machine gun fire from the slopes on the north side of the Scarpe. The 4th Division should, he said, have started their attack simultaneously with the 15th Division but they did not advance till noon. Consequently the northern flank of the 15th Division had been uncovered. One of his battalions took Monchy village yesterday and had been fighting for it all day, the Enemy having received orders to retake it at all costs . . .

Haig then visited the HQ of 17th Division and spoke to Major General Robertson.[1]

He said that his division were very fit and well having had a rest for nearly 3 months in training. They had billeted in Arras last night and had a good night's rest. He was sending up one brigade to Monchy tonight to relieve the 15th Division. I then rode out and saw some of the men of the division. They were singing and whistling as they marched out towards Monchy in spite of snow falling heavily at the time. I rode out along the Cambrai road to see the HQ 3rd Division but went beyond the Faubourg St Saveur without finding it. I saw a number of cavalrymen marching back on foot having had their horses killed . . .

The 4th Australian Division (Gough's Fifth Army) attacked at 4.30 this morning and preceded by 12 Tanks passed the Hindenburg Line between Bullecourt and Quéant. They occupied Heudecourt and Riencourt. About noon the Enemy made a strong counter-attack from the direction of Cagnicourt and drove the Anzacs back to their original line taking 400 prisoners.

Thursday 12 April

First Army report at 9.20 am that 4th Canadian Division (Hilliam's brigade –

1 Major General (later Sir) Philip Rynd Robertson ('Blobs') (1866–1936), GOC 17th (Northern) Division, 1916–19. Robertson was one of the BEF's longest-serving and most experienced divisional commanders by the end of the war; a competent and prudent commander.

late Sergeant Major in 17th Lancers[1]) attacked and captured 'the Pimple' (a small hill at the extreme north end of the Vimy Ridge) early this morning. About 50 prisoners reported captured. At the same time the I Corps (24th Division) attacked Bois en Hache successfully and took some prisoners. Total guns taken by Canadians now reported at 33 including four 8-inch and nine 5.9-inch.

I motored with Kiggell to St Pol (HQ Third Army) and saw General Bols (the Major General General Staff). He explained situation and orders given. Allenby was away seeing Corps Commanders. I pointed out that the Enemy had now been given time to put the Drocourt–Quéant line into a state of defence and to organise positions also in our immediate front. He has also brought up a large amount of guns. Our advance must therefore be more methodical than was permissible on Monday night and Tuesday after the victory. Then *great risks* might have been made without danger because Enemy had been surprised and had no reserves on the spot! Now we must try and substitute shells as far as possible for infantry . . .

I then motored to Ranchicourt (HQ First Army) and saw General Horne. He told me that the going this morning (owing to the snow and the shell holes) when the Canadians attacked 'the Pimple' was very bad indeed. Yesterday Horne had visited Thélus and found it difficult to discover where the German first line trenches had been. All had been so terribly destroyed by our shell fire. Horne thought he had used too many shells! It had broken up the soil so frightfully that all movement was made most difficult.

Owing to the amount of artillery and ammunition now available, the frontal attack on a position had become, Horne thought, the easiest task. The difficult matter was to advance later on when the Enemy had organised a defence with machine guns. He also said that many officers in the First Army had said to him that their chief joy in gaining Monday's victory was the knowledge that it would put the stopper on the disgraceful intrigue which had been going on at home in certain quarters against me. Especially was this feeling marked in the Canadian Corps, who had resented very much the attacks to which I had been subjected by certain politicians and others in England.

Message received from Nivelle, French attacks are again postponed for another 24 hours. When I think over the fine work of the Canadian 4th Division in taking 'the Pimple' notwithstanding the mud, shell holes and snow, I come to the conclusion that no other people are comparable to the

1 Brigadier General (later Major General) Edward Hilliam (1863–1949), GOC 10 Canadian Brigade, 1917; GOC 44 Brigade, 1917–18; GOC 102 Brigade, 1918. Hilliam served in the ranks of the 17th Lancers, Haig's old regiment, before emigrating to Canada, where he was a fruit rancher in British Columbia.

British race as downright hard fighters. This operation of Hilliam's brigade this morning was a fine performance.

Friday 13 April

I left Heuchin by motor at 10.00 am and visited HQ Third Army at St Pol. I told Allenby to arrange his advance steadily and sparing the infantry as much as possible: and that I would arrange the next general attack of the First, Third and Fifth Armies, in combination, for Tuesday morning...

I reached Arras about midday with General Kiggell. We visited HQ 50th Division (Wilkinson),[1] 29th Division (De Lisle) and 17th Division (Robertson) and got the exact situation, and the nature of the orders which had reached them. The latter differed in some cases in essentials from those which had been issued from Army HQ!

We lunched from the lunch box in my house in the Rue Jeanne d'Arc and then rode by the Bapaume road to Beaurains where I left the horses. I then walked over the defences eastwards to Telegraph Hill where the famous 'Harp' was situated. I was greatly pleased at the way the *wire* had been quite destroyed. This shows how effective our new instantaneous fuse (No. 106) for destroying wire is with the large heavy shells and no craters are formed. Beyond the defence wire no shell holes, showing how good our shooting was! I had a good view of Monchy (less than 6000 yards off) and of Wancourt Tower which was taken about noon today. The Enemy was bombarding Monchy fairly severely.

The battlefields had already been well cleaned up. I walked back to Beaurains and then rode via Mercatel and Ficheux to Blaireville.[2] On the way I looked at the heavy artillery which were all ready to leave their emplacements in the banks on the edge of the Bapaume road and advance to new positions further forward. It is fairly easy work moving these great heavy guns nowadays by means of tractors. The real difficulty is getting the large amount of shells forward. Luckily our railways are following our advance well. The through Albert–Bapaume main line will be open by the 18th. It is already open to Boisleux and as I passed the broken railway bridge west of Mercatel a train was on the line north of it having come from Arras.

At Blaireville I saw General Pinney (33rd Division). His HQ are in a quarry. His troops had 2 bad nights moving up in the snow, but are now as cheery as possible. He is relieving the 21st Division (Campbell) on the right of VII Corps.

---

1 Major General (later Sir) Percival Spearman Wilkinson (1865–1919), GOC 50th (Northumbrian) Division, 1915–18. Wilkinson was wounded later on in the day of this meeting.
2 Properly 'Blairville'.

On reaching Beaumetz Captain Muir[1] (17th Lancers) GSO3 Third Army met me with a telephone message from the French GQG to the effect that the French Army Group Commanders wished to postpone operations for another day but Nivelle will not approve unless I concur. The nearest telephone station was at Walrus[2] (HQ 14th Division). I left the horse at Beaumetz, and motored by back road to Walrus and was able to speak to Kiggell at Heuchin. I told him that since the French had been given the main decisive attack to carry out we must do all in our power to help them make their operations a success. I therefore concurred in whatever postponement Nivelle found necessary to attain the object in view.

Friday 13 April. Letter to Lady Haig

Your dear kind letter written on Thursday has just reached me. I am delighted to think that *you* only believe what I write to you. You are quite right – these papers publish a lot of untruths – or at any rate only publish what suits their policy!

The effect of our Victory will be great. Already the Enemy has begun to fall back from north of Vimy. He says in his 'communiqué' that we attacked him. This is not the case. Only our bombardment scattered a whole division of Guards which was forming to make a counter-attack, and they bolted according to prisoners' statements – This is all very hopeful.

I am very glad to hear from you that those serving under me have an affection for me. As you know, I don't go out of my way to make myself popular, either by doing showy things or by being slack in the matter of discipline. I never hesitate to find fault, but I leave myself a tremendous affection for those fine fellows who are ready to give their lives for the Old Country at any moment. I feel quite sad at times when I see them march past me, knowing as I do how many must pay the full penalty before we can have peace.

It is satisfactory to hear that a much larger percentage than usual are slight bullet wounds during this last battle. This is due to our dominating artillery fire.

Saturday 14 April

I met Gough at Doullens soon after noon at the mairie. There were present also Generals Kiggell and Malcolm. Gough's first objective to co-operate with

---

1 Captain (later Major) John Huntly Muir (1882–1918), 17th Lancers, killed in action on 11 April 1918 while attached to 1st Battalion King's Own Scottish Borderers.
2 Properly, 'Warlus'.

the Third Army in the capture of the Drocourt–Quéant line, particularly with artillery enfilade fire. It may be necessary for him to put in an infantry attack if Allenby is occupied on his left and his artillery is delayed in coming forward.

Gough is also to reconnoitre and prepare an attack astride the Bapaume–Cambrai road with the objective of piercing the Hindenburg Line in the direction of Marcoing.

Gough will not attack the front Bullecourt–Quéant until Allenby's advanced guards are across the Sensée River and are able to support Gough . . .

On our way back I called at HQ Third Army at St Pol and saw General Allenby who had just seen his Corps Commanders. The 29th Division which had advanced about 1000 yards on the spur east of Monchy during the night, had been heavily counter-attacked and driven back to the wood east of the village. Fighting had been going on most of the morning. Also our troops which had occupied the spur southwest of Chérisy had been forced back to the positions they were in last night near Wancourt Tower.

Allenby thought that the companies having been so long in the trenches were now like 'blind puppies' and unable to see the features of the ground and take advantage of the cover afforded for turning on to the Enemy's machine gun. Personally I think that the movement of the several divisions wants to be co-ordinated better, especially astride the Scarpe, east of Fampoux. I told Allenby what instructions I had given Gough, and I hoped that the advanced guards of Third Army would be over the Sensée in time for Gough to attack Tuesday morning. Allenby thought that there would be no difficulty about this . . .

The question of advanced GHQ was considered by Kiggell and myself. At present I and CGS with my personal Staff are at Heuchin, the whole of GHQ is still at Montreuil. The distance from the latter to the front is very great and much time is wasted in journeys in motor cars. It is necessary for me and the operations section to be in close touch with HQ of the Armies and for me to be able to visit corps and divisions without wasting time on the road.

The long-awaited French attack – the Nivelle Offensive – was launched on 16 April.

Tuesday 17 April

I could get no details from French [mission] as to results of today's fighting, which is always a bad sign [and I fear that things are going badly with their offensive.]

It seems Enemy captured during his successful attack near Sapingneul (when he took 800 French prisoners) the whole plan of attack of three [French] Corps! [Information from GQG states that] a division had published a written order which had gone down to battalions indicating the whole plan of operation! With such carelessness it seems difficult to avoid information from reaching the Enemy.

Wednesday 18 April

Letter dated April 17, received from Sir H. Wilson from Compiègne (French GQG). On morning of French battle yesterday he walked along the heights of south side of the Aisne facing German positions (on line Condé to Pont d'Arcis and Troyon). I know that ground well of course. Wilson states Enemy's position greatly strengthened in the $2\frac{1}{2}$ years since we left. So strong is this front now, that Wilson thinks that it ought not to have been attacked.

'There is no doubt, to my mind that the whole of the Sixth Army attack has been a dead failure. The Fifth Army on the other hand got on much better, etc.' 'Pétain (Fourth Army) seems doing well this morning...'

GQG is disappointed, and they will look about for some excuse. One of them will be that the whole German Army is facing them and that we have not succeeded in easing their load! This would be pure French, i.e., the woman's side of their nature, wounded vanity, jealousy and disappointment at their own failure and our success! I don't think, luckily, that the French losses are very heavy...

Major General Maurice from War Office came to dinner. He had travelled from England with the Prime Minister (Lloyd George). The latter is going to Italy tomorrow with M. Ribot[1] to take concerted action with the Italian Premier to try and prevent Russia from concluding a separate peace with Austria. LG is to be back in Paris on Saturday, and will meet the French Government. Maurice had been directed by LG to obtain my views on the situation. M. Albert Thomas, who had just passed through London on his way to Russia, had told LG that it was the intention of the French Government, if the offensive operations near Soissons by the French did not develop successfully very quickly, to stop them, and do nothing till 1918 when the Americans would be able to help.

I told Maurice to put his questions on paper and that I would address my reply to the CIGS. He could then, if the latter concurred, give it to the Prime Minister. But I must say at once that it would be the height of folly for the French to stop now, just when the Germans had committed the serious fault of retiring, meaning to avoid a battle, but had been forced to fight against their will. The Enemy should be pressed everywhere [without delay] by *all*

---

1 Alexandre Felix Joseph Ribot (1842–1923), Prime Minister of France, March–September 1917.

the Allies. If offensive operations are stopped in France, the Enemy will be given time to recover from the blows he received on the Somme, at Verdun, Arras, and now on the Aisne. He will also be able to transfer troops to other theatres, which will call for counter-measures on our part. This will mean increased demand on shipping, and help the Germans in his submarine campaign. He would also have troops available for a threat against England.

Tuesday 24 April

I left Bavincourt at 1.30 by motor for Amiens where I met General Nivelle at 3 pm. Previous to the meeting I had a talk with Sir Henry Wilson who told me of the difficulties under which Nivelle had to carry out his operations – on account of gossip and lack of confidence on the part of the President (*Poincaré) and of individual members of the Government and jealousies on the part of rival French generals. If Nivelle is replaced by another, the latter will be in the same position as Nivelle in two months' time! I also received a wire from Esher from Paris saying 'strong determination on the part of Minister of War here to make radical changes in High Command...'

I thought it best to have a private talk with Nivelle alone first of all, so we at once went to a small room upstairs by ourselves, and I put my view of the situation to him. Briefly my points were as follows:

1. The French Government had told the British Prime Minister that if a distinct success were not obtained in the first few days of attack on the Aisne, they intended to stop offensive.
2. In view of submarine campaign it was most necessary to clear the Belgian ports soon, at any rate before autumn.
3. This could be done either *directly* by operating from Ypres, or *indirectly*, by operating towards Charleroi–Liège.
4. We are at present carrying out the latter plan, and I am prepared to use every effort to break the Hindenburg Line and take Cambrai; but for this to be successful, the continued action of the French Army is essential.
5. I requested him to assure me that the French Armies would continue to operate energetically, because what I feared was that, after the British Army had exhausted itself in trying to make Nivelle's plan a success, the French Government might stop the operations. I would then not be able to give effect to the other plan, viz. that of directly capturing the northern ports.

Nivelle assured me that [neither he nor his Government had any intention] of stopping the offensive. He then told me his plan, which was to continue operations on the Aisne until Rheims was safe etc., and that he would place an Army of Reserve on Franchet's[1] left rear, which would be available to support me too, if required. Franchet would also be given many more guns.

Thursday 26 April

Haig went to Paris.

M. Painlevé was delighted to see me but he appeared quite excited, and from his conversation I gathered that he had almost persuaded himself that the French had been beaten on the Aisne! He assured me that whatever happened, the French Government and Army would loyally discharge their duties towards the British Army, that there would be no change of plan, and that the offensive would be maintained. I gathered however that he wished to replace Nivelle with Pétain. I told him of the plans agreed upon between Nivelle and myself [regarding clearing the Belgian coast before winter.] He stated definitely that there would be no delay in carrying it out. [Painlevé was evidently anxious that I should urge the dismissal of Nivelle, hence his desire to see me before I saw the Prime Minister.]

At 3 pm I saw M. Ribot (the Prime Minister) at the Quai d'Orsay (Foreign Office). He is a tall old man of eighty years of age. A dear old thing but I should think too old to deal with these tricky French politicians. He told me of the jealousies existing amongst their generals, of the [mutual] complaints made regarding their last attacks on the Aisne and in Champagne. Already 95,000 wounded had passed through their Casualty Hospitals, and he presumed there would be ... a total of over 115,000 casualties. He stated that this was no time for making a change in the Higher Command. He asked my opinion. I said any change in command during a battle was to be deprecated but that I was delighted to work with any general whom the French Government appointed as their C-in-C. He asked me about Pétain's merits, but I of course could not discuss this. I said I knew him so slightly that I had not had any means of judging.

I asked him if I could assure my Government that there was no intention to stop operations or modify the present plans agreed upon. He begged me in the strongest way possible to tell my Government that there will be no change made in the execution of plans. Nothing had yet been decided about Nivelle and he personally thought that Nivelle should remain on.

---

1 General (later Marshal of France) Louis Felix Marie François Franchet D'Esperey (1856–1942), GOC French Army Group North in 1917; as Allied GOC-in-C in Salonika after June 1918 he led his armies to the Danube. A soldier of enormous energy and indomitable spirit; known to the British as 'Desperate Frankie'.

Friday 27 April

Haig had another meeting with Painlevé.

Painlevé seemed much quieter and steadier this morning. I asked him definitely 'Can I rely on the French Army to go on with the preparations for an attack on my right as agreed between Nivelle and myself.' He assured me that there will be no change of plan in any respect. But he asked, 'Do you find any delay on the part of the French Army in making preparations?' I replied that when a Commander is uncertain about his position, the orders which he issues and the way they are carried out are never the same as if he were confident of himself and received the confidence of his Government. He replied that he would see to that but in any case there will be no delay in their preparations.

I fancy that he (Painlevé) rather looks upon himself as C-in-C now! In any case, he begged me to come frequently to Paris to see him whenever the state of the operations permitted. He for his part would also come to my HQ to see me.

Altogether my visit I think has been fruitful and I left the Minister of War much more confident of [ultimate victory] than when I saw him yesterday. At the same time I do not wish my relations to become very close with the French Minister of War, because my duties require me to work closely with the French C-in-C and the GQG! [In other words, to be on good terms with the French High Command, and not with the French Politicians.]

Monday 30 April

After lunch I explained to Gough that I am preparing for the Ypres operations, and that he would command the northern half of those operations, including the landing force. He must keep this absolutely secret but is to study the scheme which Colonel McMullen (his former Staff officer)[1] would explain to him. Admiral Bacon is attending a trial of 'Tanks' today, so I sent Gough off at once to Erin (Tank HQ)[2] to see the Admiral and McMullen.

Tuesday 1 May

*Charteris reported on the situation. Enemy's reserves have still further been drawn upon and only 10 divisions remain available on Western Front. Docu-

1 Properly Colonel (later General Sir) (Cyril) Norman Macmullen (1877–1944), GSO1 Fifth Army, 1916–17; GSO1 Operations GHQ, 1917; BGGS XIX Corps, 1917–18.
2 Haig was planning an amphibious assault on the Belgian coast, which would involve the use of tanks.

ments also captured showing that orders were issued on 7 February and 12 March to reduce infantry battalions to 650 men fit for field service and 50 men fit for duty or labour. This is a distinct sign of shortage in men. Each company will be equipped with 3 light machine guns.

An order, signed by v. Hindenburg,[1] was also captured, signed 13 April, ordering a reduction of food ration for the troops and in consequence of 'the considerable shortage of cereals' . . .

I sent memo by King's Messenger today to War Cabinet on the 'Present situation and future plans'. The guiding principles are those which have proved successful in war from time immemorial, viz. that the first step must always be to wear down the Enemy's power of resistance [and to continue to do so] until he is so weakened that he will be unable to withstand a decisive blow: then [with all one's forces] to deliver the decisive blow: and finally to reap the fruits of victory.

The Enemy has already been weakened appreciably but time is required to wear down his great numbers of troops. The situation is not yet ripe for the decisive blow. We must therefore continue to wear down the Enemy until his power of resistance has been further reduced.

The cause of General Nivelle's comparative failure appears, primarily, to have been a miscalculation in this respect, and the remedy now is to return to wearing-down methods for a further period the duration of which cannot yet be calculated.

I recommended that the pause [which is forced upon us in] vigorous offensive operations be utilised to complete measures for clearing the coast this summer.

Success seems reasonably possible. It will give valuable results on land and sea. If full measure of success is not gained we shall be attacking the Enemy on a front where he cannot refuse to fight, and our purpose of wearing him down will be given effect to. We shall be directly covering our own most important communications, and even a partial success will considerably improve our defensive positions in the Ypres salient and thus reduce the heavy wastage which must otherwise be expected to occur there next winter as in the past.

Wednesday 2 May

Held conference at 11 am with Generals Gough and Allenby and fixed zero hour at 4.45 am for tomorrow's operations.[2]

---

1 Field Marshal Paul von Hindenburg (1847–1934), Chief of the German General Staff, 1916–1918, and virtual dictator. This is a rare example of Haig mentioning 'the Enemy' individually.
2 Fifth Army's attack at Bullecourt.

The difficulty is that on Gough's right the Australians must cross some open ground *in the dark* – while on First Army front opposite Oppy there is a wood which can only be passed conveniently *by daylight*. Allenby must conform to Horne. If Gough went in early, and the others attacked later, it is almost certain that Enemy would become alarmed and barrage our front before the troops can get out of the trenches!

Thursday 3 May

I had a long talk with Pétain. He was Professor of Infantry Tactics at the French Staff College, and is a very capable soldier according to all accounts. I put my case, more or less, as follows:

Are we agreed on 'principles'? i.e. that the Enemy must first be worn out before a decisive attack is launched and a pursuit begun?

Next as to 'method'? I aim at *capturing and consolidating* as much ground as can be prepared [beforehand] by our artillery – then push on advanced guards. Meantime, bring forward guns in preparation for another advance. The advance will probably soon be held up, but as the wearing-out process of the Enemy continues, a moment will come when our advanced guards and cavalry will be able to progress [for much longer distances until a real decision is reached].

Then coming to our plan: I am disposing my troops on a front opposite the Drocourt–Quéant line, and the Hindenburg Line (as far south as St Quentin) from which I can advance to the attack, *if the French have the means and the intention to continue their present plan.*

If they can't continue, then we must evolve another plan.

General Pétain showed me his latest reports. According to these there are today only 35,000 men in the depôts to meet wastage. This [he said] must mean that each month *one* French Division must disappear, unless the Americans can be induced to send over men to enlist in French Army! I think there is very little chance of their doing so! Pétain has a scheme for this however.

Finally, I explained my plan, and stated that I hoped that the French could support me in two ways –

(a) by relieving 6 British Divisions and
(b) by continuing to press the Enemy and so hold him in their front and so prevent him sending large reserves to meet the British attack.

Pétain replied that he entirely agreed with my views and plans. The one difficulty was the question of 'effectives'. But he would consider the question and let me have his reply in writing. He would do his utmost to help me in every possible way.

I found him most clear headed and easy to discuss things with. There is always the difficulty, however (which one has always had in agreements with the French) – viz. to what extent we can depend on the French in carrying out their attacks?

In this case, if the French do not act vigorously, the Enemy will be free to transfer his reserves to oppose our attacks in the north . . .

At 9.30 pm I saw the Prime Minister with General Robertson. The former is afraid that the French Government is not going to act offensively! He is here he says to press whatever plan Robertson and I decide on. [Rather a changed attitude for him to adopt since the Calais Conference!]

Friday 4 May

At 10 am I attend Conference at General Pétain's office . . .
    We agreed:

1. To continue the offensive to full extent of our power.
2. British will make the main attack and French will support us to the utmost of their power, both by taking over some of our line, and by attacking vigorously to wear out and retain the Enemy on their front.
3. Plan to be kept a perfect secret. Governments not to be told any details concerning the place or date of any attack, only the principles . . .

After lunch I walked with LG across the Seine to the trees of the Champs Elysées, expecting Robertson to join us under the shade, for the day was very hot. 'Wully', however, found the combination of new breeches, riding boots, a big lunch and the hot sun too much for him to face a walk! So he got into a car after walking a few yards and went direct to the hotel. We accordingly went and joined him there, and the Prime Minister discussed the situation with us in the sitting room.

At 3 pm the Conference met at the Quai d'Orsay.[1] Great Britain was represented by Mr Lloyd George and Lord Robert Cecil[2] with General Robertson, Admiral Jellicoe and myself, while for France were M. Ribot, M.

1 Ribot later told Henry Wilson that he was convinced Lloyd George came to the conference in order to demand that Haig be made Supreme Commander on the Western Front! This shows a remarkable lack of understanding of the Lloyd George–Haig relationship.
2 Lord (Edgar Algernon) Robert Cecil (later Viscount Cecil of Chelwood) (1864–1958), Minister of Blockade, 1916–18.

Painlevé (Minister of War), Bourgeois,[1] Admiral Lacaze,[2] with Generals Pétain and Nivelle. The two Governments agreed to and accepted a document drawn up by Robertson giving the results of this morning's meeting to which all the generals gave their assent previously.

Mr Lloyd George made two excellent speeches in which he stated that he had no pretensions to be a strategist, that he left that to his military advisers, that I as C-in-C of the British Forces in France, had full power to attack where and when I thought best. He (Mr LG) did not wish to know the plan, or where or when any attack would take place. Briefly, he wished the French Government to treat their Commanders on the same lines.

His speeches were quite excellent.

M. Ribot replied and quite agreed, but mentioned the great losses of the French Army since the war began. M. Painlevé also spoke and said that his views had been misinterpreted. He was all in favour of an offensive, but only differed from those who planned the last attacks in the question of *methods* of execution. He concurred in the necessity for putting in large attacks but on wide fronts with limited objectives.

The Conference passed off in the most friendly spirit, and all stated that they were united in the determination to attack vigorously, and carry on the war 'jusqu' au bout'.

Saturday 5 May

In order to save shipping,[3] I directed QMG[4] recently to arrange to make hay on all possible areas which have recently been taken from the Enemy. He accordingly brought Captain Rea of Northumberland Hussars,[5] a gentleman farmer, to see me, as suitable for appointment to take charge of this work. He took a farming degree at Cambridge and is said to be energetic and a first rate businessman. So I appointed him and approved of a letter going to Armies to start an organisation.

1 Léon Victor Auguste Bourgeois (1881–1925), French politician; a leading advocate of the League of Nations.
2 Admiral Marie Jean Lucien Lacaze (1860–1955), Minister of Marine, October 1915–August 1917.
3 The German 'unrestricted' submarine warfare campaign, launched in February 1917, had caused severe losses to British and Allied shipping.
4 The Quartermaster General, Lieutenant General Maxwell.
5 Captain (later Major) John George Grey Rea (1886–1955), Northumberland Hussars Yeomanry. Rea was an authority on agricultural production. He chaired the Northumberland County Agricultural Executive Committee during the Second World War.

Thursday 10 May

We hear from American members of Belgian Relief Committee who have arrived in Switzerland, that German cavalry are now in eastern Brabant in considerable numbers.[1] Food riots took place on 1 April in Hainault. Discipline is deteriorating in German Army: 250 soldiers mutinied near Valenciennes. At Mons troops were begging for food. Rolling stock, and especially locomotives, is in an extremely bad condition...

General *Plumer came to lunch today. Afterwards he explained his plan of attack[2] and received my approval. I called his attention to the new German system of defence. The Enemy now fight not '*in*' but '*for*' his first position. He uses considerable forces for counter-attacks. His guns should be registered beforehand to deal with these. Our objective is now to capture and consolidate up to the range of our guns, and at once to push on advanced guards to profit by Enemy's demoralisation after the bombardment. No delay should take place in doing this.

Friday 11 May

Major Orpen, the artist, came to lunch.[3] I told him that every facility would be given him to study the life and surroundings of our troops in the field, so that he can really paint pictures of lasting value. The War Office already wanted to see the results of his labours in return for the pay which he is now receiving! As if he were a sausage machine into which so much meat is put and the handle is turned and out come the sausages! But war is a fickle mistress!

Saturday 12 May

I then went to HQ Third Army at Noyelle-Vion and had a talk with General Allenby. He was much pleased with a telegram of congratulations which I had sent him last night re. this morning's success.[4] He was rather opposed to making small effort with limited objectives to gain ground, but the recent successes have quite changed his views on the question! I pointed out the necessity of having a 'runabout barrage' as well as an ordinary 'rolling barrage'

1 This is a reference to German deserters; eastern Brabant is in the Netherlands.
2 For the Battle of Messines, which began on 7 June 1917.
3 Major (later Sir) William Orpen (1878–1931), a well-known portrait painter, became an official war artist in 1917. His most famous painting is probably *The Signing of the Peace*. He also painted Haig's portrait.
4 The notorious chemical works had been captured in one of the last actions of the Battle of Arras.

when we are dealing with a hostile position which is organised in depth with many machine guns.

Tuesday 15 May

In afternoon I motored to Hermanville, HQ 4th Division and had a talk with General Lambton. His GSO1 Colonel Kirke (late of the Intelligence Branch at GHQ)[1] is doing well. I went round the office and spoke to the Staff officers and some of the clerks. Brigadier General Ravenhill Commanding Divisional Artillery has not given satisfaction and is being sent home.[2] The Brigadiers have done well. They are Pritchard (Indian Cavalry)[3] Berners (Welch Fusiliers)[4] and Carton de Wiart (4th Dragoon Guards).[5] I congratulated Lambton on the determination and steadfastness displayed by his men. The division had been 3 times in the fight and captured the village of Roeux 3 days ago, after most severe fighting.

Thursday 17 May

The QMG (Maxwell) went home yesterday for ten days leave as he could not sleep. He is in the habit of doing too much himself e.g. he drafts all his instructions instead of using his Staff for the purpose. Still the QMG branch is working better than at any time previously.

Friday 18 May

Haig met Pétain, who had been appointed French C-in-C the previous day, at Amiens.

I then asked him straight 'Did the French intend to play their full part as promised at the Paris Conference?' 'Could I rely on his whole-hearted co-operation?' He was most outspoken and gave me full assurances...

As regards Pétain personally I found him businesslike, knowledgeable, and brief of speech. The latter a rare quality in Frenchmen!

1 Colonel (later General Sir) Walter Mervyn St George Kirke (1877–1949), GSO1 GHQ, 1915–17; GSO1 4th Division, 1917; GSO1 War Office, 1917–18.
2 Brigadier General Frederick Thornhill Ravenhill (1865–1935), CRA 4th Division, February–June 1917.
3 Brigadier General Aubrey Gordon Pritchard (1869–1943), GOC 10 Brigade, April–November 1917.
4 Brigadier General Ralph Abercrombie Berners (1871–1949), GOC 11 Brigade, 1916–17.
5 Brigadier General (later Lieutenant General Sir) Adrian Carton de Wiart VC (1880–1963), GOC 12 Brigade, 1917.

Tuesday 22 May

I saw Sir Herbert Plumer Commanding Second Army at 9.45 am for a few minutes. He is in very good spirits now that his Second Army occupies the first place in our thoughts! I find him a most pleasant fellow to work with and Harington[1] and all his Staff work very kindly with GHQ. All are most ready to take advice.

HQ X Corps at Abeele. Sir T. Morland seems greatly improved since July last year on Somme. He has now more knowledge and more confidence. I spent over an hour with him, his CGS (Cameron)[2] and CRA (Reed)[3] going into his plan of attack. It seems carefully thought out and sound...

On the whole a fine spirit in the Corps I saw today,[4] but I felt that the leaders have been on the defensive about Ypres so long that the *real offensive spirit* has to be developed.

Wednesday 23 May

I continued my inspection today and visited the IX Corps. I spent over an hour with General Hamilton Gordon,[5] and went carefully into all his plans. He produced a well thought out and practical scheme of attack. Every difficulty seemed to have been foreseen and provided against! In fact I felt that at every point the working of an active brain was most noticeable. His CRA (General Humphreys)[6] seemed fully alive to his work ... I then visited HQ 19th Division ... Major General Stuart Wortley.[7] I did not like his arrangements. He had broken up a brigade to provide 2 battalions as 'moppers up' to another brigade. In fact I felt that he had barely got beyond the fringe of the problem which confronted him. He was also very nervous and fussy.

1 Major General (later General Sir) Charles Harington Harington ('Tim') (1872–1940), MGGS Second Army, 1916–17; MGGS British Forces in Italy, 1917–18, and Second Army, 1918; Deputy CIGS War Office, 1918–20.

2 Brigadier General (later General Sir) Archibald Rice Cameron (1870–1944), BGGS X Corps, 1915–18; BGGS Fourth Army, 1918; BGGS XIX Corps, 1918–19.

3 Brigadier General (later Major General) Hamilton Lyster ('Paddy') Reed VC (1869–1931), BGRA X Corps, 1917; GOC 15th (Scottish) Division, 1917–19, Haig's good opinion of Reed was not shared by everyone.

4 Haig had also visited Jacob's II Corps.

5 Lieutenant General Sir Alexander Hamilton Gordon ('Sunny Jim') (1859–1939), GOC IX Corps, 1916–18. Haig retained a high opinion of Gordon from their time together at the War Office before the war, an opinion not shared by Sir Henry Rawlinson, who finally got him replaced in September 1918.

6 Brigadier General Gardiner Humphreys (1865–1942), BGRA IX Corps, 1916–18.

7 Major General (later Lieutenant General Sir) Alan Richard Montagu-Stuart-Wortley (1868–1949), Temporary GOC 19th (Western) Division, April–May 1917. Haig replaced Stuart-Wortley with Major General Cameron Shute on 24 May. Shute recast 19th Division's plans.

Thursday 24 May

1.5 pm HQ New Zealand Division in huts at Westhoek Farm. General Sir A. Russell commands.¹ He seems a most capable soldier with considerable strength of character. His problem is a difficult one but he and his officers and men are all most confident of success. I saw all his Brigadiers, his CRA and GSO1.

. . . at 2.35 pm arrived at the HQ 3rd Australian Division at Steenwerck – the Commander is General Monash, I believe an auctioneer by profession, but in my opinion a clear headed determined commander.²

Monday 28 May

Trenchard reported on work of the Flying Corps. He seemed quite satisfied that we are superior to the Enemy in the air. He thinks Enemy's losses are about 800 or more for month; ours were 420 for April.³

Wednesday 30 May

At 11 am I met General Plumer at the village of Pernes (between Lillers and St Pol) and discussed the action to be taken if the Germans vacated their front trench on the front of our attack . . . We agreed that the Germans were holding their front trenches lightly (in accordance with their Regulations). The main object at present was to cause the Enemy to disclose the position of his barrage batteries.

Thursday 31 May

After lunch I motored to Avinfer Wood where HQ 33rd Division is now established in huts, and the brigades are resting in the area to the westwards. General Pinney was on leave, but I saw the CRA (Brigadier General C. Stewart).⁴ He reported all in best of health and spirits. He did not give any

1 Major General Sir Andrew Hamilton Russell (1868–1960), the only man to command the New Zealand Division during the war; one of the finest divisional commanders of the war, much admired by Haig.
2 Major General (later General Sir) John Monash (1865–1931), GOC 3rd Australian Division; and, from June 1918, GOC Australian Corps. Monash was actually a civil engineer (and lawyer) by profession; Haig expressed a high regard for him as early as 1916.
3 April 1917 ('Bloody April') was the worst month of the war for the RFC, which was temporarily outclassed following the introduction of a new generation of German aircraft organised into the famous 'Flying Circuses' led by Baron Manfred von Richthofen.
4 Brigadier General Cosmo Gordon Stewart (1869–1948), CRA 33rd Division, 1917–18.

clear reason why a battalion of the 19th Infantry Brigade (Mayne HLI)[1] came back to its original trenches during the attack on the support trench of the Hindenburg Line south of the Sensée about a week ago. The other battalions reached and consolidated their objectives without much difficulty.

Saturday 2 June

I saw Major Lytton this forenoon regarding the state of feeling in France.[2] He takes charge of the French newspaper correspondents and so has a good opportunity of knowing what the general opinion happens to be! He said that the feeling towards the British was better than it had ever been, and that the feats of the British Army were much admired. On the other hand, there is a feeling of despondency abroad, [people say] that their losses have been very great, that the last French attack [was very badly] managed, and, altogether a certain number were wondering whether the war had not lasted long enough. There have been strikes recently, and some of the soldiers on leave sided with the women strikers. In fact the situation wants careful watching and some success is much wanted to raise the spirits of the French people. Grave doubts are felt about the ability of Russia to do anything serious this year. This is another cause of the despondent feeling in France...

The 'Major-Général' of the French Army arrived about 6.30 pm and stayed to dinner. His name is General Debeney.[3] He brought a letter from General Pétain saying that he had commissioned him to put the whole situation of the French Army before me and conceal nothing. [The French Army is in a bad state of discipline.][4]

Debeney then stated that the French soldiers were dissatisfied because leave had been so long suspended. Leave must consequently be opened at once. This would prevent Pétain carrying out his promise to attack on 10 June! The attack would go in 4 weeks later. Then I discovered by questions that the attack promised already for the middle of July was the one which would be launched. So really the attack of 10 June will not be made by infantry – only by artillery! However the Germans are now counter-attacking the French

1 Brigadier General Charles Robert Graham Mayne (1874–1944), Highland Light Infantry, GOC 19 Brigade, 1916–18.

2 Major Neville Stephen Lytton (later 3rd Earl Lytton) (1880–1951), Press Liaison Officer at GHQ; painter and tennis champion.

3 General Marie Eugene Debeney (1864–1943), GOC French First Army, 1917–18.

4 For the French Army 'mutinies', see Guy Pedroncini, *1917: Les Mutineries de l'armée française* (Paris: Julliard, 1968); see also David French, 'Who Knew What and When? The French Army Mutinies and the British Decision to Launch the Third Battle of Ypres', in L. Freedman, P. Hayes and R. O'Neill (eds), *Strategy and International Politics: Essays in Honour of Sir Michael Howard* (Oxford: Clarendon Press, 1992).

with considerable vigour in Champagne, so I hope no reserves will be able to come to Flanders to oppose my attacks!

Debeney's next point was to tell me that 6 French Divisions would be at my disposal when I wanted them for employment in the Yser sector, and they would be put under my orders.

Lastly, the coast sector would be handed over *when* I decided that the situation was suitable to make the landing.

As regards the last point, I said 6 weeks' preparation would probably be necessary on the coast. But I would state definitely as to the dates when the result of the forthcoming attack was known.

Plumer's Second Army launched its attack on the Messines Ridge on 7 June.

Thursday 7 June

Zero hour was at 3.10 am. At that hour we exploded some of the largest mines ever used in war! These were under the German front system. At that hour all our guns (over 2500) opened on the Enemy's positions and counter-battered his artillery batteries; and the infantry advanced behind a heavy barrage. Most of the infantry had got beyond their parapets before zero and lay in the open ready for zero! ...

The explosion of the mines was highly successful. 19 were exploded – all went off perfectly, though some had been charged for over a year! Altogether nearly *one million* pounds of explosives were used! The 'Tunnelling Companies' concerned deserve high praise for their endurance and perseverance for they fought the Enemy continuously underground all these many months! ...

Soon after 4 pm I visited General Plumer at his HQ at Cassel, and congratulated him on his success. The old man deserves the highest praise for he has patiently defended the Ypres salient for $2\frac{1}{2}$ years, and he well [knows] that pressure has been brought to bear on me in order to remove him from Command of Second Army.

The operations today are probably the most successful I have yet undertaken ... Our losses are reported to be very small. *Under* 11,000 for the 9 divisions which attacked. Our front of attack was about 9 miles in length.

Haig met Pétain on the latter's train at Cassel.

Pétain and I then had a private talk. He told me that 2 French Divisions had refused to go and relieve 2 divisions in front line because the men had not had leave! Some were tried and were shot. The French Government supported Pétain. They also refused to allow the Socialists to go to Stockholm for a Conference with German Socialists. The situation [in the French Army] was serious at one moment but is now quite satisfactory. [But the bad state of discipline causes Pétain grave concern.]

Sunday 10 June

General Robertson (CIGS) left after having a talk with me and Kiggell after church. A night's reflection and Duncan's words of thanksgiving for our recent victory seemed to have had a good effect on him.[1] He was less pessimistic and seemed to realise that the German Army was in reduced circumstances! I again urged the need for increased activity by the Allies *all round.* There must be no thought of staying our hand until America puts an Army in the field next year. [We must press the Enemy now, as vigorously as possible by every means at our disposal on the Western Front.]

Wednesday 13 June

Charteris reported that there are signs of Enemy being short of ammunition and guns. The supply of the latter is unequal to the demand.

German prisoners state that NCOs have lately been given special practice in what they call 'English tactics'. How far 'the invincible German Army' has already fallen!

Thursday 14 June

I presided at Conference with Army Commanders at HQ First Army, Lillers, at 11 am. Some 40 officers were present. The Agenda included

(1) General situation
(2) Situation in front of each Army
(3) Future plans.

As regards the latter, I stated that there was no departure from the plans I had outlined at the Conference of 7 May. Viz. British and French wear down and exhaust the Enemy by attacking by surprise as far as possible at points where not expected. Finally British will strike the main blow probably in the north.

Underlying the general intention of wearing out the Enemy is the strategical

---

1 Reverend George Simpson Duncan (1884–1965), Presbyterian chaplain at GHQ, 1915–19; author of *Douglas Haig as I Knew Him* (1966). See also Duncan's diary, edited by Gerard J. De Groot: 'The Rev. George S. Duncan at GHQ, 1916–1918', *Publications of the Army Record Society*, vol. 12: *Military Miscellany I* (Stroud: Sutton for the Army Record Society, 1996), pp. 266–436.

idea of securing the Belgian coast and connecting with the Dutch frontier.

The nature and size of the several steps which we take towards that objective must depend on our *effectives* and the replacement of *guns*.

Roughly these are

1. Capture bridgehead formed of the Passchendaele–Staden–Clerken ridge.
2. Push on towards Roulers–Thourout so as to take coast defences in rear.
3. Land by surprise in conjunction with attack from Nieuport.

If effectives, or guns inadequate it may be necessary to call a halt after No. 1 is gained!

Meantime it is desirable to mislead the Enemy as to our next point of attack.

Haig left for England on 17 June.

Tuesday 19 June

I saw the CIGS at 10.45 am and then walked to Lord Curzon's Office (Privy Council) for a meeting of the War Cabinet at 11 am . . .

We discussed the military situation till 1 o'clock when the Prime Minister left to marry his daughter. The members of the War Cabinet asked me numerous questions all tending to show that each of them was more pessimistic than the other! The PM seemed to believe the decisive moment of the war would be 1918. Until then we ought to husband our forces and do little or nothing, except support Italy with guns and gunners (300 batteries were indicated). I strongly asserted that Germany was nearer her end than they seemed to think, that *now* was the favourable moment, [for pressing her] and that everything possible should be done to take advantage of it by concentrating on the Western Front *all* available resources. I stated that Germany was within 6 months of the total exhaustion of her available manpower, *if the fighting continues at its present intensity.* [To do this, more men and guns are necessary.]

Wednesday 20 June

I attended the War Cabinet at 11 am at the Privy Council Office . . .

I read a paper 'On the Strategical Situation with special reference to the Comparative Advantages of an offensive in northern Belgium as against an offensive from Italy against Austria'. Much talk and many questions. We again adjourned and the PM said he wished to discuss the problem privately with his colleagues . . .

In the afternoon I visited War Office, and also saw 'Admiral' Sir Eric Geddes at the Admiralty.[1] The latter is most anxious about the state of affairs at the Admiralty. The First Lord (Carson)[2] has recently married, is very tired, and leaves everything [to] a number of incompetent sailors! Jellicoe, he says, is feeble to a degree and vacillating. Only one Admiral (Hersey)[3] is fit for his post. There is no *fixed policy*: they don't know *where* the submarines are sinking our ships, or the type of ship (whether 10 knot or 12 knot steamers) to build. It is difficult to know how to act as Geddes means to be loyal to his colleagues. We agreed that I should do my best to arrange that Lloyd George should see Geddes [when the latter would put the whole position of affairs before him], and that the King should also have an interview with him [(Geddes)].

Secret. (Not to be copied.)

[A most serious and startling situation was disclosed today.] At today's Conference Admiral Jellicoe as First Sea Lord stated that owing to [the great shortage of shipping due to German submarines], it would be impossible for Great Britain to continue the war in 1918. This was a bombshell for the Cabinet, [and all present] and a full enquiry is to be made as to the real facts on which this opinion [of the Naval Authorities] is based. No one present shared Jellicoe's view, and all seemed satisfied that the food reserves in Great Britain are adequate. [Jellicoe's words were, 'There is no good discussing plans for next spring. We cannot go on.']

Monday 25 June

I attended meeting of War Cabinet at 11.30 am . . .

As regards the main problem; Lloyd George was much pleased with my notes. On the other hand, he criticised Robertson and tried to get a more definite statement of his views out of him as to the result which he expected. Robertson would not budge! All he would say was that my plan was the only thing to do. Eventually [it was] decided that I am to go on with my preparations: that in two weeks M. Albert Thomas (who is in favour of my plan) will report on state of France and what the French Army can do. The British

1 Eric Geddes had moved from his post as Director General (Transportation) BEF in May 1917 to become Controller of the Navy, where it was hoped that his logistical brilliance would help combat the depredations of German U-boats. He was granted the rank of Temporary Hon. Vice-Admiral. He became First Lord of the Admiralty, political head of the Royal Navy, in July 1917.

2 Sir Edward Henry (later Baron) Carson (1854–1935), one of the leading advocates of his generation and the leader of the Ulster cause; First Lord of the Admiralty, December 1916–July 1917.

3 Properly Admiral Lionel Halsey (1872–1949).

Government will then meet the French Government and decide on the extent of our operations.

Thursday 28 June

I had a long talk with Sir Henry Wilson. He thinks our continuing offensive is the only way to save France. The French Army is in a state of indiscipline not due to losses, but to disappointment! . . .

Haig discussed the forthcoming attack with Gough.

I urged the importance of the right flank. It is in my opinion vitally important to occupy and hold the ridge west of Gheluvelt and cover our right flank and then push along it to Broodseinde . . . the advance should be limited until our right flank has really been secured on this ridge.

Monday 2 July

I found Anthoine[1] most anxious to help in every way, [but he seemed terribly afraid of the lack of determination to fight on the part of the men]. His relations with the Belgians are much more friendly, [I am glad to know].

Saturday 7 July

. . . I held a conference with General Gough regarding the date of attack. The guns of the XIV Corps on his left were he said suffering considerably from Enemy's fire. 27 guns out of 36 had been damaged. He asked for postponement for 5 days. I pointed out that the date of attack could not be definitely fixed now. We had first to gain supremacy in the air, and then to dominate the Enemy's artillery. Much depended on the weather. We were now engaged in the artillery battle and must expect losses . . .

    After dinner a telegram was received from War Office ordering two fighting squadrons to England tomorrow to protect London![2] I saw Trenchard about 11 pm and CGS and Davidson. The withdrawal of these squadrons at this time will have serious effect. Today was the first day of our battle for air supremacy – and the Enemy has also concentrated his fighting machines to

1 General François Paul Anthoine (1860–1944), GOC French First Army, 1917; First Army was deployed on the northern flank of the BEF throughout Third Ypres.
2 After earlier Zeppelin raids, during 1917 London had come under attack from German fixed-wing aircraft, causing public and political consternation.

oppose us. Our War Cabinet is thus playing the Enemy's game in thus withdrawing airoplanes from this front.

Tuesday 10 July

*Charteris, reporting on situation, stated that political situation in Berlin seemed critical. Confidence in their Army and in the success of the submarine blockade of England seems to be waning.

As regards our own front, Enemy still retaining inferior divisions on the Ypres front, and no reinforcements have appeared in that sector yet. On the other hand the coast sector has been reorganised, marines being detailed to guard the coast, and regular infantry the land front.

Wednesday 11 July

General Trenchard reported on the state of the RFC this morning. He seems quite confident that we will shortly have complete command of the air, notwithstanding the withdrawal of one of our fighting squadrons to England.

General Birch reported that our artillery position north of Ypres is quite satisfactory. The losses in personnel and guns have been wonderfully small.

Thursday 12 July

The BEF prepared for a major offensive at Ypres.

I held Conference at 11 am at HQ of Fifth Army ... We discussed the state of the Fifth Army preparations, and effect of delaying 3 days on Enemy as well as ourselves! I finally decided to postpone date of infantry attack for 3 days. The bombardment to begin on 15th inst. as arranged.

Tuesday 17 July

I attended practice of attack against 'Shrewsbury Forest' and 'Tower Hamlets Ridge' by the 73 Brigade ... The troops looked extremely fit and well after nearly a month out of the line.

It gave me great confidence as to the result of the attack, to talk to the officers and men. Jacob is also most confident as to the result.[1]

1 Lieutenant General Claud Jacob, commanding II Corps, which had a key role to play in the forthcoming attack.

Friday 20 July

Haig held a meeting with the senior officers of II Corps.

Looking round the faces opposite to me, I felt what fine hard looking determined men the war had brought to the front ...

About 6.30 pm General *Pershing (Commanding the American Forces in France) arrived ... I had a talk with General Pershing before and also after dinner. I was much struck with his quiet gentlemanly bearing – so unusual for an American. Most anxious to learn, and fully realises the greatness of the task before him. He has already begun to realise that the French are a broken reed.

His AG and CGS are men of less quality, and are hardly 'soldiers' in our sense of the term, and all quite ignorant of the problems of modern war. The CGS is a kindly soft looking fellow with a face of a Punchinello. The AG having served long in Manilla and other hot places, seems to be less alert mentally than the others. The ADC is a fire-eater, and longs for the fray.[1]

Saturday 21 July

I signed letter this morning to Robertson CIGS in reply to one received late on Thursday night in which he says, 'When you left Cabinet had not definitely approved of your plans. Up to the present no official approval of your plans has been given. I dare say that tomorrow or the next day I shall be told that your plans are approved.'

This is somewhat startling, so I wrote strongly and pointed out that these operations were agreed to at a conference at the War Office as long ago as 23 November 1916. And on 1 January 1917 I was again reminded of the 'great importance' attached to this operation by the War Cabinet. While on 1 December the desire of the War Cabinet that the operation should be undertaken this year was communicated to me and to General Joffre. The fact is that the Cabinet does not really understand what preparation for an attack really means [for the forces and Commanders in the field]! ...

As regards *Rawlinson's visit to London, I told him that he was not to discuss the question of the pros and cons of a landing with Admiral Jellicoe.[2] [I] had already done so with him, and if he wished to come and see me in France I shall be glad to make all arrangements for his visit, and go into the matter again with him.

1 The AG was Lieutenant Colonel Alvord, the CGS Lieutenant Colonel (later General) James Guthrie Harbord, the ADC Captain (later General) George S. Patton.
2 On 10 May Rawlinson had been appointed to command the forces to be used in an amphibious assault on the Belgian coast in conjunction with the forthcoming offensive around Ypres.

I told Rawlinson (what I had before told him) that in my opinion three situations might arise in which a landing would be justified – viz.

(a) If on our attack being launched Enemy gave way in disorder, and we were able to gain ground very rapidly.
(b) If Enemy fought a prolonged battle and in the course of it used up his Coast Garrisons.
(c) If we progressed and were by degrees advancing from the Clerken–Staden ridge against the Couckelaere–Thourout hills.

Davidson is to accompany Rawlinson to London in order to ascertain whether Jellicoe has anything to urge for my information.

Thursday 26 July

Charteris reported that situation as regards Enemy was very favourable for our main attack. Reports indicated that he was disposing his troops as if to defeat an attack against Lille from the northwest and southwest. This was shown in the increased wireless activity opposite Armentières . . . the divisions opposite our Ypres front were still of inferior quality except the 6th Bavarian Reserve Division – and after we had broken the Langemarck line, the Enemy has no other line completed yet. The Intelligence Branch considers that the Enemy will hold and fight us in his present support line, but will not counter-attack until we reach the Langemarck line (this passes east of Zonnebeke).

Friday 27 July

General Birch reported that artillery counter-battery work proceeding satisfactorily.

Saturday 28 July

General Trenchard gave his report on the work of the Flying Corps. Yesterday the fighting was *most severe* and the results highly satisfactory. Our aviators 'drove the Enemy out of the air' said Trenchard to me. It was 'a very good day' he added. We crashed 19 machines and drove down out of control 26 = 45. We lost 3 machines . . .

After lunch General Birch came to see me again. He had discussed situation with Uniacke (CRA Fifth Army). The latter is very satisfied. At 5 am a practice barrage was carried out on whole army front. We placed neutralising fire on Enemy's batteries which we had knocked out. In spite of this, there were only 210 guns active on this front! Very encouraging. In fact my artillery adviser is of opinion that 'we have already cowed the Enemy's artillery' . . .

At 7.45 pm Charteris reported that 5th and 6th German Divisions have gone to Russia and further confirmation of 1st and 2nd Guard Divisions on Eastern Front has been received. 'There seems now to be little doubt but that Germany is making a strong effort to knock out Russia.' This is all in favour of our operations here. Also it seems possible to me that she may 'knock' Russia *together* with her blows!'

Sunday 29 July

Reports indicate no change on our front. Enemy do not seem to realise that the French and our troops on the left have crossed the Ypres Canal! Enemy's patrols sent forward to reconnoitre have been allowed to come quite close and then shot down so as to prevent information of the changed position reaching Enemy HQ. We are also not mentioning any advance in this sector in the daily Press Communiqué.

Prisoners report Enemy's losses in artillery have been very heavy. One battery in the 49th Reserve Division is said to have had its gun detachments replaced nine times, and its guns five times since the beginning of our bombardment.

All Enemy's artillery except a few scattered batteries have been withdrawn east of the Steenbeek.

Charteris reports that Enemy yesterday relieved 4 of his divisions on the battle front. Possibly Enemy may have heard that the 28th was the date of our attack and so placed these new divisions close at hand for counter-attack! In any case the divisions which were relieved had suffered most severely, and the divisions now in the line will have 3 days under our artillery fire, so they too will suffer very considerably before our attack goes in . . .

At Hazebrouck I visited HQ I Anzac Corps and saw the BGGS (General White). The Australians are much upset at the large number of desertions which have taken place, particularly in the 4th Division. Birdwood is proposing to form companies of prisoners, as we cannot carry out the death penalty . . .

I replied to a kind letter from Lord *Derby in which he assured me of his friendship and support, and hoped that I would shift any additional worry on to his own and Robertson's shoulders.

---

1 This comment is not as silly as, in retrospect, it seems. Haig was a keen student of military history and was well aware that Russia had been 'knocked' together by the Napoleonic invasion of 1812, as the Soviet Union was also to be 'knocked together' during the Great Patriotic War of 1941–5.

Monday 30 July

The motor lorry drivers have been doing very well. Regularly night after night they have gone through Ypres in spite of heavy shell fire, and [suffering] a considerable number of casualties. These men have shown that they have the same spirit as the fighting soldiers!

Report received this afternoon states that of 136 Tanks to be moved up to positions east of Canal and Ypres, 133 are in position and all is well.

The Third Battle of Ypres ('Passchendaele') was launched by Gough's Fifth Army on 31 July. The actions of this day are known as the Battle of Pilkem Ridge. This was followed by the Battle of Gheluvelt Plateau (10 August), and the Battle of Langemarck (16 August). Haig spent the morning of 31 July reading reports on the progress of the attack delivered to him at his Advanced Headquarters in a camouflaged train near West Cappel.

Tuesday 31 July

Zero for all the Fifth Army except XIV Corps was 3.50 am (i.e. 2.50 Greenwich Time). For the latter Corps and the French it was 20 minutes later . . .

Fighting on our right had been most severe. This I had expected. Our divisions had made good progress and were on top of the ridge which the Menin Road crosses, but had not advanced sufficiently eastwards to have observation into the valleys beyond. Further to the west our troops had established themselves *beyond* the Steenbeek and the French had taken Bixschoote and the Cabaret Kortekeer (which was so frequently attacked in October and November 1914). This was a fine day's work. Gough thinks that he has taken over 5000 prisoners[1] and 60 guns or more. The ground is thick with dead Germans killed mostly by our artillery. I sent Alan Fletcher and Colonel Ryan[2] round the Casualty Clearing Stations. They report many slight cases, mostly shell fire. *Wounded* very cheery indeed. Some 6000 wounded have been treated in the ten hours up to 6 pm.

As regards future operations, I told Gough to continue to carry out the original plan: to consolidate ground gained, and to improve his position as he may deem necessary for facilitating the next advance: the next advance will be made as soon as possible, *but only after adequate bombardment and after dominating the hostile artillery.*

Heavy rain fell this afternoon and airoplane observation was impossible.

1 Ts diary says '3000'.
2 Colonel Eugene ('Micky') Ryan (1873–1951), Chief Medical Officer at GHQ and the only man who could safely order Haig about.

The going also became very bad, and the ground was much cut up. This has hampered our further progress [and robbed us of much of the advantage due to our great success.]

Wednesday 1 August

Haig spoke to a French officer who was going to see Pétain.

Already the 52nd Reserve Division has come from the Rheims area, the 12th Division from near Verdun, and the 51st Division was soon expected (from the Rheims front). I told him to call Pétain's attention to the certain result of the policy advocated in Paris during the May Conference, viz. to wait and do nothing serious on the Western Front this *year* until Americans arrived! 'This would have suited the Germans admirably because they would then have concentrated all their available reserves against Russia so as to gain a decision in that theatre before the winter. In my opinion now is the critical moment of the war, and the French must attack as strongly as possible and as soon as possible so as to co-operate with the British in dealing the Enemy as strong a blow as possible.' I mentioned the bad state of discipline in the 6th Reserve Bavarian Division – one of the Enemy's crack corps – and the prisoners taken yesterday suffered from malnutrition due to shortage of food.

The examination of the prisoners yesterday shows [the number of the] 1918 class [to be very large] – about 15% of the total prisoners. Prisoners of a poor stamp: 'moral' lower than any lot previously captured. An officer 52nd Division confirmed report of the bad state of the 6th Bavarian Reserve Division, and also said that his regiment had suffered from lack of artillery support during the battle.

Gough held meeting of his Corps Commanders last night after seeing me. The II Corps propose to take the rest of the Black line tomorrow. A small operation, but today being wet, may delay matters. On Saturday XIV Corps will be ready to take village of Langemarck, and the right and the centre will advance to the Green line.

Haig discussed the amphibious landing in support of the main attack.

At 11 am I saw Sir H. Rawlinson and his MGGS (Montgomery). He will be ready to start his attack on Sunday morning. I told him that if the weather continued wet he must delay in order to ensure having artillery supremacy. I approved of his plan . . .

Charteris reported at 2 pm. Enemy's divisions are being used up at a rapid rate.

In afternoon I motored to HQ of Corps in the Fifth Army as follows:

II Corps. General Jacob explained the action of yesterday in detail. His position is a good one on the ridge. His advance was stopped by hidden machine guns in concrete emplacements. Owing to dull weather these could not be located by photographs. Two German maps have luckily been captured, giving the exact positions. They can now be easily destroyed: – but a 15 inch howitzer is necessary, as the emplacements are strongly built of [reinforced] cement. Jacob is quite confident of being able to capture and hold the ridge at his next attempt. The losses of his divisions were very small . . .

XIX Corps. General Watts explained how his divisions got right forward to the extreme limit, viz. Green line, but were obliged to retire owing to artillery fire from the main ridge on the east. This confirms my view that progress cannot be made by an advance towards the Forêt d'Houthoulst until the *main* Broodseinde–Staden ridge is taken. His troops are now on the Black line.

XVIII Corps. General Maxse's troops also got right forward to the Green line, but were counter-attacked and forced back to the Steenbeek along with those of XIX Corps on their right. His Corps took 1700 prisoners besides killing great numbers. His own losses were 3200. Small considering the results gained.

At Fifth Army HQ I saw General Uniacke. He thinks artillery situation very satisfactory, but must have 2 days of good observation before the next step forward is attempted.

A terrible day of rain.[1] The ground is like a bog in this low lying country! The light railways and roads are steadily being pushed forward. Still, in view of this terrible wet, I judged that we are fortunate not to have advanced to the extreme Red line, because it would not have been possible to supply our guns with ammunition. Our troops would thus have been at the mercy of a hostile counter-attack and a check might have resulted.

Thursday 2 August

Owing to heavy rain front seems quieter, but yesterday the Enemy launched 2 big counter-attacks. One was made with a whole division. Luckily it fell on the 15th Division, which stoutly held its ground, and beat Enemy back with very heavy loss.

At 10 am I saw Gough and N. Malcolm (his MGGS) with Kiggell. I showed him on my relief map the importance of the Broodseinde–Passchendaele ridge, and gave it as my opinion that his main effort must be

---

1 The rain in the late summer and autumn of 1917 was exceptionally heavy. See John Hussey, 'The Flanders Battleground and the Weather in 1917', in Liddle (ed.), *Passchendaele in Perspective*, pp. 140–58.

devoted to capturing that. Not until it was in our possession could he hope to advance his centre. He quite agreed.

I also told him to have patience, and not put in his infantry attack until after 2 or 3 days fine weather, to enable our guns to get the upper hand and to dry the ground.

Prisoners taken by First Army near Armentières state that they have been told that a big offensive with Lille as objective was in preparation, and they believed that French troops were opposed to them!

The Enemy also bombarded Ploegsteert Wood and the roads in that area. All this proves the advantage of spreading false reports in war!

Haig visited Plumer at Cassel.

His Army has done well misleading the Enemy. We spoke about the relief of divisions now holding the line: it is necessary to be as economical as possible on his front, but this bad weather takes so much out of the men in the trenches that more frequent reliefs are necessary.

Saturday 4 August

Fifth Army is relieving all the divisions in front line on account of the wet weather.

General Charteris reported the situation as usual. Prisoners state that our gas shell bombardment was very effective. 3rd Guard Division wore their gas helmets but the gas cloud created was so thick that the helmets were apparently penetrated. Two other divisions further south were equally severely affected when carrying out a relief.

In view of the bad weather and wet ground General Gough has cancelled the orders which he issued for the continuation of the attack.

Sunday 5 August

Charteris reports that Enemy is seen to be changing his divisions in the battle front very quickly. This may be due to large losses suffered in fruitless counter-attacks. State of German troops does now not appear to be so good that they can be trusted to hold a line for a prolonged period in the recent bad weather.

After heavy shelling, Enemy attacked on both sides of Comines Canal and got a footing in Hollebeke. He was quickly driven out. Fighting said to be severe. About 9 pm Enemy again attacked here and also further north at Westhoek. Both attacks were repulsed.

I went into the state of *our reserves*, and find that they are likely to be sufficient; but divisions after having been once in the battle cannot be made up again but must go forward a second time *below* war establishment. Also divisions on the defensive fronts must be allowed to fall to 8 or 9000 Infantry. This is due to lack of Drafts.

Monday 6 August

Charteris reports that the presence of the 54th Division in the Ypres area must now be accepted. It was withdrawn from the front line in Champagne on 26th July and moved up to Flanders hurriedly on the night of 3/4 August. He thinks there must be some underlying reason for this rapid rotation of divisions, other than casualties.

Enemy's artillery fire on Westhoek prior to launching the counter-attack was most severe. His attack was completely defeated.

Tuesday 7 August

Reports show situation quiet at battle front. Enemy has brought up large reinforcements. The line which was held on the day of our attack, by 8 divisions, seems now held by 10. Zonnebeke area is the strongest, where on a front of 4000 yards, there are 5 fresh divisions, either in the line or in reserve.

Charteris considers Enemy is planning a counter-attack on a considerable scale in this area. Armies and Corps have been warned...

As regards the value of concrete dugouts, prisoners state that they are considered dangerous unless of great depth. In some cases orders have been issued forbidding troops to use certain old shallow ones. Those affording effective protection are used for officers and dressing stations...

General Nash (DGT)[1] came to see me today and reported on the Transportation Service. Everything has gone extremely well. The number of trains to rail-head has increased to an excessive number: 30 more per diem than we had calculated for, and told the French we would want! The number is now 220 per diem, in addition to L of C trains. To avoid the risk of breakdown, he is reducing the number of trains to what can reasonably run. I agreed of course...

Major General Travers Clarke (who has been QMG of Salonika Force for $1\frac{1}{2}$ years) arrived this afternoon and stayed night.[2] He has taken up duties of Deputy Adjutant General. I spoke to him regarding his duties which must

---

1 Major General (later Sir) Philip Arthur Manley Nash (1875–1936), Director General of Transportation, 1917; Haig had a high regard for Nash's abilities.
2 Major General (later Lieutenant General Sir) Travers Edwards Clarke (1871–1962), DAG France, 1917; QMG France 1917–19. Greatly distinguished himself in supplying the armies in 1918, being described as 'the Carnot of Haig's armies'.

be those of a 'deputy' helping in the work of the whole department, and *not* in charge of merely one section of it. The question of *War Efficiency* must be uppermost in his mind in dealing with AG questions.

Wednesday 8 August

General Birch's Staff officer brought map showing how our batteries are gradually being pushed forward since 31 July, so that our artillery positions are very favourable both for supporting an attack, and exploiting success.

In view of large reinforcements brought up by Enemy, and his manner of using them (viz. for counter-attack *after* our troops have reached the end of an offensive operation and are exhausted), instructions are sent to Gough by Kiggell directing him to reduce the length of his next advance to what the men can easily do in the bad state of the ground (say about 2000 yards). The Enemy will then when he counter-attacks be held up by our troops while they are still fresh! This reducing the length of our advance may make our progress slow to begin with, but will pay us later on, I hope, when the Enemy's troops are worn out, and discouraged through failures in counter-attacking . . .

At Abbeville I called at the HQ of GOC 'L of C Area' and saw Major General Asser.[1] I then went on to Rouen lunching by the wayside in the Forêt d'Eu. It was 3.30 pm when I got to the Commandant's Office (Major General McNab).[2] I went round his office and spoke to his Staff officers, Sergeant Major etc. Then I went to Major General Graham's[3] office – the B Echelon of the Adjutant General's Office, and deals with the posting of men to units, casualties, drafts etc. An immense amount of writing is done here and many hundred clerks are employed. When I arrived some 200 female clerks were going off to draw their pay. They seem a businesslike looking lot, most industrious. They have done very good work already, though they cannot stand the long hours which the men often have to do. I went round Graham's office and spoke to his officers, head clerks etc. I thought them looking much fitter than on my last visit. Graham said that he had reduced the hours of work and had arranged for everyone to go out daily for an hour or two . . .

I crossed the Seine at Rouen and reached Deauville about 7 pm. Colonel Hickson met with me on arrival, with a number of officers on his Staff.[4] In consequence of the large number of Hospital Ships sunk by the Enemy we

1 Lieutenant General (later General) Sir (Joseph) John Asser (1867–1949), GOC Line of Communications Area, BEF, 1916–19.

2 Properly Brigadier General Colin Lawrance Macnab (1870–1918), Base Commandant, Rouen, April–October 1917.

3 Major General Edward Ritchie Coryton Graham (1858–1951), DAG Base, 3rd Echelon; Graham held this mundane but vital post for the whole of the war.

4 Colonel (later Major General Sir) Samuel Hickson (1859–1928), RAMC.

are erecting large hospitals and Convalescent Camps here so as to be able to treat a larger proportion of sick and wounded in France, who are at present sent to England.

The DGMS (Sir A. Sloggett) also appeared on my arrival ... After dinner Sloggett brought up Captain Cohen and introduced him to me. I was much interested in seeing him after having had such a lengthy correspondence about him for the past 2 years nearly![1] He seemed most pleasant and quite harmless. He expressed himself very anxious to do his best to help disabled officers to get work, and is prepared to organise and work a scheme but the Committee must consist of really practical people, and not figureheads.

Thursday 9 August

At 10 am accompanied by Colonel Hickson RAMC I motored to his hospitals on the high ground about 2 miles off. Hospitals are in process of erection for 15,000 sick or wounded and convalescents. On my way I inspected about 2000 convalescents who were on a route march – all seemed very fit and happy ...

In the camps I saw a number of convalescents doing physical exercises, drill etc. All seemed in the happiest spirit possible.

Colonel Hickson has a very large command and difficult task. I came away with the highest opinion of his organising and disciplinary faculties. Even at the Cambridge Hospital, Aldershot, he showed that he was a manager above the average. I told Sloggett that he must arrange to promote him to General.

A large number of German prisoners are at work here making roads and building huts etc. for the hospitals. I told the officer in charge to insist on their discipline being kept up especially saluting when British officers pass.

Friday 10 August

The II Corps (18th and 25th Divisions) attacked this morning on a 2 mile front near the Menin Road with the object of advancing their front over the ridge in some places, and to gain points of observation in others. All objectives were gained except 'Inverness Copse'. Here our attack was held up by a strong point which the division had arranged to deal with instead by withdrawing our front line and bombarding it with artillery. The attack was most satisfactory on the whole, and, observation being good, our guns killed vast numbers of the

1 Captain (later Major Sir) (Jack Benn) Brunel Cohen (1886–1965) took up the cause of crippled soldiers after he himself was badly wounded; he was later Hon. Treasurer of the British Legion, 1921–30, 1932–46.

Enemy when forming up for counter-attacks. Six of them were attempted but all failed! We captured 2 officers and 225 other ranks. Westhoek and adjoining ridge are now completely in our hands, and our troops are established in Glencorse Wood.

I left Trouville Pier about 11 am in a steamboat belonging to our Admiral at Havre. It is dignified by name of 'Yacht'. It took almost an hour to cross the Bay and sea was rather jumpy. Brigadier General Nicholson (Commandant of Havre Base)[1] met me on arrival and motored to his office. I spent about half an hour going round his office and talking to his assistants. I then visited the Convalescent Camp ... on the ridge above the town. Much excellent work has and is done here. I saw several officers and others whose acquaintance I made on my visit last year. I noticed the Sergeant Major who had kidney trouble, but who is now fit and strong and has done magnificent work.

Saturday 11 August

Five counter-attacks reported on II Corps centre divisions and one on the left division (25th), all repulsed. Some further ground gained near Menin road, where the trees are very thick, and progress most difficult owing to tangled mass of branches ...

About two miles west of Valéry sur Somme I went round the rest camp of the Third Army. Battalions of men, with a proportion of officers and NCOs, are sent down for a fortnight's rest ... They play games and sleep all day ... I saw one young officer (Nelson, Scotch Fusiliers) who had been wounded 4 times. I have told the Military Secretary (Peyton) to arrange to employ him away from the firing line.

Monday 13 August

Kavanagh Commanding Cavalry Corps came to see me this morning. Also Sir H. Rawlinson, who stayed to lunch. He stated that Du Cane Commanding XV Corps holding Corps sector, was anxious that the landing should be made before his Corps had taken Lombartzyde. I told Rawlinson that I had no intention of changing my plan. And one of the three conditions which I had always mentioned must be complied with before I approved of the landing being attempted. We discussed dates and tides etc. and arranged that there will be ample time for training the divisions detailed for the operation.

1 Brigadier General John Sanctuary Nicholson (1863–1924), Base Commandant, Le Havre, 1916–18.

Sir W. Furse (Master General of Ordnance, War Office)[1] came with Birch to dinner. Furse assured me that the state of the production of guns (18 pdrs) is improving, and that everything is being done to meet our demands. Also I pointed out that the new 9.2 howitzer is short of ammunition and a whole battery of them cannot in consequence be used! It seems there are no cartridge cases and three weeks' delay is the result.

On the whole Furse seemed more hopeful on the output of the Munitions Department and said Churchill is doing good work in co-ordinating the work of its numerous branches.

Wednesday 15 August

At 4.25 am First Army launched an attack consisting of 1st and 2nd Canadian Divisions against Hill 70 northwest of Lens. By 9 am reports indicated that all objectives had been taken except small part at extreme limit of the attack. Here heavy machine gun fire was encountered from brickfields and Cité St Auguste. Attack was made on a front of $2\frac{1}{2}$ miles and our captures include Cité St Emilie, Cité St Laurent, Fosse 14, Hill 70, Bois Rasé, Puits 14 bis and western half of Bois Hugo. All these names were well known to us in September 1915 at the time of the Battle of Loos! Losses reported to be 'very moderate' . . .

At 10.30 am I met General Gough and his CGS (Malcolm) at Cassel. General Kiggell accompanied me. I told Gough that looking to the development of his advance, I did not wish a direct attack made on the Forêt of Houthoulst. It would be very costly and would be playing the Enemy's game to embark on a large battle in the forest. My view is that the forest should be turned on both flanks and that, at the right moment, the Belgians should launch an attack via Dixmude to capture the Clerken ridge. Gough should arrange to establish a strong flank on the southern edge of the forest and push a line of skirmishers here assisted by Tanks into the southern part of the forest to clear up the situation there. If Enemy is found in force, we can cause him great loss by our artillery: on the other hand if not strongly defended, all ground gained by the Tanks and skirmishers can be consolidated. After Gough has thought over the matter and reported to me, I will then arrange with General Anthoine what his rôle should be.

Haig later visited Horne at First Army HQ.

His attack this morning has gone very well, and losses have been small. I

1 Lieutenant General Sir William Thomas ('Bill') Furse (1865–1953), Master General of the Ordnance, 1916–19.

discussed his future plans and decided that he should arrange to capture hill southeast of Lens. This will take 3 weeks, perhaps longer. I told him that I might want some of his guns to help our attack north of the Lys but I will leave guns as long as possible with him. He agreed that it would be most unwise to keep any guns away from decisive point which could be usefully employed . . .

Sir John Cowans, the QMG, visited Haig.

He has come out with orders to reduce some of our motor lorries because 'spare parts' cannot be manufactured in sufficient quantities now, and petrol is very scarce indeed. I had a long talk with him. He hardly realised the nature of this war! The War Cabinet and the Members of the Army Council keep pressing me to make a few cheese-paring reductions (6 Divisional cavalry regiments = 2500 horses out of 450,000 in the Army, some motor lorries, work on railways for instance) but they fail to see the huge beams in their own eyes. Such as 2 Army Staffs (northern and southern) at home, which swallow up many useful subordinates and cost much money.

I felt it a waste of time speaking to Cowans: he knows so little of the essentials which make for success in war. All the same he is most anxious to be friendly: he is feeble because he listens too much to gossip – e.g. he has an idea that 'Tanks' will never be of any use, when as a matter of fact they have already accomplished so much as to show that they have come to stay!'

Thursday 16 August

Yesterday's attack by First Army was an undoubted success. Three hostile divisions almost destroyed. 5 counter-attacks were made – all failed – that made at 5.30 pm was carried out by 4th Guard Division. Enemy's losses very great.

Fifth Army attacked at 4.45 am. We heard at breakfast time that the attack was progressing well, except on right flank where the country is very wooded and much broken up by our heavy shell fire, so that progress was slow.

At 9.45 our troops II Corps were reported in Polygon Wood and flank had been formed along southern edge of Glencorse Wood.

XIX Corps and XVIII Corps had both got Green line. XIV Corps had passed beyond Langemarck.

At 10.30 a telephone message stated that our troops had been seen coming back from Nonne Boschen and Gallipoli. It is very difficult in these battles

1 This is an ungenerous account of Cowans, who appears to have been remarkably successful as QMG.

quickly to discover what the real situation is. By 4.30 pm it was known that the II Corps was on the line Clapham Junction and hence through Glencorse Wood, connecting with the right division (16th) of XIX Corps which is on line Potsdam–Vampir–Beck House. Left division on line Pommern Redoubt–Border House. XVIII Corps on line Border House–crossroads west of Winnipeg–crossroads Vieille Maison–Rat House. XIV Corps are on Red line, i.e. have taken all their objectives and 900 prisoners.

On the left of the latter Corps the French have occupied the whole of the ground up to the Marjevaart as well as the bridgehead at Drie Grachten. Also 300 prisoners. So French have done well and are in good spirits. 'Casualties extremely small' they report.

Friday 17 August

Haig visited Lord Cavan (GOC XIV Corps) at his HQ.

He had insisted on our Regulations being closely adhered to as regards 'moppers up' and the capture of strong points. He saw no reason for changing them in any detail. Owing to the mud, he made special arrangements for passing up freshly cleaned rifles to replace those clogged with mud and grit. 'Armourer shops' were sent forward for that purpose.

Next, Haig visited Gough.

He was not pleased with the action of the Irish Divisions of the XIX Corps (36th and 16th). They seem to have gone forward, but failed to keep what they had won. These 2 divisions were in the Messines battle and had an easy victory. The men are Irish and did not like the shelling, so Gough said.

At HQ XVII Corps I was told by the GSO2 (Franklyn)[1] that only the left of 11th Division got forward. Before zero, only a small number were over the Steenbeek. Most of the concrete farms and 'dugouts' had not been destroyed by our bombardment and held up the attack.

At XIX Corps I saw General Watts who gave a bad account of the two Irish Divisions (36th and 16th). Nugent[2] and Hickie[3] are the respective GOCs. But I gather that the attacking troops had a long march up the

1 Major (later General Sir) Harold Edmund Franklyn (1885–1963), GSO2 XVII Corps, 1917; GSO1 21st Division, 1917–19.
2 Major General (later Sir) Oliver Stewart Wood Nugent (1860–1926), GOC 36th (Ulster) Division, 1915–18.
3 Major General (later Sir) William Bernard Hickie (1865–1950), GOC 16th (Irish) Division, 1915–18.

evening before the battle through Ypres to the front line and then had to fight from zero 4.45 am until nightfall. The men could have had no sleep and must have been dead tired. Here also a number of concrete buildings and dugouts were never really destroyed by artillery fire, and do not appear to have been taken. So the advances made here were small.

At II Corps I saw General Jacob. The 8th Division he said did splendidly, and so did the 56th. With a little luck the success would have been greater: as it was, a certain amount of important ground was taken. The Enemy was able however to mass a concentric artillery fire on his front of attack which was small. He now intends to advance by smaller attacks e.g. 2 battalions to take Inverness Copse. Then get Nonne Boschen Wood and so on until the right flank is strongly established so as to admit of a fresh advance along the ridge in conjunction with a general attack on a wide front.

The cause of the failure to advance on the right centre of the attack of the Fifth Army is due, I think, to Commanders being in too great a hurry! 3 more days should have been allowed in which if fine the artillery would have *dominated* the Enemy's artillery, and destroyed the concrete defences! After Gough has got at the facts more fully I have arranged to talk the matter over with him.

Saturday 18 August

Trenchard reported on the work of the Flying Corps. He considers that he has enough machines to keep battle going till October. But how different would our position be now if the programme which I put forward last October had been complied with! We were then at the height of our success in the air: the Enemy was at his lowest. It was to be expected that the Enemy would put forward a large effort and build many new 'planes'. This he has done, and hence our difficulties in the air.

Yesterday the French airmen ... working under my orders attacked their first train by day. They were quite delighted by the results, and all came back safely. On the whole however the French air service is in a bad state. No [real] management, no discipline and a considerable number [of pilots] don't mean business when they go out! ...

After lunch I motored with Butler to the Machine Gun School at Camiers, on sea coast north of Etaples, and attended a demonstration of machine gun fire. Three Army Commanders, many Corps Commanders and Staff officers were present. We saw 'barrages' carried out with 4 batteries = 32 guns, at a range of 2300 yards and over. Also a 'box barrage'. I then ordered a concentration to meet a supposed attack on our right front. The barrage came down in *one minute* from the time I gave the order. The officer in charge of this Machine Gun School is a Major Barrie the amateur golfer.[1] Before the war he knew nothing about military matters! Now he is most proficient and has everything in excellent order.

Sunday 19 August

At 11.30 am I had a meeting in my room with my senior Staff officers, viz. CGS, AG, QMG, DGT, GOC L of C (Asser), *Butler, Travers Clark and Engineer in Chief – on the subject of 'manpower'. I outlined the situation, pointing out that our Army's efforts this year have brought final victory near.[2] Indeed I think that, if we can keep up our effort, final victory may be won by December. In order to keep up our effort, the strength of our divisions must be kept up.

To get men, it is necessary that every service and department should immediately give up every man who is in any way likely, by training, to become fit for service in the ranks of the infantry. The remainder must work longer hours in order to replace their comrades.

All work which is not essential for the operation must be closed down. All decided to take up the matter most seriously and I feel sure they mean to work in the proper spirit. I ordered a conference of Army Commanders for Tuesday at which I can ask them to assist.

Monday 20 August

Charteris reported on Enemy's situation. Already 29 divisions have been exhausted in the battle in Flanders and 4 divisions opposite Lens = a total of 33 divisions since beginning of August.

Trenchard reported on work of Flying Corps. The recent strong west wind has prevented our damaged machines from being able to get back to our lines, and so our losses have been heavier in consequence. The Enemy however has lost still more than we have. French had asked his permission to withdraw 'a group of machines'. I said that of course the French must do what they thought best. Personally I viewed any withdrawal from this area as a pity, because at present it is the decisive point and the Allies should be as strong as possible here.

Birch reported that our artillery had done well during last 2 days. A marked decrease in hostile artillery fire was noticed in consequence.

1 Properly Arthur Gordon Barry DSO MC (1885–1942), English Amateur Golf Champion, 1905. Barry remained in the Army after the war, retiring as a brigadier in the Tank Corps in 1938. He was Army Golf Champion in 1922 and 1925.
2 This becomes 'nearer' in the Ts diary.

The French attacked early today northwest of Verdun. All objectives were soon taken and over 4000 prisoners. This defeat should have a great effect on the Enemy because they thought the French Army had become a negligible quantity.

Tuesday 28 August

On this day Haig decided to transfer responsibility for the main offensive from Gough's Fifth Army to Plumer's Second. Plumer asked for, and was granted, three weeks to prepare for the next major attack.

Trenchard reported the work of Flying Corps. Our photographs now show distinctly the 'shell holes' which the Enemy has turned into a position. The paths made by men walking in rear of those occupied, first caught our attention. After a most careful examination of the photo, it would seem that the system of defence was exactly on the lines directed in General Sixt von Armin's[1] pamphlet on 'The Construction of Defensive Positions' viz. advanced posts, lines of defence, Support lines etc. Now that we know where the Enemy is holding out, it will be more easy to bombard him out of the 'shell hole' position, than from his old concrete dugouts! . . .

Mr Morgenthau (late American Ambassador at Constantinople) came to lunch.[2] He seems to be a great personal friend and confidential adviser of the American President (*Wilson). In the course of our conversation he indicated that Wilson was determined to go on to the bitter end and remove the Hohenzollerns. I urged that it would be a mistake to leave Germany at the mercy of Revolutionaries, and that if disorder started in Germany it would spread to France and England. He said that he agreed with me, and no doubt Wilson would have to change his mind on this as he had done on some other matters. He questioned me closely on our 'ability to hold out until America is ready'. I replied that every day we got more of the upper hand over the Enemy, and that [if the French could only support us in a moderate way] there was a chance of ending the war this autumn. My chief fear was that Germany might offer in October or November terms of peace which the Allied Governments might accept, though not giving all we *ought* to receive. To this he said Wilson would oppose such a peace to the best of his ability. I liked Morgenthau and felt he was all out to help. He says Americans are more 'brothers' than 'cousins' of England now.

1 General Sixt von Armin, Commanding German Fourth Army in the Ypres Salient.
2 Henry Morgenthau (1856–1946), US Ambassador to Turkey, 1913–16. He was a leading supporter of President Woodrow Wilson and one of the most important bankers of his generation.

Saturday 1 September

Since the attack on 31 July we have captured 10,697 prisoners (including 234 officers), 38 guns (including 6 heavy), 208 machine guns and 73 trench mortars. These numbers are exclusive of French captures in Flanders.

Since the beginning of the Ypres battle 41 German Divisions have been engaged on the Ypres front of which over 30 have been withdrawn to refit.

10 of the [German] Divisions brought in to reinforce this sector have been withdrawn from the French front.

During the same period we have engaged 23 divisions and withdrawn 13.

The result of our pressure at Ypres is shewn by the slackening of the German efforts on the Chemin des Dames, and the comparatively weak resistance which they have made to the French attack at Verdun. [The French Army has consequently had the quiet time desired by General Pétain in which to recover from the Nivelle Offensive.]

Of the 146 German Divisions on the Western Front, 122 have been engaged in heavy fighting on the British or French battle front during the past $3\frac{1}{2}$ months, many of them 2 or 3 times over. Of the remaining divisions which have not been engaged, 16 are troops of inferior value which are normally employed only on quiet parts of the line.

Documents recently captured show the heavy strain to which the Enemy's troops are being subjected owing to losses, hardship, and the moral effect of our artillery and air superiority. These factors are having a steadily increasing effect on the German troops as they did during the Battle of the Somme, though in the present case they are likely to have more important results owing to our greater superiority in material, and to the inferior value of the recruits which are now being drafted into German units.

Haig went to London to prevent Foch from persuading the War Cabinet to send 100 guns to Italy.

Tuesday 4 September

I ... attended Conference in the CIGS's room at which General *Foch, Robertson, Davidson and myself were present.

Foch asked for guns to go to Italy because the *political* effect of a success there would be greater, in his opinion, than one in Flanders. He asserted that the French guns would be doing nothing for a month in Flanders! This of course I told him was not the case. French guns [on Anthoine's front] have a wide sector, and are employed covering our left and supporting Belgians at the present moment by counter-battering hostile guns ... I explained that the decisive point was in Flanders and it was most unsound policy to withdraw a single gun from my front. I produced maps showing where the French guns were situated and how they were employed.

The Prime Minister was very anxious that [some] guns should be sent. Bonar Law was, as usual, very weak. Carson and General Smuts[1] were opposed to any guns going. Lord R. Cecil for Foreign Office 'dissociated' himself from everything the Prime Minister proposed!

Finally it was agreed that the matter should be placed in my hands. After explaining the wishes of the Cabinet that the guns should be sent if I could possibly spare them, Lloyd George spoke to me alone, and said it was very desirable to help the Italians in this question because the French were trying to supplant us in their affections! We must not give the French the power of saying that they *wanted* to send 100 guns but the British would not let them go! I said I would review the whole gun situation on the battle front and if we could possibly liberate 50 guns it would be done. He said he was very grateful.

At 4 pm General Foch arrived, and went through the same performance as this morning, viz. argued that the guns were really doing nothing on our front. The proposal of holding a conference with me and Pétain was discussed, and after I had seen Foch we agreed to meet at Amiens on Friday at 12 noon, meantime I would wire to France and direct Kiggell to discuss the gun situation with Birch and Anthoine with a view to liberating 50 French guns for Italy.

Friday 7 September

I discussed with Kiggell the wisdom of making small attacks on farms and isolated strong points, such as Gough had been doing on the Fifth Army front. In my opinion unless we have dominated the Enemy's artillery completely our troops cannot retain a small area captured because of the hostile artillery fire which will assuredly be concentrated on the spot, and also because our own guns have so destroyed the defences before our troops attack that they find little left to consolidate. These small operations are very wasteful on ammunition. I decided to stop Gough from going on with these little attacks.

Saturday 8 September

We have obtained a position from which excellent observation over the Enemy's area can be obtained, the immediate consequence being, the withdrawal of the hostile artillery to a very considerable distance. There are now

1 Jan Christian Smuts (1870–1950), South African soldier and politician; member of Lloyd George's War Cabinet.

few guns west of a line drawn north and south through Gheluvelt; the majority are grouped around Nieuwe Kruiseecke, Becelaere and east of Broodseinde Ridge.

The result in our rear areas has been very apparent. Whereas, formerly, the marshy nature of the ground west of Zillebeke Lake caused the approaches to be few in number. Those under the hostile shelling became literally the death trap of the 'Ypres salient'. Now this area is practically immune from shelling. Little hostile shelling now falls west of a north and south line through Zillebeke, with the exception of some 8-inch howitzer and a few 5.9-inch from a southeast direction.

Monday 10 September

General Kiggell reported that he is afraid that some of Gough's subordinates do not always tell Gough their true opinion as regards their ability to carry out an operation. I therefore decided to go tomorrow to see the GOC V Corps (General Fanshawe) with reference to the small attacks prepared for the 13th.

Tuesday 11 September

General Birch reported on work of artillery. Owing to haze, observation was very bad yesterday and very little artillery work was possible. Ammunition is not arriving so well as has been promised. The cause is not clear . . .

Haig visited HQ V Corps.

I had a long talk with General Fanshawe.[1] He was CRA to General Lomax during the Battle of Ypres and knows the ground on the Menin road and also about Langemarck. He reminded me how on 31 October 14 I had only a few cavalrymen left under my hand as reserve.

All the rest of the two divisions had become involved in the battle. A German officer prisoner was very astonished and excited at seeing on his way to the rear no reserves at all! While he told us that the German reserves were standing in masses in the rear of the German front. How changed the situation has become in our favour today!

As regards 'small' enterprises, Fanshawe thought that 61st Division had been in the line so long (over 3 weeks) that the troops were not fresh enough to undertake the attack on Gallipoli etc. with good prospect of success. Similarly the 42nd Division was not sufficiently trained. He was therefore

1 i.e. Edward Fanshawe.

inclined to cancel the proposed small attacks – on the other hand General McKenzie (61st Division)[1] was coming to see him and submit his proposals.

I went round the offices of V Corps and before leaving General McKenzie ... arrived and so was able to have a few words with him. He thought that his division had not suffered unduly considering the terrific shell fire experienced each day. He was anxious to take Hill 35 before going out of the line, and felt confident his men could take it. I said that it was primarily for him to decide and the Corps Commander to decide whether these small enterprises should be undertaken or not.

Lieutenant Colonel Hereward-Wake (McKenzie's GSO1)[2] accompanied his general. I thought him looking ill and nervous – hardly fit for our present fighting.

I lunched at Château Löwe (HQ Fifth Army) with Gough. Sir H. Rawlinson was also lunching. All very cheery. After lunch I spoke about the advisability of making more attacks on a small scale before the main operation is launched and said the first question to be decided was 'Were these attacks necessary for the success of the main attack?' If not then they should not be made. If a division has failed the best thing to do is withdraw it for training before it is asked to attack again. Gough is to see the Corps and Divisional Commanders this afternoon and will then report.

I next visited HQ XVIII Corps and saw General Maxse. An attack of 3 platoons against Winnipeg failed 2 nights ago, because some of our own gas shells were thrown onto one of the platoons instead of onto 'the cemetery' and 9 men were gassed. The other platoons reached their objectives but had to be withdrawn as the strong point which the gassed platoon was to capture could not be attacked. There were only three casualties (2 wounded 1 killed).

Wednesday 12 September

Report from Fifth Army. General Gough has decided to give up the minor operations which he had proposed to make before the 'main operations'.

General Horne came to see me regarding the continuation of his operations against Lens. He has all the infantry necessary: he is anxious about the number of guns which I can give him. We are sending him a large number of the new type of heavy mortar (6-inch) some with 1500 yards range, and some sections of 6-inch howitzers from England to make his batteries up to 6 guns each. I

1 Properly Major General (later Sir) Colin John Mackenzie (1861–1956), GOC 61st (2nd South Midland) Division, 1916–18.
2 Lieutenant Colonel (later Major General) Sir Hereward Wake Bt. (1876–1963), GSO1 61st Division, 1916–17; BGGS Allied Supreme War Council at Versailles, 1917–19. He greatly disliked Haig and abused him at the Supreme War Council.

told him to go on with his arrangements and that it is pretty certain that we can find the guns which he requires . . .

The AG reported some disturbances which have occurred at Etaples, due to some men of new drafts with revolutionary ideas who produced red flags and refused to obey orders. The ring leaders have been arrested, and the others sent to their units at the front.[1]

I received Mr Horatio Bottomley (editor of *John Bull* etc.)[2] and he stayed to lunch. He seems to be a true friend of the soldier, and imbued with sound patriotic ideas . . .

Maybury showed me in detail the work which is being done on the roads. He was much pleased with a letter received from Lord Cavan complimenting one of Maybury's subordinates on what had been done in XIV Corps area.

Mr Winston *Churchill arrived this forenoon and visited Messines. The Enemy started shelling the hill with a few 5.9 shells. Winston ran back down the hill in such a hurry that he forgot his hat! After dinner he, General Kiggell and I had a talk. He said that for next year he is all in favour of concentrating our efforts against the Western Front.

Saturday 15 September

I had a talk with Sir E. Carson before he went out this morning. He considers that Lloyd George has considerable value as PM on account of his driving powers, but he recognises his danger. He has no knowledge of strategy or military operations, yet he thinks that he himself is well qualified to direct his military advisers! Carson wished me to talk freely with Mr Asquith because the latter, though in opposition, has very great power.

Sunday 16 September

The weather forecast is more hopeful for fine weather than it has been for *many* weeks . . .

I discussed some operations which *Byng proposed[3] after lunch, and I told

1 This is a reference to the so-called Etaples Mutiny. The disturbances were essentially a response to the harsh training regime at the notorious 'Bull Ring'. Haig's comment is interesting in attributing political motives to the 'mutineers'; its dismissive tone does not suggest that High Command was sent into a panic by the events.
2 Horatio William Bottomley (1860–1933), the self-styled 'soldier's friend', ended his colourful career of political populism and fraud in poverty and obscurity. He founded the rabble-rousing newspaper *John Bull* in 1906.
3 These 'operations' were to lead to the Battle of Cambrai. Byng had succeeded Allenby as commander of Third Army in June 1917 after the latter's departure to command the Egyptian Expeditionary Force.

him I would give him all the help I could. He wished the following divisions made up to strength – 34th, 35th, 40th, 50th, 62nd. Each is about 3000 men short of the establishment in infantry. Davidson is to go to his HQ at Albert tomorrow to talk over details.

Monday 17 September

I visited all Corps HQ in Second Army and held a conference at which the following were present – Corps Commanders, CRA, BGGS and GOC Divisions and CRA of the divisions taking part in the attack. I went very carefully into the preparations made by each division for the attack, as well as the Corps arrangements for counter-battery work and barrages etc.

At HQ IX Corps I saw General Hamilton Gordon. He is quite a changed man since his success on 7 June at Messines – quite youthful and vigorous in mind and body as well as confident now! Only the 19th Division is attacking on this Corps front.

I next saw General Morland (X Corps) at Abeele. His CRA (Brigadier General Reed VC) is a fine officer with considerable force of character and grit...

... I visited the HQ I Anzac Corps and saw Lieutenant General Sir W. *Birdwood, Major General Walker Commanding 1st Australian Division;[1] Smyth VC 2nd Australian Division;[2] Maclagan[3] 4th Australian Division; Hobbs[4] 5th Australian Division – CRAs etc.

In every case I found the officers full of confidence as to the results of the forthcoming attack. Every detail has been gone into most thoroughly, and their troops most carefully trained.

Our artillery airoplanes had never been interfered with seriously by the Enemy and the result of counter-battery work was considered by all to be quite satisfactory. Altogether I felt it most exhilarating to be around such a very knowledgeable and confident body of leaders.

At 4.30 I reached Berquette (near Aire) and was present at a trial of two narrow-gauge railway trucks designed for carrying heavy artillery. I saw a 6 inch howitzer and a 60 pounder gun loaded and carried a short distance on

1 Major General (later Lieutenant General Sir) Harold Bridgwood ('Hooky') Walker (1862–1934), an Indian Army Regular who commanded 1st Australian Division 1915–18.
2 Major General (later Sir) Nevill Maskelyne Smyth VC ('The Sphinx') (1868–1941), a British Regular who commanded 2nd Australian Division 1916–18. He emigrated to Australia after he retired.
3 Major General Ewen George Sinclair-Maclagan (1868–1948), a British Regular who commanded 4th Australian Division 1917–19.
4 Major General (later Lieutenant General Sir) (Joseph John) Talbot Hobbs (1864–1938), GOC 5th Australian Division, 1917–18; an architect by profession.

the trucks. The trial was quite successful. My intention is to use these trucks for the rapid transfer of heavy artillery from one battle front to another. This will greatly reduce the time required for mounting an attack, and should consequently enable us to surprise the Enemy as to the point chosen for attack.

Tuesday 18 September

Mr Asquith left after breakfast to visit Somme battlefield and stay night at Amiens. He said that he had been immensely struck with all he had seen, and particularly with the grand spirit of confidence existing from top to bottom in the Army. I felt that the old gentleman was head and shoulders above any other politician who has visited my HQ in brains and all round knowledge. It was quite a pleasure to have the old man in the house. So amusing and kindly in his ways.

I visited Corps HQ of the Fifth Army today, in the same way as I visited Second Army yesterday...

I called first at HQ V Corps near Poperinghe and saw General Fanshawe ... and amongst others Brigadier General Benson (his CRA);[1] Major General Lukin (9th Division), Jeudwine (55th Division), Deverell (3rd Division),[2] Romer (59th Division). The first two are commanding the 2 divisions which are attacking. They explained their plans in detail. They seemed thorough and sound. General Benson's artillery arrangements did not seem so satisfactory. He withdrew guns from counter-battery work at zero to thicken his barrage. I pointed out that the Enemy's guns on his Corps front might then freely turn against the Anzacs on the right! It was essential in my opinion that every known hostile battery should be engaged at zero: *subsequently* guns might be withdrawn if situation permitted. His map of the Enemy's gun position was not up to date. I directed General Birch (my artillery adviser) who was with me to go into the details of the artillery plan with Fifth Army after I had finished my tour of inspection today.

All were very confident of success. But Benson and others stated that the Enemy's airoplanes had been causing more trouble than ever before and some batteries had been bombed by them.

I next visited General Maxse Commanding XVIII Corps – Generals Harper (Commanding 51st Division); Fanshawe (Commanding 58th Division) explained their plan of attack. All very thorough and satisfactory.

1 Brigadier General Riou Philip Benson (1863–1939), BGRA V Corps, 1917–18.
2 Major General (later Field Marshal Sir) Cyril John Deverell (1874–1947), GOC 3rd Division, 1918–19; a ruthless and aggressive officer who rose from captain to major general in two years.

Brigadier General Fasson[1] the CRA was as usual very clear in his explanations. Though doubled up with rheumatics he has a grand spirit and does his work as thoroughly as anyone and without a grumble about the pain which he must constantly be suffering . . .

After lunch I called on Gough and told him what I had found in V Corps artillery arrangements. Otherwise I thought everything quite satisfactory. I am inclined to think that the Fifth Army Staff work is not as satisfactory as last year. Neill Malcolm seems fatigued, and is rather inclined to allow things to take their course.

About 2.30 I called at HQ XIV Corps and saw Lord Cavan and Major General Douglas Smith[2] Commanding 20th Division and Brigadier General Wardrop, CRA etc. All full of confidence. Cavan is quite pleased with French support on the left.

On my way back I left General Birch at Fifth Army HQ to go into V Corps artillery plan, and then called at Second Army HQ at Cassel.

General Plumer was in great spirits. I told him that I had only small suggestions of detail to offer as a result of my visit to his Corps and Divisions yesterday. Everything was quite satisfactory. I could only wish him success and good luck. The old man was full of good spirits and most confident.

Wednesday 19 September

General Birch . . . reported that he fixed up the artillery arrangements of V Corps quite satisfactorily last evening.

General Trenchard stated that airoplanes were not coming as well as he hoped. The Army seems to suffer, he thinks, from the lack of someone at the War Office to press our special needs in aircraft, and to see that they are provided in proper time. In June 1916 I asked for 56 air squadrons. In November 1916 for 20 more, total 76. We today have 57 squadrons i.e. 25 short! . . .

After lunch I motored to the quarries near Marquise whence we get road stone. General Maybury (the Director of Roads) met me and took me round. The quarries are about 10 miles northeast of Boulogne; are 5 in number and employ 7 to 8000 workmen including 400 German prisoners. Maybury took over the quarry last December, in which month 47,000 tons of stone were produced. Since then he has so developed them that in August 126,132 tons of stone were dispatched. His arrangements are being further improved and increased so that the output per annum will reach nearly 2 million tons!

1 Brigadier General Disney John Menzies Fasson (1864–1931), BGRA XVIII Corps, 1917–18.
2 Major General (later Sir) William Douglas Smith (1865–1939), GOC 20th (Light) Division, 1916–17; 1917–18; GOC 56th Division, 1917.

Engines, air compressors, stone breakers etc. have been imported from England, and some of our most capable quarry managers and quarrymen are now employed. The results have been highly satisfactory. A year ago I did not know where to turn to get road stone for our roads. Now all anxiety is over on this score. We pay the French 1 fr 75 cts per ton for our stone, at first the charge was 3 frs! And it all goes back onto *French* roads!! They are truly a race of usurers! ...

In the course of talk after dinner, Lord Derby said that Lloyd George is scheming to get rid of him and Robertson from the War Office. LG and Painlevé (now PM in Paris) are desirous of forming an Allied General Staff in Paris to direct operations. This I feel certain cannot possibly work. It seems an effort of the French to retain control of operations, notwithstanding that their Army has ceased to be the main factor in the military problem, in fact [the French Army has not only] ceased to be able to take the offensive on a large scale but according to Pétain's opinion, its discipline is so bad that it could not resist a determined German offensive.

Sir Herbert Plumer's Second Army entered the Third Battle of Ypres in earnest with its attack on the Menin Road Ridge on 20 September. This was the first in a series of set-piece attacks utilising artillery barrages of crushing density on narrow fronts in support of limited objectives. It was followed by Polygon Wood (26 September), Broodseinde (4 October) and Poelcappelle (9 October).

Thursday 20 September

About midnight General Gough proposed that operations should be postponed on account of rain, but General Plumer between 1 and 2 am after consulting his Corps and Divisional Commanders decided to adhere to plan. Zero hour was 5.40 am. Attack was launched on a front of about 8 miles: from Langemarck in north to Hollebeke on Ypres–Comines Canal in south. Our attacks were everywhere successful ...

After lunch I visited HQ of Second and Fifth Armies and saw Generals Plumer and Gough. I fixed date for the next attack ...

The Enemy's counter-attacks were numerous and determined. Second Army reported at 10.20 pm all had been destroyed. The most serious was against the left brigade of the right Anzac Division about 7.20 pm. Very careful artillery preparations had been made to deal with counter-attacks. As the afternoon was very clear the plans worked well.

Fifth Army reported at 11.25 pm that 3 heavy counter-attacks were delivered against XVIII Corps front between 6 and 6.30 pm. They were all destroyed and Enemy suffered very severe losses. In fact all reports show that Enemy's losses have been *most severe*, about 20,000.

Prisoners captured are estimated at 3300. Our casualties are very slight indeed. Fifth Army about 7000, Second Army less.

Wednesday 26 September

Second and Fifth Armies attacked at 5.50 am ... Our operations were entirely successful ... At 5 pm I (accompanied by Kiggell, Birch and Davidson) met Generals Plumer and Gough with their CGS at Cassel. They explained the situation on their fronts, and I decided on the extent of the next operation – and of a subsequent one when it will be necessary for the French to join in to cover the left of the XIV Corps.

Monday 1 October

Enemy made 3 attacks this morning between 5.30 am and 8.40 am between the northeast corner of Polygon Wood and Reutelbeck. Attacks fell on right brigade of 1st Australian Division, on 7th Division, 21st Division and 23rd Division. The last 3 divisions are in X Corps (Morland). All attacks were beaten off, except on right of 21st Division near Joist Farm which the Enemy captured. Enemy attacked with a fresh division (the 45th and storm troops) specially brought up from the Woëvre and ordered to go straight in and *attack* without relieving any of the troops holding the front.

It is a piece of good fortune that Enemy attacked today, and was defeated. None of our troops for our next attack are in the line yet – so Enemy has exhausted his divisions without interfering with our own plans ...

I ... visited the HQ of Guards Division at Proven and saw General Feilding.[1] I went round his officers and spoke to Staff etc. I also called at HQ of 20th Division in the same village. This latter division is leaving by train for Bapaume area. All seem in high spirits. In spite of having been in the XIV Corps front for a month and carried out 2 attacks, the division is only 1800 men under strength.

I called in at XIV Corps HQ and had a talk with Lord Cavan. He agrees that now divisions understand the manner of making an attack, long delays are no longer necessary ...

... I saw General Godley[2] Commanding II Anzac Corps: he relieved V Corps. I spoke to him of importance of making his arrangements so as to be

1 Major General (later Sir) Geoffrey Percy Thynne Feilding (1866–1932), GOC Guards Division, 1916–18.
2 Lieutenant General Sir Alexander ('Alick') John Godley (1867–1957), GOC XXII Corps (previously II Anzac Corps), 1916–18; his nickname – 'Lord God' – is indicative of his high-handed approach, which was rarely appreciated by the New Zealanders under his command.

able to exploit any success gained without delay. Thus guns should be placed behind Grafenstafel Hill (as soon as it is captured) for dealing with Passchendaele – and the reserve brigades of attacking divisions should be used *at once* to exploit a success if the Enemy counter-attacks and fails. Further reserves will be brought up by train. This is now possible as we have 3 lines (broad gauge) beyond Ypres. So there must be no hesitation in using reserves on the spot.

At Abeele I saw Brigadier General Cameron at X Corps HQ. He told me of the Enemy's attacks this morning. General David Campbell commands 21st Division which lost ground on its right. Heavy artillery fire from Enemy's Tenbrielen group of guns. All seemed pleased at defeat of Enemy's great efforts to counter-attack.

Tuesday 2 October

I held Conference at my house in Cassel at 11 am. Kiggell, Davidson and Charteris accompanied me. Generals Gough and Plumer were also present with their senior Staff officers and General Nash (DGT). I pointed out how favourable the situation was and how necessary it was to have all the necessary means for exploiting any success gained on the 10th, should the situation admit, e.g. if the Enemy counter-attacks and is defeated, then reserve brigades must follow after the Enemy and take the Passchendaele ridge at once ... Both Gough and Plumer quite acquiesced in my views, and arranged whole-heartedly to give effect to them when the time came. At first they adhered to the idea of continuing our attacks for limited objectives.

Charteris emphasised the deterioration of German Divisions in numbers, moral and all round efficiency.

Wednesday 3 October

A great bombshell arrived in the shape of a letter from CIGS stating that the British Government had 'approved in principle' of the British Army ... taking over more line from the French, and details are to be arranged by General Pétain and myself. This was settled at a conference at Boulogne on 25 September at which I was not present. Nor did either LG or Robertson tell me of this decision at our interview. All the PM said was that 'Painlevé was anxious that the British should take over more line'. And Robertson rode the 'high horse' and said it was high time for the British now to call the tune, and not to play second fiddle to the French, etc. etc., and all this when shortly before he must have quietly acquiesced at the conference in Painlevé's demands! Robertson comes badly out of this, in my opinion – especially as it was definitely stated (with the War Cabinet's approval) that no discussion re. operations on the Western Front would be held with the French without my being present.

Second Army attacked at Broodseinde on 4 October, inflicting a serious defeat on the Germans. The Germans were themselves concentrating their infantry for an attack when they were hit by a crushing British barrage.

Thursday 4 October

Attack was launched at 6 am this morning by 8 divisions of Second Army (Plumer) and 4 divisions of Fifth Army (Gough). On right of the attack was 37th Division (IX Corps) south of the Menin road. Next on the north was X Corps with 5th, 21st and 7th Divisions. Some hard fighting took place here.

Then came I Anzac Corps 1st and 2nd Australian and next in north was II Anzac Corps with 3rd Australian and New Zealand Divisions. The right of this latter Corps was Zonnebeke station. Against the front from Zonnebeke to Polygon Wood the Enemy had concentrated 5 divisions and intended to attack about 7 o'clock. 3 of these divisions have lost prisoners of all 3 regiments, and 2 divisions lost prisoners of two regiments! Thus it is clear all five divisions were heavily engaged and large numbers of German dead are reported in front of these Corps. Enemy lost very heavily indeed . . .

The fighting was not severe against the Second Army and those of the Enemy who did not surrender ran away!

Today was a very important success and we had great good fortune in that the Enemy had concentrated such a large number of divisions just at the moment of our attack with the very intense artillery barrage.

Over 3000 prisoners and six guns are already reported captured.

In order not to miss any chance of following up our success if the Enemy were really demoralised, I met Generals Plumer and Gough with their Staff officers at my house in Cassel at 3 pm. Plumer stated that in his opinion we had only up to date fought the leading troops of the Enemy's divisions on his front. Charteris who was present thought that from the number of German regiments represented among the prisoners all divisions had been seriously engaged and that there were few more available reserves.

Gough had given orders to XVIII Corps to push on beyond Poelcappelle, but soon a report was received that 4th Division (XIV Corps) had lost '19 metre' Hill (northwest of the village). This eventually proved incorrect, but in the meantime further advance had ceased.

After full discussion I decided that the next attack should be made two days earlier than already arranged provided Anthoine could also accelerate his preparations.

At 4 pm I saw the latter. He was most anxious to do everything possible to hasten matters. Finally it was found only possible to advance the attack by *one* day.

Rain fell heavily this afternoon as I took a walk.

Trenchard reported on the result of his visit to London. All members of the War Cabinet seem to have lost their heads over the German bombing raids [against London.] He told them that London must expect bombing to continue even though we do bomb German towns.

Friday 5 October

I had a talk with Sir Eric Geddes regarding Staff work at the Admiralty. In order to have more time to devote to reorganising matters, he asked me for General Nash (my DG Transportation) to join him. He recommends Cruickshank[1] as successor. I agree to allow Nash to go, and Geddes promised to supervise certain railway returns and help me at any time should the situation require it.

I discussed future plans with Kiggell. He wishes Belgians to attack Dixmude and Beerst – but the latter is separated by inundations from the Belgians' present position and only one causeway leads across the marshes.

In my opinion when we have gained the Passchendaele ridge as far north as Stadenberg the Enemy will be forced to withdraw from Dixmude front and Forêt d'Houthoulst, because he can't risk his troops being cut off in that area. The river from Contemarcke to Dixmude is unfordable except at the bridges. My view is *first* capture the Passchendaele–Stadenberg ridge…

As regards allocation of divisions to Armies, Kiggell recommended that the Canadian Corps (4 divisions) should be sent to General Plumer and not to Gough because the Canadians don't work kindly under the latter. The idea seems to be prevalent that he drove them too much in the Somme fighting last year! I think Gough's Staff officer (Malcolm) is partly the cause.

Saturday 6 October

At 11 am I inspected 57th Division commanded by Major General Barnes[2] near Estrée Blanche. General Horne Commanding First Army was also present. The day was cold and wet. I rode round each brigade and saw them march past in turn by platoons. The physique of the men is good: they

1 Properly Major General (later Sir) Sydney D'Aguilar Crookshank (1870–1941), Deputy Director General (then Director) of Transportation, BEF, 1917–18.
2 Major General (later Sir) Reginald Walter Ralph Barnes (1871–1946), GOC 32nd Division, 1916–17; GOC 57th (2nd West Lancashire) Division, 1917–19. Barnes was a friend of Winston Churchill; he was twice wounded during the war.

handled their arms well, and stood still in the ranks. Altogether they presented a fine appearance in spite of the cold. Each brigade had chosen a piece of grass land for the march past: the ground however became very muddy and slippery, but the men marched past extremely well. Every man was doing his best, and gave one the impression of there being a fine spirit in the division.

Sunday 7 October

An order of 5th Guard Infantry Brigade was captured stating that 'at today's conference . . . there was a general complaint that the losses incurred (through counter-attacking) bear no relation to the results obtained. Experience therefore shows the importance of making the front line strong' . . . . . .

'The altered method of attack of the Enemy who fixes a limited objective for his attack, forces us to change our tactics which are based on the repulse of a deep penetration of our position with a view to further operations.'

This is very satisfactory, and shows that our tactical methods have defeated those of the Enemy!

I discussed the question of concentrating rolling stock for sending forward reserves to exploit success on the 9th (Tuesday).

In order to collect the required number of railway waggons, the vehicles used for animals and road stone must be given up. We can do without these trains for 24 hours. If however I order tonight to collect the necessary rolling stock, and owing to the wet ground or other cause the success is not exploited on the 9th, the vehicles must then be dispersed, but will have to be collected again for the 12th (next attack). Thus in one week 3 days' trains of ammunition and road stone would be lost. This would cause serious delay in ultimate advance and inconvenience . . .

In view of the heavy rain today, and the possibility of the ground on Tuesday being too wet to admit of our men going forward beyond the 'limited objective' I decided to delay issuing an order to collect waggons until tomorrow when I will again consider the question with DGT (Nash).

Monday 8 October

General Birch reported on artillery situation. Guns have been worked well forward. XVIII Corps (Fasson CRA) and II Anzac (Powell CRA)[1] have done particularly well in this respect. Owing to rain yesterday mud was very bad, and so only enough guns have been pushed forward to cover tomorrow's attack, but there are not enough to cover exploitation! It is therefore evident

1 Brigadier General Edward Weyland Martin Powell (1869–1954), BGRA II Anzac Corps, 1916–17; BGRA XXII Corps, 1917–18.

that my decision yesterday not to concentrate rolling stock was correct...

I saw the DGT (Nash) and General Davidson regarding the demands to be made on railways to carry troops to exploit a success on 9th or 12th. I decided only to ask for a certain number of tactical trains for the second date, viz. 4 for Fifth Army and 10 for Second Army. Nash could run 10 such trains in 10 hours without disturbing other traffic...

I called on General Plumer and had tea. It was raining and looked like a wet night. He stated that II Anzac Corps (which is chiefly concerned with tomorrow's attack) had specifically asked that there should be *no postponement.* Plumer was anxious lest the French should want to postpone. I told him that Cavendish (attaché to General Anthoine) had reported at noon by telephone that 'situation in First Army (French) for attack on 9th is on the whole satisfactory', though the bombardment had not been effective. But Anthoine is 'quite ready to carry out his attack as already arranged'...

Later Kiggell brought me Anthoine's letter – a very mean document. He is evidently keen to save himself and to place the risk of failure on me. I am ready to take the responsibility and have ordered him to carry on and do his best. The French appear to have lost their chivalrous spirit if it ever existed out of the story book!

Gough telephoned to Kiggell as to postponement. He said Cavan was against it, but Maxse wanted to postpone. I ordered them to carry on.

Second Army attacked at Poelcappelle on 9 October. Poor artillery preparation and appalling weather that badly affected artillery observation, communications and logistic arrangements conspired to turn the attack into something of a shambles. British casualties in October 1917 were the third highest of the war, exceeded only by July 1916 and April 1917.

Tuesday 9 October

A general attack was launched at 5.20 am today from a point southeast of Broodseinde on the right to St Janshoek on the left (1 mile northeast of Bixschoote). The results were very successful...

The ground was so bad that 8 hours were taken in marching to forming up points: troops in consequence late and barrage started before the troops were ready. Notwithstanding this the 66th Division advanced without barrage and took all objectives – 49th gained all except a small piece on the left.

Friday 12 October

At the First Battle of Passchendaele, the attackers suffered from the same problems as three days earlier, and made only limited progress.

Second and Fifth Armies continued their attack at 5.25 this morning. Troops reached points of assembly up to time in spite of the very bad state of ground ... Owing to the rain and bad state of the ground General Plumer decided that it was best not to continue the attack on the front of his Army.

Saturday 13 October

I held a conference at Cassel at noon with Generals Plumer, Gough, their Staff officers, Kiggell, Nash, Birch, Charteris, Davidson ... I said that our immediate objective was the mass of high ground about Passchendaele. Once this was taken the rest of the ridge would fall more easily. The Canadians would join Second Army at once for next attack. The Fifth Army would have 1st and 63rd Divisions. Every effort must be made to complete railways and communications in rear of the battle front. Nash asked that traffic might be reduced temporarily as much as possible. Army Commanders asked for horse transport to replace lorries on roads in front in order to save the new roads. All this will cause delay of 10 to 12 days before next attack. Enemy seems to have increased the number of his machine guns in front. This necessitates a larger bombardment. We all agreed that our attack should only be launched when there is a fair prospect of fine weather. When ground is dry no opposition which the Enemy has put up has been able to stop them. Ground is so soft in places the DGT (Nash) told us that he has light engines on the 60 centimetre railways sunk halfway up the boilers in the mud! Track has disappeared!

Monday 15 October

General Birch reported on artillery situation. Enemy is moving his guns from Tenbrielen area northeast opposite (that is east of) Passchendaele. He advises complete withdrawal from Poelcappelle before the next attack, in order to bombard it thoroughly. The two infantries are now so close that effective bombardment now is impracticable.

Charteris reports that on 12 October 2 pioneer companies of the 233rd Division 'refused to attack'. This is another direct instance of insubordination in German Army and consequent loss of fighting spirit. Yet it is stated in a note by the DMI War Office dated 1 October (WP 49) 'The moral of the troops in the field gives no cause for anxiety to the German High Command'. I cannot think why the War Office Intelligence Department gives such a wrong picture of the situation except that General Macdonogh (DMI) is a Roman Catholic and is (unconsciously) influenced by information which doubtless reaches him from tainted (i.e. Catholic) sources[1] . . .

General Byng (Commanding Third Army) came to lunch and afterwards went into his proposals for an operation on his front. I had already discussed the matter twice before with him. It was now a question of getting him some troops. Major Tandy[2] (General Staff) attended and I was able to arrange for Byng to have 4 divisions to start training at once. Viz. the 8th (now in Second Army), the 12th, 29th and 51st, the three latter are now in the Third Army. I promised before the operation is launched to concentrate a Reserve, if possible Cavan's XIV Corps including the Guards.

Friday 26 October

Second and Fifth Armies launched 'Second Passchendaele'.

The positions won by the Canadians and 63rd Division today are of the greatest importance . . .

In the evening General Gough communicated with General Kiggell CGS that he found the ground on his front so very bad that he recommended delaying further operations until frost set in! Kiggell proposed a conference tomorrow with General Plumer to discuss this question. I said 'No. Let Army Commanders go round their troops tomorrow and ascertain situation, and report to me personally on Sunday at Cassel whether they consider any delay of date fixed for next attack necessary.' In my opinion today's operations at the decisive point (Passchendaele) had been so successful that I was entirely opposed to any idea of abandoning the operations till frost set in. If wet continues, a day or two's delay may be advisable before we launch the next attack.

Friday 2 November

Trenchard reported on work of Flying Corps. 2 good squadrons are going to Italy. He attended a meeting of Corps Commanders recently in Second Army. When complaints were made about Enemy bombing our trenches, billets etc., and also that his low flying machines were a serious factor, he told them that the *only way* to stop them is to bomb more than the Enemy does and to send more low flying machines than he does!! In fact there is *no* other way of stopping them.

---

1 Some British newspapers condemned the Pope as pro-German, following the papal peace initiative of August 1917. We owe this information to Jim Beach.
2 Major (later Brigadier General) Ernest Napper Tandy (1879–1953), GSO2 Third Army.

Sunday 4 November

In Paris, Haig had a meeting with Lloyd George.

The Prime Minister first made a few remarks regarding the necessity for forming an Inter-Allied Supreme War Council and Staff and asked my views. I told him that the proposal had been considered for 3 years and each time had been rejected as unworkable. I gave several reasons why I thought it could not work, and that it would add to our difficulties, having such a body. The PM then said the two Governments had decided to form it. So I said there is no need saying any more then! . . .

We then discussed the Italian situation.[1] I urged strongly that no more troops be sent from my command in France. We could give more effective help by attacking here. LG said he would not decide to send more troops until he had seen what the situation is in Italy.

Incidentally he complained about attacks being made on him in the Press which were evidently inspired by the Military! He intended to make a speech and tell the public what courses he had proposed and how if he had his way the military situation would have been much better today but his Military advisers had prevented him from carrying out his intentions! He took special exception to articles in the *Morning Post, Spectator, Nation, Globe,* and he said one editor had come back from my Headquarters and said that I had complained that he (LG) had interfered with my Tactics! I at once said 'What is his name? because it is not true!' He said 'Spender of the *Westminster Gazette*'.[2] I said 'I will write to him', but LG at once said, 'Oh, please do not do that'!

I thought LG is like the German, who, whenever he proposes to do anything extra frightful, first of all complains that the British or French have committed the enormity which he is meditating. LG is feeling that his position as PM is shaky and means to try and vindicate his conduct of the war in the eye of the public and try to put the people against the soldiers! In fact, to pose as the saviour of his country, if he had not been hampered by bad advice given by the General Staff! One important point to bear in mind is that he has never taken the soldiers' advice and *concentrated all resources* on the Western Front.

I gave LG a good talking to on several of the questions he raised, and felt I got the best of the arguments. He seemed quite 'rattled' on the subject of Italy.

1 On 24–25 October an Austro-German force had smashed an Italian army at Caporetto, precipitating a major crisis.
2 J. Alfred Spender (1862–1942), editor of the *Westminster Gazette*, 1896–1922; an Asquithian liberal.

About 12 o'clock he asked me to go out for a walk, and I went with him up the Champs Elysées to the Arc de Triomphe. Quite a pleasant little man when one has him alone, but I should think most unreliable...

Tuesday 6 November

Canadian Corps attacked this morning at 6 am with 2 divisions (2nd Division on right, 1st Division on left) northeastwards along Passchendaele ridge and on the spur north and northwest of the village.

The operations were completely successful. Passchendaele was taken, as also were Mosselmarkt and Goudberg. The whole position had been most methodically fortified. Yet our troops succeeded in capturing *all* their objectives early in the day with small loss – 'under 700 men'! The left battalion of 2nd Division had hard fighting – 21 officers and 408 other ranks were taken prisoners. Today was a very important success.

Wednesday 7 November

Haig was ordered to send Plumer to Italy with British reinforcements.

I decide to replace Second Army HQ with the Fourth Army Staff (Rawlinson) at once. This will cause least dislocation of arrangements. Was ever an Army Commander and his Staff sent off to another theatre of war in the middle of a battle?

Friday 9 November

Gemeau also said that state of the French Army is now very good but at end of May there were 30,000 'rebels' who had to be dealt with. A whole brigade of infantry had marched on Paris with their rifles after looting a supply column. Another lot seized a motor convoy. Some others occupied a village and a brigade of cavalry had to be employed to round them up. This was not done without opening fire on the village! This shows how really bad the condition of the French Army was after Nivelle's failure, and Pétain had a very difficult job to get things in good order.

Saturday 10 November

After lunch Robertson explained the Italian situation to me – Kiggell, Butler, Davidson, Plumer and his Staff officer being also present.

I pointed out the importance of the Belgian coast to Great Britain, and urged that nothing should be done to stop our offensive next spring.

Robertson stated that the Government had decided that the saving of Italy was to take first place, and we might have to send 8 or 9 divisions in all and the French a similar number! He would write and ask for my views. I asked if even 20 divisions can save the Italians [from disaster.] The loss of that number of divisions from the Western Front might lead to the loss of war.

Attack was launched at 6.5 am today on II Corps and Canadian Corps fronts extending from north of Passchendaele village to Tournaut Farm on the west of the ridge. At 9.30 am Second Army reported all objectives taken. Very heavy rain had fallen in the night and the ground was very deep.

At 3.30 pm Second Army reports our troops had been driven out of 'Veal Cottages' and 'Vat Cottages' on the spur northwest of Passchendaele and also from Vox and Vocation Farms which are on the main ridge. 'Steps are being taken to retake these localities.' Notwithstanding these points being still in Enemy hands, our troops have improved their position on the Passchendaele ridge very greatly.

Sunday 11 November

I attended Church of Scotland at 9.30 am. Reverend Captain Duncan officiated. Text from 90th Psalm 'Oh Lord Thou hast been our dwelling place for all generations'. A most encouraging sermon at this time.

After church I saw Birch and Charteris. Then the QMG regarding the organisation of a 'Farm Directorate' to cultivate farm land in France as requested by QMG War Office – on account of shortage of shipping we must grow more in France. I wrote to Sir J. Cowans and suggested letting Americans do this! If we occupy land, many Frenchmen will say that we have come to stay, just as the Germans are prophesying that we mean to hold this part of France.

Monday 12 November

Generals Nash (DGT) and Freeland[1] came to see me regarding railway arrangements. Butler was present. It was agreed to stop extension of broad gauge lines in the Ypres area and use the men set free for narrow gauge continuation and maintenance. Men very tired and must have relief. Nash can supply ammunition to keep up bombardment for another fortnight.

Freeland (who is in charge of the railways in the Ypres sector) states that 3 months will be required to complete railways and roads there, before offensive can be resumed . . .

1 Brigadier General (later Major General Sir) Henry Francis Edward Freeland (1870–1946), Deputy Director General of Transportation, 1917–18.

Haig visited 62nd Division.

I rode on to Fosseux (Divisional HQ) and saw General Braithwaite.[1] He is very pleased with his division and satisfied that operations will be a success. I was introduced to his staff and also saw Brigadier General Lord Hampden Commanding 185 Brigade.[2] His battalions are up to a good strength and he has men spare.

I then rode to Gouy HQ 186 Brigade and saw the Brigadier. He took over command 2 days ago: his name is Bradford, aged 29 and a Lieutenant in his own regiment, the Durham Light Infantry.[3] He started war in 6th Division on the Aisne – soon got a company and latterly has had a battalion in 50th Division. Has come from battle front, Poelcappelle sector. He has won the VC and Military Cross. Quite a fine modest fellow. After he got telegram ordering him to this brigade, he was going round his piquets when 3 bullets (from a machine gun) wounded him on the right cheek and chin!! Bradford is very pleased with his brigade and feels very confident and thinks his battalions are quite good.

Tuesday 13 November

I left soon after 9 by motor and met General Scott Commanding 12th Division at Vacquerie (west of Frévent) at 10 am. The 37 Brigade (Webber)[4] then carried out an attack across country with Tanks represented. I walked with the troops for an advance of fully 3 miles. Going quite good . . .

I explained to Divisional and subordinate Commanders whom I saw today that the object of the operations of the infantry aided by Tanks [was] to break through the Enemy's defences *by surprise* and so permit the Cavalry Corps to pass through and operate in open country. This requires bold and determined action on the part of the subordinate Infantry Commanders. This was not, I thought, fully realised in all units I saw today, especially in the 6th Division.

1 Major General (later General) Sir Walter Pipon Braithwaite (1865–1945), GOC 62nd (2nd West Riding) Division, 1915–18; GOC IX Corps from September 1918. He was a friend of Haig, who had helped him to resurrect his career after the Gallipoli debacle, during which he was Sir Ian Hamilton's Chief of Staff. Braithwaite proved to be an outstanding corps commander in the final battles of the war on the Western Front.
2 Brigadier General Viscount Hampden (1869–1958), GOC 185 Brigade, August 1917–18.
3 Brigadier General Roland Boys Bradford VC (1892–1917), GOC 186 Brigade, 10–30 November 1917. Bradford was actually only twenty-five. He was the youngest British general of the twentieth century. He was killed in action on 30 November 1917.
4 Properly Brigadier General Adrian Beare Incledon-Webber (1876–1946), GOC 37 Brigade, 1917–18.

Position of hay reserves is serious. I wired to War Office on 11th that only 6 days' reserve are in hand and ships advised as probably arriving in next seven days, only carry about $5\frac{1}{2}$ days' hay for the Force in France. Situation seems likely to become worse.

General Kavanagh (Commanding Cavalry Corps) . . . came to dinner. We discussed his plan afterwards. He expressed himself as most confident of success.

Wednesday 14 November

I left at 9 am and met horses near Lucheux. Major General Ponsonby[1] Commanding 40th Division and his Staff met me and then witnessed a tactical exercise of the 120 Brigade (Willoughby)[2] against a smaller force which had orders to hold certain localities and then retire. I thought that the pursuing force was prematurely deployed, and so its advance was delayed and was slow. But the men (though many 'Bantams' amongst them), seemed quick and alert, and cleaner than when I last saw this division. Ponsonby has only had the Division 3 months and will, I am sure, quickly remedy the defects I noticed.[3]

We then motored to Albert where I arrived at 12.15 at Third Army HQ. I had an hour's talk with General Byng. Everything is going on well and up to time. I saw Brigadier General H. Elles Commanding the Tank Corps.[4] He seemed confident and satisfied.

We lunched by the roadside near Fricourt (on the Somme battlefield). The ground is now covered with long grass and bracken and looks very different to how it was this time last year.

At 1.45 I witnessed an exercise carried out by the 6th Shropshire Light Infantry (under Colonel Walsh)[5] with Tanks. This battalion is in 60 Brigade (Duncan Royal Scots),[6] 20th Division (Major General W. D. Smith). A very good battalion. The Tanks were part of Colonel Hardress Lloyd's command

1 Major General (later Sir) John Ponsonby (1866–1952), GOC 40th Division, 1917–18; GOC 5th Division, 1918–19.
2 Brigadier General Hon. Charles Strathavon Heathcote-Drummond-Willoughby (1870–1949), GOC 120 Brigade, 1915–18.
3 40th Division was originally raised as a 'Bantam' formation including men of below usual height.
4 Brigadier General (later General Sir) Hugh Jamieson Elles (1880–1945), GOC Tank Corps, 1916–19: Elles' wartime career owed much to Haig's patronage; this did not make Elles deferential, indeed he was almost pathologically outspoken.
5 Lieutenant Colonel H. E. Welch (1880–1918), CO 6th King's Shropshire Light Infantry, 1917–18.
6 Brigadier General (later Major General) Francis John Duncan (1870–1960), GOC 60 Brigade, 1917–18; GOC 61st Division, 1918–19.

(the polo player).[1] I thought the Tanks went very well, and were better manoeuvred and at a faster pace than I have seen hitherto...

Hay situation is distinctly better since I telegraphed on the 11th. *Reserves* now risen to 9 days – 2 days in the field depôts – $1\frac{1}{2}$ days en route to front [make] 12 days in all.

Thursday 15 November

At 10.30 I motored to HQ 29th Division at Basseux where General De Lisle Commanding the Division met me. We then rode towards Ransart. The scheme was based on the idea that the 29th Division will have to pass through the divisions which have gained the *first of* [*our*] *objectives*, and capture 2 villages and a system of trenches beyond a canal as *second objective*, the flanks of the division being covered by other troops.

Monchy on the right and Ransart on the left represent the 2 villages: while the ditch in the low ground between these two places was taken as the Canal and crossing places were marked with flags. The ground represented the reality very well, and the old British and German trench lines are very much like the actual defences over which our troops will have to pass.

The division advanced with its 3 brigades in line. Right brigade on Monchy, and left brigade had to capture Ransart.

I was very pleased on the whole with the way battalions worked. I noticed 2 points however of importance

1. In some cases platoon and company commanders did not arrange for *covering fire* with machine and Lewis guns to help forward the advance from stage to stage. This should have been arranged for automatically, whether it was necessary or not to support the advance, and
2. The advance should be from ridge to ridge. That is to say before leaving the line gained, all arrangements should be made for occupying the next ridge and then *everyone*, knowing his objective, should move forward on to it without any hesitation or delay. Partial advances here and there should be avoided. I also spoke of the need for Brigadiers having artillery *at their call*.

The brigades seemed to me well commanded; 86 Brigade (Cheape)[2] was

1 Colonel (later Brigadier General) John Hardress Lloyd (1874–1952), OC 3rd Tank Battalion, 1917; GOC 3rd Tank Brigade, 1917–18; No. 1 Group HQ Tank Corps, 1918–19. He was a former captain of the England polo team.
2 Brigadier General George Ronald Hamilton Cheape (1881–1957), GOC 86 Brigade, 1917–19.

on the left, 87 Brigade (Lucas)[1] in centre and 88 (Nelson)[2] on right. I was very pleased with the general appearance of the divisions and the spirit and keenness of the men.

In afternoon I motored with Kiggell to Hermanville, HQ of 51st (Highland) Division, and saw General Harper Commanding and his Brigadiers, viz. 152 Brigade (Pelham Burn),[3] 153 (Beckwith),[4] 154 Buchanan.[5] The division is now 13,000 infantry and in great form. We discussed the scheme and I called attention to importance of covering fire with machine and Lewis gun at all stages of the fight. Harper pointed out that if the 62nd Division on his left did not get on, his advance might be held up. I indicated that it is possible for him to form a defensive flank on his left, and push forward with his right as rapidly as possible and get behind the Enemy by seizing Bourlon Wood and [Hill.]

All seemed very pleased with the operation and confident of success if it is launched as a surprise.

Friday 16 November

At 11.30 am I had a conference at Villers au Flos (HQ IV Corps) with Generals Byng (Commanding Third Army), Pulteney III Corps, Woollcombe IV Corps, Kavanagh Cavalry Corps. We discussed plans of Divisions and Corps in detail. All very confident and everything so far has gone very smoothly indeed. We finished about 1 o'clock. Kiggell went off to lunch with his friend Braithwaite, Commanding 62nd Division, and Heseltine and I motored back via Arras. We lunched on the flats above Mercatel...

In view of extra work now thrown on the Transportation Branch on account of the movements to Italy I arranged with Sir E. Geddes (First Lord Admiralty) to retain General Nash's services as DGT.

Sunday 18 November

I attended Church of Scotland at 9.30 am. The Rev. Duncan officiated: he took as his text a chapter of the Acts. Christ never spoke to his disciples of dying but He said 'When I leave you I will send my Comforter to you, and

1 Brigadier General (later Major General) Cuthbert Henry Tindall Lucas (1879–1958), GOC 87 Brigade, 1915–16 and 1917–18; BGGS Machine Guns, GHQ, 1918; GOC 4th Division, 1918–19.
2 Brigadier General Herbert Nelson (1875–19??), GOC 88 Brigade, 1917–18.
3 Brigadier General Henry Pelham Burn (1882–1958), GOC 152 Brigade, 1916–18.
4 Brigadier General Arthur Thackeray Beckwith (1875–1942), GOC 153 Brigade, 1917–18.
5 Brigadier General (later Major General Sir) Kenneth Gray Buchanan (1880–1963), GOC 154 Brigade, 1917–19.

he will go with thee wheresoever thou goest'. That is *the spirit* of the Lord
Jesus...

Third Army reports 7.10 pm giving details of raids by Enemy at 6 am
around Guillemont Farm and at 5.30 am south of Havrincourt. General Byng
states that the prisoners taken by Enemy did not know of our intended
operations. I was very anxious lest they might have given away information
of these plans.

Enemy's airoplanes active today over Guillemont sector, otherwise 'hostile
aerial activity very slight'.

Monday 19 November

Charteris reported that all reports indicated that Enemy is in absolute ignorance of our preparations for tomorrow's attack. No airoplane activity: no
wireless: no listening telephone work: no artillery fire! All seems favourable!!
So far prisoners taken by Enemy have apparently told them nothing about
the attack for tomorrow.

At 9.45 am I saw Sir H. Rawlinson Commanding Second Army.[1] He told
me of his views to extend the front northwards of Passchendaele. He does
not wish to take Westroosebeke. I suggested attack by small units by night,
because up to the present nothing of this nature has been attempted by us at
the Ypres battle front. I directed Rawlinson to work out his plans, but not to
give effect to them until the result of tomorrow's attack is known, and I can
decide on our future plans.

Haig visited Horne at HQ First Army.

His Army is weak in numbers of infantry and in guns. The Canadian Corps
is back with him. General Currie (Commanding Canadians)[2] was relieved on
battle front yesterday. I explained to Horne my proposed operations and
pointed out that by crossing the Sensée River east of Arleux, I turned all the
Enemy's defences facing First Army and the Drocourt–Quéant line. I could
not expect the First Army, owing to weakness in guns and numbers, to do
more than reconnoitre until our advance from Cambrai direction caused
Enemy to withdraw from his front. Then he must do his best to follow up
and press the Enemy.

The Battle of Cambrai began on 20 November at 6.20 am. To achieve surprise,

1 Rawlinson commanded Second Army from 9 November to 19 December 1917 after Plumer
was sent to Italy; Second Army was designated Fourth Army on 20 December 1917.
2 Lieutenant General Sir Arthur William Currie (1875–1933), GOC Canadian Corps, 1917–19.

there was no preliminary artillery fire, but at zero hour about 1000 guns began a 'predicted' artillery bombardment. Some 380 tanks were employed, and considerable gains were made and many prisoners taken. The German front was penetrated to a maximum depth of 7000 yards. It appeared that a significant victory had been won and church bells were rung in celebration in Britain. But the momentum of the attack was not maintained. The cavalry was not able to exploit the breakthrough and there were no reserves of infantry available. A ferocious German counter-attack on 30 November eventually drove the British back, regaining more ground than they had lost.

Tuesday 20 November

The Third Army under Byng attacked this morning at several points between St Quentin and the River Scarpe. Operations were very successful and our casualties remarkably small.

The main attack was made on a front of about 7 miles from near Gonnelieu on right to a point about 2 miles northwest of Havrincourt on left (southwest of Cambrai). III Corps (Pulteney) on right, with divisions as follows in order from the right, 12th (Scott), 20th (Douglas Smith), 6th (Marden).[1] IV Corps (Woollcombe) on left with 51st (Harper), 62nd (Braithwaite) and a brigade of 36th (Nugent) on west of the Canal du Nord.

The attack was launched at 6.20 am. There was no artillery bombardment previous to this hour but the infantry were covered by a number of Tanks which cut lanes through the wire ... The attack was made against the famous Hindenburg lines of defence, which consist of 2 main systems, each most stiffly wired, with a reserve system in rear.

Our troops rapidly passed the first two systems of trenches and occupied the third line about Masnières and Marcoing with the Canal crossings. Havrincourt, Ribécourt and Vacquerie were taken early in the day; all were found carefully prepared for defence.

The 12th Division captured the ridge on which is Lateau Wood and formed a defensive flank to the right.

After the Hindenburg Support line had been taken the 29th Division (De Lisle) passed through and occupied the Reserve line including Marcoing and Masnières. A brigade of the 20th continued the defensive flank southeastwards from Masnières on the 12th Division left.

The 51st Division was checked in front of Flesquières, but the 62nd pressed on and took Graincourt and Anneux before nightfall and extended north to beyond the Bapaume–Cambrai main road.

To withdraw the Enemy's attention from the main attack and to keep him

---

1 Major General (later Sir) Thomas Owen Marden (1866–1951), GOC 6th Division, 1917–19.

in doubt as to our intentions two subsidiary attacks were made

(a) east of Epéhy (55th Division Jeudwine)
(b) between Bullecourt and Fontaine-les-Croiselles. These had limited objectives and all were gained.

I visited Byng at Albert at 4.30 pm and decided that, for the present, there was no room for French troops in the sector of attack. They are consequently detraining around Péronne.

Over 5000 unwounded prisoners already reported. Our casualties light; 3 battalions reached the 'Support line' with only 5 wounded for the whole three!

By the positions gained today we now threaten the rear of the Enemy's 3 systems of defence facing westwards, viz.

(1) the line Lens–Bullecourt
(2)   "   "   Drocourt–Quéant
(3)   "   "   Douai-Marquion

In my message to the CIGS tonight I asked that the 2 additional divisions now warned for Italy be placed at my disposal 'unless the situation there is critical' ...

Wednesday 21 November

62nd Division aided by 2 companies of 15th Division[1] took Anneux and the 36th Division captured Moeuvres this morning.

51st Division also took Flesquières during the night and advanced northeast. Near Crévecoeur 20th Division crossed Canal but not the river.

Between Masnières and Rumilly Enemy brought 107th Division [from Russia] and counter-attacked – Our troops held their ground. We held Support line of the German system of trenches here: this system is the *third* line of the Hindenburg defences. Noyelles was taken by 1st Cavalry Division. Cantaing was taken by infantry, cavalry and Tanks after the infantry had first been checked. Enemy's infantry then fled so quickly to Fontaine-notre-Dame with half a dozen Tanks after them, that 2 companies of the 51st Division were able to occupy the latter village without difficulty.

40th and Guards Divisions moving up to reinforce. CIGS replied to my request that War Cabinet approved of my using the two divisions (47th and

1 This should be 51st Division.

2nd) detailed for Italy but I must prepare two other divisions to take their place.

Thursday 22 November

About 10 am I left in motor with Butler and went via Bapaume to Trescault. HQ of 51st Division were in dugouts about 500 yards from road. We walked there and saw General Harper ... His leading troops are now in Fontaine-notre-Dame. I thought the Divisional HQ were very far back! But the division had done very well notwithstanding the distance from its commander.

I met General Mullens (Commanding 1st Cavalry Division)[1] just after leaving HQ 51st Division. Mullens was returning with his division in accordance with orders received from IV Corps to concentrate around Metz-en-Couture where the water supply was better. Mullens stated that the Cavalry Division and he himself were very disappointed at being ordered back! I personally would much have liked to have given him an order to return but restrained myself because it is impossible to be successful if more that one Commander is giving orders, and Woollcombe Commanding IV Corps had had the Cavalry Division under his orders.

I then got on to Bertie Fisher's horse (he is GSO1 of the division)[2] and rode with Mullens and Butler to a point overlooking Ribécourt from which I got a good view of Flesquières, Bois du Neuf etc. Mullens explained all that his Cavalry Division had done, and said that this experience had been worth very much to them and they were all as pleased as possible.

On the ridge about Flesquières were a dozen or more Tanks which were knocked out by artillery fire. It seems that the Tanks topped the ridge and began to descend the ridge into the village (which is on north side of the ridge) then came under direct artillery fire. An eyewitness stated that on the appearance of the first Tank all the personnel of a German battery (which was in a kind of chalk pit) fled. One officer however was able to collect a few men and with them worked a gun and from his concealed position knocked out Tank after Tank to a number of 8 or 9. The officer was then killed. This incident shows the importance of infantry operating with Tanks at times acting as skirmishers to clear away hostile guns and reconnoitre.

The holding up of the 51st Division at Flesquières on the 20th had far

1 Major General Richard Lucas Mullens ('Gobby Chops') (1871–1952), GOC 1st Cavalry Division, 1915–19.
2 Lieutenant Colonel (later Lieutenant General Sir) Bertie Drew Fisher (1878–1972), GSO1 1st Cavalry Division, 1915–18; GOC 8 Brigade, 1918–19. He was later a Trustee of the Estate of Lord Haig.

reaching consequences, because the cavalry were also held up and failed in consequence to get through!...

I saw Braithwaite who was very pleased at what his division had done. His division was being relieved by 40th Division (Ponsonby) tonight, and the latter was to attack Bourlon Wood at 10 am tomorrow.

I thought Braithwaite should have been closer up with his division. The head of it is now close to Bourlon Wood. At Ytres I saw Nugent Commanding 36th Division (Ulster). On the 20th he only used one brigade and their casualties had been very small. Enemy fell back quickly or surrendered. Today had been hard fighting at Moeuvres. He thought that Enemy had no infantry on their front only machine gun companies. Several of these machine gunners fought like fanatics and instead of surrendering when surrounded blew out their brains.

I next visited HQ IV Corps at Villers au Flos. I saw Hugo Depree on the road.[1] Woollcombe was out walking. I told Hugo I thought Divisional Commanders should be closer up so as to take a grip of the battle. He said that they themselves were going to have Corps Report Centre closer up tomorrow.

I reached Albert about 5 pm and saw General Byng. I urged capturing Bourlon Wood *tomorrow.* If we did not get it tomorrow, it would be harder to take the next day and in view of the demands made on me for Italy I could not continue a wasting fight. I also told him about the cavalry being withdrawn, and he said he would see to it that the division was sent forward for tomorrow's attack.

Friday 23 November

40th Division relieved 62nd Division, and at 10.30 this morning attacked Bourlon Wood supported by 51st on the right and 36th (Ulster) on the left ... About 120 Tanks took part.

Bourlon Wood and village were captured. This was a fine performance, as the Enemy intended to hold the positions at all costs, because it dominates the country all around, to the Sensée River in the north, and Cambrai with its approaches in the east.

Situation around Fontaine is not clear. The village has been burning but our troops are in a portion of it.

West of the Canal du Nord London Scottish captured the copse on the ridge about a mile west of Moeuvres: it is known as Tadpole Copse and is an important tactical feature because from it the Enemy had observation over

1 Brigadier General (later Major General) Hugo de Pree (1870–1943), BGGS IV Corps, 1915–18; GOC 189 Brigade, 1918, and 115 Brigade, 1918–19. He was a cousin of Haig and later a Trustee of his Estate.

the bridge that carries the Bapaume–Cambrai road over the Canal du Nord. It also gives good observations north and west. Low flying airoplanes also gave great assistance today . . .

Day was highly successful but I am anxious that everything possible should be done to pass our cavalry through near Bourlon to exploit our success, before the Enemy can recover and bring up fresh troops. Kiggell saw General Byng regarding this.

Officers of GHQ who accompanied General Davidson to the battle front today, think the 51st Division is tired and several other units are *very short* of sleep. Many men can hardly keep awake.

The Guards are relieving 51st today and tonight. The 47th (Gorringe) and 2nd (Pereira) are also available and the 56th (Dudgeon).[1]

Saturday 24 November

During night a hostile counter-attack drove our troops out of a portion of Bourlon village, but our position at Bourlon Wood and remainder of Cambrai battle front is unchanged . . . Over 100 guns have been taken since the operations began on 20th.

I was anxious that everything be done to exploit the success at Bourlon by utilising the cavalry and organising in commands of suitable size so I motored to Albert with Generals Kiggell and Birch and saw General Byng and his Chief Staff Officer (Vaughan). I arrived there about 11 am. I found that Byng had already arranged to place General Haldane Commanding VI Corps in charge of operations west of the Canal du Nord, while General Woollcombe continued to direct east of the Canal as far as the right of III Corps near Noyelles. Woollcombe was given the Guards Division and if the attack in Bourlon village opens the way for the cavalry he will receive more infantry to help exploit the success.

General Byng's plan this morning is to attack northwest from Bourlon Wood and village with a fresh brigade of the 40th Division (supported by a brigade of the Guards holding the hill) and two cavalry brigades of the 2nd Cavalry Division (Greenly).

Subsequent reports show that our attack as planned was not made today because the Enemy who has been considerably reinforced in this sector attacked this morning twice in considerable force, 6 or 7 battalions. The first attack was repulsed, but the second succeeded in driving the brigade of the 40th Division from the crest of the hill. A counter-attack delivered by 2 battalions 40th Division with dismounted cavalry, re-established our line on

1 Major General Frederick Annesley Dudgeon (1866–1943), GOC 56th (1st London) Division, 1917–18.

north edge of the wood, and took more ground than we had lost. The greatest credit is due to the 15th Hussars who stormed the hill and took the most important point on the ridge ...

I directed Kiggell to inform Byng that he must devote all his strength and, if necessary, the reserve divisions at his disposal in establishing our position on the Bourlon ridge, and retaking it if lost. There must be no other attacks attempted on a big scale until our positions about Bourlon are really safe.

Byng stated that his casualties only amounted to 8000 wounded and 2000 killed and missing.

Sunday 25 November

Third Army reported late last night that 40th Division reported by telephone at 9.20 pm that we are in possession of Bourlon village.

At 5.15 pm yesterday, Enemy counter-attacked for the fourth time against Bourlon Wood since we took it. The attack was made from Fontaine and drove back our right flank a short distance to the Sunken road which runs southeast from the wood to Fontaine, where 40th Division is in touch with Coldstream Guards. On west of Bourlon Wood the 40th is in touch with 36th Division.

About noon today 40th Division reported that Enemy had counter-attacked, and that fighting was going on in Bourlon village – and at 1.10 pm village had been retaken by Enemy. Later reports showed however that we still have detachments in the east end of the village and in railway cutting further east and hold line along south side of village. Bourlon Wood with the high ground is in our possession. But from a personal report which Colonel Armitage[1] gave me about 9 pm after visiting the ground, I gather that the Enemy has good observation from the shoulders of the hill (east and west of the Bourlon Wood) which are in his possession, over the area we hold on the south side of Bourlon Wood. The units on the Bourlon front are much mixed up: 40th Division – Guards – Cavalry dismounted. At the same time the Enemy is bringing forward more troops. I therefore [tell] Kiggell to communicate with Byng on telephone and urge him to go *personally* into the situation, because I am not sure that Woollcombe has a real grip of it: and I have no great confidence in his CRA (Geddes).[2] It is most important to

1 Lieutenant Colonel (later General Sir) (Charles) Clement Armitage (1881–1973), GSO1 GHQ, 1917–18. Armitage was one of the personal liaison officers who reported to Davidson (DMO) and to Haig himself; this 'innovation' is usually attributed to Field Marshal Montgomery in the Second World War. Robertson also used the system when he was CGS to Sir John French.
2 Brigadier General John Gordon Geddes (1863–1919), CRA IV Corps, 1916–18. Despite Haig's lack of confidence in him, Geddes remained in command of IV Corps' guns for the rest of the war.

secure the shoulder of Bourlon Hill and deny the observation to the Enemy.

Monday 26 November

I . . . rode to Havrincourt where I met the Third Army Commander (Byng) who had been holding a conference to decide on the plan of operations at Bourlon. The objectives were to capture and hold the best line for winter.

General Woollcombe Commanding IV Corps then explained his plan. 62nd Division attacks 6.40 am tomorrow against Bourlon village, while the Guards Division will attack the spur on the east of Bourlon Wood and Fontaine village by moving eastwards from the wood. I then spoke to Braithwaite Commanding 62nd Division who said his men were full of confidence, and he felt that they would do the job all right. I also saw Feilding and complimented him on the long march (20 miles) which the leading Guards Brigade had made yesterday to relieve 51st Division. He then explained his plan for tomorrow, and said he felt satisfied that he would be able to gain the objectives . . .[1]

Haig then went to HQ 40th Division, where he met Major General Ponsonby.

I congratulated him on success gained by his division in capturing Bourlon Wood and hill. He explained that Brigadier General Campbell Commanding 121 Infantry Brigade[2] had attacked Bourlon village on his own initiative, and that the Corps Commander had ordered the attack to be postponed till next morning, but owing to wires being cut and runners being wounded, orders never reached the brigade. Ponsonby stated that he sent in all the troops he had available to mop up the village but as events proved they were not sufficient.

Tuesday 27 November

Charteris reported no change in Enemy on Cambrai battle front since yesterday. His troops are very thin on this front except at Bourlon. In fact the situation is most favourable for us but unfortunately I have not got the necessary number of troops to exploit our success. Two fresh divisions would make all the difference, and would enable us to break out in the neighbourhood of Marcoing northeastwards.

We captured a German 'Sound ranging set'. An examination of prisoners

1 Feilding was actually unhappy with the operation and had argued about it with Woollcombe.
2 Brigadier General (later Major General) John Campbell (1871–1941), GOC 121 Brigade, 1915–18; GOC 3rd Division, 1918, 31st Division, 1918–19.

etc. shows that the Enemy is at least one year behind us in this matter. It is only in instruments for intercepting wireless that he seems ahead of us. He has one of these sets per division. We have only 1 per corps. WO cannot provide the skilled personnel we have asked for.

IV Corps attacked at 6.40 am with Guards Division (Feilding) against Fontaine village and high ground north of it. 62nd Division (Braithwaite) on left of Guards against Bourlon village. Each used about 20 Tanks ... Over 600 prisoners were reported as taken today and our position in Bourlon Wood considerably improved – a strong point being captured.

Wednesday 28 November

On the general situation, Anthoine thought that the Enemy might concentrate for an attack against the French, but not through Switzerland. The lack of railways in that country would he thought prevent the Enemy attempting it, but he knew that Pétain and GQG were anxious on the subject and doubtless they had some information to go on. We discussed the proposal made by certain people to make our plans for ending the war in 1919. Anthoine was of opinion that the war must end no later than October 1918. The people of France were already feeling the pinch of want, and could not contemplate doing nothing next year on the chance of the Americans being in force in 1919. I called his attention to the general *shortage of food all over the world,* because workmen had been withdrawn to fight and for war work. There will be shortages in 1918 but probably famine [in] 1919. So we both agreed that Enemy is at present suffering from the blows that we have dealt him this year, and is very short of men, that therefore the best plan is to continue to attack him with the utmost of our power.

General Kiggell went to see Byng this afternoon. The Guards and 62nd are being relieved tonight by the 59th (Romer) and 47th (Gorringe). Byng's plan is to consolidate his present position, reconnoitre and then improve matters as soon as the situation was thoroughly known.

Friday 30 November

At 10 am I received a report from Third Army that the Enemy attacked 55th Division (Jeudwine) at 8 am east of Villers Guislain after heavy artillery preparation. At 10.50 am report states latter village is in hands of Enemy and he was attacking in the direction of Gonnelieu. This village was captured also Gouzeaucourt.

At 8 am Enemy also attacked the line Bourbon Wood–Moeuvres, but after reaching the Bapaume–Arras road he was repulsed by our counter-attacking brigade and artillery. Enemy suffered very heavily here.

Later information shows that the attack on VII Corps (Snow's)[1] front was made by two divisions in line and one in reserve . . . The left attacking division formed a flank to the southwest while the right division captured Gonnelieu and then turned northeast along the Gonnelieu–Bonavis ridge. Our 20th Division retook La Vacquerie.

The 29th Division was also heavily attacked but held its line from Marcoing to Masnières. 6th Division filled gap between right of 29th Division and La Vacquerie.

I motored to Albert and saw General Byng a little before noon. I told him to use his reserves energetically and that I had ordered two divisions to Péronne and 2 others to Bapaume by train *in case* of the Enemy attacking in great strength. I then went on to Bucquoy where George Black met me with horses.[2] We lunched in the abandoned German defences . . . and rode home.

Saturday 1 December

About 11 o'clock Charteris brought me copy of captured order showing that Enemy has organised his attack on big lines and is employing about 12 divisions. The objective of his southern attack is stated to be Trescault. The main objective being to dislodge us from Bourlon hill and the ground recently captured by us.

I motored to Albert with Kiggell after lunch and had a talk with Byng. He was much happier over the situation than when I saw him yesterday. Indeed he had every right to be pleased! The splendid defence put up by the 2nd and 47th Divisions around Bourlon and determination of the 29th and 6th Divisions on the Masnières front quite justifies a feeling of satisfaction. Guards have retaken Gonnelieu with 3 to 400 prisoners and 40 machine guns and the cavalry with Tanks pressed the Enemy eastwards from Gauche Wood and further to the south of the latter place. The 21st Division comes up in the place of the cavalry tonight and the 61st Division relieves the troops on the right of the 29th Division. These reliefs will allow troops to reorganise.

Sunday 2 December

Second Army carried out an operation on north end of the Passchendaele ridge in the moonlight on a front of about 4000 yards by the 8th and 32nd

---

1 Lieutenant General Sir Thomas D'Oyly Snow ('Snowball') (1858–1940), GOC VII Corps, 1915–18; he was replaced in the aftermath of the Cambrai fighting.
2 Captain George Balfour Black (1889–1918) commanded Haig's personal escort of 17th Lancers. He was killed in action on 29 March 1918 while attached to 13th Battalion Tank Corps.

Divisions. The object was to obtain certain points which gave the Enemy observation westwards onto our Communications. All were captured except one and our troops are now within 100 yards of it.

Byng reports that the night passed quietly and 29th Division retook Rues Vertes (south of Masnières) which the Enemy entered yesterday afternoon. We took 50 prisoners.

During night III Corps ordered evacuation of Masnières to straighten our line. Enemy had attacked it unsuccessfully 9 times yesterday!

At 11.30 Third Army reported Enemy attacked 29th Division on their new line west of Masnières at 8.30 am and was completely repulsed – 'Situation now quiet on the III Corps front' ...

In the afternoon, and again before dinner I discussed with Kiggell the advisability of ordering Byng to fall back from the Marcoing–Bourlon salient and take up the best line we can for the winter. My view is that although Bourlon is itself a strong position, the salient will be costly to hold. Moreover its main value is for offence. Now we have not sufficient reserves to take the offensive on a large scale. Also, with the fact of Russia entering negotiations for peace before us,[1] it is possible that Germany may start a big offensive on this front [next spring]. We ought therefore to make our front as strong as possible and avoid having *weak* points. The Marcoing salient is a source of weakness and will be a constant anxiety in my opinion. Kiggell telephoned to Byng to think over this side of the problem, to select a suitable line of defence, and make all arrangements for withdrawing, but not to issue orders for the same until he has seen me tomorrow morning.

Situation about 8 pm Enemy retaken Gonnelieu. I order 4th Australian Division to move up and ask French to be ready to push up a division on our right flank tomorrow in case of necessity.

Monday 3 December

9.30 am report from Third Army that Enemy bombarding heavily from Epéhy to La Vacquerie, and attack begun. I ask the French to move forward their divisions in readiness to act if necessary on our right flank.

I visited Byng at Albert about 11 am. Kiggell accompanied me. I explained my view of the situation in regard to holding the Marcoing salient. Byng said to hold it means the employment of 2 extra divisions ... These would otherwise be in rear training etc. He stated that the rear line was very strong and quite suitable. I accordingly told Kiggell to issue an order to Third Army accordingly. Withdrawal to be carried out at the earliest moment possible. Byng said this would be tomorrow night probably.

1 The Ts diary reads 'without consulting us'.

Byng stated that he felt confident of holding his right flank and 'every moment his artillery situation there was improving'. He did not think that the attack on La Vacquerie was a serious affair. The Enemy had suffered very seriously indeed . . .

After lunch I discussed with Butler and Elles our programme of Tank construction for the coming year. Tanks had done very well in the recent counter-attack made by III Corps on 30 November and 1 December. I approved of our organisation for defence. The difficulty is to find men and officers in sufficient numbers and train them! Four months is necessary.

Evening reports state that the Enemy delivered repeated strong attacks from Gonnelieu northwest to Marcoing. His attacks were repulsed with great loss to Enemy. All our troops seem to be on west of the Canal now, and we hold Marcoing to Canal bank . . . Written orders issued to Byng in confirmation of my verbal ones this morning. We impress on him the importance of holding some position about La Vacquerie to cover his right flank. Otherwise he cannot hold Flesquières!

Tuesday 4 December

Soon after 9 am I left in motor with Kiggell and Heseltine[1] and went round Corps HQ in Third Army. I first visited V Corps at Villers au Flos, and had a talk with General Sir E. Fanshawe who took over from IV Corps (Woollcombe). He was very cheerful, stated the troops were in great heart and felt confident that they could hold the Bourlon position without much difficulty. Their guns had punished the Enemy *most severely* in all his attacks. All his arrangements were complete for withdrawing from Bourlon and were being co-ordinated with those of III Corps at a conference at III Corps HQ this morning. Bourlon Wood held the gas for a long time and as a result we had many casualties from gas in that sector, but only slight. Men will, as a rule, be back in a fortnight.

They were using as a road the Nord Canal which is a new one with cement bottom and without any water in it as yet. At one place the banks are 100 feet deep in a cutting.

Fanshawe had commanded a division in the retirement from Suvla, so had carefully studied such a problem before and also had practical experience. He saw no difficulty in the present operation but he would have liked longer time to make and leave behind 'surprises' for the Enemy.

At Templeux I saw General Pulteney, III Corps. He looked tired and had obviously passed through an anxious time. He told me about the Enemy's attack on the 30th. Apparently our patrols had gone out as usual in the early

1 Lieutenant Colonel Christopher Heseltine (1869–1944), King's Messenger.

morning, found nothing unusual and all then proceeded to breakfast. There seems to have been no warning of the attack, and the Enemy swept through the front held by the left of 55th Division (VII Corps) and parts of the 12th and 20th Divisions. The position rushed is immensely strong, but the defenders seem to have put up little or no fight at all. The Enemy attacked in great numbers preceded by some 'stoss-truppen'. Some of the latter were taken prisoner a mile west of Gouzeaucourt! Luckily the Guards Division happened to be near the latter village and were marching back to rest (i.e. westwards) with bands playing. On hearing of the trouble troops were at once faced about, and they advanced eastwards. The Brigadier (de Crespigny) Commanding 1 Brigade rode on ahead.[1] Crowds of fugitives of all branches of the service were streaming back, some without arms or equipment. By this time the Enemy were on the ridge west of Gouzeaucourt so the Guards at once deployed and after some heavy fighting cleared the ridge and retook Gouzeaucourt which is in the valley beyond.

Next morning they took Quentin ridge and Bois de Gauche, also part of Gonnelieu. The Enemy however was able to pour in troops from the north (i.e. round their left flank) and eventually they had to give up the village but held a line on the west edge of it which they consolidated.

This was a fine performance of the Guards Division, and had they not been on the spot it is difficult to estimate where the Enemy would have been checked! The mishap might have spread to a disaster!

I also went round the artillery office of III Corps, and complimented the CRA Tancred on what he had done. He looked very tired. Most of his heavy artillery had been taken, but we have managed to reinforce him with more than he has lost.

I next went to HQ VII Corps at Catelet about 3 miles east of Péronne and saw General Snow and his staff (Jock Stuart is BGGS).[2] He has very few troops to hold a wide front. The 55th Division which is weak holds 15,000 yards!! He expected the attack because the Enemy had thrown 7 new bridges etc. and he accordingly did his best to prepare his left flank to meet the blow. He personally went the day before to Villers Guislain (where he expected to be attacked) and arranged for 13 extra machine gun posts! This he and Jeudwine Commanding 55th thought would render the place unassailable. Apparently the British fugitives rushing back in front of the Enemy prevented our machine gunners firing and so all were captured without firing a shot!

1 Brigadier General Claud Raul Champion de Crespigny ('Crawly') (1878–1941), GOC 1 (Guards) Brigade, 1917–19.
2 Brigadier General (later General Sir) John Theodosius ('Jock') Burnett-Stuart (1875–1958), BGGS VII Corps, 1917; Deputy Adjutant General GHQ, 1917–19; an efficient staff officer, though somewhat highly strung.

This happened also in the case of a section of artillery I placed on the Menin road west of Gheluvelt in October and November 1914 and was the occasion of a firm order on my part. The actual loss of British life will be much less if they fire than if they wait and the position is captured by the Enemy!

I gathered that the wire and defences in front of VII Corps are poor and much remains to be done to render them a serious protection.

Wednesday 5 December

Retirement from Bourlon began at 3.15 am today and was carried on without any interference by the Enemy. Our low flying airoplanes later . . . discovered the Enemy manning his trenches in strength as usual opposite Bourlon and elsewhere on that front.

Captured documents show that the total force employed in the main attack on the 30th November by the Enemy against Bourlon–Gonnelieu front amounted to 8 divisions in front line and 5 in support = total 13. His main effort was against the Bourlon sector *not* against Gonnelieu where his success was gained really by chance.[1]

Friday 7 December

I motored with Kiggell to Doullens and presided at a conference with Army Commanders at 11 am. The main topic was the organisation of our defensive lines in view of the Russians having dropped out of the war. This will allow the Germans to employ some 30 more divisions on this front. These can be brought here at a rate of 8 to 10 per month if the Enemy so will it.

It is just 6 months today since I held the last Conference with Army Commanders at Doullens (7 May) and issued orders for the offensive against Messines etc. We expected at that time help from Russia, Italy and France!! In reality the British Army has had to bear the brunt of it all. I added that we [Commanders] might well be proud of the achievements of the Armies this year and I thanked them one and all for their help and support.

Saturday 8 December

About 11 pm Kiggell rang up Byng on telephone. Latter reported quiet day and our troops had been able to improve their defences. There seem to be ample reserves on the spot to deal with an attack should the Enemy make

---

1 Haig was mistaken. The main German effort was directed at the southern sector.

one on the Cambrai front. Byng stated that divisions fully realised that Enemy might be trying to deceive them into a sense of security by adopting an inactive attitude.

Sunday 9 December

Charteris . . . said to me that he was afraid that the Government at home was striking at me through him. He had much rather do anything than be a source of trouble to me. I told him that I alone was responsible for the opinions which I expressed to the War Cabinet and these were based not only on what Charteris told me but on what I learnt from Army and subordinate Commanders who were in close touch with the fighting troops and so were able to form an opinion of the Enemy's fighting value.

Kiggell then spoke to me about Charteris. That although he did his work well at HQ he was much disliked in Corps and Armies. I told Kiggell to see Charteris and that if what he (Kiggell) said was based on good evidence, we ought to give Charteris another appointment but that there was no question of removing Charteris because of supposed inefficiencies in his work. No one could do the Intelligence work better than Charteris but I fully realised Charteris's faults towards his [equals and his own] subordinates. At the same time in Charteris's professional interests it was a mistake for him to specialise entirely in Intelligence work.

At 10 pm General Kiggell spoke to Byng on the telephone. Latter said that he thought that 'if his troops did not hold their present line, they would not be able to hold any line'! That he was satisfied that VII Corps could hold their front with their troops now on the spot. 63rd Division will relieve 61st, and 19th Division the 6th Division, on the front north of Gonnelieu in the next few days. I asked Kiggell to send officers to see that the Staff work in Corps and Division of Third Army was all right, and that the troops were being well cared for in their journeys and reliefs.

Monday 10 December

Morning reports normal. No signs of an impending attack on Third Army front. Charteris reported that the information indicates that the Enemy had been manufacturing Tanks since April last.[1] We must arrange our defences for dealing with a Tank attack.

---

1 In fact the Germans manufactured only a handful of tanks during the war. They also used captured British tanks.

Thursday 13 December

Charteris reports situation on Cambrai front seems quieting down, but we must still expect an attack! Some reliefs are taking place on the Enemy's side...

General *Lawrence (Commanding 66th Division) arrived and stayed night. I arranged for him to take over charge of the Intelligence Branch from Charteris. The latter has made himself so unpopular with authorities at War Office and War Cabinet that in order to avoid friction I am obliged to change him. I am sorry to lose him.

Friday 14 December. Letter to Lady Haig

It is over a year ago since Derby and the War Office have set their faces against poor Charteris,[1] and although he has done his work admirably and his Intelligence Branch is in excellent order, I feel that it would be wrong of me to keep an officer at this time who seems really to have upset so many people and to have put those who ought to work in friendliness with him against him.

I have for some months been discussing a reorganisation of his Branch, and the change has nothing to do with the Cambrai battle, but really the winter is the cause, a period when fighting usually slackens.

I shall, of course, do my best to find Charteris another good job. As you know, he has lots of brains, and so in the long run it may probably turn out to have been a good thing for him to have left the Intelligence at this time, because Intelligence is rather a special kind of work which has a very small place in the Army in time of peace.

Sunday 16 December

I told General Maxwell of the decision of the Army Council to replace him with a younger man. He took it very well and said that he was pleased at any rate that I was not dissatisfied with him. He does not want further employment in England.[2]

---

1 Derby never forgave Charteris for his embarrassing failure to censor an interview that Haig gave to French journalists early in 1917.
2 Maxwell was replaced as QMG by Lieutenant General Sir Travers Clarke.

Tuesday 18 December

Charteris reported that there is an increase in wireless activity in the southeast corner of Cambrai salient. This may indicate arrival of batteries and possibly an offensive, but he thought hostile attack would be a deliberate affair when it came. A new type of wireless has also been discovered along our whole front using a very powerful wave. This our experts say is costly to work, and may possibly be used in conjunction with air attacks.

Wednesday 19 December

Charteris reports wireless activity considerable from La Bassée Canal southwards to our right. Particularly around Cambrai. There is no other indication of an immediate attack, although I consider Germans will launch large attack on the Western Front early next year.

I left by motor at 10 am with Birch for Fourth Army HQ at Cassel ... I reached Cassel soon after 12 o'clock and had a talk with General Rawlinson and Hunter Weston (Commanding VIII Corps) on the artillery situation on the Passchendaele front. There are 8 brigades of field artillery close up on that salient; 1 gun to 23 yards of front! After going fully into the matter I urged that the field guns there be reduced and the barrage obtained from 6-inch howitzers, 9.2-inch 60 pdrs in their place. Those firing at 9000 yards range or more! Rawlinson then ordered Hunter Weston to move back 4 of the field artillery brigades. I told him to do this as soon as possible because Enemy must be expected to attack before the end of the year. The Germans pay much attention to dates of events and anniversaries. I also urged them carefully to go into the condition of moral and discipline of machine gun batteries because being new units in the Army, all had not the necessary feeling of esprit de corps which encourages men to hold on even when a position is turned. Rawlinson told me that he had failed to get any troops or labour of any kind to work on the rear defences of the Ypres sector. I asked him again to speak to the King of the Belgians and Chief of Staff on the subject.

Thursday 20 December

Charteris reported this morning that Third Army were of the opinion (and he concurred) that the Enemy had stopped its offensive on the Cambrai sector for the time being. Charteris thought that Enemy's big blow would not fall until March ...

Colonel Ryan and Sir W. Herringham (Consulting Physician to Army),[1] came to lunch and afterward they examined Kiggell. They then reported to me that they found Kiggell is suffering from 'nervous exhaustion due to the very exacting nature of the work he has to perform'. There is no organic disease. Personally I think Kiggell is much better now than he was two years ago when I took over from FM French. I spoke to Kiggell. He goes on leave tomorrow and returns 28 December. We agreed that if either he feels he is not up to the work, or I think he is not fit for the work that I will ask him to go home. But at present he is better than he has been for some time. Butler too is here as Deputy CGS and is at hand to take his place if anything happens.

Friday 21 December

I motored with Heseltine and Butler to St Pol and presided at a conference with Army Commanders and their Chief Staff Officers . . . General Byng said that the Enemy's attitude seemed defensive. His own position was now much stronger. Troops were not suffering from 'Trench foot'. General Horne said there were so few cases that he had ceased to ask about it.

We discussed the organisation of 'labour' in the Armies, and the allotment of work. More method is required to avoid wasting men.

As regards 'artillery fire' and 'raids' I asked Army Commanders to adopt a passive attitude as far as possible until our defences are in a more forward state.

After the Conference I had a talk with Byng, the AG, Butler and Vaughan (Third Army) regarding the report on the Cambrai affair of 30 November. The War Cabinet are anxious for my report as soon as possible.

Sunday 23 December

General Asser reported on the L of C area. Some of the Chinamen (labourers) are giving trouble. I spoke to the AG on the question of improving the class of company officer with the Chinese, because some of the British NCOs seem to me to be rather bullies. A good class of officer would notice this (if it occurred) and at once would put a stop to it. I also spoke with the AG and Asser regarding the discussions which sometimes take place on 'reconstruction after the war'. Sometimes advanced socialistic and even anarchical views are expressed. I said that our policy should be not to stop free discussion but

1 Sir Wilmot Parker Herringham (1855–1936), Consulting Physician to St Bartholomew's Hospital; Consulting Surgeon to the British Armies in France, 1914–19; author of *A Surgeon in France* (1919).

rather to guide it by having really capable men to lecture and control any subsequent talk. It would be wrong to forbid the talk, because the views would then be driven underground, and thus eventually more harm would result.

General Maxwell left for England this morning. Travers Clarke is now QMG and reported to me on taking over. He had recently been in London regarding drafts: he is not hopeful that Government means to tackle the manpower problem in earnest. They are afraid to deal with Ireland or the Trade Unions.

Wednesday 26 December

Lord Milner arrived from Versailles and stayed the night. He seems to me a most honest and level headed man, and does very valuable work in steadying Lloyd George. Milner told me that he is more than ever impressed with the latter's ability and power of work. This no doubt is true and I assured Milner that I as C-in-C in France considered it my duty to assist the Prime Minister to the fullest extent of my power and not to countenance any criticism of the PM's actions. All this I had done and in fact had stopped criticism in the Army. On the other hand LG had warned me at my last meeting with him in Paris (end of October last) that he was going to 'retaliate on the soldiers' as he put it, because of the attacks made in the Press on him and which he thought were organised by the Military. LG had asked me what my feelings would be 'if the men were told that the attacks in Flanders were useless loss of life, and that all the suffering and hardship which they had endured were unnecessary'! I said such action would be most unpatriotic, yet the LG Press at once commenced their attack on me and other Commanders.

Milner admitted this and said he had spoken to LG on the subject. I further said to Milner that if LG did not wish me to remain as C-in-C in the interests of the Country and success in the war, it would be much better that I should go at once, rather than that LG should proceed with his policy of undermining the confidence which troops now feel in their leaders, and eventually destroy the efficiency of the Army as a fighting force. Moral in an army is a very delicate plant. Milner assured me that he believed all these attacks had ceased, and that he knew who had organised them. I said I did not want to know the name, but no patriot should lend himself to such cowardly work at this time of the Country's crisis.

Friday 28 December

Germany's peace offer appeared in last night's wireless, and a more detailed account this morning. General opinion is that it will be difficult to ignore this offer . . .

I went out for a ride immediately after an early lunch as I expected General Pershing . . . about 3 pm. But first his train was delayed (a coupling broke) and then the road from Etaples station was in bad order so he did not arrive till nearly 6.30 pm. We then discussed his arrangements for training the American Forces and my proposals. Briefly his scheme did not go beyond training a corps of 4 divisions by June. I pointed out that if peace was not made soon the crisis of the war would be reached in April and that he should aim at training an Army Staff and some Corps Staff as well as HQ of divisions in as short time as possible.

He said that *if the situation became critical he was ready to break up American divisions and employ battalions and regiments as draft to fill up our divisions.*[1]

1 These phrases are underlined in the Ts but not in the Ms diary.

1918
YEAR OF DECISION

The year 1918 began with Haig's reputation at a low ebb in London. The Government refused to allow him to proceed with a new offensive at Ypres. Lloyd George won over the Supreme War Council at Versailles to a strategy of an offensive in Palestine in 1918, while building up tanks, aeroplanes, guns and US forces on the Western Front for an attack in 1919. The Prime Minister's desire for a new C-in-C of the BEF was undiminished, and Haig's position became more precarious when The Times *and other Northcliffe papers turned against him. In January, Lloyd George sent Hankey and Smuts to the Western Front, in part to discover if there was a credible alternative to Haig. They concluded that there was not.[1] The C-in-C's hand was strengthened by the hostile reaction to Lovat Fraser's* Daily Mail *article of 21 January, which attacked GHQ. Haig's position remained vulnerable, especially after the German breakthrough in March. Only the run of victories that began with Amiens on 8 August secured Haig's position as C-in-C, but even then, Haig suspected that the Government was looking for an excuse to sack him (see diary entry of 1 September 1918).*

By that stage, the Haig–Robertson–Derby alliance had been broken up. In February Lloyd George manoeuvred Robertson out of the position of CIGS over the question of his authority vis à vis *the Supreme War Council. Robertson refused to accept a diminution of his powers, or to go to Versailles as the British representative, and was succeeded as CIGS by Henry Wilson. Derby became British Ambassador in Paris in May, being replaced as Secretary of State for War by Lord Milner. Haig welcomed Milner's appointment, and although his relationship with Wilson was never entirely easy, ultimately, their partnership must be judged as productive. In May, Lloyd George survived the Maurice Debate, potentially the most serious civil–military clash of the war. The former Director of Military Operations charged the Prime Minister with lying to the House of Commons about the strength of the Army. The suspicion was that Lloyd George was trying to shirk his share of the responsibility for the initial success of the German offensive in March, instead blaming Haig and the military.*

The German defeat of Russia released larger numbers of men for an offensive in the West, and the steady build-up of German forces in France forms the

---

1 D. French, *The Strategy of the Lloyd George Coalition, 1916–1918* (Oxford: Clarendon Press, 1995), p. 231.

backdrop to the first three months of 1918. The manpower crisis in Britain, and the paucity of reinforcements being dispatched to the BEF, forced a reduction in the strength of divisions from twelve battalions to nine, and the wholesale disbandment of 141 battalions. At the same time, Haig, against his better judgement, took over twenty-five miles of line from the French. The Supreme War Council proposed to set up an inter-Allied reserve to be controlled by an Executive War Board (in effect, by Foch). On paper this had some merit, but Haig, deeply suspicious of it and faced with the prospect of a major German offensive, was loath to part with any of his troops. Pétain, the French C-in-C, had similar objections. The matter came to a climax in March. Haig made it a resignation issue and Lloyd George, wary of provoking another confrontation with the military so soon after the Robertson affair, did not press the case.

Haig's Headquarters Staff also underwent some significant changes in early 1918. Herbert Lawrence replaced Kiggell as CGS, and Major General G. P. Dawnay became Deputy CGS vice Butler. Charteris's place as head of GHQ Intelligence Branch was taken by Brigadier General E. W. Cox. When Cox was accidentally drowned in August 1918, Brigadier General G. S. Clive took his place. Two other key appointments were Lieutenant General Travers Clarke, who became QMG in late 1917, and Major General Hugh Trenchard, who relinquished command of the RFC on the Western Front in January 1918 to become Chief of the Air Staff, being replaced by Major General J. M. Salmond.

The German Spring Offensive began on 21 March 1918 and made substantial gains, especially against Gough's Fifth Army, which was outnumbered in men and guns, with inadequate defences. Haig had been forced to make hard choices, and correctly gauged that he could more easily afford to give ground in the Somme area than further north. Nonetheless, he miscalculated the weight and axis of the German offensive. The ensuing crisis finally brought about unity of command, with Foch emerging as Generalissimo, on 26 March, with Haig taking a hand in the appointment. The German offensive failed in its objectives and represents an Allied defensive victory, in which the BEF played the principal role, and Douglas Haig could claim much credit. Despite a series of further offensives that lasted until mid-July, the Germans failed to win a decisive victory on the Western Front.

Throughout 1918 American troops poured into France. The commander of the American Expeditionary Force (AEF), John J. Pershing, was determined to create a self-contained US Army. He fiercely resisted proposals for 'amalgamation' of American units with British and French formations for any but the most temporary periods. While perfectly understandable from a US perspective, this policy caused problems for Haig, who needed troops immediately. Haig's frustration with Pershing is an important theme in his letters and diary for 1918. He also had problems with the Canadians, who insisted on their divisions together fighting as a single corps. In the process, Haig learnt the reality of the emergence of the Dominions as what has been described as 'junior but sovereign' allies.

Following the successful Allied counter-offensive on the Marne (18 July), Haig launched a major offensive at Amiens on 8 August. In a single day, the front advanced eight miles. From this point on, the Allies, with the BEF in the vanguard, steadily drove the Germans back. Haig initiated a series of offensives at various points on the British front, which denied the initiative to the Germans, forcing them to dance to the BEF's tune. Haig's relationship with Foch, spiky but productive, and characterised by mutual respect, is clearly reflected in his letters and diaries. Haig's belief that Germany might be beaten in 1918 stood in stark contrast to the views from London, and was a significant factor in the final victory. As victory drew near, the Allies began to debate what sort of terms would be offered to the Germans. Haig favoured a moderate peace, in part because he feared that to hold out for harsh terms would only prolong the fighting.

With its allies having capitulated and its army having been decisively defeated on the Western Front, Germany sued for peace. The Armistice came into force at 11 am on 11 November 1918.

Tuesday 1 January

Lord *Derby called to see me at 9.45 am. He first told me of *Lloyd George's decision to change *Robertson. This was only abandoned when Derby told him that he (Derby) would also resign if either Robertson or myself were moved. The Prime Minister apparently was afraid of a Cabinet crisis and that his Government would be forced to go. With reference to the PM's desire to change the CIGS it is interesting to note that Sir Henry *Wilson writes me *today* 'I was wired for Sunday but return (to Paris) tomorrow'. Doubtless LG intended him to succeed Robertson.

Derby then spoke to me about *Kiggell's state of health. In view of the hard times to be faced by the Army in France he considered that I was unwise to retain 'a tired man'. I said that I had *Butler on the spot to replace Kiggell if the latter was unfit to do his work. Derby at once said neither he nor the Cabinet would approve of Butler becoming CGS in France. I gathered from what Derby said that Butler was not liked by any of the 'Authorities' at home.[1]

Wednesday 2 January

After lunch I motored to Buckingham Palace and was presented with my Field Marshal's bâton by the *King. He asked me about the Cambrai mishap and he agreed that the Country and the Army must be prepared for a very

1 Haig successfully argued for Butler to be given a corps command (the III). Kiggell's replacement was Lieutenant General Sir Herbert Lawrence, who had already briefly replaced Charteris as head of the GHQ Intelligence.

hard time, for severe losses, and to be obliged to relinquish certain points and positions on our front. I told the King that it was very desirable to tell the Army in a few unambiguous sentences, what we were fighting for. The Army is now composed of representatives of all classes in the nation, and many are most intelligent and think things out. They don't care whether France has Alsace and Italy Trieste: they realise that Britain entered the war to free Belgium and save France. Germany is now ready, we have been told, to give all we want in these respects. So it is essential that some statement should be made which the soldier can understand and approve of. Few of us feel that the 'democratising of Germany' is worth the loss of an Englishman! I also pointed out that the removal of the Hohenzollerns from Germany is likely to result in anarchy just as was the case in Russia. This might prove a serious evil for the rest of Europe.[1]

Monday 7 January

I attended a meeting of the War Cabinet at 11.30 am. All were most friendly to me. The main points for consideration were the state of the British Defences in France, and the extension of front demanded by the French ... As regards the Enemy's action, I stated that I thought that the coming four months would be the critical period. Also that it seemed possible that the Enemy would attack both the French and ourselves, and hold reserves ready to exploit wherever he succeeded.

I felt too, that if the French were heavily attacked they would ask for support either in the shape of British reserves, or by our taking over some of their line in order to set free French troops. In either case the British front would be seriously weakened. In my opinion the best defence would be to continue our offensive in Flanders, because we would then retain the initiative and attract the German reserves against us. It is doubtful whether the French [will stand] for long, a resolute and continued offensive on the part of the Enemy.

Wednesday 9 January

... I lunched with the PM (Mr Lloyd George) ... We had a very cheery party. Conversation turned on the length of the war and some betting took place. Derby bet the PM 100 cigars to 100 cigarettes that war would be over by next new year. LG disagreed. I said I thought the war would be over because of the *internal* state of Germany. She could not continue after the coming autumn, because her population was degenerating so fast that even

---

1 In reality, Germany was unwilling to make peace on such terms.

if she won, there would not be the men to exploit and develop the country after the war etc. etc.

I also emphasised the critical nature of the coming 4 months on the Western Front if Germany did not make peace. Germany having only one million men as reserves for this year's fighting, I doubted whether they would risk them in an attempt to 'break through'. If they did, it would be a gambler's throw. All seemed to depend on the struggle now going on in Germany between the Military and Civil parties. If the Military won, they would certainly attack and try and deliver a knock out blow against the Western Front, probably against France.[1]

After lunch I visited General Whigham[2] in War Office, and then with Butler I called on Winston *Churchill at the Munitions Department. Churchill is really doing very well and has quite stirred up his office. He supports the Army's demands well as against the Navy.

Thursday 10 January

On this day the Army Council reluctantly ordered Haig to reduce all British divisions by three battalions, to economise on manpower. The change caused considerable disruption to the BEF at a critical time.

General Trenchard called at tea time to see me regarding his appointment as Chief of Staff to new Air Service. Lord Derby had declined to allow Trenchard to retain command of RFC in France for 4 months as I had asked. I therefore wrote a letter to Derby remonstrating in view of critical period which is before us in France.

Monday 14 January

Having heard from CIGS and also from Henry Wilson that military members of the 'Supreme War Council', Versailles, had come to the conclusion that the British should extend their line to some point between the Ailette and the Soissons–Laon road,[3] I wrote to CIGS (Robertson) both officially as well as in a private note to give my reasons against such extension. I also pointed out that this raises the whole question as to the status of the 'War Council'

---

1 In the Ts diary, Haig adds that the PM 'by cunning argument tried to get me to commit myself to an opinion that there would be "no German offensive", that the "German Army was done" but I refused to agree to his suggestions'.
2 The Deputy CIGS.
3 The British line was 95 miles long at this time, but as a result of this decision, by 4 February it had been extended to 123 miles, an increase of nearly 30 per cent.

in an acute form. The Government now have two advisers! Will they accept the advice of the Versailles gentlemen (who have no responsibility), or will they take my advice? Wilson has arrived at his conclusion [so he writes] as the result of a War Game and on mathematical calculations. The whole position would be laughable but for the seriousness of it . . .

The Engineer-in-Chief[1] reported that by the middle of February our 'battle' and 'forward' zones of defence should be very strong. He explained in detail all that is being done as a result of my last orders.

Monday 14 January. Letter to *Lady Haig

I am still corresponding with Derby over Trenchard. Derby is a very weak minded fellow I am afraid, and, like the feather pillow, bears the marks of the last person who has sat on him! I hear he is called in London 'genial Judas'!

Friday 18 January

Colonel Bacon (at one time American Ambassador in Paris)[2] arrived as head of the American Mission and I had a long talk with him. He is most keen for the American troops to join the British, and he told me that their relations with the French were 'most critical' at the present time. I impressed on him the importance of getting the Commanders and Staffs organised and functioning, and I told him of the offer which I had made to *Pershing to train 6 Divisional HQ, 3 Corps, and I Army HQ (Commanders and Staffs). He said that he was most anxious to see my proposals accepted, and he knew Pershing would do his utmost in the matter. The difficulty was French feeling and the Government of USA. The French policy is to prevent Americans and British from amalgamating.

Sir Edward Kemp (Agent for Canada in London)[3] came to lunch and I had a long talk afterwards with him. He asked my opinion about General Turner and he agreed that he must keep him in charge of the Canadian organisation in England and that General Currie (now Commander Canadian Corps) should command in the field. He agreed not to reduce the Canadian Divisions to 9 battalions until our scheme for getting 3 American Battalions for each British Division is settled one way or another.

1 Major General (later Sir) Gerald Moore Heath (1863–1929), Engineer-in-Chief, BEF, 1917–19.
2 Robert Bacon (1860–1919), US philanthropist who had privately organised American humanitarian relief in France, 1914–17; US chief Liaison Officer at British GHQ after American entry into the war; he had been US Ambassador in Paris, 1909–12.
3 Hon. Sir (Albert) Edward Kemp (1858–1929), Minister of Overseas Military Forces of Canada, 1917–20.

Tuesday 22 January

*Lawrence reported as CGS this morning and Brigadier General Cox[1] from War Office took over Intelligence Branch. The latter has had charge of the German Austrian section in London, and seems most capable...

I gathered from Smuts that the Austrian Government has notified Great Britain that she will not send large forces against the Allies on the Western Front. This I presume must be in return for Great Britain supporting the integrity of Austria-Hungary.

I also inferred that Great Britain might have peace at once with the Central Powers on Lloyd George's terms, with the exception of handing over Alsace-Lorraine.[2]

Saturday 26 January

Letter received from Robertson from Paris stating that 'Versailles Military Council have just sent in a paper advocating an offensive in Palestine' – 'I have told the War Cabinet they cannot take on Palestine' and he says he will resign if overruled. [In this proposal Wilson is playing the tune called by Lloyd George.]

General Trenchard ... came to report how things are developing at home. Lord Rothermere[3] (brother of Lord Northcliffe) who is Air Minister is quite ignorant of the needs or working of the Air Service, and is in great terror of newspaper criticism. Money is being squandered and officers and men wasted by being employed in creating units for performing work hitherto done by the Army (or Navy) for the Air Service. For example, Hospitals, Detention Barracks, etc. All this is very sad at a time when officers and men are so badly needed. Trenchard thinks that the Air Service cannot last as an independent Ministry, and that air units must again return to Army and Navy.

Mr *Asquith (who had come to France to see his son Brigadier General Asquith, recently wounded[4]) lunched on his way to catch the packet at

1 Brigadier General Edgar William Cox (1882–1918) took up the post of BGGS (Intelligence) on 24 January 1918; he was drowned while swimming near Le Touquet on 26 August 1918.
2 On 5 January 1918 Lloyd George gave a speech in which he put forward moderate war aims. In response to Lord Esher's speculations about Lloyd George's intentions, Haig noted: 'Personally I have received no hint from the PM that his policy is "peace", and not war until we get a "*victorious* peace"': Diary, 30 January 1918. The provinces of Alsace and Lorraine had been annexed by Germany in 1871, and their return was a key French war aim.
3 Viscount Rothermere (1868–1940), British newspaper magnate, brother of Lord Harmsworth, publisher of the *Daily Mirror*, Air Minister in Lloyd George's Coalition Government, 1917–18.
4 Brigadier General Arthur Melland ('Oc') Asquith (1883–1939) rose from civilian to brigadier general in three years, but was badly wounded a few days after taking command of 189 Brigade, eventually losing a leg.

Boulogne. He told me that the recent attack against me had failed at once, and that LG had found it would not pay him to attack me. He was not sure but thought the attack on Robertson might be continued. The Press man (Lovat Fraser) who wrote the article in *Daily Mail* starting the attack on War Office is said to have spent a Sunday with LG.[1] I had pointed out the similarity of certain expressions in the article with what LG had said to me in Paris in November last. So this visit no doubt accounts for it. Asquith said that those who recently spoke against me in the House of Commons are of no account. The old man was most friendly.

Saturday 26 January. Letter to Lord Derby[2]

You ask me for my opinion as to you being 'able in Paris to be of more help than Bertie has been'! Without wishing to judge the latter as an ambassador, I can honestly say he has been of very little help to us, and I feel sure that you might be a real help to the Army in France if you were at the Head of the Embassy in Paris.

Sunday 27 January

After dinner I received a copy of a paper compiled by War Council at Versailles in which certain offensive projects were recommended to the Allied Government. All their proposals are based on theory and hard facts are ignored. I had a long talk with Lawrence on the personnel situation which seems to me likely to be very serious in the autumn owing to lack of men. Auckland Geddes[3] only asks for 100,000 men for the Army. We must therefore look forward to having to reduce 16 to 18 divisions; against this we may put 7 or 8 American Divisions at the most. The French if attacked must reduce some 50 divisions, and at most can put only a dozen American Divisions in their place. Yet with these facts before us, the Versailles War Council writes a volume advising an offensive to annihilate the Turks in Palestine, as well as a great combined Franco-British one on the Western Front.

1 This article was a fierce attack on Haig and GHQ's conduct of the war.
2 Viscount Bertie of Thame was old and ill, and Lloyd George was dissatisfied with Derby's performance as Secretary of State for War.
3 Auckland Campbell Geddes (1879–1954), a surgeon turned wartime administrator; Minister of National Service, 1917–18; brother of Eric Geddes.

Repington has certainly stated the true case in his articles in the *Morning Post*, yet few seem to believe him.[1]

The problem seems to me to be how to bring home to our Prime Minister's mind the seriousness of our position and to cause him to call up more men while there is yet time to train them.

Tuesday 29 January

Haig attended the Supreme War Council at Versailles from 29 January to 2 February.

The 'Supreme War Council' is housed in a great new hotel building, the 'Trianon Palace Hotel'. An air of unreality prevailed, looking at the place from a war point of view!

I was shown upstairs and into Sir H. Wilson's room, where Lloyd George, Lord *Milner, Wilson, Hankey, Robertson were in consultation with Generals *Pershing, Bliss[2] and Captain Boyd (ADC). The arguments seemed heated, and I gathered that Pershing had stated that he was opposed to giving a battalion of Americans to each British Brigade. Evidently something had happened to upset him since I saw him at Compiègne. I gathered that the people in America were [criticising] their Government because there seemed to be no results to show what America is doing![3] No troops in the field, no airoplanes, no guns, no nothing yet in fact! After a time I pointed out that the battalions would come to me for training, and would then be grouped together into American Regiments and Divisions. At once Pershing's attitude changed, and he said that he was quite agreeable to send 150 battalions to the British Army on the lines I had indicated.

I also took the opportunity of stating definitely my opinion that the situation of the Allies in France would become very serious in September unless steps were *at once* taken to raise more men for the British Army as well as to bring as many American troops as possible to Europe. Calculating on $\frac{1}{2}$ a million casualties in the British and French Armies respectively the British would in 9 months be reduced by 30 divisions, and the French by 53 divisions . . .

[A]t 2.30 pm attended a conference at the HQ of the Supreme Council

---

1 Repington had attacked the Government for failing to keep the BEF up to strength, using figures that Lloyd George suspected had been leaked by the military. In January, Repington had resigned from *The Times* in an editorial dispute.

2 General Tasker Howard Bliss (1853–1930), US military representative on the Allied Supreme War Council at Versailles.

3 In the Ts diary, Haig amends this sentence to refer to the money spent by the USA.

with the PM and Lord Milner. We first discussed the demand of the French to extend the British front, and I gave the PM detailed reasons why we should not extend our front. Sir H. Wilson insisted that *Pétain was 'not playing straight', but said one thing to me and another to his Government. I can't believe this, but think Wilson has never forgiven Pétain for having him (Wilson) sent away from being the head of the British Mission at French GQG.

We also discussed the question of a General Reserve for the Western Front. I said that I could not spare troops for that; troops in Italy and elsewhere should be set free for the purpose!

Wednesday 30 January

*Clemenceau began by asking us to discuss the Allied plans for next year. Foch led off with a speech of generalities; Robertson followed, then I was called upon.

I pointed out that before we could make plans, we must know what means we had at our disposal. In my opinion, the situation was now serious on the Western Front, and might become grave in September...[1]

I pointed out that the American Army could not be trained sufficiently to operate in divisions this year.

General Pétain followed and supported me in every way. He said that *without* fighting, and allowing only for normal wastage, he must reduce 25 divisions by the autumn.

I was very pleased at the way Pétain backed me up, and this without any preliminary talk or argument. Lloyd George followed and asked for detailed figures. This no doubt to give him time to think over the situation which he admits is serious.

Thursday 31 January

Certain tables of the effectives of the Allies and Germany had been prepared. These were discussed and *Foch began an indictment of England for not [providing] more men...

Lloyd George answered well, pointing out that England had to hold the seas, carry the food in ships, build the latter, produce the coal for the Allies, etc. etc.

Much time was wasted over this, and the Conference did not break up till 6.30 pm. *Work done* showed our shortage of men and Lloyd George [had shown himself] anxious to prove by figures that we had ample men.

---

1 A reference to the impending manpower crisis.

Thursday 31 January. Letter to Lady Haig

It was dinner time before I got back here from Versailles tonight, and we meet there again tomorrow at 10 to discuss 'our plans for 1918'! So you see that although there have been floods of words and words, we are still at the beginning of our work. I find that Clemenceau (the French Premier) though 76 is the soundest and pluckiest of the lot. He is a grand old man, full of go and determination. LG cannot touch him in practical sound sense! I hope that Clemenceau will succeed in preventing any faulty decision being taken. In any case today he gave LG a real good dressing-down! but unfortunately LG does not understand French, and the translator missed a good deal of the force of the speech though he gave the general meaning all right.

Friday 1 February

After some more talk it was agreed to accept the recommendations of the Military Members of the Supreme War Council to adopt a defensive attitude for the present until the situation developed, with a request that Commanders-in-Chief should prepare offensive projects suitable for the forces at their disposal. Nothing should be done to weaken the Allied forces on the Western Front, but LG insisted on going on with his scheme for the destruction of the Turks. Clemenceau said that he could not prevent Great Britain doing what she thought best in this matter but he got LG to agree that nothing should be done for two months. After that time Clemenceau hoped to have situation again discussed by the Versailles Council.

On that understanding the Turkish project was passed. Robertson then put in a minute of dissent to the effect that the Military Members of this War Council did not know all the factors of the problem on which they had made a recommendation. Robertson considered the scheme was quite unsound and gave his advice against it. [I am strongly of the same opinion, but LG never asked my opinion.]

I saw LG was much annoyed but he said nothing at the time. Later he told Robertson that, having given his advice in London it was not necessary for him to have repeated it here.

Saturday 2 February

M. Clemenceau had a private meeting (as usual) with LG half an hour before in order to settle privately the decisions at which it was intended to arrive in full conference.

As the result of the night in which to think, several proposals were produced on the question of the General Reserve. Amongst these was one from Lloyd

George which appointed Foch as President of the Committee of the Versailles Military Members to deal with the matter, and issue orders to Commanders-in-Chief as to when and where the Reserve is to be used and to decide (in consultation with C-in-Cs) the strength of the General Reserves.

This was the proposal which was accepted after some discussion, and a few amendments. To some extent it makes Foch a 'Generalissimo'. But although Pétain and I get on very well and no co-ordinating authority is necessary for us, on the other hand, the Italian front needs a central authority. At the present Conference the Italians seem ready to come to Versailles to beg for something they want, but they never have the smallest intention of parting with anything for the general good!

When the 4 representatives (Clemenceau, Lloyd George, Orlando,[1] Bliss) had approved of the resolution, I asked the following question, 'By what channel am I to receive orders from this new body?' This was rather a poser, because this resolution to appoint an international Committee involves a change in Constitutional procedure. Finally, LG said 'Orders would be issued by the members of the body nominated by the Supreme Council.' I asked that the exact position might be made clear to me in writing.

The next question discussed was the extension of the British front. Clemenceau had previously told me that he persisted in raising this point on account of the necessity of getting more men from England to make sure of holding the front until the Americans could take their share of the fighting.

So I made a few remarks and stated that, with my present strength, it was quite out of the question for me to extend my line. Notwithstanding the table of figures compiled for the Conference, my statement of Wednesday last holds good, viz. that we must expect to have to reduce 30 divisions in nine months, if Enemy attacks us heavily. Eventually it was agreed to accept the proposed extension *in principle*, but it was left to Pétain and myself to decide when to carry it out. After this Pétain came along to me and said that 'he had no intention to "taquiner" (worry) me over this'.

The Italians were asked to send some divisions to France to replace the British and French Divisions now in Italy, but Orlando and Sonnino[2] had every sort of reason for refusing! . . .

After dinner Robertson came to see me. He has no intention of resigning but means to make Derby take up the question as Secretary of State.

1 Vittorio Emmanuele Orlando (1860–1952), Prime Minster of Italy, 1917–19.
2 Baron (Giorgio) Sidney Sonnino (1847–1922), Foreign Minister of Italy, 1914–19.

Monday 4 February

... I motored to Camiers, the Machine Gun School, north of Etaples and saw about 150 officers. About a third of these are about to be appointed to command battalions of machine guns. This is a further development in machine gun organisation so I went to see the selected officers. I shook each one by the hand and asked him a few questions. They seemed a splendid lot of officers. I afterwards gave a short address in which I rubbed in the importance of 'esprit de corps' for the new units and also explained the nature of the forthcoming fighting, viz. defensive first of all, and when we are strong enough, offensive. I emphasised the fact that material resources are not sufficient to give victory. Ethical factors, discipline, a strong will to direct the whole [unit] and power of thought to point the way to success.

The instructional staff of the school (except the Commandant) is composed of New Army officers entirely, a Cambridge Professor of Mathematics, another from St Andrews, and others of similar type.

Monday 4 February. Letter to Lady Haig

... [A]s far as I am concerned the Versailles Conference went off quite well.

In the first place, the demand for me to extend my line was not pressed.

Secondly, although it was decided to form an Inter-Allied Reserve, before the Committee can handle it they must form it! Now I cannot part with any of my troops. So if they want a Reserve it must be found from French and British troops in Italy. The five divisions I sent there are really the reserves of the British Forces in France – or bring troops from Salonika or elsewhere.

I, like you, am sorry for Robertson, but then it seems to me (and I can write it to you privately) that he has not resolutely adhered to the policy of 'concentration on the Western Front'. He has *said* that this is his policy, but has allowed all kinds of resources to be diverted to distant theatres at the bidding of his political masters. So I think he ought to have made a firm stand before. Anyhow don't let the Versailles Conference trouble your little head. The machinery there is so big and clumsy it will take some time before it can work fast enough to trouble me. So I don't mean to be influenced by it against my better conscience.

Saturday 9 February

Doris and Lord Derby met me at Victoria Station. The latter then drove me to Downing Street – by a circuitous route so as to have a talk and explain the situation. Briefly, the Cabinet had decided on the previous day to replace Sir William Robertson as CIGS. On that my opinion would not be asked. He then produced a copy of draft instructions arranging for the new order of things on the following lines:

The Secretary of State for War was again to assume full responsibility for the War Office, and CIGS's position was to return again to what it was before Robertson was appointed in Lord *Kitchener's time. The CIGS is to continue to be the 'Supreme Military Adviser of the Government'. 'The Military Representative at Versailles to be a member of the Army Council' and to be a 'Deputy CIGS'. It was proposed that orders should be sent to me regarding the handling of the 'Inter-Allied General Reserve' by the latter. I told Derby of the draft letter which Henry Wilson had sent me this morning on the question of forming a General Reserve, and which clearly showed that he and Foch were practically in the position of a Generalissimo . . .

The PM then explained his views and difficulties. I pointed out the tremendous powers now given to Versailles, that the 'Military Representative' there had full powers to commit the Government possibly against my opinion, and take decisions which the British Government ought alone take. He said as PM he was anxious to get into more direct touch with me as C-in-C in France, and that under the present system he always felt that in seeing me he was going behind the back of the CIGS! I also pointed out that only the Army Council or a Field Marshal senior to me, could give me orders. I suggested that Robertson's original proposal, by which he (as CIGS) after consultation with Foch, should send me orders re. reserves was probably the best solution of the difficulty. The PM said he had come to the same conclusion and he proposed to send Robertson to Versailles as Military Representative and to make Henry Wilson CIGS.

This came as a pleasant surprise to Derby, who evidently was much exercised in his mind as to how to get out of his present difficulty with Robertson. The latter had lately become most difficult to deal with and lost his temper quickly, he told me.

The draft decision was accordingly revised so as to make the Military Representative at Versailles 'absolutely free and unfettered on the advice which he gives', but he is to report to CIGS the nature of advice given for information of the Cabinet, and CIGS will advise Cabinet thereon.

I warned the PM and Derby of the distrust in which Henry Wilson is held by the Army. Derby said that he would issue instructions in the War Office to ensure that Staff appointments are fairly made!

The PM also said that he considered that the best solution of their present difficulties would be to make me 'Generalissimo' of all the British Forces. Derby concurred and I was asked what I thought of the proposal. I replied that with a serious attack impending in France, I considered that no change should be made in the Command there.[1] I knew every detail of the situation, and it would not be fair to the Army to suddenly put on a new Commander such a serious responsibility. PM agreed and said he 'ought to have made me Generalissimo last September'.

Monday 11 February

... I saw Lord Derby. He said that Robertson had declined to see Macpherson[2] and he (Derby) had told Robertson of the Cabinet's decision to replace him etc. Robertson had refused to go to Versailles so the situation was still uncertain.

I then went to Robertson's room. Robertson said he had no intention of accepting appointment to Versailles. The position would be impossible for all information was in hands of CIGS in London. I disagreed, and said that, as member of Versailles Committee, he was in the position of Generalissimo and further that this was no time for anyone to question where his services were to be given. It was his *duty* to go to Versailles if the Government wished it. I am afraid that in the back of his mind he resents Henry Wilson replacing him in London, and means to embarrass the Government to the utmost of his power.

I then went to Buckingham Palace and saw the King at 12 o'clock ... We also discussed Robertson's attitude and I urged HM to insist on Robertson going to Versailles. In the first place it was necessary for all soldiers to work together at this time, [and secondly, Robertson might save us from defeat by opposing Lloyd George's desire to send troops to the East against the Turks].

Friday 15 February

Cipher personal telegram from Lord Derby arrived 1 am. It stated that Robertson had been offered choice of Versailles, or remaining where he is, but had decided to resign claiming that it is necessary to be both CIGS and Government Representative on the Council at Versailles. Government is now offering position to *Plumer. He would like to see me as he thinks a talk would be an advantage.

I replied that I consider only permanent solution of difficulty is that CIGS should have his Deputy at Versailles in same way as French have Foch [with] a subordinate General at Versailles. And I added that I would come to London tomorrow afternoon to see him.

1 However, Haig no doubt remembered that Joffre in 1916 had been 'kicked upstairs' and lost all effective power, despite being given an exalted title.
2 Under Secretary of State for War.

I sent Sassoon[1] to Montreuil to arrange for my journey. Everything arranged when Derby's Private Secretary states the PM would rather that Derby comes to Boulogne to see me. I reply that I am coming to London and desire to see the PM.

I decide on this course because the latter is stating that I am 'in agreement with the Government'. I am anxious not to embarrass Government at this time, but I am not in agreement on all the decisions passed at Versailles. For instance, I agree on the need of forming a General Reserve, but not on the system of control which has been set up.

Sunday 17 February

Sir William Robertson came to see me at 9.30 am. He told me his story . . . [A]t 11.30 Lord Derby called and motored me to Mr Lloyd George's house at Walton Heath . . . In the course of our talk, I made it quite clear to the PM that I had never approved of any of the arrangements now under discussion. When asked I had stated my reasons for disagreeing, but once the Cabinet had given its decision, I had loyally done my best to make the system run . . . LG told me of the efforts of the Government to come to terms with Turkey. We could not give up Mesopotamia or Palestine or Syria (if we took it) but we offered Turkey a large sum of money, and to recognise her flag as supreme in those countries just as we did for many years in Egypt. He spoke freely about Austria. She had already been told that we want to leave her quite strong. And now Czernin[2] was desirous of meeting Lloyd George at Geneva. He asked me what I thought of the suggestion. I said he ought certainly to meet him and to leave no stone unturned in order to arrive at a settlement with Austria . . .

The PM had asked me to see Henry Wilson at once and decide on who was to be the Military Representative at Versailles . . . Henry Wilson came to see me at Eastcott about 4.30 pm. After talking over the matter I decided that Henry *Rawlinson would be the best man.[3] I could spare him provided that Plumer and his General Staff Officer (Harrington)[4] were sent back to me at once. This he agreed to do.

About 6.30 pm Lord Derby came from London to see me! He was tired and harassed. He did not know whether to resign or stay on as Secretary of State for War. I told him that in the interests of the Army there should be no

1 Sir Philip Albert Gustave David Sassoon Bt. MP (1888–1939), private secretary to Sir Douglas Haig, December 1915–18.
2 Ottokar, Count von Czernin (1872–1932), Austrian Foreign Minister, 1916–18.
3 Rawlinson was appointed to the post on 18 February 1918.
4 Actually, 'Harington'.

change, and that he should remain on. He said he would accept my advice. If he left, Lord Northcliffe would probably succeed him. This would be fatal to the Army and the Empire!

Monday 18 February

Haig visited Bonar Law.

He[1] received me at once, and stated as his reason for wishing to see me, that he was to be asked certain questions on the military situation and might be cross-questioned as to my views and attitude and so wished to be clear as to what to say. I explained, as I did yesterday to the PM, that my opinion as to the merits or otherwise of the proposed organisation had never been asked, only whether I was satisfied with the proposed channel of communication between the Government and myself. That the General representing the British Government on the Versailles Committee being now a member of the Army Council, rendered any instructions which I received from him 'lawful commands' (in meaning of Army Act). My objections were therefore satisfied.

He spoke very freely and I told him that difficulties might arise between me and Versailles if I were ordered to earmark certain divisions as 'General Reserve'. This could not be done without upsetting existing plans for the defence of my front, and I would rather be relieved of my command than do it.

Mr Law said that the PM had asked him to read a statement of the position of affairs as he (the PM) was ill. Law was not going to do it, but he would like my opinion on what was down regarding myself. The document stated that I 'thought it a workable scheme'. I said that was not my opinion, because I thought it a bad scheme and unsound since it set up *two* authorities who would give me orders, i.e., dual control. 'He must not say that I thought the scheme workable, but that I will do my best to work under it.' He said that he quite saw my point, and would make that clear if asked.

Robertson's appointment to Eastern Command, an administrative post in Britain, was announced on 18 February.

1 Andrew Bonar Law (1858–1923), Leader of the Unionist Party, 1911–23; Chancellor of the Exchequer and Leader of the House of Commons in the Lloyd George Coalition Government; an unobtrusive but leading wartime political figure.

Tuesday 19 February

I think I can *fairly* claim as the result of my visit to London that generally a saner view is now taken of the so-called military crisis, and the risk of a quarrel between 'civilian and soldier' (which last Saturday seemed imminent) was avoided.

Thursday 21 February

Commandant Gemeau told me that a group of 5 German Divisions had been training near Chimay in wood fighting and in passing difficult ground. Does this mean that the Germans hope to pass through difficult wooded country about St Gobain? Another group of 3 divisions had been exercised in long 30 kilometres night marches followed by attacks until noon the following day. A 'breakthrough' to a depth of 12 miles practised. All this reminds one much of Nivelle's methods of this time last year.

Monday 25 February

General Sir Aylmer Hunter Weston VII Corps came to lunch. He had seen some MPs who had been visiting the front and to whom some men had spoken and asked if they were 'Labour MPs'. The men then expatiated on the horrors of the war, and said that they wanted to know for what they were fighting; [and hoped that the horrors of war would be made to cease!]

I thought the best remedy was to let the MPs see some of the best and most thoughtful of our soldiers. There is no doubt that we have, in this very large Army, men of all opinions – ultra Socialists, pacifists and conscientious objectors, as well as real hard fighting patriots.

Sir H. Wilson (the new CIGS) arrived from England and stayed the night. Rawlinson is also here ... Wilson pressed me to earmark certain divisions as an 'Inter-Allied General Reserve'. I pointed out that I had only 6 divisions under my hand, and with the prospect of an early attack by the Enemy, I could not agree to place any of my divisions under the hand of another person, without grave risk to the plans of defence which had been most carefully drawn up in accord with General Pétain and his Staff: Rather than run such risk at this time, I would prefer to be relieved of my Command. Wilson argued that the Inter-Allied Reserve is being formed really to help me! It is difficult to discover what Wilson has at the back of his mind. Now that he has become CIGS in London, he did not appear so anxious to make the Versailles Staff under Rawlinson very strong. Indeed, differences between these two have already begun to show themselves on the matter of the organisation of Versailles. Had Wilson remained on at Versailles, there was every chance of the General Staff, London, becoming reduced to a local office for *Home* Defence. Now that is all changed with his advent to power as CIGS [But I still fear that he means to help Lloyd George to detach troops from my Command to fight against the Turks].

Thursday 28 February. Letter to Lady Haig

I spent some time today with the Canadians. They are really fine disciplined soldiers now and so smart and clean. I am sorry to say that the Australians are not nearly so efficient. I put this down to *Birdwood, who, instead of facing the problem, has gone in for the easier way of saying everything is perfect and making himself as popular as possible. We have had to separate the Australians into Convalescent Camps of their own, because they were giving so much trouble when along with our men and put such revolutionary ideas into their heads!

Saturday 2 March

... [A]t 10 am I presided at Conference of Army Commanders...
The usual statement on the position of the Enemy was made by my Intelligence Officer (Cox). He gave reasons why we think the Enemy is preparing to attack on the fronts of our Third and Fifth Armies. I emphasised the necessity for being ready as soon as possible to meet a big hostile offensive of prolonged duration. I also told Army Commanders that I was very pleased at all I had seen on the fronts of the 3 Armies which I had recently visited. Plans were sound and thorough, and much work had already been done. I was only afraid that the Enemy would find our front so very strong that he will hesitate to commit his Army to the attack with the almost certainty of losing very heavily. There was a tendency in some divisions to place all the brigades in line instead of keeping one under the hand of the GOC Division. I pointed out that this should be the rule, and it should only be departed from for some good reason as for instance in front of Armentières. All Commanders should retain some part of their force to meet the unforeseen! ...

Sunday 3 March

The AG[1] reported this morning. General Godley has been most unfairly attacked in the New Zealand House of Representatives, and compared with Birdwood, commanding the Australians, to the disadvantage of the former. I sent a strong letter in reply supporting Godley and incidentally enclosed a

1 Adjutant General, Lieutenant General Sir George Fowke.

graphic showing the numbers of men per thousand in prison, because Bird-wood was held up as an excellent disciplinarian. This table shows:

9	per thousand	Australians in prison
1.6	" "	Canadians, NZ South African
1	" "	British (excluding above)

That is to say nearly one Australian in every hundred men is in prison. This is greatly due to the fact that the Australian government refuses to allow capital punishment to be awarded to any Australian.

Before we introduced the '*suspended* sentence' in February 1915, the British had 5.1 men per thousand in prison. By June that year the numbers fell to 1.2 and in August to .7 per thousand. Really the absence of crime in this Army is quite wonderful.

Sunday 3 March. Letter to Sir Charles Kavanagh[1]

The situation with regard to manpower has made it necessary to convert to other uses certain units now in the field, and, in consequence, the Army Council, with the consent of His Majesty the King, have issued orders that the three Household Cavalry Regiments are to be dismounted and converted into Army Machine Gun Battalions.

I feel confident that since this reorganisation has become necessary, it will be accepted with the loyalty and devotion with which every turn of fortune has been met by British officers and men throughout the war, and that the Household Cavalry Regiments will in their new rôle as Machine Gun Battalions maintain their old esprit de corps and add further honours to their very distinguished record.

On the eve of this change, I wish to express to all belonging to these regiments my admiration of the fine services they have rendered since the beginning of the war.

Monday 4 March. Letter to Lord Derby

Are you and the Cabinet really playing the game by me? On Sunday 17 February to help the PM and you out of your political difficulties, I agreed *at once* to the transfer of Rawlinson to Versailles. But it was also agreed by the PM that Plumer should replace Rawlinson as soon as possible! As you

---

1 Letter is in the War Diary of the Royal Horse Guards, Household Cavalry Museum, Windsor. Earlier, Kavanagh had claimed, 'The men are very heavy and use up a large number of horses; also these regiments are not getting as good Officers as the others': Diary, 15 January 1918.

know signs are accumulating of an attack being likely at an early date, it is therefore most important that Plumer and his staff take over command hitherto held by Rawlinson, and get settled down. A week lost now may never be regained.

Tuesday 5 March. Letter to Sir Henry Wilson[1]

Peyton goes London tomorrow to explain my views about moving Corps Commanders. I am all for it, but in view of enemy's threatening attitude I must go carefully and thus replace those who go by officers who know the local conditions.

I can send 2 Corps Commanders home at once (Woollcombe and McCracken) and promote Harper and De Lisle.

Thursday 14 March

Haig visited Downing Street.

I ... had a long talk with the PM and Mr Bonar Law ... I pointed out the deficiency of men would make the situation critical by June if the Enemy attacked ... They did their best to get me to say that the Germans would not attack! The PM remarked that I had 'given my opinion that the Germans would only attack against small portions of our front'. I said that 'I had never said that. The question put to me was: if I were a German General and confronted by the present situation, *would* I attack?'

I now said that the German Army and its leaders seem drunk with their success in Russia and the Middle East, so that it is impossible to foretell what they may not attempt. In any case we must be prepared to meet a very strong attack on a 50 mile front, and for this drafts are urgently required ...

An Anglo-French conference then took place.

Before we sat down, M. Clemenceau came to me and said, 'It is all arranged about the reserves, I have seen M. Lloyd George' ...

Lloyd George opened the discussion and put my case very well. He finally proposed that, although neither I nor Pétain could contribute towards the General Reserve at once, the intention to form a Reserve should still be maintained, and that as the American troops arrived and set free British and French units, the decision should be given effect to.[2]

1 IWM: Wilson papers, HHW 2/7A/5.
2 The meeting eventually agreed to this proposal despite Foch's objections.

Saturday 16 March

Haig visited Buckingham Palace, and then returned to France.

The King received me at once ... He was delighted at the news of the birth of our son.[1] He said that his sister (Princess Victoria) had kept him constantly informed of the progress of things at Eastcott and how Doris was etc.

We then had a long talk on the general state of affairs. The King considers that the feeling in the country is good, and wherever he has been, he has met with the friendliest welcome.

Monday 18 March

Cox reported Enemy has 187 divisions now on West Front: of these 80 are believed to be in reserve ... Plumer has not yet realised that the situation on this front is much changed since he left here last November for Italy. There are indications that public opinion in Germany has yet to be convinced of the necessity for an offensive in the West, and of the likelihood of its success. But the Enemy has concentrated already adequate means for a large attack here, and so we must expect an attack at short notice, and make our plans accordingly. Plumer would like to continue the attack in Flanders like last year but neither our manpower situation, nor the strength of the Enemy admits our acting on the offensive.[2]

Tuesday 19 March

The Minister of Munitions, Winston Churchill, visited GHQ.

Churchill has written a paper urging the reorganisation of the Army so as to employ mechanical appliances to take place of men, because we are lacking in manpower. He stated that with the approval of the War Cabinet, he was proceeding with the manufacture of a large number of Tanks (4000). This is done without any consideration of the manpower situation and the crews likely to be available to put into them! He asked my views on making peace. I stated that from the point of view of British interests alone, if the Enemy will give the terms Lloyd George recently laid down, we ought to accept them at once; even some modification of our demands for Alsace-Lorraine might be given way on. At the present moment, England is in a stronger position than she has ever been and by continuing the war she will get weaker

1 The present Earl Haig was born on 15 March 1918.
2 Earlier in 1918 Haig too had wanted to take the offensive.

[financially and in manpower]. On the other hand, America will get stronger, and finally will dictate *her* peace which may not suit Great Britain . . .

After dinner Lawrence brought me the reports on the examination of certain prisoners showing that Enemy's intention is to attack about the 20 or 21 March. Batteries have received their allotment of ammunition for battle, 1200 rounds including 300 of gas shell. Large air forces have been concentrated on this front, but these will not be fully disclosed till day of the battle.

Thursday 21 March

Numerically superior in guns and men, the Germans launched Operation Michael, *a massive blow against British Fifth and Third Armies. Aided by dense fog, German forces made significant gains and took large numbers of prisoners, especially on Fifth Army's front.* Michael *reopened mobile warfare and initiated the greatest crisis Haig had faced since October–November 1914.*

Foggy morning with sun trying to come through.

About 8 am General Lawrence came to my room while I was dressing to tell me that the German attack had begun.

At 4.43 am Enemy opened heavy bombardment on the whole of Fifth Army front except between the Oise and Vendeuil.

Bombardment was continued northwards along the Third Army front . . . to the Sensée River . . .

Very severe fighting on the Third and Fifth Army fronts continued well into the evening. Our men seem to be fighting magnificently.

About midday *Byng seemed very anxious because reports showed that Enemy had got Bullecourt and penetrated into the 'battle zone'. But by 2 pm he found that Enemy had not got as far as had been reported at first.

By evening Byng had his troops of the VI and IV Corps generally on the rear line of the 'battle zone' and (with my approval) ordered the withdrawal of the V Corps from the Flesquières salient back to the battle zone (including Havrincourt) during the night. This gives us an extra division in reserve.

*Gough's Army were very heavily attacked all day. From opposite La Fère northwards to Benay our III Corps held the battle zone all day and inflicted great losses on the Enemy. Next in the north the XVIII Corps held its front except Massemy (on north of Bois d'Holnon). The XIX Corps also held the battle zone, except on the north of its sector where it had to withdraw from Hargicourt, after Ronsoy¹ was vacated by our troops (16th Irish Division). The latter corps (VII) held its battle zone intact to the junction with Third

¹ Properly Ronssoy.

Army. But the fighting was extremely heavy and the Enemy came on in *dense waves*, 9 divisions were identified on a 10,000 yard front.

With my approval, Gough decided to withdraw from the sector between La Fère and the Somme to the St Quentin Canal. I asked the French to place some troops on Gough's right here in the Oise Valley. Two divisions and 1 dismounted Cavalry Division were ordered to Noyon area.

Enemy attacked on a front of over *fifty miles*. According to a captured map the final direction of the 111th Division was Boiry St Martin 5 miles west of Croisilles: we still hold Croisilles! . . .

Having regard to the great strength of the attack (*over* 30 extra divisions having reinforced those holding the original German front line for the battle) and the determined manner in which the attack was everywhere pressed, I consider that the result of the day is highly creditable to the British troops: I therefore sent a message of congratulation to the Third and Fifth Armies for communication to all ranks.

Thursday 21 March. Letter to Sir Henry Wilson[1]

This morning at 4 am the enemy started his attack on the wide front we expected. It is hardly necessary to urge the CIGS (for I have repeatedly done so) to insist on the Government producing men for drafts! – The 63rd Division alone has lost in last 10 days, chiefly from gas 77 officers, and 2440 other ranks.

Friday 22 March

All reports show that our men are in great spirits. All speak of the wonderful targets they had to fire at yesterday. Enemy came on in great masses. Our 16th (Irish) Division which was on the right of VII Corps and lost Ronsoy village, is said not to be so full of fight as the others. [In fact, certain Irish units did very badly and gave way immediately the Enemy showed.]

Our Flying Corps did wonders yesterday. They crashed 16 Enemy machines and we only lost one. They too had marvellous targets; masses of infantry on roads, horses, guns, etc. Into these they fired with machine guns, and spread consternation and disorder . . .

Also on Fifth Army the Enemy continued to work up the Omignon Valley north of Bois d'Holnon, and at 8 pm Gough telephoned 'parties of all arms of the Enemy are through our Reserve Line'.

I concurred in his falling back to line of Somme and to hold Péronne Bridgehead in accordance with his orders.

1 IWM: Wilson papers, HHW 2/7A/9.

I at once sent to tell General Pétain and asked his support to hold line of Somme and Péronne Bridgehead. I expect big attack to develop towards Arras. He [Pétain] had already agreed to send 3 divisions to the Crozat Canal, and to hold that portion of our front.

Saturday 23 March

Haig visited Byng, commander of Third Army.

He reported on situation. Troops have fought very well indeed. He was anxious about Nurlu, but on the whole was quite satisfied with the situation.

I then went on to Villers Bretonneux and saw General Gough Commanding Fifth Army. [I was surprised to learn that] his troops are now behind the Somme and the River Tortille. Men very tired after two days fighting and long march back. On first day they had to wear gas masks all day which is very fatiguing [but I cannot make out why the Fifth Army has gone so far back without making some kind of a stand] . . .

General Pétain arrived about 4 pm. He has arranged to put 2 Armies under General Fayolle on my right, to operate in Somme Valley and keep our two Armies in touch with one another. Pétain is most anxious to do all he can to support me. The basic principle of co-operation is to keep the two Armies in touch. If this is lost and the Enemy comes in between us, then probably the British will be rounded up and driven into the sea! This must be prevented even at the cost of abandoning the north flank.

I arranged with Plumer to thin down his front; then I shall be glad to see the divisions thus set free near the Somme! It is most satisfactory to have a Commander of Plumer's temperament at a time of crisis like the present.

Sunday 24 March

I attended the Church of Scotland at 9.30 am. The Rev. Mr Black of Edinburgh preached an excellent sermon, indicating why we can and should rely on the gospel of Christ to guide us in the present and future.

The situation this morning was better, but by this afternoon, reports in succession had arrived showing that the Germans had taken Morval, then Delville Wood. The latter report was later reported to be untrue. By night the Enemy had reached Le Transloy and Combles. North of Le Transloy our troops had hard fighting; the 31st, Guards, 3rd, 40th and 17th Divisions have all repulsed heavy attacks and held their ground.

On the Somme, south of Péronne, our troops with the French, drove back parties of the Enemy which had crossed.

I sent Lawrence to see Gough and the Fifth Army [and fix on some line on which to halt his troops and make a stand. He is also to] meet General Fayolle, Commanding French Group of Armies on my right, [and will arrange for close co-operation.] . . .

I dined with Byng at Beaurepaire at 8.30 pm. All [at Third Army Head-quarters are] in good heart. I told him to hold on with his left at all costs to the right of First Army near Arras, and if forced to give ground, to do so by throwing back his right on to our old trench system from Arras via Ransart etc. along our old defence line. My intention being to concentrate all reserves I can by thinning my line in the north. With these reserves to strike south-wards when the Enemy has penetrated to Amiens . . .

I went on from Beauquesne to Dury. General Pétain met me there at 11 pm.[1] I explained my plans as above and asked him to concentrate a large force near Abbeville astride the Somme to co-operate on my right. He said he expected every moment to be attacked in Champagne, but would give Fayolle all his available troops . . .[2]

Situation seems better, but we must expect these great attacks to continue.

Monday 25 March

Got back from Dury with General Lawrence and Heseltine about 3 am.

[Lawrence at once left me to telegraph to Wilson (CIGS London) request-ing him and Lord Milner to come to France at once in order to arrange that

1 The Ts diary adds a paragraph that reads: 'Pétain struck me as very much upset, almost unbalanced and most anxious. I explained my plans as above, and asked him to concentrate as large a force as possible about Amiens astride the Somme to co-operate on my right. He said he expected every moment to be attacked in Champagne, and he did not believe that the main German blow had yet been delivered. He said he would give Fayolle all his available troops. He also told me that he had seen the latter today at Montdidier, where the French reserves are now collecting, and had directed him (Fayolle) in the event of the German advance being pressed still further, to fall back southwestwards to Beauvais in order to cover Paris. It was at once clear to me that the effect of this order must be to separate the French from the British right flank, and so allow the Enemy to penetrate between the two Armies. I at once asked Pétain if he meant to abandon my right flank. He nodded assent, and added, "It is the only thing possible, if the Enemy compel the Allies to fall back still further." From my talk with Pétain I gathered that he had recently attended a Cabinet meeting in Paris and that his orders from his Government are to "*cover Paris at all costs*". On the other hand to keep in touch with the British Army is no longer the basic principle of French strategy. In my opinion, our Army's existence in France depends on keeping the British and French Armies united. So I hurried back to my headquarters at Beaurepaire Château to report the serious change in *French strategy* to the CIGS and Secretary of State for War, and ask them to come to France.'

2 Pétain gave Haig a copy of an order he had issued at 9 pm. This stated that the primary task was to maintain the unity of the French armies and 'Secondly, if it is possible, to maintain liaison with the British forces' (J. E. Edmonds, *Military Operations France and Belgium, 1918*, vol. I (London: Macmillan, 1935 pp. 448–50.))

General Foch or some other determined general, who would fight, should be given supreme control of the operations in France. I knew Foch's strategical ideas were in conformity with the orders given me by Lord Kitchener when I became C-in-C, and that he was a man of great courage and decision as shown during the fighting at Ypres in October and November 1914] ...

General Wilson, CIGS, arrived about 11 am from London. I gave him my views on the situation in the presence of General Lawrence. Briefly, everything depends on whether the French can support us *at once* with 20 divisions at least *north* of the Somme. A far reaching decision must be taken at once by the French PM so that the *whole* French Army may take turns in supporting my force.

After lunch I visited Abbeville at 4 pm, to meet M. Clemenceau, Lord Milner, and Foch but none of them arrived yet[1] only General Weygand (Foch's Staff officer). I gave him a note [for Clemenceau] containing my view of the situation – briefly that the only chance of saving a serious disaster is for the French to act at once, and concentrate as large a force as possible north of the Somme about Amiens.

Tuesday 26 March

An emergency Anglo-French conference at Doullens resulted in the critical decision to appoint Foch as Allied Supreme Commander.

We must estimate enemy has 25 divisions still in reserve ...

I attended Conference at Doullens at 11 am with Plumer (Second Army), *Horne (First), Byng (Third) ... I explained my object is to gain time for the French to come and support us. To this end we must hold our ground, especially on right of Third Army (near Bray) on Somme, where we must not give ground. The covering of Amiens is of first importance to the success of our cause. On the other hand, I must not so extend our line, through Enemy pressing our centre and making it bulge, as to risk its breaking ...

About 12 noon I had a meeting (also at Doullens) between Poincaré (President of France), Clemenceau (Premier), Foch, Pétain and Lord Milner, General H. Wilson (CIGS), my CGS (Lawrence) and myself. We discussed the situation, and it was decided that *Amiens must be covered at all costs*. French troops are being hurried up as rapidly as possible and Gough has been told to hold on with his left at Bray. It was proposed[2] that Foch should be

---

1 The Ts diary has 'turned up by train as expected'.
2 These words replace 'We also decided', which are crossed out in the Ms diary.

appointed to co-ordinate the operations at *Amiens*.[1] I at once recommended that he should co-ordinate the action of all the Allied Armies on the Western Front. Both Governments agreed to this. Foch goes to Dury as his HQ (3 miles south of Amiens) . . .

I rode about 5 pm – as I was going out I met Milner and Wilson. They spoke to me about Gough. I said that whatever the opinion at home might be, I considered that he had dealt with a most difficult situation very well. He had never lost his head, was always cheery and fought hard.

Wednesday 27 March

We learn from prisoners that their units were put straight into battle after long marches – no objectives were given, but companies were told to go as far as possible. A good deal of discontent is reported amongst divisions near Bucquoy because of want of food: the troops had over marched their supply arrangements . . .

I told Birch (Artillery Adviser) to organise as powerful artillery as possible on Byng's front. There must be no retirement . . .

Heavy fighting took place all day north and south of Somme. Enemy attacked in large forces estimated at 15 divisions in first line north of Somme supported by a further 10 to 13 divisions. Enemy made progress at Chipilly, Méaulte, Dérnancourt, deployed on west of Albert and attacked Bucquoy and Ablainzeville. Our troops vigorously counter-attacked so that our line is approximately as last night. We intercepted an order on Enemy's wireless directing their objective today as Talmas (north of Amiens) for their right, and Querrieu as left. In spite of attacks repeated 10 and 11 times against certain parts of our line, no progress was made, and wherever the Enemy did make ground our men counter-attacked and forced him back.

Thursday 28 March

Operation Mars, *the second phase of the German offensive, began in the Arras sector. Unlike on 21 March, the British defenders won a significant victory.*

Early this morning the Enemy opened a heavy bombardment south and

1 The Ts diary reads: 'It was proposed by Clemenceau that Foch should be appointed to co-ordinate the operations of an Allied force to cover Amiens and ensure that the French and British flanks remained united. This proposal seemed to me quite worthless, as Foch would be in a subordinate position to Pétain and myself. In my opinion it was essential to success that Foch should control Pétain, so I at once recommended that Foch should *co-ordinate the action of all the Allied Armies on the Western front* . . . Foch seemed sound and sensible but Pétain had a terrible look. He had the appearance of a commander who was in a funk and has lost his nerve.'

north of the Scarpe and is (11 am) attacking vigorously opposite Arras against our 3rd, 15th and 4th Divisions' front...

Telegram dated yesterday received War Cabinet 'today cordially endorsed arrangement reached yesterday at Doullens'.

North of the Sensée River Enemy attacked with 5 divisions in line and 2 in support [against First Army (Horne) and left of Third Army (Byng)]. Our 56th Division met this attack very well, and repulsed it with slaughter.

Friday 29 March

The King visited GHQ.

I left at 10.30 and met General Foch at Abbeville about noon. The King remained at Beaurepaire for about half an hour after I left. I thought HM looked as if he has been suffering from anxiety and 'funk'! I told him that I thought the Allies were fortunate that the attack had fallen on the British and not on the French because the latter could not have withstood it. I also pointed out

1. British Infantry in France at the beginning of the battle were 100,000 less than a year ago!
2. We now had 3 times as many Germans on our front as we had last year.
3. We had also extended our line (by order of the British Government) fully ⅕th more than it was last autumn. This may have been necessary, because the French had inadequate numbers and the Americans had not arrived, but it rendered our front precarious.

The French Army we relieved was to have remained in rear of left flank of French ready to support at point of junction of the Allies if necessary. Apparently only the Army Headquarters went to Clermont, but the divisions were dispersed.

The King said he was *opposed* to forcing conscription upon Ireland. I strongly pressed the contrary view not only in order to get men but for the good of Ireland.

Foch met me at Abbeville about 20 minutes late, as usual, and full of apologies. He is doing all he can to expedite the arrival of French Divisions, and until they come we can only do our best to hold on to our present positions. It is most important to prevent the Enemy from placing guns near enough to shell the troop sidings near Amiens (Longeau) on east of the town.

By 2 April, I gather that the French should have sufficient troops concentrated to admit of them starting an offensive.[1]

I think Foch has brought great energy to bear on the present situation, and has, instead of permitting French troops to *retire* southwest from Amiens, insisted on some of them relieving our troops and on covering Amiens at all costs. He and I are quite in agreement as to the general plan of operations . . .

General Gough and Sir John Simon[2] came to dinner. I told the former I wanted him and his Staff out of the line in order to reconnoitre the Somme Valley from Amiens to the sea. It may be necessary for me to hold such a line if French do not hold on! So a Reserve Army Staff is necessary.

Saturday 30 March

I visited Sir Henry Rawlinson at Dury about 1 o'clock today. He with the old Fourth Army Staff is relieving Gough and Fifth Army Staff. Rawlinson explained the situation. There are nearly 20,000 remnants of divisions in the Villers–Bretonneux sector. The majority are very tired indeed, most having been fighting since the beginning of the battle . . .

I saw General Kavanagh, Commanding Cavalry Corps and M. Clemenceau (French Premier) at Dury . . . Clemenceau is in full accord with me and gave orders for the French to support us energetically and cross the Avre River, so as to hold the high ground where the Canadian Cavalry now is. I sincerely hope that Clemenceau will get his order carried out! Clemenceau spoke most freely about Foch's position. He had no fears about me loyally doing my best to co-operate. It was Pétain and Foch who he feared would squabble. 'Pétain', he said, 'is a very nervous man and sometimes may not carry out all he has promised.' Personally, I have found Pétain most honest and straightforward, but in the present operations he has been slow to decide and slower still in acting! Hence the troubled position of affairs about Amiens.

Monday 1 April

I left Beaurepaire about 11 am and motored to Dury, where I met M. Clemenceau. I again pointed out the importance of the Villers–Bretonneux position both for covering my right as well as Amiens and the French left. In order to enable me to hold that position, the French must take over the front from Moreuil to the village of Hangard . . . This sector includes the defence of the Luce valley.

---

1 The Ts diary adds, 'But will they?'
2 Sir John Simon (1873–1954), Liberal politician who had resigned as Home Secretary in January 1916 because of his opposition to conscription; he was nevertheless a supporter of the war.

Clemenceau said we must get Foch, and settle the point at once between us, so Foch was telephoned for . . . Foch arrived about 3 pm, and after a few words to him privately by Clemenceau and an explanation from me of my wishes, Foch quickly put his name to a document ordering General Fayolle to take over the line I wanted. Half to be taken over tonight, and half tomorrow night.

Wednesday 3 April

Haig, Lloyd George, Pershing, Foch, Wilson, Clemenceau and Pétain met at Beauvais.

M. Clemenceau proposed to modify the agreement come to at Doullens, which gave Foch authority to 'co-ordinate the action of all Allied Armies on Western Front'. After considerable discussion it was agreed to entrust to Foch 'the strategical direction of military operations. The C-in-C of British, French and American Armies will have full control of the tactical action of his respective Armies. Each C-in-C will have the right of appeal to their Government if in his opinion his Army is endangered by reason of any order received from General Foch.'

I was in full agreement and explained that this new arrangement did not in any way alter my attitude towards Foch, or C-in-C French Army. I had always [in accordance with Lord Kitchener's orders to me] regarded the latter as being responsible for indicating the general strategical policy and, as far as possible, I tried to fall in with his views.

Before the meeting broke up, I asked the Governments to state their desire that a French offensive should be started *as soon as possible* in order to attract the Enemy's reserves and so prevent him from continuing his pressure against the British. Foch and Pétain both stated their determination to start attacking *as soon as possible*. [But will they ever attack? I doubt whether the French Army as a whole is now fit for an offensive.]

Haig shared a car with Lloyd George.

The PM looked as if he had been thoroughly frightened and seemed still in a funk . . . LG is a fatiguing companion in a motor. He talks and argues so!

I gathered that LG expects to be attacked in the House of Commons for not tackling the manpower problem before, also for sending divisions to the East at a critical time [against the advice of his military adviser, viz. the CIGS (Robertson)]. He is looking out for a scapegoat for the retreat of the Fifth Army. I pointed out that 'fewer men, extended front and increased hostile forces' were the main causes. He was much down upon Gough. I championed his case ... LG said he had not held the Somme bridges, nor destroyed them, and that Gough must not be employed. To this I said I could not condemn an officer unheard, and that if LG wishes him suspended he must send me an order to that effect.

Thursday 4 April

Haig received a telegram from Derby, ordering Gough's removal from command.

I replied that decision of War Cabinet would be complied with at once, and I recommended that Cavan should take over command of Army and be replaced in Italy by Haking.[1]

Friday 5 April

General Asser, Commander Lines of Communication area, explained to me his arrangements for holding succession of lines in the event of the Enemy succeeding in capturing Amiens and advancing to Abbeville, with the object of covering Rouen and Havre ...

General Gough came to lunch, and I told him of the orders received from Secretary of State for War for him to go home. He quite understands, that I have supported him to the utmost of my power, and that it is the Cabinet which has now taken action.

Saturday 6 April

Enemy's intentions seem still to be the capture of the Vimy position by turning it in the south of Arras as well as in the north (south of the La Bassée Canal). At the same time a surprise attack by 3 or 4 divisions against the Portuguese front is also to be expected. The First Army is quite alive to these possibilities and is prepared to meet them.

Sunday 7 April

Haig consulted with Foch.

Foch quite agreed that the British must be prepared for a very heavy attack. His plan was first to block the door to Amiens. To this end the French were

---

1 On this day Haig wrote to Derby, offering to resign. Lloyd George decided against accepting: 'Gough became the army's sacrifice to appease the government's critics'. French, *Strategy of the Lloyd George Coalition*, p. 233.

going to attack from Moreuil southwards, and he wished the British Fourth Army to co-operate. I pointed out the very limited means at Rawlinson's disposal.

When the door to Amiens was barred, then he (Foch) would consider the advisability of putting in a large attack from the south towards Roye. [Personally, I do not believe that Foch or Pétain has any intention of putting French Divisions into the battle.]

As regards my requests for either taking over British front south of the Somme, or placing a French Reserve near St Pol, Foch said he was unable to do either; but he had ordered a Reserve of 4 divisions and 3 Cavalry Divisions of the French Army to be located southwest of Amiens [i.e. in a very safe place]. This was the best that he could do at present, and he thought that the presence of the French reserves near Amiens would enable me to move my own reserves from the right flank if the battle required them further north. I wired to the CIGS result of my meeting with Foch, and suggested that he (Wilson) should come out to discuss the situation [and try to get better arrangements from Foch.]

Monday 8 April

A German aviator captured by French states that the mass of the German reserves are in the Tournai–Douai–Cambrai area, that is opposite the Armentières–Arras front.

I saw General de Laguiche,[1] and asked him to request General Foch to arrange to relieve 6 British Divisions in the Ypres sector, i.e. as far south as the Ypres–Comines Canal. This would enable me to form an effective reserve on my left ... General Weygand came to see the CGS this afternoon, but was unable to agree to our proposals.

Tuesday 9 April

The Germans launched Operation Georgette, *a major offensive in Flanders. If successful, this German thrust threatened to cut off the BEF from the coast. The British called this phase of fighting the 'Battle of the Lys'.*

After an intense bombardment from the La Bassée Canal northwards to the neighbourhood of Armentières, Enemy attacked the Portuguese and British holding this front. Enemy's strength estimated at 8 divisions. Thick mist made observation impossible.

Our flanks at Givenchy in south, and Fleurbaix in north held firm, though

1 Head of the French Mission.

at one time Enemy had occupied Givenchy as far as the church. The 55th Division retook the whole village in fine style.

As previously arranged, British Divisions in reserve moved up on each side and rear of the Portuguese. The latter retired [or to be more exact, 'ran away'] through the British taking their guns with them . . .

The state of the Portuguese has been reported as bad, and yesterday a battalion refused to go into the trenches. So it was arranged to relieve them with British troops tonight! The difficulty was to know what to do with them. They are very discontented chiefly because their officers have had leave to Portugal, but no men have gone. The recent revolution in Portugal has also upset them. We don't want to quarrel with Portugal because they have many suitable submarine bases for the Enemy! On the other hand, the Portuguese troops with their Portuguese officers are useless for this class of fighting.

General Foch came here about 1 o'clock and we had a long talk together. He declined to take over any part of the British line, but is determined to place a reserve of 4 French Divisions with their heads on the Somme immediately west of Amiens . . . I pointed out the very great inconvenience caused by the insertion of these troops into the area of the Fourth Army.

Haig reluctantly agreed to the proposal, but told Foch:

I do not consider that a satisfactory solution of our difficulties. The Enemy aims at the destruction of the British Army. We ought therefore at once to reduce the front which we are now holding in order to

1. Form a British Reserve to keep the battle going, and preserve the Channel ports, the Bruay coal mines and Amiens.
2. Give the Enemy a smaller target to strike at, and so reduce the wastage of British units.

I . . . motored to Hesdin (HQ Third Army) where I saw General Byng. He . . . thinks all indications point to his being attacked tomorrow.

Foch agreed today to receive General John Du Cane on his Staff to represent my views. He declined 2 days ago when I saw him at Aumale. [Henry Wilson did not help us at all in our negotiations with Foch. His sympathies almost seem to be with the French.]

Wednesday 10 April

General Horne has gone (9 am) to see Plumer regarding placing reserves at his disposal. Yesterday we had drawn on Plumer to help Horne. Now we are strengthening Plumer by moving Reserve Divisions from First Army to the left and replacing them from Third Army.

The Fourth Army (Rawlinson) has been told that, in view of the development of Enemy's attacks in the north, no troops will be available for his proposed offensive except the 5 Australian Brigade to cover the French left near Hangard village. I also order Cavalry Corps less 1 division to be moved to the St Pol–Doullens area in GHQ Reserve.

Cox reported that attack north of the La Bassée Canal was made on an 11 mile front by 8 divisions in front line and 2 in reserve.

At 11.30 am I wrote to General Foch, called his attention to the situation north of the La Bassée Canal and in process of development north of Armentières. I requested him to arrange to take over *some portion* of the British line in order to set free reserves and enable me to continue the battle etc. . . .

About 10 pm General Foch with Weygand (his Chief of Staff) came to see me from his HQ . . . He had carefully considered my letter: he agreed that the Enemy's objective was the British Army, and that his main effort would be between Arras and the Somme. So he had decided to move up a large force of French troops ready to take part in the battle . . . I am glad that the French at last are beginning to realise the object of the Germans. The French losses in this battle are about 20,000 to 25,000, ours are 160,000 and will be more. This shows their share in the fight so far! [But personally I have come to the conclusion that Foch is afraid to put any French Division into the battle, and that he won't do so until force of circumstances, as a last resort, compel him.]

Thursday 11 April

Haig visited HQ of Second Army.

On leaving Plumer I motored straight back to Montreuil and saw Lawrence, Davidson and Cox regarding the necessity of sending Plumer more reserves. It seems to me that Enemy will do his utmost to exploit his success towards Hazebrouck and Calais. So it is very necessary to give Plumer sufficient troops to hold up the Enemy's advance. On the other hand, I have only the 1st Australians and 4 Canadian Divisions, which have not been heavily engaged: so my reserves are very few indeed.

The most important thing is to keep connection with the French. With this end I must be strong at, and south of Arras.

I must also cover Calais and Boulogne. I cannot spare another division today, but when the French advance north from the Somme tomorrow I might let the 57th Division go north to Plumer.

In view of the possibility of the Enemy's advancing on Hazebrouck, and my shortage of reserves, I write to Foch asking him to concentrate a force of *at least* 4 French Divisions between St Omer and Dunkirk in readiness to support the British. I send my letter by Davidson, who will explain the situation of our troops to Foch. The latter says to hold our front and try to form a pocket round the area where the Enemy has broken through. This is already being done by us. Foch is to send a French Cavalry Corps to Cassel to support Plumer. It will be at Hesdin tomorrow night. We must expect Enemy to press his attacks to the coast, and I am still anxious for French support about Cassel, [since Foch refuses stoutly to take over any line from us, and so set free British Divisions for this purpose.]

The situation seemed so grave that Haig issued an Order of the Day, part of which read: 'Every position must be held to the last man: there must be no retirement. With our backs to the wall and believing in the justice of our cause each one of us must fight on to the end.' Haig's diary does not mention him writing this Order.

Friday 12 April

... I had a talk with General Byng (Third Army). He expects to be attacked shortly, but says all are confident and in good heart.

I reached Doullens at noon, and spent ¾ hour with M. Clemenceau in his train. M. Loucheur was present. Clemenceau was anxious about our covering the Bruay coal mines effectively. He had seen Horne this morning, and had formed the opinion that the British were going back at once to the La Bassée Canal! There are only 5 days reserve [of coal] now at the French munition factories, and as 70% of their coal comes from the Bruay district, it is of very great importance to cover the mines as long as possible. I assured him on this point.

I next pointed out the urgent necessity of the French reinforcing the British, and of getting the latter on to a shorter line *in order to be able to continue the battle.* My troops are fast getting worn out. I urged that 3 measures should be taken at once:

1. Hasten move of French Divisions by road from the Somme on Doullens etc.
2. Inundate the Dunkirk area.
3. Send troops (French and *American*) to the St Omer–Dunkirk line to support our Second Army.

Clemenceau left by train to visit Foch and is to press my points. He told me that I could depend on him to support me, even though the French Army holds from Amiens to Switzerland. To this I replied that the decisive point is the British Army, and it is of the greatest importance to the Allied cause to preserve the British forces and *keep the war going*...

Haig then visited the HQs of Harper's IV Corps, Monash's Australian Corps and Fanshawe's V Corps.

I was greatly struck with the fine spirit of confidence and cheerfulness which existed everywhere.

All spoke of their present positions being very good and strong, and their ability to hold it against hostile attacks. I got many stories of what happened during the retreat. White of the Australians is a fine cheery fellow, and assured me that the Australians would do their best for me. They might lose a little ground here and there, but all meant fighting. At every Corps Headquarters everyone I met expressed disgust with Lloyd George's speech (which I have not read) but which they stated contained untrue statements of our *fighting* strength in France.[1] Harper stated that his present front is on a circle and so envelops Enemy to a great extent; in this salient the Enemy has lost *enormously*, especially about Serre on 5 April, when our gunners fired at great masses of the Enemy without being interfered with at all by hostile artillery fire.

It gave me a great feeling of confidence seeing these Commanders and Staffs so well after all their trying times, and so confident!

I returned via Auxi-le-Chateau to St André HQ Flying Corps. I had a talk with Generals Salmond[2] and Festing[3] and hear of the satisfactory results of today's work in the air. I also rang Davidson up on telephone. He said Plumer was anxious about the situation at Bailleul. Enemy is attacking northwest, but seemed to be held opposite Merville.

I rode back to Beaurepaire and had a talk with Lawrence and Davidson before dinner. I said my policy was the same. – Keep touch with the French on the right *at all costs*. Therefore we cannot reduce any more our reserves from Arras to Amiens. Plumer must keep in touch with First Army at all costs. If French send reserves to Cassel he may be able to hold on to Pilkem line for a time but, in view of Enemy's very large available reserves, he should be prepared to withdraw slowly to the line in front of Dunkirk (Hondschoote) [and thence] to Forêt de Nieppe. Inundations *must* be made in north at once.

Lawrence went off at 8.30 pm to see Plumer.

---

1 In a speech to Parliament on 9 April, Lloyd George claimed that the BEF was stronger in January 1918 than twelve months earlier.
2 Lieutenant General (later Marshal of the RAF Sir) John ('Jack') Maitland Salmond (1881–1968), became GOC Royal Flying Corps in January 1918 aged only thirty-six.
3 Colonel (later Brigadier General) Francis Leycester Festing (1877–1968), RAF staff officer.

Saturday 13 April

Lawrence got back at 1.30 am from Plumer's HQ. He explained situation. We have now withdrawn from Passchendaele salient leaving only a force of outposts on it. We hold the Pilkem ridge on the lines arranged some months ago.

Sunday 14 April

A conference took place at Abbeville. As well as Haig and Foch, Milner, Lawrence, Weygand and Du Cane attended.

I explained urgent need for French to take a more active share in the battle, because the British Divisions were fast disappearing and our men were very tired. Foch spoke a lot of nonsense, that as we were in the battle, there must be no divisions withdrawn for rest and spoke about what the British did at Ypres in 1914. He then asked for my proposals. I asked him to order his 4 leading Reserve Divisions under General Maistre now on the line Doullens–Acheux to continue their march towards Lillers, and be disposed between Pernes and Bruay to act as Reserve to my First Army either towards Hinges and Béthune, or towards the Vimy ridge. The next group of four divisions to be disposed north of Somme to act as a Reserve towards Albert (i.e., for my Third and Fourth Armies).

Foch said he would consider my proposal. I incidentally pointed out that the Enemy was likely to continue his effort to reach Calais, because by taking that place he might be able to dictate peace to England! The present position of Foch's reserves was too distant to admit of their affecting in any way the advance of the Enemy on Calais.

I also pressed Foch to send as many troops as he could to the Hazebrouck–Cassel area. He said that he would see what the situation was when the present movement of troops was finished ... Foch seems to me unmethodical and takes a 'short-view' of the situation. For instance, he does not look ahead and make a forecast of what may be required in a week in a certain area, and arrange accordingly. He only provides from day to day sufficient troops to keep the railway accommodation filled up! Also, as at Ypres in 1914, he is very disinclined to engage French troops in the battle.

Monday 15 April

Field Censor reports that judging from the letters written by the men, the moral of the troops is extremely good. 'It can safely be said that it has never been higher.' 'As soon as the German offensive started, the tone of the letters improved and grousing ceased' and was 'replaced to a great extent by a confident tone'.

Tuesday 16 April. Letter to Rev. G. S. Duncan[1]

One line to thank you most truly for your letter. I am very grateful for you thinking of me at this time, and I *know* I am sustained in my efforts by that great unseen Power, otherwise I could not be standing the strain and am doing. I missed my Sunday morning greatly. But it could not be helped.

Thursday 18 April

Haig visited XV Corps.

De Lisle replaced Du Cane in command of this Corps and is very satisfied (as usual) with himself. He took great credit for the position of the 1st Australian Division covering Hazebrouck 'which' he said 'saved the situation'! (It is interesting to note that I ordered the division to that position before De Lisle had anything to with operations in this area!) . . .

I then went to Ranchicourt, HQ First Army, and discussed the situation with General Horne. He feels very confident. Currie (Commanding the Canadians) is suffering from a swollen head Horne thinks! He lodged a complaint when I ordered the Canadian Divisions to be brought out of the line in order to support the front and take part in the battle elsewhere. He wishes to fight only as a 'Canadian Corps' and got his Canadian representative in London to write and urge me to arrange it. As a result, the Canadians are together holding a wide front near Arras, but they have not yet been in the battle! The Australians on the other hand have been used by divisions and are now spread out from Albert to Amiens and one is in front of Hazebrouck . . .

The French attacked on our right to improve their positions near Hangard and made some progress, but they are still a long way from the Demuin–Moreuil road which is necessary for us to hold to cover our flank. This is the first active steps taken by French since battle began on 21 March.

Friday 19 April

After lunch Commandant Gemeau brought me a letter from Foch stating that he was anxious to maintain 15 French Divisions in reserve behind the British Army. To enable him to obtain these divisions it would be necessary

---

1 NLS: Duncan Papers, Acc. 7706.

to put tired British Divisions in the positions now held by the French Divisions which he wants.

I at once replied that I would do anything necessary to help to win the battle, but it was desirable to tell Foch that any idea of a permanent 'Amalgam' must be dismissed from his mind at once, because that would never work. I also reminded Gemeau of the proposals made at the Calais Conference, February 1917, by which the British GHQ was to disappear. He assured me that I could implicitly depend on Foch's good faith. So I told Gemeau that I would send a favourable reply and have the question studied at once.

Lord Milner arrived about 3 pm on his way to London to take up his duties as Secretary of State for War.[1] He expressed his intention to do his best to guard the interests of the Army, and he hoped that the Army would treat him in a kindly spirit.

I showed him Foch's letter. He agreed that it was necessary to meet his request but only as a temporary measure. He was entirely opposed to mixing up units of the French and British. The needs of this great battle had made intermingling of units for a time necessary, but he would never approve of a permanent 'Amalgam' . . .

I signed a letter to Foch telling him I was prepared to send four tired divisions at once to a quiet sector on the French front, and would send a Staff officer to study the question in detail.[2]

Wednesday 24 April

Ludendorff launched a fresh offensive, this time towards Amiens. The thrust was halted by a counter-attack by Australian and British troops which recaptured Villers-Bretonneux.

After violent bombardment, Enemy attacked about 6.30 am our front south of the Somme. Attack was at first repulsed, but aided by two groups of Tanks (3 in each group) Enemy pierced our line north of Hangard at two points, and captured Villers-Bretonneux . . . I motored to HQ Fourth Army at Flixécourt and saw Sir H. Rawlinson about 12.30. By my instructions he telephoned to J. Du Cane, who is with Foch, to urge the latter to direct the French Moroccan Division to co-operate with our troops in order to retake Villers-Bretonneux by a counter-attack.

I then went on to Dury HQ III Corps. I found Butler living in my chateau there, and I lunched out of the lunch box in his dining room. Butler explained

1 Milner replaced Derby, who became Ambassador in Paris.
2 On hearing of Foch's scheme, Wilson, alarmed at the implications, sent a telegram to Haig. The C-in-C replied defending his decision on military grounds: Diary, 20 April 1918.

the situation. I felt very pleased at the quiet methodical way in which he was arranging for a counter-attack to retake the village of Villers-Bretonneux.

Butler was in command, with Heneker[1] Commanding 8th Division and Hobbs Commanding 5th Australian Division by telephone. A combined attack by two Australian Brigades and one of the 18th Division was arranged to go in at 8 pm...

Counter-attack to retake Villers-Bretonneux was launched at 10 pm.

Friday 26 April

I arrived at Advanced HQ Second Army at Cassel about 1.30 pm and had a long talk with Generals Plumer and Harington (his MGGS). The French 28th Division did not fight well. We all thought Kemmel almost impregnable. Yet the place was abandoned after 2 hours' fighting. General De Mitry[2] Commanding the French Corps in Second Army had to employ French cavalry to collect the French fugitives from Kemmel, and prevent a rout.[3]

Our 25th Division (which acted under orders of the Commander of the 3 French II Cavalry Corps, General Robillot)[4] attacked as ordered, took all objectives, but was not supported on its right by the French. The latter were to attack at the same time but they did nothing!...

Plumer reported to me that Enemy had taken Voormezeele and were north of Kemmel. In view of this, he had decided to withdraw to the Ypres Canal line, leaving outposts on the Pilkem Ridge line. I told him that my Army Commander on the spot could decide when the moment had come to retire. Looking at the points already reached by the Enemy south of Ypres, I considered that the time had come to retire from the salient and I concurred in the dispositions that he had ordered...

I next ... visited the HQ of the American Division which has recently arrived. I saw the Chief of Staff (Colonel Booth).[5] The General (Johnston)[6] was out. I was told that the division *must* have 30 days' training before they move at all. There is a considerable percentage of recruits in each battalion who joined just before the division sailed. I asked if they could not send the battalions to join British Brigades with their fit men sooner, and leave the recruits to continue their training at the depôt. This was considered impossible. I found all very pleasant, but very ignorant of the present situation.

1 Major General Sir William ('Billy') Charles Giffard Heneker (1867–1939), GOC 8th Division, 1915–18.
2 General M. Henri De Mitry (18??–19??), later GOC French Ninth Army.
3 The German capture of Mont Kemmel proved to be their last success in Operation *Georgette*.
4 General Robillot (1857–1924).
5 Colonel E. Booth, Chief of Staff 77th US Division.
6 Brigadier General Evan M. Johnston.

Saturday 27 April

Haig attended a high-level conference at Abbeville.

Clemenceau began by complaining that he had learnt from General Foch that the British and American Governments had concluded an agreement (unknown to the French) by which all American troops now arriving were to go to the British, etc., etc. Milner quickly explained that he had merely bound General Pershing down in writing to sending 120,000 infantry and machine-gunners (for which Great Britain had found the ships) to the British during May. If he had not done so, Pershing would have sent over divisions complete with artillery, transport, etc., which are not wanted at this moment. Clemenceau at once acquiesced, but said he would like subsequent arrangements with the Americans settled by the three Governments together. This was concurred in by Milner . . .

The question of the transfer of tired British Divisions to a quiet sector in the French front was brought up by Milner, who said that the British Army must not be 'scattered all over the French front'! To this Foch and Clemenceau said nothing would be done without my approval, and in any case divisions would be kept together as a corps . . . Wilson tried to get an expression of opinion from Foch as to whether he intended to defend the Channel ports, or fall back on the Somme if the Allied Army were pressed back after suffering heavy losses. Foch would not say any more than that he intended to keep the two Armies (French and British) united.

Sunday 28 April

Haig met Milner.

I gave the latter a note with reference to a statement by Mr Bonar Law in the House of Commons in which he declared that the extension of the British lines had been arranged between the Commanders in France without interference by the British Government. My note showed clearly how on 25 September last a conference (at which I was not present) was held at Boulogne, and the British and French Governments decided on *the principle* that the British should take over more line! To this I protested. Today I told Lord Milner I did not wish to embarrass the Government at this time, but I must ask that a true statement of the facts be filed in the War Office. Milner said he would be glad to do this, and that he recollected very well 'how all along I had objected to any extension. And that it was his opinion that if we had not taken over some line from the French, the blow would have fallen on them and the war would now have been well-nigh lost!' He (Milner) wishes to throw the blame on no one, but is quite ready to accept all blame himself. 'Unfortunately,' said he, 'some of the members of the Cabinet are not so constituted'!!

Milner has given me a very favourable impression as Secretary of State for War. He spent all yesterday afternoon and this morning in the offices at GHQ learning all he can; his one idea seems to be to be as helpful as possible.

Wednesday 1 May

Lunched early and arrived Abbeville in time for Conference at 2 pm. Lloyd George did not turn up till nearly 3 pm. I was therefore able to have a meeting with Foch at which Weygand, Pétain, Lawrence and Du Cane were present. Foch and I were in complete agreement. I recognised the difficulty he was in to find reserves at the *decisive* point, and said I would do my best to exchange tired British Divisions for fresh French ones which would be brought to the battle area as soon as possible. I said that I would detail 4 divisions to go to the French front as soon as possible. Then 2 more, but after that it would depend on the development of the situation whether I could spare any more.

At the Conference of the Supreme War Council a great deal of time was wasted discussing the agreement made by Lord Milner and General Pershing regarding bringing 120,000 American Infantry to France in May to join the British Army. I thought Pershing was very obstinate, and stupid. He did not seem to realise the urgency of the situation.

Finally, the arrangement for May is to hold good and Pershing is to decide in a fortnight whether the same arrangement will continue for June. He hankers after a *'great self contained American Army'* but seeing that he has neither Commanders of Divisions, of Corps, nor of Armies, nor Staffs for same, it is ridiculous to think such an Army could function alone in less than 2 years' time!

Thursday 2 May

Haig attended a conference at Abbeville.

We discussed the strategical objectives of the Allied Armies in France. We were all agreed that: (1) touch with the French and British Armies must be maintained, and (2) that the Channel ports must be covered. If, however, circumstances required the C-in-C to decide between the two objects, then rather than allow the Armies to be separated, a retirement would be made southwards towards the Somme. But Foch expressed himself as quite certain that this would not be necessary. He was most confident, but asked for more labour to dig lines of defence.

I then left. M. Clemenceau, Lloyd George and Lord Milner were to discuss privately who was to succeed Foch if anything happened to him. I told Milner that the best arrangement would be to decide that the C-in-C of the French Army would be *ipso facto*, 'Generalissimo' (because the latter must be a Frenchman in France). Foch then would be C-in-C French Army as well as 'Generalissimo' and have the GQG under him. At present he lacks a Staff, and in consequence he and Weygand are over worked. Having given Foch a Staff we get continuity. Then the French Government should be asked to nominate (privately) either Anthoine or Pétain to be Foch's successor in case of necessity. Milner agreed and said he would express my views . . .

The PM, Lord Milner and General Wilson stayed the night. General Hankey came to dinner, also AG and QMG.[1] I thought Lloyd George looked less worried than when he last visited France. Indeed, he seemed in good spirits and made himself most pleasant to all. I gathered from a talk with Wilson and Milner, that Clemenceau would not consider the question of a possible successor to Foch, and further the French have ideas of increasing Foch's responsibilities by giving him charge of operations in Salonika, Egypt, Palestine, Mesopotamia, etc. This would be very foolish in my opinion, because Foch's strength is already severely strained with his duties on the Western Front. The Italians are ready to place their Army under him, but they get something from the French in exchange!

Sunday 5 May

I received Sir E. Kemp (agent of the Canadian Government in London) . . . The Canadian Government is anxious to have a Canadian *Army* and to this end hopes that the four Canadian Divisions will be employed *together*. I told him that my intention was to keep them united, and only extreme urgency would make me depart from that principle. Kemp was very friendly, but from some of the remarks which fell from him inadvertently I could not help feeling that some people in Canada regard themselves rather as 'allies' than fellow citizens in the Empire!

Tuesday 7 May

All . . . indications point to an attack as imminent – say on Saturday 11th if weather in the meantime is fine. I estimate that the enemy might attack

1. From about Albert to Neuville Vitasse, a front of 18 miles (about) with say 18 divisions in front supported by 12 = 30

---

1 AG (Fowke) and QMG (Travers Clarke).

2. Astride the Scarpe, 7 miles of front, say 7 divisions supported by 4 = 11
3. Givenchy and astride La Bassée Canal, say 5 divisions = 5

Roughly 50 divisions for an attack. Of these only 16 will be fresh and will not have been engaged in battle.

Our troops are very confident, positions have been well organised, troops are fairly fresh on this front, know the ground, and reserves are at hand. None of us are therefore anxious about the result.

General Bonham Carter (Director of Training)[1] reported on the arrangements made to receive and train the Americans. We are using the cadres of our 39th, 66th, 30th and 34th Divisions to help in the training of the infantry of 4 American Divisions. I impressed on Bonham Carter that our officers are not to command, and order the Americans about, but only to *help* American officers by their advice and experience to become both *leaders* in the field, as well as *instructors*. For the moment, *training as leaders* should take the first place.

Tuesday 7 May. Letter to Lady Haig

Major General Sir Frederick Maurice, until recently the Director of Military Operations, wrote to The Times *accusing Lloyd George of lying to Parliament on 9 April about the manpower available to the BEF. Maurice believed that the Prime Minister was not merely attempting to protect himself from blame for the German successes in France, but was attacking Haig as a preliminary to dismissing him.*[2]

Reuter states General Maurice has written to the papers. This is a grave mistake. No one can be both a soldier and a politician at the same time. We soldiers have to do our duty, and keep silent, trusting to Ministers to protect us.

Wednesday 8 May

Haig visited formation HQs, and drew the following conclusions:

1. Latest Drafts are young, but men have been well trained. They lack muscle, but have fought well. One officer said they are 'like the young soldiers at Waterloo, and will again save the Empire'. Artillery are fresh.

1 Major General (later General Sir) Charles Bonham Carter (1876–1955), BGGS (Training) GHQ, 1917–18.
2 N. Maurice (ed.), *The Maurice Case* (London: Leo Cooper, 1972), p. 132.

2. Our positions are strong, and all would like the Enemy to attack!
3. The divisions I visited are all in V Corps (General Shute).[1] They have been directed by him to hold their fronts with portions of 3 brigades, instead of having 2 brigades in front line, and one in reserve. *I think it is unsound to have 3 brigades all in front*, because the 3 battalions in reserve belong to different brigades and there is no Brigade Staff to command there in case of necessity. Also it is not possible to rest a Brigade Staff with all 3 in the line.

Saturday 11 May. Letter to Lady Haig

Many thanks for telling me what the gossips say about my being selected to succeed Field Marshal *French as C-in-C Home Forces. As you know I am ready to serve wherever the Government thinks fit to send me, and I don't want to stay here a day longer than the Government have confidence in me. At the same time, I think that they will find it difficult to find a successor *at this moment.* I only say this to you of course.[2]

Poor Maurice! How terrible to see the House of Commons so easily taken in by a clap trap speech by Lloyd George. The House is really losing its reputation as an assembly of common sense Britishers. However, I don't suppose that Maurice has done with LG yet.[3]

Tuesday 14 May

Haig visited Horne at First Army.

He spoke to me about Maxse who commands the XVIII Corps. When he arrived he made difficulties: and after his troops had been in the line a few days, he said that unless he got 2 more divisions he would not be responsible for the front. Horne told him that his Corps was considerably stronger than the Canadians whom he had relieved, and that there were no more troops to give him. If his dispositions were not satisfactory, it was his (Maxse's) fault, and if he still felt that he could not hold his front let him say so, and another Corps Commander would be put in to relieve him at once. Maxse's tone at

1 Lieutenant General (later General Sir) Cameron Deane Shute ('Tiger') (1866–1936), GOC V Corps, 1918–19.
2 Haig was correct: the absence of an heir apparent was an important factor in staying the hand of the Government.
3 In the 'Maurice Debate' of 9 May 1918 Lloyd George deployed all his oratorical brilliance and sophistry to destroy the case against him. The PM thus turned a situation that threatened his hold on power into a rout, not only of Maurice, but also of his political opponents such as Asquith.

once changed! I asked Horne not to judge Maxse too quickly but if he found he could not work in sympathy with Maxse, I would arrange to change him.[1]

Thursday 16 May

Cox reports Enemy's divisions on Western Front have now risen to 208 ... Cox considers Enemy is training, getting up ammunition etc. and possibly waiting for Tanks.

General Foch and Weygand arrived a little before 12 o'clock. Foch is very anxious that no divisions should be reduced: he is sure that, out of the 1,400,000 men wearing khaki in England, 100,000 could be obtained to fill out nine divisions sufficiently to hold a quiet part of the front, and release fresh French Divisions for the General Reserve. So I agree to write a letter to our War Office men for men of the lower class than 'A' men for this purpose. Clemenceau is also to press on the Prime Minister the urgent need of sending soldiers to France.[2]

Friday 17 May

I motored with Lawrence to HQ Fourth Army at Flixécourt and had a long talk with Rawlinson ... He thinks the Enemy will attack from Albert northwards as far as Arras. I told Rawlinson to begin studying in conjunction with General Debeney the question of an attack eastwards from Villers-Bretonneux, in combination with an attack from the French front south of Roye. I gave him details of scheme.[3]

At Bertangles (HQ Australian Corps) I saw General Birdwood, and had a long talk with him and his Staff. The Australian Corps is diminishing owing to lack of drafts. He does not think Enemy means to attack his front at the present time.

It was now about 1.30 and I lunched in a field near Allonville. At 2.15 I attended parade of the 10 Brigade 3rd Australian Division east of the latter village. General Monash commands division and McNicoll[4] the brigade. About 2 miles further on, I inspected the 11 Brigade under Brigadier General

1 Maxse left XVIII Corps on 23 June to become Inspector General of Training, a post he filled with some distinction.
2 Clemenceau believed, erroneously, that the British were holding back fit soldiers from the front line.
3 This scheme eventually bore fruit as the Battle of Amiens in August.
4 Brigadier General Walter Ramsay McNicoll (1877–1947), GOC 10 Australian Brigade, 1916–18; a headmaster by profession.

Cannan.¹ In both cases I walked down the front rank and returned through the centre of the masses, i.e. between the 2nd and 3rd platoons. I thus got an additional view of the men. Troops then marched past. It was a grand sight. Troops marched well, and were well turned out. The transport too was well cleaned and animals well groomed and in good condition. The Australian is a different individual now to when he first came, both in discipline and smartness. Altogether it was a most inspiring sight. I said a few words to each of the Battalion Commanders after the parade, and urged tactical training of Battalion and Company officers.

At St Gratian HQ 2nd Australian Division, I saw General Smyth and his Staff officers. This division holds front from Ancre to Somme [running along the] high ground. All very fit and in good heart.

Saturday 18 May. Letter to Sir Henry Wilson²

As regards the refusal of the Army Council to permit me to make use of the Fifth Army HQ and Staff by declining to sanction an Army Commander, I wired to WO yesterday. Additional reasons must be apparent, such as great fatigue produced in Army Commander and Army Staffs by these long continuous battles, so that even if my line was not the length it is, a spare Army Commander and Staff is a necessity. The fact too of having so many French Divisions moving about and cantoned in our Army areas, also adds to Staff work very much and obliges us to reduce Army areas if possible.

Monday 20 May

At Pernes I spent ¾ hour with General Currie (Commanding Canadian Corps) and his Staff. Three [Canadian] Divisions are now out of the line in reserve, and Currie fully realises the need for putting them into the battle as required, even though the whole Corps may not be [employed] together. He assured me that I could rely on him and his divisions to do their best, however employed! The divisions are now training and are 50 per cent better than when they first came out of the line...

Headquarters 3rd Division at La Beuvrière. Major General Deverell, Commanding Division, told me of his fighting south of Arras and then north of Lys. He spoke of the fine performance of the last drafts of young soldiers. [Our] main difficulty now is the lack of trained Battalion and Company Commanders.

1 Brigadier General James Harold Cannan ('The Bull') (1882–1976), GOC 11 Australian Brigade, 1916–18.
2 IWM: Wilson Papers, HHW 2/7A/27.

That evening Wilson, the CIGS, visited GHQ.

He seems anxious to do the right thing. He told me that Cabinet would not consider Robertson for appointment as C-in-C Home Forces vice French (Lord Lieutenant of Ireland) because Robertson is thought to be mixed up with Maurice and the letter he wrote to the papers, as well as with Repington and others hostile to the present Government. Nor did the Cabinet desire to replace me in France and give me the Home Command. So no one has been chosen yet!

Tuesday 21 May

On a visit to 77th US Division, Haig spoke to Brigadier General Wittenmyer.[1]

An old regular officer of 30 years' service: he was at West Point in 1887 and is very old for his years both physically and mentally. At first he spoke to me as if he felt that he was being hurried in the training and pressed to go into the battle before his men were adequately trained. But after I had been with him half an hour he saw that I did not want him to do impossibilities. For he then said that he was ready to do whatever I thought right, only he begged me to leave my officers and NCOs (who were helping his troops) 'because it would be little short of murder to send his men into the trenches in their present state, without them!' ... This division comes from New York State, and I was told that there are 18 nationalities represented in it.

Monday 27 May

Four British divisions, tired from battles in the north, were sent down to the French sector to hold a supposedly quiet area near the Aisne. Along with French forces, they faced a major German offensive. The Allies were mal-deployed by Duchêne, the commander of French Sixth Army. The British fought well, but the Germans broke through and headed for the Marne.

Our IX Corps (Hamilton Gordon) on Aisne reported at 11.45 pm last night indications pointed to strong hostile attack at dawn.

At 1.30 am he reported heavy shelling on whole Corps front began at 1 am.

At 3.30 am Enemy attacked upon the whole of our IX Corps front, and on front of the French Divisions on our right and left ... Cox in his report on the situation commented on the failure of French GHQ to get early news

---

1 Brigadier General (later Major General) Edmund Wittenmyer (1862–1937), later GOC US 7th Division.

of the coming attack on the Chemin des Dames ... The French air service does not seem to be very energetic or persevering at the present time, because yesterday, in spite of our warnings, GQG replied that there were no signs of an impending attack! and the blow fell at 3.30 am today!

Tuesday 28 May

Cox considers that we must expect a small attack on the Hazebroucke[1] front, possibly combined with a renewal of the attack on the Scherpenberg etc. I am inclined to think this opinion is based on evidence received before Enemy succeeded in breaking in the Aisne front. Now he will, in my opinion, devote all his energy and divisions to exploiting his success. While securing his flank towards Rheims, he will press vigorously west against French flank, in combination with frontal attacks (as progress is made) towards Compiègne.

Friday 31 May

I saw Military Secretary who gave me an advanced copy of *London Gazette* (King's Birthday). Very little attention had been paid to my recommendations, and some few officers have been promoted by *seniority*: not by selection with a view to getting the best men to the top ...
 ... [A]fter lunch I had a talk with Foch. Present were Lawrence, Weygand and Du Cane. We spoke of the possibility of supporting the French with some divisions. I said it all depended on the situation on my front and read a translation of my note on the question. Foch also said that Pétain had asked for American Divisions to be sent him (no matter how untrained), to hold long fronts (25 kilometres) on the Swiss frontier, and release French Divisions. I gave some good reasons against the proposal, but said I would consider the matter and reply on Saturday (tomorrow). I also promised to go into the possibilities of forming a corps of 3 divisions as a Reserve to support the French in case of grave emergency.
 While we were talking a message came from Pétain asking Foch to meet him near Meaux, and stating that M. Clemenceau, the French Prime Minister, would be there too. Foch told me that the situation was anxious: the reserves which had been sent forward had 'melted away very quickly' and I gathered that the French troops were not fighting well. Foch and Weygand started at once. I thought Foch looked more anxious than I have ever seen him.

Lloyd George, Sir Eric Geddes (First Lord of the Admiralty) and Admiral Wemyss (First Sea Lord), visited Haig at a hotel in Paris.

1 Properly, 'Hazebrouck'.

After dinner they came and discussed the holding of Dunkirk till I was thoroughly tired of them. Fortunately an air raid started and the lights went out. After a period (as I am a privileged visitor) my lights were put on again and Geddes left!

Saturday 1 June

The Supreme War Council met at Versailles.

We discussed the size of American Army and it was agreed that President of USA should be asked to aim at having 100 divisions! By when? As soon as possible. I suggested a definite *organised force* by 1st May next.

The French suddenly asked Lloyd George last night to agree to send all American troops now with British to hold extended sectors in French area and relieve French Divisions for battle. I said that it would be very wrong to employ these new troops in the way proposed by the French, because, being on so wide a front, the companies would never get a chance of getting together and training. I hoped to quicken up the training of the Americans, and to render 4 divisions fit for the line by the middle of June.

In discussing this problem, I pointed out that the most important fact to know was whether the French Army was fighting or not. From what I heard from Foch and Weygand I inferred that French reserves once in the battle did not last out but 'melted away': this was due to coddling them last summer, and to want of discipline [and to the lack of reliable officers and NCOs].

In view of the doubtful condition of many French Divisions I thought it a waste of good troops to relieve French Divisions by Americans . . .

About 2.30 a meeting took place in M. Clemenceau's room, at which the following were present: Lloyd George, Milner, Wilson, Hankey, Lawrence, and self for England. France was represented by Clemenceau, Foch, Weygand and Clemenceau's Military Secretary.

The question of 'effectives' was discussed at length. Foch quoted some of my statements at last Conference to the effect that if the Enemy attacked the British Army would be reduced by the autumn by 30 divisions unless something was done at once to obtain reinforcements. 'Nothing had been done', said Foch. Lloyd George denied this strongly and insisted that the British Government had made great efforts to get men before the battle of 21 March began. And so these people went on wrangling and wasting time. Finally, Foch asked 'What number of divisions will the British Government maintain?' I reminded Milner that I had been told only 28 by War Office. He said this was pessimistic. Then Lloyd George agreed that Foch should send an expert to look through the British manpower figures. This quite satisfied Clemenceau.

As regards our American Divisions going to the French, Foch said he and

I would easily settle together what was the best thing to do. So the matter was not discussed. The strength for Americans to aim at was agreed to be 100 divisions.

It was now past 4.45 pm. The large meeting which had been convened for 3 pm then took place – numerous Italians and Americans took part, and Mr Balfour (Secretary for Foreign Affairs) joined the British ...

The only subject discussed was the appointment of a Supreme Commander to control all the fleets in the Mediterranean. The Italians objected! Their object seemed to be to stay in port and keep their fleet safe. I was disgusted with their attitude. Admiral Wemyss (First Sea Lord)[1] agreed with the French Admiral. Nothing could be settled ...

Just before I came away, Wilson told me that in a conversation he and Foch had just had with Pershing, they discovered that the Americans had nearly exhausted their supply of trained men! For 2 or 3 months recruits had not been enlisted. Really the ignorance of the Americans in all things connected with an Army is appalling.

Monday 3 June

Letter arrived from Foch stating that he, with General Pershing's approval, proposed to move some of the American Divisions now in the British area to relieve French Divisions, and asking me to send an officer to GQG to discuss details ... My views are that it is a waste of valuable troops to send half trained men to relieve French Divisions. In 3 weeks' time these Americans will be fit for battle. I doubt if the French Divisions they relieve will ever fight! However, I told Foch that the American Divisions were at Pershing's disposal to do what he liked with them. The British cadres would remain with me of course, but the equipment could go if wanted.

At noon I had a meeting at Blendecque with General Plumer ... We ... discussed action to be taken if French called upon us for more troops. Plumer was opposed to falling back: and in view of possibility of Germans advancing and isolating Paris, the importance of holding a line far enough east of Dunkirk to allow port to be used fully for supplies, is apparent. I agreed that Plumer must hold his present line, but to have all plans for withdrawal worked up, and to be put into effect only if situation requires.

1 Admiral Roslyn ('Rosie') Erskine Wemyss (1864–1933), First Sea Lord, 1917–19; British representative at the Armistice negotiations.

Monday 3 June. Letter to Major S. G. Sanders, Superintendent at Remount Depot[1]

I have recently received through the Director of Remounts a particularly nice horse . . . it is thanks to your skill and care that the horse is so well broken and in good condition. I am most grateful to you for all the trouble you have taken, and am exceedingly pleased to have him. Please accept my very best thanks.

Tuesday 4 June

Telegram received from Foch asking me to place a reserve of 3 divisions astride the Somme ready to support British or French. I replied that I am complying with his order at once, but I wished to make a formal protest against any troops leaving my Command until the bulk of the reserves of Prince Rupprecht's[2] Armies had become involved in the battle. Foch has already withdrawn all French reserves, and four American Divisions are under orders to go. I repeated my telegram to Secretary of State for War for information of War Cabinet together with copy of Foch's wire . . .

The DGT (Cruickshank)[3] reported on Transportation work . . . I told Cruickshank to keep ample rolling stock for British needs in case Paris shortly comes under shell fire and French draw off our waggons to evacuate Paris etc.

Losses of our 5 divisions in the Aisne battle between 27 May and 11.30 am 2 June, amount to 24,414. One division (the 19th) has had three French Divisions relieved on each side of it since it went into battle. Our troops are being used up to the last man in order to give the French courage and fight! Hamilton Gordon commanding our IX Corps gives a dismal picture of the French troops. But this I knew in August 1914; the Somme battle confirmed my view that much of the French good name was the result of newspaper puffs! Then came *Nivelle's fiasco in the spring of 1917, and for the rest of last year the French 'rested'. And now when the result of the war depends on their 'fighting spirit' many of their divisions won't face the enemy . . .

Friday 7 June

Haig attended a conference at the French Ministry of War.

Lord Milner explained why the British PM had asked for this meeting; briefly,

1 LHCMA: Sanders Papers.
2 Crown Prince Rupprecht of Bavaria (1869–1955). As commander of the German Sixth Army and, in 1918, of Army Group Rupprecht, he often found himself opposite the BEF.
3 Actually Major General (later Sir) Sidney D'Aguilar Crookshank.

Foch had moved many reserves (French and American Divisions) from behind the British front, and, in view of the large number of Enemy reserves still available for action against the British, the Government had become genuinely anxious.

I then read my memo stating I was in full accord with Foch as to the necessity for making all preparations for moving British troops to support the French in case the necessity for doing so might arise, but I asked that I should be consulted before a definite order to move any divisions from the British area were given. [I had reported to London the telegram which I had sent to Foch] in order to warn the Government that the situation was quickly reaching a stage in which circumstances might compel me to appeal to the British Government under the Beauvais Agreement,[1] because in my opinion, the order about to be issued imperilled the British Army in France. I hoped that everything that forethought could do would be done now and in the immediate future to prevent circumstances arising which would necessitate such an appeal.

Foch stuck out for full powers as Generalissimo to order troops of any nationality wherever he thought fit and at shortest notice. Milner and Clemenceau agreed that he must have these powers, and the latter urged Foch and myself to meet more frequently. Clemenceau strongly forbade any orders being sent direct from French HQ moving French or any units in my area, without passing through my hands first of all. This was with reference to the departure of certain French Divisions and guns from DAN[2] which had been ordered direct, without even notifying General Plumer on the subject.

The effect of the Beauvais Agreement is now becoming clear in practice. This effect I had realised from the beginning, namely, that the responsibility for the safety of the British Army in France could no longer rest with me because the 'Generalissimo' can do what he thinks right with my troops. On the other hand, the British Government is only now beginning to understand what Foch's powers as Generalissimo amount to. This delegation of power to Foch is inevitable, but I intend to ask that the British Government should in a document modify my responsibility for the safety of the British Army under the altered conditions.

Tuesday 11 June

At 10 am I presided at Conference at Hesdin with Army Commanders and principal Staff officers. All Commanders were present including Birdwood

1 Of 3 April 1918.
2 *Détachement d'Armée du Nord*: a French force commanded by General De Mitry, serving with Plumer's Second Army.

Commanding Fifth Army.[1] We followed the usual procedure. First Cox gives an account of the Enemy's numbers and positions etc. Secondly, Generals Commanding Armies dealt with the situation on the front of their Army. Then I asked Army Commanders for their opinions on a memo I had issued on the principles of Defence. All agreed the principles were most sound, and had no criticism at all to offer. Lastly, I pointed out that infantry had been taught to rely too much on strong artillery barrages [to cover their advances]. They must be taught to depend more on their rifles and machine guns. I advocated tactical exercises without troops for training Company, Battalion and Brigade Commanders.

Thursday 13 June

Gemeau spoke with sadness about the poor resistance offered by the French Divisions. In his opinion the French infantry is now inferior to the German. I said 'No – only *some* French units. These want discipline and training.' He agreed, and said last year Pétain ought to have shot 2000 instead of only 30 when so many mutinied this time last year. The situation of the French Army was very grave then, and required severe measures to remove the canker. Instead of training, the men were given leave and 'repos'.

Sunday 16 June. Letter to Lady Haig

As regards Gough – I am sorry that he is talking stupidly: but I don't think it would be any use writing to him. Some of his friends are advising him to keep quiet. I am doing all I can to help him, but, as a matter of fact, some orders he issued and things he did were stupid – and anything of the nature of an enquiry would not do him any good. In my report, of course, I will give him every credit for being in a very difficult situation, and will stick up for him as I have hitherto done.

Monday 17 June

Lawrence and Sassoon returned from London. The former had seen the PM and Milner and got to understand their views. Sir Henry Wilson (CIGS) also explained their intentions. Briefly these are:

1. To support Foch to the utmost of their power, with drafts, by allowing him to move British Divisions as he deems right, etc. The Government are in full accord with all I have done, and regret greatly that we have to

---

1 Birdwood had taken command on 23 May.

subordinate our Armies in France to a French Generalissimo: but it is only a temporary arrangement, and is necessary because it is the only means of holding our own [diplomatically] at present!

2. When the present crisis is over, the Government mean to assert themselves and put the British Army on a sound footing, but the *first essential* for England is *supremacy* at sea and to secure our position in India and the East. They are prepared to leave to France and America the settlement of Luxemburg [and the Rhine frontier] and concentrate on sea power.

3. The Government has no wish at all to replace me as C-in-C in France.

Tuesday 18 June

Foch was in good form. He was pleased with the Italian situation and with the fighting qualities shewn by the American Divisions. I gathered that Pershing by his obstinacy has carried the day and that he will concentrate all his American Divisions somewhere! By next April, Pershing is to have 80 American Divisions in France. The question of providing efficient Divisional Commanders will be a difficult one for the Americans to solve...

Foch is to keep strong French reserves to cover Paris ... We also discussed the principles of defence and how to meet German methods of attack ... Foch laid great stress on holding 'the second system' (i.e. our Reserve Zone) with fresh troops, as soon as the bombardment commences. I told him that was our arrangement also, but sometimes we had not had sufficient troops for the purpose!

Saturday 22 June

QMG brought letter re. Transportation Service received from War Office. Army Council hope I will arrange to place it under QMG at early date. I replied that I proposed first to reorganise Transportation Directorate etc., and asked Sir Sam Fay (from War Office Transportation)[1] to visit my HQ and discuss one or two points. Fay is a railway manager (LNW Railway) of experience, and as we have some first rate railway officials in my Transportation Directorate it seems desirable that he should see them and arrange what should be done...

French have now 14 American Divisions with them. We have 5 divisions = total 19 American Divisions in France. Other divisions are arriving quickly.

Engineer in Chief informed me that reports have reached him regarding

1 Sir Sam Fay (1856–1953), railway administrator (general manager of the Great Central Railway since 1902) who – together with Sir Guy Granet – effectively ran Britain's temporarily nationalised wartime railways. Haig was mistaken in attributing a LNW Railway connection to Fay.

the action of the French Higher Command in the Aisne battle. Permission was refused to our IX Corps to mine the bridges over the Aisne, and prepare them for demolition until the battle began! Then our Engineers had to do this work under the fire of the Enemy, with the result that we lost some splendid officers and men, and some of the bridges were not destroyed. How little this French Army Commander seems to have known of *war*! The only sure way of acting is to prepare all bridges for destruction beforehand, and leave to the man on the spot the decision as to when to explode the mine. It is impossible in such circumstances for an order from Army Headquarters to reach the bridges in time! The Army Commander (Duchesne)[1] has been removed.

Monday 24 June

Haig inspected some units of 40th Division (23rd Lancashire Fusiliers, 10th King's Own Scottish Borderers, 18th Royal Irish Rifles, 13th Royal Inniskilling Fusiliers) which, he wrote, 'had been made up with men of "B class"'.

I saw some at drill, others musketry, one whole battalion was on parade in open order. The latter presented arms and handled their rifles well. I was greatly surprised and pleased with the class of men in the ranks. They can shoot and will hold a position, but cannot march very far, say, 5 miles slowly is the normal.

COs said that they were very pleased with their officers. Equipment is coming in well. Some few points call for attention. Some Irishmen in the KOSB. Latter regiment quelled disturbances in Dublin before the war! Highlanders in Fusilier Battalions anxious to wear their kilts again! Some are anxious as to the meaning of this measure! I told them that they are to fight to help us to prevent the Germans from getting to Calais. I think these divisions of old veterans will be a very great strength to us as they can hold 'Support lines', and if the front becomes quiet can relieve a division (for training) in the line...

Tuesday 25 June

I approved of a small offensive plan sent in by Rawlinson to improve his front south of Somme and take advantage of the low moral of the German Divisions opposite the Australians. But I told CGS to arrange for some American troops to take part: to have an adequate reserve of Tanks: and 1 Cavalry Division at hand in case Enemy is caught unawares and some units bolt.

1 Properly, General Denis Auguste Duchêne (1862–1950), GOC French Sixth Army.

Friday 28 June

Haig conferred with Foch.

Foch seemed in the best of spirits owing partly to the delay in the Enemy's
attack, partly to the success of the Italians, and largely to speech recently
made by Kühlmann in Berlin,[1] which stated that there was no hope of the
Germans ending the war by military means alone and foreshadowing the
German Government's intention of opening direct communications with the
Allied Governments.

The first question raised by Foch was the relief of the whole of the
Détachement de l'Armée du Nord as soon as possible. He said that the French
Government was alarmed about Paris and wished to have adequate reserves
to protect the capital. I pointed out that I could only relieve the DAN at
once by depleting my reserves on part of my front, that this would mean
running extra risks; if, however, Paris was really in danger the risk must be
taken. Foch said that the French Government insisted on the DAN being
withdrawn *on account of Paris.* I therefore agreed to release the divisions of
the DAN as soon as possible, and would let him have the exact dates on my
return to GHQ.

I asked Foch to arrange to place one or two good French Divisions near
Dunkirk so as to be in a position to support the Belgians in case of necessity.
He agreed with me that such a disposition was desirable, and he would try
and arrange it, but for the moment no French troops could be spared.

He asked me to arrange for an offensive at the end of August. The French
would also carry out an offensive, but not the Montdidier–Noyon project,
because it was now more important to drive the Enemy back elsewhere. I
told Foch of two small offensive projects which I contemplated carrying out
if the military situation allowed. He was pleased at my holding offensive
intentions at the present time.

Saturday 29 June

*Rawlinson, once again commanding Fourth Army, and Major General George
Read, commanding II US Corps, visited Haig to outline the plans for the
forthcoming operation.*

I suggested that one American company should be attached to each of the
attacking battalions i.e. 9 companies in all. Reed[2] at once agreed. I also dealt

1 Richard von Kühlmann (1873–1948), German Foreign Minster, July 1917–1918.
2 Properly, General George Windle Read (1860–1934). As GOC US II Corps Read collaborated
closely with the BEF.

with the concentration on airoplanes for defeating Enemy in air, and for bombing...

Letter from Pershing that all American Divisions go this month to the American area. This is referring to my letter offering to take 2 more American Divisions to equip and train.

Monday 1 July

Haig visited Australian Corps HQ.

I spent about an hour with Monash and went into every detail with him of an operation which he is shortly to carry out with the Australian Corps. Monash is a most thorough and capable Commander who thinks out every detail and leaves nothing to chance. I was greatly impressed with his arrangements. A company of American infantry (33rd Division) will be attached to each of the ten Australian Battalions detailed for the attack.

Wednesday 3 July

In Paris, Haig visited Pershing.

I was with him for well over an hour and we got on very well indeed ... We agreed about necessity for Foch having an adequate Staff [with headquarters] located in a central position, say at Chantilly. Also that Foch should have periodical meetings with his three C-in-Cs to discuss our plans. Pershing is most anxious that I should visit him at his HQ at Chaumont; I promised to do so when things are quieter. He said the French are always 'buzzing about' and he wished that the British C-in-C would come and see him!

As regards his troops taking part in operations with Australians tomorrow morning, he thought them insufficiently trained and had told Rawlinson yesterday that he did not wish them used. I asked him if he wished me to interfere in the matter, but he said 'no, that all had been settled between him and Rawlinson...'

Before dinner and again at 11 pm Lawrence (my CGS) spoke to me regarding the Americans taking part in the Australian operations ... Some 6 companies had been withdrawn; about 4 could not be withdrawn; was the operation to be stopped in order to do so? I said 'No'. 'The first essential is to improve our position east of Amiens as soon as possible. The attack must therefore be launched as prepared even if a few American detachments cannot be got out before zero hour.'

Mr Serjeant, the painter,[1] came to dinner and stayed the night.

Thursday 4 July. 'American Independence Day'

The action at Hamel was a model operation that, by intelligently combining all arms, prefigured the major battle fought a month later near Amiens.

The attack by 10 battalions of the Australian Corps preceded by some 60 Tanks was entirely successful this morning. Reports up to midday state that over 1100 prisoners taken and [our] casualties under 500. Our line has been advanced on a front of 4 miles to a depth of $1\frac{1}{2}$ miles, and village of Hamel and the ridge to the east of it captured. This greatly strengthens our positions on the Villers-Bretonneux ridge.

Cox reported on the situation. Enemy's preparations for an attack on Kemmel front are still being pushed [forward], and also on the Scarpe front. We estimate that his arrangements cannot be ready for another ten days about. Enemy's vigorous counter-attacks on the hill northwest of Albert which we took and he retook 2 days ago seem to show that he attaches much importance to his present bridgehead on the Ancre. So I fancy he intends to attack *sometime* on the front Arras–Albert. South of Albert the Enemy does not seem to be in force though he is working on his narrow gauge railways. French expect to be attacked on the 6th in Champagne.

Friday 5 July

I presided at a conference of Army Commanders at Hesdin at 10 am. I saw Sir Henry Rawlinson $\frac{1}{4}$ hour before the Conference. He wished me to approve of him making another attack south of the Somme to advance his line still further. I did not approve of his proposal, because it would result (if successful) in extending our line, and also because my present reserves are small! I told him however to study the problem, and prepare a plan, in case troops should become available.

At the Conference . . . we considered the work of the new Inspector General of Training and his Staff. I pointed out that this appointment in no way affected the responsibility of the various 'Commanders' for the efficiency of their units in every respect: the IG was there to assist and to report. All agreed that the IG and his Staff were much needed and they would do all they could to help him in his work . . .

1 Properly John Singer Sargent (1856–1925). Sargent, whose parents were American, had been commissioned to paint a large canvas symbolising British–US collaboration; instead he painted the famous *Gassed*.

I spoke to General Horne (First Army) re. putting the Canadians back into the line. Two divisions have been out of the line for nearly two months ... I subsequently saw Generals Byng and Horne together and told them to consider a plan for retaking Orange Hill (west of Monchy le Preux near Arras) ... The attacking troops will consist of 4 Canadian Divisions and 3 or 4 more divisions with Tanks etc. The attack will be under one Army Commander probably First Army, but this and the modification of the Army boundary will be settled when I have received Byng's and Horne's reports.

Haig went home on leave on 6 July.

Saturday 6 July. Letter to Sir Hubert Gough

My dear Hubert,

I duly received your letter of June 21, and am sorry that I have not been able to reply to it before now as we have been having rather busy times here.

You ask me regarding my report on the operations of the Fifth Army in the month of March last. I was asked by the War Office on 6 April, to send in answers to certain questions, such as the distribution of my reserves, condition of the defences, causes which led to the rapid passage of the Crozat Canal and the Somme, the arrangements made for the destruction of certain bridges, for co-operation with the French, state of discipline and training of the troops, etc. To these questions I replied on the 12 May, and I see that in my reply I never once mentioned your name. Briefly, I stated that detailed reports had been called for, but had not, at the time I wrote my report, been received. These will be embodied in a despatch which is now nearly complete, and will, I presume, be published in the newspapers.

As regards my report which I sent in on May 12, I may say, for your own personal information, that I stated that the following facts stand out: Both on the morning of 21 March and the morning of 22 March there was a thick mist. This mist masked the fire of our infantry and machine gunners, and prevented the signals of batteries and observers being seen. The very dry season had rendered the valley of the River Oise fordable in many places. There were, moreover, insufficient troops to hold our defences continuously. Under these circumstances, the enemy was able to penetrate our line in certain places unseen, and to these reasons may be attributed the enemy's initial success and our inability to hold our battle defences until the scheme for bringing up French reserves on to the battlefield could be put into execution.

I hope this will put your mind at rest regarding the nature of my report. I send you this for your personal information and not for publication of course. When my despatch is published, you will, naturally, be free to do what you like, but I strongly recommend you to remain quiet and not stir up an agitation, because, even though an officer has right on his side, it does not in the least mean that he will get what he wants. The Government has a perfect right to send any one of us away at a moment's notice without giving us any reason beyond saying that they are not satisfied with us. Indeed, if any authority finds he does not work in sympathy with any of his subordinates, he is perfectly justified, in the interests of the Country, to dispense with the services of that subordinate. I regard the conduct of the Government towards you in that light.

During the winter I was on several occasions cross-questioned as to your military qualities, and, as I told you, always replied that I was thoroughly satisfied. The failure of the Fifth Army to hold its position on 21 March, even though there are many good reasons why it was forced to fall back, has furnished the Government with a reason for ordering me to send you home. That being the case, I strongly recommend you to remain quiet until more history is made and the events of 21 March and following days have faded somewhat from the memory of the people at home. Then, I hope, there may be a chance of getting you back to some active appointment.

With every good wish and hoping it won't be long before we are soldiering again together.

Friday 12 July

Haig visited Lord Esher.

Incidentally he mentioned that soon after Foch was appointed Generalissimo, the French were anxious to abolish all Commanders-in-Chief and to create instead Commanders of 'Army Groups'. It seems they feared that as the American Army increased in numbers, so Pershing would become more dictatorial and Foch's position would become very difficult. At the outset too the French knew that there would be friction between the GQG (i.e. Pétain) and Foch, and it was never thought that I and Foch would get on as well as we do. Now, the Allied Governments are quite determined to retain their Commanders-in-Chief, in addition to the Generalissimo.

Sunday 14 July

Apparently, without any definite facts to go on, Foch has made up his mind that the Enemy's main attack is about to fall on the French in the east of Rheims. Lawrence saw him at his HQ at Bombon last Friday and, as a result of their talk, a second British Division was moved south of the Somme as a reserve to the left of the French.

But before Lawrence could get back to GHQ, Foch, evidently becoming still more anxious, ordered by cipher wire (about midday Saturday) a first instalment of British reserves to be sent to the Champagne sector. This is to consist of a Corps HQ and 4 divisions. Two divisions are leaving today and will detrain southeast of Châlons. Foch also asks me to prepare for the dispatch of a second group of 4 divisions! And all this when there is nothing definite to show that the Enemy means to attack in Champagne. Indeed Prince Rupprecht still retains 25 divisions in reserve on the British front.

But Foch has completely changed his view of the situation and strategical plan. On 1 July he issued 'Directive Générale No. 4'. In this he stated that 'Paris and Abbeville' were to be covered before anything else. 'The advance of the Enemy must be stopped at all costs in these two directions.' Consequently we must concentrate our force on the front 'Lens–Château-Thierry ...' And now we are sending our reserves (of which we have very few) right away to the east of France, by Foch's bidding on Saturday 13th.

I at once arrange to see Foch as soon as possible in order to find out what has happened to him or his Government! I also write a letter to General Foch in which I set out the position on the British front and end up by saying that 'I am averse to dispatching any troops to Champagne at the present moment. I adhere to my previous opinion [that we ought to be prepared to meet] minor operations in Champagne and Flanders to disperse and absorb Allies' reserves, and subsequently the main blow in the centre, i.e. between Lens and Château-Thierry.'

Monday 15 July

The Second Battle of the Marne, the final German offensive of 1918, began near Rheims.

Telephone message from CIGS was received during the night to the following effect: War Cabinet had discussed Foch's orders for moving British reserves to east of France. They feel anxiety that Rupprecht has large reserves left and will attack the British front, and it is directed 'that if you consider the British Army is endangered or if you think that General Foch is not acting solely on military considerations, they (the War Cabinet) rely on the exercise of your judgement, under the Beauvais Agreement, as to the security of the British front after the removal of these troops. General Smuts on behalf of the Imperial War Cabinet will proceed to GHQ today (Monday) to confer with you on your return from Beauvais' ...

I note that the Government now tells me 'to use my judgement' in obeying *orders* given me by 'the Generalissimo of the Allied Armies'. On 7 June at the Conference in Paris of the Secretary of State for War (Milner) with Foch and

Clemenceau, we were confronted by a similar concrete case, and I put the definite question, 'If General Foch orders me to move my reserves south of the Somme, is it permissible for me to delay to carry out Foch's orders until I have referred to the British Government?' Foch objected and said he could not be Generalissimo on such terms. And so I was directed to obey all his orders at once, and notify War Cabinet if I took exception to any of them.

On the other hand, Milner's instructions to me dated 22 June 1918, lay down, 'You will carry out loyally any instructions issued to you by the C-in-C Allied Forces. At the same time, if any order given by him appears to you to imperil the British Army, you should appeal to the British Government before executing such order.' This is a case of 'heads you win, and tails I lose'! If things go well, the Government take credit to themselves and the Generalissimo: if badly, the Field Marshal will be blamed!

What I have done in the present case is to start to carry out the order with two divisions and Corps HQ and to prepare 2 more divisions to follow, but I forbid the latter move to be carried out until I have seen Foch.

Gemeau translates my letter to Foch into French, and about 10 am I leave with Lawrence for Mouchy le Châtel. We get there just after 1 o'clock and lunch with Foch who had sent on a special meal from his HQ at Bombon for us. Foch was in the best of spirits. He told me that after three hours' bombardment, the Enemy had attacked at 4 am this morning on two fronts east and west of Rheims. East of Rheims on a front of 26 miles, and west of Rheims on a front of 29 miles. A front of 16 miles about Rheims itself was not attacked. The total front attacked seems therefore to be about 55 miles. East of Rheims the attack was held and the Enemy only gained the 'outpost zone'. Southwest of Rheims the Enemy crossed the Marne, and had advanced three to five miles in places. Château-Thierry was strongly held by Americans, and further eastwards an American Division had counter-attacked and driven Enemy back into the river, taking 1000 prisoners. So altogether the situation was satisfactory, and a weight was taken off Foch's mind who feared an attack as far east as Verdun, where he had no reserves. The British 4 divisions had first of all been ordered to detrain near Châlons: now that the Enemy's attack had been defined, the divisions were ordered to detrain further west, at Ronille and Pont sur Seine.

I put my case strongly to Foch why I was averse to moving my reserves from my front until I knew that Rupprecht's reserves had been moved to the new battle front ... Prisoners and deserters stated that an attack on the Lys salient was to be ready mounted by the 18th inst. ... these facts and many others pointed to the *intention* of the Enemy to attack the British some time soon.

Foch agreed with me but said his first object was to hold up the present attack at all costs as soon as possible. He only wanted my divisions as a reserve in case of necessity, and they would be in a position *ready to return to me at once* in case the British front was threatened. Under these circumstances, I agreed to send the next 2 divisions as arranged. I read my letter to Foch and left him a copy so that he could have my statements on record in writing.

Tuesday 16 July

Haig visited HQ of Fourth Army, and spoke to Rawlinson.

I told him of the orders which I had given to Horne and Byng this forenoon, to prepare to make certain attacks. The preparations for these attacks, I hoped, would attract the attention of the Enemy from the *main operation* on my front, which would be carried out by his (the Fourth) Army. It was my intention, if the situation became favourable, that the Fourth Army's right should be pushed forward to the River Luce, say near Caix. Thence the line would run northwards through Harbonnières to Chipilly on the Somme. I proposed to ask Foch to order the French Army on our right to co-operate by an attack advancing northeastwards on the south of Moreuil, so as to co-operate with us and pinch the salient formed by the Rivers Luce and Avre between the villages of Caix and Pierrepont.

Wednesday 17 July

General Du Cane came from General Foch's HQ ... Du Cane brought me a letter from Foch asking my opinion on the situation ... All reports showed that an attack on the Meteren–Ypres front might be expected in the near future. After doing my utmost to collect troops I would only have 9 divisions in front, and 6 in support to meet the Enemy's attack. I therefore requested the return of the 4 British Divisions now with the French in the Marne battle area, as well as the brigade of airoplanes. Two of the divisions in support were half trained Americans, and another division was one of the 2nd class category B men.

On 18 July two French armies, which included some US divisions, counter-attacked on the Marne and achieved major success. British XXII Corps entered the fighting on 20 July. By 2 August, the strategic initiative had passed decisively to the Allies.

Friday 19 July

Major General Newbourn[1] (Minister for Defence) and Colonel Ballantyne[2] (Minister of Marine) Canada, came to see me about 1 o'clock, and stayed to lunch. Both well meaning but second rate sort of people: at least the Major General is that, Ballantyne seemed to me a superior type to him. After talking on general topics for a short time, Newbourn said to me that he wished to let me know privately 'that there is a good deal of feeling amongst Canadians because the Canadian Corps is not altogether under their Corps Commander Currie' ... The 3rd Canadian Division, though next to the other Canadian Divisions, is in Third Army area, and so not administered by the Canadian Corps.

I at once told the Canadian Minister that the British Army alone and unaided [by Canadian troops] withstood the first terrific blow made by 80 German Divisions on 21 March until 27 May when the Aisne attack was launched: that since March units of the British Army had been constantly engaged until the present moment, when 4 British Divisions are fighting in the battle on the Marne. *During all this severe fighting the Canadian Corps has not once been engaged.* Why? Because the Canadian Government only wished it to be engaged as a corps! I was on the point of employing Canadian Divisions in the battle: they would have had to go into the fight separately to start with; but a wire arrived from the War Office emphasising Canadian Government's desire to fight together, so I at once put the Canadian Divisions back into the line, and employed British Divisions!

These remarks of mine at once made the Canadian Minister of Militia shut up, and he became quite bearable. I sent them off to start their lunch, while I went upstairs and washed my hands. When I joined them again in the dining room, I found Newbourn a changed individual! and when he was going away he said 'My only object is to do all Canada can to support Great Britain at this time of trial.'

Friday 19 July. Letter to Lady Haig

Very pleased to get yours of Wednesday, and to see that the Government at last means to look after the claims of Disabled Officers, although they cannot yet decide how exactly they will proceed in the matter. The Officer Class is now very different to what it was in the case of the old regular Army. Now the Officer in many cases has risen from the ranks, and in most cases is quite

---

1 Properly Major General Hon. Sidney Chilton Mewburn (1863–1956), Canadian Minister of Militia and Defence, 1917–20.
2 Hon. Charles Colquhoun Ballantyne (1867–1950), Canadian Minister of Marine and Fisheries, 1917–20.

without means outside his pay. They are also very numerous, about 90,000 in France alone. So you will thus see that the suffering after the war will be very great indeed unless something is arranged soon for their benefit. You are doing splendid work my darling, in interesting yourself so intensely in their claims ... I still expect to be attacked on the Hazebroucke–Ypres front. But we ought to hold the Enemy all right I think.

Sunday 21 July

Yesterday our XXII Corps (51st and 62nd Divisions) attacked by passing throughout the front of the Italian Corps and took Marfaux village (southwest of Rheims). Very hard fighting took place ... Our troops attacked although tired and without any delay in order to take advantage of the situation. Enemy's primary object seems to be to keep the base of the Château-Thierry salient as wide as possible, and with this object he has been counter-attacking southwest of Soissons, and southwest of Rheims, about Marfaux village, where our XXII Corps is engaged ... Evening reports state our 'troops have done their job well'.

General Henry Wilson arrived from England in time for dinner. Also General Du Cane from General Foch's HQ. The former told me that War Office had decided to retain battalions at 900 strong. It was not known what number of divisions could be kept up; he thought about 40 more or less.

He thinks LG means to stop 'combing out' the home industries very soon, and will have an election in the autumn.

I had a talk with Du Cane and Lawrence, and explained my plans in reply to a letter received from Foch. In view of Rupprecht's large reserves, I cannot attack on the Kemmel front unless the Enemy first attacks and is repulsed. If his reserves remain on my front, I will carry out local attacks: if they go, I am preparing an operation in the south, which I would launch if Enemy's reserves are drawn off.

Tuesday 23 July

As we are fairly well prepared to meet an attack by Rupprecht upon my Second Army, it is most likely that the attack won't be delivered. So I am prepared to take the offensive, and have approved of an operation taking place on Rawlinson's front, and steps have been taken to make preparations very secretly in order to be ready (should the battle, now being fought out on the Marne, cause the situation to turn in our favour).

Sir Henry Wilson arrived from Versailles at 1 o'clock ... I gave back to

Wilson a proposed draft of an amended letter of Instructions to me as C-in-C France. The change was to the effect that I should proceed to carry out *all* orders received from Foch, even though the safety of the Army should be endangered thereby, and complain afterwards! I pointed out that if an officer was fit to be given the appointment of C-in-C[1] he ought to be able to use his discretion in a question of this nature. So he decided to leave the Instructions as they now are.

Wednesday 24 July. Letter to Sir Henry Wilson[2]

Just a line to tell you that nothing startling happened at the meeting at Foch's HQ today.

Pétain and Pershing were also present. I dined with the latter last night. He is forming 2 American Armies at once – one a 'Battle Army' on the Marne; the other an Army of 'repos' near St Mihiel. I expect that their rôles are likely to change with one another!

Pershing is also ready and keen to employ all his Americans in a *vigorous* offensive this autumn . . .

. . . Foch . . . outlined the *general* plan for the next few weeks, to which each of us could agree at once, namely

a) regain the initiative, and
b) clear the main railway lines, with a view to further operations. Certain points were indicated which it is best to not put on paper.

Then on to next year's plan, Foch asked for answers to certain questions regarding our reserves.

We of course have the number of divisions which each Army will be able to keep up next January and next March! This I will send on to you officially of course.

I thought them all in great spirits.

The General Staff of the War Office issued a document, dated 25 July 1918, entitled British Military Policy 1918–1919. *This concluded that there was little chance of breaking the stalemate in France before mid-1919, and that prospects in other theatres were better. On the cover of his copy, Haig wrote, 'Words! Words! Words! Lots of words! And little else.'*

1 At this point the Ts diary contains the words 'of the Allied Armies', which changes the sense of the original. The word 'Allied' is probably a mistake for 'British'.
2 IWM: Wilson Papers, HHW 2/7B/3.

Friday 26 July

At 2 pm I attended a conference with Foch. The following were also present. Generals Rawlinson and Montgomery, Weygand, Du Cane, Debeney ... The latter proposed to carry out a small operation south of Hangard on the River Luce. But Foch decided on a larger operation on the lines which I had proposed. Rawlinson and Debeney are to meet at 10 am tomorrow to settle details of area of concentration etc. Rawlinson was very anxious to carry out his operation alone, without French co-operation, but in view of our limited number of divisions I agreed that Debeney should operate on our right. This is also the more desirable in view of the reserves which Foch is moving to the Beauvais area ... No sign yet reported of divisions leaving the sector of Rupprecht's Army for that of Crown Prince.

Sunday 28 July

General Weygand ... arrived from Bombon with a letter from Foch to me. In it he asked me to take command of the First French Army (General Debeney) and combine its action with my Fourth Army in the operations which we are now planning. I said, 'Yes,' and sent Foch a letter of thanks. Foch wishes operations hurried on. I said I will try and gain two days if my XXII Corps can be sent back two days earlier than I asked for on Friday last. This will be arranged. I am pleased that Foch should have entrusted me with the direction of these operations.

Monday 29 July

Having last night modified draft of orders to Fourth Army (Rawlinson) and First French Army (Debeney), I gave my approval to final draft after breakfast this morning ...

At 12 noon I received Army Commanders except Rawlinson ... who is preparing for forthcoming operations. I met the Army Commanders alone with my CGS and had a general talk for $1\frac{1}{2}$ hours. They appreciated the opportunity of being able to state their views to me personally instead of before a number of Staff officers as on one of the regular periodical conferences with Army Commanders and Staffs.

I explained the policy and future plans of the Generalissimo (Foch). He intends to keep the initiative, etc. and felt that we had 'turned the corner'! As regards Tactics, I called attention to divisions being side by side in the line following different principles and ignoring those laid down by my orders. Corps Commanders must be held responsible that these principles are followed by *all*, and Army Commanders must be responsible for supervising the Corps Commanders' [methods.]

Then, as to offensive tactics, Army Commanders must do their utmost to get troops out of the influence of *Trench* methods. We were all agreed on the need for the training of Battalion Commanders, who in their turn must train their Company and Platoon Commanders. This is really a 'Platoon Commanders' war' . . .

About 2.30 pm Rawlinson came to see me. He has had a meeting with his Corps Commanders. The date would be advanced 2 days, as requested by me. All his arrangements were being pushed forward satisfactorily. His relations have been most cordial with Debeney since our meeting at Sarcus with Foch last Friday.

Wednesday 31 July

I motored via Fléxicourt to Vaux-en-Amenais, and witnessed troops practising with Tanks. Remarkable progress has been made since Cambrai, not only in the pattern of Tank, but also in the methods of using them. Tanks now go first, covered by shrapnel barrage, and break down all opposition. Enemy in strong points and machine gun nests are then flattened out by the Tanks. The latter then signal to infantry to 'come on', and these then advance in open order and mop up the remaining defenders, and collect the prisoners. During consolidation Tanks zig-zag in front to cover the operation. Australian infantry were used to demonstrate first of all, and then the onlookers from another battalion were put through similar exercises on the same course.

The result of these methodical exercises has been to render a Tank attack more effective and much less costly to us. Sir Henry Rawlinson, General Hugh Elles and Staff of Tanks met me at the Tank ground . . .

At Bertangles Château, I saw General Monash Commanding Australian Corps. He came back from leave yesterday: he was recalled: said he was delighted to return though he had only had 4 days in England but he 'had all the threads of the operation in his hands'. We discussed the situation. I told him he must have some cavalry under his Command, and suggested getting a brigade from the Cavalry Corps as he said his own Corps mounted troops were not well enough trained for this work.

Thursday 1 August. Letter to General John J. Pershing

In accordance with General Foch's wishes I am arranging to carry out certain offensive operations on the British front.

I write to ask you what your wishes are as regards American troops taking part. At the present moment I am of course adhering to your instructions given in your letter of 7 July viz. that *during the training period* of American Divisions, no American unit is to be employed in active operations without your personal sanction.

I do not wish you to modify this decision. I am anxious however to know definitely what your wishes are, when the training period is terminated. Can I then use your divisions in the battle or not?

I hope to carry out an offensive operation during the early days of September ... Before that date I can arrange for American Corps Commander and Staff to take over a sector on my front, and command a portion of the troops in the operation to which I have referred.

Saturday 3 August

Foch and Haig met at Mouchy le Châtel.

After lunch he and I took a short walk in the grounds. More than once he expressed the opinion that the 'Germans are breaking up', and was anxious lest they should fall back before I could get my blow in.

Later that day Haig received a telegram from Henry Wilson in which the CIGS proposed exchanging communications 'in which opinions expressed would not be regarded as having official character'. Haig's autograph comments read: 'An extraordinary proposal. It is impossible for a CIGS to exchange opinions on military matters with a C-in-C in the field in personal *telegrams!* His telegrams will be official!'

Sunday 4 August

This date marked the fourth anniversary of Britain's entry into the war.

I attended a Special Service of Thanksgiving at 9.30 am in the Square in the 'Ecole Militaire' in which GHQ Offices are established ... The service was carried out by the Rev. Duncan (Church of Scotland) and Bateman Champain (Church of England). The Roman Catholic priests were not allowed by their regulations to take part in the ceremony, but many RC officers attended. The attitude of the RC clergy over this service should open our eyes to what the RC religion really is. They are RC first and Englishmen afterwards, if their Church permits.[1]

1 Sir Philip Sassoon recorded Haig's anger over this matter. Diary, 31 July 1918, Sassoon papers, Houghton Hall, Norfolk. We owe this reference to Jim Beach.

Monday 5 August

Haig conferred with Rawlinson, Kavanagh and Debeney.

I thought that the Fourth Army orders aimed too much at getting a *final* objective on the old Amiens defence line, and stopping counter-attacks on it. This is not far enough, in my opinion, if we start by surprising the Enemy! So I told Rawlinson (it had already been in my 'orders') to arrange to advance as rapidly as possible and capture the old Amiens line of Defence ... [and to] put it in state of Defence; but not to delay – at once reserves must be pushed on to capture the line Chaulnes–Roye ... I said that the cavalry must keep in touch with the battle and be prepared to pass through *anywhere* between the River Somme and the Roye–Amiens road.

Tuesday 6 August

Reports state Enemy quiet on our front except just north of Somme, in angle between that river and the Ancre. Here Enemy attacked our III Corps (Butler), Fourth Army with 3 battalions of 27th Württemberg Division: at a time when the 18th Division was side-slipping to its right in preparation for attack on 8th inst. The Enemy penetrated about 1500 yards and took some prisoners including an artillery officer and sergeant who knew of the forth-coming attack.

A counter-attack regained some of the ground which had been lost. General Butler has been told that as far as his Corps is concerned, the battle has begun, and he must carry out his orders as best he can, so as to cover the left of the Australian Corps when they advance.

Wednesday 7 August

The King arrived at 12.15 from Traucourt Château where he is staying ... HM looked well and very cheery. So different to his frame of mind on the occasion of his last visit in March.

He brought me a message from the Prime Minister Lloyd George! The latter, the King said, now talks about 'poor Haig' and 'the excessive length of line which he had to hold'. The Government is now determined to support me as against the French Government. LG wishes me to insist strongly on having our front reduced before the autumn comes, so that men can be given leave and troops be rested and trained.

The PM also wants 2 American Armies to be formed – one on our right – then will come a French section covering Paris, and on its right a second American Army in the Vosges. From my point of view the idea is very excellent, but both the French and the Americans will be against us. Pershing wants to form one large American Army, while, of course, the French desire to keep the Americans as far away from the British as they can! [However, I expressed the belief that the British front would be much further forward before winter arrived! – and I explained in detail on the map in my study our forthcoming operations.] . . .[1]

At 2.45 pm I left for Fléxicourt, where I had a talk with General Rawlinson. Everything is going on without a hitch and the Enemy seems in ignorance of the impending blow! I then went on to HQ Canadian Corps at Dury and saw General Currie commanding the Corps. The latter said it had been a hustle to be ready in time, but everything had been got in except 2 long-range guns. The platforms were ready for them and they would be got in by tonight. Last night was our most critical moment. If the Germans had bombarded the Canadian zone, we could not have retaliated last night. Tonight the situation is quite different, and we are ready!

Canadians are very keen to do something. Up to date they have not had a hand in the battle. I reminded Currie that 55 British Divisions had withstood the attack of 109 picked German assault divisions from 21 March to 27 April! . . .

The move of some Canadian Battalions and Casualty Clearing Stations to Second Army front seems to have quite misled the Canadian troops, and many spoke of the coming offensive to take Kemmel!

On leaving Dury, I motored . . . to Wiry au Mont Station where my Advanced Headquarters is established in my train.

Thursday 8 August

The Battle of Amiens was the BEF's greatest victory of the war. Famously, Ludendorff described it as 'the black day of the German army'.

Glass steady. Fine night and morning – slight mist in the valley. An autumn feel in the morning air.

7 am Fourth Army reported 'Generally quiet night until zero, 4.20 am. We attacked from southern boundary (south of Domart en Luce) to Morlancourt (near Ancre) in conjunction with French on right. Attack apparently complete surprise and is progressing satisfactorily.' . . .

Soon after 12 noon I motored to Fléxicourt with General Davidson and saw Sir H. Rawlinson. Some hard fighting was then going on near Morlancourt (north of the Somme). But Butler Commanding III Corps was fully

---

1 Haig then had lunch with President Poincaré, whom he described as 'a mediocrity', and the King. Haig commented 'HM can't stop talking!'

alive to the situation, and had an adequate number of troops to deal with the situation.

Everywhere else the situation had developed more favourably for us than we had dared even to hope![1] The Enemy were completely surprised, 2 reliefs of divisions were in progress, very little resistance was offered, and our troops got their objectives quickly with very little loss!

I told Rawlinson ... to continue to work on the orders already given, namely, to organise his left strongly; if opportunity offers, to advance it to line Albert–Bray. With his left strongly held he will push his defensive front out to line Chaulnes–Roye. Reconnaissance to be pushed forward to the Somme River, while his main effort is directed southeastwards on Roye to help the French. The cavalry should work on the outer flank of the infantry, and move on Chaulnes–Roye as soon as possible.

I returned to train for lunch, and about 4 pm I called at HQ First French Army at Contay. Debeney was pleased with himself though 3 battalions of Colonial Infantry had bolted before a machine gun.[2] I told Debeney to do his utmost to join hands with the British at Roye: his; cavalry should be sent forward as soon as possible to operate on the right of the British *as soon as possible*...

At 6 pm Marshal Foch[3] came to see me. He is very delighted at our success today, and fully concurred in all the arrangements I had made for continuing the battle ... Situation reports at 4.30 pm stated Canadian Corps had captured Beaucourt, Caix and the Amiens outer defence line east of Caix. Cavalry Corps south and east of Caix; Canadians in touch with French at Maison Blanche. Australians on final objective all along their front. III Corps on ridges northeast of Chipilly.

Enemy blowing up dumps in all directions and streaming eastwards. Their transport and limbers offer splendid targets for our airoplanes.

Thursday 8 August, 10.30 am. Letter to Lady Haig

Our attack started at 4.20 this morning and seems to have taken the enemy completely by surprise ... I hear. Two of our armoured motor cars being sent on to round up German Corps Headquarters!

Who would have believed this possible even 2 months ago? How much easier it is to attack, than to stand and await an enemy's attack!

As you well know, I feel that I am only the instrument of that Divine

---

1 In the Ts diary, Haig amended this to '... than I, optimist though I am, had dared even to hope!'
2 In the Ts diary Haig has Debeney 'much distressed' at this occurrence.
3 Foch was appointed as Marshal of France on 6 August 1918.

Power who watches over each one of us, so all the Honour must be His.

Friday 9 August

Debeney's orders are framed for covering the British right: not for exploiting yesterday's success. I therefore send for him to come to a conference in order to find out what his troops are really capable of doing.

Attack was renewed on our whole front south of the Somme, Canadians at 10 am – Australians at 11. The III Corps did not attack till 4 pm.

Good progress was made, in spite of increased opposition. Canadians took Bouchoir–Folies, Beaufort–Warvillers–Vrély–Rouvroy–Méharicourt–Rosières. Australians captured Vauvillers–Framerville.

By dark III Corps had taken Morlancourt and Chipilly, and advanced their line to the high ground from west of Etinehem to Dérnancourt on Ancre. This relieved me of all anxiety for our left flank.

The French met with no opposition owing to the determined advance of the British in front of their left, [having cut in on the Enemy's communications.]

General Debeney arrived about 4 pm[1] ... Owing to the hard fighting north of the Somme and the great extension of the battle front of Fourth Army, as compared with its original front, the Fourth Army front is *thin*, if a serious hostile attack has to be met! So I asked Debeney to include in his front of advance, Roye and 5 kilometres north of it. He said, this would upset all his plans! I accordingly asked him to take Roye, and the village of Goyencourt (northwest of Roye) to give him an adequate area in which to move round to envelop Roye. This he agreed to do ...

Fourth Army have taken 16,000 prisoners to date.

Saturday 10 August

General Foch came to see me at 11 am. He wishes the advance to continue to the line Noyon–Ham–Péronne, and to try to get the bridgeheads on the Somme. I pointed out the difficulty of the undertaking unless the Enemy is quite demoralised, and we can cross the Somme on his heels. At the same time I outlined my proposals for advancing our front on Aubers ridge and so freeing the Béthune coal mines [together with movements against Bapaume and Monchy le Preux. Byng and Horne's Armies.]

He quite agreed, but said, 'You will be able to carry out the Aubers Ridge plan, all the same.'

I agree if the Enemy's opposition on the present battle front is not stiffening.

1 Haig added that French successes were aided by the fact that 'all opposition had been [removed] by the British advance of course!'

[In any case, we must expect German reserves to arrive very soon in order to check our advance. My plan to advance my left on Bapaume and on Monchy le Preux will then become necessary.] In Foch's opinion the fact of the French First Army's and now the Third [French] Army's getting on without meeting serious opposition shows the Enemy is demoralised. [I agree that *some* German divisions are demoralised, but not *all* yet!]

I accordingly issue orders to continue the advance on Guiscard–Ham–Péronne, and occupy passages of the river below Ham. I also ordered General Byng (Third Army) to raid, and if situation favourable to push forward advance guards to Bapaume. ... Afterwards we went on through Villers-Bretonneux to Marcelcave [and] to Demuin. HQ Canadian Corps are here in some dugouts to southeast of the village below a little hill, the plan for the capturing of which caused us some anxiety before the 8th! I saw General Currie: he explained the situation. He wished to keep one or two of his divisions fresh to meet a counter-attack. I pointed out the advantage of crossing the Somme on the heels of the Enemy, if we could! It would save us many casualties later on if it became necessary to force the passage of the river in the face of the Enemy. A message arrived from the Cavalry Corps timed 2.25 pm stating that 'Enemy's opposition was diminishing'. One division was accordingly ordered to high ground northeast of Roye, and another to Nesle.

General Rawlinson arrived when I was with Currie. I explained my intentions and orders ...

... I visited the Headquarters of our 32nd Division, which had relieved the 3rd Canadians in the early morning. I met General Lambert (Commanding Division).[1] He had just returned from visiting his brigades at the front. His opinion was that the Enemy's opposition had stiffened up. There were many hostile machine guns, [much intact wire] and the old battlefield ground [between the German and French lines] with numerous holes favoured delaying tactics and prevented the action of our cavalry. He had therefore decided to stop the attack till tomorrow morning, when he would put in his remaining brigade, which was fresh, with all available Tanks.

Sunday 11 August

Haig took notice of the concerns of Currie and Lambert about continuing major operations on Fourth Army's front. On 11 August Rawlinson added his doubts.

About 10 pm Marshal Foch came to see me ... After a talk he approved (in view of the increased opposition) of me reducing my front of attack, and

---

1 Major General Thomas Stanton Lambert (1871–1921), GOC 32nd Division, 1918–19; killed in action during the Anglo-Irish war, 20 June 1921.

aiming at reaching the Somme on the front Brie–Ham (exclusive) instead of Péronne–Ham ... He urged me to attack with my Third Army (Byng). I told him that 3 weeks ago I discussed with Byng the possibility of the Third Army co-operating and today I had seen Byng [and given him definite orders to advance as soon as possible on Bapaume].

Monday 12 August

At 1.45 General Pershing (C-in-C American Army) came to see me. He stated that he might have to withdraw the 5 American Divisions now with British. I pointed out to him that I had done everything to equip and help the American Army, and to provide them with horses. So far, I have had no help from these troops (except the 3 battalions which were used in the battle near Chipilly in error). If he now withdraws the 5 American Divisions, he must expect some criticism of his action not only from the British troops in the field but also from the British Government.

All I wanted to know was *definitely* whether I could prepare to use the American troops for an attack (along with British) at the end of September against Kemmel. Now I know I cannot do so.

Pershing said he would not withdraw his divisions as long as the present battle was in progress. When he was going he thanked me for being quite outspoken to him. 'At any rate, I always know when I am dealing with you what your opinion is on the question at issue. [This is not always the case with the French.]'

I then motored to Fléxicourt (HQ Fourth Army) and held a conference at 3.30 pm with Generals Rawlinson, Debeney and Byng ... I explained the situation, gave objectives viz: Chaulnes – and high ground east of Roye. After gaining these objectives a fresh dividing line between Armies would be given and movement to be northeast, with left on the Brie crossing over the Somme. As regards date, I fixed it for the 15th at dawn, because Fourth Army could not be ready before, but Debeney said he would be able to attack on the 14th if I wanted.

I then spoke to General Byng. His objective is to break the front, and advance on Bapaume. He would be reinforced with 4 divisions and the Cavalry Corps (of 2 divisions) – also some 200 Tanks. My plan is to break the front, operate towards Péronne so as to [outflank and] force Enemy back in front of Fourth Army – [at the same time he¹ will try and] widen the gap northwards, and get Monchy le Preux back into our hands. This would greatly improve the Arras position. General Elles, Commander Tank Corps

1 i.e. Byng.

was present. As regards date – this depends on railway movement, but I fixed the 20th (Tuesday week) [as the date to work for.]

HM the King ... then presented the KCB to General Debeney ... We were then photo'd – Marshal Foch in his new hat, the King, self, Pétain, Fayolle and a host of others. The Cinema running all the time while we were forming up.

Prisoners captured since August 8 by Fourth Army exceed 20,000; 5 Regimental Commanders, over 20 Battalion Commanders, 3 Army Brigade Commanders, about 600 officers in all. Over 400 guns, 3 complete railway trains and vast stocks of engineer material and stores.

First French Army (Debeney) has taken over 8500 prisoners and 250 guns.

Tuesday 13 August

General Kavanagh explained to me the nature of the operations carried out by the cavalry. These were highly successful, and I feel sure that without the rapid advance of the cavalry the effect of the surprise attack on the 8th would have been much less and very probably the Amiens outer defence line would not have been gained either so soon or so cheaply ... The 17th Lancers reached their objective ('blue dotted line') 4 hours before the infantry came up! The latter were able to advance 5000 yards without a shot being fired at them in consequence.

At the same time I consider that at least a whole Cavalry Division should have moved on the north side of Harbonnières village as far as Framerville before turning south in order to outflank the Enemy, who was in strength on the front Cayeaux–Harbonnières and in the woods there, which were unfavourable for cavalry action. The rule that reinforcements should be sent to where we are gaining ground and *not* where opposition is strongest is equally true of the action of cavalry as infantry! ...

It is interesting to note that the old German position (which the Enemy now holds) in front of Roye was considered a model one by the French and kept up for the instruction of young officers and others in order to show how to organise a defensive position; positions of machine guns, wiring etc. Such a position cannot be taken without very careful preparation! I therefore have decided to order counter-battery work and wire cutting, and step by step advance, with the object of holding the Enemy to his position, or causing him to vacate it. Meantime, the attack by our Third Army is being hurried on.

Wednesday 14 August

At 10 am Sir Henry Rawlinson came to see me and brought photos showing the state of the Enemy's defences on the front Roye–Chaulnes. He also showed me a letter which he had received from General Currie Commanding the Canadian Corps stating that to capture the position in question would be a very costly matter. He (Currie) was opposed to attempting it . . .

I accordingly ordered the date of this attack to be postponed, but preparations to be continued with vigour combined with wire cutting and counter-battery work.

Thursday 15 August

Haig conferred with Horne, Byng and Kavanagh.

Enemy continues to fall back on the front of Third Army and our troops are already in outskirts of Beaucourt; have taken Puisieux and are near Courcelles.

The divisions holding the line have done well in following up the Enemy at once. I directed Byng to continue to press the Enemy as much as possible. Today the leading lot of tanks arrived, he will also receive some cavalry and 4 extra divisions. He must press on as fast as he possibly can even before these reinforcements arrive, in order to prevent the Enemy from destroying bridges, roads etc. His objective is Bapaume, thence the advance will be continued to threaten Péronne, and thus withdraw pressure from the Chaulnes–Roye front.

I directed Horne to be ready to profit by advance of Third Army, to attack and capture Orange Hill and Monchy-le-Preux. He can deliver an attack with 3 divisions in addition to others in the line: about 100 Tanks are being sent to him.

The Cavalry Corps is being put under Byng's orders for advanced guard work to save the infantry, and if the enemy stands to fight, to exploit the success after the Enemy has been dislodged from his position.[1]

Cox reported on the situation. The Enemy seems to have only one division left in reserve on the front Arras–Albert. Between the sea and the Oise, the Germans only have 10 divisions fit to fight, in reserve.

I visited Foch at Sarcus at 3 pm . . . Foch had pressed me to attack the positions held by the Enemy on the front Chaulnes–Roye. I declined to do

1 That day Haig wrote to Wilson that Byng had been sent mobile troops in 'order to press the Enemy back quicker than he would like!' It is not clear whether the 'he' refers to Byng or the enemy. IWM: Wilson Papers, HHW 2/7B/5.

so because they could only be taken after heavy casualties in men and Tanks. I had ordered First French and Fourth (British) Armies to postpone their attacks, but to keep up pressure on that front [so as to make the Enemy expect an attack on this front,] while I transferred my reserves to Third Army [and also prepared to attack with the First Army] on the front Monchy le Preux–Miraumont. Foch now wanted to know what orders I had issued for attack: When I proposed to attack? Where? and with what troops? I think he really wanted a written statement to this effect from me for his records! . . .

I told Foch of my instructions to Byng and Horne; and that Rawlinson would also co-operate with his left between the Somme and Ancre when Third Army had advanced and withdrawn some of the pressure which was still strong in that sector.

I spoke to Foch quite straightly, and let him understand that I was responsible for the handling of the British Forces. Foch's attitude at once changed and he said all he wanted was early information of my intentions, so that he might co-ordinate the operations of the other Armies, and that he thought I was quite correct in my decision not to attack the Enemy in his prepared position.

Saturday 17 August

From talking to various officers, I gather that Enemy's resistance has stiffened on the Ancre, and the villages of Beaucourt, Puisieux, Bucquoy. It seems strange that Enemy should have begun his retirement and then reinforced his line recently! It almost looks as if the Enemy Higher Command had changed its plan of operations since our attack on the 8th. Two plans in my opinion seem open to him,

(a) to fall back on the Somme line from Péronne to Ham etc., and retain his reserves on the defensive, or
(b) to concentrate his reserves in a sector not blocked by his retreating troops, and then counter-attack. The area from the Scarpe to the Somme seems favourable for this kind of operation. Enemy might counter-attack left flank of our Fourth Army if it advanced eastwards, without having [adequate] supports on its left from our Third Army.

Plan (b) seems more in keeping with German views and strategy. But has he the necessary force? and will they fight? In any case we cannot expect the Germans to own defeat until they have played their last card! So we're right to be prepared for a counter-attack.

Monday 19 August

Haig met Byng.

He explained his plan, which I thought was too limited in its scope. I told him that his objective was to break the Enemy's front, and *gain Bapaume as soon as possible.* Rawlinson would operate between Byng's right and the Somme in the direction of Péronne. His right was therefore well protected; at the same time a force of three divisions of the First Army would be concentrated in rear of Byng's left, and would be available either to develop Byng's operation northeastwards towards Monchy[-le-Preux] and Quéant (in this case under Byng's orders) or to break the front east of Arras and capture Orange Hill (this operation would be under Horne's orders). At present there are signs that the Enemy is withdrawing on the south of Scarpe from Orange Hill.

Byng had only arranged to use about a brigade of cavalry. I told him that the Cavalry Corps is 100 per cent better than it was at Cambrai. He must use the cavalry to the fullest extent possible. Now is the time to act with boldness, and in full confidence that, if we only hit the Enemy hard enough, and continue to press him, that he will give way and acknowledge that he is beaten.

... At Merieux, HQ IV Corps I saw General Harper and went into his plans. Colonel Dill of GHQ[1] happened to be there, so I sent him to see General Byng and direct him to detail a cavalry regiment to each corps taking part in the attack, because the Enemy's 'line of resistance' may have been withdrawn some distance from our front trenches, and it will be necessary to push forward advanced guards of all arms to reconnoitre, and prepare the way for the attacking troops. Advanced guards of *all arms* will also be necessary, when the Enemy's line of resistance has been pierced.

Wednesday 21 August

The Battle of Albert began. This offensive carried the BEF across the old Somme battlefield of 1916 in a matter of days.

Third Army attacked at 4.55 am on the front Beaucourt-sur-Ancre (inclusive) to Moyenneville (inclusive). Prisoners report that attack was a complete surprise...

Mr Winston Churchill (Minister of Munitions) came to see me about

1 Colonel (later Field Marshal Sir) John ('Jack') Greer Dill (1881–1944), GSO1, then BGGS (Operations) GHQ, 1917–19; Dill's 'emergence' in 1918 owed much to Sir Herbert Lawrence.

noon and stayed to lunch. He is most anxious to help in every way, and is hurrying up the supply of '10 calibre head' shells, gas, Tanks, etc. His schemes are all timed for completion in next June! I told him we ought to do our utmost to get a decision this autumn. We are engaged in a 'wearing-out battle' and are outlasting the Enemy. If we have a period of quiet, he will recover, and the 'wearing-out' process must be recommenced. [In reply, I was told that the General Staff in London calculate that the decisive period of the war cannot arrive until next July.]

In the afternoon I visited HQ VI Corps at Lucheux. General Haldane's divisions were over the Arras–Albert railway, but the 63rd Division on the left of the adjoining corps had not taken Achiet le Grand. Haldane was holding back the right of his line in consequence. I told him that he must order his troops to push on and turn Achiet le Grand by working to the east of it from the north. Reinforce where we are winning, not where we are held up!...

About 10.30 pm CGS reported that Byng had decided not to continue the operation against Achiet le Grand tomorrow morning. Troops had suffered much from the heat, and were in disorder. Guns too had to be advanced. I expressed the wish that the attack should be resumed at the earliest possible moment.

Thursday 22 August

Fourth Army came into action on the right flank of Third Army.

Tonight I issued a Note to Army Commanders asking them to bring to the notice of all subordinate leaders the changed conditions under which operations are now being carried out. 'It is no longer necessary to advance step by step in regular lines as in 1916–17 battles. All units must go straight for their objectives, while reserves should be pushed in where we are gaining ground.'[1]

Friday 23 August

Total prisoners captured by British during last fortnight amount to over 29,000 up to yesterday...

I then rode on to Fonquevillers. Ground much cut up with trenches – the old German system prior to the spring of 1917 ran along here. All the men as

---

1 In this order (OAD 911) Haig also declared that 'Risks which a month ago would have been criminal to incur, ought now to be incurred as a duty'.

I passed ran out of their bivouacs to see me and salute. Every one in the best of spirits . . .

All Divisional Commanders said hostile machine guns causing us much trouble. Tanks had come [on] well but had gone back at end of their day's petrol supply. I told them to use sections of field artillery with battalions or even single guns against machine gun nests.

Saturday 24 August

Brigadier General *Charteris came to see me. He had been ordered to Baghdad in a position with less pay than he had on leaving India in 1911 with me! I told him to state the facts in a letter to me, and I will forward it with my remarks to War Office. He seems almost a sort of Dreyfus in the eyes of our War Office authorities!

I received news of George Black's death yesterday. No details, only that he was badly wounded with his Tank and died in the Casualty Clearing Hospital at Daours . . . He was with me from April 1915 until the beginning of this year in charge of 17th Lancers troops (my mounted escort). He insisted on going to the Tank Corps as 'he wanted to fight'! He is a great loss to me and all of us. Always so cheerful and happy even when things looked darkest . . .

Haig went to Canadian Corps HQ and consulted with Horne and Currie.

I explained that I wished the First Army to advance by surprise and attack as rapidly as possible astride the Cambrai road with left secured on the River Scarpe . . . If all went well and the advance was accomplished rapidly the Enemy might still be holding his positions in front of the Third Army. It would then be the rôle of the First Army to operate against the right flank of this part of the Enemy's forces.

Sunday 25 August

I directed CGS to augment Cavalry Corps by the addition of good infantry brigade in buses,[1] and extra machine gun batteries in motors, with the object of exploiting situation which I hope will arise after we get the Marquion–Canal du Nord line. We might get the chance of pushing on the Cavalry Corps to the Bois de Bourlon to intercept the Enemy's retreat! . . .

I then motored on to HQ III Corps and saw General Godley. Sir H. Rawlinson and Sir H. Wilson (CIGS) were at tea. We had a long talk on the situation.

---

1 4th (Guards) Brigade was used for this purpose.

We must aim at having an equal number of divisions in the front line [and] in support. This will enable troops to rest, and operations to be continued without intermission. In reply to a request from Rawlinson for more divisions as his troops were tired, I regretted I could not comply with his request because in my opinion the decisive point was the Arras–Cambrai road, and all my reserves would be better employed in attacking in the direction of Cambrai than on the Fourth Army front! He fully concurred.

The Battle of the Scarpe began on 26 August when Horne's First Army attacked north of Arras, and made good progress.

Tuesday 27 August

I saw AG. In accordance with WO decision we must purpose to reorganise the Army in view of shortage of men. The number of active divisions to be maintained will be 32 British and 10 Dominion = total 42. In addition there will be 12 Replacement Divisions for some time. 7 will be broken up, 42 + 19 = 61 our present number of divisions.

Tuesday 27 August. Letter to Sir Henry Wilson[1]

I hope you will get the Despatch I sent home at the beginning of the month published soon to stop stupid questions and unfounded stories which are now in circulation . . .[2]

John Du Cane was here last night. I sent back by him a letter to Foch recommending the immediate distribution of American Divisions amongst British and French to enable a concentric movement being begun without delay on Cambrai, on St Quentin, & from the south on Mézières. The attack on St Mihiel will lead to nothing (a) because it is eccentric, and (b) Germans have already taken steps to make a new line across the salient. A *small* attack in this salient would educate the American Higher Command and might be allowed for purposes of camouflage! The main attack should be launched between Rheims and Verdun in direction of Mézières etc. under French direction.

---

1 IWM: Wilson Papers, 2/7B/7.
2 The despatch concerned the German Spring Offensive. It appeared in November 1918, with considerable deletions and emendations (concerning the BEF's shortage of manpower) insisted upon by Lloyd George.

Tuesday 27 August. Letter to General John J. Pershing[1]

As regards the movement of your divisions from the British area, I was glad to be able to meet your wishes at once, and I trust that events may justify your decision to withdraw the American troops from the British battle front at the present moment, for I make no doubt but that the arrival in this battle of a few strong and vigorous American Divisions, when the enemy's units are thoroughly worn out, would lead to the most decisive results.

Thursday 29 August

Memorial service at 10 am for General Cox, who was drowned in the sea bathing 3 days ago. I could not go as Foch asked me to meet him at Mouchy le Châtel . . .

We discussed the whole situation. Foch was very pleased with what the British Army had done. As regards future plans, he is 'in full agreement with me'. I noted however that *since he received my letter*, he has decided to put in the American attack down the left bank of the Meuse towards Mézières instead of against the St Mihiel salient. Pershing is still preparing for the latter operation. Foch will tell him as soon as possible of the change. Mangin[2] with Tenth French Army began an attack yesterday eastwards on the north bank of the Aisne north of Soissons, with the object of getting the Craonne position, and opening the road to Laon. This fits in well with my operations, and with the new plan for the American Army under Pershing.

Haig's strategic vision helped win Foch over to the idea of a far-reaching offensive. This was to materialise at the end of September 1918.

Friday 30 August

The Australian Corps of Fourth Army forced a crossing of the River Somme.

At 10.30 I held meeting with 5 Army Commanders and my CGS. I told them of the general plan decided on by Foch yesterday (*secret and for their personal information*) in order that they might realise that the Enemy would be engaged by the Allied Armies [on a very wide front] from now on, and that there was no risk of any *heavy attack* by the Enemy. We were therefore justified in taking

---

1 Library of Congress Manuscript Division: Pershing Papers, Container 86. We owe this reference to Mitch Yockelson.
2 General Charles Marie Emmanuel Mangin ('The Butcher') (1866–1925). Mangin had been sacked by Nivelle after the failure of the Aisne attack in May 1917, but Foch, who admired his aggression, restored him to active service.

full risks in our forthcoming operations. Our objective being to reach the
front Cambrai–St Quentin, the area from the Scarpe to Somme is our
main sector, and other sectors would be denuded of troops as circumstances
required to keep the battle going ... I also spoke to Army Commanders re.
handling of Tanks. 'Tanks must join the Army' and manoeuvre on similar
lines to infantry, i.e. in accordance with FSR Vol. I! I spoke about the
importance of advanced guards [of all arms].

Saturday 31 August

First Army's advance carried it towards a major German defensive position.

I sent Lawrence to see Horne and Currie and tell them that I have no wish
to attack the Quéant–Drocourt line, if they are in any doubt about taking it.

Sunday 1 September

I attended Church of England at HQ Third Army at 9.30 am. Afterwards I
had a talk with Byng ... He was disinclined to agree to give Horne support
by attacking, which Horne asked for. I told him that owing to shortage of
men I was opposed to doing more attacking than was absolutely necessary.
Our object is to keep the battle going as long as possible, until the Americans
can attack in force ...

   General Lawrence discussed with me the position in front of Fourth Army
about Péronne. The Australian and III Corps had had a great success today.
The Enemy's troops near St Quentin are in great disorder. We have taken
prisoners from 17 different regiments today! He consequently advised sending
a Cavalry Division to exploit the success there. I did not agree, because our
object at the present time is to wear out the Enemy by continually attacking
him, and so to prevent him from settling into a strong position. The decisive
moment will arrive when the Americans attack in force. The British Army
must still be able to attack then, and to have the means of exploiting the
victory and making it decisive. I therefore wished the Cavalry Corps to be
kept as strong as possible, and at the present time merely to detach the
minimum number of squadrons necessary for Divisional and Corps requirements. By this procedure I hoped to have an efficient Cavalry Corps ready to
act vigorously when the decisive moment comes ...

*The following passage does not appear in the Ms diary. However, it echoes some
earlier comments noted by Haig on a telegram from Wilson (3 August 1918)
suggesting an exchange of unofficial messages, and repeats verbatim some of Haig's
autograph comments on Wilson's telegram.*

The following telegram from Wilson (CIGS) reached me this morning. It is marked 'H.W. Personal' and was sent off yesterday. 'Just a word of caution in regard to incurring heavy losses in attacks on Hindenburg Line as opposed to losses when driving the enemy back to that line. I do not mean to say that you have incurred such losses, but I know the War Cabinet would become anxious if we received heavy punishment in attacking the Hindenburg Line WITHOUT SUCCESS.' Signed 'Wilson'.

[It is impossible for a CIGS to send a telegram of this nature to a C-in-C in the field as a 'personal' one. The Cabinet are ready to meddle and interfere in my plans in an underhand way, but do not dare openly to say that they mean[1] to take the responsibility for any failure though ready to take credit for every success! The object of this telegram is, no doubt, to save the Prime Minister (Lloyd George) in case of any failure.[2] So I read it to mean that I can attack the Hindenburg Line if I think it right to do so. The CIGS and the Cabinet already know that my arrangements are being made to that end. If my attack is successful I will remain on as C-in-C. If we fail, or our losses are excessive, I can hope for no mercy! I wrote to Henry Wilson in reply. What a wretched lot of weaklings we have in high places at the present time!]

Sunday 1 September. Letter to Sir Henry Wilson[3]

With reference to your wire re. casualties in attacking the Hindenburg Line. What a wretched lot! And how well they mean to support me!! What confidence!

Please call their attention to my action 2 weeks ago when the French pressed me to attack the strong line of defence east of Roye–Chaulnes front. I wrote you at the time and instead of attacking south of Somme I started Byng's attack.

I assure you that I watch the 'Drafts' most carefully . . .

Sunday 1 September. Letter to Sir Herbert Plumer

Admiral Keyes was here last night.[4] I explained to him the military situation on the Western Front, and I gave the opinion that it is quite possible that the enemy may be forced to fall back in the near future eastwards from the

1 Presumably this is a slip for 'do not mean'.
2 Lloyd George lied when he later claimed that he had nothing to do with the sending of this telegram; see David R. Woodward, *Lloyd George and the Generals* (Newark, NJ: University of Delaware Press, 1983), p. 331.
3 IWM: Wilson Papers, HHW 2/7B/11.
4 Vice Admiral (later Admiral of the Fleet) Roger John Brownlow (later Baron) Keyes (1872–1945), commander of the Dover Patrol; an aggressive commander in the Nelson tradition.

Hindenburg Line. He may also be obliged shortly to retire from western Belgium and the coast.

I asked Keyes to consider the possible situation from the Naval point of view, so as to be able to co-operate immediately with you and the Belgians *whenever the situation becomes favourable...*

I asked him to consider the possibility of landing troops on the Belgian coast. *Not in the face* of the enemy,[1] but as a means for rapidly reaching Bruges and placing our left flank on the Dutch frontier. In view of the small number of German troops now opposing the Belgians, I hope that you may be able to induce *them* to make a move forward!

Monday 2 September

The Canadian Corps broke through the Drocourt–Quéant line.

The 1st and 4th Canadian Divisions with 4th Division attacked the Drocourt–Quéant line south of the Scarpe at 5 am today. Reports at 10 am show that the attack is progressing well, and prisoners from *seven* different divisions have been taken. General Brutinel's force[2] (a Canadian regiment, motor machine guns, armoured cars, cyclists, etc.) was on the main Arras–Cambrai road southwest of Dury at 8.5 am and the British 1st Division was advancing from the old German front line east of Arras, to occupy the Drocourt line and push on to the Canal du Nord if all goes well.

After lunch I motored to Noyelle Vion (Headquarters of the Canadian Corps) and saw the BGGS (Webber).[3] He told me that the position had been captured without much loss, thanks mainly to the Tanks. After getting the position, our troops came under fire from many machine guns as they advanced, and losses became severe in the case of the 4th Canadian Division. The Enemy had done his utmost to hold his position, and had moved forward many reinforcements. The Canadian Corps had taken prisoners from 10 different divisions. Enemy had local superiority in the air, and prevented our airoplanes from observing over Ecourt St Quentin. Eight of our machines were destroyed here.

I went on to HQ 4th Division, which was established in dugouts on main Cambrai road near Monchy le Preux. General Matheson had gone forward with his brigades,[4] but I saw the GSO1 and the CRA.[5] Enemy was holding

1 'Keyes was opposed to any landing on the beach': Diary, 31 August 1918.
2 Brigadier General Raymond Brutinel (1882–1964). His formation was unique.
3 Brigadier General Norman William Webber (1881–1950), BGGS Canadian Corps, 1918.
4 Major General (later General Sir) Torquhil George Matheson (1871–1963), GOC 4th Division, 1917–18; GOC Guards Division, 1918–19.
5 Lieutenant Colonel L. Carr (GSO1) and Brigadier General C. A. Sykes (CRA).

a wood east of Etaing with machine guns; these fired up the valley, and caused much damage.

The officer examining the prisoners stated that the moral of German officers was terribly low. He had at no period of the war seen such a despicable state. The prisoners I saw seemed well fed but badly drilled.

Near Wancourt I visited HQ of 4th Canadian and 1st Canadian Divisions. General Watson[1] commanding the former corroborated what Webber had said re. taking the position with little loss; and he added that the Tanks had been sent off after getting the Enemy's defences in order to economise Tanks and save loss in them. Now his infantry was having a bad time from Enemy machine guns which were scattered on the lower slopes east of the Drocourt line. Watson seemed disturbed at the report of the losses he had had, but on enquiry I found that they did not amount to many. Watson also stated that the German private soldiers abused their officers and NCOs and would not obey their orders...

At Bretencourt I saw General Fergusson Commanding XVII Corps.[2] He explained how the 52nd and 57th Divisions had taken Riencourt and an immensely strong 'triangle' of trenches and wire to the east of it in the early morning without trouble. The right of 52nd was held up by machine-gun fire from Lagnicourt direction but left of division go right on, and moved eastwards on north side of Quéant. The 63rd Division then passed through and got along the railway from near Quéant to Buissy. This was well done, and the whole day had been a great success. He too said of the prisoners, that his Provost Marshal reported that they would not obey their officers. Discipline in the German Army seemed to have gone! If this is true, then the end cannot now be far off, I think.

Tuesday 3 September

During the night Third Army took Rocquigny and occupied Quéant. This morning Enemy is said to be retreating on the front of our Third and First Armies. Our troops have reached (9 am) the line Bertincourt, Doignies, Pronville. First Army is on hill south of Buissy. Thence line passes west of the latter village, Dury and Etaing, both inclusive. Advance is continuing to Canal du Nord. I expect that the results of our success in yesterday's great battle should be very far reaching...

Lastly I rode to Ervillers and had a talk with General Haldane

1 Major General (later Sir) David Watson (1871–1922), GOC 4th Canadian Division, 1916–18; a journalist by profession.
2 'Division' in the Ms diary. Sir Charles Fergusson's XVII Corps was part of Third Army, which made some important gains on 2 September.

Commanding VI Corps. He has an advanced HQ here. Today he is employing the 2nd Division and the Guards. These he kept fresh for the 'pursuit', he said. They know the ground too over which they are now advancing. All ranks are in the very highest spirits.

The Enemy seems in full retreat today on the whole front from Lens to Péronne. I am inclined to think that the Enemy will be unable to remain on the Hindenburg Line for any time, but will seek for rest and peace behind the Meuse and the Namur defences, in order to refit his shattered divisions.

I received a letter from General Henry Wilson in explanation of a personal wire which he sent me 3 days ago stating that Cabinet were anxious lest I sacrificed many men in attacking the Hindenburg Line. 'Police strike and other cognate matters make Cabinet sensitive to heavy losses, especially if these are incurred against old lines of fortification.' How ignorant these people are of war!! In my opinion it is much less costly in lives to press the Enemy after a victorious battle than to give him time to recover and organise afresh his defence of a position! The latter must then be attacked in the face of hostile artillery and machine guns, all carefully sited.

Wednesday 4 September

I left soon after 9 am with Lawrence for Mouchy le Châtel, where Marshal Foch met me at noon. He was particularly pleased with the results of the operations carried out by the British. He spoke of 'la grande bataille' won by us on Monday, and thought that it would produce a great effect on the Enemy's plans. I explained the situation on the British front. Foch then produced a 'Directive' dated 3rd September. This did not affect the task of the British, but ordered certain moves by the Americans and by the French in combination with our attacks. Foch had a great deal of trouble in getting Pershing to agree to attack *at once*. Pershing looks forward to the creation of a great American Army, and will only allow his American Divisions to fight in American corps. However, Foch managed to bring Pétain and Pershing together and fixed up all details for a combined attack under Pétain.

I lunched with Foch after our talk, and after lunch took a little walk with him. He is most hopeful, and thinks the German is nearing the end. Reports came in that the Enemy is in full retreat on the Vesle and Ham fronts ... Since 1 August, we British alone have captured over 72,000 prisoners and more than 700 guns.

Thursday 5 September

General Plumer came to see me about 11 am re. the instructions I sent him for co-operating with Belgian Army. He was inclined to continue his efforts to press Enemy back between Ypres[1] and Armentières and retake Messines. I told him the most important object was to get the Belgians to advance! With this in view he was to employ 2 good divisions on his left to co-operate with Belgian right. First objective should be Clerken Ridge–Forêt d'Houthoulst and Passchendaele. Then when main attacks of Allies developed, he should be prepared to move a division by sea to Ostend and occupy Bruges with left on the Dutch frontier, and connecting with Anglo-Belgian Army on the line Thourout–Roulers ... Plumer said that he had every confidence that Belgian troops would do well once they started.

Saturday 7 September

DGT explained the rail situation. He has laid over 200 miles of track since last battle (8 August) began. He asks for 120 miles of rails (broad gauge) every month from now on to enable him to follow up the Armies through Belgium. The railways have kept up with the advance of the troops in a most praise worthy way.

Sunday 8 September

Colonel Butler[2] reported on the situation ... Evidence from prisoners indicates that Enemy is preparing to fall back to the Passchendaele Ridge...

Mr Winston Churchill (Minister of Munitions) came to see me at 12.30. I told him that I considered that the Allies should aim at getting a decision, *as soon as possible.* This month or next, or next spring,[3] and that our greatest effort should be made at once so as to take advantage of the present disorganised state both of the German Army and of the German plans. Our reserves of ammunition and programmes of construction should also be reviewed in this light. Further that it would be a mistake to provide the Army with a new form of weapon after 31 December if any new form of training were required. Churchill agreed and said that he would go into the matter and do his best to set free men from Munitions.

Sir Henry Rawlinson came to lunch ... He urged me to give him the 6th Division which is now in GHQ Reserve. I said my objective was to strike as heavy a *blow as possible in co-operation with the other Allies.* If I was to reinforce him now, my reserves would become used up before the time for combined action had come.

1 In the Ts diary this is amended to 'the Yser'.
2 Colonel S. S. Butler, Cox's temporary replacement as Haig's Intelligence chief.
3 In the Ts diary, Haig amended this to 'This month or next, not next spring or summer as the Cabinet proposed'. It is possible that the second 'or' in the Ms diary is a slip for 'not'.

Monday 9 September

Haig met Foch at Cassel.

He first of all had a private talk with myself and Weygand. He told me that he saw the King of the Belgians this morning; and that although the Belgian Staff opposed any advance by the Belgian Army, the King was all in favour of action. Foch had accordingly made a plan. Practically the same one as Plumer had put forward and I approved.

The King of the Belgians[1] would command in person with a French general (De Goutte) as Chief of the Staff,[2] but under another title. I agreed that Plumer should take orders from the King regarding the operations but I declined to give 3 Cavalry Divisions.

Haig then crossed to England.

Tuesday 10 September

At the War Office, Haig conferred with Milner.

I stated that the object of my visit was to explain how greatly the situation in the field had changed to the advantage of the Allies. [I considered it to be of first importance that the Cabinet should realise how all our plans and methods are at once affected by this change.]

Within the last four weeks we had captured 77,000 prisoners and nearly 800 guns! There has never been such a victory in the annals of Britain, and its effects are not yet apparent. The German prisoners now taken will not obey their officers or NCOs. The same story is told me [of the prisoners] from our hospitals. The discipline of the German Army is quickly going, and the German officer is no longer what he was. It seems to me to be the beginning of the end. From these and other facts I draw the conclusion that the Enemy's troops will not await our attacks in even the strongest positions.

Briefly, in my opinion, the character of the war has changed. What is wanted now at once is to provide the means to exploit our recent successes to the full. Reserves in England should be regarded as Reserves for the French front, and all yeomanry, cyclists etc. now kept for civil defence should be sent to France *at once*.

If we act with energy now, a decision can be obtained in the very near future.

1 Albert I, King of the Belgians (1875–1934).
2 Properly General Jean Marie Joseph Degoutte (1866–1938).

As regards next year, aim at having all our units full up by 1 April. To consider that 1 July is 'time enough' is thoroughly unsound. All reserves of ammunition, airoplanes, etc. should be reviewed in the light of the present situation. These reserves may well be reduced in order to set free men for the Army: men already marked for the Navy should for the next 6 months be sent to Army. It is all important to provide the Army with infantry drafts and *mobile* troops to exploit success.

Lord Milner fully agreed and said he would do his best to help. He also spoke to me about my recent Despatch (20 July). He (Milner) had read it, and was willing to publish it as it was. But the PM (Lloyd George) took exception to certain phrases. These Milner had marked and suggested omitting a few words in certain paras. Their omission did not affect the facts as recorded in the Despatch. I read the proposed modification, and agreed to what Milner suggested. Lawrence, who was present, also read the alterations proposed and concurred.[1]

I then visited the QMG (Cowans). The PM had tried to put in a civilian as Adjutant General, but Milner had defeated him . . .[2]

About 7 pm General Seely (now in Munitions Department) came to see me. I told him we ought to aim at finishing the war *now* and not to delay the provision of Tanks until experiments showed we had a *perfect* design. I felt it was a waste of time talking to Seely.

Wednesday 11 September

At 1.30 I lunched with the King at Buckingham Palace . . . The King was in the best of spirits, but I saw that he had not yet realised the magnitude of our recent victory. He is determined to continue the war till the Germans are completely broken. He spoke with bitter hatred of the Germans!

Byng and Rawlinson's forces captured the outer positions of the Hindenburg Line (12–26 September).

Sunday 15 September

I held a conference with the 3 Commanders of Armies on my right, viz. General Rawlinson (Fourth) on right; Byng (Third) next and Horne (First)

---

1 See entry for 27 August 1918.
2 General Sir (Cecil Frederick) Nevil Macready (1862–1946), Director of Personal Services, War Office, 1910–14; Adjutant General BEF, 1914–16; Adjutant General to the Forces, 1916–18; Chief Commissioner of the Metropolitan Police, 1918–20. Macready had been moved from the post of AG in response to the Police Strike.

on the Scarpe with right on Canal du Nord, west of Bourlon Wood. Conference took place at Third Army HQ at Villers l'Hôpital at 11 am. Army Commanders in turn explained the situation on their front. I then told them of the general situation, and outlined the general plan. We then went into the actions of each Army.

Rawlinson's Army is now in close touch with the Enemy's 'outpost zone' of defence in front of the Hindenburg Line. Enemy seems to have strengthened his force holding the line of heights from Le Verguièr to Epéhy. On the other hand in all combats which our troops have recently had with the Enemy, the latter has not really fought. The First Army (Horne) stated the same thing, but Byng (Third Army) said the fighting at Trescault and Havrincourt had been severe: Enemy had put in five divisions there in last 3 days.

As result of our discussion, I decided that Rawlinson should attack in force as soon as possible to capture the Enemy's outpost zone on the Le Verguièr–Epéhy ridges, and if possible push his right forward to get the rising ground about Fayet and Gricourt northwest of St Quentin. The possession of this height is important for gun positions to attack the main Hindenburg Line subsequently . . .

After Rawlinson's attack has taken place (probably on 18th) we should know more about the nature of the Hindenburg Line and how it is now held. My present view is that main attack will be made by Rawlinson against the Canal Tunnel with the object of reaching Bussigny.[1] The Third Army will support him (Rawlinson) and advance on Solesmes. Horne will take Bourlon Wood and cover left of Third Army by holding a front on the [Rivers] Scarpe and Scheldt as far as Valenciennes. Kavanagh with Cavalry Corps and a brigade of infantry in buses etc. will be ready to pursue. On Tuesday I am holding an exercise for the Cavalry Corps against a marked enemy, in order to practise all ranks in the pursuit.

Monday 16 September

Haig had a meeting with Foch.

After a general review of the situation on the British front, and outlining my plans, I asked that Debeney's French First Army should be reinforced so as to co-operate with Rawlinson on Wednesday by taking the village of Fayet, northwest of St Quentin. Foch said that Debeney was very weak, and his guns had been taken for other Armies, but he would see that Debeney was strengthened sufficiently to enable him to cover Rawlinson's right. The

---

1 Actually, 'Busigny'.

dividing line was moved 1000 yards to the south, thus giving the village of Fayet to Rawlinson.

As regards the operations in Flanders, Foch agreed with me that it was not necessary or desirable for Plumer to attack Messines–Wytschaete position. Plumer's attack by 2 divisions should be towards Zandvoorde and Gheluvelt, and these divisions should be well supported in order that the flank of the Belgians should be adequately covered, and the exploiting force enabled to move out at once. Foch gave me the details of the movements of the other attacks, dates, etc. He expressed the wish that I should continue my activity for another week. I explained that Rawlinson's attack would commence on Wednesday, and that the rest of the front to Bourlon Wood would be pressing the Enemy hard all the time.

Wednesday 18 September

Fourth Army fought the Battle of Epéhy.

Our front of attack was about 18 miles in length. We met and defeated 13 Enemy divisions in front line together with three more divisions brought up from Reserve = total 16 divisions. The 6th Division from Thourout in Flanders was identified in the battle! It was the only remaining Enemy division in reserve north of the Lys . . .

At 3 pm I had a meeting with the King of the Belgians at La Panne . . . I explained our plan and why I was opposed to attacking Messines . . . The King said that the Belgian Army was in the very best spirits and meant to fight well.

As regards a 4-hours bombardment which the Belgian General Staff proposed, I stated that the objection was that it would at once prepare the Enemy for attack, and he might be able to put down a counter-preparation with gas upon the troops when concentrated for the attack. This might have serious consequences.

Thursday 19 September

All reports indicate that yesterday's battle was a great success. Enemy did his utmost to hold on to his positions, but was defeated and driven back. Our troops are now [within] about 6000 yards of the front line of the Hindenburg main system west of Bellicourt.

General Clive[1] reported on the situation. Reports of the last 48 hours

1 Brigadier General (later General Sir) (George) Sidney Clive (1874–1959), Haig's new, permanent, Intelligence chief.

indicate clearly that the Enemy is about to fall back on the front from Armentières to Lens ... Third Army report that the losses suffered by the Enemy in his counter-attack yesterday afternoon against Trescault and Havrincourt were the heaviest ever seen by our troops ... two divisions advanced in great masses. The attack came against our 37th, 3rd and Guards Divisions. All first rate troops, and well trained in musketry ...

Three officers of the South African Defence Force, who are spending a few months with the Army to learn our administrative system came to dinner. Their names were Major W. Nussey, Major C. Brink, Major W. Klerck.

I found them most pleasant and full of enthusiasm for the British Army and our people. General Botha had sent them to England.[1] When they arrived, they were very anti-British! Brink, however, very frankly told me how his feelings and those of all Colonials had changed as the result of their visit to England and the kindness they had received and life with our Army. The war has broken down the feelings of prejudice which existed mutually between Colonials and English men in the old Country! This is all most satisfactory.

On 19 September Wilson wrote to Haig, 'Well done! you must be a famous general!'

Friday 20 September. Letter to Sir Henry Wilson[2]

My dear Henry

Very many thanks for your kind little note of yesterday. – No, certainly not! I am not, nor am I likely to be a *famous* general'. For that must we not have pandered to Repington and the gutter Press? But we have a surprisingly large number of *very capable* generals. Thanks to these gentlemen, and to their 'sound military knowledge built up of study and practice until it has become an instinct', and to a steady adherence to the principles of our FSR Part I are our successes to be chiefly attributed.

Friday 20 September. Letter to Lord Stamfordham[3]

In view of the events which are taking place in France, and the possibility that greater events may take place in the near future, possibly the King might think it desirable that the Prince of Wales should be in this Theatre of War at the present time ...

I would suggest that the Prince should visit the Australian and Canadian

1 Louis Botha (1862–1949), Prime Minister of South Africa, 1910–19.
2 IWM: Wilson Papers, HHW 2/7B/16.
3 RA: PS/GV/O 1382/7.

Corps in turn, and join whichever Army HQ happens to be engaged in the most interesting operations at the time . . .

Saturday 21 September

I had another talk with Milner. He states recruiting is bad, and that if British Army is used up now, there will not be one for next year. He was quite satisfied that I should do what I deemed best in the matter of attacking or not. I pointed out that the situation was most satisfactory and that *every available man should be put into the battle at once.* In my opinion it is possible to get a decision *this* year: but if we do not, every blow that we deliver now will make the task next year [much easier] . . .[1]

I then motored to Bavincourt where I held a conference with Army Commanders . . . Plumer considered that Enemy knew nothing of his and Belgian preparations. Enemy was preparing to go back to Passchendaele ridge, and shorten his line southwards also.

Birdwood also thought Enemy was preparing to go back on front as far south as Lens.

Horne agreed also to this. As regards the rest of our First Army front Enemy would not move back until attacked.

On Third and Fourth Army fronts, Enemy must hold on at all costs to Cambrai–St Quentin front until his troops on the Champagne and Laon fronts can be got back [otherwise their retreat will be cut off.]

As regards our own operations, the objective of the main British effort will be the line Valenciennes–Le Cateau–Wassigny. We were confronted by a strong well sited series of defences, and the Enemy appears to have collected a certain number of reserves behind the Cambrai–St Quentin front. I therefore did not propose to attack until the American–French attack has gone in. This latter attack *might* draw off some of the Enemy's reserves from our front. I therefore would like to attack 2 or 3 days *after* the main Americo–French attack. If we could arrange this, there was a chance of the Enemy's reserves being unavailable for either battle . . .

All were quite pleased with my arrangements. Before my intervention, Byng and Rawlinson were each inclined to try to get the better of the other!

---

1 In his diary for 23 September, Henry Wilson noted that Milner thought Haig was 'ridiculously optimistic and is afraid that he may embark on another Passchendaele', and other generals he spoke to were 'all most optimistic'. Milner was concerned about the manpower situation. Callwell, *Field-Marshal Sir Henry Wilson*, II, p. 126.

Wednesday 25 September

Haig visited Third Army HQ near Bapaume.

I found Byng in an improvised railway train and quite comfortable. He had
gutted the inside of an International Sleeping Car, and put his various
requirements into two compartments of it. I also saw Vaughan his CSO. I
thought that they were afraid that our troops will meet strong Enemy reserves
on Cambrai–St Quentin front, and that in consequence they are desirous for
me to wait and do nothing for some days, so as to allow the other attacks to
have an effect and cause Enemy to withdraw some of his reserves from before
us. I therefore told Byng of the dates fixed for the various attacks by Marshal
Foch, viz. the Franco–American attack with *right* on Meuse and advancing
northwest will be on Thursday 26th; my attack with First Army and left of
Third Army will take place as I arranged last Saturday, namely on Friday
27th. The Flanders attack will go in on Saturday 28th, and then my Fourth
Army on Sunday 29th. The delay in the Flanders attack is due to the lack of
reserves behind it: it is therefore desirable to engage the Enemy in force
elsewhere, and so fix his reserves before the Flanders attack goes in.

I then motored on to Bois du Hennois, HQ V Corps and had a talk with
Lieutenant General Shute. He said his divisions were full of cheer but were
very 'sleepy'. A few days' rest and they would be as fit as ever again. The 21st
Division (David Campbell) had, after the first start, done splendidly. He also
spoke about the difficult task which confronted him in attacking Gouzeaucourt and the Gonnelieu spur. I told him my plan was to cross the Canal
at Marcoing, and by the Bellicourt tunnel, and then the centre of the Enemy's
position (opposite which [is his corps]) would fall of itself. All he would be
wanted to do would be to advance sufficiently to counter-batter the Enemy's
artillery) . . .

This morning reports of railway strike in England are serious. Our supply
of ammunition would be affected. I ordered no change to be made, however,
as I have full confidence in the good sense of our railwaymen at home. Some
means will be found to keep up our supply of ammunition even if the worst
happens. If strike continues, I ordered all leave to be stopped from tomorrow.

Thursday 26 September

*The first phase of Foch's sequential Grand Offensive began with a Franco–
American attack between the River Meuse and Rheims.*

I first visited HQ Fourth Army in huts near Eterpigny–Villers Carbonnel
road. General Rawlinson explained his plan in detail. Byng came in during

my talk ... Both assured me that everything was satisfactorily arranged and that they were fully confident of success in the forthcoming attack, but Byng insisted that the fighting is sure to be hard and that Haldane's estimate of crossing at Marcoing on Friday is too optimistic!

I next visited HQ Australian and II American Corps in hutments off the Barleux–Asservillers road. General Monash had about 40 or 50 officers gathered together for a conference ... Monash begged me to go in and see them all even at the risk of delaying matters! So I went into the room, and shook the senior officers by the hand and said a few words of encouragement. I told them that the biggest battle of the war had started this morning – the Enemy would be attacked by 100 divisions in the next 3 days. The French and Americans had attacked with right on the Meuse this morning, and were getting on extremely well, etc. etc. ...

At Villers Carbonnel, HQ IX Corps, I had a talk with General Braithwaite ... Braithwaite is satisfied now with the positions he is holding for starting his attack on Sunday. In one sector his men have to cross the Canal: for this every conceivable device has been provided, including life protecting jackets from the Channel leave steamers. The French took Hill 138, or Manchester Hill today. This gives observation over St Quentin and is important because the Enemy has many guns in the outskirts hidden in buildings and yards.

Friday 27 September

First Army attacked at 5.20 am today. General Horne arranged for demonstrations by XXII and VIII Corps who attacked Fresnes–Rouvroy line from River Scarpe to midway between Gavrelle and Oppy. Lens was bombarded, and 8th and 20th Divisions took Arleux and German front system 2000 yards north of Arleux, to a depth of 500 yards. This greatly misled Enemy, because his artillery fire was all concentrated on the Canal crossings astride the Arras–Cambrai road, whereas our advance was made on the south of that ...

After lunch I visited First Army ... I explained to Horne my views as to the employment of the Cavalry Corps, viz. that First Army should continue to form a defensive flank on right bank of Scheldt while the Cavalry Corps passed beyond and took (if possible) Valenciennes and (if Plumer and Belgians are successful) moves down river towards Ghent. I told Currie that with Enemy in his present state there was nothing to fear as to his flank!

At Ervillers, HQ VI Corps (Lieutenant General Haldane). This Corps did very well today ... Haldane reported that 2nd Division had pushed on through the Guards and was close to the Canal. He regretted that Harper and Byng had not accepted his opinion that his advance would be fast, and now his progress was being delayed because his right was in the air! ...

I personally corrected communiqué and put General Horne's name in with doings of his Corps in detail. Byng's name had to go in also though he has done nothing particular *today*.

Saturday 28 September

Second Army attacked this morning in conjunction with the Belgians in the Ypres area. The Allied line has been advanced between 2 to 5 miles on a front of 20 miles. The object of the day's operation is to get the Clerken–Passchendaele ridge as a base for further operations.

Reports from Cambrai sector are also most satisfactory. The enemy seems to be falling back without offering much resistance to the east of the Scheldt. Over 13,000 prisoners taken since yesterday.

I visited HQ Third Army before lunch and had a talk with Byng. He is very pleased at the progress which his troops have made since yesterday morning. Now his VI Corps have been able to advance well and he has directed Harper to cross at Crève-Coeur[1] and get the rising ground northeast of the Canal tonight if possible. He thinks that the Enemy on his front shows signs of 'cracking' . . .

At 3 pm I visited HQ Australian Corps and found Monash in what he called 'a state of despair'. The cause of it was that some detachments of Americans had yesterday attacked and taken a few advanced points on the ridge west of the Canal, but had not been heard of. Airoplane observers said that they were in possession of the positions in question; on the other hand, ground observers said that Germans were between these positions and our main line, and were firing machine guns against us! I told him that probably both reports might be correct and that the Americans had gone forward to the positions as ordered but had not mopped up the intervening trenches. In any case it was not a serious matter and he should attack tomorrow morning in force as arranged.

I went on to American II Corps HQ which is close to Australian HQ as the latter are nursing the 2 American Divisions. I saw General Read. He is a good honest fellow, but all this class of warfare is quite new to him, and he was genuinely very anxious. I did my best to cheer him up and told him that the reality was much simpler than imagination pictured it to his mind . . .

Haig later visited the HQs of US 27th and 30th Divisions.

The Generals had gone on to their battle stations, so I only saw some of the Staff, and an Australian officer who is looking after the supply arrangements

---

1 Properly, Crèvecoeur.

of the 2 American Divisions. No easy job! He told me all are very ignorant but most keen and quick, and never have to be told a thing twice. The Americans are very ignorant of war requirements and insist on each man carrying 5 bombs! I said $\frac{1}{2}$ a bomb per man was now our average in the attack.

Sunday 29 September

General Kavanagh and his CGS (Home) came to lunch. He mentioned that an Army Commander (I gather Byng) stated in August that we would never get beyond the Hindenburg Line! Now we *are* through that line. The Fourth Army can give him [Kavanagh] facilities to have his head on the line Bellicourt–Bellenglise across the Canal by noon tomorrow. His objectives will be to

(a) occupy the railway junctions Busigny and Le Cateau
(b) operate against the flank and rear of the enemy now opposing our 3rd and 1st Armies' advance
(c) cut the Enemy's communications at Valenciennes

I explained my orders and he quite understood what is intended. He left fully confident that there is a great opportunity offering for the cavalry.

Situation at 10 pm: IX Corps on right of Fourth Army has done very well – 46th Division has taken over 4000 prisoners and 40 guns! Its losses very slight. Right of Australian Corps is also satisfactory, but no one seems to know what has happened to the left of the Corps where two American Divisions are operating . . .[1]

Rawlinson reports to CGS that Americans are very ignorant of their duties, and are now greatly disorganised. These two divisions are quite unfit to operate as a corps under an American Corps Staff.

As Rawlinson's left did not get on, Byng did not press with his right about Gonnelieu. He is quite satisfied with progress on his left which is well across the Scheldt and in outskirts of Cambrai.

46th (North Midland) Division's assault crossing of the St Quentin Canal, thus breaking one of the most formidable sections of the Hindenburg Line, was arguably the single most important action of the Grand Offensive.

1 Several weeks later Haig visited the canal and described the German defences as 'admirably sited . . . had the German Army been in a good state of moral, the position would have been impregnable': Diary, 15 October 1918.

Monday 30 September

Marshal Foch came to see me at 9.30 am. He was with the King of the Belgians yesterday at La Panne. Much pleased with position in Belgium and progress made by the Allied Armies there, as well as on British front. As regards the American operations west of Meuse, he says Americans have employed too many troops on that front, and have blocked one another's advance. In fact they have not been able to feed so many divisions in that area. But they are going on attacking and are 'learning all the time'. Pétain is now using some American troops to push on towards Machault (southeast of Rethel). I asked Foch to send 3 American Divisions to Plumer. Foch said it was not possible at present as 'their amour propre made the Americans determined to press on to Mézières'! But later on 'he would see what could be done when Pershing has learnt the difficulty of creating an army' . . .

Foch told me that the 'Bulgarians had agreed to all our terms for peace'. Foch was of opinion that the Germans cannot much longer resist our attacks against their whole front and that 'soon they will crack'.

Tuesday 1 October

I motored with CGS to HQ Third Army at Ligny Thilloy (near Bapaume) and had a talk with Generals Byng and Rawlinson. Both consider that Enemy has suffered very much, and that it is merely a question of our continuing our pressure to ensure his breaking. They agreed that no further orders from me were necessary, and both would be able to carry on without difficulty. The French on Rawlinson's right seem to be hanging back so Lawrence telephoned to Foch's HQ to ask him to urge Debeney to action! . . .

We have adopted the 24 hour clock system since the 1 October. This is a great convenience. [I advocated it when producing Field Service Regulations at the War Office. But my proposal was turned down.]

Reports from Americans (west of the Meuse) and from Belgian HQ state that their roads and communications are so blocked that the offensive has had to stop and cannot be recommenced for 4 or 5 days. What very valuable days are being lost! All this is the result of inexperience and ignorance of the needs of a modern attacking force.

Thursday 3 October. Letter to Winston Churchill[1]

My dear Mr Churchill,

Very many thanks for your kind letter of October 1, and for your friendly

---

1 CCC: Churchill Papers, CHAR 27.32/38.

remarks on the doings of our splendid Army. I am more than grateful for the kindly sympathy which you extended to me during the anxious time we passed through in the spring, and for the immense vigour with which you set about providing us with munitions of war.

I have read the memorandum you enclose with great interest, and I hope everything will be done to *maintain* this Army at full strength in order to beat the enemy as soon as possible. In my opinion, it is of the highest importance to keep on pressing the enemy at every possible point: because if we allow him any breathing time at all, he will be able to reorganise his forces, to construct new defences, and make new plans, and much of the work of 'wearing him out' will have to be started afresh.

On his copy of a memorandum by Churchill, against a paragraph calling for conservation of resources 'for the decisive struggles of 1920', Haig noted, 'What rubbish: Who will last till 1920? Only America??' In a separate note dated 3 October 1918, Haig recalled his visit to London on 9 September to explain the new conditions on the Western Front, and the need for maximum reinforcements to 'win this autumn or early next year'.

On 4 October Fourth Army captured the last section of the Hindenburg Line, triggering a major German retreat; not only on Rawlinson's front, but eventually opposite Third, First and Fifth Armies as well. At long last, the BEF began to advance into open country.

Saturday 5 October

The QMG came to see me. General David Henderson was present,[1] and I fixed up his duties so far as I am concerned. I signed letter to War Office re. supply of Box cars and Fords during next 6 months. I asked QMG to experiment with Ford car arranged with a body like an Irish outside-car [for carrying] infantry men, as lorries are very cumbersome near the front...

Brigadier General Charlie Grant[2] arrived from Foch's HQ and stayed the night. He states that Foch's Staff are terribly disappointed with results of American attack west of the Meuse. The Enemy is in no strength in their front, but the Americans cannot advance because their supply arrangements have broken down. The divisions in the front line are really starving, and have had to be relieved in order to be fed! There are many fine divisions there and cannot be used owing to incapacity of American HQ Staff. General

1 Lieutenant General Sir David Henderson (1861–1921), father of the RFC and of the Intelligence Corps, who had been appointed British Military Attaché in Paris.
2 Brigadier General (later General Sir) Charles ('Charlie') John Cecil Grant (1877–1950), BGGS HQ Allied Forces in France, 1918–19.

Weygand (Foch's Chief of Staff) spent 5 hours with Pershing recently explaining the situation, but Pershing won't allow any of his divisions to be transferred to another sector, where they might produce decisive results.

Recognising that defeat was inevitable, the German Government resigned, and the liberal-minded Prince Max of Baden became Chancellor on 3 October.

Sunday 6 October

Haig visited Foch.

He had a Paris morning paper opened out on the table, in which in large type was printed a note from Austria, Germany, and Turkey, asking for an armistice at once, and stating their readiness to discuss conditions of peace on the basis of President Wilson's 14 points.[1] 'Here' said Foch, 'here is the immediate result of the British piercing the Hindenburg Line. The Enemy has asked for an armistice.' His opinion is that the Enemy should be told to retire to the Rhine as a guarantee of good faith, before any negotiations are begun.

I explained to Foch the position on the British front and said that if we get sufficient artillery and ammunition forward we proposed to attack tomorrow morning on front from Cambrai to right of Fourth Army. If ammunition not up in sufficient quantities, then attack will not take place till [Tuesday] morning. Foch said he was very pleased with all we had done, and was in complete agreement with what I proposed to do now. He then explained the situation on the other battle fronts...

I told Foch that with 3 fresh American Divisions it would be possible to reach Valenciennes in 48 hours! Foch said it was impossible to get any troops from Pershing at this moment.

Monday 7 October

Major General Salmond reported on work of Flying Corps. In reply to my question as to whether he was ready to support the Cavalry Corps with large numbers of low flying machines, in the event of the enemy breaking; – for instance, how many machines could he concentrate about Busigny? – he replied that all were quite ready to act, and he could concentrate 300 machines practically at once!

1 Idealistic terms for the settlement of the conflict, announced in January 1918.

Tuesday 8 October

At 5 pm Haig met with the commanders of Fourth, Third and First Armies at Byng's HQ.

The day had been most successful. We had driven Enemy from his last defensive line east of the St Quentin Canal, and had taken some 8000 or more prisoners ... I directed operations to continue tomorrow – or rather they will continue without intermission on front of Fourth Army and right of Third *only* on left of the latter Army to organise an attack.

Wednesday 9 October

[Telephone message from General Vaughan,[1] Third Army at 8.15 am. The Germans appear to have vanished. The V Corps are beyond Selvigny, which is full of civilians. The IV Corps are approaching the railway, meeting with very little opposition, and picking up a few stragglers. The VI Corps are through Wambaix, and on the line of the railway, without much opposition.][2]

I motored on by Gouzeaucourt–Welch Ridge–Bois Lateau and the Bonavis Spur, so famous during the Battle of Cambrai last November and December. We crossed the Scheldt Canal by the sluice bridge near Vaucelles and then up the hill, turning northwards to Bel Aise Farm ... The farm acted as a kind of 'keep' to the trenches, machine gun nests, and wire in front. It was only yesterday that the Enemy was driven from this great fortress, and yet I was able to walk about today, 24 hours later, almost out of the hearing of the guns. The dead were still lying about and one was able to see where the struggle had been fiercest. [How well] our '106 fuse' had cut the wire, as if it were thread (but brittle!) and how our gallant fellows had pushed through by the gaps thus made ...

Thursday 10 October

I motored to Mouchy le Châtel where I met Marshal Foch at midday. I sent him a message by wire last night recommending that my advance on the battle front should now be between the Scheldt and Sambre with the object of joining hands with my Second Army and the other troops under King of the Belgians ...

I found Foch in very good spirits and highly complimentary at what British

1 Chief of Staff, Third Army.
2 This passage is not in the Ms diary, yet the degree of detail suggests that it is contemporaneous. Also, it is difficult to discern what advantage Haig would gain by adding this passage to the Ts diary unless he simply wanted to set down as full an account as possible.

Army had done. He produced a new 'Directive'. In this he said that the success of the British Armies is to be exploited to the full, and with this object Debeney's First French Army is to be reinforced. Besides covering my right Debeney will also operate to clear Laon by advancing southeast from Guise. The French attacks on the Rheims and Verdun fronts will be continued, but all available reserves and resources in Tanks, guns, etc. will go first to Debeney and then to the French force in Flanders . . .

After lunch Foch gave me a paper which he had handed to the Allied Conference in Paris on the subject of an armistice . . . His main points were:

1. Evacuation of Belgium, France and Alsace-Lorraine.
2. Hand over to Allies to administer all country up to Rhine with three Bridgeheads on the river. The size of each of latter to be 30 kilometres from the crossing drawn in semi-circle.
3. Germans to leave all material behind, huts, supplies, etc., etc., railway trains, railways in order.
4. Enemy to clear out in 15 days from signing of agreement.

I remarked that the only difference between his (Foch's) conditions and a 'general surrender' is that the German Army is allowed to march back with its rifles, and officers with their swords. He is evidently of opinion that the Enemy is so desirous of peace that he will agree to any terms of this nature which we impose . . .

After dinner, I handed over Foch's 'Directive' to Lawrence. He seemed in a pessimistic mood and foresaw many dangers ahead. He said 'the British Army is doing all the fighting, the French will do nothing, and the American Army is quite incapable of doing anything' and so on. If the Enemy were to counter-attack us, we should find ourselves in a difficult position!

I assured him that the Enemy has not the means, nor the will-power, to launch an attack strong enough to affect even our front line troops. We have got the Enemy down, in fact he is a beaten Army, and my plan is to go on hitting him as hard as we possibly can, till he begs for mercy.

Lawrence has a cold and so is looking at things in a gloomy way tonight. I think the situation highly satisfactory, and the results of our victories will be *very far reaching*: it may take a few days for its results to begin to show. The Enemy is in such a state that we can run all kinds of risks without any chance of Enemy hitting back in any force.

Friday 11 October. Letter to Lady Haig

I enclose a copy of a number of telegrams which I have received congratulating the Army on the recent successes. The Prime Minister's shows the least understanding of the great efforts made by the *whole* British Army. He speaks of the 'success' of the last '*two* days'. In the papers I see some friend of his has altered the word to '*few* days'. Then, as the message originally reached me, no mention at all was made of Horne and the First Army, when the Canadian Corps actually were in Cambrai, and have had such hard fighting for Monchy le Preux, the Drocourt–Quéant line etc.

Foch told me yesterday how, at a conference in Paris two days before, at which all the Prime Ministers were present, he told them of the great successes gained by the British, and said that a message of congratulation should be sent to me. M. Clemenceau at once said 'Of course the French Government will wire to me,' ditto was said by Orlando for Italy, and so on. 'No,' said Foch, 'that would never do because the Prime Ministers of the Allies were not always in session.' And if he wanted sometime to congratulate the French Armies, they would feel aggrieved if the message only came from their own Government! So he said, Mr Lloyd George alone must congratulate the British Commander-in-Chief. LG agreed at once, and drafted this clumsy wire of which I enclose a copy.

Saturday 12 October

At 11 am I held a conference with Army Commanders and General Kavanagh, Commanding Cavalry Corps ... I explained Foch's *general plan* and told them how I proposed to operate with the British Army. For the moment the important thing was to complete our railway communications on the Cambrai–Le Cateau front. These were being pushed on very satisfactorily. As soon as these enabled adequate ammunition to be brought up, *our main advance* will be made between the Scheldt and the Sambre Rivers, with the object of joining hands with our Second Army and cutting off the Lille salient. Birdwood was of the opinion the Enemy is ready to evacuate Lille at an early date ...

Later Haig visited HQ V Corps, where he saw Lieutenant General Shute.

Such check as has taken place here today is due to Enemy suddenly strengthening his rear guard and taking the offensive. This must always be expected in operations of this nature, when advanced guards are pushing on to keep touch and press the Enemy. We seem to be in presence of a hostile rear guard, and as soon as we organise an attack with an adequate artillery support the Enemy will fall back.

Monday 14 October

The Prince of Wales with Major Thompson left for HQ Canadian Corps, where Prince will be attached for a month. He seems a good sporting lad, natural and sincere, but rather faddy over his diet. Eats no breakfast, but has jam in large quantities with 'morning tea'. His small stature makes me think he was starved as a baby...

AG reported ... AG brought no Courts Martial. The fighting of the past few weeks has prevented any crime from being committed.

Thursday 17 October

The Battle of the Selle began.

Fourth Army met with considerable opposition but made good progress ... On the right we advanced over 2 miles across the high wooded ground east of Bohain, and captured Audigny les Fermes. Further north line of Selle River taken up to and including Le Cateau, and ridge to east of the river. Villages of La Vallée Mulatre and L'Arbre du Guise taken. On left of attack, the line of railway east of Le Cateau captured. Front of attack about 9 miles. This was held by Enemy with 7 divisions disposed in depth. They were thus able to dispose of large reserves which counter-attacked vigorously. All were repulsed, and Enemy lost many killed. About 4000 prisoners taken by Fourth Army, and several guns, including two complete batteries.

Enemy continued his withdrawal in the Lille sector. Fifth Army is now round Lille ... First Army occupied Douai today after pressing Enemy's rear guards back from the Haute Deule Canal. Opposition ceased at 12 noon, and the Enemy went off...

Mr Dawson (Editor of *The Times*) arrived for dinner and stayed the night. After dinner CGS, Davidson and I had a discussion with him and called his attention to the very small support given by the English Press to the British Army. Papers seem to vie with each other in cracking up the French, and running down the British military methods and Generals! Even now, few seemed to realise the tremendous successes won by the British Army. Dawson assured us that he is most anxious to help in every way. Before going to bed I had a talk with Lawrence over the nature of an armistice. He is of opinion that it should not be too exacting because it is in the interests of Great Britain to end the war this year. Lawrence is to give me a note tomorrow morning embodying his views.

Haig crossed to England on 18 October.

Saturday 19 October

I visited the War Office soon after 10 am and saw Wilson. He gave me his views on conditions of armistice. He considers that 'the Germans should be ordered to lay down their arms and retire to the east bank of the Rhine'.

I gave my opinion that in that case there would be no armistice, and the war would continue for at least another year!'

We went over together to 10 Downing Street, and found Mr Lloyd George, Lord Milner and Bonar Law discussing. General Davidson accompanied me. The PM asked my views on the terms which we should offer the Enemy if he asked for an armistice. I replied that they must greatly depend on the answers we give to two questions:

1. Is Germany now so beaten that she will accept whatever terms the Allies may offer?
2. Can the Allies continue to press the Enemy sufficiently vigorously during the coming winter months as to cause him to withdraw so quickly that he cannot destroy the railways, roads, etc.?

The answer to both is in negative. The German Army is capable of retiring to its own frontier, and holding that line if there should be any attempt to touch the *honour* of the German people [and make them fight with the courage of despair.]

The situation of the Allied Armies is as follows:

French Army worn out, and has not been fighting latterly. It has been freely said that 'war is over' and 'we don't wish to lose our lives now that peace is in sight'.

American Army is disorganised, ill equipped and ill trained. Good officers and NCOs are lacking.

The British Army was never more efficient but has fought hard, and it lacks reinforcements. With diminishing effectives, moral is bound to suffer.

French and American Armies are not capable of making a serious offensive *now*. British alone cannot bring the Enemy to his knees.[2]

In the coming winter, Enemy will have some months for recuperation and absorption of 1920 class, untouched as yet. He will be in a position to destroy

1 In the Ts diary Haig amended this to: 'I gave my opinion that our attack on the 17th inst. met with considerable opposition, and that the Enemy was not ready for unconditional surrender. In that case ...' His relative pessimism was reflected in a memo sent to Foch on 23 October (OAD 945).
2 In the Ts diary, Haig amended this to: 'The British alone might bring the enemy to his knees. But why expend more British lives – and for what?'

all communications before he falls back. This will mean serious delay to our advance next year.

I therefore recommend that terms of armistice should be:

1. Immediate evacuation of Belgium and occupied French territory.
2. Metz and Strassburg to be at once occupied by the Allied Armies, and Alsace-Lorraine to be vacated by the Enemy.
3. Belgian and French rolling stock to be returned, inhabitants restored etc.

When I had finished my remarks, Hankey (the Secretary of War Cabinet) came in and I had to repeat most of what I had said for him to note down.

The Prime Minister seemed in agreement with me. Wilson urged 'laying down arms'. Lord Milner took a middle course between my recommendations and those of Foch, i.e., in addition to what I lay down he would occupy the west bank of the Rhine as a temporary measure until the Germans have complied with our peace terms.

About noon Mr Balfour (Secretary of State for Foreign Affairs) came in, and the whole story was gone over again.

I was asked what the attitude of the Army would be if we stuck out for stiff terms, which Enemy then refuses, and war goes on. I reminded the PM of the situation a year ago when there were frequent demands for information as to what we were fighting for. He (the PM) then made a speech and stated our war aims. The British Army had done most of the fighting latterly, and everyone wants to have done with the war, *provided* we get what we want. I therefore advise that we only ask in the Armistice for what we intend to hold, and that we set our faces against the French entering Germany to pay off old scores. In my opinion, under the supposed conditions, the British Army would not fight keenly for what is really not its own affair.

Mr Balfour spoke about deserting the Poles and the people of Eastern Europe. But the PM gave the opinion that we cannot expect the British to go on sacrificing their lives for the Poles! Admiral Wemyss, 1st Sea Lord, then came in and the views of Navy for an armistice were stated. They seemed most exacting and incapable of enforcement except by a land force.

Monday 21 October

Doris and I motored to London about 10 am and I visited War Office. General Davidson met me; I also saw General Macdonagh,[1] AG. I showed him my note on proposals for armistice. He agreed with me entirely. As regards manpower, he stated that latest figures showed that we are not

1 Properly 'Macdonogh'.

able to maintain more than 36 divisions next year. At present we have 61 divisions.

I then saw the CIGS. I gathered that the main reason why he was in favour of a 'complete surrender' for terms of an armistice is on account of Ireland. He is most keen that conscription should be applied to Ireland at once in order to get us more men, and as a means of pacifying Ireland.

We went over to 10 Downing Street together, and met the Prime Minister at 11.15 as directed. Lord Milner, Mr Bonar Law, and Mr Balfour were present as members of War Cabinet, and Admiral Beatty (Commanding the Grand Fleet)[1] and Admiral Wemyss represented the Navy.

We discussed the Naval proposals for an armistice. They calculated that if the German High Sea Fleet came out and gave battle, our Grand Fleet would defeat it entirely, but we would lose 6 or 7 ships. So they now recommended that *all* modern ships should now be handed over to the British *because they would have been* destroyed in the battle, if it had taken place!

Another point discussed was a request by the new Turkish Government to make Peace. It was sent by General Townshend,[2] a prisoner-of-war captured at Kut. He had arrived at Mudros. All the Cabinet were agreed that no time should be lost in discussing terms of armistice, and that if we got the Dardanelles open and free passage into the Black Sea for our troops etc., hostilities with Turkey should be stopped. Delay in making actual Peace must occur, as we have to consult our Allies . . .

In the afternoon the German reply to Wilson's note was received. Feeling was strong against the President. He does not seem to realise our requirements. So a telegram was sent him pointing out that in addition to retreat to pre-war frontier, Enemy must hand over territory as guarantees, and at least Alsace-Lorraine.

As regards my advice on armistice, the PM and Milner agreed that it was very sound. But the effect of Turkey going out of the war might enable us to demand more, because we could bring in Roumania and the Checo-Slovaks.

On 22 October Haig returned to France.

---

1 Admiral (later Admiral of the Fleet) Sir David Beatty (later Earl Beatty) (1871–1936).
2 Major General Sir Charles Vere Townshend (1861–1924), captured at the surrender of Kut to the Ottomans, April 1916.

Wednesday 23 October

Pershing visited Haig.

He also asked my views on an armistice. He said that he agreed with me both as to state of Enemy, and state of Allied Armies, and as to what our demands should be. As to American Army, he also concurred in thinking that it would be next autumn before it could be organised and sufficiently trained to be able to play an important part.

Pershing promised to keep the two American Divisions now with British up to strength and I urged on him to make this American Corps up to 4 divisions. He said that he had not the divisions available for the purpose, as his losses had been heavy: though not so great as British and French had been accustomed to suffer.

Thursday 24 October

With the BEF continuing to advance steadily, Haig visited HQ of French First Army.

Foch said that he insisted on having bridgeheads across the Rhine, and on occupying all German territory on left bank as a guarantee to ensure that the Enemy carries out the terms of peace imposed upon her ... On the whole, Foch's reasons were political, not military, and [Lawrence and I] were both struck by the very unpractical way in which he and Weygand regarded the present military situation. He would not ask himself 'What does the military situation of the Allies admit of their demanding?' 'What terms can we really enforce?'

We then dealt with the question of the Second Army which I asked last week should be again placed under my orders. On the 9th September I agreed that it should co-operate under the King of the Belgians for a specific purpose, namely, to cover the right of the Belgian Army on the River Lys, and enable the Belgians, supported by French, to advance on Bruges and Ghent. That phase of the operation is over, and all the five Armies of which the BEF is composed are either along or approaching the line of the Scheldt and are confronted with the same problem, viz., the passage of that river. The manner in which the line of the Scheldt can most easily be forced is to cross it in its upper course where my Fourth, Third and half of the First Armies have already crossed it. From Oudenaarde downwards the minimum number of troops should be employed as a menace. To force a passage there, in the face of hostile opposition, would be most costly.

Foch declines to return the Second Army to me because he says of the political value of having the King of the Belgians in command of an Allied Army, when he re-enters his capital, Brussels! His real object is to use the British Second Army to open the way for the 'dud' divisions (of which the rest of the King's Army is composed) and ensure that they get to Brussels. France would then get the credit for clearing Belgium and putting the King back in his capital. De Goutte is nominally Chief of Staff to King Albert: really he is the Army Commander.

I explained the military reason why the Second Army must now be under my orders. If there were political reasons requiring the Second Army to remain under King Albert, then the British Government must direct me on the subject. Until I was so informed, I must continue to view the situation from a *military* standpoint, and insist on the return of the Second Army without delay. Foch asked me to submit my request in writing. He would then let me have his views.

I am disgusted at the almost underhand way in which the French are trying to get hold of a part of the British Army – and so ungenerous too, because in the first instance, I handed over all the troops of that Army at once to operate under the French Staff of the King of the Belgians, without raising the smallest difficulty. I felt annoyed at the attitude of Foch and Weygand over this question. I told them a few 'home truths' for, when all is said and done, the British Army has defeated the Germans this year, and I [alone] am responsible to the British Government for the handling of the British troops *not* Foch.[1]

Friday 25 October

General Clive reported on general situation. The enemy has now no fresh divisions left. He considers that the internal situation of Germany is serious, and that the German Government fears Bolshevism may get the upper hand in the country, and all law and order be at an end. Clive is of opinion that it would be an error to demand excessively hard terms for an armistice because the result would be that the Government of Prince Max would have to go and all their schemes of reform would be upset. The militarists would return to Power, and begin a life and death struggle...

I also saw the AG. I told him to keep in closer touch with the Australians. The Premier of Australia (Hughes) had told the Australian troops that they would not be used in the line again for some months! I want them to go into a sector very soon. It is said that 2 divisions are

1 Haig wrote to Foch arguing that his refusal to return Second Army struck 'at the very foundation of my position' as the BEF's commander. Haig to Foch, 27 October 1918. NLS: Haig Papers.

likely to decline to go into the line if ordered. The casualties since 21 March (infantry only) are:

		average
English, Scottish, Welsh, Irish per battalion	45 officers	1088 other ranks
Australian	36	704
Canadian	42	956

The Australians have the least claim of any therefore for consideration on account of losses ...[1]

... I attended a conference at Marshal Foch's HQ ... Foch stated that he had been directed by his Government to obtain the views of the Commanders-in-Chief on the terms of an armistice ... I gave practically the same as I had given to the War Cabinet in London last Saturday. Pétain followed, and urged the same terms as Foch, viz. left bank of Rhine with bridgeheads. Pershing, although 2 days previously, he had acquiesced with my views, now said ditto to Foch ...

I felt that Enemy might not accept the terms Foch proposed because of military necessity only – and it would be very costly and take a long time (2 years) to enforce them, unless the internal state of Germany compels the Enemy to accept them. We don't know very much about the internal state of Germany – and so to try to impose such terms seems to me really a gamble which may come off or it may not. It struck me too that the insistence of the 2 French Generals on the left bank of the Rhine means that they now aim at getting hold of the Palatinate as well as of Alsace-Lorraine! Pétain spoke of taking a huge indemnity from Germany, so large that she will never be able to pay it. Meantime, French troops will hold the left bank of the Rhine as a pledge![2]

Saturday 26 October

President Wilson's representative, Colonel House, visited Haig.

House[3] struck me as natural, sincere and capable. He criticised the President's note to Germany, and said that had he been at home he would have advised

---

1 In September, the 1st and 59th Battalions of the Australian Imperial Force, in 'mutinies of exhaustion', refused to return to the front line.
2 Haig had political support for his views: he wrote that Derby and Milner 'agreed that the demands of the English Press (led by Lord Northcliffe) for a humiliating peace for Germany were against the best interests of the British Empire': Diary, 26 October 1918.
3 Colonel Edward Mandell House (1858–1938), President Woodrow Wilson's confidant and *éminence grise*.

the President to have merely replied that he was passing the German request for an armistice to his Allies for consideration.[1]

I asked him how the President interpreted 'Freedom of the Seas'.[2] He replied by saying that the President took him aside and told him what Geddes had said to him on the subject, and similarly Geddes told him what the President had said to him. And it all amounted to nothing!

We discussed the objects of Great Britain and America, and the possible terms of an armistice. I found that he viewed the situation very much as I do. He knew that the French were not fighting, also that the Italians were keen to stop fighting! And he seemed to take a reasonable view of what should be demanded from the Germans.

Sunday 27 October

At Versailles, Haig consulted with Milner and Henry Wilson.

Milner stated that the Cabinet had decided that the Second Army was to return to my Command! It was merely a question of how to arrange it without making too much fuss.

I gathered from Wilson that the Cabinet were glad of a chance of supporting me against the French, because in *every theatre* they are doing their utmost to get control of everything! Consequently, there is much friction in the Balkans and in Palestine and in the fleet in the Mediterranean! It is odd that the French should be so greedy of power!

Report received that Ludendorff has resigned his post as Chief of Great General Staff.[3] Clemenceau thinks this means a return to active operations in the field under Hindenburg's directions. Time will show, most of us think it means a retreat to the German frontier and an armistice...

On the way back to Paris I met Lord Derby in the Park of St Cloud. He had seen Clemenceau and explained my point of view as to the Second Army remaining under the King of the Belgians. Clemenceau at once said that the French Government as well as the British would be behind me in demanding the return of the Second Army to my Command. Derby thought the whole matter was settled, but Clemenceau was going to see Foch in the afternoon, and would settle the question if Foch was in a reasonable mood! It seems that

1 Some resentment was caused by President Wilson's exchanges with Berlin, which excluded the British and French.
2 This was one of the Fourteen Points promulgated by President Woodrow Wilson on 8 January 1918. The Fourteen Points became the basis of Wilson's 'Peace Without Victory' diplomacy. Britain objected to the proposal for 'Freedom of the Seas'.
3 Erich Ludendorff (1865–1937), German First Quartermaster General, but *de facto* Commander-in-Chief.

Clemenceau and Foch are not on good terms. Foch is suffering from a swelled head, and thinks himself another Napoleon! So Clemenceau has great difficulties with him now.[1]

Monday 28 October

Colonel Bacon reported that General Pershing had misunderstood some of my remarks at the Conference at Senlis last Saturday.[2] I had spoken in French, and what I had said was then translated into English. Pershing, who is in bed with 'flu, imagines now, though he said nothing at the time, that I had disparaged the American Army.[3] Nothing was further from my thoughts. I was anxious that the Allied Commanders should not deceive themselves as to the difficulties which confront us before we can make the Germans accept 'Unconditional Surrender'. It is necessary to realise the time required to create *several* American Armies to replace the dwindling numbers of the French and ourselves. So I wrote to Pershing and explained my views. The Americans have been so criticised by the French that they are very touchy.

Tuesday 29 October

I saw the Prime Minister (Lloyd George) at Château Romaine at 11 am by appointment. He spoke about the necessity for having a strong Army after the war for at least a year. We should decide now what classes of men we should keep. South Wales miners should be sent away, but North Wales, being farmers, can be retained. He evidently feels that we may have to face both internal troubles, as well as difficulties with some of our present Allies.

As regards terms of Armistice: I advised him to insist on strong Naval terms from the Enemy because our existence depends on 'Sea Supremacy', i.e., all Enemy submarines should be destroyed, and a large part of the High Sea Fleet to be sunk. On the other hand, although the collapse of Austria makes Germany's position hopeless, I advised more lenient terms on land, i.e. stick to the terms I suggested 2 weeks ago, although the military situation is more in our favour today. LG was very pleased that I had spoken out about the real state and [present military] value of the American Army at the Conference of Commanders-in-Chief at Senlis last Saturday. He said that Foch reported in the same tenor to him but would [not] tell Pershing to his

---

1 At a meeting on 28 October, Foch agreed Second Army would return to Haig once the Scheldt was reached, i.e. after the next operation: Diary, 28 October.
2 A slip for 'Friday'.
3 See Library of Congress: Pershing Papers, Container 86. Haig to Pershing, 27 October 1918, and reply of 29 October.

face what he really thought of the American Army and its present fitness for war...

There seems some doubt as to the proper procedure now. I advised to keep the roles of civilians and soldiers distinct, i.e., the soldiers will arrange the Armistice. As soon as that is concluded, the Diplomatists should take their places and arrange Peace.

The Allies should first settle amongst themselves what terms they will give Germany. These will be notified by some Plenipotentiary at a meeting with German representatives. Once Peace has been signed, then a *conference* must be held for the settlement of the World! Germany may be admitted to this.

Thursday 31 October

Haig held a conference at Cambrai with the commanders of First, Third, Fourth and Fifth Armies.

Each explained his views on the situation. The Enemy is fighting a very good rear guard action and all are agreed that from a military standpoint, the Enemy has not yet been sufficiently beaten as to cause him to accept an ignominious peace. Neither on our right or on our left are the French Armies really fighting...

At Escadoeuvres I visited HQ XXII Corps and had a talk with Lieutenant General Godley. He states that Enemy is fighting a very good rear guard action, but he hopes no Armistice will be arranged until after his next 2 operations, viz. tomorrow and 4 November! From what I heard today the Enemy's machine gunners are most capable in occupying positions, and are fighting until killed. Hostile guns are disposed in depth, and on the whole are not very effective though the losses of our gunners are much greater than earlier in the year. This is due in great measure to the Enemy placing his guns in small scattered groups. It is difficult to find them, as time and good weather are lacking for photography; consequently our counter-battery work cannot be carried out very effectively.

Friday 1 November

Valenciennes fell in the course of an offensive by First and Third Armies.

I was present at the Supreme War Council at Versailles. The paper embodying the proposed terms for an armistice which had been approved in general by the Prime Minister was read. The terms are very stiff and include retirement beyond the Rhine with a strip of 40 kilometres on the eastern bank. The surrender of 5000 guns (heavy and field), railway waggons, locomotives, etc. The fact that Turkey and now Austria have abandoned Germany seems most important and means the early downfall of Germany. So probably the Allied Governments may be justified in demanding stiff terms. On the other hand, the determined fight put up by the Enemy today shows that the German Army is not yet *demoralised*!' The Austrian Army, on the other hand, is in quite a different state.

Sunday 3 November

The Enemy is withdrawing in the Valenciennes sector, and our advanced troops are in touch with him on the general line Villers–Pol–Jenlain–Etreux–Onnaing. I am anxious lest he withdraws before our attack can catch him tomorrow morning!

Monday 4 November

This day marked the beginning of the last major British offensive of the war, the Battle of the Sambre.

This morning, at time varying from 5.30 to 6.15 the Fourth, Third and First Armies attacked between the Sambre Canal at Oisy and the River Scheldt north of Valenciennes. A front of over 30 miles. The First French Army (Debeney) also attacked in co-operation on our right and made satisfactory progress. The British took over 10,000 prisoners and 200 guns. The French 3000 prisoners about to 5 pm.

At 8 pm Fourth Army reported 'Attack is being pressed and progress made along the whole front of the Army. Resistance which was stiff all morning is weakening, except south of Landrecies, where stubborn fighting is still taking place.' 'Our casualties have been light ... Attack on so big a scale was not expected.'

At 8.40 pm Third Army reported over 6000 prisoners and 125 guns ... 'There has been considerable opposition on whole Army front today' ... First Army does not report much progress after midday. The troops of the XXII Corps had very hard fighting on the last 3 days. So this may account for the slowness of their progress.

The weather has been very favourable – a fog in valley until 8 am. This enabled our troops to get across the Canal de la Sambre without being seen. This part of the country is much enclosed with high hedges which have not

1 In the Ts diary, this becomes '... shows that all the divisions in the German Army are not yet demoralised'!

been trimmed for the period of the war at least. The barrage only advanced at the rate of 6 minutes to 100 yards.

The Enemy seems to have placed all his strength in his front line. Consequently when this was overcome he had no reserves in rear with which to oppose our advance.

Tuesday 5 November

General Clive reported that we engaged and took prisoners from 25 divisions yesterday. Reports continue to indicate that Enemy means to fall back from the line of the Scheldt at an early date . . .

I had a long talk with General Byng . . . He finds that our men are fighting better than they have ever done, and are 'killing more Germans'. He has noticed many more German dead after a battle. He ascribes this to our men feeling that they are better men than the Germans, and now always fight it out. A few months ago this was not always the case, and sometimes a platoon in close fighting would 'hands up' if the Enemy did not immediately give in . . .

In reply to my question whether, in view of the Enemy's opposition being so slight, he would like the Cavalry Corps (to operate against Mauberge for instance, by turning it etc.) he replied that the roads were so congested, and railways had been broken by hostile mines with delayed action fuses, that it would be most difficult to get cavalry forward or to feed them if they were pushed on.[1]

Wednesday 6 November

Haig was visited by General Degoutte, the French Chief of Staff to the King of the Belgians.

I told him that owing to my success in the direction of Maubeuge, I thought it unlikely that the Enemy would remain on the Scheldt in force. I therefore proposed to force the passage of that river (if the Enemy remained!) by my Fifth and Second Armies on Monday next, and then to push forward the Cavalry Corps as soon as possible. De Goutte quite agreed with me, and said he would co-operate on the same day.

1 Later that day Rawlinson also politely declined Haig's offer of the Cavalry Corps, citing similar concerns as Byng: Diary, 5 November 1918.

Saturday 9 November

Guards and 62nd Division have captured the whole of the fortress of Maubeuge. Enemy south of the Condé Canal seems to be falling back without
offering much opposition. North of that Canal he is also falling back, and
detachments of Second and Fifth Armies have crossed the Scheldt. I sent
orders to General Birdwood Fifth Army to push the whole of the Cavalry
Corps across the Scheldt and follow up the Enemy if he judges the situation
on his front sufficiently favourable, i.e. that the Enemy is falling back as on
the south of the Condé Canal without offering serious resistance.

3 pm	Second Army reports	'No opposition on 40th Division front'.
2 pm	Fifth " "	'Enemy offering no opposition'.
1.30 pm	First " "	'Advance continued on whole Army front without opposition'.
"	Fourth " "	'Enemy retreating rapidly on whole of Army front followed by our cavalry patrols' ...

Intercepted German Wireless states:

1. The Kaiser has abdicated and the Crown Prince has renounced his claim
   to the Throne. Max of Baden remains in office etc.
2. Another message from 'The Soldiers Council at Metz' appeals to the Army
   to continue fighting and to maintain order as everything depends on their
   attitude at the present moment.

Meanwhile our troops are pushing on as fast as they can. All Corps
Commanders are anxious for more cavalry as advanced guards of all arms are
being organised to keep touch with the retreating Enemy, and the question
of 'Supply' is difficult for big forces owing to railheads being back on the line
Le Cateau–Solesmes.

Monday 11 NOVEMBER

Fine day but cold and dull.
    Reports from Foch's HQ state that meeting with the German delegates
(which took place in train in the Forest of Compiègne, not in Château as
previously reported) began at 2 am and at 5 am the Armistice was signed. The
Germans pointed out that if the rolling stock and supplies of the Army (which
have to be handed over by the terms of the Armistice) are given up, then
Germans east of the Rhine will starve. Report says Foch was rather brutal to

the German delegates, and replied that that was their affair!

The Armistice came into force at 11 am.

The state of the German Army is said to be very bad, and the discipline seems to have become so low that the orders of the officers are not obeyed . . .

At 11 am I had a meeting in Cambrai with the 5 Army Commanders and General Kavanagh, Commanding Cavalry Corps. I explained that for the moment my orders are to advance on to a sector of the German frontier 32 miles wide extending from Verviers (exclusive) to Houffalize in the south. The northern half of this sector would be held by the Second Army; southern half by Fourth Army. The other Armies would for the present either stand fast, or send back behind railheads such divisions as could not be easily supplied. Each Army sent forward would consist of four corps = 32 divisions. The remaining 28 divisions would be under the command of the First, Third and Fifth Army Commanders. The selection of divisions had been made for reasons of manpower and recruiting, but I should be glad of any suggestions from Army Commanders on the subject.

I then pointed out the importance of looking after the troops during the period following the cessation of hostilities. Very often the best fighters are the most difficult to deal with in periods of quiet! I suggested a number of ways in which men can be kept occupied. It is as much the *duty* of all officers to keep their men amused as it is to train them for war. Staff officers must [attend to this]. If funds are wanted, GHQ should be informed, and I'll arrange for money to be found.

After the Conference, we were all taken on the Cinema! General Plumer, whom I told to 'go off and be cinema'ed' went off most obediently and stood before the camera trying to look his best, while Byng and others near him were chaffing the old man and trying to make him laugh . . .

We heard this morning that the Kaiser is in Holland. If the war had gone against us no doubt our King would have had to go, and probably our Army would have become insubordinate like the German Army! cf. John Bunyan's remark on seeing a man on his way to be hanged, 'But for the Grace of God, John Bunyan would have been in that man's place!'

Friday 15 November

Marshal Foch came to lunch . . . Foch explained very graphically how the Conference with the German delegates regarding an armistice went off. They said that they expected 'hard terms, but these were very hard'. After the first meeting, they asked to have informal meetings with one of Foch's Staff, so General Weygand worked all day with them over the details. Weygand learnt that the German Army was so disorganised that it was well nigh a rabble. On this, Foch bases the opinion that 'if operations had continued for another week' there would have been a disaster for the Germans on a far vaster scale than Sedan!¹ It was to avoid this disaster that the Germans were so anxious to conclude an armistice as soon as possible. But it must be recollected that of the 3 Allied Armies, only the British were fighting and pressing back the Enemy! The French had stopped fighting being exhausted, and divisions very weak in numbers. The Americans had lost the greater part of their trained personnel, and their administrative arrangements had [completely] broken down. I therefore come to the conclusion that there remained only the British Army sufficiently strong and determined to get a decision. If *we* stopped, the Enemy would be given time to reorganise. And since our divisions had been fighting hard since spring, it would have been necessary soon to call a halt for rest and training. Foch's hope of a disaster happening in a week or fortnight if hostilities continued was, like most French calculations in the war, doomed to certain disappointment.

Major General Sir John Adye visited GHQ on 16 November. He later recorded his impressions: 'I fancy the Commander-in-Chief and his personal staff were still under the influence of the tremendous strain they had been through'. A month later, Haig 'seemed a different man, with a load of care and responsibility lifted from him'.²

Friday 15 November. Letter to Sir Henry Wilson³

I ought really to have congratulated *you*. And I now do so with all my heart. For have we not *one* Army? and without your wholehearted support what a mess I would have been in on many a time! You have really done splendidly and I am never tired of telling all and sundry this. And I know a little about the difficulties with which you have had to contend ...

Wednesday 20 November. Letter to Lord Milner⁴

I held a conference with Army Commanders yesterday, and I feel I must tell you how one and all expressed the hope that, whatever the result of the forthcoming General Election, you would still remain on as Secretary of State for War ... it is so vitally important that there should be no change in the supreme direction of the Army in the very critical period which must super-

1 Sedan was the scene of a crushing Prussian defeat of the French in 1870.
2 J. Adye, *Soldiers and Others I Have Known* (London: H. Jenkins, 1925), p. 293.
3 IWM: Wilson Papers, HHW 2/7B/23.
4 National Archives of Scotland: Unsigned, TS copy, Lothian Papers, GD40/17/61/179.

vene between a state of war and the time when the Army assumes a peace-footing.

Wednesday 27 November

The King arrived at Boulogne at 1 o'clock ... On the way to Montreuil, the King said to me that he had told the PM to offer me a peerage. I replied that I had been offered a Viscountcy, but had requested leave to decline accepting any reward until adequate grants for our 'disabled' had been voted ... He also said that the Kaiser wished to surrender to me: he would have nothing to do with the French. He was prevented from doing so by those around him telling him that he would be shot if he attempted such a thing.[1]

Saturday 30 November

Lloyd George asked Haig, via the CIGS's office, to participate in a victory parade in London along with Foch, Clemenceau and Orlando.

Later I heard that I was to be in the fifth carriage along with General Henry Wilson. I felt that this was more of an insult than I could put up with, even from the PM. For the past 3 years I have effaced myself, because I felt that to win the war it was essential that the British and French Armies should get on well together. And in consequence I have patiently submitted to Lloyd George's conceit and swagger, combined with much boasting as to what *he* had accomplished, thanks to his foresight in appointing Foch as C-in-C of the Allied Forces, sent Armies to Egypt, Palestine, Mesopotamia, Salonika, etc., etc. Now, the British Army has won the war in France in spite of LG and I have no intention of taking part in any triumphal ride with Foch and a pack of foreigners, through the streets of London, merely to add to LG's importance and help him in his election campaign. So I had a message to the following effect sent by telephone to War Office.

First that I could not come to London tomorrow to take part in any ceremonial procession unless I was ordered to do so by the Army Council (tomorrow is a *Sunday*). Second, was I wanted for any discussion by the War Cabinet or merely for a ceremonial pageant?

General Lawrence telephoned to War Office on my behalf and later in the afternoon he stated that he had spoken with General Harrington[2] who fully

---

1 Haig also saw the offer as a snub from Lloyd George, as when French was removed from command of the BEF '*for incompetence*, he was made a Viscount!' Diary, 19 November 1918.
2 Properly Harington.

realised my views on the matter, and that this matter was closed so far as the War Office and I were concerned.

Meantime, Lord Stamfordham (who is at Buckingham Palace) took it upon himself, on hearing of the proposed ceremony, to telephone to GHQ to beg me not to come to England tomorrow, as he felt sure that the King would be much displeased that any reception of the kind should be held during his absence.

Evidently this pageant of Lloyd George's is causing a great stir all round. Further details of the proposed triumphal progress show that the procession is to go to the French Embassy at Albert Gate for a reception to which I am not invited. A motor car, however, is to be in waiting for me there, to take me 'wherever I like!' Was there ever such an insult prepared for the welcome of a General on his return from commanding an Army in the field during 4 long years of war? Yet this is the Prime Minister of England's view of what is fitting.

Sunday 1 December. Letter to Sir Clive Wigram[1]

You have already heard of the almost impertinent message which was sent me from Downing Street yesterday, viz. to take part in a triumphal procession with a lot of foreigners through the streets of London on a Sunday! This too after all I have done to keep the peace with Foch and the other French Supreme Commanders during 3 years.

As you know I hate ovations and nothing will induce me to receive a welcome (as C-in-C of the King's Forces in France) in combination with a pack of foreigners. The welcome must be purely British.

Monday 16 December: 'I crossed the Rhine'

My train reached Cologne about 2 am and a little before 9 am I received General Plumer (Commanding Second Army) and Lieutenant General Sir Charles Fergusson whom I had appointed Governor of Cologne and to supervise the occupied area administratively under Plumer.

At 9 am I left the train and was received by a Guard of Honour, found by the 2nd Guards Brigade (Sergisson Brooke)[2] ... As I passed through the station, all the German officials saluted most respectfully. After inspecting the Guard outside the station, I entered my car with Plumer and, escorted by a squadron of cavalry of the 9th Lancers, went on to the Hohenzollern Bridge

---

1 RA: PS/GV/K1387/7.
2 Brigadier General (later Lieutenant General Sir) Bertram Norman Sergison-Brooke ('Boy') (1880–1967), GOC 2 (Guards) Brigade, 1917–18.

which crosses the Rhine to Deutz. 25 Press Correspondents were collected here under Major Lytton for me to bid them goodbye. I left my car and shook hands with each one, then made them a short address, and finally presented a small Union Jack to each one in memory of this historic occasion.

Haig's 'short address' included these words: 'For my part I sincerely hope that in our time of victory we may not lose our heads, as the Germans lost theirs after 1870 – with the result that we are here'.[1]

Thursday 19 December: 'Day of my Welcome Home by Dover and London'

The train reached Charing Cross at 1 o'clock exactly. The Duke of Connaught and the Prime Minister (Lloyd George) were opposite the door of the railway carriage as the train stopped. The first named welcomed me on behalf of the King. A fine Guard of Honour from the Grenadier Guards (of which regiment the Duke is Colonel) presented arms. I was asked to inspect the Guard before shaking hands with the *many* who had come to the station to welcome me. As I got to the right of the Guard which was close to a small party of spectators, I saw Henrietta[2] close by so I gave her a kiss and then turned and went round the Guard. On the left of the Guard were the members of the War Cabinet, Admiralty, Army Council and a host of others, Mr Asquith, Sir Evelyn Wood etc.

I was not given any time for conversation but was hustled off to the Royal Carriages which were in waiting ... Doris had warned me to look for Queen Alexandra at Marlborough House so when we came opposite I told the carriage to stop, and Queen Alexandra with Doris and our two girls came forward to the carriage, and Queen Alexandra gave me some flowers from her dress ... The route was not lined with troops. The reception was essentially a *welcome by the people*, without any official interference, and I could not help feeling how the cheering from great masses of all classes came from their hearts. As ADC to King Edward, I have taken part in many functions, but never before have I seen such crowds, or such wholehearted enthusiasm ... It was indeed most touching to take part in such a ceremony.

At Buckingham Palace, I was at once received by the King. I thanked him for the splendid welcome which had been given me, and which was made possible by the King's thoughtfulness and his personal intervention...

Lord Stamfordham spoke to me about accepting a Peerage – he argued that Beatty would be made an Earl and Plumer a Viscount, and what reason could they give for not rewarding me. I said that an excellent excuse had been

1 O. Elton, *C. E. Montague, a memoir* (London: Chatto & Windus: 1929) p. 230.
2 Haig's sister.

given as to why I had not come over with Foch! (they said the King required my presence in France) and I felt sure an equally good reason could be given now, but why not state the truth and say I wished no reward until the Army had been provided for. I then told him that Government had neglected its duty to the *Disabled*, and outlined some of the reports of hard cases which had reached my ears . . .[1]

It was past 5 pm before Doris and I got to Eastcott. I was hoping for a quiet evening with her but at 8.30 pm a mass of people, probably 10,000 in all, with torches, and 3 bands, mostly workmen and women from the Sopwith Airoplane Works, came to salute me and welcome me home to Kingston. I was asked to go to the gate and say a few words and see them march past. I complied of course and thanked them for turning out to greet me. The people were all in their best clothes except some who were in fancy dress, and all were most orderly and cheery.

Today was indeed a red letter one in my life. To receive such a *spontaneous* welcome all the way from the coast to my house at Kingston Hill shows how the people of England realise what has been accomplished by the Army and myself. This more than compensates me for the difficulties put in my way and the coldness towards me by the Prime Minister (Lloyd George).

Saturday 28 December

Haig and Doris went to London to hear President Wilson speak.

He seemed to me to be rather an idealist, and pointed to the advantages of a 'League of Nations' . . . At lunch we found ourselves sitting opposite the President and the Lady Mayoress, and on the President's right was the Prime Minister. During lunch, the results of the Election kept coming in. Lloyd George was perfectly delighted at the news which reached [him]. And further down the table was Asquith, who evidently knew that he had been rejected by East Fife. The President's speech seemed more natural after lunch and was well received. There was less rubbish talked about the League of Nations ['self-determination'] and Democracy . . .

At night I dined at 10 Downing Street with the Prime Minister to meet the President of the USA . . . The magnitude of the victory of the Coalition was just becoming apparent. Several said that the majority was too great to last. Bonar Law said that he would have great difficulty in keeping such a large majority together, and Mr Balfour deplored the disappearance from the

---

1 Haig gave evidence before a parliamentary committee on pensions in July 1919, which was instrumental in inducing the Government to increase pensions. Once this had been achieved, in October 1919 Haig accepted a peerage.

House of so many who understood the ways and traditions of the House of Commons.[1]

Monday 30 December

I was entertained to dinner on Monday night 30 December by Lord Milner, Secretary of State for War. The dinner took place at 'The Senior' in Pall Mall and we sat down 34. It was intended to be a 'Military family party' and consisted of the Army Council and heads of the War Office, with myself and Army Commanders. Only 3 of the latter were able to be present as Generals Plumer and Rawlinson had returned to France. My AG (Fowke) and QMG (Travers Clarke) were present.

It was a very friendly gathering. After dinner Lord Milner made a very charming speech in which he gave as 'a sentiment' 'the greatest British Army which the Empire had ever produced' coupled with my name.

I replied. My speech was very well received. I alluded to the work of the War Office [during the war], especially of the 4 Military Members (whom I alluded to by name), the unchanging civilians, and Lord Milner. All were very pleased.

It was nearly midnight before I got back to Kingston Hill.

1 Voting in the 1918 general election had taken place on 14 December. The Coalition, led by Lloyd George, won a crushing victory. The Asquithian Liberals were reduced to a rump, and the Labour Party emerged as a major electoral force. Despite his antipathy to Lloyd George, Haig voted for Coalition candidates: Diary, 14 December 1918.

BIOGRAPHICAL SKETCHES

Those listed below are identified by an asterisk (*) before the first mention of their names in each year of the diary.

Allenby, General Sir Edmund Henry Hynman (later Field Marshal Viscount Allenby of Megiddo) (1861–1936) GOC Cavalry Division, 1914; GOC Cavalry Corps, 1914–15; GOC V Corps, 1915; GOC Third Army, 1915–17; GOC-in-C Egyptian Expeditionary Force, 1917–19. Edmund Allenby was the son of a Nottinghamshire squire-parson. He did his regimental soldiering with the 6th Dragoons and then with the 5th Lancers (which he commanded), seeing active service in Bechuanaland, Zululand and South Africa. He was Inspector General of Cavalry at the Horse Guards from 1910 until the outbreak of war, when he took command of the Cavalry Division. Allenby and Haig were colleagues at the Staff College, Camberley, in 1896. The popular Allenby's election as Master of the [Staff College] Drag Hounds in preference to Haig is considered by some to have been the start of a professional rivalry in which Haig was driven by jealousy. Haig's relationship with Allenby, who was the last Army commander to be appointed under Sir John *French, was never warm but it was always professional. Haig's diary and letters to Lady *Haig pay tribute to Allenby's great initial success at Arras. They are less candid about Allenby's removal.

Allenby's problem in 1917 was not so much Haig as the loss of confidence in him expressed by his subordinates, who objected to the way in which he handled the Arras fighting once it entered an attritional stage. Three of his divisional commanders appear to have registered their protest directly with Haig over Allenby's head. In situations like this something has to give, either the divisional commanders or the Army commander. In the event, the vacancy created by the sacking of General Murray as GOC-in-C Egyptian Expeditionary Force made it convenient to send Allenby to the Middle East. He regarded his transfer as a badge of failure, but he more than redeemed his reputation by defeating the Turks in 1917–18. Allenby was a sensitive man who hid this under an intimidating physical exterior and manner that earned him the nickname 'The Bull'. Some thought that this bluster was due to shyness, others to deep-seated feelings of professional inadequacy. Allenby's only son, Captain Michael Allenby MC, was killed in action in 1917.

Asquith, Herbert Henry (Earl of Oxford and Asquith) (1852–1928) British Liberal Prime Minister, 1908–16, leader of HM Opposition, 1916–18. Until Margaret Thatcher beat his record, Asquith had occupied 10 Downing Street for the longest unbroken period in twentieth-century British history. His time there was a turbulent one, marked by domestic social, political and constitutional unrest that some (then and since) believed to be revolutionary, by the threat of civil war in Ireland and, of course, by the outbreak of one of the most destructive wars in history. Despite this, he managed to drive forward a reform agenda at home while seeking to secure Britain's position abroad. His governments rebuilt the Royal Navy, winning the naval arms race with Germany. They also completed the post-South African War reform of the British Army and greatly improved Britain's reserve military forces.

Asquith's formidable intelligence, unflappability and political cunning dominated an Edwardian House of Commons with no shortage of political giants. He is generally considered to have been a better peacetime than wartime Prime Minister, but this is to simplify the dilemmas he faced between 1914 and 1916. His preference for waiting upon events generally served him well in peacetime, but in war gave the increasing impression of vacillation and inaction. He perhaps also made the fatal mistake of believing himself indispensable. Even so, his fall in December 1916 and his replacement by David *Lloyd George was surprising, even shocking. Certainly, he was shocked.

Asquith's governments arguably took all the key decisions of the war: the decision to intervene; the decision to send the British Expeditionary Force to fight on the flank of the French armies in France; the decision to raise a mass volunteer army; the decision to start and then to end the Gallipoli campaign; the creation of a Coalition government in May 1915; the mobilisation of British industry; and the introduction of conscription. Asquith always allowed his ministerial colleagues a free departmental rein and he applied the same licence to his generals. This suited Haig, who also admired Asquith's sharp mind and his ability to keep it clear despite imbibing large quantities of alcohol (see letter to Lady Haig, 8 September 1916). Although his wartime prime ministership has been heavily criticised, Asquith – like Lloyd George – has largely escaped moral responsibility for the war's casualties, with which he was all too familiar. His eldest son, Raymond, was killed in action on the Somme in September 1916; his youngest, son, Arthur ('Oc'), rose from civilian to brigadier general in three years before being wounded and losing a leg in 1917.

Birdwood, General Sir William Riddell (Field Marshal Lord Birdwood) ('Birdy') (1865–1951) GOC I ANZAC Corps, 1916–18; GOC Fifth Army, 1918–19. Birdwood was an Indian Army cavalry officer, from a family with long Indian connections, and a protégé of Lord *Kitchener. Haig's diary entries are rarely complimentary about Birdwood, whose elevation to Army command seems somewhat surprising. Haig was critical of Birdwood's indulgent command of the Australians, believing that he sacrificed discipline to popularity, and was distrustful of his shameless self-publicity. This indulgence, however, perhaps rendered Birdwood's promotion less objectionable. Haig was aware that Birdwood left the day-to-day running of the formations he commanded to his exceptionally able Australian Chief of Staff, Brudenell White. The removal of Birdwood to Army command also allowed the redoubtable John Monash, whom Haig much admired, to command the Australian Corps, despite an attempt to prevent this by some of Monash's fellow countrymen. To be fair to Birdwood, it is doubtful whether the imposition of a more authoritarian 'British regular' style of command on the Australians would have been more effective. Fifth Army did not play a leading part in the Great Advance and, other than at the formal Army commanders' meetings, Birdwood and Haig rarely seem to have met. Birdwood wrote two volumes of autobiography, *Khaki and Gown* (1941) and *In My Time* (1946).

Butler, Lieutenant General Sir Richard Harte Keatinge (1870–1935) GSO3, Aldershot Command, 1911–14; CO 2nd Battalion Lancashire Fusiliers, 1914; GOC 3 Brigade, 1914–15; BGGS, First Army, February–June 1915; MGGS, First Army, June–December 1915; Deputy CGS, GHQ, British Expeditionary Force, 1915–18; GOC III Corps, 1918–19. Richard Butler was the son of a colonel in the Army Medical Service. Haig had a high regard for him. He was GSO3 in Haig's Aldershot Command from 1911 until June 1914, when he was fast-tracked from his regiment, the Dorsetshire, to command 2nd Battalion Lancashire Fusiliers. He did not get his wish to take the battalion to war, however; instead, he was retained at home to help with the deployment of the BEF. The value put on Butler's staff skills by higher authority was something about which Butler himself was decidedly ambivalent. In December 1915 Haig wished to take Butler to GHQ as his Chief of Staff after he was appointed Commander-in-Chief, but this was vetoed by *Robertson on the grounds that Butler was 'too junior'. At GHQ Butler performed for Haig the role of 'flak catcher', a role in which he was often resented, not least by the Army commanders. He also became something of an unofficial tank expert. J. F. C. Fuller, the influential advocate of tank warfare, derided Butler's views, dismissing him as 'an intensely stupid man'. This dismissal, altogether characteristic of Fuller, is not only unfair but also absurd. In the light of recent scholarship, Butler's views seem entirely prudent and practical. Butler was aware of the resentment he caused and frustrated by being kept in the staff ghetto, from which he regularly petitioned for release. But when he was given a field command, as GOC III Corps in 1918, he was not a success.

Byng, Hon. Sir Julian Hedworth George (Field Marshal Viscount Byng of Vimy) ('Bungo') (1862–1935) GOC 3rd Cavalry Division, 1914–15; GOC Cavalry Corps, 1915; GOC IX Corps, Mediterranean Expeditionary Force, 1915–16; GOC XVII Corps, France, 1916; GOC Canadian Corps, 1916–17; GOC Third Army, 1917–19. Julian Byng was the seventh son of the 2nd Earl of Strafford; his wife, Evelyn Moreton, was an author. He did his regimental soldiering with the 10th Hussars, which he commanded from 1902 to 1904, including active service in the Sudan and South Africa. He was Commandant of the Cavalry School at Netheravon from 1904 to 1905. When the war broke out he was GOC-in-C British forces in Egypt. As GOC Canadian Corps, Byng captured the Vimy Ridge in April 1917, the first really striking British success in trench warfare. As GOC Third Army at Cambrai in November 1917 he pioneered important artillery techniques that restored surprise to the battlefield and used tanks *en masse* for the first time in war. He successfully avoided responsibility for the success of the German counter-attack at Cambrai and did much to restore his reputation by Third Army's resolute defence of Arras during the German Spring Offensive of 1918. During the Great Advance Third Army was the largest of the five British armies, playing a key role in the defeat of Germany, a role for which neither he nor his troops have – as yet – received sufficient recognition. Byng divided contemporary opinion. Some thought him an inveterate intriguer; others, notably the perceptive Australian Brudenell White, thought him unusually selfless for a general. After the war Byng served as Governor General of Canada (1921–6) and Chief Commissioner of the Metropolitan Police (1928–31).

Charteris, Brigadier General John (1877–1946) Assistant Military Secretary to GOC Aldershot (Douglas Haig), 1912–14; ADC to GOC I Corps, 1914; GSO2 (Intelligence), I Corps, 1914–16; BGGS (Intelligence), GHQ, 1916–18; retired, 1922. A fellow Scot from a clerical and academic family, Charteris's career owed much to Haig's patronage. This was invariably bestowed for professional reasons and – in Charteris's case – despite the expressed dislike of Lady *Haig, who considered him to be 'dirty and vulgar'. Haig had a high regard for Charteris's abilities and hard work that he never surrendered. As Haig's chief Intelligence Officer Charteris has been blamed for reinforcing Haig's attacking instincts by giving him a deliberately false picture of German military decline. This may be doubted, and Haig specifically acquitted Charteris of such 'wrongdoing'. Charteris may have been mistaken in his assessments of the state of German fighting capacity but his opinions were honestly given. Charteris's intelligence appreciations were only one element – and not the most important one – in the formulation of Haig's strategy. As author of *Field-Marshal Earl Haig* (1929), *At GHQ* (1931), and *Haig* (1933), Charteris was one of the most important post-war defenders of Haig's reputation.

Churchill, Winston Spencer (1874–1965) First Lord of the Admiralty, 1911–15; Chancellor of the Duchy of Lancaster, 1915; Minister of Munitions, 1917–18. Churchill's war was almost on the scale of Greek tragedy. He began it as political head of the Royal Navy, one of the most powerful instruments of international relations since the Roman army, and one that he wielded with total self-confidence. The failure of the attack against the Dardanelles and the subsequent stalemate on the Gallipoli peninsula in the spring of 1915, however, saw the long-standing doubts about Churchill's character resurface and he was banished to the post of President of the Duchy of Lancaster in *Asquith's Coalition Government. After a period as a battalion commander on the Western Front (Haig refused to give him a brigade), Churchill was brought back into the political fold as Minister of Munitions by *Lloyd George in July 1917. Although Haig generally shared contemporary doubts about Churchill, he grew to appreciate his outstanding achievements at the Ministry of Munitions (see, for example, diary, 9 January 1918, and letter, 3 October 1918). Churchill's time at Munitions saw him focus – unusually for him – on his departmental brief. Perhaps for this reason his achievements there, which were vital to British military success in 1918, have largely dropped out of sight.

Clemenceau, Georges ('The Tiger') (1841–1929) French Prime Minister, 1906–9, 1917–20. Clemenceau's return as Prime Minister in November 1917, at the age of seventy-six, and at the end of a traumatic year for France, was a political expression of French determination to see the war through to a victorious conclusion. Clemenceau was clearly the right choice. He galvanised the French home front, waging war on defeatism, persecuting pacifists, simultaneously coercing and conciliating the work force. His presence in office at the height of the German Spring Offensive was a guarantee that the Entente would not shatter under the German blows. In *Foch, whose elevation to Allied Supreme Commander he did much to effect, and in Haig, whom he described as 'the greatest general in the world', he found two soldiers who shared his courage, aggression and optimism.

Derby, 17th Earl of (1865–1948) Director of Recruiting, 1915–16; Secretary of State for War, 1916–18; Ambassador in Paris, 1918–20. Derby is best remembered for his official and unofficial roles in recruiting the great volunteer armies of 1914 and 1915, especially for his sponsorship of the famous 'Pals' battalions whose experience on the Somme has come to dominate British perceptions of the war, often to the exclusion of everything else. As Secretary of State for War in the *Lloyd George Coalition Government Derby did his best to support the Western Front strategy and to protect Haig from the interference of the Prime Minister, though Haig often believed that Derby's best was not good enough. Lloyd George distrusted Derby and disliked his advice. By the time Derby was replaced by *Milner in April 1918 his influence was marginal. He was British Ambassador in Paris from 1918 until 1920. Lord Derby was godfather to Haig's son in 1918.

Foch, Marshal Ferdinand (1851–1929) Foch was one of France's leading military intellectuals, often seen – wrongly – as a doctrinaire advocate of the offensive. He played a key role in the defence of Ypres in 1914. In 1915 he co-ordinated French forces on the northern part of the Western Front. His career was temporarily derailed after the fall of *Joffre in December 1916, but he returned as French Chief of Staff in the aftermath of the *Nivelle Offensive. In 1918 he became *de facto* Allied Commander-in-Chief ('Generalissimo'), an appointment in which Haig's role is much disputed. Haig and Foch had their differences in 1918, but on the whole they worked well together. Foch took the German surrender in the forest of Compiègne on 11 November 1918. He was a man of boundless courage and energy, vital to the Allied victory.

French, Field Marshal Sir John Denton Pinkstone (1st Earl of Ypres) (1852–1925) GOC-in-C British Expeditionary Force, 1914–15; GOC-in-C Home Forces, 1915–18; Lord Lieutenant of Ireland, 1918–21. 'Johnny' French established a dashing reputation as a cavalry commander in the South African War, in which Douglas Haig was his Chief of Staff. In the years before the outbreak of the Great War, French held a series of important posts, including C-in-C Aldershot (1907), Inspector General of the Forces (1907–12), and Chief of the Imperial General Staff (1912–14), from which he was forced to resign in 1914 over the 'Curragh Incident'. French was a notorious ladies' man and much given to the company of politicians. He and Haig were, nevertheless, friendly until the painful parting of the ways over the issue of the reserves at Loos (diary, 27 September 1915, and following). French is charitably described as 'mercurial'. Haig, less charitably but rather accurately, compared him to a bottle of soda water, given to frothing unpredictably when shaken. There is no doubt that by the end of 1915 French had lost the confidence of many of his senior military commanders and of leading political figures. The vendetta that French pursued against Sir Horace *Smith-Dorrien, which resulted in Smith-Dorrien's dismissal in April 1915, virtually ensured that Haig would succeed him as GOC-in-C BEF. French's memoir, *1914*, helped perpetuate the split with Haig (and Smith-Dorrien) beyond the war. Haig tried to repair the relationship, not least by asking French to be godfather to his son (an invitation that French accepted), but the two men were never fully reconciled. In Haig's case the dominant feeling was sorrow rather than anger.

George V (1865–1936) King of Great Britain and Emperor of India, 1910–36. George V was not a man of great intellectual gifts, but he was well endowed with common sense and patriotism. These characteristics came to the fore during the war, in which he became a symbol of national unity and determination. He set an example of modest living that was admired even if it was not followed by many of his subjects, especially his ministers. He showed himself to his people at home by visiting factories and hospitals and to his soldiers abroad, where he made five visits to the Western Front. He was very aware that officers held the King's Commission. He took a personal interest in the Army and its commanders, several of whom (including Haig) were invited to correspond with him. Haig's supposed royal patronage has been much exaggerated, however, and so has the King's influence over military appointments. Haig's pre-war royal connections were with Edward VII rather than George V, to whom other generals, notably *Smith-Dorrien, were much closer. The King's decision to give up his German titles and to change the name of the royal family from Saxe-Coburg-Gotha to Windsor not only reflected the pragmatic need to respect public opinion but also George's own increasing hatred of Germany. The warmth of his reception during his Silver Jubilee year of 1935 surprised him. He was one of the few monarchs whose throne was strengthened by the Great War.

Gough, General Sir Hubert de la Poer ('Goughie') (1870–1963) GOC 3 Cavalry Brigade, 1914; GOC 1st Cavalry Division, 1914; GOC 2nd Cavalry Division, 1914–15; GOC 7th Division, 1915; GOC I Corps, 1915–16; GOC Reserve Corps, 1916; GOC Reserve Army, 1916; GOC Fifth Army, 1916–18. Hubert Gough was the son, brother, nephew and cousin of Victoria Cross winners. His pre-war career was almost terminated by his involvement in the 'Curragh Mutiny', in which he and his brother, John (later Haig's Chief of Staff at I Corps), emerged as the leading champions of the Ulster cause within the army. Gough's wartime rise was, nevertheless, dramatic – from cavalry brigade commander in August 1914 to Army commander in May 1916, at the very early age of forty-four. This rise owed much to Haig, who admired Gough's high sense of professionalism, optimism and aggression. Haig seemed more comfortable in the company of Gough than that of his other Army commanders, responding warmly to the younger man's energy and wit. Haig has been much criticised for his patronage of Gough and, especially, for his choice of Gough to lead the attack in Flanders in 1917. Gough had many qualities associated with successful commanders, but he was also impetuous and inclined to run before he could walk. These were serious handicaps in trench warfare, which put a premium on careful preparation and modest objectives. Gough's often withering sarcasm also alienated many sub-ordinates. *Kiggell left Haig in no doubt about how unpopular Fifth Army was among the troops, though Haig believed that much of this was due to Gough's acerbic Chief of Staff, Neill Malcolm, whom he replaced at the end of 1917. It was Gough's misfortune to face the full force of the German Spring Offensive in March 1918. Public opinion needed a scapegoat and Gough was it. No one recognised this more clearly than Haig. Gough was therefore denied the opportunity to test his skills in the semi-mobile warfare of the Great Advance, to which temperamentally he was much more suited.

Haig, Dorothy Maud (Countess Haig)('Doris') (1879–1939) Dorothy Vivian, twin second daughter of the 3rd Lord Vivian, was a Maid of Honour to Queen Alexandra, wife of King Edward VII, when she met Douglas Haig in 1905. They married after a whirlwind courtship, much of it spent on the golf course. The marriage was a happy one; Haig was a uxorious husband and a loving father. Lady Haig was the recipient of Haig's manuscript diaries and it was she who was responsible for forwarding extracts from them to the *King. Other than this requested transmission, she let slip nothing of the diaries' contents, a trust to which Haig paid tribute in the inscribed copy of his *Despatches* that he gave her in 1919. She was a vital emotional support to her husband during the war as well as providing an outlet for his frustrations through their correspondence. After his death Lady Haig became a doughty defender of her husband's reputation as well as the author of a memoir, *The Man I Knew* (1936), an act for which she has been widely derided.

Horne, General Sir Henry Sinclair (Lord Horne of Stirkoke) (1861–1929) BGRA I Corps, 1914–15; GOC 2nd Division, 1915; GOC XV Corps, 1916; GOC First Army, 1916–19. Horne began the war as Haig's artillery adviser at I Corps. He was promoted to corps command (XV Corps) shortly after Haig became C-in-C and succeeded to Haig's old command at First Army in September 1916. Horne had much in common with Haig. Both were Scots. Both were religious. Both had a strong sense of duty. Horne was also ascetic, living a life of almost monkish restraint. He was not a great soldier – the claim that he was responsible for the 'creeping barrage' is ill founded – but he was careful and thoroughly professional. He had a good knowledge of the ordinary soldier and well understood the human costs of war. He was blessed with a talented staff with whom he did not interfere once he had made up his mind to trust them. Despite commanding an army for two years in the greatest land war Britain has ever fought, he has never been the subject of a biography.

Joffre, Marshal Joseph Jacques Césaire (1852–1931) Joffre was the eldest of eleven children of a Pyrenean barrel-maker, socially and geographically remote from the centre of French power. He rose to prominence in the politically fractious pre-war French Army largely because of his sound 'Republican' credentials, but in 1914 his imperturbability under extreme stress allowed him to rescue his country, his army and himself from the disastrous initial deployment of the French Army and achieve the 'miracle of the Marne'. Joffre was a formidable man and a demanding ally. Throughout 1915 and 1916 France bore the brunt of the fighting, something that Joffre was not slow to point out to his British allies, from whom he demanded more and more. The longer the war lasted the more power Joffre drew to himself and he exercised a control over strategy that Haig could only dream of. But after two years of unprecedented military effort had failed to drive the Germans from France he fell victim to French war weariness and was replaced at the end of 1916 by *Nivelle. Haig often referred to Joffre as 'the old man' and sometimes disparaged his military abilities, but he also often admired his resolution and 'soldier-like' qualities. Their collaboration, however fractious and argumentative, was always real and in practice close.

Kiggell, Lieutenant General Sir Launcelot Edward ('Kigge') (1862–1954) Kiggell was Haig's Chief of Staff from December 1915 until January 1918. He was not Haig's first choice – that was Richard *Butler – but he nevertheless welcomed Kiggell's appointment. Kiggell had risen in the Army on merit, with no advantage of birth or wealth (he did not go to public school). Haig admired Kiggell's professionalism, dedication, hard work and loyalty. Whereas *Charteris has been accused of having a 'malign' influence on Haig, Kiggell has been charged with having no influence at all, dismissed as a tidy-minded clerk incapable and unwilling to offer any intellectual challenge to his Chief's ideas. One student of British High Command has described him as 'the invisible man'. Kiggell was undoubtedly self-effacing and donnish. But where his influence and ideas are discernible – for example, in relation to the most effective employment of tanks and in the authorship of the important pamphlet, *SS135: The Training of Divisions for Offensive Action* – he emerges as a thoroughly prudent and able soldier.

Kitchener, Field Marshal Earl (1850–1916) Secretary of State for War, 1914–16. Few men exercised more influence over the British conduct of the war than Kitchener. It was Kitchener who insisted on the raising of a mass volunteer army. This decision, made even before the professional BEF had been deployed, fundamentally changed the nature of the war for Britain. Kitchener believed the war to be about the long-term safety and security of the British Empire, an institution he had done much to create and to which he had dedicated his life. Imperial security required not only an Allied victory on the battlefield but also a decisive British presence at the conference table. Such an outcome would be best achieved by the British Army inflicting the *coup de grâce* some time in 1917 on a German army rendered ripe for defeat by the French and Russian Armies. In the event this was not to be. Kitchener's armies were committed to a bloody 'wearing-out fight' on the Somme a year before they were ready because the German Army had rendered the French Army ripe for defeat. This could not be allowed to happen. Kitchener could not envisage an outcome to the war satisfactory to the interests of the British Empire that acquiesced in the defeat of France. This became one of the war's strategic realities and one that Haig fully shared. Kitchener died in June 1916 in the loss of HMS *Hampshire* while on a diplomatic mission to Russia.

Lawrence, General Sir Herbert Alexander ('Lorenzo') (1861–1943) Herbert Lawrence was the son of the last Governor General and first Viceroy of India and he had about him something of a regal aspect. His emergence, in 1918, as Haig's Chief of Staff was a remarkable turnaround for both men. Lawrence had retired from the Army on 12 May 1903 after Haig had been brought in from outside as CO of Lawrence's regiment, the 17th Lancers, an appointment to which Lawrence felt himself entitled. Lawrence used his family connections – his wife belonged to the Mills banking dynasty – to forge a career in the City, where he was remarkably successful. He was recalled from the Reserve of Officers in 1914, serving on Gallipoli and in Egypt. In the summer of 1916 he inflicted a significant defeat on a German–Turkish force at Romani, winning back control of the Sinai. But he then resigned for a second time, disbelieving in the wisdom of invading Palestine. One resignation was usually enough to end a career, but two was inviting oblivion. Oblivion, however, is not what happened. Lawrence received another field command, the 66th (2nd East Lancashire) Division, in February 1917, deployed to the Western Front in March. In February 1918 he succeeded *Kiggell as Haig's Chief of Staff. He was much more obviously independent minded than Kiggell, bringing his own men on to the GHQ staff, and always prepared to use his initiative and judgement. This took a considerable burden from Haig, who paid testimony to his 'right arm' in his Final Despatch of 1919, commending Lawrence's 'unfailing insight, calm resolution and level judgement which neither ill-fortune nor good was able to disturb'. Two of Lawrence's sons were killed on the Western Front.

Lloyd George, David (Earl Lloyd-George of Dwyfor) (1863–1945) Chancellor of the Exchequer, 1908–15; Minister of Munitions, 1915–16; Secretary of State for War, July–December 1916; Prime Minister, 1916–22. Lloyd George and Haig are invariably portrayed as stereotypical opposites (the nature of the stereotype depending on the writer's prejudice): 'the dour Scot' and 'the mercurial Welshman', 'the rigid soldier' and the 'imaginative politician', the 'straight dealer' and the 'devious intriguer'. Few books have done more to damage Haig's reputation than Lloyd George's *War Memoirs*, in which the index entries on Haig alone constitute a systematic assault on the Field Marshal's character and professional abilities. Although the animosity between Lloyd George and Haig was real, it disguises the issues of policy that were at the heart of the differences between them. Lloyd George came to power because he seemed to offer a better prospect than *Asquith of taking the war seriously. At home, Lloyd George was prepared to slaughter any number of sacred cows on the altar of victory but abroad he recoiled from the human costs of military success. Although he disliked the military advice he was receiving, he was unwilling or unable to change his advisers (at least until he replaced *Robertson in February 1918) and so to convince his allies that there was a quicker and cheaper road to victory that led away from the Western Front. Lloyd George, like Haig, has been accused of self-interested ambition, but his rise to power was the result of an act of considerable political courage – leaving the Chancellorship of the Exchequer for the Ministry of Munitions – and he seems to have done remarkably little to secure his accession to the prime ministership during the crisis of December 1916. His resolve during the German Spring Offensive of 1918 was of immeasurable value to the Allied cause.

Milner, Alfred, Viscount (1854–1925) The German-born Milner made his reputation as a colonial administrator and imperial pro-consul in Egypt and South Africa. A brilliant academic, he had been much influenced at university by the views of Arnold Toynbee on the rise and fall of civilisations. He was determined to prevent the fall of British civilisation. This made him an advocate of social reform at home and imperial efficiency abroad. He was co-opted into government in 1914 to organise coal and food production and, in December 1916, joined *Lloyd George's small new executive War Cabinet. He became Secretary of State for War in April 1918. Milner played a key part, with *Clemenceau, in the creation of an allied unified command in March 1918. Haig welcomed his appointment as Secretary of State for War and collaborated closely and effectively with him for the rest of 1918.

Monro, General Sir Charles Carmichael (1860–1929) GOC 2nd Division, 1914; I Corps, 1914–15; Third Army, July–October 1915; First Army, February–August, 1916; Commander-in-Chief, India, 1916–20. Monro is the least known of the BEF's Army commanders. He is best remembered for being the butt of Churchill's withering dismissal – 'he came, he saw, he capitulated' – following Monro's recommendation that the Gallipoli peninsula should be evacuated. Monro was descended from an old Scottish family, best known in medicine, but his mother was Irish. It was said of him that he 'was Scottish on duty and Irish off duty'. He was an outstanding regimental officer with the Royal West Surreys and, as Commandant of the School of Musketry, 1903–7, made an important contribution to the Army's outstanding rifle skills. His career as an Army commander was relatively uneventful, though First Army helped to perpetrate XI Corps' bungled attack at Fromelles in June. But Monro showed himself adept at spotting talent and encouraging initiative, not least in the development of Army Schools, which were taken up by other armies and became an important feature of improved British training. J. F. C. Fuller was one of the officers who blossomed in Monro's Third Army. He was an outstanding C-in-C India, his thorough reorganisation of the Indian Army making possible the 'Indianisation' of the Palestine and Mesopotamia campaigns.

Nivelle, General Robert Georges (1856–1924) Commander-in-Chief of the French Army, December 1916–May 1917. Nivelle's rise was dramatic; he was a mere artillery regiment commander in 1914. He made his reputation at Verdun, where his III Corps recaptured Forts Vaux and Douaumont. By the end of 1916 the French Government was war-weary and appalled by the prospect of more colossal attritional battles. *Joffre paid the price and was replaced by Nivelle, whose self-confidence and optimistic assurance that there was an easier but certain path to victory captivated the French Prime Minister, Aristide Briand. Despite Nivelle's possibly disingenuous role in *Lloyd George's intrigues at the Calais Conference (diary, February 1917), Haig did his utmost – as he always did – to assist the Nivelle plan. When Nivelle failed to deliver the expected 'victory in forty-eight hours', the French Army was brought to the point of mutiny, leaving the BEF as the only reliable Allied Army in the field. He was sacked on 15 May 1917.

Pershing, General John Joseph ('Black Jack') (1860–1948) Commander-in-Chief of the American Expeditionary Force, 1917–19. Pershing had fully absorbed what limited military experience the pre-war United States Army had to offer, including combat in the Spanish–American War (1898), the Philippines insurrection (1899–1903) and the expedition against Pancho Villa (1916–17). Pershing was a cold professional soldier, acutely aware of his responsibilities as a 'national contingent commander'. Haig was impressed by Pershing, being 'much struck with his quiet gentlemanly bearing – so unusual for an American' (diary, 20 July 1917) and initially found him easy to deal with. But in 1918, he regarded Pershing's refusal to allow American formations to take their place in the Allied line with increasing exasperation. He was not alone in this.

Pétain, Marshal Henri-Philippe (1856–1951) Commander-in-Chief of the French Army, 1917–19. Pétain was the son of a peasant from the Pas-de-Calais. Throughout his long life he retained the virtues and vices of the French peasantry. In 1914 he was an elderly colonel of infantry and his career appeared to be moving towards an undramatic conclusion; by the end of 1916 he had become 'the hero of Verdun' and 'the saviour of France'. He was the obvious choice to replace *Nivelle after the disastrous failure of the French offensive in May 1917. Pétain skilfully dealt with the mutinies of the French Army and restored its operational effectiveness. Haig found Pétain 'businesslike, knowledgeable, and brief of speech' (diary, 18 May 1917) and had no difficulties working with him in 1917. During the German Spring Offensive of 1918, however, their relationship reached a controversial crisis point, at which *Foch was appointed *de facto* Allied Commander-in-Chief. Haig's view of Pétain as 'defeatist' was shared by the French Prime Minister, Georges *Clemenceau.

Plumer, General Sir Herbert Charles Onslow (Field Marshal Viscount Plumer of Messines) ('Plum') (1857–1932) GOC II Corps, 1914–15; GOC Second Army, 1915–17; GOC-in-C Italy, November 1917–March 1918; GOC Second Army, March 1918–19. Haig often referred to Plumer as 'the old man', even though he was only four years his senior. Haig frequently reminded himself that he might have sacked Plumer after Second Army's loss of a position known as 'The Bluff' in February 1916 and congratulated himself for not having done so. Perhaps for this reason Plumer was, arguably, the most loyal of Haig's Army commanders and far less independent-minded than *Byng, *Gough or *Rawlinson. Haig's diary testifies to his growing regard for Plumer's qualities and for those of Second Army, which owed much to the meticulous planning and preparation of Plumer's Chief of Staff, 'Tim' Harington, a Haig appointee. Haig has been severely criticised for failing to entrust the 'Passchendaele' campaign to Plumer after his stunning success at Messines in June 1917. John Terraine described the handing over of the battle to Gough's Fifth Army as 'Haig's greatest and most fatal error'. Haig and Gough have since borne the brunt of the criticisms of the Flanders fighting, but the battles fought by Plumer from late September onwards were never cheap and, in October, Second Army's troops had to endure some of the worst conditions of the war.

Poincaré, Raymond Nicolas Landry (1860–1934) President of France, 1913–20. As a native of the 'lost province' of Lorraine, Poincaré was an ardent patriot who favoured a strong military (not always the case among Republicans). Although he was a very 'interventionist' President, he had real difficulty in influencing the conduct of the war, which was increasingly dominated by *Joffre between 1914 and 1916. Poincaré's decision to abandon the politics of coalition in November 1917 and appoint *Clemenceau as Prime Minister was a courageous one, but it eventually marginalised him. Clemenceau dominated the conduct of the war in 1918 and even succeeded in excluding Poincaré from the Paris Peace Conference.

Rawlinson, General Sir Henry Seymour Bt. ('Rawly') (1864–1925) GOC 4th Division, 1914; GOC IV Corps, 1914–15; GOC Fourth Army, 1916–18; British Representative Supreme War Council, 1918; GOC Fourth Army, March 1918–19; GOC-in-C India, 1920–5. Henry Rawlinson was the son of a distinguished Assyriologist and MP. He did his regimental soldiering with King's Royal Rifle Corps and the Coldstream Guards. He served as ADC to Lord Roberts in India and was Kitchener's DAAG in the Sudan. As Commandant of the Staff College, 1903–6, he was instrumental in modernising the curriculum and making it more relevant to the needs of a modern army. Rawlinson was the first Army commander to be appointed under Haig. He was, perhaps, the most experienced commander available, having led IV Corps in all First Army's attacks of 1915. Principal responsibility for planning the Somme campaign fell to Rawlinson. He favoured a cautious approach, based on the method of 'bite and hold', but this found little favour with Haig, who wished to leave open the possibility of a more decisive advance. Their failure to resolve their differences played a part in the disasters of 1 July 1916. 'Bite and hold' was no panacea, however. The success of the method in 1918 was achieved under very different conditions and with a very different army. Rawlinson's piecemeal attacks on narrow fronts with inadequate forces in July and August 1916 were very costly. He was sidelined for much of 1917, planning an amphibious landing on the Belgian coast that never took place. But the defeat of Fifth Army and the replacement of Hubert *Gough gave Rawlinson his chance. His Fourth Army spearheaded the Allied counter-attack, inflicting a major defeat on the Germans at Amiens on 8 August. Haig was wholly appreciative of Rawlinson's achievements and their relationship developed a warmth that had not always characterised it.

Robertson, General (later Field Marshal) Sir William Robert ('Wully') (1860–1933) QMG British Expeditionary Force, 1914–15; Chief of Staff, BEF, January–December 1915; Chief of the Imperial General Staff, 1915–18. William Robertson was the son of a Lincolnshire village tailor who ran away at the age of seventeen to join the Army as a private soldier, much to his mother's disapproval. His subsequent rise to field marshal is unique in the history of the British Army. This was possible only because Robertson was a formidable man, highly intelligent, supremely analytical, with a flair for languages and a capacity for hard work. He made his reputation as an Intelligence Officer, but broadened into more general staff work, especially military administration ('logistics'). He was the first officer promoted from the ranks to enter and pass Staff College; in 1910 he became its Commandant. Robertson distinguished himself as QMG in 1914, especially during the Retreat from Mons. In 1915 he brought order and purpose to Sir John *French's staff. In December 1915 he became Chief of the Imperial General Staff, professional head of the British Army. His appointment was a deliberate ploy by the Government to curb the influence of Lord *Kitchener.

Robertson drove a hard bargain and entered the office of CIGS with unprecedented powers, backed by an Order-in-Council. His view of the war was coherent and bleak. Unlike Kitchener, he did not believe that the war could be fought on terms of limited British liability and realised that the BEF would have to participate fully in the wearing-out fight against the German Army. He was under no illusions about the human costs. He believed that the war could only be won (and lost) on the Western Front and argued that British military strength should be fully concentrated there. This he never achieved, but his advocacy of it brought him into increasing conflict with *Lloyd George, especially after the latter became Prime Minister in December 1916. He believed that the Ottoman Empire could be taken out of the war by diplomatic means and feared the consequences of the Empire's dissolution. In this he showed more judgement than his Prime Minister. He was appalled by Lloyd George's behaviour at the Calais Conference of February 1917 and increasingly saw it as his role to protect Haig and the Army from misconceived political interference. Despite this, he never shared Haig's operational optimism and continually counselled him against making exaggerated claims. During 1917 Robertson's perennial realism hardened into something like pessimism. By the end of the year Haig felt that Robertson had lost the faith. This was one of the reasons why he refused to 'walk the plank' with Robertson when the latter was forced into resignation by Lloyd George in February 1918.

Smith-Dorrien, General Sir Horace Lockwood ('S.D.') (1858–1930) GOC II Corps, 1914; GOC Second Army, 1914–15. Smith-Dorrien succeeded to the command of II Corps after the sudden death in transit of its original commander, Sir James Grierson. It was, perhaps, an unfortunate choice. Smith-Dorrien and his Commander-in-Chief, Sir John *French, had a poisonous relationship, not improved by Smith-Dorrien's volcanic temper and French's vindictiveness. Haig's diary is often critical of II Corps in 1914. Some of this was justified. II Corps, unlike Haig's I Corps, was an *ad hoc* organisation with no peacetime existence. It took some time to 'bed in' and was required to do this while bearing the brunt of the early fighting. Smith-Dorrien's unsanctioned stand at Le Cateau on 26 August is now generally recognised to have 'saved' the BEF. But French came increasingly to believe that Smith-Dorrien had recklessly risked the existence of the Army. When Second Army retreated under the German gas attack in April 1915, French saw his opportunity to get rid of his hated subordinate, leaving Douglas Haig as the only realistic alternative as Commander-in-Chief.

Wilson, General (later Field Marshal) Sir Henry Hughes (1864–1922) Sub-Chief of Staff, BEF, 1914–15; Chief Liaison Officer with the French Army, 1915; GOC IV Corps, 1915–17; Chief Liaison Officer with the French Army, 1917; GOC Eastern Command (in the UK), 1917; CIGS, 1918–22. As Director of Military Operations, 1910–14, Wilson had played a leading part in the administrative preparation of the British Expeditionary Force for war. His trouncing of naval opinion at the meeting of the Committee of Imperial Defence in August 1911 is often regarded as key to the Government's adoption of the 'Western Front' strategy. Wilson's importance as an instigator of British belligerency must, however, be consigned to legend. Neither Wilson nor any other British soldier played a significant part in Britain's decision to go to war. Wilson would have been Sir John *French's choice as Chief of Staff, but the central part played by Wilson in the 'Curragh Incident' put him beyond the pale as far as *Asquith's Government was concerned. He had to content himself with being Sub-Chief of French's staff, a role in which he undermined the authority of the actual Chief of Staff, Sir Archibald Murray.

Wilson was widely distrusted in the Army. Haig shared the opinion of Wilson as an 'intriguer'. He was also disturbed by Wilson's pro-French leanings, describing him in 1914 as 'more French than the French' (diary, 18 November 1914). Haig advised *Kitchener not to choose Wilson as Murray's successor, advancing instead the name of *Robertson (diary, 18 December 1914). Wilson was not a success as a corps commander and was effectively sidelined for much of the war as 'Chief Liaison Officer' at French GHQ. But while back home in 1917 as GOC Eastern Command he reinvented himself as 'unofficial military adviser' to Lloyd George and he was the Prime Minister's choice as CIGS after Robertson was forced into 'resignation' in February 1918. Haig and Wilson, however, generally worked well together and, towards the end of the war, there appears an unusual intimacy in their relationship, Haig addressing his letters to Wilson 'My dear Henry' (letter 20 September 1918). Wilson was assassinated by the Irish Republican Brotherhood on 22 June 1922 outside his house in Eaton Square. He had just returned from unveiling the war memorial at Liverpool Street Station and was therefore wearing his field marshal's uniform. He died sword in hand.

Wilson, (Thomas) Woodrow (1856–1924) President of the United States of America, 1912–20. Although a political reformer at home, Wilson showed no reluctance to wield what Theodore Roosevelt called the 'big stick' abroad, authorising military interventions in Nicaragua, Haiti, the Dominican Republic and Mexico. The decision to intervene in the European War was drawn out and painful. Wilson declared US neutrality on 19 August 1914 and won the 1916 presidential election on the slogan 'He kept us out of the War'. Wilson saw himself as a 'peacemaker' rather than a 'warmonger', but when his attempts to broker a peace failed in December 1916 he gradually realised that if the US was to have an influence on any peace settlement, his country would have first to go to war. US belligerency was eased considerably by the collapse of Tsarist autocracy in Russia. The USA joined the war as an Associated Power rather than as an Ally. Wilson made it clear from the outset that the United States' aspirations were of a 'higher' and 'purer' kind than the reimposition of a discredited diplomatic abstraction like the European balance of power. He wished to make the 'world safe for democracy'. Wilson figures less in Haig's diary than other 'Allied' political leaders. He did not come to Europe until 1919, preferring to operate through his personal representative, Colonel Edward M. House, whom Haig described as 'natural, sincere and capable' (diary, 26 October 1918). Wilson's presence can nevertheless be felt, especially in the autumn of 1918 when the question of surrender terms came to the fore. Haig did not share the President's grandiose ambitions, favouring a more limited and practical settlement.

APPENDIX ONE

Instructions of the Secretary of State for War (Lord Kitchener) to the Field Marshal Commanding-in-Chief, British Armies in France (Field Marshal Sir John French), August 1914

1. Owing to the infringement of the neutrality of Belgium by Germany, and in furtherance of the Entente which exists between this country and France, His Majesty's Government has decided, at the request of the French Government, to send an Expeditionary Force to France and to entrust the command of the troops to yourself.

2. The special motive of the Force under your control is to support and co-operate with the French Army against our common enemies. The peculiar task laid upon you is to assist the French Government in preventing or repelling the invasion by Germany of French and Belgian territory and eventually to restore the neutrality of Belgium, on behalf of which, as guaranteed by treaty, Belgium has appealed to the French and to ourselves.

3. These are the reasons which have induced His Majesty's Government to declare war, and these reasons constitute the primary objective you have before you.

4. The place of your assembly, according to present arrangements, is Amiens, and during the assembly of your troops you will have every opportunity for discussing with the Commander-in-Chief of the French Army, the military position in general and the special part which your Force is able and adapted to play. It must be recognised from the outset that the numerical strength of the British Force and its contingent reinforcement is strictly limited, and with this consideration kept steadily in view it will be obvious that the greatest care must be exercised towards a minimum of losses and wastage.

5. Therefore, while every effort must be made to coincide most sympathetically with the plans and wishes of our Ally, the gravest consideration will devolve upon you as to participation in forward movements where large bodies of French troops are not engaged and where your Force may be unduly exposed to attack. Should a contingency of this sort be contemplated, I look to you to inform me fully and give me time to communicate to you any decision to which His Majesty's Government may come in the matter. In this connection I wish you distinctly to understand that your command is an entirely independent one, and that you will in no case come in any sense under the orders of any Allied General.

6. In minor operations you should be careful that your subordinates understand

that risk of serious losses should only be taken where such risk is authoritatively considered to be commensurate with the object in view.

7. The high courage and discipline of your troops should, and certainly will, have fair and full opportunity of display during the campaign, but officers may well be reminded that in this, their first experience of European warfare, a greater measure of caution must be employed than under former conditions of hostilities against an untrained adversary.

8. You will kindly keep up constant communication with the War Office, and you will be good enough to inform me as to all movements of the enemy reported to you as well as to those of the French Army.

9. I am sure you fully realise that you can rely with the utmost confidence on the whole-hearted and unswerving support of the Government, of myself, and of your compatriots, in carrying out the high duty which the King has entrusted to you and in maintaining the great tradition of His Majesty's Army.

APPENDIX TWO

Instructions of the Secretary of State for War (Lord Kitchener) to the General Commanding-in-Chief, British Armies in France (General Sir Douglas Haig), 28 December 1915

1. His Majesty's Government consider that the mission of the British Expeditionary Force in France, to the chief command of which you have recently been appointed, is to support and co-operate with the French and Belgian Armies against our common enemies. The special task laid upon you is to assist the French and Belgian Governments in driving the German Armies from French and Belgian territory, and eventually to restore the neutrality of Belgium, on behalf of which, as guaranteed by Treaty, Belgium appealed to the French and to ourselves at the commencement of hostilities.

2. You will be informed from time to time of the numbers of troops which will be placed at your disposal in order to carry out your mission, and in this connection you will understand that, owing to the number of different theatres in which we are employed, it may not always be possible to give the information definitely a long time in advance.

3. The defeat of the enemy by the combined Allied Armies must always be regarded as the primary object for which the British troops were originally sent to France, and to achieve that end, the closest co-operation of French and British as a united Army must be the governing policy; but I wish you distinctly to understand that your command is an independent one, and that you will in no case come under the orders of any Allied General further than the necessary co-operation with our Allies above referred to.

4. If unforeseen circumstances should arise such as to compel our Expeditionary Force to retire, such a retirement should never be contemplated as an independent move to secure the defence of the ports facing the Straits of Dover, although their security is a matter of great importance demanding that every effort should be made to prevent the lines which the Allied Forces now hold in Flanders being broken by the enemy. The safety of the Channel will be decided by the overthrow of the German Armies rather than by the occupation by our troops of some defensive position with their backs to the sea. In the event, therefore, of a retirement, the direction of the retreat should be decided, in conjunction with our Ally, with reference solely to the eventual defeat of the enemy and not to the security of the Channel. Notwithstanding the above, our Expeditionary Force may be compelled to fall back upon the Channel ports, or

the circumstances may be such that it will be strategically advantageous that, while acting in co-operation with the French Army, it should carry out such a retirement. The requisite steps required to meet this contingency should therefore receive due attention.

5. In minor operations you should be careful that your subordinates understand that risk of serious losses should only be taken where such risk is authoritatively considered to be commensurate with the object in view.

6. You will kindly keep up constant communication with the War Office, and you will be good enough to inform me regarding all movements of the enemy reported to you as well as those of the French Army.

7. I am sure that you fully realise that you can rely with the utmost confidence on the whole-hearted and unswerving support of the Government, of myself, and of your compatriots.

APPENDIX THREE

Instructions of the Secretary of State for War (Lord Milner) to the Field Marshal Commanding-in-Chief, British Armies in France (Field Marshal Sir Douglas Haig), 21 June 1918

In consequence of the concurrence of His Majesty's Government in the appointment of General Foch as Commander-in-Chief of the Allied Forces on the Western Front, it has become necessary to modify in some respects the instructions given to you in War Office letter No. 121/7711 dated 28 December 1915.[1]

1. The general objects to be pursued by the British Armies in France remain the same as those set forth in the first and second paragraphs of that letter.
2. In pursuit of these objects you will carry out loyally any instructions issued to you by the Commander-in-Chief of the Allied Forces. At the same time, if any order given by him appears to you to imperil the British Army, it is agreed between the Allied Governments that you should be at liberty to appeal to the British Government before executing such order. While it is hoped that the necessity for such an appeal may seldom, if ever, arise, you will not hesitate in cases of grave emergency to avail yourself of your right to make it.
3. It is the desire of His Majesty's Government to keep the British forces under your command as far as possible together. If at any time the Allied Commander-in-Chief finds it necessary to transfer any portion of the British troops to the French area in order to release French troops for purposes of *roulement*,[2] it should be distinctly understood that this is only a temporary arrangement, and that as soon as practicable the troops thus detached should be re-united to the main body of the British forces.
4. You will afford to the American troops forming part of the Allied Armies in France such assistance in training, equipment, or administrative matters as may from time to time be required of you by the Commander-in-Chief of the Allied Forces.
5. Subject to any special directions you may receive from the Commander-in-Chief of the Allied Forces, the principles laid down in the fourth paragraph of War Office letter No. 121/7711 of 28 December 1915, are to be regarded as holding good.
6. The fifth, sixth and seventh paragraphs of that letter are maintained in their entirety.

1 See Appendix Two.
2 Rotations.

APPENDIX FOUR

An Extract from Sir Douglas Haig's Final Despatch, 21 March 1919

In this my final Despatch, I think it desirable to comment briefly upon certain general features which concern the whole series of operations carried out under my command. I am urged thereto by the conviction that neither the course of the war itself nor the military lessons to be drawn therefrom can properly be comprehended, unless the long succession of battles commenced on the Somme in 1916 and ended in November of last year on the Sambre are viewed as forming part of one great and continuous engagement.

To direct attention to any single phase of that stupendous and incessant struggle and seek in it the explanation of our success, to the exclusion or neglect of other phases possibly less striking in their immediate or obvious consequences, is in my opinion to risk the formation of unsound doctrines regarding the character and requirements of modern war.

If the operations of the past four and a half years are regarded as a single continuous campaign, there can be recognised in them the same general features and the same necessary stages which between forces of approximately equal strength have marked all the conclusive battles of history.

There is in the first instance the preliminary stage of the campaign in which the opposing forces seek to deploy and manoeuvre for position, endeavouring while doing so to gain some early advantage which might be pushed home to quick decision. This phase came to an end in the present war with the creation of continuous trench lines from the Swiss frontier to the sea.

Battle having been joined, there follows the period of real struggle in which the main forces of the two belligerent armies are pitted against each other in close and costly combat. Each commander seeks to wear down the power of resistance of his opponent and to pin him to his position, while preserving or accumulating in his own hands a powerful reserve force which he can manoeuvre, and, when signs of the enemy becoming morally and physically weakened are observed, deliver the decisive attack.

The greatest possible pressure against the enemy's whole front must be maintained, especially when the crisis of the battle approaches. Then every man, horse and gun is required to co-operate, so as to complete the enemy's overthrow and exploit success.

In every stage of the wearing-out struggle losses will necessarily be heavy on both sides, for in it the price of victory is paid. If the opposing forces are approximately equal in numbers, in courage, in moral and in equipment, there is no way of avoiding payment of the price or of eliminating this phase of the struggle.

In former battles this stage of the conflict has rarely lasted more than a few days, and has often been completed in a few hours. When armies of millions are engaged, with the resources of great Empires behind them, it will inevitably be long. It will include violent crises of fighting which, when viewed separately and apart from the general perspective, will appear individually as great indecisive battles. To this stage belong the great engagements of 1916 and 1917 which wore down the strength of the German Armies.

Finally, whether from the superior fighting ability and leadership of one of the belligerents, as the result of greater resources or tenacity, or by reason of higher moral, or from a combination of all these causes, the time will come when the other side will begin to weaken and the climax of the battle is reached.

Then the commander of the weaker side must choose whether he will break off the engagement, if he can, while there is yet time, or stake on a supreme effort what reserves remain to him. The launching and destruction of Napoleon's last reserves at Waterloo was a matter of minutes. In this World War the great sortie of the beleaguered German Armies, commenced on March 21, 1918, lasted for four months, yet it represents a corresponding stage in a single colossal battle.

The breaking down of such a supreme effort will be the signal for the commander of the successful side to develop his greatest strength, and seek to turn to immediate account the loss in material and moral which their failure must inevitably produce among his opponent's troops.

In a battle joined and decided in the course of a few days or hours, there is no risk that the lay observer will seek to distinguish the culminating operations by which victory is seized and exploited from the preceding stages by which it has been made possible and determined. If the whole operations of the present war are regarded in correct perspective, the victories of the summer and autumn of 1918 will be seen to be directly dependent upon the two years of stubborn fighting that preceded them.

THE LENGTH OF THE WAR

If the causes which determined the length of the recent contest are examined in the light of the accepted principles of war, it will be seen that the duration of the struggle was governed by and bore a direct relation to certain definite factors which are enumerated below.

In the first place, we were unprepared for war, or at any rate for a war of such magnitude. We were deficient in both trained men and military material, and, what was more important, had no machinery ready by which either men or material could be produced in anything approaching the requisite quantities. The consequences were twofold.

Firstly, the necessary machinery had to be improvised hurriedly, and improvisation is never economical and seldom satisfactory. In this case the high-water mark of our fighting strength in infantry was only reached after two and a half years of conflict, by which time heavy casualties had already been incurred. In consequence, the full man-power of the Empire was never developed in the field at any period of the war.

As regards material, it was not until midsummer 1916 that the artillery situation became even approximately adequate to the conduct of major operations. Throughout the Somme battle the expenditure of artillery ammunition had to be watched with the greatest care. During the battles of 1917, ammunition was plentiful, but the gun situation was a source of constant anxiety. Only in 1918 was it possible to conduct artillery operations independently of any limiting considerations other than that of transport.

The second consequence of our unpreparedness was that our armies were unable to intervene, either at the outset of the war or until nearly two years had elapsed, in sufficient strength adequately to assist our Allies. The enemy was able to gain a notable initial advantage by establishing himself in Belgium and Northern France, and throughout the early stages of the war was free to concentrate an undue proportion of his effectives against France and Russia.

The excessive burden thrown upon the gallant Army of France during this period caused them losses the effect of which has been felt all through the war and directly influenced its length. Just as at no time were we as an Empire able to put our full strength into the field, so at no time were the Allies as a whole able completely to develop and obtain the full effect from their greatly superior man-power. What might have been the effect of British intervention on a larger scale in the earlier stages of the war is shown by what was actually achieved by our original Expeditionary Force.

It is interesting to note that in previous campaigns the side which has been fully prepared for war has almost invariably gained a rapid and complete success over its less well prepared opponent. In 1866 and 1870, Austria and then France were overwhelmed at the outset by means of superior preparation.

The initial advantages derived therefrom were followed up by such vigorous and ruthless action, regardless of loss, that there was no time to recover from the first stunning blows. The German plan of campaign in the present war was undoubtedly based on similar principles. The margin by which the German onrush in 1914 was stemmed was so narrow, and the subsequent struggle so severe, that the word 'miraculous' is hardly too strong a term to describe the recovery and ultimate victory of the Allies.

A further cause adversely influencing the duration of the war on the Western Front during its later stages, and one following indirectly from that just stated, was the situation in other theatres. The military strength of Russia broke down in 1917 at a critical period when, had she been able to carry out her military engagements, the war might have been shortened by a year.

At a later date, the military situation in Italy in the autumn of 1917 necessitated the transfer of five British divisions from France to Italy at a time when their presence in France might have had far-reaching effects.

Thirdly, the Allies were handicapped in their task and the war thereby lengthened by the inherent difficulties always associated with the combined action of armies of separate nationalities, differing in speech and temperament, and, not least important, in military organisation, equipment and supply.

Finally, as indicated in the opening paragraph of this part of my Despatch, the huge numbers of men engaged on either side, whereby a continuous battle front was rapidly established from Switzerland to the sea, outflanking was made impossible and manoeuvre very difficult, necessitated the delivery of frontal attacks.

This factor, combined with the strength of the defensive under modern conditions, rendered a protracted wearing-out battle unavoidable before the enemy's power of resistance could be overcome. So long as the opposing forces are at the outset approximately equal in numbers and moral and there are no flanks to turn, a long struggle for supremacy is inevitable.

THE EXTENT OF OUR CASUALTIES

Obviously, the greater the length of a war the higher is likely to be the number of casualties in it on either side. The same causes, therefore, which served to protract the recent struggle are largely responsible for the extent of our casualties. There can be no question that to our general unpreparedness must be attributed the loss of many thousands of brave men whose sacrifice we deeply deplore, while we regard their splendid gallantry and self-devotion with unstinted admiration and gratitude.

Given, however, the military situation existing in August 1914, our total losses in the war have been no larger than were to be expected. Neither do they compare unfavourably with those of any other of the belligerent nations, so far as figures are available from which comparison can be made.

The total British casualties in all theatres of war – killed, wounded, missing and prisoners, including native troops – are approximately three millions (3,076,388). Of this total, some two and a half millions (2,568,388) were incurred on the Western Front. The total French losses – killed, missing and prisoners, but exclusive of wounded – have been given as approximately 1,831,000.

If an estimate for wounded is added, the total can scarcely be less than 4,800,000, and of this total it is fair to assume that over four millions were incurred on the Western Front. The published figures for Italy – killed and wounded only, exclusive of prisoners – amounted to 1,400,000 of which practically the whole were incurred in the Western theatre of war.

Figures have also been published for Germany and Austria. The total German casualties – killed, wounded, missing and prisoners – are given at approximately six and a half millions (6,485,000), of which the vastly greater proportion must have been incurred on the Western Front, where the bulk of the German forces were concentrated and the hardest fighting took place.

In view of the fact, however, that the number of German prisoners is definitely known to be considerably understated, these figures must be accepted with reserve. The losses of Austria-Hungary in killed, missing and prisoners are given as approximately two and three-quarter millions (2,772,000). An estimate of wounded would give us a total of over four and a half millions.

The extent of our casualties, like the duration of the war, was dependent on certain definite factors which can be stated shortly.

In the first place, the military situation compelled us, particularly during the first portion of the war, to make great efforts before we had developed our full strength in the field or properly equipped and trained our armies. These efforts were wasteful of men, but in the circumstances they could not be avoided. The only alternative was to do nothing and see our French Allies overwhelmed by the enemy's superior numbers.

During the second half of the war, and that part embracing the critical and costly period of the wearing-out battle, the losses previously suffered by our Allies laid upon the British Armies in France an increasing share in the burden of attack. From the opening of the Somme battle in 1916 to the termination of hostilities the British Armies were subjected to a strain of the utmost severity which never ceased, and consequently had little or no opportunity for the rest and training they so greatly needed.

In addition to these particular considerations, certain general factors peculiar to modern war made for the inflation of losses. The great strength of modern field defences and the power and precision of modern weapons, the multiplication of machine guns, trench mortars, and artillery of all natures, the employment of gas and the rapid development of the aeroplane as a formidable agent of destruction against both men and material, all combined to increase the price to be paid for victory.

If only for these reasons, no comparisons can usefully be made between the relative losses incurred in this war and any previous war. There is, however, the further consideration that the issues involved in this stupendous struggle were far greater than those concerned in any other war in recent history. Our existence as Empire and civilisation itself, as it is understood by free Western nations, were at stake.

Men fought as they have never fought before in masses.

Despite our own particular handicaps and the foregoing general considerations, it is satisfactory to note that, as the result of the courage and determination of our troops, and the high level of leadership generally maintained, our losses even in attack over the whole period of the battle compare favourably with those inflicted on our opponents.

The approximate total of our battle casualties in all arms, and including Overseas troops, from the commencement of the Somme battle in 1916 to the conclusion of the Armistice is 2,140,000. The calculation of German losses is obviously a matter of great difficulty.

It is estimated, however, that the number of casualties inflicted on the enemy by British troops during the above period exceeds two and a half millions. It is of interest, moreover, in the light of the paragraph next following, that more than half the total casualties incurred by us in the fighting of 1918 were occasioned during the five months March–July, when our armies were on the defensive.

WHY WE ATTACKED WHENEVER POSSIBLE

Closely connected with the question of casualties is that of the relative values of attack and defence. It is a view often expressed that the attack is more expensive than defence. This is only a half-statement of the truth. Unquestionably, unsuccessful attack is generally more expensive than defence, particularly if the attack is pressed home with courage and resolution. On the other hand, attack so pressed home, if skilfully conducted, is rarely unsuccessful, whereas, in its later stages especially, unsuccessful defence is far more costly than attack.

Moreover, the object of all war is victory, and a purely defensive attitude can never bring about a successful decision, either in a battle or in a campaign. The idea that a war can be won by standing on the defensive and waiting for the enemy to attack is a dangerous fallacy, which owes its inception to the desire to evade the price of victory.

It is an axiom that decisive success in battle can be gained only by a vigorous offensive. The principle here stated had long been recognised as being fundamental, and is based on the universal teaching of military history in all ages. The course of the present war has proved it to be correct.

To pass for a moment from the general to the particular, and consider in the light of the present war the facts upon which this axiom is based.

A defensive role sooner or later brings about a distinct lowering of the moral of the troops, who imagine that the enemy must be the better man, or at least more numerous, better equipped with and better served by artillery and other mechanical aids to victory. Once the mass of the defending infantry become possessed of such ideas, the battle is as good as lost.

An army fighting on enemy soil, especially if its standard of discipline is high, may maintain a successful defence for a protracted period, in the hope that victory may be gained elsewhere or that the enemy may tire or weaken in his resolution and accept a compromise. The resistance of the German Armies was undoubtedly prolonged in this fashion, but in the end the persistence of our troops had its natural effect.

Further, a defensive policy involves the loss of the initiative, with all the consequent disadvantages to the defender. The enemy is able to choose at his own convenience the time and place of his attacks. Not being influenced himself by the threat of attack from his opponent, he can afford to take risks, and by greatly weakening his front in some places can concentrate an overwhelming force elsewhere with which to attack.

The defender, on the other hand, becomes almost entirely ignorant of the dispositions and plans of his opponent, who is thus in a position to effect a surprise. This was clearly exemplified during the fighting of 1918. As long as the enemy was attacking, he obtained fairly full information regarding our dispositions. Captured documents show that, as soon as he was thrown once more on the defensive and the initiative returned to the Allies, he was kept in comparative ignorance of our plans and dispositions. The consequence was that the Allies were able to effect many surprises, both strategic and tactical.

As a further effect of the loss of the initiative and ignorance of his opponent's intentions, the defender finds it difficult to avoid a certain dispersal of his forces. Though for a variety of reasons, including the fact that we had lately been on the offensive, we were by no means entirely ignorant of the enemy's intentions in the spring of 1918, the unavoidable uncertainty resulting from a temporary loss of the initiative did have the effect of preventing a complete concentration of our reserves behind the point of the enemy's attack.

An additional reason, peculiar to the circumstances of the present war, which in itself compelled me to refuse to adopt a purely defensive attitude so long as any other was open to me, is found in the geographical position of our armies. For reasons stated by me in my Despatch of July 20, 1918, we could not afford to give much ground on any part of our front. The experience of the war has shown that if the defence is to be maintained successfully, even for a limited time, it must be flexible.

THE END OF THE WAR

If the views set out by me in the preceding paragraphs are accepted, it will be recognised that the war did not follow any unprecedented course, and that its end was neither sudden nor should it have been unexpected. The rapid collapse of Germany's military powers in the latter half of 1918 was the logical outcome of the fighting of the previous two years.

It would not have taken place but for the period of ceaseless attrition which used up the reserves of the German Armies, while the constant and growing pressure of the blockade sapped with more deadly insistence from year to year at the strength and resolution of the German people. It is in the great battles of 1916 and 1917 that we have to seek for the secret of our victory in 1918.

Doubtless, the end might have come sooner had we been able to develop the military resources of our Empire more rapidly and with a higher degree of concentration, or had not the defection of Russia in 1917 given our enemies a new lease of life.

So far as the military situation is concerned, in spite of the great accession of strength which Germany received as the result of the defection of Russia, the battles of 1916 and 1917 had so far weakened her armies that the effort they made in 1918 was insufficient to secure victory. Moreover, the effect of the battles of 1916 and 1917 was not confined to loss of German man-power.

The moral effects of those battles were enormous, both in the German Army and in Germany. By their means our soldiers established over the German soldier a moral superiority which they held in an ever-increasing degree until the end of the war, even in the difficult days of March and April 1918.

ACKNOWLEDGEMENTS

The editors would like to thank Lord Haig and the rest of the Haig family, especially Douglas Scott. Michael Orr was hugely helpful and supportive. John Hussey's contribution was in a class of its own. Ronald Cullen deserves special thanks for his assistance with the '1917' chapter.

Quotations from material held in the Royal Archives appear by gracious permission of Her Majesty Queen Elizabeth II. Crown Copyright material appears by kind permission of The National Archives.

We would like to thank the following for permission to quote from material for which they hold the copyright:

* Lord Haig (Haig papers)
* The Trustees of the Imperial War Museum (Wilson papers; French papers, IWM Special Miscellaneous, J5)
* The Trustees of the Liddell Hart Centre for Military Archives (Howell papers, Sanders papers)
* Lord Kitchener (Kitchener papers)
* The Household Cavalry Museum (War Diary of the Royal Horse Guards)
* Keele University Library (Wedgwood papers)
* The Library of Congress (Pershing papers)

We would also like to thank the Trustees of the National Library of Scotland for allowing access to material housed in the Library.

It has not proved possible to trace the holder of copyright in the Lomax papers held in the Imperial War Museum. To anyone whose copyright we have unwittingly infringed we offer our sincere apologies.

The views expressed in this book are our own and do not represent those of the Joint Services Command and Staff College or any other organisation or body.

We also wish to thank Dr Stephen Badsey, Dr Niall Barr, Major Jim Beach, the late Lord Blake, Professor Brian Bond, Dr Wyn Bowen, Dr Bob Bushaway, Dr Chris Collins, Dr Mark Connelly, Dr Jeremy Crang, Dr Alan Dearn, Mrs Andrea J. P. De Pree, Wing Commander Peter Edwards, Professor David French, Dr Giles Gasper, Bryn Hammond, Professor Richard Holmes, Dr David Jordan, John Lee, Nick Lloyd, Dr Jenny Macleod, Dr Bill Philpott, Captain Chris Page RN, Stephen Prince, Dr Chris Pugsley, Major General Jonathon Riley, Andy Robertshaw, Professor Peter Simkins, Dr Andy Simpson, Dr Michael Snape, William Spencer, Kathy Stevenson, Professor Hew Strachan, Carolyn Sweet, the late John Terraine,

Rob Thompson, Dr Dan Todman, Richard van Emden, Brigadier Barney White-Spunner, Professor Andy Wiest, Keith Wilson and Mitch Yockelson.

A number of people read through all or part of the manuscript and made many helpful suggestions. Any errors that remain are, of course, the responsibility of the editors. We would be pleased to receive comments or corrections that could be incorporated in a future edition.

Gary Sheffield would like to thank the Arts and Humanities Research Board for granting him a Research Leave award, which allowed him an additional period of sabbatical in which to complete the book; the Douglas Haig Fellowship for their generous support; and the Defence Studies Department, King's College London, for several small grants. He would like to thank the various seminars where he has tried out some of his thinking on Haig, especially at the University of Kent, the Joint Services Command and Staff College, the Institute of Historical Research, University of Birmingham, and the National Army Museum.

Producing a book like this has put the editors in the debt of archivists and librarians. Our principal debt is to the National Librarian and the staff at the National Library of Scotland, who have been enormously helpful and supportive from the very beginning of the project. We would especially like to thank Colm McLaughlin. Thanks are also due to the staff at the Imperial War Museum; the National Archives of the UK (Public Record Office); the Liddell Hart Centre for Military Archives; Churchill College, Cambridge Archives Centre; the Bodleian Library; the Household Cavalry Museum; the library of the Joint Services Command and Staff College; the library of the Royal Military Academy, Sandhurst; and the library of the University of Birmingham.

Our editor at Weidenfeld & Nicolson, Ion Trewin, has been an exemplary mix of wisdom, patience and good advice, and his assistant, Anna Hervé, has been very helpful. Gary Sheffield's literary agent, Simon Trewin, has been a tower of strength.

As ever, our wives, Viv and Barbara, and our families deserve our thanks for their tolerance and support.

G.S. and J.B.

SELECT BIBLIOGRAPHY

Printed Primary Materials

R. Blake, (ed.) *The Private Papers of Douglas Haig 1914–1919* (London: Eyre & Spottiswoode, 1952)

M. & E. Brock (eds), *H.H. Asquith, Letters* to *Venetia Stanley* (Oxford: Oxford University Press, 1985)

J.H. Boraston, *Sir Douglas Haig's Despatches* (London: Dent, 1919)

J. Charteris, *At GHQ* (London: Cassell, 1931)

D. Dutton (ed), *Paris 1918: The War Diary of the 17th Earl of Derby* (Liverpool: Liverpool University Press, 2001)

K. Jeffrey, *The Military Correspondence of Field Marshal Sir Henry Wilson 1918–1922* (London: Bodley Head for Army Records Society, 1985)

D.R. Woodward (ed), *The Military Correspondence of Field-Marshal Sir William Robertson Chief Imperial General Staff December 1915 – February 1918* (London: Bodley Head for Army Records Society, 1989)

Books and Articles about Haig

G. Arthur, *Lord Haig* (London: Heinemann, 1933)

S. Badsey, 'Haig and the Press', in B. Bond & N. Cave (eds), *Haig: A Reappraisal 70 years On* (London: Leo Cooper, 1999)

N. Barr & G. Sheffield, 'Douglas Haig, the Common Soldier, and the British Legion', in B. Bond & N. Cave (eds), *Haig: A Reappraisal 70 Years On* (London: Leo Cooper, 1999)

I.F.W. Beckett, 'Haig and French', in B. Bond & N. Cave, *Haig: A Reappraisal 70 Years On* (London: Leo Cooper, 1999)

B. Bond & N. Cave (eds), *Haig: A Reappraisal 70 Years On* (London: Leo Cooper, 1999)

J.M. Bourne, 'Haig and the Historians', in B. Bond & N. Cave (eds), *Haig: A Reappraisal 70 Years On* (London: Leo Cooper, 1999)

N. Cave, 'Haig and Religion', in B. Bond & N. Cave (eds), *Haig: A Reappraisal 70 Years On* (London: Leo Cooper, 1999)

J. Charteris, *Field Marshal Earl Haig* (London: Cassell, 1929)

J. Charteris, *Haig* (London: Duckworth, 1933)

M. Crawshaw, 'The Impact of Technology on the BEF and its Commander', in B.

Bond & N. Cave (eds), *Haig: A Reappraisal 70 Years On* (London: Leo Cooper, 1999)

J. Davidson, *Haig Master of the Field* (London: Peter Nevill, 1953)

G. J. De Groot, *Douglas Haig 1861–1928* (London: Unwin-Hyman, 1988)

G. J. De Groot, 'Ambition, Duty and Doctrine: Haig's Rise to High Command', in B. Bond & N. Cave (eds), *Haig: A Reappraisal 70 Years On* (London: Leo Cooper, 1999)

G.A.B. Dewar & J.H. Boraston, *Sir Douglas Haig's Command 1915–1918* (2v. London: Constable, 1922)

A. Duff Cooper, *Haig* (2v. London: Faber and Faber, 1935–36)

G.S. Duncan, *Douglas Haig As I Knew Him* (London: Allen and Unwin, 1966)

K. Grieves, 'Haig and the Government, 1916–1918'. in B. Bond & N. Cave (eds), *Haig: A Reappraisal 70 Years On* (London: Leo Cooper, 1999)

Haig, The Countess, *The Man I Knew* (Edinburgh & London: The Moray Press, 1936)

Haig, Major the Earl, *My Father's Son* (London: Leo Cooper, 2000)

J.P. Harris, 'Haig and the Tank', in B. Bond & N. Cave (eds), *Haig: A Reappraisal 70 Years On* (London: Leo Cooper, 1999)

J. Hussey, 'Portrait of a Commander-in-Chief', in B. Bond & N. Cave (eds), *Haig: A Reappraisal 70 years On* (London: Leo Cooper, 1999)

J. Marshall-Cornwall, *Haig as Military Commander* (London: Batsford, 1973)

J. Peaty, 'Haig and Military Discipline', in B. Bond & N. Cave (eds), *Haig: A Reappraisal 70 years On* (London: Leo Cooper, 1999)

W.J. Philpott, 'Haig and Britain's European Allies', in B. Bond & N. Cave (eds), *Haig: A Reappraisal 70 years On* (London: Leo Cooper, 1999)

T. Secrett, *Twenty-Five years with Earl Haig* (London: Jarrolds, nd)

P. Simkins, 'Haig and the Army Commanders', in B. Bond & N. Cave (eds), *Haig: A Reappraisal 70 Years On* (London: Leo Cooper, 1999)

K. Simpson, 'The Reputation of Sir Douglas Haig', in B. Bond (ed), *The First World War and British Military History* (Oxford: Clarendon Press, 1991)

E.K.G. Sixsmith, *Douglas Haig* (London: Weidenfeld & Nicolson, 1976)

J. Terraine, *Douglas Haig the Educated Soldier* (London: Hutchinson, 1963)

P. Warner, *Field Marshal Earl Haig* (London: Bodley Head, 1991)

D. Winter, *Haig's Command: A Reassessment* (London: Viking, 1991)

D.R. Woodward, 'Sir William Robertson and Sir Douglas Haig', in B. Bond & N. Cave, *Haig: A Reappraisal 70 Years On* (London: Leo Cooper, 1999)

Books and Articles on Other Key Figures

R.J.Q. Adams, *Arms and the Wizard: Lloyd George and the Ministry of Munitions 1915–16* (London: Cassell, 1978)

R.J.Q. Adams, *Bonar Law* (London: Murray, 1999)

J. Baynes, *Far From a Donkey: The Life of General Ivor Maxse* (London: Brassey's, 1995)

I.F.W. Beckett, *Johnnie Gough VC* (London: Tom Donovan, 1989)

I.F.W. Beckett, *The Judgement of History: Sir Horace Smith-Dorrien, Lord French and* 1914 (London: Tom Donovan, 1993)

I.F.W. Beckett, 'Hubert Gough, Neill Malcolm and Command on the Western Front', in B. Bond (ed), *The First World War and British Military History* (Oxford: Clarendon Press, 1991)

G.H. Cassar, *Kitchener: Architect of Victory* (London: Kimber, 1977)

G.H. Cassar, *Asquith as War Leader* (London: Hambledon, 1994)

J.J. Cooke, *Pershing and his Generals* (Westport, CT: Praeger, 1997)

A Farrar-Hockley, *Goughie: The Life of General Sir Hubert Gough* (London: Hart-Davis, MacGibbon, 1975)

P. Fraser, *Lord Esher* (London: Hart-Davis, MacGibbon, 1973)

K. Grieves, *Sir Eric Geddes* (Manchester: Manchester University Press, 1989)

J. Grigg, *Lloyd George: From Peace to War 1912–16* (London: Methuen, 1985)

J. Grigg, *Lloyd George: War Leader 1916–1918* (London: Allen Lane, 2002)

R. Holmes, *The Little Field Marshal: Sir John French* (London: Cape, 1981)

A.M.J. Hyatt, *General Sir Arthur Currie* (Toronto: University of Toronto Press, 1987)

F.B. Maurice, *Rawlinson of Trent* (London: Cassell, 1928)

P.A. Pedersen, *Monash as Military Commander* (Melbourne: Melbourne University Press, 1992)

G. Powell, *Plumer: The Soldier's General* (London: Leo Cooper, 1990)

R. Prior & T. Wilson, *Command on the Western Front: The Military Career of Sir Henry Rawlinson* (Oxford: Blackwell, 1992)

G. Sheffield, 'An Army Commander on the Somme: Hubert Gough', in G. Sheffield & D. Todman (eds), *Command and Control on the Western Front 1914–1918: The British Experience* (Staplehurst: Spellmount, 2004)

P. Stansky, *Sassoon: The Worlds of Philip and Sybil* (New Haven & London: Yale University Press, 2003)

J. Walker, *The Blood Tub: General Gough and the Battle of Bullecourt, 1917* (Staplehurst: Spellmount, 1998).

J. Williams, *Byng of Vimy* (London: Leo Cooper, 1983)

D.R. Woodward, *Field Marshal Sir William Robertson* (Westport, CT, & London: Praeger, 1998)

Books and Articles on the First World War – General

N. Barr, 'The Elusive Victory: The BEF and the Operational Level of War, September 1918', in A.A. Wiest & G. Jensen (eds), *War in the Age of Technology* (New York: New York University Press, 1999)

I.F.W. Beckett & K. Simpson (eds), *A Nation in Arms* (Manchester: Manchester University Press, 1985)

I.F.W. Beckett, *The Great War 1914–18* (Harlow: Longman 2001)

S. Bidwell, S. & D. Graham, *Fire-Power: British Army Weapons and Theories of War 1904–1945* (London: Allen & Unwin, 1982)

B. Bond (ed), *The First World War and British Military History* (Oxford: Clarendon Press, 1991)

B. Bond et al, *'Look To Your Front: Studies in the First World War'* (Staplehurst: Spellmount, 1999)

B. Bond, *The Unquiet Western Front: Britain's Role in Literature and History* (Cambridge: Cambridge University Press, 2002)

J.M. Bourne, *Britain, and the Great War* (London: Edward Arnold, 1989, 1991, 1994)

J.M. Bourne, 'British Generals in the First World War', in G.D. Sheffield (ed), *Leadership and Command: The Anglo-American Military Experience since 1861* (London: Brassey's, 1997)

J. Bourne, P. Liddle & I. Whitehead (eds), *The Great World War 1914–45* (2v. London: HarperCollins, 2000, 2001)

J.M. Bourne, *Who's Who in World War One* (London: Routledge, 2001)

Ian Malcolm Brown, *British Logistics on the Western Front* (Westport, CT: Praeger, 1998)

G.H. Cassar, *The Forgotten Front: The British Campaign in Italy, 1917–1918* (London: Hambledon, 1998)

H. Cecil & P. Liddle (eds), *Facing Armageddon: The First World War Experienced* (London: Leo Cooper, 1996)

P. Dennis & J. Grey (eds), *1918: Defining Victory* (Canberra: Department of Defence, 1999)

J.E. Edmonds (ed and comp) *Military Operations France and Belgium* (14v London, published variously by HMSO and Macmillan, 1922–47)

D. French, *British Strategy and War Aims 1914–1916* (London: Allen & Unwin 1986)

D. French, *The Strategy of the Lloyd George Coalition 1916–18* (Oxford: Clarendon Press, 1995)

D. French & B. Holden Reid (eds), *The British General Staff: Reform and Innovation* (London: Cass, 2002)

J.G. Fuller, *Troop Morale and Popular Culture in the British and Dominion Armies 1914–1918* (Oxford: Clarendon Press, 1991)

P. Griffith, *Battle Tactics of the Western Front* (London: Yale University Press, 1994)

P. Griffith (ed), *British Fighting Methods in the Great War* (London: Cass, 1996)

J.P. Harris with N. Barr, *Amiens to the Armistice* (London: Brassey's, 1998)

J. Horne (ed), *State, Society and Mobilization in Europe during the First World War* (Cambridge: Cambridge University Press, 1997)

M. Hughes & M. Seligmann, *Leadership in Conflict 1914–1918* (London: Leo Cooper, 2000)

P.H. Liddle (ed), *Passchendaele in Perspective: The Third Battle of Ypres* (London: Pen & Sword, 1997)

M. Middlebrook, *The First Day on the Somme* (London: Allen Lane, 1971)

M. Middlebrook, *The Kaiser's Battle* (London: Allen Lane, 1978)

B. Millman, *Pessimism and British War Policy 1916–1918* (London: Cass, 2001)

J. Nicholls, *Cheerful Sacrifice: The Battle of Arras 1917* (London: Leo Cooper, 1990)

A. Palazzo, *Seeking Victory on the Western Front: The British Army and Chemical Warfare* (Lincoln, NA, & London: University of Nebraska Press, 2000)

Ian Passingham, *Pillars of Fire: The Battle of Messines Ridge June 1917* (Stroud: Sutton, 1998)

W.J. Philpott, *Anglo-French Relations and Strategy on the Western Front, 1914–18* (London: Macmillan, 1996)

R. Prior & T. Wilson, *Passchendaele: The Untold Story* (New Haven: Yale University Press, 1996)

B. Rawling, *Surviving Trench Warfare: Technology and the Canadian Corps 1914–1918* (Toronto, University of Toronto Press, 1992)

S.B. Schreiber, *Shock Army of the British Empire: The Canadian Corps in the Last 100 Days of the Great War* (Westport, CT: Praeger, 1997)

G. Sheffield, *Leadership in the Trenches: Officer-Man Relations, Morale and Discipline in the British Army in the Era of the Great War* (London: Macmillan, 2000)

G. Sheffield, *Forgotten Victory: The First World War – Myths and Realities* (London: Headline, 2001).

G. Sheffield, 'The Australians at Pozières: Command on the Somme', in D. French & B. Holden Reid (eds), *The British General Staff: Reform and Innovation* (London: Cass, 2002)

G. Sheffield, *The Somme* (London: Cassell, 2003)

G. Sheffield & D. Todman (eds), *Command and Control on the Western Front 1914–1918: The British Experience* (Staplehurst: Spellmount, 2004).

P. Simkins, *Kitchener's Army* (Manchester: Manchester University Press, 1988)

A. Simpson, *The Evolution of Victory* (London: Tom Donovan, 1995)

H. Strachan, *The Politics of the British Army* (Oxford: Clarendon Press, 1997)

D. Stevenson, *The First World War and International Politics* (Oxford: Oxford University Press, 1988)

H. Strachan (ed), *The Oxford Illustrated History of the First World War* (Oxford: Oxford University Press, 1998)

H. Strachan, *The First World War: To Arms* (Oxford: Oxford University Press, 2001)

J. Terraine, *The Western Front 1914–1918* (London: Hutchinson, 1964)

J. Terraine, *To Win a War: 1918* (London: Sidgwick & Jackson, 1978)

J. Terraine, *The Smoke and the Fire: Myths and Anti-Myths of War 1861–1945* (London: Sidgwick & Jackson, 1980)

D. Todman, 'The Grand Lamasery Revisited: General Headquarters on the Western Front, 1914–1918', in G. Sheffield & D. Todman (eds), *Command and Control on the Western Front 1914–1918: The British Experience* (Staplehurst: Spellmount, 2004).

J. Turner (ed), *Britain and the First World War* (London: Unwin-Hyman, 1988)

T. Travers, *The Killing Ground* (London: Allen & Unwin, 1987)

T. Travers, *How The War Was Won* (London: Routledge, 1992)

T. Travers, 'The Evolution of British Strategy and Tactics on the Western Front in 1918: GHQ, Manpower and Technology', *Journal of Military History,* 54 (1990)

A.A. Wiest, *Passchendaele and the Royal Navy* (Westport, CT & London: Greenwood Press, 1995)

A.A. Wiest, 'Haig, Gough and Passchendaele', in G.D. Sheffield (ed), *Leadership and Command: The Anglo-American Military Experience since 1861* (London: Brassey's, 1997)

C. Wilcox (ed., assisted by J. Aldridge), *The Great War: Gains and Losses – ANZAC and Empire* (Canberra: Australian War Memorial & Australian National University, 1995)

T. Wilson, *The Myriad Faces of War* (Cambridge: Polity Press, 1988)

D. R. Woodward, *Lloyd George and the Generals* (Newark, NJ: University of Delaware Press, 1983)

INDEX